Information Science
in theory and practice

Information Science
in theory and practice

Brian Vickery
Professor Emeritus
University College London
School of Library, Archive and Information Studies

Alina Vickery
formerly Senior Information Officer
University of London
Central Information Service

Bowker-Saur

BOWKER
SAUR ●   London ● Melbourne ● Munich ● New York

First published 1987
Reprinted 1989
Revised edition 1992
Reprinted 1994

British Library Cataloguing in Publication Data

Vickery, B.C.
    Information science in theory and practice
    1. Information science
    I. Title   II. Vickery, A.
020   Z1001

ISBN 1-85739-017-2

Library of Congress Cataloging-in-Publication Data

Vickery, B.C. (Brian Campbell)
    Information science in theory and practice.

    Bibliography: p.
    Includes index.
    1. Information science. I. Vickery, A.
II. Title.
Z665.V73   1987   020   86-29913
ISBN 1-85739-017-2

Published by Bowker-Saur, Maypole House, Maypole Road, East Grinstead,
West Sussex RH19 1HH
Tel: +44(0)342 330100 Fax: +44(0)342 330191
Bowker-Saur is a division of REED REFERENCE PUBLISHING

ISBN 1-85739-017-2

Printed on acid-free paper
Printed and bound in Great Britain byAntony Rowe Ltd, Chippenham

Preface

It is nowadays a commonplace that we are living in an 'information society'. The practical importance of information to problem solving, decision making, and just plain coping with life is clear to all. The communication of information in society is an immensely variegated and complex phenomenon, and the more understanding of it we can achieve, the more effective can it become.

This book is an attempt to present and discuss a scientific understanding of the processes of information transfer. This transfer is a human, social activity: it is the transfer of meaning from one person to another, through whatever apparatus of media, machines, and intermediaries that may exist. This is the central principle that has guided our selection of subject matter for the book and that has shaped our presentation of the subject.

In seeking scientific understanding of the processes of information transfer we have had to go considerably outside the subject limits within which 'information science' as an academic subject is normally constrained. In doing this we are following the same path as current advanced research in the field. It has become increasingly clear that only by widening its 'knowledge base' can information science establish a solid foundation for future development.

Our title mentions both theory and practice. There is a good deal of theoretical research and discussion embedded in the text, and we are very conscious of the need for theory development. But we have also sought to relate theory both to experimental studies of information processes and to the practical environment of information provision.

We should make clear what the book does not seek to provide. It is not a manual of information practice or information management—though we hope that it contains insights that can be put to use by the practitioner in this field. It is also not a handbook of techniques for the design and development of information systems, though once again we hope that the data and principles presented can be of value to the systems engineer.

Further, we would not claim that the book is a manual of research methods in information science—neither experimental techniques nor mathematical analyses are presented in any detail—though we hope that our literature references give guidance to readers who want such detail.

Again, the text does not describe information technology and its application to information provision, though we have tried to indicate ways in which modern technology influences provision, and the implications of this for access to information.

Finally, the information problems explored are restricted to those of the industrial society in which our experience lies (most examples being drawn from the UK and the USA). We are well aware of the many different, more difficult, and—from a world viewpoint—more important information problems of less industrialized countries, but our competence does not extend to these.

The authors both graduated in chemistry, each spent some time working on journals of industrial chemistry, and each has had long experience in the provision of library and information service, and in research, development, education, and training in information science. At a number of places in the book we have drawn directly upon this personal experience. Over the years we have had the immense benefit of personal contact with a number of the investigators on whose work we have reported—too many to be mentioned here, but, hopefully, all included in the References—and it is to them, as well as to those whom we know only through the printed word, that our thanks must go. Our attempt to integrate all this work has considerably strengthened our faith in the future of information science as an academic discipline and a professional practice. We hope that the book can contribute to this development.

For this revised edition we have added a short appendix on intelligent search interfaces, but made no other changes. Although the factual data in Chapter 10 is now not up-to-date, we hope that this does not impair our broad description of UK information provision, and that our overall survey of information science will continue to be of service.

B.V.,A.V.

Contents

Frontispiece　xiii
1　Information science: emergence and scope　1
　1.1　Factors creating information demand　4
　1.2　The study of information transfer　6
　1.3　The information system and information science　9
2　A social approach to information　13
　2.1　Aspects of industrial society　14
　2.2　Communication in society　16
　2.3　Information needs　17
　2.4　The information environment　18
　2.5　The recipients of information　20
　2.6　Sources of information　22
　2.7　Channels of communication　23
　2.8　The information system as a whole　25
3　Wider contexts of information transfer　28
　3.1　Information transfer in nature　29
　3.2　Machines and their interactions　33
　3.3　Relations between documents　36
　3.4　Human information processing　37
　3.5　Conclusion　41
4　People and information　44
　4.1　Selectivity of attention and exposure　45
　4.2　Linguistic charcteristics of messages　46
　4.3　Media of communication　48
　4.4　Linking sources and recipients　51
　4.5　Groups and organizations　53
　4.6　Diffusion within a community　57
　4.7　The study of people and information　60
　4.8　Variables, categories, and data　61
　4.9　Analysis of variables　64
　4.10　The development of indicators and indexes　68
　4.11　Professional orientation and information channels　70
　4.12　The use of existing records　73
　4.13　Population, sample, and unit　79
　4.14　Collecting data from people　82
　4.15　Case studies　84
　4.16　Scientific research and communication　84

4.17 Studies in psychological science   86
4.18 Journal publication   89
4.19 Secondary announcements   90
4.20 Reception of information   91
4.21 The information needs of practitioners   94
4.22 Characteristics of practitioners   95
4.23 Sources of new-practice knowledge   98
4.24 The importance of informal communication   100
4.25 The relation between formal and informal sources   101
4.26 Information flow in the construction industry   106
4.27 The information needs of 'Everyman'   107
4.28 Conclusions and implications   112

5 **Information retrieval**   116
5.1 The entities to be stored and retrieved   116
5.2 Tools, techniques, and agencies   117
5.3 Design problems in information retrieval   118
5.4 Information analysis   119
5.5 Record and file structures   124
5.6 Query formulation and searching   127
5.7 Evaluation of information output   129
5.8 Query modification   130
5.9 Primary information store   131

6 **Semantics and retrieval**   133
6.1 Transfers of meaning   135
6.2 The practice of subject retrieval   136
6.3 Research in information retrieval   140
6.4 Structures of public knowledge   141
6.5 Personal knowledge   145
6.6 Studies of memory   146
6.7 Language and logic   150
6.8 A global model of personal knowledge   154
6.9 Knowledge representation in artificial intelligence   158
6.10 Information wants and their expression   162
6.11 The origin of designations   164
6.12 Criteria for message designation   166
6.13 The standardization of designations   168
6.14 The semantic structure of retrieval systems   171
6.15 Studies of index languages   175
6.16 Conclusions   177

7 **Intermediaries and interfaces**   180
7.1 The reference process   180
7.2 What the intermediary should know   181
7.3 The nature of questions   182
7.4 Questions and answers   185
7.5 Questions and problem solving   186
7.6 Questions in discourse   187
7.7 Cooperative dialogue   188
7.8 Models of the other   189
7.9 The reference interview   190
7.10 Interviews for online search   191

7.11 Interview techniques   193
7.12 Characteristics of enquirer/intermediary interaction   197
7.13 Machine interface for online search   198
7.14 Parsing   199
7.15 Expert systems in general   203
7.16 The MYCIN story   204
7.17 Expert system for referral   207
7.18 Conclusion   209

8 Information systems   210
8.1   Typology of information systems   210
8.2   The interconnection of systems   215
8.3   The impact of electronic technology   216
8.4   General system features   217
8.5   System development   222
8.6   Relevant data   225
8.7   The measurement of system use   229
8.8   Sources and recipients   229
8.9   Use of message stores   243
8.10 Access to information stores   247
8.11 Probability distributions and modelling   249
8.12 Queueing   252
8.13 Collisions of demand   253
8.14 Stock retention and discard   255
8.15 Distributed storage   256
8.16 Hierarchical provision   259
8.17 Some information system principles   260

9 The evaluation of systems   261
9.1   Criteria of evaluation   262
9.2   A framework for evaluation   263
9.3   Relevance and its assessment   265
9.4   Service qualities   266
9.5   Evaluating performance   266
9.6   System efficiency: cost and cost effectiveness   268
9.7   Coverage in acquisition search   270
9.8   Retrieval from store   272
9.9   The evaluation of MEDLARS   273
9.10 Operational current-awareness services   280
9.11 Online search service   282
9.12 Experimental study of retrieval   283
9.13 Availability on demand   287
9.14 Variables affecting availability   288
9.15 Document-delivery test   291
9.16 The effect of service delay   293
9.17 Degradation of performance   296
9.18 The value of information   297
9.19 The perceived value of information service   298
9.20 Conclusion   299

10 Information in society   300
10.1   Information-transfer channels   301
10.2   Publication and distribution   302

10.3   The press and broadcasting   305
10.4   Abstracting and indexing services   305
10.5   Libraries and information services   305
10.6   Public libraries   308
10.7   Educational libraries   308
10.8   Special libraries and information services   310
10.9   Interlending and library cooperation   310
10.10 Access to information   312
10.11 Some lessons from educational research   314
10.12 Information technology   316
10.13 Institutional agencies   321
10.14 Databases and database hosts   323
10.15 The context of information provision   328
10.16 The economics of information provision   330
10.17 Economic trends associated with telematics   332
10.18 Factors affecting access to information   336
10.19 The differential impact of new technology   339
10.20 Some final questions   341
References   344
Appendices   361

1   Criteria for information science   361
2   Areas of study in information science   365
3   Data questionnaire for chemists   370
4   MYCIN at work   374
5   TEIRESIAS explains   377
6   Intelligent search interfaces   379
Index   383

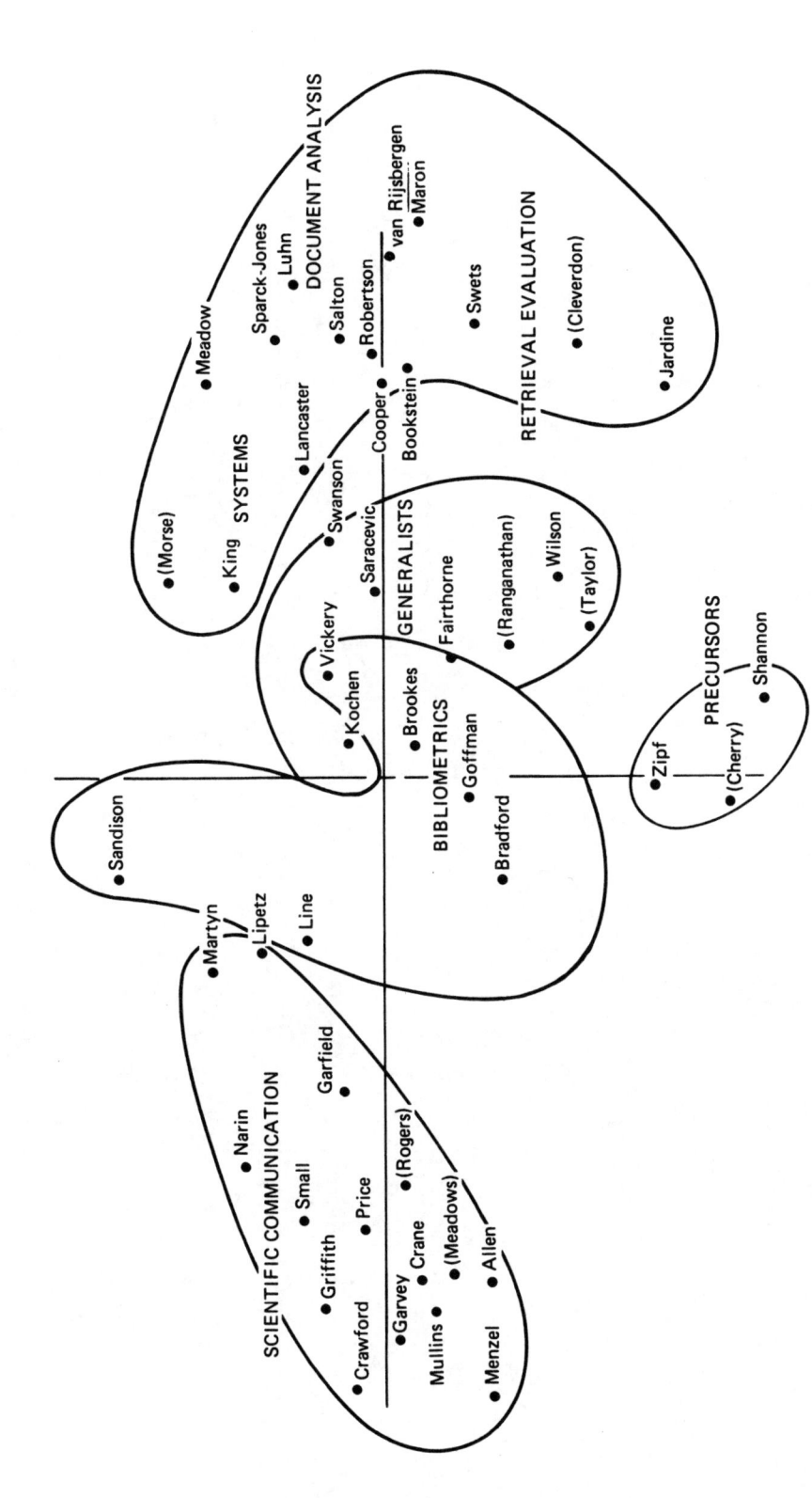

Frontispiece

A map of some major information science writers

The following text and the accompanying 'map' are. adapted from *Key Papers In Information Science*, edited by Belver Griffith.

Howard White and Belver Griffith generated this figure based upon the co-citations of the entire work of some major writers in information science. Distances between pairs of authors were estimated through a procedure which starts with counts of co-citations of the entire published work of pairs of authors by any citing paper covered in seven years (1971-1978) of SSCI. Raw co-citations across the matrix of thirty-nine authors were then subjected to Pearson product–moment correlation procedure correlating pairs of authors (after a suitable transform was employed to create diagonal scores). The resulting correlation coefficients were subjected to Kruskal's MDSCAL method of non-metric multi-dimensional scaling. All normal criteria for this procedure indicate that the spatial model fits the data well.

The author list was taken from *Key Papers* after first eliminating persons who were too rarely cited to generate reliable results. To that was added a list of well-known writers, including some precursors (e.g. Luhn) whose work is not included therein. While certainly not complete, the resulting map tells us where most 'missing' persons would go.

The regions were delineated through another clustering procedure, the labels coming from the mappers' imagination. The origin is set by procedure; most generalists, as for example Brookes and Kochen, lie nearby. The axes are arbitrary, being set to run horizontally between the centres of the scientific communication group and the information-retrieval group. The vertical axis seems to represent different variables on the left, centre, and right sectors of the figure. At the left, lower writers use only behavioural measures to study scientific communications; higher writers, only citation measures. In the centre there is some broad opposition of theory (Shannon and Zipf) and practice (Sandison and those persons involved in system design and evaluation). At the far right, persons who evaluate retrieval seem to oppose those who develop methods of document analysis.

The figure is a unique attempt of a field to display itself using its own methods. [The authors of this book have taken the liberty of adding a few names in brackets.]

Chapter 1

Information science: emergence and scope

Information science is identified in this book as the study of the communication of information in society. This meaning is only beginning to emerge from its practical background, the social activity of facilitating information transfer. The social practice itself has a very long history. It emerges from the social environment that gives rise to demands for information. Let us consider the urban environment, in which information transfer has developed and flourished.

Cities are large in comparison with other forms of social organization. Size has implications that go beyond the influence of numbers *per se*. The capacity to invent, for example, is relatively scarce in any population. Perhaps only one in a thousand or one in ten thousand people has the potential for true innovation. The larger the population, the greater the number of persons who are generating new ideas, new products, new information. Larger populations also present more complex problems of social control. Small groups, characterized by face-to-face interaction, permit simple social arrangements. Large collections of population force the development of specialized government, law, socialization, and other techniques for coordination and control.

Cities encourage trade. They cannot provide their own food and must trade for it. They must have a hinterland which they dominate, and so broaden their influence beyond their own boundaries. Trade also promotes travel and communication. People begin to specialize and to trade for life's necessities and luxuries. Cities come to have a complex division of labour, which grows out of trade but then goes on to exert an independent influence of its own. Specialists appear in the performance of most tasks. As a consequence, cities offer diversified goods and services. They are places with markets, shops, warehouses, banks, merchant associations, offices, factories, law courts, archives, property taxation, police, libraries, museums, theatres, observatories, schools, parks, plazas, parade grounds, citadels, temples, arenas, auditoriums, hospitals, fire brigades, rental services, pawnshops, brothels, gymnasia, public baths, laundries, funeral establishments, beauty salons, and hotels (all these were to be found in both Imperial Rome and medieval London).

Cities are therefore heterogeneous. As trade centres, they attract strangers and foreigners. Some of these settle there, and the city becomes full of people who differ from one another in language, dress, religion, eating habits, family structure, architectural preferences, and so on. These differences create demand for diverse goods and services. The city falls heir to the variety of cultural traditions that its residents bear. It selects, blends, and cherishes features of them all.

Cities are in contact with the outside world. The constant stream of travellers brings contact with the city's hinterland and with other cities of which it may be a hinterland. Highways, waterways, and airports have cities at their hub. Cities are located at the intersections of transport routes and at breaks in transportation where goods or passengers change from ship to rail, rail to truck, and so on. The city becomes a centre of communication (Lenski and Lenski, 1978).

Finally, cities are changing. Something is always happening in the city; change is rapid. All the preceding characteristics induce change and in turn are furthered by change. The last few thousand years have seen more significant alteration in the condition of human life than did the preceding hundred thousand. These changes germinated and flowered in urban centres. All these features give urbanism its special qualities and distinguish it from non-urban life. The diffusion of urban culture into even the most rural areas means that some elements of urban culture become known to most of the people of the world. One of the distinctive features of

Table 1.1 An approximate time chart (after 1500, the emphasis is on UK developments)

−3000	Writing: clay tablets, papyrus rolls
	Temple and palace archives
−2000	Horse transport
	The alphabet
−1000	Clay tablets in Assyria
−500	Official couriers in Persia
	Scholarly libraries (e.g. Alexandria Museum)
	Parchment roll, manuscript trade
	Private libraries in Rome
0	Roman roads facilitate transport
	'Public' libraries, *Acta diurna* in Rome
	Paper in China
	Encyclopedias
	Codex book
500	Monasteries and scriptoria
	Block printing in China
1000	Spread of papermaking
	Movable type in China
	Cathedrals and their libraries
1250	Universities, manuscript trade
	Humanist scholars
	Commercial couriers
	Printed book
1500	Bibliographies
	Legal and medical libraries
	State archives
	Pamphlets, patents, newsletters
1600	Royal libraries
	Town libraries
	Postal service

Table 1.1 continued

	Royal Society of London
	Periodicals
1700	Newspapers
	Circulating and subscription libraries
	Agricultural and other societies
	National libraries (e.g. British Museum)
	Roads and canals, mail coaches
1800	Trades unions
	Abstracts journals, annual reviews
	Lithography
	Parliamentary reform
	Steamships, railways
	Government libraries
	Public Record Office
	Photography
	Telegraph
1850	Public Libraries Act
	News agencies
	Professional societies
	Microfilm
	Rotary printing press
	Education Act
	Telephone, typewriter
	Parliamentary reform
	Civic universities
	Major library classifications
	Punched records
	Disc audio records
	Linotype, Monotype
1900	International associations
	Office duplicators
	Cine films
	Industrial research
	Aircraft
	Photostat
	Women's franchise
	Radio broadcasts
	Interlending, special libraries
	Facsimile transmission
	Tape records
	Television broadcasts
	Information centres
	Technical reports
	Phototypesetting
	Xerography
	Education Act
	UNESCO
1950	Digital computer
	New universities and polytechnics
	British Library
	Communication satellites
	Timesharing computers
	Computer typesetting
	Databases, databanks
	Computer networks
	Videotapes
	Microprocessors
	Video discs
	Expert systems

this culture is the generation, dissemination, and search for information. As Mumford (1966) puts it:

> The city, as it develops, becomes the centre of a network of communications: the gossip of the well or town pump, the talk at the pub or the washboard, the proclamations of messengers and heralds, the rumours of the exchange and the market, the guarded intercourse of scholars, the interchange of letters and reports, bills and accounts, the multiplication of books—all these are central activities of the city... It is no accident that the emergence of the city coincided with the development of permanent records... [This development] not merely held together a larger body of people and institutions than any other kind of community, but it maintained and transmitted a larger portion of their lives... This condensation and storage, for the purpose of enlarging the boundaries of the community in time and space, is one of the singular functions of the city... As Emerson well observed, the city lives by remembering.

In the earliest known cities formal provision for information transfer already existed—written records on clay tablets or papyrus, temple and palace archives, professional scribes, official couriers. Ever since the early archive stores, libraries of one kind or another have been a permanent feature of the community—whether private, scholarly, royal, ecclesiastical, or public. A succession of new forms of documentary record has emerged: parchment rolls, codexes, printed books, periodicals, newspapers, microforms, and many more. Telecommunications have annihilated distance. A bird's eye view of these developments is shown in *Table 1.1*.

1.1 Factors creating information demand

The characteristics of cities indicated above already identify factors that have stimulated the need for formal information channels. In *Figure 1.1* we try to suggest how social developments lead to increased information demand.

The coming together of people in larger groups creates a need for administrative information. This is not only a matter of administrators requiring information about the community but also of the citizen needing to know the laws, regulations, policies, and decisions of the administration. These information needs have steadily increased, on the one hand as a result of ever-greater involvement of the government in the life of the community (taxation, social welfare, and planning), and on the other because of the growth of democratic participation in administration.

The growth of commerce—which is itself stimulated by technological innovation and improved transport—immediately creates information needs: traders have to identify potential markets and sources of supply, to be aware of new products and new consumer requirements, to learn about the activities of competitors and regulatory constraints that administrators may impose. The diversification of trades and occupations began very early in the life of the city: even in Ancient Mesopotamia we know of bakers, boatmen, brewers, butchers, carpenters, cartwrights, fishermen, fowlers,

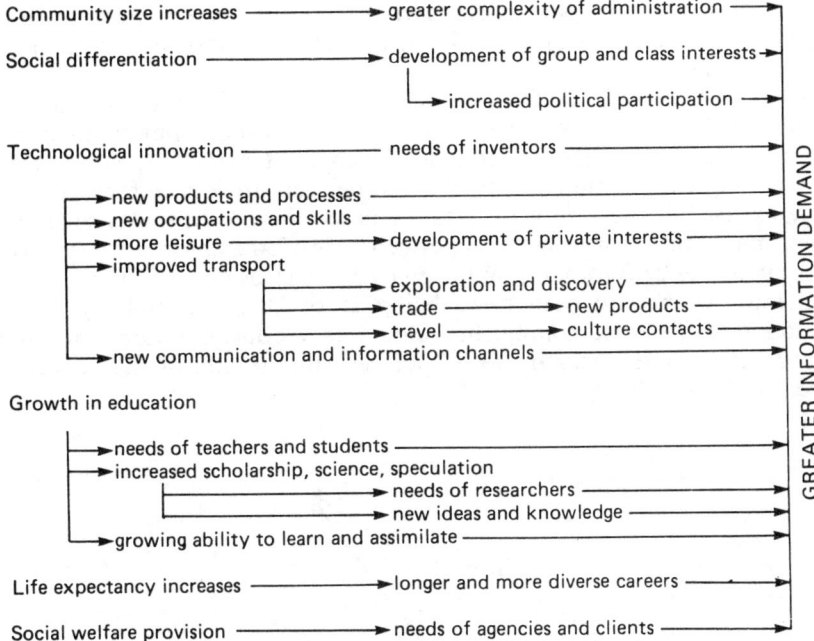

Figure 1.1 Social developments leading to increased information demand

innkeepers, joiners, musicians, night-watchmen, potters, shipwrights, smiths, stonemasons, street vendors, tanners, and weavers—as well as astronomers, interpreters, physicians, priests, and scribes (Oppenheim, 1964). Each specialist occupation in time develops information needs. In turn, the citizen as consumer or job-hunter requires to know of the services and opportunities that each trade offers.

Running parallel to such social developments—the growth of cities, of social welfare and planning, of democratic government, of commerce, the division of labour into innumerable occupations and specializations, increase in leisure and general interests—there has been the expansion and extension of education. This creates information needs among teachers and their administrators. Even more, of course, it lays a foundation for later information demand among those who have been educated.

One important result of schooling is the ability to read and write. Although writing has existed for over 5000 years, only recently has literacy been widespread in any community. The further back we go in history, the more indirect is the evidence whereby we can judge the extent of literacy within a community. In Ancient Mesopotamia the ability to read a complicated script was probably restricted to professional scribes, priests, and some administrators. In Classical Greece and Rome, a simpler (alphabetical) script and increased democratization extended the ability widely enough to make possible a commercial trade in manuscripts. Literacy in Europe declined drastically after the fall of Rome, but by the fourteenth century a new reading public was being formed. As well as priests, nobles, and a handful of scholars there were lawyers, administrators of all kinds, rich merchants, and master craftsmen who began to make active use of the written word.

Even so, the overall literacy rate was still low. In fourteenth-century England it is likely that not more than 3 per cent of the population could read, but thereafter it began to increase. By about 1650 it is estimated that literacy among Englishmen averaged 25-30 per cent (evidence for women scarcely exists, but the rate was certainly much lower). In towns such as London, male literacy was up to 50 per cent. By 1750 English literacy was perhaps 55-60 per cent for men, but even by 1850 it was only 65-70 per cent (the rate for women in both cases being 15 or 20 per cent less). The introduction in 1870 of compulsory elementary education brought the literacy rate for both sexes up to 97 per cent by the end of the century (*Figure 1.2*, Stone, 1969).

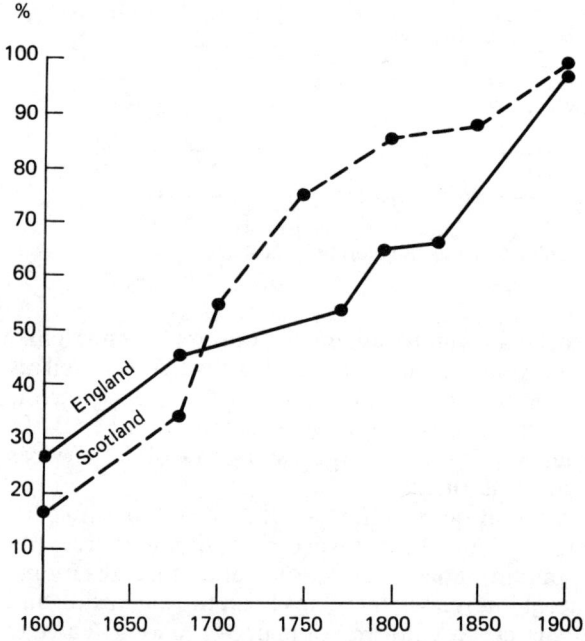

Figure 1.2 Estimated adult male literacy, 1600–1900

These, then, are some of the social factors that have created demand for information and hence for formal mechanisms of information transfer. Once again, we draw attention to *Table 1.1* that briefly chronicles the growth of response to this demand.

1.2 The study of information transfer

Information transfer is concerned with all the processes involved in transferring information from sources to users. In many cases there is some form of document associated with some stage of the transfer, even though other stages may be by word of mouth. The volume and variety of documents are immense, and consequently procedures of handling them are often pragmatic. Nevertheless, principles emerge that may be applied in practice. The field of documentation is most helpfully characterized if we take its scope to be all forms of document (i.e. any physical carrier of symbolic messages) and all aspects of their handling, from production to delivery. The document system then includes publication and printing, distribution, some forms of telecommunication, analysis, storage, retrieval, and delivery to the user. This widening of scope is in accord with actual practical developments, since there is increasing institutional overlapping and merging of the various functions.

Practice in these fields has always been a craft, with skills often learnt by apprenticeship. As we have noted, it has a long history, during which it has developed its own techniques and technologies—printing, indexing, systems for storage, retrieval, and delivery, etc. Intimations that scientific investigation could contribute to the practice have appeared only during the last half century. We will note three areas in which this development occurred.

Perhaps the earliest claim to an intellectual content for the craft came from those concerned with the subject organization of recorded knowledge. The theory and practice of classification has a long philosophical history. When H. E. Bliss in 1929 published his studies in the organization of knowledge, preparatory to developing his bibliographic classification, his book was published with an introduction by the philosopher John Dewey. A second area of intellectual investigation in documentation was the quantitative study of bibliographic production. An early exposition of 'statistical bibliography' was that by E. W. Hulme, of the British Patent Office Library, in 1922, and in 1934 Bradford and Lancaster Jones at the Science Museum Library first drew attention to a bibliometric distribution that has since been widely studied. Third, during this same period, social survey methods were first applied to studying the use of books and libraries, an early publication being that of Waples.

About the same time, the Indian mathematician Ranganathan—after a spell at University College London School of Librarianship—began to formulate his five 'laws of library science'. As he himself stressed, they were not scientific generalizations but norms, precepts, guides to good practice: 'Books are for use; every reader his* book; every book its reader; save the time of the reader, and of the staff; a library is a growing organism'. These principles became valid guides to practise in the wider field of documentation and information transfer.

Every document serves some immediate use when first created—even if only that of satisfying some inner need of the author. The documentation system—by preserving, replicating, storing, retrieving, distributing it, etc.—seeks to extend its potential and actual use. The methods employed in replication, storage, distribution, etc., and the amount of effort put into these processes, should logically be related to expected use. Thus

---

*Here and throughout, wherever we write 'he' or 'his', the reader may substitute 'she' or 'her'.

expectations of the use of documents should guide their practical handling. From this principle has ensued all the many studies of uses and users that have been undertaken to aid information system development.

'Every reader his book' (which Ranganathan also expressed as 'books are for all') served as a continual reminder to practising documentalists and information scientists against exclusive or excessive concentration on service to one particular group of users or potential users. Though individual services have to specialize so as to be effective and efficient, the information system as a whole has to take account of all potential users and their great variety of needs. Today indeed we must include non-readers as well as readers among those who have a need for documents, since the establishment of literacy is a prior condition for access to the world of books.

The principle 'every book its reader' stressed the dynamic aspect of documentation practice: the system should not wait passively for a document to be demanded—'it should leave no stone unturned to secure readers for every book'. The aim of the system should be to link authors (or, at any rate, their products) to users. As well as giving service to all potential users the information system should seek to disseminate all documents.

There was more hidden within these precepts than issues of 'universal bibliographic control', active promotion of the use of documents, user education, creating the reading habit, etc. They also implied that the documentation system should impartially serve all readers and all authors—that the system should impose no censorship on who reads or what they read.

The principle 'save the time of the reader and staff' is now most actively pursued within documentation, in such guises as the evaluation of the performance of services, cost effectiveness, and cost benefit. In stressing 'time', Ranganathan pointed to an element of system performance which is often of crucial subjective importance to the user (and indeed to the author): the time involved in getting documents published, distributed, processed, located, delivered: the 'timeliness' with which a document reaches a user. There is also the trade-off between the time of the user and the time of the information staff—a faster service may demand more staff effort.

That a 'library is a growing organism' has been amply demonstrated since Ranganathan formulated the 'law'. What to do about the 'information explosion' has been a constant theme within documentation. The inherent tendency of each document collection towards cumulative growth is an inescapable management problem. The expansion starts from the ever-growing mass of available documents and the ever-increasing number of current potential users. No individual information service, if it is to be cost effective, can keep pace with these expansions. The system as a whole can only cope with growth if it adopts a corollary principle, 'no library (or other information service) can stand alone'. This theme—cooperation, resource sharing, overall system development—is increasingly taken as a central guide to action.

Ranganathan's use of the term 'organism' was a healthy reminder that, though we strive to design, develop, and operate information 'systems', they take on lives of their own, changing continually under the influence of their external environment and their own internal dynamism. Not only authors and readers but also librarians, documentalists, publishers, booksellers, and all others involved are *people*. The system is not a clockwork mechanism, but a multiplicity of human activities influenced by the hopes, fears, prejudices, ambitions, skills, knowledge, and ignorance of the participants, and by the pressures of social forces acting on them. Information transfer is essentially a relationship between people.

1.3 The information system and information science

The terms used in Ranganathan's model—book, use, reader, staff, library—covered only some of the elements of the whole information system, whose wider scope has already been noted. Between the generation and reception of information are many social activities as indicated in *Figure 1.3*. Authors and editors produce documents, which are published, distributed, stored, and retrieved. Document analyses (indexes, abstracts, catalogues, etc.) are prepared, published, distributed, stored, and searched. To aid these processes, guides of many kinds are produced. At the bottom of *Figure 1.3* we have the 'mediating' function—personal information transfer by such agents as advisers, consultants, librarians, translators, and information scientists. It is with this whole cycle that information science is now concerned.

A new stage in the development of a scientific approach to the study of the information system began in 1948, when the Royal Society of London brought together an international Scientific Information Conference, at which a number of research papers were presented. Ten years later the field received even greater impetus from the International Conference on Scientific Information, organized by the United States National Science Foundation. Since 1966 progress has each year been surveyed by the Annual Review of Information Science and Technology.

By 1970 research had developed sufficiently for Tefko Saracevic (1970) to produce a survey of information science in the form of a carefully edited book of selected papers that reflected the emphases of the preceding decade. His first section was devoted to 'basic phenomena': notions of information, the behaviour of knowledge, of literature and of users, and the concept of relevance. The second section on 'information systems' focused mainly on the functions referred to in *Figure 1.3* as 'preparation of analyses', 'guides' (such as classifications and thesauri), and 'retrieval'. The third section of his book was primarily concerned with the evaluation of retrieval systems.

The term 'information science' first appeared in the guise of 'information scientist'. Particularly in industry during recent decades, some qualified scientists moved out of research, development, or production into a new occupational role, that of providing an active information service to their colleagues. They regarded themselves as 'information' scientists rather than 'research' scientists. As this kind of work expanded and became formalized the need was seen to provide training for those who would enter the occupation. In time, the content of this training came to be called 'information science'.

10

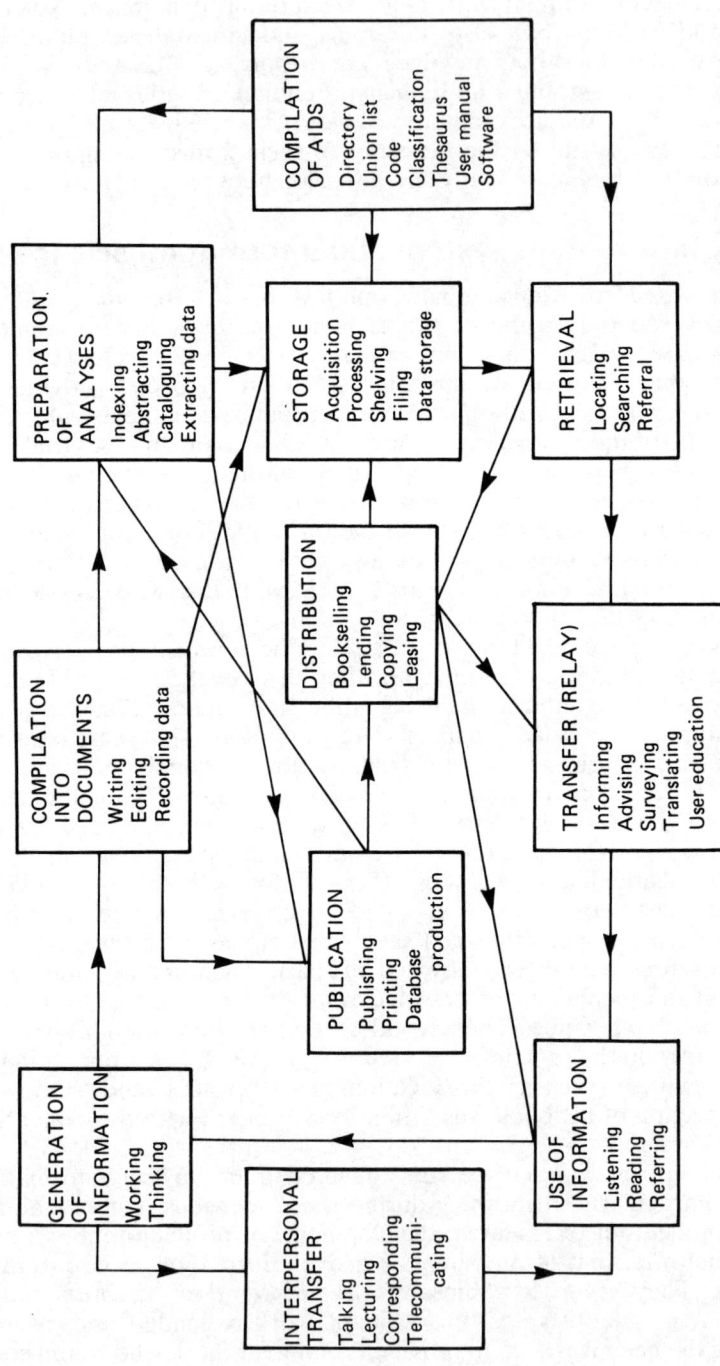

Figure 1.3 Main information functions

At first, this content emphasized the practical skills needed in giving information service—knowledge and experience of information sources, the organization of documentary sources by means of indexing and abstracting, the handling of enquiries, etc. In due course these skills and the tools available to the information specialist have become more sophisticated. In particular, computers and telecommunications have come to play an ever-greater role in information handling. Technical sophistication in turn has led to an increase in the scale of information facilities: as well as small, specialized 'centres' there have developed large, dispersed 'systems'. It has become necessary for information scientists to acquire the skills of systems analysis, design, and evaluation as well as management skills.

The potential content of 'information science'—even if still seen as training or professional education for a practical occupation—has steadily widened. The Institute of Information Scientists in 1976 developed a set of criteria for information science, as a 'guide to topics that might usefully and justifiably be included in a course of instruction'. The latest version of these criteria is reproduced in Appendix 1. The topics were grouped into two sets of six sections: knowledge and its communication, sources of information, organization of information, retrieval, dissemination, and management of information. These six were regarded as the core topics, the remainder being complementary, namely data processing, research methods, some aspects of mathematics, statistics, and linguistics, knowledge of foreign languages, and some 'advanced' topics such as associative techniques and machine translation.

The initial topic (knowledge and its communication), and the supplementary study of research methods, already imply some recognition of an underlying field of scientific study that might contribute insights for the practical information scientist. This possibility is more explicitly recognized in some notes on 'areas of study in information science', prepared some years ago by one of the present authors (reproduced in Appendix 2). In part reflecting the historical development of the field, four areas were identified:

(1) The particular problems of the communication of information in science and technology—better called 'science information';
(2) The use of technology, particularly computers and telecommunications, in information handling—'information technology';
(3) The application of scientific method to practical information problems—'information systems study'; and
(4) The scientific study of the communication of information in society—'information science' in the sense of an academic discipline.

The emphasis in the present book is on information science in this last sense, and its implications for practical information service. Since 'science information' has been the object of much study by 'information science', illustrations from scientific and technical communication inevitably play a part in our account. However, it is essential to stress that information science is not solely concerned with science information, nor indeed only with the provision of information to academic and professional workers, but with all forms of information transfer in society (*Figure 1.4*). From

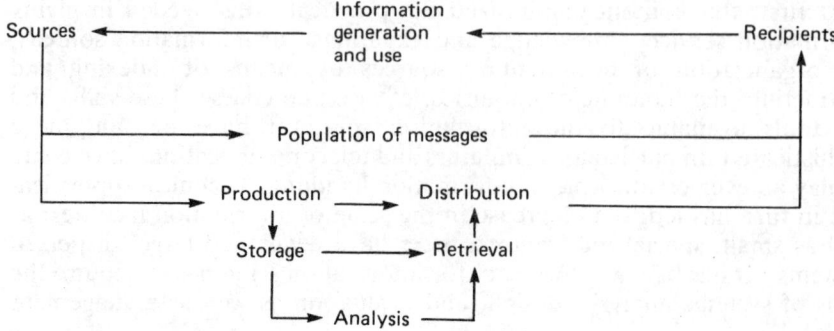

Figure 1.4 Information transfer cycle

sources to recipients, messages pass in the form of books, articles, letters, memoranda, conversations, lectures, broadcasts, and a great variety of other forms. The information system provides channels involved in producing, distributing, storing, retrieving, and analysing these messages.

Information science seeks to increase our understanding in such areas as the following:

(1) The behaviour of people as generators, sources, recipients, and users of information, and as channel agents;
(2) The quantitative study of the population of messages—its size, growth rate, distribution, patterns of production, and use;
(3) The semantic organization of messages and of channels that facilitates their identification by sources and recipients;
(4) Problems particularly associated with the functions of information storage, analysis, and retrieval;
(5) The overall organization of information systems and their performance in transfer;
(6) The social context of information transfer, in particular its economics and politics.

These are the topics taken up in this book. Chapter 2 offers a general introduction to our view of the social nature of the process of information transfer and in Chapter 3 we look at information transfer in contexts other than that of human communication. Chapter 4 provides an overview of how people generate, seek, and use information and of the ways in which informative communication has been studied. Chapters 5 and 6 are devoted to aspects of information retrieval—the current practice (in particular, as influenced by the use of electronic technology) and an extended discussion of the semantic aspects of retrieval. Chapter 7 continues with the retrieval theme, exploring the role of human intermediaries in information search and their possible replacement or supplementation by machine interfaces. Chapters 8 and 9 turn to information systems, in particular to the quantitative understanding of their characteristics that can aid system design and to methods of evaluating their performance. The concluding chapter looks at information in society, providing practical data on the UK information system and a discussion of the problems of achieving adequate access to information.

Chapter 2

A social approach to information

A unit act of communication can be represented as the interconnection:

Source—Channel—Recipient

The channel can be the sound waves of speech, a written letter, or the most complex chain of information-transfer processes. It is to be noted at once that the links between the elements in the chain are not represented as directed arrows. Although the net result of communication is a transfer from source to recipient, communication itself is often interactive, two-way. Communication can take place if a source has information and emits it, if a recipient wants the information and accepts it, and if an appropriate channel is available to both.

One focus of interest in communication is on people as sources and recipients. It is equally important to note that people are also involved in channels. This involvement can be direct (when the channel is a human 'linker' of some kind) but it can also be indirect. The characteristics of any channel, however much physical technology plays a part, are determined by the people who manage, design, and operate it, the channel 'agents'. That is the reason that we can study the willingness of a channel to transmit a message—one way or another, human decisions are made as to what messages can be transmitted. Exactly the same point can be made if we are considering non-human sources and recipients (for example, machines). These too have been designed, produced, operated, and controlled by people.

The essence of the unit act of communication is therefore a set of relations between the people who act as, or who are associated with, sources, recipients, and channels. Communication acts thus take place in a social context—indeed, it is the existence of society that gives rise to the communication of information. From the social viewpoint we can represent the unit act of communication as

Social element	Social channel	Social element
S ————————	C ————————	R

Viewed in this way the social elements that are communicating can be individuals, groups, organizations, or any other constituents of society. One focus in the study of information is on their social relations.

Information *systems*, at any level of complexity above that of speech, necessarily involve technologies such as printing, telecommunications, or computers. However, to information *science* technical potentialities and constraints are of importance mainly in that they affect the social relations concerned.

Any study of social relations must itself be conducted in the light of assumptions about the nature of these relations. These assumptions will control what aspects of communication will be selected for analysis. Our assumptions can be expressed as follows:

(1) Each individual person, group, organization, or other element occupies a certain social position, and enters into varied social relations with other persons, groups, organizations, etc.

(2) Each individual undergoes a lifelong change in his social position and social relations, associated with childhood, maturity, and old age, and with career.

(3) Each group or organization undergoes a similar development, changing in activities, personnel, internal structure, social position, and social relations.

(4) Society as a whole is similarly changing in evolutionary fashion (that is, changing cumulatively to a state previously unknown, not just in a fluctuating or cyclical fashion). The structure of society and the interrelations of its elements are therefore continually altering.

Some consequences of these assumptions can be set out. Since communication is essentially a social act, we may expect it to be affected by many aspects of the social positions of the participants (source, recipient, and channel). It is unlikely that an analysis confined to the unit act itself will give us full understanding. It is necessary to explore what social influences affect information resources and wants, channels and their availability, and other aspects of the transfer process.

Second, we may expect that the communication behaviour of each source or recipient will depend strongly on the stage he has reached in his life and career development, and that it will change continually as his social position and environment changes. Similarly, it is likely that the communication activity of a group or organization will be related to the stage that the ensemble has reached in its development.

Third, we may expect to find a continually evolving pattern of informative communication within society as a whole, strongly dependent on changes in the underlying social structure and relationships.

2.1 Aspects of industrial society

The characteristic features of life in an industrial society are obvious enough. Most of us live—or have lived—in a nuclear family group, visited from time to time by more distant kin. We meet friends and acquaintances on social occasions. Some of us join associations to indulge special interests—sports, music, politics, etc. To earn a living, mostly we work in organizations—commercial, industrial, educational, administrative, etc.

We are acutely aware of the great variety of occupations to which the social division of labour has led; for example, to name a few:

Medical Officer of Health	Policeman
Company Director	Carpenter
Chartered Accountant	Bricklayer
Solicitor	Commercial Traveller
Business Manager	Insurance Agent
Works Manager	Newsagent and Tobacconist
Farmer	Routine Clerk
Nonconformist Minister	Tractor Driver
Civil Servant	Dock Labourer
Jobbing Master Builder	Agricultural Labourer
Elementary School Teacher	Shop Assistant
News Reporter	Carter
Chef	Railway Porter
Coalminer	Barman
Fitter	Roadsweeper

Our daily lives bring us into contact with many other organizations—such as shops, schools, the Post Office, gas and electricity supply, transport services, departments of local and national government, the police, health and welfare services, trades unions and professional associations, banks, solicitors, insurance companies, and estate agents. We receive the outputs of organizations concerned with communications—the press, publishing, broadcasting.

We are aware that the multiplicity of individuals, groups, associations, and organizations is highly interdependent, that there is a continual flow between them of money, goods, energy, information, people, and other resources, a flow without which the life of society cannot exist. Even a local and temporary disruption of a service (such as the electricity supply or the buses), or a strike by bakers, can cause social havoc, and we live continually oppressed by the fear of widespread and long-term economic or political crisis.

This interdependence to a degree enforces cooperation and accommodation between the multiplicity of interests, but we know that the result is no heavenly harmony. All the interests are also, to a degree, competing, in conflict. Individuals may compete for jobs or for status in their social groups and associations. Economic organizations and services compete for a share in the market. Government departments compete for limited budget resources. Within industrial organizations the broader conflict between capital and labour may be observed. At the world level, competition and conflict among nations is far more evident than intermittent cooperation.

We are also increasingly aware that the dynamic interweaving of flow processes that constitutes society is not a 'steady state', with an unchanging overall pattern. Every association and organization in society seems to be either growing or declining, developing or decaying, in continual change. Almost every year sees the emergence of a new nation state, and sometimes the disappearance of an old one. Organizations are created, merge, divide, or go bankrupt. Their relative strengths, status, and influence continually alter. Overall, as well as random perturbations and cyclical oscillations, the flow patterns display secular trends—slow or dramatic changes in particular directions. These upheavals are in part initiated by perpetual innovation—the production of new goods and services, the introduction of new techniques, new styles of behaviour, new ideas. The innovations are themselves in part a consequence of increases in the speed, extent, and variety of communications between individuals and between communities.

One effect on the individual of social change is increased social mobility—changes of job and even of occupation, changes of residence and hence of neighbours, friends, and associates, changes in income and status. Even if none of these apply, our work and leisure environments are steadily altering. The times they are a-changing.

2.2 Communication in society

In whatever social situation we find ourselves—whether with the family or with friends, at work or at play, shopping, or driving a car—the elemental social process is communication. It is the social technique upon which all social processes depend. In all situations, we communicate intentions, instructions, advice, information, attitudes, opinions, agreement or disagreement, feelings, beliefs, hopes, and fears. We communicate to command, to inform, to instruct, to persuade, to amuse, to encourage others, to encourage ourselves, to avoid thinking, to understand what we are thinking, to air our knowledge, to work ourselves into a mood or out of one. Though rarely *homo sapiens*, we are inherently *homo loquens*. The variety of communicative interactions typically found in a group discussion has been categorized by Bales (1951) as follows:

 (1) Shows solidarity, raises other's status, gives help, reward;
 (2) Shows tension release, jokes, laughs, shows satisfaction;
 (3) Agrees, shows passive acceptance, understands, concurs, complies;
 (4) Gives suggestion, direction, implying autonomy for others;
 (5) Gives opinion, evaluation, analysis, expresses feeling, wishes;
 (6) Gives orientation, information, repeats, clarifies, confirms;
 (7) Asks for orientation, information repetition, confirmation;
 (8) Asks for opinion, evaluation, analysis, expression of feeling;
 (9) Asks for suggestion, direction, possible ways of action;
(10) Disagrees, shows passive rejection, formality, withholds help;
(11) Shows tension, asks for help, withdraws out of field;
(12) Shows antagonism, deflates other's status, defends or asserts self.

Leaving aside the more personal reasons for communicating, we can identify the main functions as informing, instructing, commanding, and influencing. Pure types of each may be found—when we are informed as to the time of the next train, or instructed in the use of a washing machine, or told to sit down, or persuaded to have one for the road. However, many communications are of multiple aspect: we are often persuaded by information provided; commands may include elements of information and instruction; and the dividing line between informing and instructing is difficult to draw. In fact, in this case we really need to look at the social context in which the act occurs.

An informative communication alters the state of knowledge of the recipient. This is certainly one of the aims of all education and instruction. However, it is helpful to distinguish the activity of instruction from that of 'informing' *tout simple*. By and large, an informational act is initiated by the recipient, who seeks (or at any rate recognizes when he encounters it) information that is of use in his daily life and work. In contrast, instruction imparts—in advance—information that is intended to be of later use in life and work: the choice of this information is largely determined by the sender. We might say that from the sender's point of view the giving of information is often instructional, but this is true for the recipient only if he is in an explicitly educational context, adopting the role of a student or trainee.

There is another aspect to this difference. Since, in the informational act, it is the recipient who determines the relevance and acceptability of the information, he does not necessarily require that the sender should understand or even be aware of the use that the recipient intends to make of the information. Unlike the student, the recipient does not have to assume that his informant knows his future information needs. The immediate informant, indeed, can be an intermediary, a link between ultimate source and recipient, with only a limited understanding of the information itself.

Although granting that in many real-life situations the distinctions made will not be clear-cut, nevertheless it is the informative act of communication as an 'ideal type' that is to be explored here. Let us now look back at the characteristics of industrial society and consider the occasions on which the need for information arises.

2.3 Information needs

The *citizen* in his daily life from time to time needs to know about the availability, quality, and cost of many things, for example:

Consumer goods and services
Health and welfare services
Education and training facilities

For the daily running of a household he (or she) may need practical information on cooking, gardening, house maintenance, and many other crafts. He will want all kinds of general information to satisfy intellectual curiosity. He will keep up with current affairs, social and political events. He will want to learn about possible occupations and their prospects, about currently available jobs, and about local, national, or even international associations and their current activities. He may seek legal, financial, and other advice. A good picture of the kinds of current information likely to be of interest to the citizen is provided by that which is commonly listed in a local newspaper:

Public notices
Forthcoming events, club notices

Directory information
  Telephone services
  Health and social security offices
  Member of Parliament
  Rent Officer, Rent Tribunal
  Special refuse collection
  Local hospitals
  Baths
  Car breakdown services
  Chamber of Commerce
  Town Hall services
  Animal dispensaries
  Chemists on duty
  Legal advisory services
  Community Relations Council
  Emergency services (police, fire, ambulance, water, gas, electricity)
  Samaritans, Alcoholics Anonymous
Personal announcements
Property (sale, lease, wanted, mortgages)
Holiday accommodation
Property maintenance
Goods and services for sale
Job vacancies

In an *occupational* capacity each citizen needs 'technical' information about work procedures—whether the work is manual, clerical, technological, supervisory, managerial, educational, scholarly, or whatever; 'administrative' information about the work environment, its rules and regulations; 'personal' information about career and working conditions; and information about his or her occupational association—whether it is a trade union or a professional society.

If the occupation is to provide a *service*, in addition there is needed information about the customers for that service (the potential market), about suppliers of goods associated with the service, and about regulations governing the service. Those who act as *advisers* also need information about laws and regulations, about sources and possibilities of finance, and case histories that can act as guiding precedents. Those concerned with public *administration* need access to a wide variety of social data.

Lastly, those working in *product* organizations, that make goods for sale, have a wide range of information needs concerning the market, competing products, raw materials and equipment, new technical and administrative methods, legal and financial regulations, sources of finance, labour, and services such as power, water, and transport.

2.4 The information environment

Let us now look in more detail at the act of informative communication from the viewpoint of the recipient. Each of us is bombarded with potential information. In an industrial society, if we consider only recorded messages, the volume is very high. Toffler (1971) estimates that

...in the US the median time spent by adults reading newspapers is 52 minutes per day. The same person who commits nearly an hour to newspapers also spends time reading magazines, books, signs, billboards, recipes, instructions, labels on cans, advertising on the back of breakfast-food boxes, etc. Surrounded by print, he 'ingests' between 10 000 and 20 000 edited words per day of the several times that many to which he is exposed. The same person also probably spends an hour and a quarter per day listening to the radio, and several times that viewing television. If he listens to news, commercials, commentary or other such programmes, he will, during this period, hear about 113 000 preprocessed words or so, plus a sequence of carefully arranged, highly purposive visuals. (See also Pool, 1983.)

We do not pay attention to all the messages from our environment— if we did, their volume and variety would totally disrupt our consciousness. We are selective in our attention. Moreover, each recipient is also a source of messages, both giving and soliciting information. Each of us can be pictured as in *Figure 2.1*. In this figure the rectangle Z represents a person.

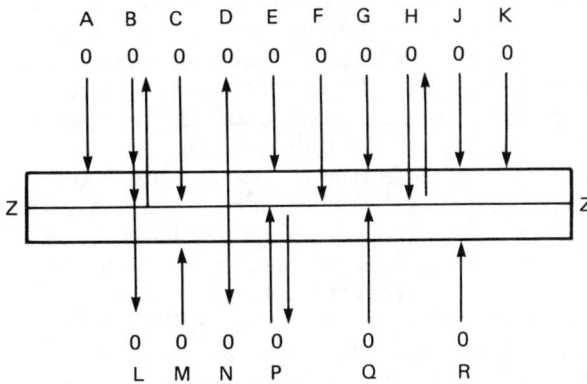

Figure 2.1 Message inputs and outputs

The circles A to K are potential sources of information, and L to R are potential recipients of information. Messages are received from sources A B C E F G H J K, but we pay attention only to B C F H (the remaining arrows do not penetrate the outer lines to our 'inner consciousness'). We solicit information from B D H, but D does not respond. We send information to L N P, and receive requests from M P Q R—but we attend only to P Q, and in fact respond only to P. Each of us from time to time also acts as a channel—passing a message from B to L, perhaps.

The fact that we are bombarded by information messages, many of which catch our attention, in itself constitutes a barrier to our receiving the information most relevant to our needs. It is clear, as Thayer points out, that we are in a dilemma:

...while our technological abilities to generate and disseminate potentially useful data have increased manyfold in the past few years, man's physical capacity to register and to process potentially informative data has probably increased very little, if indeed at all. The sheer volume of data that crosses the typical executive's desk today should serve to spotlight the inadequacies of the education and development of his acquisition strategies and practices. But no gain in ability could offset the widening gap between the exponentially-increasing quantity of data available for consumption and man's very limited capacity for acquiring and processing useful information.

2.5 The recipients of information

In any social situation, whether communication takes place and what information is assimilated may depend upon the information want of the recipient, his willingness to seek or accept information, his access to a channel, and his ability to assimilate the information from a message.

An expressly felt information want arises if one can foresee some use for the information. 'Use' must be interpreted widely. It should not be restricted to the use of information 'for decision making', or 'for problem solving', or 'to reduce uncertainty'. These and other specific types of use will certainly be applicable in particular situations, but the 'uses' to which people put information are as varied as human motives in general. It is used to further some activity—any one of the multifarious practical or mental, private or public activities that men, women, and children pursue. The activity served by any particular act of informative communication is individual and unique, but we may expect that types of activity can be related to the social positions occupied by those concerned—in fact, social position is partly specifiable in terms of the activities in which a person is engaged. So we have a chain of influences: social position—activities—information uses—information wants—communication behaviour.

Even if we have a felt information want, we may not be willing to seek or accept information. This can arise because of personal motives (a wish not to appear ignorant, wanting not to have to rely on an external source, judging that the benefits will not justify the effort or expense, a fear that the information will be unpalatable or will create more problems than it solves, etc.). A second reason for failure to seek or accept available information is simply the surfeit of messages to which we have already referred. Behaviour in this situation is affected in a variety of ways, relating not only to acceptance but also to assimilation of information.

Responses to information overload include omission (failing to attend to or assimilate some proffered information) and error (assimilating it incorrectly). Omission is necessarily selective—we may omit what is difficult or unpalatable to assimilate, even though it may be highly relevant to our current activities. We may pay inadequate attention to what we think is of minor importance, and so misinterpret the message. We may queue messages received during periods of peak load, hoping to catch up during a lull—which never comes. We may selectively filter out certain types of information according to some preconceived ideas of their relative importance to us—which may prove wrong.

These responses to overload from the flood of messages directed at us are related to the nature of the information that they contain. We will only pay attention to a message—indeed, we will only regard it as informative—if we find it comprehensible, credible, relevant to our needs, and usable. If the information is difficult to understand, or we cannot accept its validity, or do not see its relevance or how it could be applied in our situation, we are likely to ignore it.

Such responses are therefore in part related to the recipient's attitude to the source. Can the source be accepted as reliable, credible, relevant, authoritative? Judgements about this are likely to be made in line with the recipient's general social orientation—which kinds of source he regards as a 'reference group', whose problems, interests, viewpoints, methods, etc. he considers most relevant to himself. Clearly, such an identification with one or more reference groups is, again, an aspect of and related to the social position of the recipient. So we have a second chain of influences: social position—reference groups—authority of source—acceptability of message—communication behaviour.

Overload responses are also related to the recipient's ability to assimilate the information from a message. In order to absorb new information we have to assimilate it to our own knowledge structure. This is more than just a matter of understanding other people's jargon and mastering difficult technical material. Our own particular knowledge structure includes the whole set of concepts, categories, and values with which we are familiar and that we use as tools to tackle problems. These knowledge structures evolve and diverge according to the social background, education, and work environment to which each of us is severally exposed. It is often our limited knowledge fund that imposes omission, selection, and distortion upon incoming messages. Each individual's knowledge structure has been built up from two kinds of source. One is by the assimilation of information from messages received from human sources—a multifarious series of communicative events that begins soon after birth. Knowledge is also derived from all sources other than the humanly intended message—that

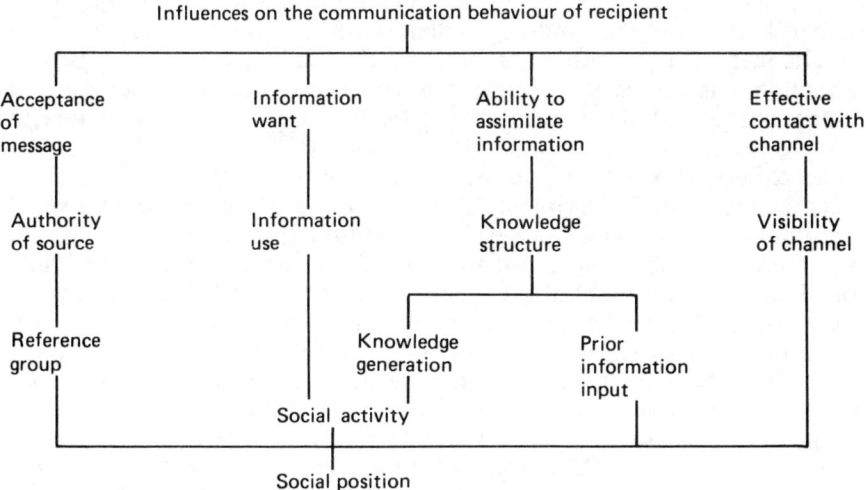

Figure 2.2 Influences on recipients

is, by interaction with the natural and man-made environment. Indeed, the second type of act is obviously the basic source of socially new knowledge, previously unknown to any individual. To distinguish it from informative communication it may be called 'knowledge generation'. Knowledge structures thus arise from a lifetime of information input, education, and social communication generally. Once again, we may expect that the pattern of life experience is related to social position. So we have a third chain of influences: social position—activities—knowledge generation and information input—knowledge structure—ability to assimilate—communication behaviour.

All the previous discussion of the recipient assumes that he is in effective contact with an appropriate channel that can transmit messages containing wanted information. This may not be the case. To the illiterate, direct use of written channels is effectively closed. So are Chinese-language channels to most English-speaking people. So are the stocks of printed messages in libraries to which one does not have access. In general, access to channels may be expected to be related to social position.

We have tried to indicate some of the complex ways in which the general social position of a recipient can influence his acts of informative communication. The main features of the pattern are summarized in *Figure 2.2*.

2.6 Sources of information

Information comes to a recipient from an 'informant' that may be either a person or a document. A personal informant may be the true source of the information (he knows something and he tells it) or he may be acting as a channel (he has been told something and he passes it on). The recipient may not distinguish between these roles. If the information is from a document—say, a cookery book—the recipient may identify its author as a source, but takes for granted the channels through which the document reached him—publisher and bookseller. In other cases, he may visualize the channel as the source ('it says in the daily paper that...'). The distinction—as far as the recipient is concerned—between source and channel is thus not always clear. Analytically, however, it is necessary to separate the two roles.

The expert who provides information in response to a question is in direct contact with the recipient. This situation is still common in a small community—for example, a research institute. However, in society at large there are innumerable potential sources, separated in space and time from innumerable potential recipients. Communication often only takes place through the mediation of a channel. The immediate target for each source message is then this channel—the source indeed may never know who ultimately uses the information he emits. Information output has therefore to a considerable extent developed in the same direction as ordinary trade—instead of face-to-face barter, we now have production for an anonymous market. An analysis of the communication behaviour of the source must therefore take into account his perception both of channels and of intended or imagined recipients.

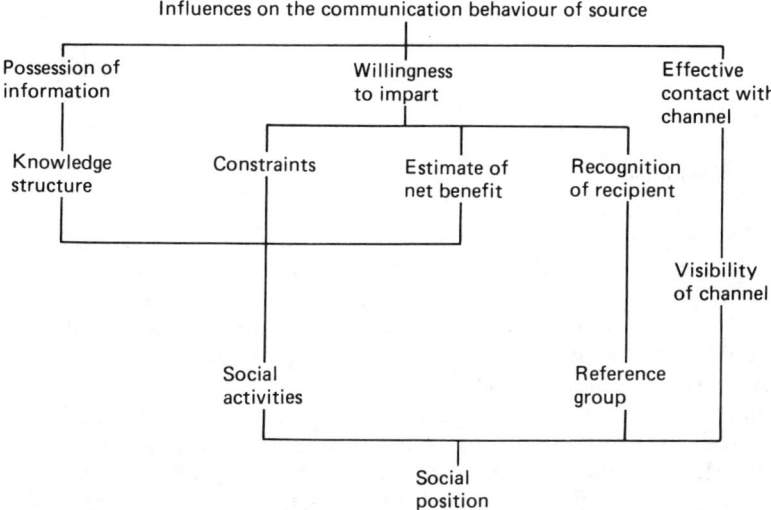

Figure 2.3 Influences on sources

In such a 'market' situation the emission of information will depend on the information stock of the source, his willingness to proffer it, and his access to an appropriate channel. The main pattern may be summarized as in *Figure 2.3*.

In this figure, it is 'willingness to impart information' that needs consideration. By 'recognition of recipient' is implied two things: the source must recognize that there are people who do—or could—want the information he can provide, and also recognize that they have some justification in expecting him to provide it. His awareness of the want will depend upon the extent to which his own social activities bring him understanding of potential recipients, and his attitude to these people will be related to those of his reference groups. Further, even though personally willing to impart information, the source may be constrained from doing so if the information is considered relevant to and confidential to any group, association, or organization of which he is a member.

To impart information involves effort and even expense—to formulate it appropriately, to find a suitable channel, etc. There may be some return for this effort (an exchange of information, financial recompense, enhanced reputation) and there may be some loss (one no longer has exclusive use of the information). These factors will be taken into account by the source in estimating the net benefit to be gained by imparting the information.

2.7 Channels of communication

It is now necessary to be more specific about the channels linking information sources and recipients. There are a number of social functions that together make up the information system, which may be broadly summarized as in *Figure 2.4*.

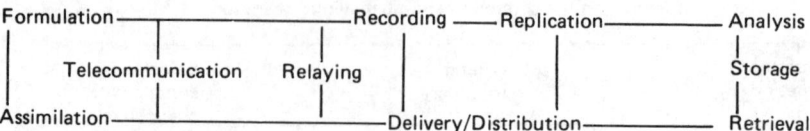

Figure 2.4 Social information functions

After a message carrying information is formulated by a source, it may be emitted face to face with a recipient who assimilates it. Alternatively, message transfer may be via a telecommunications system (for example, by telephone) and this is our first example of a channel. The problem of effective contact with the channel—can both source and recipient get to a telephone?—is immediately evident.

A second mode of transmission is named in *Figure 2.4* as 'relaying'. This term is used here to cover all human intermediaries who pass on information from source to recipient. They can be friends, colleagues, advisers, consultants, agents of all kinds. Their existence reveals most explicitly that people are involved in channels. Communication takes place only if the relay linker plays his part as well as the source and recipient. He has both to accept information from an appropriate source and impart it to an appropriate recipient. Much 'relaying' activity is incidental. In the course of other activities we assimilate information of interest to ourselves, and from time to time pass it on to others. However, there are an increasing number of social roles which inherently involve such linking.

For the citizen, in the past the priest, teacher, physician, druggist, solicitor, and banker have been traditional advisors. Today they are supplemented by social workers of various kinds, health visitors, youth employment officers, etc., as well as Citizens' Advice Bureaux. Agriculture and industry have various kinds of technical liaison staff. Consultants are active in many areas of industry and construction.

All the other channel functions in *Figure 2.4* relate to recorded messages. Recording can be in the familiar form of ink on paper (written, typed, or drawn) or in audio, visual, or digital mode. A recording such as a letter can then be delivered via a private or public mail service. Replication (by printing or other means) is followed by distribution and delivery. Single recordings, or replicated copies such as books, or analyses of them (catalogue entries, abstracts, summaries, etc.) may then be stored for retrieval.

Each channel function may be carried out by an agency, an organization devoted to the purpose. We have already indicated some examples of these, and a fuller (but by no means comprehensive) list is given below:

Telecommunications: PTT (telephone and telegraph), agencies such as Western Union or Tymnet;
Relaying: Citizens' Advice Bureaux, technical liaison, consultancies;
Recording: Typing agencies, database producers;
Replication: Printers, publishers, audiovisual suppliers;
Distribution: Booksellers, subscription agents, clearing houses, information brokers;
Delivery: Post Offices;

Analysis: Bibliographic services of various kinds;

Storage and retrieval: Libraries and other depositories, correspondence registries, archive and record offices, database processors, patent searchers.

Some communication channels are concerned to act as 'common carriers' and are largely unselective as to the information messages carried (the postal service is the prime example). Most agencies, however, are selective, and make choices as to the kinds of source and recipient for whom they will cater. Indeed, they may set out quite deliberately to act as a channel linking defined groups of sources and recipients.

The choices will be influenced by the 'recognition' of sources and recipients by the channel. Such 'recognition' has a number of aspects:

(1) Awareness of the existence of S and R;
(2) Acceptance of them as within the field of interest of the channel;
(3) Acceptance of their 'quality' according to some criteria judged to be relevant.

Choice may also be subject to policy constraints—for example, that information from certain types of source is inadmissible or that certain types of information should not be made available to certain types of potential recipient. The fact that each channel is of limited capacity acts as a further restrictive factor. Moreover, in one sense or another, channels must recover costs; the transfer of information must be paid for from some fund; in many cases, it is a commercial operation that must show a profit. So the willingness of a channel to transmit information is subject to an estimate of net benefit.

2.8 The information system as a whole

We can picture the social transfer of information of all kinds in the following way:

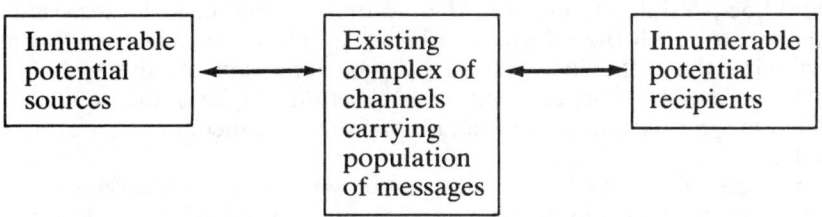

Sources and recipients seek each other. The complex of channels is the essential link between them in our industrial society, but it is at the same time a filter through which informative communications must pass. Without the channels, information transfer would be crippled, with catastrophic consequences for society. However, not all the proffered or wanted messages are equally acceptable to the system of channels, and there remain unsatisfied potential sources and recipients.

Channels, as already noted, are not neutral 'message-carrying' organs. The agencies are separate organizations with their own places in society, their own objectives to pursue, their own power and institutional dynamics. They offer many alternative information paths to sources and recipients, and are thus often—indeed, usually—in competition with each other. This can benefit information transfer, as each agency tries to improve performance to retain its position, but competition is not always beneficial.

We want to emphasize here the increasingly powerful economic determination of the transfer process. The context for the operation of every channel is the market. The pressure of rising costs causes all channels to attempt to maximize their audience. An agency that aims to provide information to a specific type of recipient must try to reach as many individuals as possible. The resulting population of users may still not be large enough to ensure continued economic viability, so the agency is tempted to widen its scope so as to win a larger audience. In this case, it tries to cater for several types of potential recipient instead of the original one, thus losing its specific focus and becoming less effective as a channel. So sources and recipients with specific information interests may find that they can only be served by channel agencies inadequately catering for a wider population.

Another way of coping with economic pressure is for channels to reduce costs even at the expense of a loss in quality—which may in turn lead to a loss in audience. There is strong incentive to seek for multiple usage of input messages—a situation particularly evident in the case of channels transferring bibliographic records, which are output in a variety of different information products. A further approach to maximizing the audience is to aim at an international market. This extends the scale of operations required but also lowers the possibility of diversity and specificity because of the need for a product that can satisfy several national markets simultaneously.

Books have been written about the information system to celebrate 'the remarkable and stimulating fact that the whole of knowledge is available for everyone to use' (Holmstrom, 1956). It is true that, in principle, it should be possible for any individual to find his way through the system of channels to reach the information he seeks. However, analysis must also recognize the difficulties caused by the complexity of the system, its deficiencies, the barriers and constraints it imposes on source and recipient, and the consequent failure in practice to meet many information wants.

Agencies concerned with information are social institutions—either independent organizations such as a commercial publisher, bookseller, or database processor, or a service within a parent organization (for example, a citizens' advice bureau, the library of a university, or the correspondence registry of a firm). Each independent or parent organization involved is pursuing its own objectives, and only rarely can this be described as 'the transfer of information'. The primary motive of the organization may be to provide education (the provision of information being seen as supplementary to this); to promote certain actions, opinions, and interests (using information to supplement persuasion); to exercise social control or to improve social welfare; or simply to make money—having chosen certain information products as a commodity likely to be profitable.

Information is a peculiar commodity. When transferred from source to recipient, or from seller to buyer, it remains available to both. Unlike the sale of a material product, information transfer does not give the recipient the right of exclusive use, nor is there usually any effective bar to his deliberately sharing the information with others (in spite of copyright laws). Moreover, information is rarely required for itself alone—it is usually only wanted because of its potential contribution to some human activity. These characteristics have the effect that the estimate of demand for information is always rather uncertain, so that information transfer is often not profitable and often needs subsidy from some other source of funds.

There are many consequences of these facts that information science may explore. The first is that solutions to system problems that are technically acceptable—for example, a cost-effective network design— may be heavily constrained by the economic and policy considerations that loom large in the thinking of the organizational agencies involved. A second consequence is that effective communication channels are only likely to be created when other—primary—interests are strongly involved and are backed up by adequate finance. Information wants—however socially worthy—that do not receive such support will be left unsatisfied. Inequalities of wealth, power, and opportunity in society will be reflected as inequality in access to information.

As social institutions, channel agencies participate in the same evolutionary development as all other elements in society. Some of these developments are technological—for example, the impact of computers and telecommunications—and determine the kinds of channel that are technically feasible and cost effective. Other developments are economic, and affect the whole institutional pattern of information transfer. In the past, the communication of information was essentially a personal service, and even the commercial publisher, bookseller, or library—though under the necessity of making a living—retained this flavour. In modern industrial society there is an increasing tendency for services to be 'industrialized', to be provided *en masse* by large-scale, impersonalized, standardized, and mechanized producers whose central objective is profit or at least cost recovery. There are, of course, counter-tendencies: small-scale intermediary services also arise to 'retail' the output of major suppliers. The details and implications of such developments need careful study by information science.

In this chapter we have sought briefly to set information transfer into a social context. Later chapters will examine some of the issues in more detail, but very much more remains to be done to expand our understanding of the functions and contexts of informative communications.

Chapter 3

Wider contexts of information transfer

The last chapter started out from a simple model of communication (source—channel—recipient) and considered its elements from the viewpoint of social interaction. We now wish to broaden the context of informative communication, basing our discussion on *Figure 3.1*.

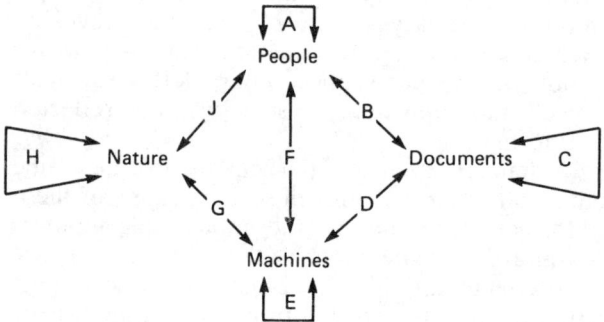

Figure 3.1 Model of informative communication

People communicate directly with each other (path A). They may do so through the medium of 'documents', by which we mean any physical carriers of symbolic messages in some conventionally agreed code or language. They may communicate via machines, man-made devices capable of interacting with people, documents, other machines, or 'nature'. By 'nature' we mean any part of the human environment that is not one of the other three elements shown. In exploring the interactions between these elements we will see that the concept of information transfer is widely applicable, and these examples will help to clarify its characteristics.

We need to give some consideration to path H, communication within nature, of which animal communication is the most obvious example. Path J relates to perception and cognition of the human environment and human action on it: this form of interaction is what we have called 'knowledge generation' and, although we distinguished it from informative communication, some understanding of it is very relevant to information transfer. Some interaction with nature is mediated through machines, path G—for example, monitoring environmental conditions—and this gives rise to data that enter into informative communication. Man–machine communication, path F—particularly where the machine is one that can transmit or process data—is of increasing relevance in information transfer. The machines may be instructed by or provide outputs in the form of documents (path D). Path E is the transfer of information from one machine to another. Path B is concerned with the writing and reading of documents—or more generally, with the generation and assimilation of the information encoded in them. Path C refers to a transformation of one document into another, in which a person or a machine (or both) must play a part.

3.1 Information transfer in nature

Anyone who lives in the country or regularly sees wildlife programmes on television is well aware of the immense variety of animal communication. Fascinating though it is, we are not going to report at length on it here. In most cases, animals signal emotional states—the distress of a lost cub, the hunger of a nestling bird, readiness to court and mate, a threat to rivals, an awareness of danger, reassurance. The information conveyed by signals is usually very general and non-specific ('danger!') but is sometimes more detailed. For example, it is said that the American ground squirrel has three distinct warning cries, for hawks, snakes, and large mammals, respectively. Black-headed gulls are said to transmit at least thirty different messages. The honeybee, by varying the pattern, speed, and direction of a 'dance', can indicate the distance and direction of a source of nectar.

Apart from this social communication all animal behaviour shows innumerable examples of acting upon information received. The spider waits motionless until a tremor in its web indicates the possible trapping of a victim, then scurries towards the source of the movement. Before dancing, the honeybee must itself have absorbed information about the spatial relationship between the nectar source and the hive. We have the general picture of an animal with the potential power to change and to act, the change or action being triggered off by receipt of a signal. A signal may determine the direction of change or action—for example, the word 'Cosmo' triggers off in our dog a specific series of actions (looking through window, then sniffing at door, excited barking and leaping), all in expectation of the arrival of a neighbour's dog. However, if the animal has only a limited range of actions it can perform, quite a variety of different signals may elicit the same action—no matter what you say to a parrot, it may simply reply 'Pretty Polly'.

This situation is common in inanimate nature. Suppose we have a metastable situation, a boulder delicately balancing on the edge of a cliff. Any 'signal' that upsets the balance (an earth movement, a strong wind, a push) has the same result—the boulder tumbles down the side of the cliff. The boulder–cliff 'system' can change in only one direction, and any appropriate 'input signal' sets the change in motion. In chemistry we have the example of two chemicals that can react to produce others: $A+B \rightarrow C+D$. The two chemicals may co-exist together until a particular 'signal', a catalyst, is brought into contact with them, then the reaction occurs.

These various examples may help us to generalize the concept of information. We start with an organism or a system that has the capacity to change—the potential energy needed is already present. 'Information' is any input into the system that initiates a change of state. If we represent the states before and after as $(K1)$ and $(K2)$, we may write $(K1)+I{\rightarrow}(K2)$, where I is an information input. These inputs are extracted from physical signals of some kind that have a source so the fact of information transfer may be represented as follows:

$$S \rightarrow M \rightarrow I + (K1) \rightarrow (K2)$$

A source, S, emits a signal or message, M, from which information, I, is assimilated by a receiver, whose state is consequently changed from $(K1)$ to $(K2)$.

Information transfer of this kind is, of course, proceeding continuously within a living organism such as the human body. An external stimulus to a sense organ (S), such as the eye, causes transmission (M) through the nervous system, from which the brain extracts information to form a percept—an image is perceived, the initial state $(K1)$ of the brain is changed to $(K2)$. If the skin is cut, the damaged tissue releases into the blood a chemical thrombokinase; here it meets a normal constituent of the blood, prothrombin, and converts it into thrombin; this further reacts with the blood constituent fibrinogen to form fibrin, which is the substance of the clot that prevents bleeding from the wound. We can regard this as a series of information transfers (*Figure 3.2*).

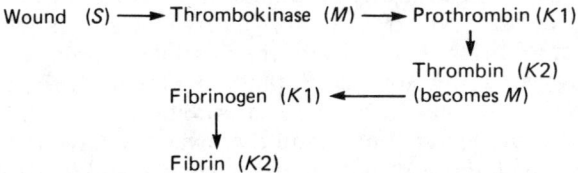

Figure 3.2 Information transfer in clotting

As another example, the female pituitary gland at intervals secretes into the blood a hormone 'FSH', which is carried to an egg sac in the ovary, stimulating it to mature and in its turn to produce a hormone oestrogen; this then stimulates the uterus wall to change so as to be ready to receive an egg. Meanwhile the pituitary has begun to secrete another hormone 'LH', which causes the sac to rupture, to release the egg (which travels to the uterus wall), and to produce yet another hormone, progesterone, which acts so as to continue the preparation of the uterus. If no fertilization occurs, the ruptured sac (*corpus luteum*) disintegrates, progesterone is no longer produced, the uterus ceases to develop, and the egg is expelled (menstruation occurs). If fertilization takes place, a placenta develops on the uterus wall, and this produces a hormone which stimulates the *corpus luteum* to continue production of progesterone and thus continue uterine development. We have a complicated set of messages (the fertilized case is shown in *Figure 3.3*).

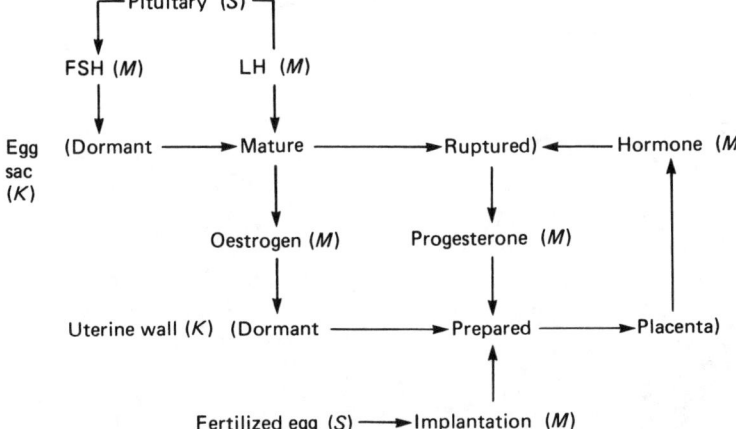

Figure 3.3 Information transfer in fertilization

The development of an organism is controlled by transfer of information coded in the chromosomes of cell nuclei. A very simplified example of this may be examined. One basic component of the organism is the group of substances known as proteins. These in turn are built by combinations of about twenty simpler chemicals, the aminoacids. How does the production of proteins take place?

The chromosomes consist primarily of very long chains of deoxyribonucleic acid (DNA). The elementary units of DNA are four relatively simple molecules, nucleotide bases. A triplet of three particular bases forms a code that will result in the production of a particular aminoacid. The course of events seems to be as follows:

(1) Along the DNA chain there are constructed a series of shorter molecules, known as RNA; the structure of each corresponds to the structural code of that part of the DNA from which it was derived.
(2) The RNA is detached from the DNA and travels to another part of the cell, where it picks up appropiate aminoacids and from these produces proteins; the aminoacid pattern of each protein again corresponds to the initial DNA code.

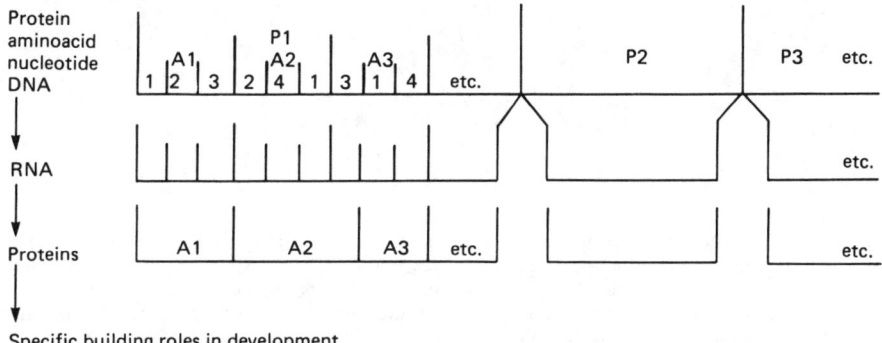

Figure 3.4 Protein building

32

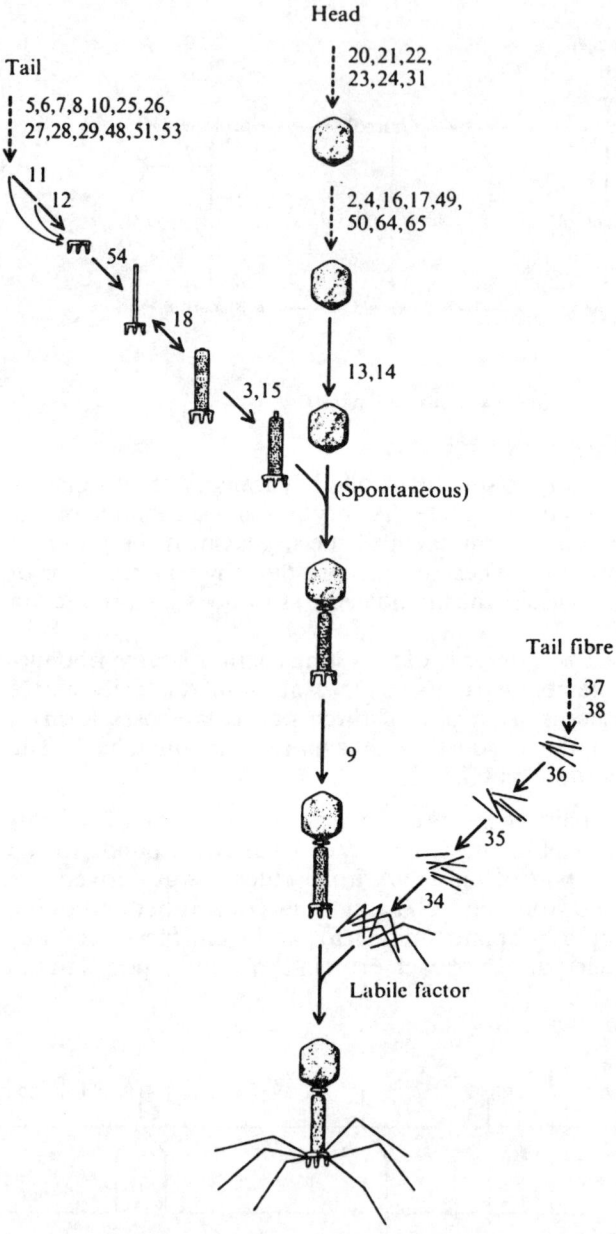

Tail

Head

Figure 3.5 Assembly of bacteriophage. Each step involves a number of genes. There are three principal branches leading independently to the formation of heads, tails, and tail fibres. Thus the primary structure of the head depends on genes listed to the right of the arrows. In the absence of these genes the culture makes only tails and fibres. Union of the finished heads and tails is spontaneous and does not need genetic material. The numbers refer to the genes at each step

(3) Particular proteins play specific roles in the building of the organism. The pattern of information transfer can be represented as *Figure 3.4*.

To simplify again, we can for our purposes equate P1, P2, etc. in the chromosome with genes, so that each gene makes a specific contributuon to development. For example, in the very simple organism known as the T4 bacteriophage over fifty genes have been identified. The way each contributes to the structure of the bacteriophage is shown in *Figure 3.5* (Young, 1971). The genetic code in the chromosome is transmitted—via RNA and proteins—to create an organism with a particular body structure:

$$DNA(S) \rightarrow RNA(M) \rightarrow proteins\ (M) \rightarrow body\ (K)$$

As is well known, during reproduction the chromosomes with their coded information are carefully passed on to the offspring of an organism.

3.2 Machines and their interactions

Any physical work task involves four elements:

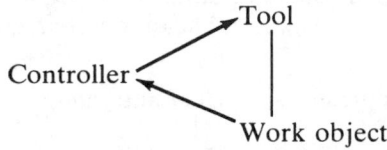

In the simplest case (say, weeding a garden) the hand is the tool, powered by muscle and controlled by mind, weeds and earth are the work object. In cutting wood, a true tool is used, the saw. To cut trees, an electric saw may be needed, and so the power source is transferred to a machine, but control remains with the man.

The control of a tool, whether power assisted or not, is in essence a transfer of information: the mind guides the action of the hand, the tool or the machine. In any work task, there is in fact a two-way information transfer:

Controller ⇄ Tool
Work object

The controller observes the action of the tool on the work object and modifies the further action accordingly. The flow of information back to the controller is now widely known as 'feedback'. It is in fact relevant in many fields of information transfer. A biological example has already been cited: in the diagram of animal fertilization on page 31, the cycle on the right shows a message feeding back from the placenta, to stimulate the ruptured egg sac to continue its production of progesterone, that controls the further development of the uterine wall.

An element of automation is introduced as soon as any aspect of control is built into the machine. For example, pushing the 'start' lever on a record player sets in motion a series of movements that are automatically controlled (rotation of turntable, release of disc onto turntable, movement of pickup arm to position over disc, descent of arm to rest, and stoppage of turntable). This is a fixed pattern of action, and incorporates two elements of feedback:

(1) If there is no disc on the central spindle of the turntable the pickup arm returns to rest at once and the action ceases,
(2) It is the advance of the pickup arm towards the spindle that eventually signals the end of the play.

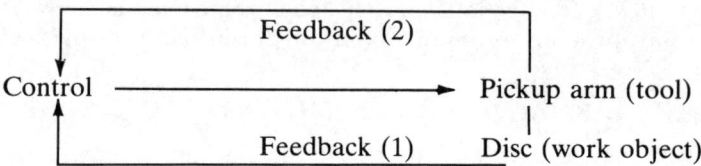

The pickup arm mechanism can respond in two different ways according to a feedback message about the work object (presence or absence of a disc on the spindle). Some automatic mechanisms are capable of more complex responses to feedback. Others respond by sending a signal to a human controller, and await his instruction. For example, an interactive search of a computer database may be represented as follows:

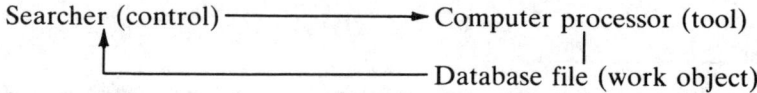

The searcher transmits a query; the processor matches it against the file, and reports the result; the searcher takes this into account in formulating a second query; etc.

Instead of responding to a human or built-in controller machines can be set in motion by signals received from 'nature'—their environment. For example, a photoelectric eye reacts to any interruption of the light beam shining on it, and opens an automatic sliding door. In other cases a mechanism picks up a signal from the environment and either records it or immediately transmits it to a human controller, in either case for some subsequent action. The flow of information in a central heating system may be represented as follows:

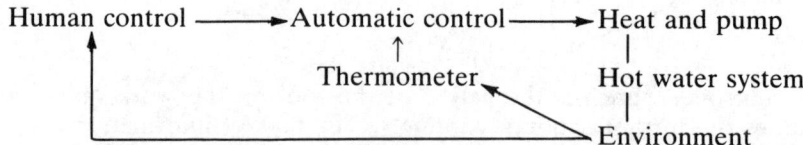

In many cases the messages passing between controller, machine, and environment are very simple—switching on a machine, a pickup arm reaching a certain position, an interruption of light, a certain temperature level being reached. However, as the actions to be undertaken by machines have grown more complex, so have the messages to and from them. The messages in fact come in the form of documents, that we have defined as physical carriers of symbolic messages in some agreed code or language. The instruction program of a computer is usually put into the machine as a document—cards or tape or disc bearing punched or magnetic encoding.

Messages from the computer about its processing may emerge as printout or a display on a video screen.

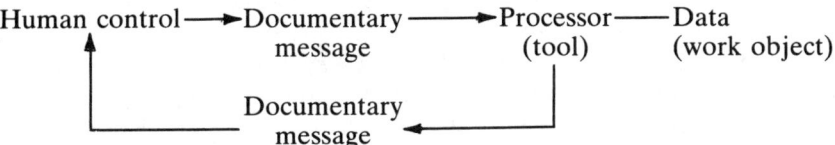

Communication with a machine—or between machines—can be modelled as follows:

Source— Encoder— Channel— Decoder— Receiver
S   M(S)   signal   M(R)   R

A source message is encoded as $M(S)$ and is transmitted through some means (channel) as a physical signal. The message $M(R)$ received for decoding may differ from $M(S)$ because the signal has been disturbed by 'noise' of one sort or another (transmission errors, losses in transit, unwanted additions to the signal, etc.). Applied to the use of punched cards to instruct a computer this model reads:

S   M(S)   M(R)   R
Program— Cards— Manual— Cards— Computer
            punched transfer   read

Noise could arise from cards being lost or disturbed in sequence during the transfer.

Even in a sophisticated machine there is usually a limit to the number of actions it can perform. We can regard the configuration it adopts for each action as a 'state', equivalent to the states of the brain or of the animal organism discussed earlier. If there is a fixed set of possible states, $K(1)-K(n)$, then there is a fixed repertory of messages, $M(1)-M(n)$, to which the machine can respond. We may then regard the act of receiving information as the identification of one message out of the possible set of n, and the act of sending information as a matter of selecting the appropriate message from this set.

The concept of the information process as selection from a repertory of possible messages has proved fruitful in communication studies of all kinds. It is clearly applicable to any decoding process. A code for the representation of information must consist of a limited repertory of conventionally agreed signs (letters of the alphabet, numerals, Morse code, the nucleotide base triplets to which we have referred, the commands of a programming language, etc.). Reading the written message ROSES ARE RED involves the identification of each letter in turn from the alphabet repertory, then of each word from a dictionary repertory, and then perhaps the phrase as a whole from a repertory of allowable sentence forms. The message RO£ES ANE ROD would present difficulties at each step.

The concept has further been of use in the design of codes: there is a mathematical relation between the number of items in a repertory, the number of available signs, and the number of signs that need to be combined to represent an item. For example, the quarter million words of the English language could all be represented by codes containing no more than four of 26 letters (there are 456 976 four-letter combinations from AAAA to ZZZZ). In fact, the maximum and even the average length of English words is greater than four letters—partly because they need to be pronounceable, partly because they have grown historically with added prefixes and suffixes (as in press, compress, compression, decompression).

This redundancy in spelling means that the code is uneconomic, and especially in communicating with machines ways of 'word compression' are sought. However, a redundant code is less liable to disruption by noise in transmission—few readers will fail to recognize this estraorbinary misprinted word, or fail to guess the missing letters in ENCYC--------. Indeed, some redundancy may be built into machine codes to minimize the chance of undetected error.

3.3 Relations between documents

As already defined, a document is a physical medium modified so as to carry marks that are signs in some agreed code. The marks can be images that we recognize or accept as representing some visual aspect of the world; they can be recordings of natural or man-made sound, similarly recognizable; or they can be conventional signs that are accepted as symbols for any mental concept or its referent in the world. The conventional signs can be the letters and words of a natural language, and thus be related to its spoken form, or they can be a special-purpose code (for example, Morse code, Braille, codes for computers, chemical symbolism).

Here we want to concentrate on relations between documents. One document can only relate to another through the active agency of a person or a machine, but this process can conveniently be considered as another variant of 'information transfer'. In the following analysis we will take a natural language text as the source document. Such a document can be subject to the following processes:

(1) Reproduction, by manual copying, retyping, or by any reprographic means; the output document can be of the same size, reduced or enlarged.
(2) Transliteration: this can simply be a change of font, or transliteration to a different script (such as Cyrillic to Roman), or transcription into code form (say, a punching code).
(3) Translation into a different language.
(4) Reformatting: we use this term to describe any rearrangement of the text sequence or layout.
(5) Extraction: the formation of a new document containing only part of the original text. We may couple with this the process of merging two or more texts into a single new document.
(6) Concordance: a form of reformatting in which the individual words of a text are arranged alphabetically and the position of each in the text is shown.
(7) Indexing: here we are thinking of a detailed index to the text, by

extraction or selection of significant words and their arrangement as a concordance.

(8) Summarization: the preparation of a summary, précis, or abstract of the text.

(9) Commentary or review: this may include a summary, but goes on to relate the text to matters external to it.

(10) Designation: the assignation to the text of a 'meta-text' that states succinctly what the text is 'about'. Typical designations are subject headings, descriptors, and class numbers.

The general process of transition from source document $M(S)$ to product $M(R)$ can be represented as:

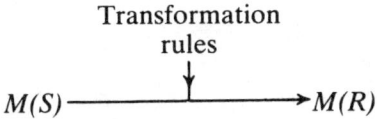

The transition rules can be purely formal and clerical, such that they can be applied by a machine: an example is optical character recognition, to transliterate between a printed text and a machine code. At the other extreme, the transformation may be intellectual and unformalized, as in a free translation or review. All degrees of formalization between the two extremes are to be found. Any such transformation is subject to corruption by 'noise'—imperfect reproductions, errors in transliteration, mistranslation, etc.

3.4 Human information processing

Standing in Piccadilly Circus a companion remarked 'Look, there's a sheik'. Let us examine some aspects of this event.

(1) It implies a selectivity of attention. Of all the myriad visual and auditory signals assailing the senses in Piccadilly Circus, certain ones caught the eye and ear.

(2) It implies a prior learning experience: on earlier occasions, certain characteristic features of the environment have been perceived and associated with the concept 'sheik'. The concept and associated attributes have been stored in the memory.

(3) On perceiving similar features in Piccadilly Circus a matching process against stored attributes has taken place, and the associated concept has been recognized and recalled (*Figure 3.6*).

Let us continue the scene in Piccadilly Circus. 'Never mind the sheik,' I replied, 'We've got to find George.' We scanned the crowds. 'There he is!' said my companion (*Figure 3.7*).

Human information processing at this level may thus involve a series of activities:

(1) Perception itself;
(2) Formation of concepts from percepts;
(3) Storage in memory;

38

Perceived environmental features

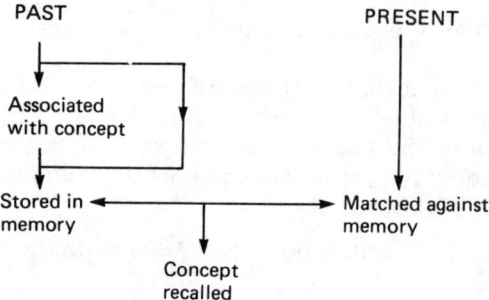

Figure 3.6 Recognition and recall (1)

Perceived environmental features

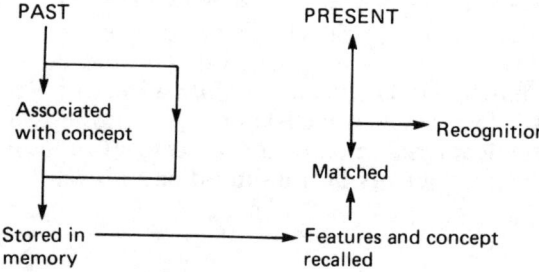

Figure 3.7 Recognition and recall (2)

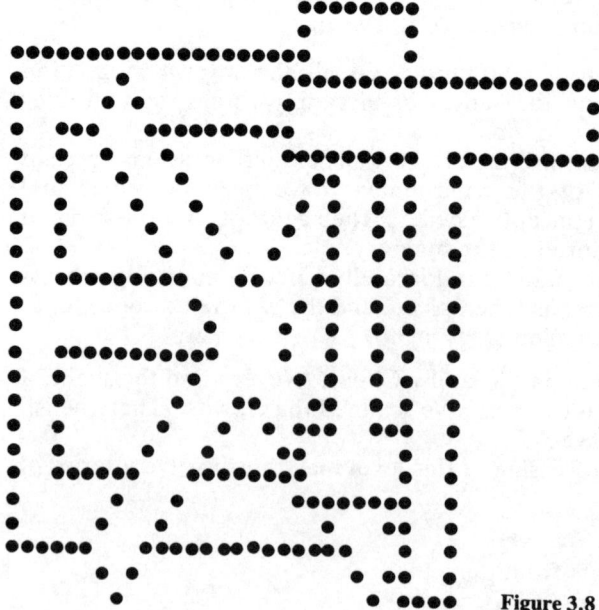

Figure 3.8 A pile of letters

(4) Recall from memory;
(5) Matching percepts against memory;
(6) Matching stored attributes against the environment.

That these activities occur is a valid deduction from the observed facts. The mechanisms involved are another matter—still imperfectly known, the subject of much scientific study. All we will do here is to indicate broadly some of the current views on human information processing and assess their relevance to information transfer in general.

Perception is not a simple photographic imprinting. It is generally agreed that it is an interactive process, with contributions coming both from the perceived environment and from the existing contents of the mind. What and how we perceive depends on what we already know. Sloman (1978) presents *Figure 3.8*, and suggests that most English readers will see it as a pile of letters—T upon I upon X upon E—making up the word EXIT. Yet note how many processes he says are involved in this:

(1) Discerning features in the sensory array (or discerning points of high contrast in the visual field);
(2) Deciding which features to group into significant larger units (for, example, which dots to group into line segments in the figure);
(3) Deciding which features to ignore because they are a result of noise or coincidences, or irrelevant to the present task;
(4) Deciding to separate contiguous fragments which do not really belong together (for example, adjacent dots which are parts of the boundaries of different letters);
(5) Making inferences which go beyond what is immediately given (for example, inferring that the edge of one bar continues behind another bar);
(6) Interpreting what is given, as a representation of something quite different (for example, interpreting a flat image as representing a scene in which objects are at different depths; the figure is a very simple example);
(7) Noticing and using inconsistencies in an interpretation so as to re-direct attention or re-interpret what is given;
(8) Recognizing cues which suggest that a particular mode of analysis is appropriate, or which suggest that a particular type of structure is present in the image or the scene depicted, i.e. detecting the *style* of a picture—this can enable an intelligent system to avoid a lot of wasteful searching for analyses and interpretations.

The activity of perception is analysed by Lindsay and Norman (1977) along the following lines. Innumerable stimuli from the environment continually reach the human organism. Clearly, only a proportion of these can be sensed, since we are receptive to only a limited range of radiations, sounds, and other stimuli. A further selection takes place; at any one moment of time we are directing attention to relatively few signals. The choice may arise from the mind's current purpose or motive, or because a signal is highly significant for action, or simply because it is very intense. The most active analysis work of the mind is directed towards the signals to which most attention is being paid.

The intertwining of all the processes involved in perception is already clear. It may be argued that a signal cannot be analysed until it has been selected for attention—yet it cannot be chosen for attention unless it has been at least partially analysed. We must envisage the mind as probing, exploring the environment, analysing, interpreting, changing the direction of attention, its activities continually modified by feedback.

The analysis process has been shown to be complex. The first stage appears to be analysis of the details of the signal. For example, it has been shown that shape recognition by the monkey depends upon analysis of an incoming visual signal by over fifty cells in the brain, each responding to the movement across the visual field of an edge at a particular orientation (see *Figure 3.9*). There are many other cells in the visual cortex of the

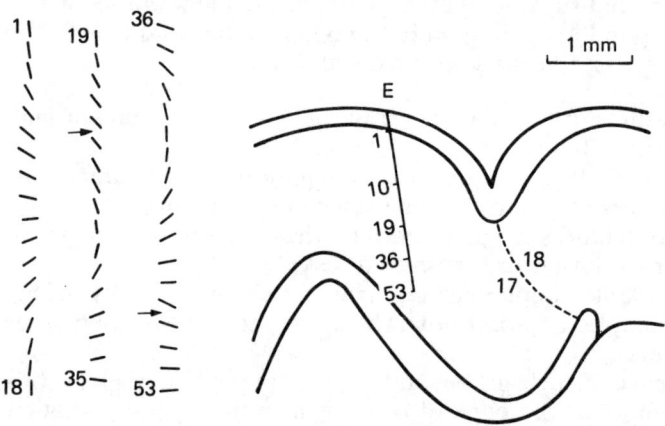

Figure 3.9 Visual responses to images. Experiment by Hubel and Wiesel to show the responses of cells of the visual cortex of the monkey. The animal is anaesthetized and an electrode (E) introduced through the surface of the cortex. It is connected to an amplifier and oscilloscope, which records the action potentials of the cells. Each cell responds only when a dark bar set at a particular angle is moved in the visual field of the opposite eye. The electrode was pushed through the cortex and cells 1–53 were encountered, giving responses to the orientations shown on the left

brain, each presumably tuned to detect a particular micro-feature. In ways not yet discovered their combined action provides information as to the image perceived.

Simplifying the reality of features analysis, Lindsay and Norman set up a hypothetical analysis system for distinguishing between letters of the roman alphabet. Let us assume that individual brain cells (or groups of cells) can respond to:

(1) Vertical lines;
(2) Horizontal lines;
(3) Oblique lines;
(4) Right angles;
(5) Acute angles;
(6) Discontinuous curves;
(7) Continuous curves,

and can count the number of occurrences of each feature. Each capital letter can then be coded by a unique set of features: for example, the letter K is 1 vertical, 2 oblique, 1 right angle, 2 acute angles. A received image is analysed for features. The result of analysis is matched against a memory store in which each set of features is linked in some way to its 'concept'—a particular letter.

The process of perception is more complex than this. A visual image has more characteristics than shape—it may be coloured, of varying tone and texture, with characteristic markings, of varying size etc. The 'feature analysis' activities brought into play will themselves be selected, again partly depending on purpose or on feedback from early trials at analysis. Perceptions immediately prior to the one currently analysed provide a context, and may localize the subset of the memory against which features are matched or stimulate speculative suggestions as to possible matches.

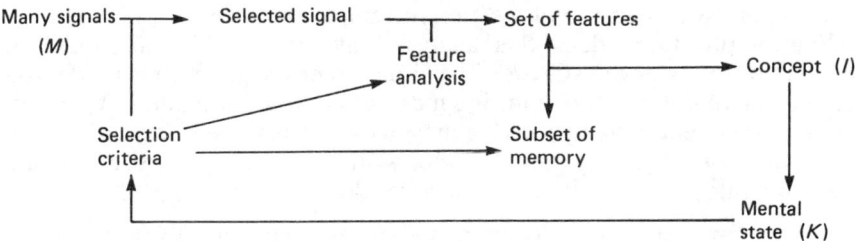

Figure 3.10 Human information processing

For example, if the two immediately preceding signals have been analysed as letters the mind is predisposed to perceive the next as a letter. (This can lead to perceptual error—for example, the next signal 8 may be perceived as B.) We have at least the interplay of processes as shown in *Figure 3.10*.

Using the symbolism employed earlier, the information (I) extracted from the message (M) to modify the mental state (K) is as dependent upon the initial state K as it is upon M. As Lindsay and Norman (1977) put it, human information processing is both 'data driven' (by M) and 'conceptually driven' (by K).

3.5 Conclusion

Figure 3.11 seems to sum up various aspects of information transfer as we have surveyed it in this chapter. A source emits a message $M(S)$. This is transmitted via a channel and during this process it may be modified to $M(R)$. This message reaches the recipient, and from it information I is assimilated. As a consequence, the state of the recipient is altered from $K(1)$ to $K(2)$.

Three feedback loops are shown. The short loop (a) from $K(1)$ implies that the information extracted from $M(R)$ is dependent upon the state K, so that I is not simply a function of $M(R)$. The upper loop (b) from $K(2)$ implies that as a result of information received the recipient may try to modify the relation between $M(S)$ and $M(R)$—for example, turn up the

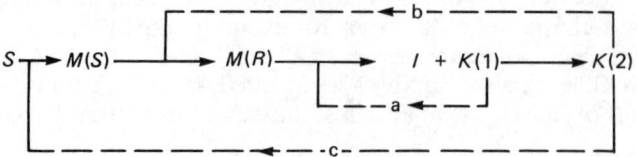

Figure 3.11 Model of information transfer

volume of a radio, ask the source to speak more clearly, get a translation made. The longest loop (c) from $K(2)$ implies that the recipient may try to modify the emitted message: human alteration of the automatic control of a central heating system is an example of this, since the intention is that the environment will then signal a different temperature.

What implications does this analysis have for our initial model of information transfer, S—C—R? The situation envisaged in this model is a human source deliberately emitting messages that are intended to inform, a human recipient actively seeking messages that may be informative, and a channel controlled by people who wish to bring some sources and recipients into contact. We may conclude that:

(1) The information actually extracted from a message by a particular recipient will be strongly dependent upon his current knowledge state and the kinds of change of knowledge state that are possible for him and desired by him.
(2) The extracted information may be only marginally related to what the source intended to convey in $M(S)$—either because the source information was not clearly expressed in $M(S)$, or because it was distorted by the channel and was not fully available in $M(R)$, or because of the focus of attention of the recipient.
(3) The relation between I emitted and received will be closer according as feedback loop (a) is open-minded, receptive, and loops (b) and (c) are active, This situation is clearly most likely to occur in informal face-to-face communication, less likely in other modes of information transfer.
(4) The model at the beginning of this chapter, linking people, documents, machines, and nature, further illustrates the meaning of 'channel' in the S—C—R model. Using the path labels on the earlier diagram, let us consider a situation in which a source writes a text (path B) that is printed (D); an abstract of it is prepared (C) and printed (D); this is read (B) by a recipient who relates it to the text (C) and reads the latter (B). Between S and R is a whole intervening series of written and printed documents, the printers, the abstractor, to say nothing of the distributors of printed text and abstracts, and perhaps the libraries in which they were consulted. All this collectively forms the channel between S and R. Within the channel, decisions have been made by people on what messages to print, what printed texts and printed abstracts to collect in what libraries. The influence of the channel on information transfer is very evident.

We have earlier stressed that communication is pervasive in social processes. The brief review in this chapter makes clear that in a wider sense information transfer is pervasive in nature. Matter, energy, and information are, in fact, the three basic features of our world.

Chapter 4

People and information

People communicate in every form of social interaction. The focus of our attention in this book is on those occasions on which information is transferred, but it is necessary to remember that many factors are at work in any social interaction. Social interaction is affected by factors relating to:

(1) The participating individuals;
(2) The occasion for the communication;
(3) The environment in which the interaction occurs; and
(4) The attitudes of the participants to each other, to the communication event, and to the environment.

As regards the participating individuals—whether recipient, source, or channel agent—their age, sex, educational level, occupation, status, etc. can all affect their interaction. Differences between the participants in any one of these characteristics can be relevant. The prevailing relations between them can affect interaction—are they strangers, casual acquaintances, regular colleagues? The occasion for the communication will influence information transfer. Is it idle interest, information urgently needed to complete a pressing task, another link in a slowly developing depth study, or an item to be remembered because it might later be useful? The environment can be an equally important factor: the encounter between recipient and source can be on the recipient's ground, or the source's, or on common ground; other people may be present, as at a meeting or conference; the physical conditions of communication may be good or bad; access to a channel agent may be simple and informal, or a struggle with bureaucracy. Finally, we come to attitudes—particularly those of the recipient. How does he/she regard the source or the channel agent? Do their characteristics affect him positively or negatively? Is the recipient at ease or not? Is he eagerly interested in the information sought, or is the search a necessary but distasteful chore? How does he react to the communication environment? Past experiences, motives, and moods affect the participant's behaviour relative to the other persons, to the requirement for information, and to the communication location.

In sum, communication activity—like any other behaviour—is the outcome of a complex interaction of factors. We may (following Sherif and Sherif, 1969) sum it up as follows:

44

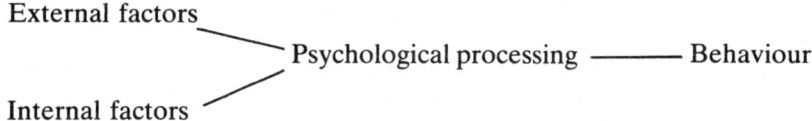

External factors include other people present and cultural products (documents, channels, the environment). Internal factors include states of knowledge, attitudes and opinions, motives and moods. In any act of communication, any or all of these factors interact in psychological processing to give a resultant behaviour.

4.1 Selectivity of attention and exposure

Faced as we are with an immense variety of informative messages, internal and external factors determine which we will attend to, and indeed what information we will extract from a message. The following report by Dearborn and Simon (1958) is a good illustration of selective cognition.

A group of twenty-three executives, enrolled in an executive training programme, were the subjects of the study. The departmental affiliations of the executives were as follows: sales (six); production (five); accounting (four); miscellaneous (eight). The executives were asked to read a standard textbook case, the 'Castengo Steel Company', which gives a great deal of factual detail about the organization and activities of the company. Before discussion of the case the executives were asked to indicate in a brief written statement 'what they considered to be the most important problem facing the Castengo Steel Company—the problem a new company president should deal with first'. The findings are given in *Table 4.1*.

Table 4.1 Analysis of a company's problems

Department affiliation	N	Number who gave as most important problem		
		Sales	*Clarify organization*	*Human relations*
Sales	6	5	1	0
Production	5	1	4	0
Accounting	4	3	0	0
Miscellaneous	8	1	3	3
Total	23	10	8	3

Note that five of the six sales executives (83 per cent) mentioned sales as the most important problem facing the company. In contrast, only five of the remaining seventeen executives (29 per cent) mentioned sales. Moreover, of the five non-sales executives who mentioned sales, three were in the accounting department in positions that involved the analysis of product profitability. Organization problems were mentioned by four of the five production executives (80 per cent) and by only four of the remaining eighteen executives (22 per cent). Only three executives mentioned human relations problems; these were executives in the public relations, industrial relations, and medical departments of their companies.

Industrial executives looking at exactly the same information selected for emphasis those aspects of a complex problem which related to the activities and goals of their particular departments. The selective organization of cognition shapes organization planning and policy. In more general terms, people are inclined to pay attention to communications that are congenial to them, that appear to have relevance to their personal goals and objectives, and that fit into their own particular knowledge structures.

Social groups develop different modes of life and outlook. Modern societies are made up of a bewildering variety of different 'social worlds', each with an organized outlook, built up by people in their interaction with one another. Common types of social world consist of associations of various kinds—the world of medicine, of organized labour, of the theatre, etc. These are held together not only by work cooperation and by voluntary association but also by sharing published communications (for example, magazines and newspapers). As Shibutani (1955) puts it, each social world is a culture area, the boundaries of which are set by the limits of effective communication. Within each area there develops a special language of discourse, a jargon or an argot. Common communication channels thus help to create such social worlds, and to reinforce them once created, so that the members of a group are selectively exposed to only a certain range of informative messages.

4.2 Linguistic characteristics of messages

The results of this multiplicity of social worlds, or linguistic subcultures, is that the messages from one group to another may not be readily understood. This is most obvious when two different natural languages are concerned, and the 'foreign-language barrier' is a very real one in information transfer. However, even within one language community there are barriers to comprehension. People vary in regard to the size, range, and richness of their vocabularies, the simplicity or complexity of their grammar, and the formality of their speech or writing. The texts they produce therefore differ in readability, and a number of measures of this quality have been developed and used to assess different types of document.

Most readability measures are based on the frequency in a text of long words and long sentences. For example, Williams (1976) describes the Fry readability graph: in this, a count of the average numbers of syllables and of sentences per hundred words of text is converted into a grade expressing difficulty of comprehension, and this in turn is related to the 'reading age' of the text. Some typical printed materials likely to be encountered by adults have the Fry grades shown in *Table 4.2*. The average hire-purchase agreement needs a reading age so high that it lies outside the Fry graph. The Flesch readability test also uses counts of words and sentence length but combines them into a different formula. On this test, the reading ages

Table 4.2 Fry grades

Grade	Reading age	Text
8	13–14	Highway Code
9	14–15	Instructions on pastry mix
10	15–16	Income tax form
11	16–17	Instructions on action if splashed by bleach
12	17–18	Trades union application form
12	17–18	Supplementary benefit form

Table 4.3 Reading ages given by the Flesch test

Reading age	Text
12	Green Cross Code
13	'Your rights when buying goods'
14	International money order leaflet
16	Bus timetable
19	Premium bonds application
22	Save as You Earn form
24	Bank of England notice to travellers

of some other materials are given in an Open University course book by Hoffman and Williams (1977) (*Table 4.3*).

These reading ages may at first sight not seem too high, but when we remember that 'functional literacy' is defined as a reading age of 9 years it is clear that the materials might fail to convey information clearly to all potential recipients.

Quite apart from long words, long sentences, and a formal style, texts present barriers to comprehension arising from specialist vocabularies. Many of the texts whose readability has just been considered are from 'official' sources. Within bureaucratic organizations, specialized activities give rise to specialized vocabularies. Gowers and Fraser (1973) quote the following (imaginary but realistic) example from an internal memorandum: 'These are all time-expired clause 4 optants and delay in referral would distort the quarterly submission-ratio.' The cited authors comment:

> This passage is, in the strict sense of the word, jargon. But it is entirely justifiable, ugly though it is, because it is doing efficiently what it sets out to do. Both writer and reader know precisely what a time-expired clause 4 optant is, and what special meanings attach to referral and submission-ratio. . . To put the passage in a form intelligible to the uninitiated would probably take at least five times the space and render it, if anything, less clear to the initiated—to whom alone it is addressed . . . The danger for the official, or for anyone else who habitually uses private language of this kind for internal communication, is that he may slip into using it for external communication too,

and thus become wholly or partly incomprehensible.

Writing generally about special languages Hertzler (1965) comments:

> Every work group of a trade, craft, calling or profession; every art, science, technology, business, industry, sport or game, hobby, or

religious group; every ideological group or cult of whatsoever kind; every school of thought, and standardized organization activity—all these have their special terminology. This consists of names and other descriptive and definitional words, of idiomatic phrases, and other symbols for the objects, conditions, facts, interests, values, ideas, principles, processes and techniques, relations, combinations, purposes, pursuits, products and other technicalities and specialties with which the group personnel is concerned. Unequivocal names are given to objects and to events that ordinary language does not always describe adequately; sometimes ordinary words are specially used or are employed with a special meaning; sometimes special terms are borrowed from other languages or are invented.

When a specialist communicates to another in his own speciality the use of special language is an aid to comprehension. As soon as his information is needed by a recipient outside the speciality, difficulties ensue. Even if a specialist attempts to write for those who are laymen with respect to his subject, he may not be able to make himself fully intelligible. The ready flow of scientific information into technology, of biological and chemical information into medical practice, or of behavioural information into social welfare is often hindered by the 'jargon barrier'.

4.3 Media of communication

In conveying information the most common form of communication is natural language, though this can always be supplemented by pictorial illustrations, sound recordings, or actual objects (samples, specimens, working models, etc.). In some cases these supplementary means are more important than any accompanying verbal description. Leaving aside such objects and also recordings of non-verbal sounds (such as birdsong), we may classify media as in *Table 4.4*.

Various combinations are possible; for example, from *Table 4.4*:

(A) and (C) Audio record plus slides; picturephone;
(B) and (C) Text with illustrations;

Table 4.4 Classification of media

Natural language		Pictorial image	
(A) Oral	(B) Textual	(C) Still	(D) Motion
Conversation	Letter	Drawing	Silent film
Lecture	Manuscript	Painting	Videotape
Audio record	Typescript	Photograph	
Telephone	Duplicated text	Print	
Radio broadcast	Printed text	Slide	
	Photocopy	Filmstrip	
	Microform text		
	Digital text		
	Computer printout		
	Teletype output		
	Television output		
	Facsimile		

(A) and (D) Sound film; television broadcast; audio/video record;
(A) and (B) and (C) and (D) Multimedia recording.

Duncan (1964) has set out a selection of media in hierarchical form (*Table 4.5*). As we go down the table, unit costs, difficulty of provision, and potential size of audience increase while ease of use and specificity decrease.

Table 4.5 Information media

Left axis (bottom to top): INCREASING PRIME COST—DIFFICULTY OF PROVISION—GENERALITY— POTENTIAL SIZE OF AUDIENCE

Right axis: INCREASE IN EASE OF USE—EASE OF PROVISION—SPECIFICITY—CHEAPNESS

Personal
Manuscript notes by lecturer or participant
Duplicated notes, bibliographies and references
Duplicated pictures

Complete or with deliberate gaps

Real group
Wall displays (including chalkboards)
Specimens (natural, i.e. real objects)
Working models, formalized models, enlarged models

Reproduction
Epidiascopes
Printed textbooks, workbooks
Programmed sheet and book texts

Audio tapes, local or general, disc recordings
Language laboratories (audio only)

Reproduction group
Still slides, filmstrips, overhead projection
Audiovisual tutorials, augmented language laboratories
Stereograms
'Moving' overhead projection systems

Reproduction group
Silent films, specially cassetted loops
Sound films with magnetic (changeable) sound
Sound films with optical (built-in) sound

Programmed texts in machine formats
Radio vision (broadcast sound plus in-house visuals)
Videotape-recordings (CCTV)
Audience-response systems
Live TV programmes (CCTV)
Computer-based instructional systems
Sound broadcasts
Television broadcasts

Schramm (in Pool *et al.*, 1973) has discussed differences among communication media from six points of view:

(1) The senses affected: face-to-face communication (whether conversation or lecture) gives the opportunity for all the senses to be stimulated, and for all media to be used—oral and textual language, pictures, sounds, objects. Television and sound film reach eye and ear, radio only the ear, texts only the eye. Multimedia recordings are both audio and

video. The telephone currently reaches only the ear, but the picturephone is on the way.

(2) Opportunity for feedback: this is maximal in conversation, lessened as the face-to-face group grows larger. A telephone attenuates the amount of feedback, and with broadcasting or with recorded material feedback is minimal.

(3) The amount of recipient control: in face-to-face communication, the recipient can ask questions and help to steer the conversation or discussion. A person reading text or using recorded material can set his own pace. A listener to radio or a viewer of film or television has no such control.

(4) The type of message coding: the ratio between verbal and non-verbal communication varies considerably between the media. Text alone is wholly verbal—whereas oral language is supplemented by facial expression and gesture. Television and film can be mainly non-verbal. In printed media it is possible to abstract easily, in audiovisual media to illustrate concretely.

(5) Multiplicative power: the distribution of a message through space and time—by reproduction and transmission—clearly has a major effect on the number of potential recipients.

(6) The power of message preservation: face-to-face communication and broadcasting are themselves evanescent, and messages can only be preserved if recorded in some form. The printed media can preserve text and picture.

As Schramm concludes: 'The importance of libraries, archives and encyclopedias testifies to the significance of this function today. Now that the glut of information is so great, new retrieval systems are needed to supplement the storage of information. Now that the audiovisual media are so important in our lives, new storage and retrieval mechanisms are needed for them also.'

We may call the kind of media used to convey any particular information the 'mode of presentation'. We may hypothesize that the reaction of a particular recipient to a particular presentation, and the degree to which the information is assimilated, will be affected by characteristics of the subject matter:

(1) Its perceived complexity and novelty;
(2) Its position on an abstract/concrete continuum;
(3) Whether it is of personal interest to the recipient or only of general interest and by characteristics of the recipient;
(4) Whether he handles words easily or is more at home with objects or with pictures;
(5) Whether he reads easily, with difficulty, or not at all;
(6) His need for interaction and feedback to amplify understanding;
(7) The pace at which he assimilates information;
(8) The urgency of his need for information,

to say nothing of the quality of the presentation itself. There is evidence that if subject matter is perceived by the potential recipient as complex, novel, or abstract, or if the need for it is urgent, he is more likely to seek an interactive mode of communication such as face-to-face contact with the man who knows (Wolek, 1970; Rogers and Shoemaker, 1971; Gralewska-Vickery, 1976).

4.4 Linking sources and recipients

We have distinguished between the ultimate source of an informative message and any intermediary agent through which it may reach a recipient, but in the act of information transfer this distinction is often not clearly evident to the recipient.

The extent to which a recipient will pay attention to, assimilate information from, and give credence to a message that comes his way depends in part on his reaction to its immediate or ultimate source. As McQuail (1975) puts it:

> One factor is the expertise of the source, as perceived by the receiver, and this may be mixed with judgements about the status and authoritativeness of the source ... Another fact is the believed objectivity and reliability of the source... Finally, there are the factors of source likeability and similarity to the recipient.

The transfer of information is most likely to successfully occur between a source (or intermediary) and a recipient who are alike or similar. This quality of likeness is called 'homophily' by Rogers and Shoemaker (1971), the opposite being heterophily. Homophily is the degree to which pairs of interacting individuals share beliefs, values, educational background, social status, etc. Two individuals from the same social group are clearly more likely to be homophilous and to communicate effectively.

Problems in information transfer arise if the immediate or ultimate source and the recipient are heterophilous. The source can, for example, be much more knowledgeable in a subject than the recipient, and this may be correlated with differences in educational background and social status, and —as we have seen—with the use of special language. All this may lead to ineffective communication. Recipients often seek sources that are slightly more technically competent in the relevant subject than themselves, but not too much so, in order to minimize the heterophily.

Anyone can, from time to time, act as an intermediary between an ultimate source of information and a recipient. Havelock et al. (1969) identify a whole series of situations in which different groups of people are acting as intermediaries, 'knowledge linkers' or 'relays', such as the following:

(1) Transferring knowledge from those who produce it to those who use it—for, example, teachers, trainers, demonstrators, science reporters, agricultural extension workers, systems engineers.
(2) Assisting users to identify problems and soures, linking them to appropiate sources—for example, change agents, consultants.
(3) Effecting linkage by influence and example—for example, opinion leaders, 'gatekeepers'.
(4) Aiding users to see how knowledge may be applied—for example,

applied research and development workers, clinical researchers, engineers.

Let us concentrate our attention on occupations whose central function is to be a relay or linker, an intermediary between source and recipient. Some of those mentioned by Havelock can be seen in this light, such as change agents, consultants, teachers, reporters. Alfred Smith (1980) has particularly singled out journalists, translators, teachers, and librarians as intermediaries or 'relay men'. He sees them as potentially able to store, stretch, and control information as well as to link, in ways that are indicated below.

Linking source and recipient is not a simple function. The linker often has to make an adjustment between the two—perhaps modifying the source message to make it comprehensible and acceptable to the recipient. Where the intermediary is essential (that is, when S and R cannot make direct contact) he can either make the link or avoid doing so—he is in a position to exercise some control over communication. The intermediary stores messages, and by this means links sources and recipients separated not only in space but also in time. Besides linking and storing, 'relay men' also 'stretch' communications. In adapting a source message to the supposed needs of a recipient they may misinterpret and distort it. The intermediary often has to analyse meanings, to reveal meanings we had not been aware of, and thereby he changes meanings so that he can relay them.

As a linker he values flexibility and adjustment between an ever-changing array of sources and recipients, but his other activity, storing, Smith sees as 'the most precious conservative agent in society', making the intermediary value the *status quo*. In acquiring, processing, and delivering information the intermediary often has too much to do, and Havelock identifies some of his specific overload problems as in *Table 4.6*.

Both Smith and Havelock stress the 'marginality' of the intermediary. He cannot be assimilated by either of the linked sides—he has to remain a man in the middle. He may not be closely homophilous with either source or recipient, and may thus not communicate easily with either. To compensate for this feeling of marginality—which may be sensed as

Table 4.6 Specific overload problems

Quantity	Complexity	Difficulty
Information has to be assembled from too many sources	Sources are highly technical, requiring high degrees of scientific competence	Information is inaccessible
Too many pieces of information need to be assembled	Information has to be taken from a highly technical form to a highly simplified and packaged form	The forms into which the knowledge must be assembled require a great expenditure of effort (e.g. construction of a complete training course)
Information has to be distributed to too many people	Information which is complex and difficult to understand must be communicated to the user	Users are very hard to reach and to influence

inferiority—the intermediary may overemphasize the element of control in his function.

4.5 Groups and organizations

As we have already noted in commenting on 'social worlds' and specialist jargons, society is highly structured. Work and personal interests separate us into a multitude of groups, associations, organizations, and communities. Much information transfer takes place within such structured contexts. In this section we will look particularly at communication within primary groups and organizations, and will deal later with information flow within wider communities.

A primary group may be defined in communication terms as 'a number of persons who communicate with each other often enough over a span of time and who are few enough so that each person is able to communicate with all the others, not at secondhand through other people but face to face' (Homans, 1951). Information transfer is particularly relevant for those groups that have a collective task to perform, and such 'work groups' are usually components in a wider organization.

Within a group, some individuals communicate more than others. In an experimental study of a group of six people, Bales et al. (1951) found the pattern of communication shown in *Table 4.7*.

Table 4.7 Communication within a group

Person originating act	To individuals						Total to individuals	To group as a whole	Total initiated
	1	*2*	*3*	*4*	*5*	*6*			
1		1238	961	545	445	317	3506	5661	9167
2	1748		443	310	175	102	2278	1211	3989
3	1371	415		305	125	69	2285	742	3027
4	952	310	282		83	49	1676	676	2352
5	662	224	144	83		28	1141	443	1584
6	470	126	114	65	44		819	373	1192
Total received	5203	2313	1944	1308	872	565	12205	9106	21311

It can be seen that person number 1 both originates and receives the most communications and number 6 the least. Within almost every row and column of the table the same ranking 1–6 prevails.

Interaction within some larger and real-life working groups has been explored by Allen *et al.* (1970), by questioning the members of the group about their technical information contacts. For example, 'who contacts whom' among the 77 members of an engineering R&D laboratory is shown in *Figure 4.1*. There are persons whom many others contact (e.g. number 59); others who both receive and initiate contacts (e.g. number 32); some who are consulted by only one other person (e.g. numbers 47, 9, 12, 70, 3, and 16); some with whom no-one initiates contact (e.g. numbers 20 and 31); and two or three subgroups (at the corners) who are tenuously or not at all interacting with the rest of the laboratory.

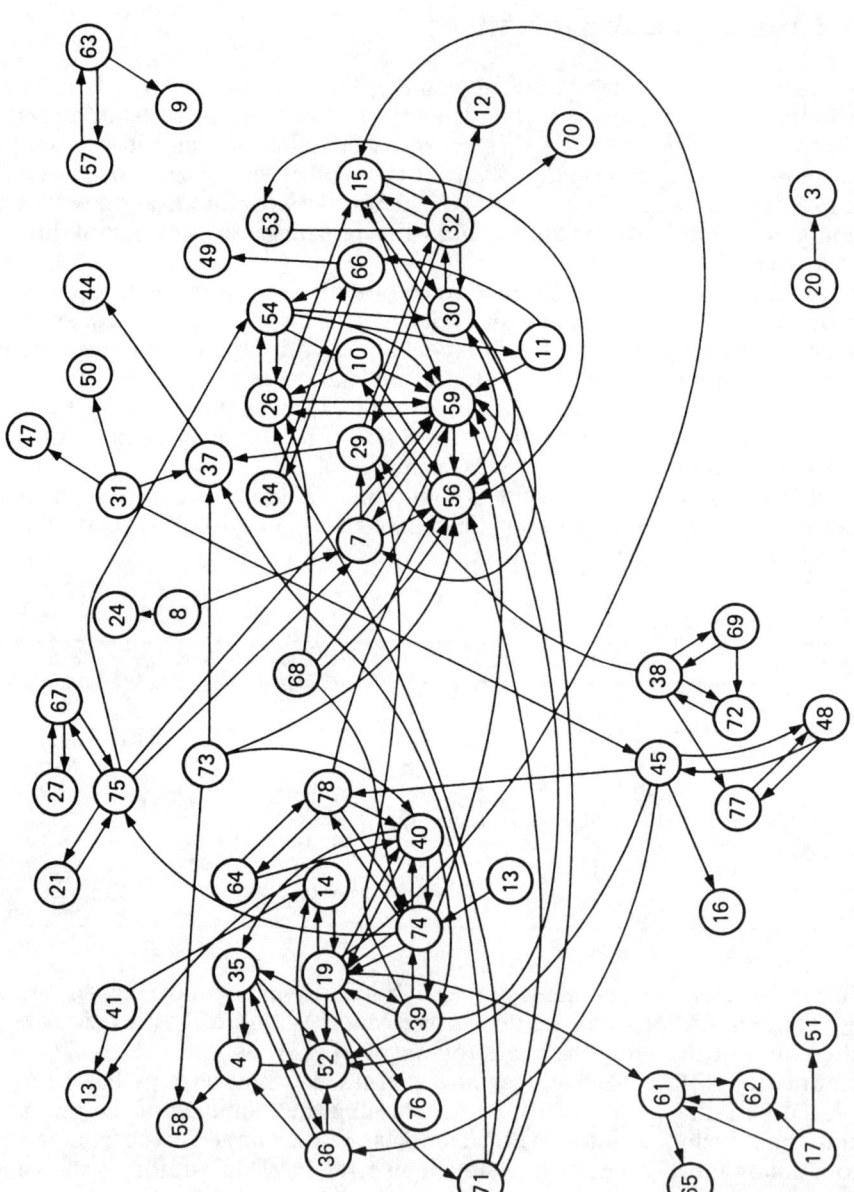

Figure 4.1 Communication network in research department

This engineering laboratory was one of eight departments in an R&D organization with a total staff of four hundred. Overall, within each departmental laboratory four groups of people were found:

(1) 'Gatekeepers', who were much consulted by others ('communication stars') and who also had many links with information sources outside the organization ('cosmopolites'). This group overlapped to a small extent with

(2) 'Liaisons', who were often consulted by others, and who had links with other departmental laboratories.*

(3) The bulk of the research engineers.

(4) 'Isolates', with whom no-one initiated contact.

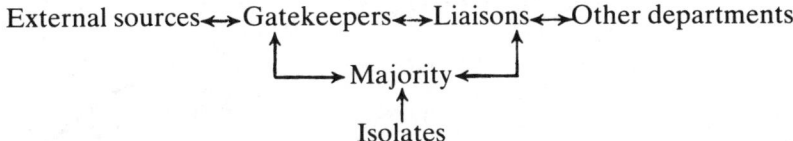

The information communication pattern within a work group may therefore be complex. In this example it bore little relation to the formal organization structure, which was basically of the normal hierarchical kind. In other situations the two structures may overlap more, and in general tend to complement each other. One reason for their distinctness is that they may be serving different functions. Within an organization the formal structure of departments and sections, with communications down and up the line, tends to be mainly concerned with operational and administrative information: job instructions and background data related to the job, guidance on procedures and practices, reports on work done and problems encountered, etc. Information needed for problem solving and decision making need not necessarily be best sought from line-of-command superiors or subordinates—it may be available elsewhere within or outside the organization. In a basically problem-solving situation such as an R&D laboratory many informal communication channels will develop as individuals seek out others who can aid their work.

Communication channels in organizations are in part deliberately planned (specialized communication units may be set up—internal telephones, teletype unit, record keeping, market intelligence, libraries and archives, etc.). In part, however, they develop through usage. The more effective they prove to be, the more they are used. Conversely, usage tends to be self-reinforcing. In particular, formal hierarchical channels tend to become general purpose, used whenever no special-purpose or informal channel exists or is known to the communicator. The existing pattern of communication will determine the relative frequency with which

---

*Care must be taken in comparing the work of investigators who refer to 'gatekeepers' and 'liaisons', for their usages differ. The 'liaison persons' of Farace and Danowski (1973) seem to have characteristics closer to Allen's gatekeepers. In Rogers and Rogers (1976), it is not their 'gatekeepers' but their 'cosmopolites' who appear to be closer to Allen's gatekeepers. All these roles and others have been classed together by McClure (1978) as 'the information-rich employee' in a useful review article.

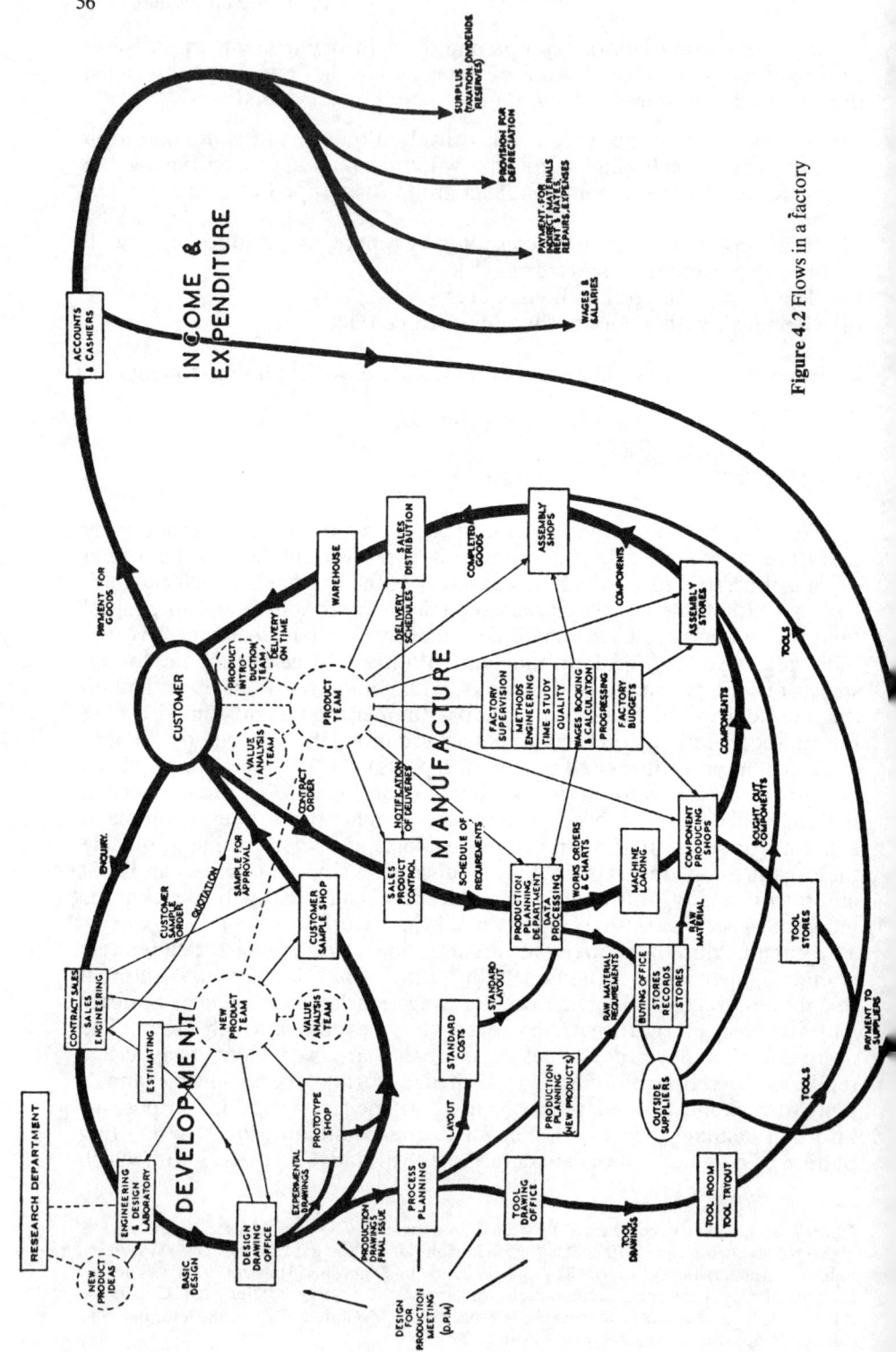

Figure 4.2 Flows in a factory

particular members of the organization make contact with each other, and hence affects the range of information to which each is exposed. The division of labour within an organization inevitably fosters separateness, with each unit developing its own 'subculture', and this can impede information transfer between units. Some idea of the complexity of information transfer in a large manufacturing organization—and of the potential barriers that division of labour may erect—can be gained by contemplating *Figure 4.2*.

4.6 Diffusion within a community

Within a community—whether people at large or those with a special shared interest—information or news diffuses through two types of channel: word of mouth and formal media. The media of particular relevance are broadcasting (radio and television) and printed publications of all kinds, including newspapers. Several studies have explored how news events with a wide impact have diffused. For example, D. C. Miller (1945) surveyed how news of Roosevelt's death was learnt among students at an American university: within half an hour of its radio announcement, 90 per cent had learnt the news. Only a minority heard the radio—85 per cent learnt by word of mouth. Each radio listener on average told seven other people. However, a later study by Deutschmann and Danielson (1960) of the spread of major news items within various US cities found that between 77 per cent and 98 per cent of the respondents learnt through television, radio, and newspapers. Within a Californian town, news of Kennedy's assassination was known to 90 per cent of the community within one hour of its broadcast and to 99.8 per cent within five hours: about half learnt via radio or television, the rest by word of mouth (Greenberg, 1964)

'News' in general, as relayed by the mass media, consists of a series of unrelated items, often transient and ephemeral. As Park (1967) has put it, 'even the most trivial happening, it seems, provided it represents a departure from the customary ritual and routine of everyday life, is likely to be reported'. The news that is relayed is inevitably enormously selective. Cutlip (1954) provides *Figure 4.3*, which shows that of all the news items flowing into an international press agency (AP), only about 2 per cent is read by the average reader. At each step along the way, selection and 'gatekeeping' is in operation. Even before news reaches AP there has been an equivalent amount of selection: the person who 'saw it happen' will report selectively; the journalist who interviews him will decide what will be worked up into a news story, and how; his editor decides whether to send the story to a wire service; this service selects what it will pass on to AP. Overall, perhaps one 'news event' in 2500 reaches the reader. It is evident that the many 'gatekeepers' involved are collectively exercising great influence on the flow of information.

We may turn now to the diffusion of information within a specialized community. One aspect of this that has been extensively explored is the spread of innovative ideas and practices—for example, new farming methods. The adoption of an innovation takes place over time—indeed, it is possible in retrospect to recognize within a community a small group of

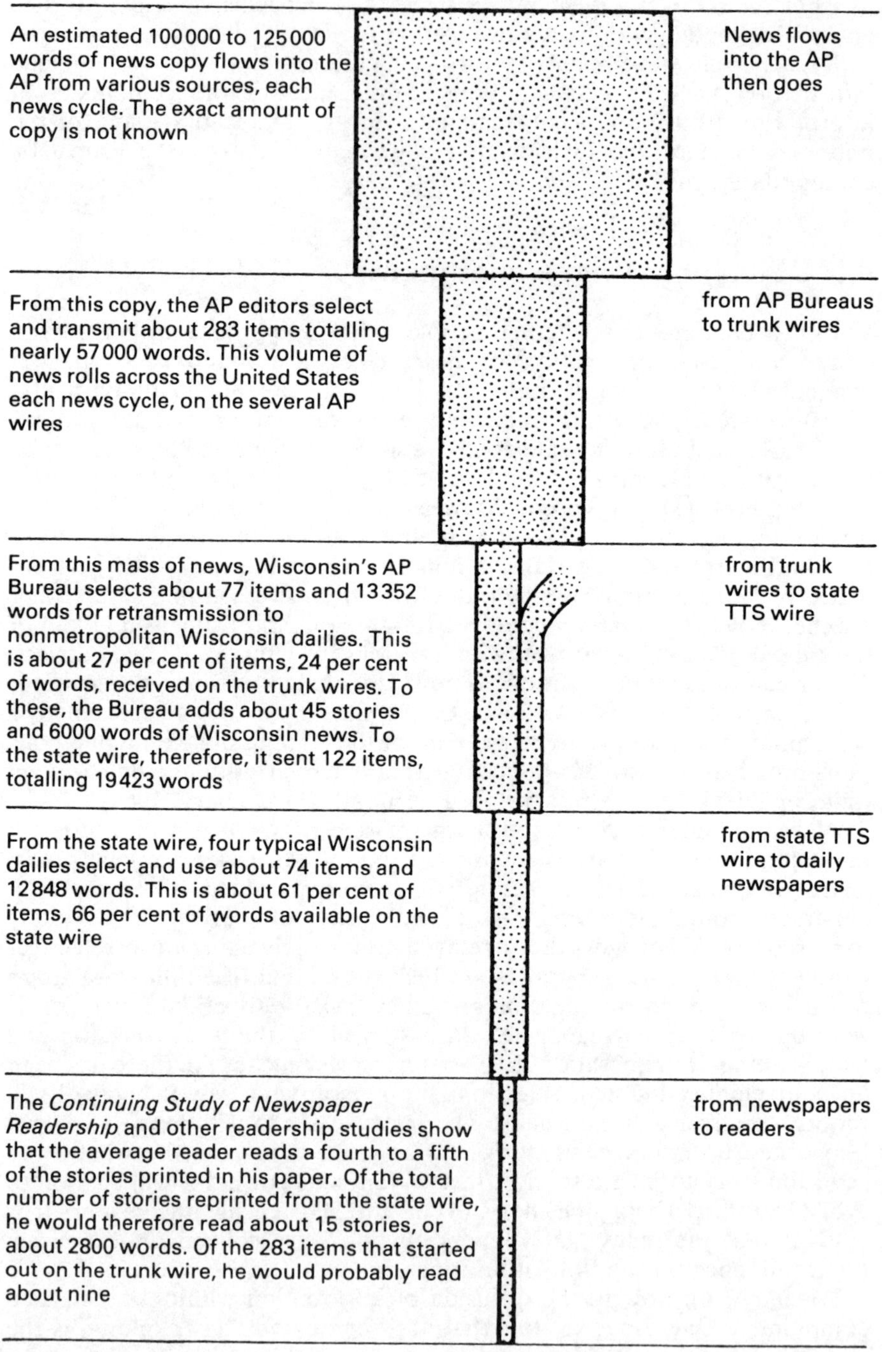

58

An estimated 100000 to 125000 words of news copy flows into the AP from various sources, each news cycle. The exact amount of copy is not known

News flows into the AP then goes

From this copy, the AP editors select and transmit about 283 items totalling nearly 57000 words. This volume of news rolls across the United States each news cycle, on the several AP wires

from AP Bureaus to trunk wires

From this mass of news, Wisconsin's AP Bureau selects about 77 items and 13352 words for retransmission to nonmetropolitan Wisconsin dailies. This is about 27 per cent of items, 24 per cent of words, received on the trunk wires. To these, the Bureau adds about 45 stories and 6000 words of Wisconsin news. To the state wire, therefore, it sent 122 items, totalling 19423 words

from trunk wires to state TTS wire

From the state wire, four typical Wisconsin dailies select and use about 74 items and 12848 words. This is about 61 per cent of items, 66 per cent of words available on the state wire

from state TTS wire to daily newspapers

The *Continuing Study of Newspaper Readership* and other readership studies show that the average reader reads a fourth to a fifth of the stories printed in his paper. Of the total number of stories reprinted from the state wire, he would therefore read about 15 stories, or about 2800 words. Of the 283 items that started out on the trunk wire, he would probably read about nine

from newspapers to readers

Figure 4.3 Flow of news

'innovators' who make the running, a larger group of 'early adopters', then the bulk of the community, followed by a group of 'laggards' or even 'non-adopters' (Rogers and Shoemaker, 1971). The process of adoption by an individual goes through four phases:

(1) Knowledge—the person learns of the new idea or practice;
(2) Persuasion—he forms a favourable (or unfavourable) attitude towards it;
(3) Decision—he carries out activities leading to a choice to adopt or reject (for example, he may try out the innovation); and
(4) Confirmation of the rightness of his choice.

At the knowledge or awareness stage, formal media are of at least equal importance to word-of-mouth information transfer, particularly for 'innovators' and 'early adopters', though interpersonal advice and discussion becomes dominant at the persuasion and decision stages. Early adopters tend to be younger, better educated, more exposed both to formal media and to personal contacts, and more active in information search than the average.

An interesting case study of the adoption of an innovation was carried out by Coleman et al. (1966). They examined the adoption of a new drug among 216 physicians in US communities. More personal sources than printed were mentioned as the initial source of information about the drug. Within the communities studied, communication among the physicians hastened the diffusion of knowledge. The doctors could be divided into two groups—those who had many interpersonal links with other physicians and those who were relative 'isolates'. The first group had a faster rate of adoption, the pattern being consistent with a chain of interactions within the group. The isolates were slower to adopt, and their pattern was more consistent with each independently learning of the drug from the manufacturer's representative or literature.

Within a scientific research community again we find both formal media and interpersonal communication at work. As has already been seen, in a research organization there is much interaction, and gatekeepers link their colleagues to external sources of information. The formal communication system of science includes research papers in journals, monographs, and meetings of various kinds. Informal processes include preprints of articles, correspondence, and face-to-face interaction. As one example of the interplay between formal and informal processes we cite a study by Garvey and Gottfredson (1976) of about 1800 scientists. Each was queried concerning his knowledge of particular published journal papers that were known to be relevant to his work (about 3600 sample papers were used in all). Some 79 per cent of the scientists were aware of a relevant paper and 75 per cent had examined one, but only 21 per cent said they had acquired useful information from it. This was certainly due in part to the fact that 63 per cent knew of the relevant research before it had been published as a paper—through having met the author (40 per cent), through correspondence (13 per cent), by having received a preprint (20 per cent), and in other ways. At least half the scientists surveyed had acquired useful information by informal means approximately a year before the relevant papers were formally published. We will look at this study again later, and comment on its interpretation.

4.7 The study of people and information

In this chapter we have already illustrated our discussion with various examples of information study: the assimilation of information from messages, the characteristics of different media, communication patterns in groups, and information flow in a community. The variety of aspects from which people and information may be approached is already evident. In this section we wish to provide a more general analysis of this field of investigation.

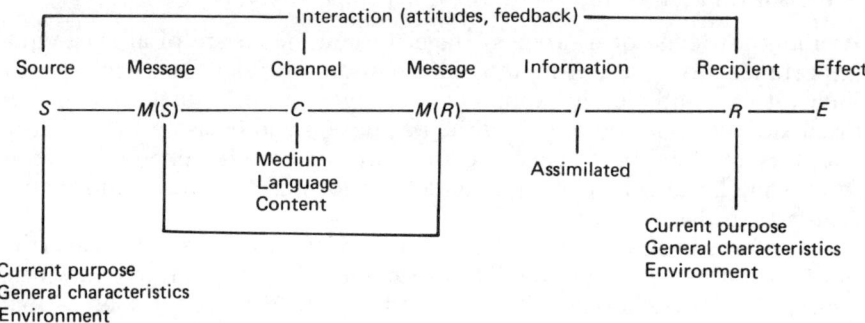

Figure 4.4 An act of informative communication

The act of informative communication can be analysed as in *Figure 4.4*. The source emits a message; it is transmitted via a channel that may modify the message; from this, the recipient extracts information. What the source and channel emit and the recipient assimilates depends upon their current purposes, general characteristics, and environments. Their attitudes towards and interaction with each other will also affect information transfer. The main characteristics of messages affecting communication are the content, the medium and the 'language', using this in the wide sense discussed earlier. Any behaviour of R as a result of receiving information is indicated here as an 'effect'.

All studies of people and information must start with individual acts of communication: specific instances of items of information sought, specific sources used, specific texts read, specific media used, specific attitudes expressed, specific contacts made in a research laboratory, specific drug promotion attended to. It is by aggregation of such specific data that 'information needs', 'information flows', etc. are concocted.

It is only possible to study the whole transaction in *Figure 4.4* if both source and recipient are accessible to the investigator (say, by his observing an interpersonal communication). More usually study is restricted to S-$M(S)$, or to $M(S)$-C-$M(R)$, or to $M(R)$-I-R, or to I-R-E. Even within these limits, further restrictions are often applied: the study is confined to a certain area of information content (say, medicine), or to a certain medium (say, printed publications), or to a certain purpose (say, information for decision making), or to a certain environment (say, research laboratories).

Having defined the scope of a study, analysis is possible at several levels. The focus of attention can be on the person: for example, if we study

$M(R)$-I-R, where $M(R)$ = publications, I = economic data, and R = industrial managers, we might ask 'through what publications is what economic data transmitted to managers? And how is this affected by the varied purposes, characteristics, and environments of managers?' By aggregation we may arrive at 'typical' economic information publications for an industrial manager, or a distribution of publications according to managerial attributes, or even some tentative generalizations relating (say) type of publication to managerial status.

We can, however, analyse at higher levels. For example, all the informative communications received or emitted by people within each individual department of an organization can be brought together to build up pictures of (1) internal communication within departments and (2) communication between departments. The unit of analysis here is the work group, not the person. We can similarly go one level higher, using the organization as the unit of analysis. Still higher, attempts are made to generalize about the transfer of information in a whole field of activity, as from 'science' to 'technology'.

There are two other dimensions that need to be considered. The first concerns the general approach of the investigator, which may be 'analytical' or 'synthetic'. The second relates to the time frame of the study—is it a 'still' picture at one point in time or does it aim to show development over time? Both aspects have a decisive influence on the conduct of an investigation.

The 'analytical' approach is that which is typical of the natural sciences. The investigator seeks to formulate and test a limited number of hypotheses, and for this purpose aims to collect specific data that will have a bearing on these hypotheses, if possible excluding, controlling, or otherwise allowing for any other variables that may disturb the situation. As an example of this, in one study Wolek (1970) tested the single hypothesis that the perceived complexity of information sought will influence the choice of medium by an engineer. In the information field, the structured survey and (less frequently) the controlled experiment are the methods used to provide data for 'analytical' investigations.

The 'synthetic' method is more akin to engineering than to natural science, and its typical forms are the case study and operational research. The investigator has before him a 'case', a social situation, an ongoing communication activity, a slice of observed reality. He examines it from many points of view, if necessary using more than one unit of analysis, drawing on all sources of data to interpret the observed phenomena, and fits all this together to form an intelligible synthesis. It is this kind of 'system study' that often precedes recommendations for action to improve communication facilities. Though not necessarily establishing firm generalizations, such case studies can provide rich material for further research.

4.8 Variables, categories, and data

Concentrating on the recipient end of the communication transaction, we can draw together some of the variables mentioned in this and earlier chapters, and relate them as in *Figure 4.5*.

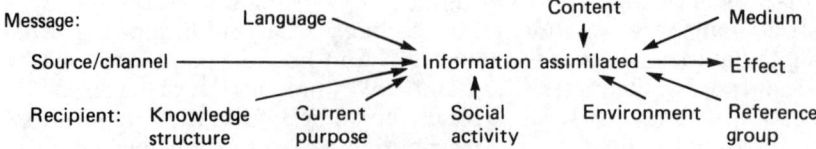

Figure 4.5 Variables in informative communication

The assimilation of information is influenced by characterististics of the message, of the source/channel, and of the recipient. The ultimate dependent variable is the effect on the recipient: to achieve some effect, even if only in the knowledge structure and not expressed in any subsequent behaviour, is, after all, the reason why R, S, and C are participating in the communication act. The immediately proximate dependent variable is the information assimilated.

To carry out a study of informative communication data are needed about some or all of these variables as related to a series of communication acts. As regards messages and channels, two types of data are needed: objective or, at any rate, consistent assessments of their characteristics and the subjective reactions of recipients to them. If the investigator can examine an adequate sample of messages and channels, he can assemble objective data. The subjective effects can only be assessed by asking or perhaps observing the recipient reacting to the messages and channels. If the investigator has only the recipient's description of messages and channels it is not possible to disentangle the objective and subjective aspects. For assessing the information extracted from a message, the investigator is wholly dependent on a statement by the recipient, unless a particular message content can be unambiguously related to an observed effect (this rarely occurs).

Data on the characteristics of the recipient (and of the source, if also studied) are much more difficult to acquire. A statement of social activity and current purpose can be obtained from the recipient, but an adequate picture of his environment can only be obtained if it can be explored. To reveal his reference groups and knowledge structure could require an in-depth study. As a result, very few investigations of people and information have been able to take into account the range of variables suggested above.

Many of these investigations have been undertaken to obtain data that might improve the performance of information channels, and so we have had library-use studies, publication-readership surveys, audience research, etc. For each variable examined, categories have been employed that spring fairly directly from the practical activities of the channel. To comment critically on these we will draw examples from a survey of metals information by Vickery *et al.* (1969).

Respondents to the survey were asked to indicate one of the following as an answer to the question. How did they find a certain item of information?

(A) By contacting a person expected to have the information;
(B) From a talk at a meeting, conference, etc.;

(C) In casual conversation;
(D) From radio, television, or film;
(E) From a publication currently scanned;
(F) By searching in documents expected to contain the information.

This list is partly drawn up according to media (oral, textual, broadcast), and partly by the occasion of the communication (person deliberately contacted or casual conversation, publication deliberately searched or currently scanned). If the respondent answered (A), (B), or (C) he was asked to specify the personal source as follows:

(1) Colleague in own establishment;
(2) Information officer/librarian in own establishment;
(3) The same in another establishment;
(4) Sales representative of another organization;
(5) Someone else in another establishment.

This is a very crude categorization of people with whom a scientist or engineer might be in contact and its use in analysis could not be expected to yield very illuminating insights into the mechanism of information transfer. If the respondent answered (E) or (F) in the first list above, he was asked to specify the type of publication from a categorization that included:

(1) Textbook, monograph;
(2) Handbook, manual, book of tables;
(3) Standard, specification, code;
(4) Scientific periodical;
(6) Newspaper;
(7) Report.

This listing by bibliographic form is perhaps typical of the approach that a librarian or publisher might adopt to channels, but it offers little scope for generalization. Earlier in this chapter we cited the categorization of media by Schramm (1964) according to senses affected, opportunity for feedback, recipient control, message coding, etc. In a similar way we need to categorize the typical messages in different publication channels, for example, their positions on such continua as theoretical/practical, introductory/advanced, general/detailed, discursive/structured. Little work has been done to test the value of such scalar characteristics.

Work-activity data in the metals survey were collected by asking the respondent to indicate on which occupation he was 'primarily engaged'. The list offered included:

(1) General management;
(2) Technical management;
(3) Research and development;
(4) Planning, O&M;
(5) Production;
(6) Technical sales;
(7) Teaching, education;
(8) Design, draughting.

Quite apart from the problem of whether these categories were consistently understood and assigned by respondents, it is far from easy to see how they could lead to generalizable results. Once again, there is a need to develop scalar categories of occupation that are relevant to differences in information transfer behaviour. A possibility to explore might be the extent to which the occupation is concerned with products, designs, concepts, or decisions.

4.9 Analysis of variables

Let us suppose that in a study of informative communication a series of records is collected (for example, questionnaire responses), each of which includes one or more values for a number of variables. For example, a category of recipient ($V1$, value a), his current purpose ($V2$, value d), message content ($V3$, value g), medium ($V4$, value k), etc.

Analysis can first look at a single variable, such as recipient, and examine the variety of categories. For example, visitors during a certain week at 33 public reference libraries in Britain were recorded by Clements (1967) as in *Table 4.8.*

Table 4.8 Use of public reference libraries

	Number	%
Industrial employment	2778	10.7
Commercial employment	2130	8.2
Staff of university or college	1392	5.4
Civil Service	742	2.8
Local government	1079	4.2
Research association, society	1114	4.3
Self-employed	820	3.2
Students	13680	52.6
Retired or unemployed	944	3.6
Other occupation	795	3.0
Multiple entries, no answer	516	2.0

Table 4.9 Loan of periodicals

Rank	Title	Loans
1	*Proc. of Royal Society, A*	382
2	*Journal of Physical Chemistry*	250
3	*Science*	244
4	*Philosophical Magazine*	240
5=	*Proc. of Inst. of Electrical Engineers*	223
5=	*Transactions of Faraday Society*	223
7	*Product Engineering*	200
8	*Biochemical Engineering*	198
9	*Journal of Chemical Society*	188
10	*Journal of Inst. of Mechanical Engineers*	184
11	*Mechanical Engineering*	180
12	*Proc. of Physical Society*	177
13	*Naturwissenschaften*	175
14	*Journal of American Chemical Society*	173
15	*Electronics*	170
etc.		

The survey may be of such a kind that the same recipient, source, channel or even message occurs in a number of records—for example, the borrowings from a library during a certain period of various periodicals. The list of periodicals (channels) can be ranked in frequency of use (*Table 4.9*).

The average use per title may be estimated, expressed in various ways (mean, median, mode), and the dispersion around the mean. The use pattern recorded in the table may conform to a mathematical distribution. Such data give a feel for the variety and variation within each variable.

The next stage of analysis is to examine relationships between pairs of variables. The aim is to discover whether the variety within one is in any way associated with the variety of the other. The study of metals information by Vickery *et al.*, previously cited, provides *Table 4.10* as an

Table 4.10 Variation in method of obtaining information

Method of obtaining information	Institutional environment of recipient					Totals including 'other'
	(A) Private firm	(B) Nationalized industry	(C) Government establishment	(D) University	(E) Technical college	
Contacting person	331 (36)	72 (38)	25 (31)	30 (15)	14 (15)	497 (32)
Current scanning	191 (21)	40 (21)	7 (9)	30 (15)	17 (19)	299 (19)
Literature search	345 (37)	63 (34)	35 (47)	128 (62)	58 (64)	666 (42)
Totals including 'other'	920	187	74	205	91	1570

example (percentage figures in brackets). This table reports partial data on how recipients obtained specific items of information. For example, of the 920 recipients working in private firms, 331 (36 per cent) had received information by contacting someone likely to know, 21 per cent in the course of scanning current publications, and 37 per cent by a deliberate search of the literature. If we look at the bracketed percentages in any row, we see that in environments (A) and (B) the percentages contacting a person were appreciably higher than the overall average (32 per cent), and the percentages undertaking literature search were somewhat lower than the overall average (42 per cent). For environments (D) and (E), the reverse situation applies. The core pattern of *Table 4.10* can be brought out if we combine (A) + (B), also (D) + (E), and remove both (C) and 'current scanning' to give *Table 4.11*.

Table 4.11 Variation in environments

Method	Industrial (A)+(B)	Academic (D)+(E)	Subtotals
Contacting person	403 (49)	44 (19)	447 (43)
Literature search	408 (51)	186 (81)	594 (57)
Subtotals	811 (100)	230 (100)	1041 (100)

The information searches within industry were almost equally divided between personal contact and literature search, and in the academic environments literature searches were four times more common than personal contacts. The only other point that *Table 4.10* tells us is that current scanning accounted for 19 per cent of the recorded acts and made lower-than-average appearance among the government establishment recipients.

The association in the sample between environment and method of information search—particularly as presented in the core pattern—looks convincing. There are statistical ways of testing the 'significance' of an apparent association, and a test of this particular association indicates that it is most unlikely to be due simply to a chance fluctuation of the sample figures. Our preliminary conclusion is that the sample suggests that characteristics of the two environments have a differential effect on the preferred medium of communication. We are free to speculate as to what these characteristics may be.

A first possibility is that literature may be more accessible in the academic environment. About 20 per cent of all respondents claimed to be working in an institution without a library, but the survey report did not analyse the data according to type of institution. Common experience tells us that all academic institutions have libraries that would be known to respondents, so it is likely that some proportion of the industrial recipients (not more than 15 per cent) had no access to a local library. *Table 4.12* from the survey suggests that this may have some influence on the frequency of literature search.

Table 4.12 Effect of library on frequency of literature search

	With library (%)	No library (%)
Contacting person	31	34
Literature search	45	32

An alternative possibility could be that persons willing and able to provide information are more accessible in industry. An analysis of personal contacts is presented in *Table 4.13* according to whether they were categorized by respondents as 'colleagues' or in 'another establishment' (excluding contacts with librarians).

Table 4.13 Analysis of personal contacts

Person contacted	Industrial	Academic	Subtotals
Colleague	98 (33)	26 (50)	124 (35)
Another establishment	202 (67)	26 (50)	228 (65)
Subtotals	300 (100)	52 (100)	352 (100)

It was certainly not locally available colleagues who attracted the most personal approaches from industrial recipients, so there is no evidence that local accessibility of persons is a factor in choice of medium. Is it possible that the kinds of information required in the two environments were different, so that industrial respondents turned to personal contacts in

Table 4.14 Information sought and use of literature search

Information sought	Academic (%)	Literature (%)
Theory, concept, or mathematics	66	55
Metal constitution or property	28	67
Metal defect, corrosion, protection	19	56
Economics, costs, statistics	18	37
Production method or process	16	54
Testing, analysis, inspection, control	15	59
Metal use or application	12	51
Equipment	9	46

other establishments and academics searched the literature? The information sought was categorized, and in *Table 4.14* we present (1) the ratio of academic to industrial reports in each category and (2) the ratio of literature search to personal contact in each.

The first column of figures in this table shows that the ratio of academic to industrial interest varies markedly according to subject, but the second column does not suggest that the search medium is correlated with this.

There are other potential factors that could be influencing the medium used for information search—the current purpose of the recipient (for example, urgency of information need), his knowledge structure (is he seeking information within or outside his own field of specialization?), and his general attitude to different channels and sources. The metals survey does not provide data to explore these possibilities.

So far we have illustrated how analysis may proceed by examining association between pairs of variables. We may find that $V1$ (say, medium used) appears to be associated with $V2$ (say, institutional environment) and also with $V3$ (say, highest academic qualification). Are $V2$ and $V3$ independent? Might not the institutional association simply be a reflection of the fact that academics may be more highly qualified than industrials? To test this, we must analyse for the qualification association within different institutional environments. The data for this are not available in the metals survey report, so we will use another example, drawn from Lazarsfeld (1972).

A group of US farmers were characterized as having a high, medium, or low orientation towards work. Their farming practices were examined, and it appeared that highly work-oriented farmers were somewhat more likely than the others to use a two-row corn planter (*Table 4.15*: bracketed figures give percentages).

Table 4.15 Work orientation related to use of two- and four-row planters

Work orientation =	High	Medium	Low
Two-row planter	38 (57)	64 (49)	25 (47)
Four-row planter	29 (43)	65 (51)	28 (53)
Totals	67 (100)	129 (100)	53 (100)

An analysis by size of farm gave the results in *Table 4.16*. Here it appeared that the corn planter used was a function of farm size, with the two-row being most used by and known to be more suitable for the small

Table 4.16 Analysis by farm size

	Under 60 acres	60 acres or more
Two-row planter	83 (72)	44 (33)
Four-row planter	33 (28)	89 (67)
Totals	116 (100)	133 (100)

Table 4.17 Work orientation by farm size and use of planters

	Under 60 acres			60 acres or more		
	High	Medium	Low	High	Medium	Low
Two-row	23 (62)	39 (71)	21 (87)	15 (50)	25 (34)	4 (14)
Four-row	14 (38)	16 (29)	3 (13)	15 (50)	49 (66)	25 (86)
Totals	37 (100)	55 (100)	24 (100)	30 (100)	74 (100)	29 (100)

farm and the four-row for the large. Was the work-orientation association independent of this?

In *Table 4.17* we see that the highly work-oriented farmer on small farms was the *least* likely to use the two-row, and on large farms was the *most* likely to use it. In each case it was the farmers with low work orientation who most frequently used the planter appropriate to their farm size. Evidently, work addiction clouds the judgement.

4.10 The development of indicators and indexes

The initial data collected in studies of informative communication are often explicit and reasonably well defined: a named document, an institution, a personal source, etc. Classing a specific response into a category is sometimes a little ambiguous—like all classification. However, we have already suggested that in order to generalize beyond the particular situation investigated we may need to categorize variables in ways that are no longer explicit and well defined. For example, we referred to some message characteristics that could be useful in analysis: complexity, or position on such continua as abstract/concrete, theoretical/practical, introductory/advanced, general/detailed. We cannot get consistent categorizations of this kind by questioning sources or recipients—by asking, for example, 'How complex is this message?' Each respondent will have his own criterion of complexity.

We also could not ask, 'How readable is this text?' Instead, we have to devise an indicator or index of readability, and earlier in this chapter the Fry and Flesch readability measures have been noted. The essence of the approach is to choose characteristics that are objectively observable and are believed to express the quality that is of interest. The readability measures are based on two characteristics: word length and sentence length. Each of these variables we regard as an 'indicator' of readability. The formulae combine them into readability 'indexes'.

Another group of non-explicit categories already mentioned is that of 'communication roles' that may be ascribed to people: intermediary, relay or linker, gatekeeper, liaison, isolate, cosmopolite, and indeed source, channel agent, and recipient. A 'gatekeeper' in Allen's (1970) study was defined objectively as 'a person who was approached more than average by others in his laboratory for technical discussion, who read professional journals more than average, and who had more than average personal contacts outside the laboratory' (in each case 'more than average' was quantitatively defined). The concept 'gatekeeper' was thus expressed by an index formed by combination of three specific measured indicators.

Hagstrom (1965) developed a typology of scientists as communicators, and this may be seen as a series of categories for which objective indicators are needed:

(1) Scientific statesmen. Men with established reputations who have made contributions to their own field in the past and now communicate primarily with specialists in other fields and with non-scientists. Presumably they now have fewer informal contacts within their field than before.

(2) Highly involved leaders. Men who participate a great deal in all the communication channels within the field, both formal and informal. Much of their available time is occupied with travel, meetings, colloquia, professional duties, etc. So much time is given over to communication that they spend little time in research itself.

(3) Informal leaders. Men with many informal contacts but few formal ones. They visit, correspond, and discuss work within their departments, but they avoid the formal activities of scientific societies. These men tend not to read the literature in their fields.

(4) Student-oriented leaders. Men who have somewhat less contact with their colleagues but spend a disproportionate amount of time with their students. They often retain contact with former students. Sometimes they are regarded as leaders of 'schools', consisting of former and present students, which express their distinctive points of view.

(5) Student-oriented scientists. Less eminent men noted not for their own work but for the work of their students, who are their primary links with the scientific community.

(6) Intradepartmentally oriented scientists. Some men, lacking prestige necessary to approach scientists outside their own departments, rely on departmental colleagues both for communication and for collaboration. In effect they depend on others in the department for assistance in publishing research.

(7) Productive isolates. Usually men who are alone in a research speciality within their departments. They are isolated only in terms of informal discussion; they use formal sources extensively.

(8) Non-productive isolates. When specialization does not account for isolation it may just be that the scientist is turning from research to other interests, such as teaching.

(9) Marginal scientists. Men nominally engaged in research who communicate disproportionately with non-scientists. Unlike the 'scientific statesmen', who also communicate with non-scientists, men in this group do not have established reputations within their fields. They seem to be serving as consultants or popularizers of their specialties in order to obtain recognition not accorded them within their fields.

Lazarsfeld *et al.* (1955) wished to categorize social scientists in terms of 'eminence', and constructed two indexes, as follows:

Honours Index
(1) Has PhD;
(2) Has published three or more papers;
(3) Has held office in a professional society;
(4) Has worked as a consultant.

Productivity Index
(1) Has written a dissertation;
(2) Has published one or more papers;
(3) Has presented three or more papers at meetings;
(4) Has published a book.

Both indexes correlated well with academic advancement to full professorship.

We have already noted another type of implicit variable, work orientation in farmers. The brief report to which we referred did not spell out the way in which the index was constructed. There is, however, a full account of the way in which Rosenbloom and Wolek (1967) developed an index to the concept of 'professional orientation', and we will report this in detail.

4.11 Professional orientation and information channels

Their study collected data using self-completed questionnaires. These were sent to 2000 engineers and scientists in 13 establishments of four large US industrial corporations. The establishments were chosen arbitrarily but were intended to cover a variety of manufacturing areas. Within each establishment a questionnaire was distributed to all 'professionals engaged in research and development work, or their first-level superiors' (presumably from lists supplied by the establishment). Altogether 2900 questionnaires were distributed, with an overall response rate of 71 per cent (80 per cent if one low-response establishment was excluded).

The questionnaire had originally been designed for an earlier survey of 430 respondents, and at that stage had been pre-tested with a small sample and further tested in post-survey interviews. The revised version used in the survey now reported was also pre- and post-tested. A great deal of effort therefore went into ensuring that the questions would be understood.

The questionnaire was in three parts. The first started with the request 'Please think of the most recent instance in which an item of information, which you received from a source other than someone in your immediate circle of colleagues, proved to be useful in your work'. There then followed a dozen questions exploring this instance: whether a need for the information had been recognized before its receipt; if yes, the purpose for which it had been sought; if not, the occasion on which it came to the attention; the channel through which the *substance* of the information was first encountered; the nature of the immediate source (whether oral informant or author of document); if the information came via a *lead* rather than direct, the channel through which it was received; the specific subject field of the information; the class of work task for which it was useful; the task to which it was actually applied (defined by three questions); the primary manner in which the information had affected the respondent's work.

The second part of the questionnaire asked about the respondent and his environment: job title, age, length of current employment, profession, highest level of education attained, number of society meetings attended in the last year, number of periodicals regularly read, number of publications and patents in the last five years. The third part asked the respondent to agree or disagree (on a five-point scale) with a series of statements about professional work (for example, 'A competent specialist is so busy that it is unrealistic to expect him to set aside more than 5 per cent of his time for extending and developing his technical or scientific knowledge and skill'). He was also asked to indicate the occupations of three people who had influenced his work (an assessment of his 'reference groups') and the extent to which he regarded himself as a specialist relative to his work colleagues. The questionnaire was highly structured, almost every question providing a list of seven to ten categories (including 'other') of which one was to be chosen.

The communication incidents selected generally were recent (40 per cent within the last two days, 60 per cent within a week, 80 per cent within three weeks). After an interval of three weeks there was a noticeable bias towards recollection of formal literature as a source and away from local, oral, informal means—this has implications for the use of retrospective descriptions of incidents that are not very recent.

In presenting their basic results, Rosenbloom and Wolek combined the answers to a number of questions, in the following ways:

Question 20: Profession
(1) Programmer, electrical or mechanical or metallurgical or other engineer = Engineer;
(2) Chemist, mathematician, physicist, metallurgist, or other scientist = Scientist.
Questions 5 and 6: Channels and sources
(1) Conversation; telephone or meeting with person in own establishment = Interpersonal local;
(2) The same with person elsewhere in own corporation = Interpersonal corporate;
(3) The same with person outside the corporation—another company, university, government agency, etc. = Interpersonal external;
(4) Report of own corporation = Document corporate;
(5) Trade magazine, supplier catalogues, industrial reports outside the corporation = Document trade;
(6) Books, articles, conference papers = Document professional.
Question 4: Occasion of receiving information
(1) While searching specifically = Specific search;
(2) Someone told me, reviewing current literature = Pointed out;
(3) While brushing up, trying to learn a new field = General competence.

They then presented percentage tabulations (*Table 4.18*). These results

Table 4.18 Channels used by scientists and engineers

Channel		Scientists	Engineers
Interpersonal	local	18	25
	corporate	9	26
	external	16	11
Document	corporate	6	12
	trade	9	11
	professional	42	15
Interpersonal total		43	64
Corporate total		33	63
Specific search		42	53
Pointed out		33	30
General competence		25	17

suggested that, relative to engineers, scientists used interpersonal channels less (so documents more) and corporate sources less (so external sources more), engaged in somewhat less specific search and were more concerned with their general competence.

Rosenbloom and Wolek extended the distinction between scientist and engineer into the concept of 'professional/operational orientation'. Four indicators of this were used, the first being Scientist/Engineer as already categorized. The second was place of work—whether 'central laboratory ' (which was more research oriented) or 'operating division'. The third indicator was based on answers to the question on the task to which the received information was applied: the answers were subjectively categorized as Research, Development, or Design. The fourth indicator was based on the third part of the questionnaire—reactions to statements about professional work and 'reference group ' influences—as well as on level of formal education, extent of attendance at professional meetings, number of periodicals read, and papers published: the factors were combined to give an 'Index of professional orientation'.

The investigators were then able to categorize 110 respondents as 'highest professional orientation' (Scientists working on Research in central laboratories, with high Index) and 178 as 'highest operational orientation' (Engineers working on Design in operation divisions, with low Index). For these 288 respondents *Table 4.19* was then produced.

The contrasts in the use of interpersonal channels and corporate sources were even more pronounced. Rosenbloom and Wolek were thus able to develop interesting categorizations of channels and an index characterizing

Table 4.19 Professional orientations

Channel		Professional	Operational
Interpersonal	local	10	27
	corporate	5	30
	external	26	12
Document	corporate	6	11
	trade	7	11
	professional	46	9
Interpersonal total		41	69
Corporate total		21	68

a certain group of people (scientists and engineers in industry), and to show how personal orientation was related to the use of channels. One minor criticism would be that the orientation index was, in small part, based on channel use (attendance at professional meetings and periodicals read), so that the two categorizations were not wholly independent.

4.12 The use of existing records

We have already given some examples of data collection, but we wish now to review more fully the ways in which data may be obtained about acts of communication:

(1) By examination of existing records of information transfer: purchase or loan of publications, enquiries answered, consultations given, books written or read, online searches made, letters written and received, meetings attended, etc.;
(2) By having people complete structured questionnaires about their information activities;
(3) By less structured but directed personal interviews with people;
(4) By having people keep personal records of communication activities (diaries, tape recordings, etc.);
(5) By actual observation of people communicating.

In this section we will concentrate on the use of existing records.

Acts that are related to informative communication may be recorded by channel agencies such as libraries and booksellers, information and advisory services, bibliographical organizations, conference organizers, correspondence registries, etc. as well as by individuals in diaries, citations, and personal record systems. Such records often do little more than link a specific message (publication, answer to enquiry, lecture, letter, etc.) to a specific recipient: M and R were in contact, the link implies, and we can—if we wish—infer that the result was a transfer of some unspecified information. Sometimes, by following through a series of records, we can get firmer evidence of the transaction: an article recorded as borrowed turns up as a citation in a paper written by the recipient; a letter received is discussed in a reply; a diary records the recipient's reaction to a television presentation.

The records themselves usually do not include the actual messages (a correspondence file is an exception), so that extra investigation must be made to establish their characteristics, if required. The channel agencies may have some personal data about the sources or recipients in their records, but this may not be adequate for the investigator's needs. There are usually few data about the environment.

Another serious deficiency of any such records is that they include only such acts as need to be recorded for the purpose of the channel agency or individual concerned: a library records loans, but not in-library consultations; an information service may keep note only of 'major' enquiries; conference organizers may record who attended a conference but not which lectures each attendant listened to; the individual author cites only some of the publications he has read and perhaps some that he has not read; etc.

Use records are limited in two other ways: they are restricted to recipients who have in fact made appropriate use of a channel, and this group may be an unrepresentative sample of a community on whom data are required; and even for this sample, they record only acts related to that particular channel, and provide no evidence about any other kinds of communication act.

As examples of the use of existing records we will look at some studies of widely differing scope—three exploring national samples of communication acts, two examining records relating to particular organizations, and one concentrating on the communication of an individual.

4.12.1 Example A

During three months in 1975 every sixth postal loan request for a serial received at the British Library Lending Division was analysed by Bower (1976) according to serial title, date, language, type of requesting organization (academic, governmental, industrial, foreign, other) and broad subject (science/technology, social science, humanities, other). Over 60 000 requests were recorded for nearly 15 000 titles—an average of about four requests per title—but the distribution was heavily skewed: about one third of the titles accounted for 80 per cent of the demand. This third comprised only 10 per cent of the serials currently received by the library and only 5 per cent of all serial titles held. The paper reporting the survey analysed the demand by language (87 per cent for English publications) and by date, showing a decline in demand with age:

	1975	1974	1973	1972	1971	1970	1960–1969	1930–1959	1900–1920	<1900
%	2	25	12	7	6	5	26	14	2	1

The only characterization of the recipients was by title of institution, and one tabulation analysed the requests from each institutional type by subject (*Table 4.20*).

Table 4.20 Analyses of institutional type by subject

	Academic %	Governmental %	Industrial %
Science/technology	74	85	94
Social sciences	18	11	5
Humanities and other	8	4	1
	100	100	100

Do the results of this survey have a significance beyond their potential value for BLLD management? They certainly illustrate types of distribution pattern (by serial title, by language, and by date) that recur in all analyses of serials use, and in this way give a general indication of user preferences. However, can the patterns be said to reflect usage in the UK as a whole? We cannot argue as follows:

(1) The demand on BLLD from each institution is a representative sample of serials use in that institution;
(2) Recipients in borrowing institutions are a representative sample of all UK readers of serials likely to be held by BLLD, therefore
(3) Demand on BLLD is representative of UK reading of such serials.

Proposition (2) is plausible but unproven, and proposition (1) is certainly false: in general, institutions resort to interlibrary loan for documents peripheral to their locally held core material, on which reading attention is concentrated. Instead of (1), it is argued that:

(4) Each institution's peripheral literature is another institution's core; and
(5) A national summation of peripheral demands will approximate to a summation of core demands.

These assumptions are beguiling but untested.

The analysis by type of institution versus subject suggests that the distribution of subject interests differs from one institutional type to another. Common observation confirms this, but the percentages shown can only be accepted as valid if we assume that all potential recipients in the three subject areas are equally likely to make demands that result in serials requests to BLLD, a proposition that is unlikely as well as untested.

4.12.2 Example B

A 10 per cent sample of 1965 UK books and periodicals in the social sciences was analysed by Earle and Vickery (1969) according to broad subject, and all citations in that sample were analysed according to broad subject, bibliographic form, country of origin, language, and date. The numbers of source documents used were 256 books and the year 1965 issues of 75 periodicals. The number of citations in these sources was 23000. Distribution patterns for language, date, and serial title were comparable in type with those at BLLD. Here we will concentrate on the subject analysis. Subject assignment was at a fairly general level—politics, economics, education, social psychology, law, etc. Analyses were made in two directions, that we will illustrate using the subject 'education'.

In the source items categorized as education were 4326 citations, and 1550 of these citations were also categorized as education. We may express this result by saying that the extent to which the subject 'education' appears to draw upon its own literature in citation is $1550/4326 = 36$ per cent (self-citation). Other subjects appreciably cited by education sources in this sample were politics (207 citations), psychology (464), law (335), and geography (196). Apart from the 1550 self-citations to education some sources assigned to other social science subjects also contained citations categorized as education—105 citations in all. We may express this result by saying that the extent to which the subject 'education' appears mainly to contribute to itself is $1550/(105 + 1550) = 94$ per cent (called self-derivation in the paper)—contributing very little to other social science subjects. Similar analyses were made for each subject. Economics, for example, had a self-citation of 38 per cent, and a self-derivation of 62 per cent, contributing more to other social science subjects than did education.

Can these results be taken as valid indicators of relations between subjects, and thus give evidence of subject relations between sources and recipients in the social sciences? (Note that a 'source' in the citation sense is a recipient in a communication act.) Their validity depends on assuming (1) that the sample was representative of UK social science writing, (2) that the sample size was large enough to justify the detailed analysis (there is doubt about this), and (3) that citation reliably indicates the pattern of communication. This last point is discussed in the next example.

4.12.3 Example C

In 1969, Vickery compared four types of indicator of the use of UK science serials: (1) Citations by a sample of British authors; (2) requests to the BLLD (then the National Lending Library for Science and Technology), (3) holdings of British libraries as recorded in the *World List of Scientific Periodicals*, and (4) number of items published annually in each periodical. The comparison was used to explore some likely biases in each indicator. Because the true national pattern of science serials use is unknown, the interpretation of the results can only be tentative, but the comparison did suggest the following:

(1) Library holdings had been proposed as an indicator on the grounds that the library purchasing decisions they embodied would match the reading habits of users. However, the *World List* may not give a true picture of national library holdings, and it seems likely that the subject distribution of serials in libraries did not fully match the subject interests of users—particularly as regards the availability of technological and medical journals.
(2) The BLLD demand appeared to be distorted towards technology, to make up for the local deficiencies noted in (1).
(3) The citation indicator was inadequate because the relation between citation and reading appeared to vary from one subject to another.
(4) To take the number of items published per year as a measure of the use of a serial implies that each published item has an equal chance of being used. However, it is likely that the average readership of a published item varies from one subject to another.

4.12.4 Example D

Analyses of reference question records were undertaken within two UK petroleum company libraries. Cole (1958) examined 410 queries submitted to his library over a period of nine years. The queries were put by 171 members of the company staff, distributed as follows:

Queries:	1	2	3	4	5	over 5
Staff	93	31	17	12	5	13

No information is provided as to whether all 171 staff were employed throughout the nine years, a factor that could have affected the distribution. The types of answer supplied were analysed thus:

%
(1) Single fact or figure, very limited information on one topic.   18
(2) Medium coverage of narrow well-defined subject by few pamphlets, journal articles   69
(3) Intensive coverage of narrow subject by bibliography, specially prepared review   8
(4) Intensive coverage of wide subject   1
(5) Light coverage of major subject by textbook   2
(6) Other   2

The main documentary sources used were journals (58 per cent), textbooks, handbooks, etc. (21 per cent), pamphlets (14 per cent), and internal reports (12 per cent). The number of journal references per answer was distributed as follows:

References: 1   2   3   4 5 6   7 8 9 10 11–15 16–20 >20
Answers: 93 41 27 20 6 8 10 2 3   1   6   3   7

In another investigation, Mote and Angel (1962) analysed 622 queries answered by their company research library over a period of three years. The number of documents (not only journal references) per answer was:

Documents: 1–3   4–7   8–15   >15
Answers: 349   171   60   42

The queries were analysed according to the subject area (engineer, physicist, chemist) and status (division head, group leader, research worker) of the enquirer (*Table 4.21*).

Table 4.21 Variation in number of queries

	Number of queries	Number of staff	Relative use	Relative use by		
				Division heads	Group leaders	Research workers
Engineers	266	68	3.9	4.1	5.4	2.8
Physicists	53	23	2.3	7.0	2.8	1.1
Chemists	198	111	1.8	8.3	2.5	0.9
Overall	517	202	2.55	6.2	3.7	1.5

The 'relative use' is the number of queries per staff member which averaged 2.55 overall. Engineers used the enquiry service the most heavily, and the authors ascribed this not necessarily to higher information use but to a greater tendency to delegate information search to the library. The analysis by status showed the greatest relative use by division heads, presumably also because of more delegated search.

In a second article, Mote (1962) categorized the 178 graduate scientists at his research centre into three groups, drawing upon his knowledge of their work:

(1) The first group comprised occupations in a subject of which the underlying principles were well developed, the literature was well organized, and the width of the subject area was well defined. A typical example of such an activity would be the search for the structure or the synthesis of a complex organic polymer (i.e. the scientists engaged in the

activity were all organic chemists, and they were concentrating on just one aspect of organic chemistry.

(2) In the second group the subject area was wider and the information less well organized. The same hypothetical chemist as before could now be thought of as joining a firm engaged in research into the application of lubricants where the pure science aspect of the work previously described was, to some extent, left behind; the work was now concerned with both chemistry and physics in an engineering environment. The literature was now less clearly organized for his purposes than before; relevant information would be found, to a greater extent, in the unpublished reports of industrial firms and government departments, in the proceedings of many more professional societies, workshop manuals, specifications, etc., in addition to that contained in the published literature.

(3) The third group was really an exaggerated form of the second, in which the number of different subjects was greater, the type of problem to be faced by the scientists being subject to greater variation, and the organization of the literature being almost non-existent. This is not to say that the literature itself did not exist, but the degree of organization for the intended purpose was, to say the least, unhelpful. An example would be an inquiry into the thermal properties of frozen soils.

The information queries put by members of these groups were then examined, and their relative uses were estimated as 1, 3, and 15, respectively (median numbers of queries per member). This result might be interpreted to mean that each successive group is more likely to delegate information search, because of the increasing variety of information sought and the difficulty of access to it. It could also imply that Group (3) in particular made more information searches, but no data are presented to distinguish between these interpretations. Figures on the relative use of other library services (such as loans) could have thrown light on the matter.

4.12.5 Example E

Our last example of using existing records of communication relates to the work contacts of a single person, an active scientist engaged in teaching, research, administration, and consultancy. Over five months in 1973 a professor of rock mechanics kept a detailed diary of personal contacts (name of contact, status, subject), and his correspondence files for a period of three years were analysed in the same way. In all, 121 personal encounters and 800 letters were recorded (Gralewska-Vickery and Roscoe, 1975). Between them, these contacts covered 1786 topics. Their subject matter was analysed by percentage (*Table 4.22*). The contacts included other professors, lecturers, students, industrial researchers, managers, consultants, engineers, publishers, librarians, and reporters. Industry used personal contact proportionately more than academics.

A review of these examples of using existing records of communication confirms that such studies give only a partial view of the information behaviour of the sources and recipients involved; there is often uncertainty

Table 4.22 Contacts made by a scientist

	Corresp. (%)	Personal (%)
Educational (courses, students, staff, research, funds, etc.)	21.4	35.8
Government committees, professional organizations	1.3	2.2
Conferences and meetings	7.4	1.5
Visits (as host or guest)	10.3	10.0
Publication activities	6.1	1.5
Advice and consultancy	16.7	48.6
Information transfer (relating to reports, references, current research, departmental information service)	36.8	0.4

as to how representative is the sample of the population from which it is drawn; usually only general data are available to characterize recipients— the use of additional data by Mote shows how much more illuminating the study can then become. Despite these defects, examination of existing records of communication acts can give insight into patterns of information transfer.

4.13 Population, sample, and unit

Some of the defects just discussed can, in principle, be overcome by deliberate data collection in a survey, whether by structured questionnaire, interview, or personal diary, though other problems may thereby be introduced. The population of sources and/or recipients of interest can be specified in advance and identified; procedures can be established to draw a representative sample of their communication acts; data can be collected on any relevant variables associated with each act. All this in principle—many obstacles exist in practice to a successful survey. The main problems are:

(1) Defining in operational terms the population to be studied;
(2) Devising a method of obtaining a representative sample of the population and its communication acts;
(3) Deciding on the units of communication behaviour to be sampled.

The population of sources and/or recipients to be studied is often specified in advance as a way of limiting the scope of an investigation—to a particular social group (as in 'the information needs of social workers') or to recipients in a certain subject field (as in 'the use of metals information') or to a particular environment (as in 'information transfer in the hospital').

Since surveys are often primarily undertaken for information management purposes, the actual population studied may be restricted to people in a particular institution (a specific hospital, industrial firm, professional association, university, etc.), but with the hope that the results may be of more general relevance. It is still rare in our field for an investigator to start with a conceptual problem in informative communication—say, interrelations among the uses of various media—and then choose a suitable population within which it may be explored.

It is one thing to specify a population, it is often another to define it operationally. There usually exists an enumeration—more or less accurate—of the members of a specific institution or of residents in a specific locality. There is no such ready list of 'chemists employed in British industry', or of 'potential users of information about metals' or of 'people who need economic information for decision making'. Often, indeed there is not even a reliable list of institutions in which people of a certain kind may be found—for example, in times past Aslib Research Department had to go to much trouble to establish an adequate list of UK libraries of all kinds. The 'potential users of information about metals' were, in the survey by Vickery *et al.* (1969), defined operationally (and imperfectly) as 'members of seven professional institutions in the metals field', and the membership lists of these institutions were used as an enumeration of the population.

Given that we have established a known population of sources and/or recipients, or indeed of intermediaries of any kind, we can most effectively survey them by obtaining data from each member of the population. If the population is large, limitation of resources may necessitate a sampling. We will most convincingly be able to argue from sample results to population characteristics if every member of the population has a known chance of being included in the sample, and selection is wholly by chance. In simple random sampling a sample is drawn by lottery from an enumerated list of the population. If the sequence of names in the list has no structure likely to bias a selection, the method of systematic random sampling can be used: if a sample of 1 in N is required, a starting point between 2 and N in the list sequence is chosen randomly, and then every Nth name therafter is selected.

The population may be known or suspected to be heterogeneous with regard to characteristics that are believed to be relevant to informative communication—for example, each of the seven metal institutions may be regarded as having special characteristics. Each individual membership list may then be regarded as a separate stratum of the population, to be sampled separately. It is not essential to select the same proportion of each stratum—for example, a higher proportion may be taken of strata with relatively few members.

If the population to be studied is geographically dispersed—say, working in industrial firms throughout the UK—and data collection necessitates that the investigators visit each member of the sample, then 'cluster' sampling may be used to reduce travel. If we can assume that the firms are reasonably similar to each other, we can sample randomly from a list of firms, and then select all members of the population 'clustered' in the chosen firms. If the firms are themselves variable in ways thought to be relevant to information transfer (say, of varying size) then it may be necessary to stratify them before sampling.

A further method of sampling that is not fully random is 'quota' sampling, which makes a deliberate attempt to include a cross section of the study population, even if the exact enumeration of it cannot be made in advance. Suppose the population were the staff of British universities, and we stratified them according to status (professor, senior lecturer, lecturer, research staff), faculty and institution, and wished to collect data on N

members of each subcategory (for example, N professors of science from each university). Members of the population would be contacted in turn in as random a manner as possible until the 'quota' of people in each subcategory had been filled.

The size of sample to be selected by any of these methods depends upon (1) the variability of the population, (2) the number of variables on which data are to be collected, (3) the number of categories within each variable, and (4) the level of accuracy required in the results.

Studies of informative communication often aim to collect data on the contacts of sources and recipients with channels; for example, does the respondent read a particular journal? How often has he read it? How many messages have been received as a result? How many actions have arisen from receiving the messages? These studies raise the question of what constitutes an appropriate unit of information behaviour that can be sampled, observed, recorded, described, counted, and aggregated for comparison with other forms. In this section we draw on the discussion by Menzel et al. (1960) in their review of studies of the flow of information among scientists.

Simple exposure data (answers to questions such as 'Do you use the library, yes or no?') are ambiguous. Does a positive answer relate to one distant remembered visit or to a daily contact—and are these to be equated? The specification of time intervals ('Have you used the library—Today? Within the last week? Within the last month? etc.') reduces the ambiguity. 'How many times within the last week (month, etc.) have you visited the library?' aims to provide data on the frequency of occurrence of a particular act of communication. Data extracted from records, as we have seen, permit similar frequency counts.

The use of communicative acts as units has much to commend it, since such activities as writing a book, visiting a library, reading an article, giving or listening to a lecture, meeting a colleague, searching an index, etc. are likely to be remembered or recorded, and associated with the reception of information. Menzel mentions that ambiguities may remain. Does reading the same book on five separate occasions count as five acts or one? Does an all-day literature search in the library equate with a visit to look up a train timetable? 'The difficulty is not that ambiguities cannot be prevented, but that their prevention requires separate definitions, instructions and provisions for various forms of exposure to information ... which adds to the labor of both the investigators and their human subjects.' If the duration of each act were recorded, some of these difficulties would be lessened.

Another unit of information-receiving behaviour is what Menzel calls the 'message' but in our terminology is I, the information assimilated from a message. The use of this unit is particularly associated with what has been called the 'critical incident' technique (there is nothing 'critical' about it, and the terminology 'specific incident' is much more appropriate). This focuses on the reception of some particular item of information and explores the source, channel, occasion, duration, consequences, etc. associated with it. Berul et al. (1965), studying scientists and technologists, focused on the information 'chunk', defined as 'the smallest quantity of information required to answer a task-related question'.

4.14 Collecting data from people

In any survey of informative communication essential data to be collected concern the information received or emitted, as we have just seen. The source, recipient, or intermediary is being observed or asked to report as to his *behaviour* and actions with respect to this information. Second, we may wish to inquire about his reasons or *purposes*. Third, we need some background data about the person surveyed—job, rank, education, age, etc.—often known as *demographic* information. We will want *factual* data from him, about messages received or emitted, their source, medium, and channel, and on aspects of his environment. It may be useful to assess his *knowledge* of some aspects of the information system. Lastly, his *opinions* of and *attitudes* towards information, sources, channels, his environment, etc. may be required.

There are many obstacles to valid data collection. The person surveyed may not accurately remember his actual behaviour or the factual data we seek. If asked to record such data, he may—through time pressure or other reasons—do so incompletely or inaccurately. An obvious conclusion for the investigator is to reduce to a minimum the time interval between an act and its report. Sometimes the 'facts' that the respondent reports—for example, about locally available information resources—may simply reflect his ignorance of the situation. Questions about frequency of action ('How often do you do X?' 'When did you last do X?') may be answered inaccurately, either through faulty memory or because the respondent wishes to present a certain 'image'.

A question as to purpose may elicit a straightforward answer, but many factors can make the answer unreliable. A respondent may not like to admit, say, that in choosing a source he was searching randomly, so he concocts a reason for his choice. The reason given for using a certain source may be that it is the most useful or valuable—the real reason may simply be habit, or easy accessibility. A search may have been ill defined, 'just browsing', but if it resulted in obtaining certain information the outcome may be presented as the intended purpose.

Expressed opinions may be genuinely held or once again be coloured by the image that the respondent wishes to present. The investigator may hope to infer attitudes from opinions and from behaviour—and the evidence from these two types of data may conflict (for example, expressions of enthusiasm for an information service but little evidence of use). The only way that the effect of these and other obstacles can be diminished is for the investigator to collect data in various ways and from different angles, so that cross checks can be made.

The use of an observer or interviewer to obtain data may offset some obstacles but can introduce other difficulties. Behaviour can deviate from the normal under observation. Answers to an interviewer will be coloured by the respondent's reaction to the situation. An observer can misinterpret what he sees or hears and will not notice all that is going on. An interviewer may allow his own views to bias his questions and his interpretation of answers. These problems can be countered by careful prior training of observers or interviewers, with detailed instructions to them.

Earlier in this chapter five ways of collecting data about communication were noted. We have already dealt with the examination of existing records, and here we will comment on the other four methods: questionnaires, interviews, diaries, and observation.

Self-completed questionnaires, distributed through the mail or offered to people at some service point, have been much used in information studies. They can be distributed in large numbers at relatively low cost, they can provide responses in standard format that are readily analysed, there are no problems of interviewer bias or interaction, and the respondent can complete the form in his own time and—if he wishes—remain anonymous. On the other hand, the response is often both slow and low, so that a representative sample of the population is not obtained. Questions may be misunderstood, some may not be answered. The set of alternative answers often offered for a question may not fit in with the respondent's view of the topic. There may be uncertainty as to who has actually completed the questionnaire, which usually requires appreciable reading skill.

Interviews can be simply oral presentations of a structured question-naire, but often allow for more flexibility both in question and answer. They permit the adjustment of a question to the understanding of the respondent, developing a question to probe for more responses, and an opportunity to identify the mood of the response—serious, jesting, cynical. They can therefore make finer discriminations and handle more complex topics. The interviewer may be in a position to see something of the respondent's environment and even his communication behaviour. Even illiterate respondents can be included, and response rate is usually high. On the other hand, all this flexibility may make analysis difficult, there are the problems of interviewer bias and interaction already mentioned, recording responses may not be easy, and the use of interviewers is time consuming and therefore costly.

The keeping of diaries by a person studied has some of the advantages and disadvantages of the questionnaire. A free-wheeling diary can be full of insights but very difficult to analyse. One problem with diaries is that busy respondents will not keep a running record of communication acts but will try to catch up periodically by recalling their activities over an elapsed time. The number of entries made by each diarist is likely to vary: for example, in a survey by Fishenden (1959), two people provided 10 per cent of all the communication acts recorded, another 12 people the next 40 per cent, and the remaining 50 per cent of the acts were spread over 49 people. This distribution is, no doubt, partly a reflection of differing intensities of communication, but may also spring from differing degrees of conscien-tiousness in completing the diaries. The technique is not suited for recording information that does not come in well-defined 'packages' like books read or meetings attended.

'Participant observation' is a mode of data collection that is sometimes contrasted with survey methods, since it is usually not based on a statistically valid sampling of a population specified in advance. Its essence is that the investigator spends a considerable time in direct contact with the situation under examination—say, communication within an organization. In some cases, the observer is a true 'participant', actually joining in the activities being studied, but more generally he simply acts as a 'field observer'. A variety of data-collection methods are used besides direct observation—some interviewing of people in the organization about their activities; the use of chosen 'informants' within the organization to provide background data and to report on activities at which the observer was not present; and analysis of documentary material available within the organization. The limitation of such an observational approach is that the data are not often useful for statistical treatment to yield generalizations—such field enquiries will suggest hypotheses to be tested but seldom provide the data for testing them. They are in fact more applicable in the 'synthetic' mode of studying people and information that we have mentioned earlier. By way of compensation we should note that the direct involvement of an observer is virtually indispensable to gain a detailed insight into the complex communication activity of an organization.

The brief notes we have provided here on methods of data collection are intended only as an introduction to the techniques. Those who wish to go into more detail will find it helpful to consult such books as those of Gardner (1978) (a plainly written and helpful introduction to survey methods), Moser and Kalton (1971) (a fuller and more authoritative text), Simon (1978) (wide-ranging, with a vivid use of illustrative examples), Madge (1953), and on participant observation, McCall *et al.* (1969). An example of data collection is presented in Appendix 3.

4.15 Case studies

In the following sections of this chapter we will report at some length the results of studies of the communication behaviour of various social groups—in particular, of research scientists, of practitioners including engineers and the construction industry, and of 'Everyman'. These results will give a more vivid impression of the extent to which scientific understanding of 'people and information' has now been advanced.

4.16 Scientific research and communication

The research scientist is engaged in the solution of a sequence of intellectual problems. Using the terminology and analysis developed by Ravetz (1971), we may show the main steps of a particular research project as in *Figure 4.6*.

The observation and experience of practical life, or the internal development of science itself, gives rise to situations which are seen to present intellectual problems. At this stage the scientist collects facts and possible explanations to see whether the problem situation can be resolved, to specify the problem in a form that can be operationally investigated, and to assess its significance—how important to practice or to science would its solution be? Having specified a problem relevant data must be collected, and to design his investigation the scientist needs to learn of methods, techniques, and tools, and in general to assess whether

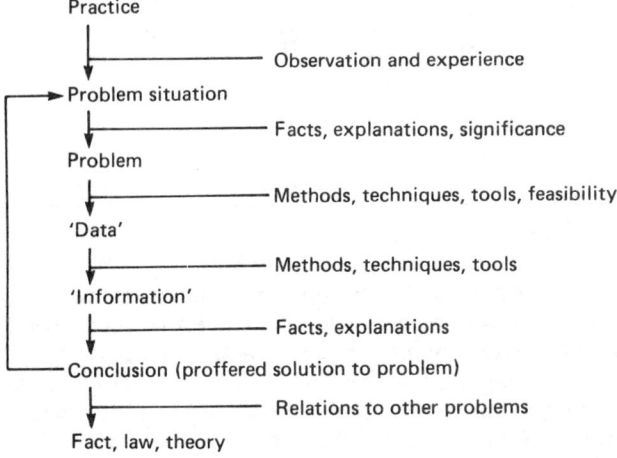

Figure 4.6 Steps in research

his project is feasible. Once the raw data have been collected they must be worked up by analysis into what Ravetz calls 'information'—for example, the results of statistical analysis. This process also requires an input of analytical methods, techniques, and tools (for example, statistical computer programs). In order to come up with a solution to the originally proposed problem the scientist uses the 'information' he has produced as evidence in a logical discussion that may also draw on the evidence of other research (facts, explanations). The conclusions of a particular project are, in the course of time, tested by use as evidence in other projects and are eventually accepted by the scientific community as facts, laws, or grand theories.

It should be noted that 'information' in the sense that we use the term embraces not only 'worked up data' but all the other categories used by Ravetz—fact, explanation, theory, law, method, technique, tool, even problem, and more besides: whatever, indeed, that can modify the state of knowledge of the scientist or other recipient.

To carry out his work the laboratory scientist thinks and plans, sets up and uses equipment to collect data, treats and analyses the data, discusses, reads, and writes. A detailed study of how some scientists allocated their time among these activities was carried out in 1957-1958 by Halbert and Ackoff. They reported on an investigation of about 1000 chemists in US industry, a proportionate stratified systematic random sample of industrial chemists in the metropolitan areas of the United States. The investigators observed each chemist at randomly selected moments of time, once in the morning and once in the afternoon, for nine working days, yielding 18 observations per chemist. Summing all the 18000 observations gave the results in *Table 4.23* for percentage time allocation.

On average, a chemist spent nearly a half of his time (43.8 per cent) in communication related to his work (some of the 'other activities' included

Table 4.23 Percentage time allocation

	Minimum	Mean	Maximum
Thinking or planning alone	0	6.0	>25
Equipment set-up and use	0	29.6	>70
Data treatment	0	6.4	>30
Communication	16.5	43.8	>70
Other activities	0	14.2	>30

personal or social communications). The 'minimum' figures show that during the observation period some chemists were not seen to spend any time thinking alone, handling equipment, or on data treatment, but no chemist spent less than 16.5 per cent of his time communicating. The 'maximum' figures show that some chemists were observed to spend over 70 per cent of their time communicating, others over 70 per cent with equipment. The wide ranges from minimum to maximum are due to:

(1) The accidents of sampling—for example, it could occur that even a regular user of equipment happened not to be using it on any one of the 18 occasions on which he was observed;
(2) The stage of each chemist's project—some could be at the planning stage, others collecting data, others treating it, others writing up results; and
(3) Differences in style of work, as between the theorist and the bench experimentalist.

Communication was categorized as in *Table 4.24*. On average, each chemist spent one third of his time in scientific or technical communication (the maximum recorded was over 60 per cent). Reading on average occupied 8.8 per cent of the working day (maximum recorded, about 20 per cent).

Table 4.24 Categories of communication

	Mean (%)
Business (related to work but not scientific or technical)	10.4
Scientific or technical	33.4
General group discussion	10.3
Non-discussion oral	9.2
Reading	8.8
Writing	5.0

4.17 Studies in psychological science

During the 1960s, Garvey and Griffith (1972) conducted a long series of investigations into communication among US psychologists, paying

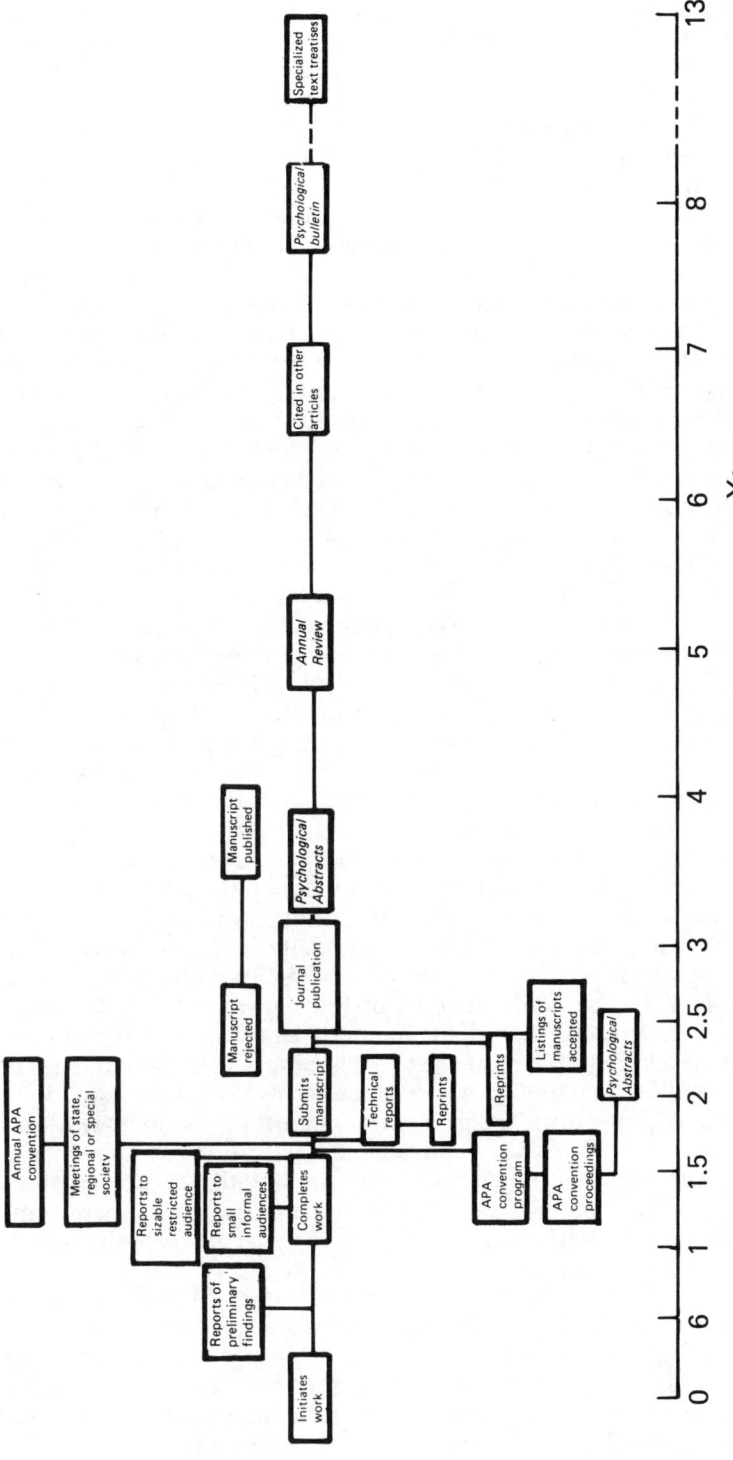

Figure 4.7 The dissemination of research results

particular attention to the way in which the results of individual research projects were disseminated to the scientific community. The investigators developed a typical or average time schedule of communication events, starting from the moment when work is formally started on a project, and stretching forward for over ten years (*Figure 4.7*). Garvey and Griffith gave a summarizing account of the picture they had formed, and we closely follow it here.

During the first 12-18 months from the time the work begins until the researcher believes he can give a complete and defensible report of it to colleagues working in the same subject-matter area, the scientist is relatively uncommunicative about his work. Exceptions, of course, are the casual, but often fruitful, discussions with immediate colleagues. Very shortly after the researcher feels he can report his work, he begins to disseminate his findings, a process that continues for many months, usually until he has submitted a manuscript reporting his findings to a journal. Usually the first reports are informal ones, presented to small, relatively sympathetic audiences at gatherings such as colloquia within the scientist's own institution. Next, the researcher launches out into broader territory, perhaps responding to a request that he present his work at a conference sponsored by the agency funding his research. Or, if he is recognized by his peers as being among the top researchers in his field, he may be invited to speak at a small conference of specialists working in the same field.

Up to this point, scientist's dissemination of information on his work is minor and primarily concerns persons who are already aware of the areas or problems he is working on and who may need only the briefest communication to understand what he has accomplished. If all has gone well, the scientist, having tested his findings and their interpretation on fellow workers, is now ready to disseminate his work to increasingly larger segments of the scientific community.

Within a few months, about one productive scientist in four will report his work to a fairly large audience at a meeting of a state, regional, or national professional society. The American Psychological Association national meeting was found to be an especially important medium in the dissemination process. The meeting occurs 15-18 months prior to journal publication of the contents of most of the papers presented there, and includes a sizable proportion of the annual scientific information output of American psychology. The published programmes of these meetings often constitute the first genuinely public announcement of the completion of a particular research effort. Consequently, almost all persons who present papers at APA conventions (and also at the major regional meetings) receive requests for copies of their presentations. These requests sometimes number more than a hundred. The majority of these requests come from persons who did not attend the meeting at which the paper was presented. The typical requester is a very young researcher. He exerts considerable effort to gain access to recent research findings through such early-alerting media as published programmes, probably because he is unlikely to have received this information earlier through the special, restricted informal networks which the author first uses to disseminate his work. At the meeting itself, a number of those attending will also contact and discuss particular points arising from the presentation.

During this period in the information flow process, about one author in ten will also produce and distribute a technical report. Another informal dissemination medium is the preprint (a prepublication draft of the manuscript which is submitted to a journal). In 1963, for example, about half the authors of articles published in major psychology journals distributed an average of ten preprints.

4.18 Journal publication

Once a manuscript is submitted to a journal the information it contains is effectively obscured from the scientific public until journal publication. The author, having submitted his manuscript, has no further personal need to disseminate its content. Once the manuscript goes to a journal, the research cycle is, in effect, complete; the active researcher then begins the cycle anew, concentrating on information exchange associated with new work. Seventy per cent of the authors studied by Garvey and Griffith had, in fact, started new work in the same areas as their articles by the time their articles were published.

In US psychology, during the 1960s an average lag of 9 months existed between manuscript submission and journal publication. Approximately one fifth of the articles published in the main psychology journals have been previously rejected by one or more journals. The most frequent reason given for rejection is inappropriateness of subject matter for the journal; this may be, however, a socially acceptable way of stating that the manuscript is of poor quality. In any discipline, there is apparently a hierarchy of journals to which authors submit their manuscripts. At the top are the most prestigious, with high rejection rates and long publication lags. These publish the core of the discipline's literature. At the next level the journals are usually less prestigious, have lower rejection rates, and are less central to the literature in the field. At the lower level the journals share few of the characteristics of the main or core journals and may be unrefereed.

The most crucial point in the process of dissemination of *scientific* information is the transfer of information from the informal to the formal domain, which occurs with the journal publication of the article. During the 2 months after publication the audience for most articles is very small. About half of the research reports in core psychology journals are likely to be read (partially or entirely) by 1 per cent or less of a random sample of psychologists. When we extrapolate this to the population studied (approximately 20 000 psychologists) we find that half the articles have a total of 200 or fewer readers. This is well within the range of some other forms of distribution (copies of meeting presentations, technical reports, reprints) which, since they are distributed mainly to interested persons, may have very high rates of readership. The journal article in psychology is no longer the only medium for disseminating *current* scientific findings to researchers active on the research front, but it remains relevant to the assimilation of research findings. Current reading in itself is only a minor portion of the use to which journal articles are ultimately put.

The article, part of the primary literature of science, becomes a permanent record of completed research; that is, it becomes part of the 'archives' of science. Next begins the procedure by which the article is assimilated into the established scientific literature of the field, and the flow from here on is slow but steady. Related findings, repetition, and further research, plus continued informal and formal evaluation (for example, in reviews), eventually establish the scientific credibility and originality of the work. An insignificant or poor piece of research will usually fade away through inattention, and will do no more harm than clutter up libraries.

4.19 Secondary announcements

The information in the article moves into secondary sources, where scientific 'information' is processed into 'knowledge'. Separate items of information from separate journal articles are interrelated, and these clusters in turn become compounded into a self-consistent meaningful body of knowledge which eventually represents the most acceptable and coherent scientific understanding of a subject matter at that time. About 7-8 months after a psychology aricle is published it will be abstracted in *Psychological Abstracts*. The abstract places the article in a public secondary source along with other contemporary works on the same subject. No item of scientific information is likely to proceed efficiently through the remainder of this process without going through this comprehensive cataloguing, without which most articles would be randomly stored, to be discovered by chance.

Evidence that this integrative and evaluative process is in motion usually appears some 2-5 years after the article is published, when it is cited by another author. Here the scientific information in the article is built upon, evaluated in the light of new information, and linked to new information which has been generated since its publication. Because of publication delay encountered by the *citing* article the general scientific public is not aware of this integrative step until some months later (and by then it is 3 years after the *cited* article's publication).

Some 2 or 3 years after publication the article, if it shows evidence of potential scientific importance, reappears in a subject-matter chapter of the *Annual Review of Psychology*. Another major source of reviews in psychology is the *Psychological Bulletin*, though at the time of the study the average age of an article cited in the *Bulletin* was over 5 years old. Reviews synthesize and evaluate recent progress in an area. Good reviews are explicit accounts of what the vast majority of experienced scientists in a field consider to be the acceptable facts and the significant relationships among these facts. Good reviews precisely identify, but do not necessarily exclude, that which is still regarded as speculation and may provide other experienced researchers in the field with strong indications of what is ripe for scientific inquiry. Reviews are an essential part of the continuous reassessment of the current stage of scientific knowledge in a field, and such reassessment is not simply a matter of retrieving and synthesizing piecemeal, discrete facts. The important thing to be noted here is that analysis, evaluation, and synthesis have been proceeding ever since the work first appeared in the journal literature, in a process so central to science as to be virtually indistinguishable from it.

The researcher who has been following the progress of his own work may get the impression that little happens to it after it is cited in a review. Earlier in the process his article may have been cited by the author of another article, but henceforth the review article will usually serve as an appropriate reference to his contribution. If his work has survived the process up to now, however, and if it subsequently proves to be an important contribution to his field, then a decade or more after he has published it he might find reference to his article in a treatise or specialized text. During the last half of the first decade after an article has been published, near the end of that process by which scientific 'information' is transformed into scientific 'knowledge', lies the final goal of all the accumulation of research data and of all the scientific communication that we have encountered up to now, that is, the synthesis of existing scientific information into erudite, general accounts of the current scientific understanding of a subject-matter area. The treatise or specialized text are major media used during this final stage. For the experienced psychologist who is actively involved in research in a particular area, a treatise or specialized text may serve only to reinforce or to reorganize his own conceptual framework of the subject matter. Information disseminated through such media is more generally understandable, and now, after years of critical evaluation and synthesis, scientific knowledge may be readied for dissemination beyond the active research community—to the non-expert, to the inexperienced student, to the applied worker, to the practitioner, etc. Garvey and Griffith conclude:

> The major dissemination events through which the work of the accomplished research psychologist evolves, from the time the work is initiated until it is deposited in the great archival reservoir of scientific knowledge, thus typically occur over a 12-15 year period. We thus have a picture of the long, slow, cautious process of creating, evaluating, re-evaluating, integrating, synthesizing, and transforming scientific information into scientific knowledge.

4.20 Reception of information

In the late 1960s, Garvey and colleagues at the Johns Hopkins University carried out a long series of studies on communication in the physical sciences, social sciences, and engineering. Their investigations in part extended the picture of dissemination reported above. They also examined information transfer from the recipient's point of view, and some of their result are given in a report by Garvey and Gottfredson (1976), to which we have already referred. They started from the published papers of 3676 scientists and engineers (group (A)). From each author they sought the names of other scientists and engineers in the same field of work as the author (group (B)), and made contact with them. They obtained from group (B) the names of yet other scientists and engineers in the same field

Table 4.25 Information needed by scientists

Stage of scientific work

Nature of information needed	(A) Preliminary planning (general)	(B) Specific planning: Theoretical/conceptual	(C) Preparation of written research proposal	(D) Preliminary experimentation/ field trials or mockups	(E) Calibration, pretesting, etc.	(F) Design and development of equipment/apparatus	(G) Formulation of experimentation/study design	(H) Collection of data	(I) Analysis of data	(J) Interpretation of results	(K) Preparation of report of work
To aid in perception or definition of problem	X	X	X	X							
To formulate a scientific or technical solution		X	X				X				
To place work in proper context with similar work already completed			X	X			X	X	X	X	X
To relate work to ongoing work in area	X	X	X	X			X	X	X	X	X
To select a design/strategy for data collection					X		X	X			
To select a data-gathering technique					X	X	X				
To design equipment or apparatus					X	X					
To choose a data analysis technique					X				X		
To enable full interpretation of collected data				X					X	X	X

Table 4.26 Information needs and sources (percentages)

Stage of work	Needed information during stage	Sources from which needed information was obtained						Formal sources	
		Informal sources				Technical reports	Preprints	Journal articles	Books
		Local colleagues	Non-local colleagues	Students	Meeting presentations				
Initial stage									
To aid in perception or definition of problem	53	27	18	7	11	18	8	33	22
To formulate a scientific or technical solution	43	19	11	4	5	14	6	24	16
Intermediate stage									
To select a design/strategy for data collection	31	16	7	4	3	7	3	11	8
To select a data-gathering technique	27	14	6	3	2	8	3	11	7
To design equipment or apparatus	24	12	6	3	2	7	2	10	6
To choose a data-analysis technique	32	16	7	2	2	9	3	15	12
Final stage									
To place data in proper context with existing data	57	15	16	3	13	18	11	44	19
To enable full interpretation of collected data	40	20	14	5	8	11	6	23	14
To integrate findings into the current state of knowledge in area	46	16	17	3	13	15	10	36	17
Any of above stages	92	53	40	15	29	41	23	70	44

of work (group (C)). Groups (B) and (C) together totalled 1816 individuals, and these were then questioned about their knowledge of the work contained in the published papers.

Among groups (B) + (C), 79 per cent were aware of a paper in their field of work published by one of the group (A) authors, and 75 per cent had in fact examined such a paper. However, only 21 per cent said that they had acquired useful information from the paper. The reason was that 63 per cent had already—before publication—learnt something about the research reported in the paper, and 50 per cent had acquired useful information at that stage, on average approximately 1 year before publication. About 52 per cent of (B) + (C) had maintained regular contact with relevant authors in group (A), and as a result 40 per cent had obtained prepublication information through face-to-face contact, 13 per cent through correspondence, and 25 per cent through receiving a preprint or technical report. Other channels found useful were 'informed by colleague' (9 per cent) and 'heard author speak at meeting' (11 per cent). The total exceeds 50 per cent because an individual received information through more than one channel.

We may analyse recipients in the following way. Out of every 100 individuals in (B) + (C), 63 had prepublication contact with group (A), and only six of these found in the published paper any useful information they had not already acquired: for them, the less formal and interactive prepublication mechanisms were the main source of new information. However, among the 100 in (B) + (C), 22 had no prepublication contact with group (A), and 15 of these found useful information in the paper: for them, the journal was the source of new information. We must remember that all 1800 members of group (B) + (C) were named individuals, known to be in the same fields of work as the authors. Between them they only account for 0.5 readers per paper in the relationship studied, whereas the total number of current readers per paper is considerably more (see the earlier figures for psychology). For many of these other readers, journal publication may be a major channel of current information.

Garvey and his colleagues also explored the information needs and behaviour of about 1600 of their scientist and engineer authors, asking them to describe their current work, information especially needed and/or sought, and sources in which it was found. The survey enable them to identify eleven typical stages of scientific work, and to relate to each of these various types of information need (*Table 4.25*). Further, the type of need was related to source of information (*Table 4.26*). Information is constantly needed throughout all stages of scientific and technical work, and quantitatively seems to be greater during the initial and final stages. Different sources and media serve different needs.

4.21 The information needs of practitioners

'Practice' has here been interpreted broadly as the production or provision of goods or services to consumers or clients. It has thus been distinguished from (1) 'research' or 'science', which is focused on the generation of new knowledge, either for itself alone or because of its potential relevance to practice, and from (2) 'consumption', the private utilization of goods and services.

Information need can only be studied as it arises in the course of the daily activity of people. The title of this section implies that there are specific groups of people engaged in 'practice' who can collectively be called 'practitioners'. To a first approximation this is true—an industrial engineer, an architect, a nurse, are each contributing to providing goods or a service. However, in the course of that practice a practitioner may also be generating new knowledge and may be consuming goods or services from other areas of practice. A study of the information needs of a particular practitioner group is therefore likely to uncover aspects of need that are related to 'research' and 'consumption' activities that are incidental to the practice centrally concerned.

The actual work of any particular practitioner may be a mix of practice, research, and consumption. Within an organization whose primary function is the provision of goods or services—for example, an industrial firm, a social service department, or a hospital—there may be individual 'practitioners' whose main activity is research, and others (such as purchasing officers of various kinds) who are acting as the 'consumers' of other organizations' products. For these reasons it is not always easy to single out 'practitioners' in the narrow sense and assess their information needs. Obviously, the concrete provision of an information service to a particular practitioner group has to take into account their total information requirements.

Any human activity has an information input, and in this sense all operatives in a production or service organization have information needs. However, the term 'practitioner' is usually reserved for those operatives who have had formal training in practical skills and background knowledge needed in their work, often associated with a formal qualification and registration. Though in their primary function practitioners do not generate new knowledge, their activity requires the application of specialized knowledge. Since knowledge in all fields is continually being extended, the successful practitioner needs a regular or intermittent supply of new information so that his practice may develop. There is therefore a necessary link between 'research'—or, at any rate, the outcome of research—and practice.

As an illustrative example of the range of information needed in practice let us look at rural occupational groups in countries where agriculture is still of major importance. *Table 4.27* comes from Coombs and Ahmed (1974). They were writing from an educational point of view, and stressing learning needs, but the exercise of learned skills requires the same continual support of current information in these subject areas.

4.22 Characteristics of practitioners

Each practitioner group has its own set of distinguishing characteristics but it also shares some features with other groups. We have drawn the following account from a review of practitioner information needs by Wilkin (1977).

Table 4.27 Rural occupations and their needs

Groups	Types of learning needs (at varying levels of sophistication and specialization)
(A) Persons directly engaged in agriculture (1) Commercial farmers (2) Small subsistence and semi-subsistence farm families (3) Landless farm workers	Farm planning and management; rational decision making; record keeping; cost and revenue computations; use of credit Application of new inputs, varieties, improved farm practices Storage, processing, food preservation Supplementary skills for farm maintenance and improvement, and sideline jobs for extra income Knowledge of government services, policies, programmes, targets Knowledge and skills for family improvement (e.g. health, nutrition, home economics, child care, family planning) Civic skills (e.g. knowledge of how cooperatives, local government, national government function)
(B) Persons engaged in off-farm commercial activities (1) Retailers and wholesalers of farm supplies and equipment, consumer goods and other items (2) Suppliers of repair and maintenance services (3) Processors, storers and shippers of agricultural commodities (4) Suppliers of banking and credit services (5) Construction and other artisans (6) Suppliers of general transport services (7) Small manufacturers	New and improved technical skills applicable to particular goods and services Quality control Technical knowledge of goods handled sufficient to advise customers on their use, maintenance, etc. Management skills (business planning; record keeping and cost accounting; procurement and inventory control; market analysis and sales methods; customer and employee relations; knowledge of government services, regulations, taxes; use of credit)
(C) General services personnel: rural administrators, planners, technical experts (1) General public administrators, broad-gauged analysts at subnational levels (2) Managers, planners, technicians, and trainers for specific public services (e.g. agriculture, transport, irrigation, health, small industry, education, family services, local government, etc.) (3) Managers of co-operatives and other farmer associations (4) Managers and other personnel of credit services	General skills for administration, planning, implementation, information flows, promotional activities Technical and management skills applying to particular specialities Leadership skills for generating community enthusiasm and collective action, staff team work and support from higher echelons

The demands of work settings are such that practitioners are under considerable pressure to get on with the job of providing services/products for use by consumers/clients. Typically, practitioners initiate actions and make decisions within a context of imperfect knowledge, and they search for satisfactory solutions rather than 'best' solutions. They are not necessarily under pressure to make heavy use of new, professional information. Older knowledge and skills are valued because these allow a person to avoid delays associated with searching for (and validating) new knowledge. Practitioners may contribute to their body of professional knowledge, but they tend to regard this contribution as a by-product of their activities rather than intertwined with them.

There is great variation in the way that practitioners' work is organized. At one extreme, the work of managers and social workers is characterized by fragmentation, brevity, and variety, and it draws heavily on information of local interest. At the other extreme, the work of development engineers is characterized by being project based and involving a lengthy prototype testing phase in which the engineer gradually closes his mind to new ideas so that he is not diverted to new possibilities.

Isolation from other members of their profession and/or from organized professional activities and information resources is a problem for some practitioners. For instance, many small manufacturers and general medical practitioners work alone or in small groups. Similarly, practitioners engaged on field work of one type or another may have little contact with professionals outside their immediate group (for example, social workers, rural physicians or site engineers).

It seems that most practitioners are affected by controls of one type or another. These include standards, codes of practice, procedural controls, building regulations, and legislation. Within these controls, the scope for individual decision making is greater in some professions than others. For example, medical practitioners are expected to make decisions on, and take responsibility for, the care of their patients, and to do so within moral and professional codes of practice. Traditionally, however, nurses have had little opportunity for individual problem solving, particularly in hospitals where their work is subject to the authority of senior nurses, procedural rules, and physicians' decisions.

The need for confidentiality in many areas of practice has a constraining influence on communication patterns. Sometimes confidentiality is related to the competitive nature of the marketplace which affects, for example, architects, designers and planners, engineers, and managers. In other work it is related to government security, as in the case of government social scientists, or to the rights of the individual for privacy, as in social welfare. On the other hand, local government officers must make many of their decisions and activities available for public scrutiny through public enquiries, consultations, etc.

The need to combat professional obsolescence by some form of lifelong education has been recognized by the leading members of most practitioner groups. Forces which combine to make continuing education an important issue include changes in professional practice and attitudes, the continuing increase in specialization of work, and the growth of complex technologies. In some professions, continuing education is closely intertwined with everyday practice. For example, general practitioners must deal with a wide range of medical conditions, information on which is recorded in the professional literature and drug information sheets, and presented in courses, meetings, and conferences. In contrast, the view has been expressed that the work of practising engineers is so highly specific that they gradually lose touch with the theories and principles of their profession.

4.23 Sources of new-practice knowledge

Havelock *et al.* (1964) point out that new-practice knowledge is generated from various sources. First, it grows out of (and is embedded in) existing practice knowledge, and in this sense it is only partly 'new'. New knowledge simply is not practical if it takes no account of the practice knowledge already in use. Changes in practice are likely to come about through an evolutionary process, an integration of new elements into a pre-existing whole, rather than through revolution or wholesale substitution. Existing practice also has an important impact in another sense, when it represents the diffusion of good practice from one practitioner to another. Usually the term 'practice innovation' is a relative one; that is, the practice is new only to the practitioner who makes the decision to adopt for the first time. He may, however, learn of this 'innovation' from another practitioner who has already used it for years.

New-practice knowledge is also based partly on inputs representing user demand in its various forms, expressions of need and reactions to previous practical knowledge, and immediate feedback to the practitioner on the effectiveness of his craft. Finally, we have the input from research, whether 'basic' or 'applied' or in the form of 'developed' prototypes. Research inputs are undoubtedly an important and unique contribution to practice and represent knowledge which is not only new but also validated according to specified rules.

Basic research knowledge is mainly transmitted between scientists—in ways that we have already discussed—but some is also transmitted directly to the practitioner, typically in his early training for his profession (for example, biochemistry for the pre-medical student, sociology for the pre-law student). Probably very little of what is transmitted actually gets translated and transformed into practice, but the effort to transmit continues to be made largely with the rationale that it provides a foundation for later, more applied learning. Undoubtedly some basic knowledge also gets transferred into operating principles or even values which the well-grounded practitioner can apply to problems in his everyday work.

Applied research knowledge may come to the practitioner in the form of a 'prototype', which represents a complex package of data, applied theory, and method, which is in some sense the end product of the research and development process. As the prototype is tested and adapted in more and more practice settings it gradually becomes practice knowledge.

Practical innovations frequently come not from research or development but from other practitioners. Moreover, there is a frequent blending of various types of practice knowledge. New products may require the development of new practices; an artificial heart (hardware) obviously must be accompanied by surgical skills (practice) and procedures (software), and possibly new surgical instruments and supplies (more hardware) before it can be meaningfully utilized; a teaching machine (hardware) requires new teacher skills on how to introduce it to the classroom (service) and programs to be used in it (software).

One other source of practice knowledge identified by Havelock is the information received from other fields of practice. In a complex multi-professional society, different types of practitioners, with entirely different formal training and background, found themselves working side by side in production or service activities. A complex example of this will be noted later. Such proximity and teamwork provide opportunities for informal transfer of information from one to another, though the 'heterophily' of the contact may impede ready communication.

Running through all the potential ways in which the practitioner can add to his knowledge is the impact of personal experience. Most fields of practice begin as crafts. For example, the engineering profession places enormous emphasis on practical experience. It is a commmonplace belief that university education of itself does not make an engineer.

Work experience includes direct experience of the work object, observation of other people's work behaviour, and interactive communication with them. It also includes feedback from the practitioner's own attempts to tackle jobs and make decisions. The development of work experience depends upon the ability to observe accurately and comprehensively, and to draw conclusions from these observations. A distinction has been drawn between figurative and non-figurative modes of perception. Figuratively, we 'see' phenomena in our mind's eye, using stored knowledge and imagination. In order to develop the ability to see figuratively, experience must be gained by frequent non-figurative observation and manipulation, seeing, touching, handling, even smelling the work object. All these aspects of work experience are of vital importance to the development of the practitioner and greatly influence his modes of communication.

It is for this reason, for example, that engineers place such emphasis on visits to other sites and institutions. One engineer told Gralewska-Vickery (1976):

It's the only way to find out what's going on. You'll never get the same amount of information unless you go and look for yourself. You can read about an ore body in a magazine, but if you go and look at a core, and talk to a geologist, you get a much better idea of what is involved.

And again:

Seeing means applying. You see a method or piece of equipment, sometimes a very simple arrangment, and suddenly you think, this is exactly what I need. Very often you see a technique or an instrument which you don't need today. But one day it will come to you as an application to your new situation. Sometimes at first you don't even realize you have seen it—you may consider it as your own development.

4.24 The importance of informal communication

The characteristics just discussed make it easy to understand why practitioners value personal communication highly. In the following discussion, we will draw upon the survey of engineers by Gralewska-Vickery and Roscoe (1975). Particularly in industry, most engineers work in teams (close knit or loosely grouped). Among 90 respondents, the size of these teams ranged as follows:

Size of team	1–5	6–10	11–20	21–50	>50
No. of respondents	23	23	25	14	5

Team work naturally facilitates discussions, both formal and informal. As one interviewee put it:

> I like to work in a team, I am dependent on each of the team members. We interact freely and discuss each particular point of the project. I benefit from being acquainted with interpretation of facts by the more mature professional staff, but also they listen to me sometimes as a recent graduate.

Personal communication makes for ease of perception and mutual evaluation. There is immediate to-and-fro feedback. The words are supplemented by gesture and tone of voice. The precision of interaction can be much higher. Statements may be less guarded, more revealing. Such informal communication is invaluable during the process of gaining experience, as in the apprenticeship of the junior engineer. Even for the experienced it is an important way of learning about new methods and equipment, the characteristics of which are difficult to convey in writing, and also of receiving feedback about their own ideas and theories. Assessment of the quality of another person can often be aided by conversation with him. Oral communication is usually the most effective mode in a crisis, when time is pressing.

When a novel, non-routine problem occurs in engineering—particularly if it creates a crisis situation—the resulting information search activity may be considerably different from the day-to-day acquisition of current information or background knowledge. The degree of difference will depend on the time pressure. A problem for a scientific researcher will suggest a project—careful investigation and elucidation—and may lead only to a quantitative increase in his formal literature search. For a practitioner, a problem will often demand quick remedial action. Responses to the question put by Gralewska-Vickery and Roscoe, 'What do you do if you have a problem?', were as follows:

Try to solve it myself	86%
Inform my supervisor	39%
Try to find somebody who knows the field	87%
Study the relevant information	90%

Percentages total more than 100% because multiple responses were made.

Interviewees provided more insight into the engineer's reaction if time presses. Crisis is the most important stimulant of information search—

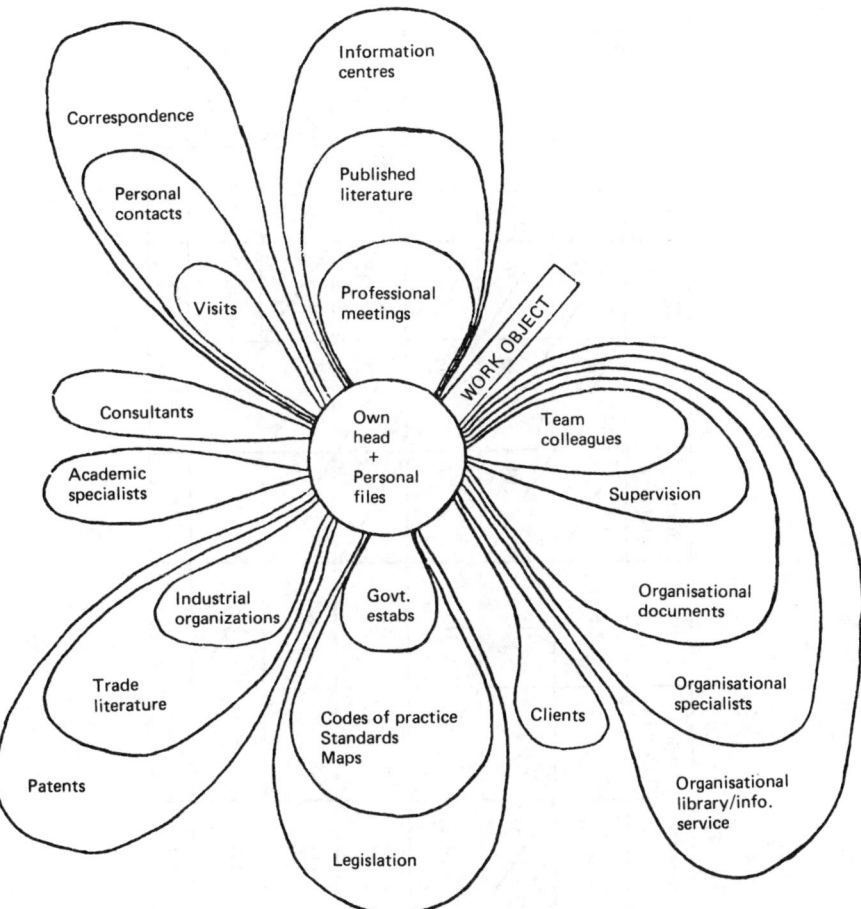

Figure 4.8 The engineer's information sources

when the system does not work, the method does not work, the machine is not working. The engineer asks himself, 'Can I solve it myself; if not, is there somebody else who can help me? Where can I find this man?' Nearly all interviewees agreed that when problems arise, if the engineer's own intervention is not helpful the first step is to contact someone who has had previous experience—a colleague, supervisor, friend, consultant. To look for and consult a written record may be too time consuming (see *Figure 4.8*).

4.25 The relation between formal and informal sources

Engineers, like other practitioners, vary considerably in the amount of time they give to the use of documentary information. Gralewska-Vickery and Roscoe reported that enhanced reading activity in an engineer was

Table 4.28 Correlations between oral and written communication (%)

	Books	Journals	Reports	Trade literature	Abstracts	Bibliographies	Reviews	Theses	Patents	Standards
Talk to colleagues outside orgn	92 / 64	NS	61 / 31	44 / 23	NS	34 / 12	44 / 21	27 / 12	NS	27 / 3
Attend meetings	84 / 68	100 / 80	54 / 34	NS	NS	31 / 10	43 / 18	26 / 10	NS	NS
Visits	90 / 73	NS	73 / 37	53 / 27	NS	40 / 17	50 / 27	NS	NS	NS
Contact manufacturer	95 / 74	NS	NS	74 / 26	NS	47 / 18	63 / 27	42 / 15	21 / 5	47 / 15
Contact consultant	95 / 74	NS	NS	65 / 27	NS	50 / 17	60 / 27	40 / 15	20 / 6	55 / 13
Contact librarian	96 / 73	NS	NS	NS	60 / 38	NS	NS	NS	NS	36 / 16
Overall use by 120	78	95	46	33	43	23	33	19	8	20

NS = not significantly related

usually not at the expense of personal, oral communication. On the contrary, there was likely to be greater use of many channels of technical information. This may be illustrated by a tabulation from their questionnaire analysis (*Table 4.28*). The table relates the uses of oral and written sources. In each cell, the upper left figure is the proportion of those respondents using the oral source who also use the written source, and the lower right figure is the proportion of those *not* using the oral who use the written. In each case, use of the oral is associated with enhanced use of the written—i.e. those more actively searching for information both speak and read more.

The same authors presented another chart (*Figure 4.9*) which displays the complexity of interaction between information search based on reading and that based on oral communication. Engineers who did relatively more reading also wrote and lectured more. The use of written information tools

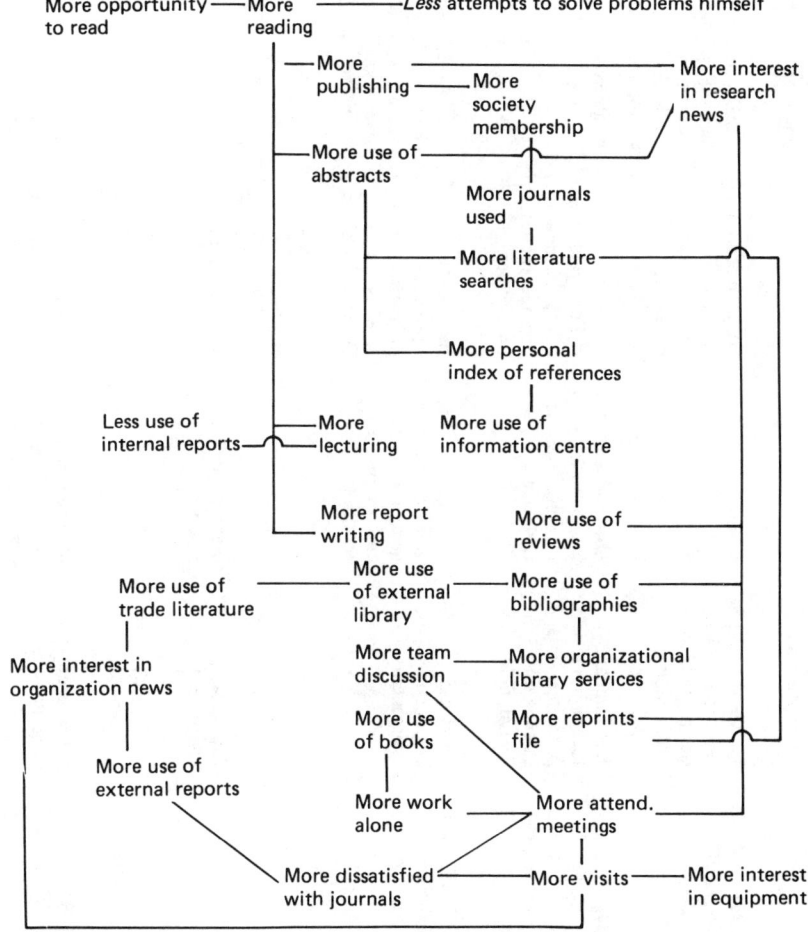

Figure 4.9 Correlations between communication activities

Table 4.29 Engineers' information needs and sources

	Duties	Degree of supervision	Decisions and leadership	Types of information most needed	Sources of information most used
STUDENT	Acquire background knowledge and some practical skills	Close	No professional decision making	Basic science and engineering knowledge, experimental and design procedures, computer programs, case histories	ORAL—lectures, tutorials, colleagues WRITTEN—textbooks, handbooks, recommended papers
JUNIOR ENGINEER (recruit)	Undertake routine technical work in design, field work, production laboratory	Close	Routine decisions within defined procedures. May supervise technicians	Local technical data, design methods, physical data, computer programs, model studies, case studies, regional site information	ORAL—supervisor, colleagues WRITTEN—handbooks, manuals, codes of practice, textbooks, maps
(later)	Use standard techniques to solve problems, assist in calculations, design, field tests	Oral and written instructions on methods. Results reviewed	Decisions within defined guidelines. May guide new engineer recruits on common project	As above	ORAL—supervisor, colleagues WRITTEN—as above plus recommended papers and reports, reviews, bibliographies
INTERMEDIATE ENGINEER	Carry out engineering assignments	Not supervised in detail but receives general guidance and review of results	Independent studies, analysis, judgements, conclusions. Difficult decisions referred up. Supervises junior engineers	As above, also specialized knowledge (e.g. rock mechanics), new methods, government regulations, equipment information, who is who	ORAL—senior engineers, colleagues, clients, contractors, contacts at meetings and conferences, manufacturers WRITTEN—as Junior, also abstracts, literature search, SDI, trade catalogues, directories
(later)	Supervise assignments	General decisions reviewed	Work assigned in terms of objectives. Responsible for success of assignment	As above	ORAL and WRITTEN—as above
SENIOR ENGINEER	Administer work programme	May be none, unless in large organization and where large expenditure is	Decisions on policy and finance. Coordinates work, appoints staff	Particularly case studies, new methods, regulations, equipment information, who is who, business and general economic information	ORAL—as Intermediate, also administrators, government departments, educators WRITTEN—as above, also government publications

such as abstracts, reviews, and bibliographies was particularly associated with an interest in research news, as was the possession of a personal file of references or reprints file. However, those with such interests also tended to go to more meetings, and this associated with more visits and more team discussion. Once again, we have the picture that all forms of enhanced communication activity tend to be correlated.

Factors favouring the use of an oral, personal, informal source of information among practitioners appear to be the following:

(1) Complexity of information sought (relative to existing knowledge of the seeker);
(2) Unfamiliarity of information sought;
(3) Time pressure;
(4) Lack of accessible and usable written sources;
(5) Lack of experience in using such sources;
(6) Ready accessibility of personal contacts.

There is also a clear variation of practitioner communication patterns according to career stage, which we will again exemplify through the engineer (*Table 4.29*).

A young graduate may enter industry or government service, and this initial stage of professional life may be described as that of junior engineer. He has background knowledge but little or no practical experience, and at first works under supervision. He is entrusted with routine decisions within defined procedures, and may assign and check the work of technicians. He is involved in routine technical work or design, field work or production operations. His duty is to forward the day-to-day work of his unit, and to gain experience—both of the technical work involved and of the art of taking engineering decisions. If he is uninspired, he may stay at this stage, never becoming more than a superior technician himself. However, if he develops, both the range and responsibility of his technical work will widen.

After several years of experience the stage we categorize as intermediate engineer is reached. The engineer is now responsible for the work of some junior engineers as well as technicians. He has begun to make more independent decisions, though these may still be reviewed by his superiors. He is using standard engineering techniques to solve problems, he assists more senior engineers by calculations, design work, field tests. He is beginning to communicate with a wider spectrum of other engineers. He has gained experience, but may feel that his theoretical knowledge needs updating and deepening. It is at this time that aspiring engineers may decide to take a higher degree.

The next stage is that of senior engineer, and now, in addition to technical skills, there is an increasing need for administrative and business skills. The engineer will now be responsible for large groups of professional and technical staff. He may be a mine manager, a senior engineering consultant, or even a partner of a consulting company. He makes policy and financial decisions. His contacts widen still further, and are not confined to technical matters—he meets administrators, government representatives, manufacturers, educators.

Associated with these successive stages of seniority, responsibilities, and duties there are changes in the types and sources of information required by the engineer, summarized in *Table 4.29* from Gralewska-Vickery and Roscoe.

4.26 Information flow in the construction industry

In industry many different practitioner groups are interacting with each other. A particularly complex example of this is the construction industry. Its information problems have been extensively studied in recent decades by working parties set up by the UK Department of the Environment, as well as by other investigators.

A construction project brings together a client (who commissions the construction), architects and other designers, quantity surveyors, engineers, consultants, building contractors and subcontractors, suppliers of materials, suppliers of services (water, gas, electricity, roads, etc.), and local authorities. Within a contracting organization there are many levels of function: project manager, estimators, site agents, gang or trade foremen, building operatives, etc. In order to translate the needs of the client and the vision of the architect into a material construction at every stage information must be handed on from one group to another.

In exploring these information flows the Department of Environment Working Parties found it helpful to think of three categories of information:

(1) Specific to a project (project information); for example, client's brief; production drawings; conditions of contract; heating calculations; correspondence, etc.: all particular to that project, and available only to those engaged on it.
(2) General information; for example, codes of practice; manufacturers' catalogues; building regulations; research reports; standard methods of measurement; etc.: all of them not particular to the project but applicable to any project, and available to everybody.
(3) Specific to an organization or firm (organization information); for example, office standard details; cost and output records; manufacturing techniques; etc.: available only to members of particular firms engaged on the project, but some of it relevant to other projects.

Clearly, there is a flow between these three categories. Experience of a particular project contributes to office standard details; research reports to project drawings; etc. Project information may become general information on completion of the project and be fed back to data stores. There is also interchange *within* a particular data store: between client's brief and production drawings; between manufacturers' catalogues and building regulations; etc. We illustrate this in simple diagrammatic terms in *Figure 4.10*.

The flow of information is shown in greater detail in *Figure 4.11*. The heavy black boxes in the second column show the procedures by which the industry performs its tasks. In doing so it draws upon the stores of general information shown in the three right-hand columns and generates

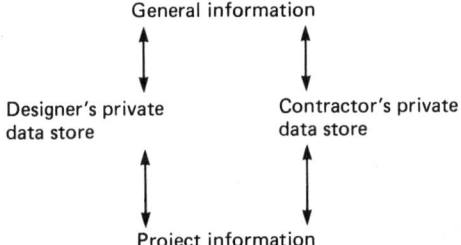

General information

Designer's private
data store

Contractor's private
data store

Project information   **Figure 4.10** Construction information

information specific to the project—the project information. Firms and
organizations engaged in the process also draw upon their own private data
stores for information specific to their own organizations to serve the
management information systems indicated in the left-hand column.

During the initial stages of a project the architect/designer receives a
brief from the client about his requirements, and draws upon generally
available past experience of such clients (user studies). Space and
environment standards to which the construction will have to conform are
ascertained from regulations and codes of practice. Prices and costs soon
begin to be needed, as well as technical data on materials and components.
As the project proceeds, it begins to generate its own abundance of
information—drawings, specifications, schedules, bills of quantities,
estimates, etc. This project information works its way along from designer
to contractor to foreman to operative, and indeed, in one form or another
to a multitude of people concerned with the project. Some picture of the
complexity of information flow in the industry is suggested by the listing of
occupations associated with large construction projects in *Figure 4.12*.

The information transfer is often hindered because successive recipients
have different knowledge structures and organize their own information
stores in different ways. For example, the information in a bill of quantities
(summarizing the materials needed for a job) is rarely organized on the
same basis as information in the working drawings, and neither of these
corresponds to the structures of manufacturers' catalogues or of building
regulations. A great deal of time has to go into 'translating' information
from one structure to another—the 'relay' function to which we have
referred earlier.

4.27 The information needs of 'Everyman'

As a final case study of people and information we will report some
American investigations of the needs of the general citizen. We draw
attention also to studies reported by King and Palmour (1980) and by Chen
and Hernon (1982).

In broad terms, 'Everyman' needs information relating to home and
family, employment, leisure, his/her activity as a consumer, and general
community involvement. Home and family needs include information on
housing, health care, education, social welfare, private insurance, savings,
banks, investment, legal matters, cooking, repairs to the home and to
domestic appliances. Employment information needs relate to jobs,

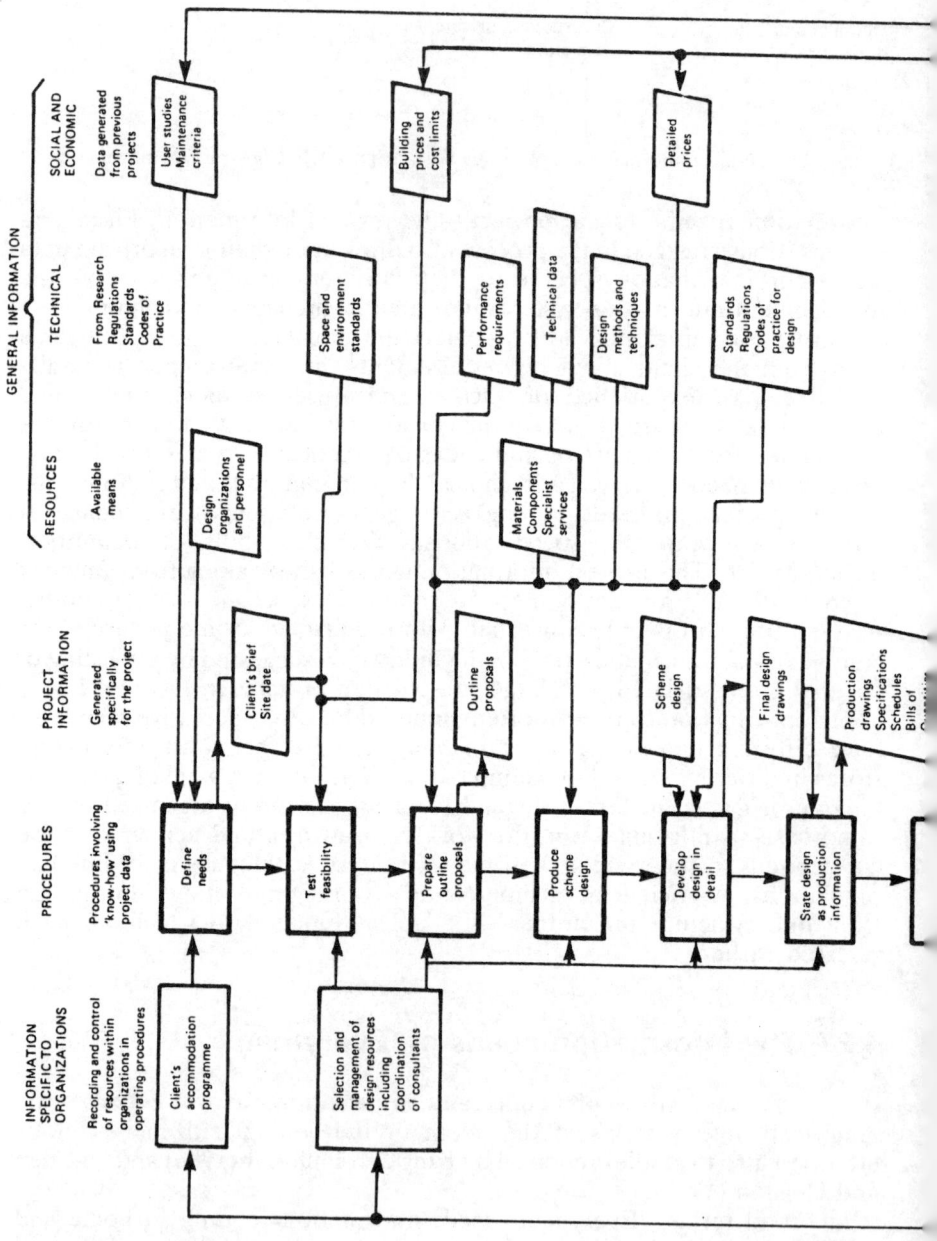

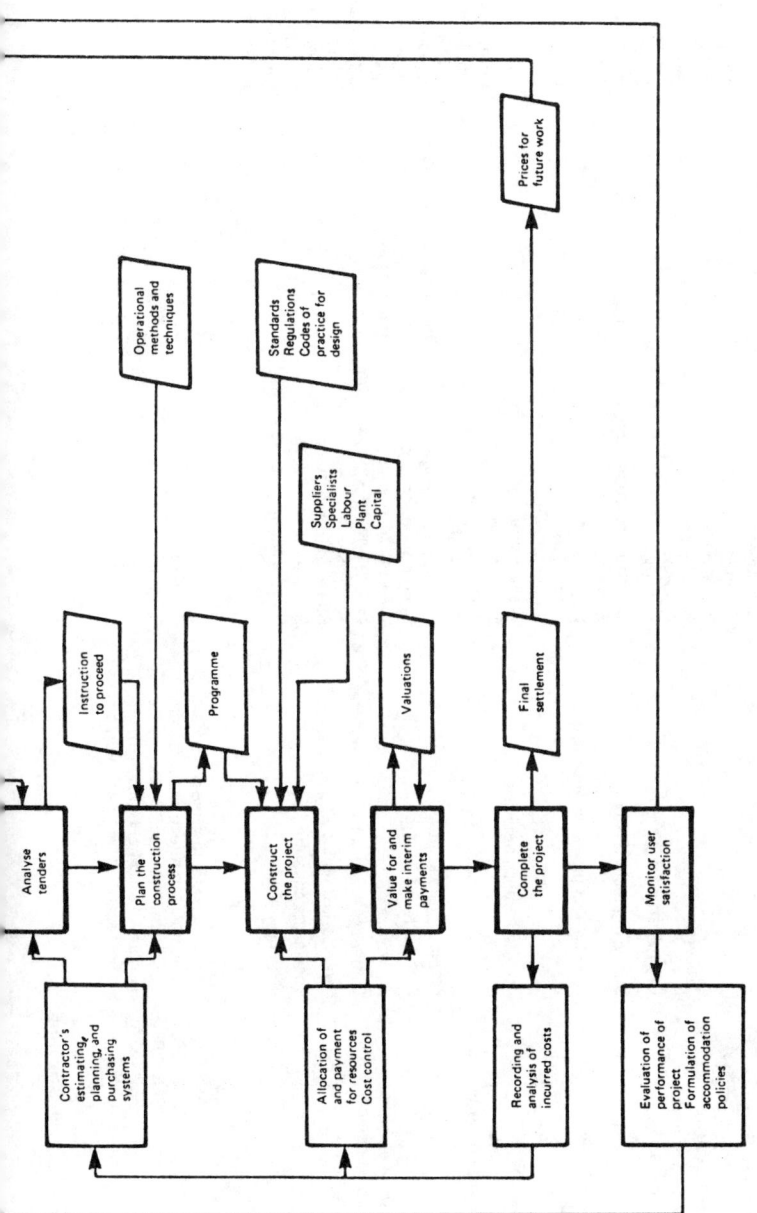

Figure 4.11 Information flow in construction

Level	Occupations
Level	
1 OPERATIVES — No formal qualifications, on the job training, unskilled/semi-skilled	Craftsmen's labourers; Scaffolders; Pipe layers; Crane drivers; Painters and decorators	Messengers; Print room workers; Filing clerks; Machine operators; Clerks
2 CRAFTSMEN — Skilled, college trained/apprenticed, practical training	Tilers; Joiners; Bricklayers; Plumbers; Electricians; Carpenters; Gangers; Foremen	Typists; Library assistants; Telephonists; Receptionists; Secretaries; Bookkeepers; Senior clerks
3 CRAFTSMEN (ADVANCED) — Experienced, qualified, skilled, with supervisory duties	Tracers; Draughtsmen	Construction supervisors; Storemen; Buyers; Estimators; Safety officers; Welfare officers; Clerks of work; Personnel staff; Training officers	Model makers; Sales representatives	Work study technicians; Assistant librarians; Administration assistants; Private secretaries
4 TECHNICIAN — Formal scientific/technical education, skilled	Surveying technicians; Structural engineering technicians	Building technologists; Building economists; Quantity surveyors; Site engineers—civil, structural, services; Site architects; Site managers/management	Computer operators; Librarians; Graphic designers; Work study staff; Operations research staff; Systems analysts; Office managers; Information officers; Accountants; Lawyers; Contract managers; Public relations officers
5 TECHNICIAN (HIGHER) — Trained, qualified, skilled, responsible work, supervisory duties	Architectural technicians	Building control officers
6 TECHNOLOGIST — Qualified to degree level, high level of scientific and technical knowledge, management education	Project administrators; Architects; Surveyors; Engineers—civil, structural, services; Landscape architects	Interior designers
7 PROFESSIONAL — Professionally qualified, experienced, management	Specialists consultants; Planners

ASSISTANT engineer/architect/surveyor, etc.
JUNIOR engineer/architect/surveyor, etc.
SENIOR engineer/architect/surveyor, etc.
PRINCIPAL engineer/architect/surveyor, etc.
CHIEF engineer/architect/surveyor, etc.

Figure 4.12 Occupations in construction

Table 4.30 Daily reading of US population

Activity	Percentage of readers	Time (min)	Notes
Newspapers	73	35	Main news, local news
Magazines	39	33	Including advertisements
Books	33	47	Bible allegedly most frequent
Mail	53	5	Often bills
At meals	42	3	Menus, etc.
At work	33	61	Manuals, instructions
Around house	46	7	Labels on food, recipes
At school	5	68	Tests, papers, notes
Travelling	70	3	Street and traffic signals
Shopping	33	7	Price, weight, labels
Club, church	10	16	—
Entertainment, sport	4	7	Programmes
Recreation	54	7	—

Table 4.31 Documents looked at by US readers

Books
Fiction, non-fiction, reference (including telephone directories, etc.)
Periodicals
Journals, magazines, television/radio programme guides
Newspapers
Local, regional, national, daily, weekly
Booklets
Pamphlets, leaflets, prospectuses, catalogues, guides, regulations, timetables, circulars, maps, brochures
Documents
Guarantees, insurance policies, credit agreements, contracts, wage slips, bank statements, cheques

Forms
Applications (jobs, credit, insurance, etc.)
Returns (income tax, car tax, census, electoral roll, football pools)
Questionnaires (medical, political, etc.)
Order (routine supplies, special equipment, items from a catalogue)
Notices
Directions, labels, store signs, bus indicators, traffic signs and symbols, menus, instructions, advertisements, posters, safety regulations, street names, price tickets, 'you are here' maps
Correspondence
Letters, postcards, telegrams, invitations, bills, circulars, official notices, propaganda
Other
Recipes, patterns (knitting, etc.), bus/train tickets, puzzles (crosswords, etc.), score sheets (games), voting papers, music scores

pensions, income tax. Leisure includes gardening, entertainment, hobbies, sport, holidays and travel generally.

Often, information on these matters can be obtained by consulting those who know—housing officers or estate agents, doctors, schoolteachers, welfare workers, insurance agents, bank managers, solicitors, local do-it-yourself shops, builders, employment exchanges and agencies, clubs of various kinds, travel agents, etc. However, even personal consultation may lead to the provision of some document or other to fill in the details. A study reported by Murphy in Hoffman and Williams (1977) explored the amount and kind of reading that occurred during the general daily activities of a representative sample of the US population aged 16 and over. The average results (subject, of course, to very considerable variation within the sample) were as shown in *Table 4.30*.

The average overall time spent reading was 90 minutes daily. The range of documents looked at is shown in *Table 4.31*.

4.28 Conclusions and implications

In this chapter many specific research results have been reported concerning the communication activities of various social groups, in particular for scientists, engineers, the construction industry, and even the 'general public'. The implications of these studies for the practising information scientists concerned with such groups are usually self-evident. Here we want to consider studies of 'people and information' in more general terms. We would also draw attention to a valuable review by Faibisoff and Ely (1976).

(1) In modern industrial society there are negligibly few people who do not, from time to time, occasionally or frequently, have a requirement for information. The task of facilitating information transfer is therefore not just a specialization involving a relatively small group of 'information workers'. It is an essential accompaniment of almost every social activity. Principles find application within the most diverse fields of life.

(2) The increasing complexity and interdependence of social activities mean that the information required by any individual grows in diversity. 'Everyman' and 'Everywoman' are ever more likely to encounter requirements for information whose potential sources are unknown to them. There is an increasing need to aid people to tap the resources of the information system.

(3) There is great variation among individuals with regard to the content, intellectual level, frequency, and volume of information required. The information system needs to have maximum flexibility to cater for the potential variety of demand.

(4) The three conclusions stated above apply with equal force to the information requirements of special groups of all kinds—whether these be voluntary associations, industrial firms, government agencies, educational institutions, learned societies, or any other. Each requires information, of increasing variety, and of great diversity in content, level, frequency, and volume. Informal procedures of information acquisition will be found in all groups, and formal information services are increasingly necessary to provide flexible aid.

(5) The information requirements of an individual—or of a social group—change continually as he, she, or it grows, develops, advances in a career or a sphere of activity. Sources found useful at one stage lose their value at a later one, and new sources must be identified. An information channel set up to link set $R1$ of recipients to set $S1$ of sources is likely to find, sooner or later, that its occupation is gone. The information system must cater for the continual rise and decline of channels as the pattern of S-R links changes. For the channel agents concerned—librarians, information officers, publishers, and the like—this can be a painful adjustment.

(6) Within a particular activity—say, scientific research—there are various phases or stages of work which have different information requirements. The formal information system must be aware of this differentiation of need within a particular group of potential recipients, so as to provide the flexibility of service we have already emphasized.

(7) Like most human activities, the information-seeking behaviour of an individual or a group tends to conform to an habitual pattern: particular sources are used for particular information requirements. The implications for the information system are either (a) that new services be designed to match the habitual search patterns of their intended recipients or (b) that if a new pattern of behaviour is called for the innovation must be very effectively promoted.

(8) A marked feature of communication behaviour is that accessibility is a most potent factor in determining whether a particular source or channel will be used by a recipient. A source or channel locally available and close at hand is more likely to be used (physical accessibility). If the potential source is another person, there is also the need for psychological accessibility—Is the recipient willing to approach the source, is the source willing to respond? (Homophily plays a part here.) For the information system there is the obvious implication that only a channel that is both locally available and clearly visible to the recipient has a chance of being used.

(9) The environment of a potential recipient is therefore of decisive importance in determining his or her communication behaviour. 'Environment' here includes people habitually met, the communication pattern within his or her primary group, information channels regularly encountered (both locally available—for example, an institution library, job documentation—and general channels such as newspapers and television), and also the intellectual environment: the reference group with whom the recipient habitually identifies. To provide an effective service to a particular social group, the information system must adequately understand these environmental features.

(10) The mode of presentation of a message (medium, language) affects the readiness with which information is assimilated from it. The medium and the language must be such as to match the knowledge structure, learning abilities, and practical situation of the recipient. Coupling this with our conclusion (2), we see an increasing need for 'relaying' work, to change the mode of presentation of a message to what is acceptable to a particular recipient.

(11) We have provided considerable evidence in this chapter of the varied mix of media and channels to which people are habitually exposed. Although our last conclusion suggests that individuals have preferences as to media—clearly, only the literate will use the written word—yet it seems also that active communicators are likely to make use of many media and channels. Information managers need to be aware of this diversity and to avoid exclusive emphasis on one medium or channel to the exclusion of others.

(12) In most situations of informative communication there is an interplay of formal and informal channels. Their relative importance in each particular situation needs to be assessed, so that the formal system does

not attempt to do what the informal can do better—and so that it can develop services that seem to be poorly handled by informal communication.

(13) Information transfer from source to recipient takes place in time, and we have seen in relation to science over what a long period of time research results are being worked into established knowledge. There is no guarantee that a requirement by a recipient for information will coincide in time with its availability from an accessible source or channel. The information system needs to be well aware of such time relations in information transfer, and to pay especial attention to 'timeliness' in information provision.

(14) There can be no argument that conclusion (3) is valid—in a given social group (researchers in a laboratory, students on a course, doctors in a town) there will be wide differences in the frequency and volume of information search. This may be ascribed to internal, personal factors. However, if we compare ostensibly similar people from different environments (different laboratories, courses, towns), we cannot exclude the influence of external factors. More particularly, it may be that inequality in the use of information sources and channels may arise from inequality of access.

(15) Exploration of this problem may be aided by the distinction that Line (1974) has drawn between information need, want, demand, and use. 'Use' represents the actual reception of a desired document; 'demand' includes unsatisfied requests for documents; 'want' goes further, expressing desires for documents (or information) that have been formulated in the consciousness of a potential recipient but which do not all result in a formal demand to the documentation system. 'Need' cuts across 'want'—it implies the possibility of objectively examining the context and environment in which information wants arise, so as to identify information and documents that would be of use and used if made accessible. The analysis points to the existence of various reasons for unequal access—system deficiencies leading to unsatisfied demand, as well as psychological or social factors that inhibit the expression of wants as demands and the individual perception of needs. While some factors leading to high unsatisfied demand or undemanded want may be personal—for example, inappropriate choice of information source, inability to express demand clearly, lack of search skills, reluctance to approach information systems—there are also structural factors that cannot be overcome simply by changes in the skills or attitudes of individuals. Such structural problems of the information system will be taken up in a later chapter.

(16) Most of the conclusions that can be drawn from studies of people and information are either very general—as set out in this section—or specific to particular social groups or even to a particular organization. As already noted, information science needs to develop and to experiment with 'middle-range' categorizations of its variables, with appropriate indicators and indexes for each. We have earlier made suggestions as to categories that might be used for media, message types and recipient occupations. There are established indexes of readability. Categories of environment and of search purpose could be sought. By

moving in this direction there would open up the possibility of more effectively comparing findings from different investigations, and of establishing more firmly based and more widely applicable generalizations about the act of communication.

Chapter 5

Information retrieval

Information retrieval is the process of selecting information from a store. The process is becoming increasingly dependent on physical mechanisms—in particular, on computers and telecommunications—and the design of information-retrieval systems based on these physical devices has become an important area of applied information technology. In this chapter we present a brief factual review of information-retrieval practice, as a background to the two following problem-oriented chapters.

5.1 The entities to be stored and retrieved

The information required by enquirers may be factual and conceptual—the value of a physical property, the details of a technical method, the description of a device, an equation for a relation between variables, the ideas behind a physical theory, etc. As such facts and ideas are mentally absorbed, they become 'information' for the recipient.

In contrast to this, the 'information' stored in a retrieval system is in the form of 'messages', physical records bearing graphic markings (number, text, drawings, etc.) which carry meaningful content that the recipient can interpret. The records in retrieval systems can be of several kinds, for example:

(1) Quantitative and qualitative data about variables of interest;
(2) Texts (including illustrations) on every kind of subject;
(3) Drawing, graphs, charts, maps, and other graphics material;
(4) Computer programs;
(5) Descriptions of objects—for example, of minerals, laboratory apparatus, industrial equipment;
(6) Names and locations—of people, institutions, manufacturers;
(7) Bibliographic references—i.e. indicators of the identity and location of texts where any of the above types of information may be found.

The total process of information retrieval is often multi-stage. To give a complex example, a search for some quantitative data on the properties of a manufactured material might require a series of steps:

(1) Search bibliography for references to texts about the material;

(2) Locate the texts and find one that gives the name of a manufacturer and another that mentions a computer databank that could include data on the material;
(3) Search directories to locate the manufacturer and the databank;
(4) Contact manufacturer and receive a brochure containing relevant data;
(5) Access databank and retrieve further data.

The entities stored and retrieved are therefore 'messages' of the kinds indicated above. Incorporated within each message are one or more 'keys' or 'index terms' by which the content of the message is designated and through which it may be retrieved.

The technical problems of information retrieval are concerned with the efficient organization of stores of messages and the choice and manipulation of search keys. The variety and complexity of these problems have increased with the development of retrieval systems based on computers.

5.2 Tools, techniques, and agencies

The conventional tools of information retrieval have been and still are printed materials of various kinds:

(1) Books with chapter headings and indexes;
(2) Handbooks and manuals with section headings and indexes;
(3) Catalogues and bibliographies of books and other printed materials;
(4) Abstracting and indexing publications, arranged by topic and with indexes, giving references to journal articles, technical reports, patents, etc.;
(5) Printed directories to people, institutions, manufacturers, etc.

Increasingly, the various kinds of message stores are becoming available in machine-readable form. Readers of this book will be broadly familiar with conventional retrieval tools. In this background chapter we will concentrate on 'electronic' tools and techniques, based on machine-readable stores. Our basic reference is to Salton and McGill (1983).

The essence of electronic retrieval is that a collection of messages is stored in some computer-readable medium—currently the preferred medium is magnetic disc—and is accessed by software run on a computer to which the store is linked. A system may be personal (using a microcomputer and small-scale disk storage) or institutional (using a mini- or mainframe computer to which a number of users have wired access from terminals), or public (with the store and software housed in a mainframe with many ports to telecommunications networks to which any telephone has access). Computer hardware and telecommunications are not dealt with in this book. It is the use of these technologies for retrieval purposes that is of concern here.

There are now many publicly available systems, such as the DIALOG Information Service in Palo Alto, California, or Pergamon Infoline in London, England, or Datastar in Zurich, Switzerland. Each of these 'data processors' or 'hosts' has powerful computing facilities and stores a considerable number of databases. Each database is produced by a publisher and leased to processors. The machine-readable database is often linked to—and indeed may be the source of—a printed version of the messages in it. For example, the Institution of Electrical Engineers in London owns the database publisher INSPEC, which is responsible for producing databases in physics, electrical engineering, computers,and control, and for publishing printed abstracts and current titles periodicals. Each database may be leased to more than one processor—for example, the INSPEC databases are available not only from DIALOG and Pergamon Infoline but also from other hosts. These databases are accessible through terminals linked by modem to the national and international public telecommunications systems.

5.3 Design problems in information retrieval

The central problems of information retrieval arise from the nature of the messages stored as records in the system and the relation of these messages to the queries likely to be put to the system.

The messages are not generally of uniform structure, in contrast to the situation in, for example, database management systems. These normally process files of data described by a small set of prespecified attributes— their record structure is uniform and restricted, each attribute may be expected to carry only one of a small number of specific values and the search keys required are largely specified in advance. In information-retrieval systems the 'values' (for example, the texts) stored are of unlimited variety, the search terms presented in queries are unpredictable, and the relationships between messages stored and queries processsed are often ambiguous. The overall structure of the storage and retrieval process can be represented as in *Figure 5.1* (INFO stands for INFORMATION).

Information is input to the system in any of the forms previously noted. The information is placed in a primary information store that may be a

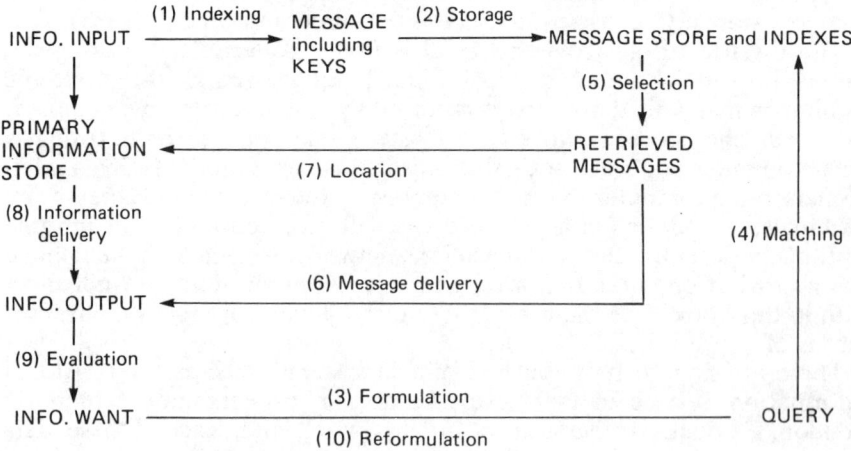

Figure 5.1 Information storage and retrieval

collection of documents (library, filing cabinet, microform collection, etc.) or a machine-readable store. It is indexed (process (1)), that is, its content is analysed to determine what will be the possible search keys. This process can take one of three forms:

(1) The information can be humanly inspected to decide on index keys;
(2) The information can be put into machine-readable form and keys extracted by computer program; or
(3) The machine-readable information can be itself used as a message for storage in the retrieval system.

The storage of messages and indexes (process (2)) completes the input phase.

Output begins when an enquirer approaches the system with an information want—a desire to fill some gap in knowledge. A query expressing this want is formulated (process (3)). This formulation process may be assisted by a human intermediary or by a computer interface. The query is matched against index keys (process (4)), resulting in the selection of certain messages from store (process (5)). In modern retrieval systems these processes are carried out by a computer program. This immediate output may be delivered to the enquirer (process (6)) for evaluation of the information carried by the messages retrieved.

Alternatively, if the retrieved messages do not themselves include the primary information they may be used to locate the primary information (process (7)) for delivery (process (8)) and evaluation (process (9)). If the enquirer appears to be satisfied by the information delivered, the output process ends. Otherwise, there may be a reformulation of the query (process (10)) and an iteration of the search.

5.4 Information analysis

Human analysis of a primary information message consists of a scan to select from it terms, phrases, and other expressions that are believed best to express its information content. The structure of the primary message itself often guides the human indexer—for example, the title of a paper, or a summary provided by the author, or his conclusions. There is considerable evidence of inconsistency in analysis—both as between two indexers of the same input and by one indexer over time.

To achieve at least some terminological consistency (though this does not prevent the selection of different concepts) many retrieval systems used a standard terminology—a list of indexing terms known as a 'thesaurus'. A typical example is shown in *Figure 5.2*. The terms acceptable for indexing are listed alphabetically. Terms not used in indexing are included with a direction to USE another term (see, for example, the term 'Lyophilization' in *Figure 5.2*). Under each accepted term are listed terms that are related in meaning and use. Three kinds of relationship are indicated: 'Lyases, BT Enzymes' indicates that Enzymes is regarded as a wider term that may be used if the initially chosen term is too specific; the narrower term (NT) 'Aldolase' is a specific kind of lyase and RT indicates a term that is related in some less definite way to the thesaurus term. The UF links (as in 'Lysergic acid') points to unacceptable terms at which USE

UF   Lutecium
BT   Metals
     Rare earth elements
RT   Lutetium isotopes
Lutetium compounds 0702
Lutetium isotopes 1802
BT   Isotopes
     Nuclides
RT   Lutetium
Luxembourg effect 1702
RT   Ionospheric propagation
     Manmade radiofrequency
     interference
Lyapuniv functions 1201
BT   Analysis (mathematics)
     Differential equations
     Functions (mathematics)
     Nonlinear differential equations
     Real variables
Lyases 0601
BT   Enzymes
NT—Aldehyde lyases
     Aldolase
     Carbonic anhydrase
     Carboxy lyases
     Hyaluronidase
     Hydrolases
Lycra®
USE Spandex
Lyman alpha radiation 2006
BT   Electromagnetic radiation
     Far ulraviolet radiation
     Ionizing radiation
     Ultraviolet radiation
Lymph 0616
BT   Body fluids
RT—Lymphatic system
     Lymph vessels
Lymphatic diseases 0605
NT   Hodgkin's disease
     Lymphedema
—Lymphomas
     Lymphosarcoma
     Reticulum cell sarcoma
     Thymoma

RT—Lymphomas
Lymph vessels 0616
BT   Cardiovascular system
     Lymphatic system
RT—Blood vessels
     Lymph
     Lymph nodes
Lyophilization
USE Colloiding
Lysergic acid diethylamide 0615 0703
UF   LSD
BT   Amides
RT—Ergot alkaloids
     Psychedelic agents
Lysimeters 1402
BT   Measuring instruments
RT   Evapotranspiration
     Fluid infiltration
     Permeameters
     Porosimeters
—Precipitation (meteorology)
—Runoff
Lysine 0601 0703
BT   Alpha amino carboxylic acids
     Amino acids
     Carboxylic acids
     Organic acids

M

Macadam pavements
USE Flexible pavements
Macaroni tubing
USE Multiple completion
and Tubes
Macerating 0701 1308
RT   Beating
—Blending

USE = Use preferred term; UF = Used For; BT = Broader Term; NT = Narrower Term; RT = Related Term.

Figure 5.2 A retrieval thesaurus

directions exist. These thesaurus relations can be used to aid the indexer in allocating terms or to help the searcher in choosing terms.

Indexers are required to translate the concepts selected from the information input into terms chosen from the thesaurus, where possible, otherwise tagging them as additional indexing terms.

The very act of selecting concepts and terms assigns to them a greater importance than those not selected. In addition, the indexer may give a greater 'weight' to some terms than to others. In some retrieval systems, selected terms are tagged as more or as less important; in a few systems, weights from 10 to 1 have been used.

Computer-based indexing systems have, in general, not tried to emulate the mental functions of a human indexer. To program a computer to select 'significant' terms from natural-language text requires that the program incorporate much linguistic understanding and a knowledge of the subject being analysed—too great a task at present for any but the most specialized of retrieval systems. Instead, automatic indexing has relied on methods based on the relative frequencies of the words in the text.

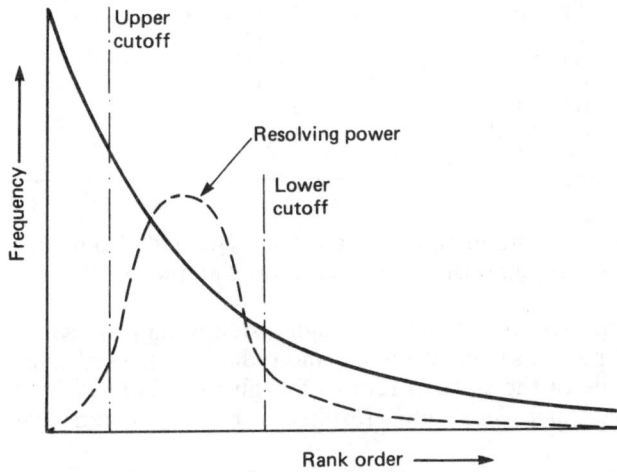

Figure 5.3 Word-frequency distribution

Word analysis of information text displays the distribution shown in *Figure 5.3*. There is a group of very frequently occurring non-significant words (for example, a, the, to, for, not, from, by, who, when, is, it); there is a group of very infrequently occurring words that may be regarded as not significantly representative of the information content of the text; and there is an intervening group of words of appreciable frequency of occurrence that are regarded as having high 'resolving power'—best able to represent the information and discriminate between information texts. It is from this central group that automatic analysis seeks to select.

Several term-weighting functions have been derived from these basic considerations. The simplest is the inverse document frequency weight. This assumes that the importance of a term in a particular text is proportional to its frequency of occurrence (F) in that text and inversely proportional to the total number (T) of texts in which it occurs (a term which occurs widely has little resolving power). A derived term weighting function is $W = F (\log N - \log (T + 1))$, where N is the number of texts analysed and logarithms are to the base 2.

In practice, automatic indexing usually operates as follows:

(1) The texts analysed are often not the full primary information: an abstract, précis, or summary of the primary text is humanly produced and a machine-readable version of this is analysed by computer.

Table 5.1 Excerpt from typical stop list

A	AMONGST	BECOMES
ABOUT	AN	BECOMING
ACROSS	AND	BEEN
AFTER	ANOTHER	BEFORE
AFTERWARDS	ANY	BEFOREHAND
AGAIN	ANYHOW	BEHIND
AGAINST	ANYONE	BEING
ALL	ANYTHING	BELOW
ALMOST	ANYWHERE	BESIDE
ALONE	ARE	BESIDES
ALONG	AROUND	BETWEEN
ALREADY	AS	BEYOND
ALSO	AT	BOTH
ALTHOUGH	BE	BUT
ALWAYS	BECAME	BY
AMONG	BECAUSE	CAN
	BECOME	

(2) The very frequent non-significant words are removed from this summary text by matching against a 'stop list', an example of which is given in *Table 5.1*.

(3) The remaining words are then passed through a stemming process, to remove suffixes (and perhaps some prefixes) and reduce each word to its root stem. An example of the suffixes removed is given in *Table 5.2*. It has been found that such stemming results in improved retrieval performance.

(4) The occurrence frequencies of the stems in the text collection analysed are then computed to derive weighting functions for each stem.

(5) Each stem with a weighting function greater than some arbitrary threshold value is assigned as an index key to the text in which it occurs. In some systems the key may be assigned a weight proportional to its weighting function value.

If the threshold value is put too high, infrequently occurring terms will not be selected as keys, yet these may on occasion have significant

Table 5.2 Excerpt from typical suffix list

ABILITIES	ACIDOUS	AIC
ABILITY	ACIDOUSLY	AICAL
ABLE	ACIES	AICALLY
ABLED	ACIOUSNESS	AICALS
ABLEDLY	ACIOUSNESSES	AICISM
ABLENESS	ACITIES	AICISMS
ABLER	ACITY	AICS
ABLES	ACY	AL
ABLING	AE	ALISATION
ABLINGFUL	AGE	ALISATIONAL
ABLINGLY	AGED	ALISATIONALLY
ABLY	AGER	ALISE
ACEOUS	AGES	ALISED
ACEOUSLY	AGING	ALISEDLY
ACEOUSNESS	AGINGFUL	ALISER
ACEOUSNESSES	AGINGLY	

'resolving power', although normally they are too specific to be useful in retrieval. One compromise is to select them, using a low threshold value, but to associate them with other terms in 'term clusters', similar to the grouping of 'narrower terms' in a thesaurus. If the term 'Aldolase' in *Figure 5.2* were such a low-frequency term, it could then be searched either as itself or as a member of the broader group 'Lyases'. Such term clusters can be constructed humanly, as a thesaurus, or automatically.

The automatic method is to follow step (5) above by the construction of a text/term association matrix, as shown in *Figure 5.4*. A similarity measure is then computed between each pair of terms. For example, if t_{ik} indicates the weight of term k in text i, then a measure of the similarity of terms k and h is $S = \Sigma t_{ik}\, t_{ih}$ (summed for $i=1$ to n).

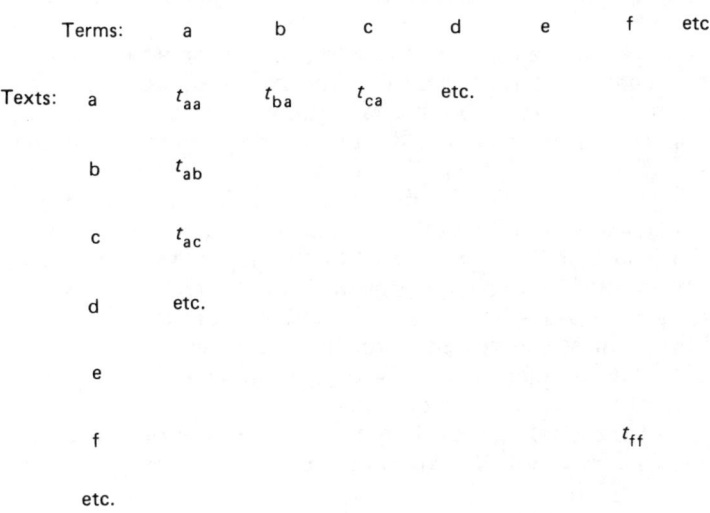

Terms:	a	b	c	d	e	f	etc.
Texts: a	t_{aa}	t_{ba}	t_{ca}	etc.			
b	t_{ab}						
c	t_{ac}						
d	etc.						
e							
f						t_{ff}	
etc.							

Figure 5.4 Text/term association matrix

Terms:	a	b	c	d	e	f	etc.
a	P_{aa}	P_{ab}	P_{ac}	P_{ad}	etc.		
b		P_{bb}	P_{bc}	P_{bd}	etc.		
c			P_{cc}	P_{cd}	etc.		
d				P_{dd}	etc.		
e					P_{ee}	etc.	
etc.							

Figure 5.5 Term/term association matrix

When all pairs of terms have been thus compared, a term/term association matrix may be constructed (*Figure 5.5*). A variety of automatic classification or clustering methods can now be used to construct clusters of terms (equivalent to thesaurus groups) by collecting into a common cluster all terms whose similarity values exceed an arbitrary value.

The stop list removes high-frequency non-significant words from the text, but there will remain other high-frequency words that are characteristic of the text (not occurring too much in other texts) and so become keys for retrieval: for example, in the present chapter the terms 'information' and 'retrieval' will be of this type. As single words (or rather, stems), they may have insufficient resolving power, but could be a useful retrieval key if compounded into a phrase, 'information retrieval'. As can be seen in *Figure 5.2* such phrases are common in humanly constructed thesauri.

There are automatic phrase-generation methods. For example, from the term/term matrix can be derived values of the pair frequency P_{kh}, the number of texts in which two terms k and h jointly occur. If C_k and C_h represent the collection frequencies of the two terms, then the 'cohesion' of the term pair is proportional to $P_{kh}/C_k.C_h$. Word-pair phrases may then be chosen which have a sufficiently high cohesion. Refinements of this approach are possible, in which simple co-occurrence of terms in text is replaced by criteria such as the adjacency of the terms, but this, of course, requires that information about word positions in the text be recorded during the prior analysis. As will be seen, this kind of information is indeed often included in the messages stored in retrieval systems.

Note that only the simpler processes of automatic indexing—word extraction, the use of a stop list, and stemming—have so far been generally implemented in operational retrieval systems. The use of term/term association matrices is rare outside experimental studies.

5.5 Record and file structures

In information-retrieval systems there is usually only one set of records carrying messages, each record having the same basic structure, a set of fields. The elements to be included as fields are of the following kinds:

(1) Generally a unique record-identification number;
(2) A set of fields that together carry the information content of the message;
(3) Fields carrying specifically assigned search keys, whether humanly or automatically derived.

The content and format of the record naturally vary according to the type of message in the system. Unlike the situation in database-management systems, many of the fields are likely to be of variable length, to cope with the variations in length of the values of some data elements—for example, book titles. In the record, the fields follow each other sequentially. The boundaries between fields may be indicated

(1) By markers—field separators;

(2) By recording the length of each field and/or the starting position of each field in the record;

(3) By starting each field with a tag that is a coded indication of its name.

For bibliographic files, the International Standards Organization has developed a standard communication format, upon which record formats in large bibliographic retrieval systems are often based (*Figure 5.6*). There

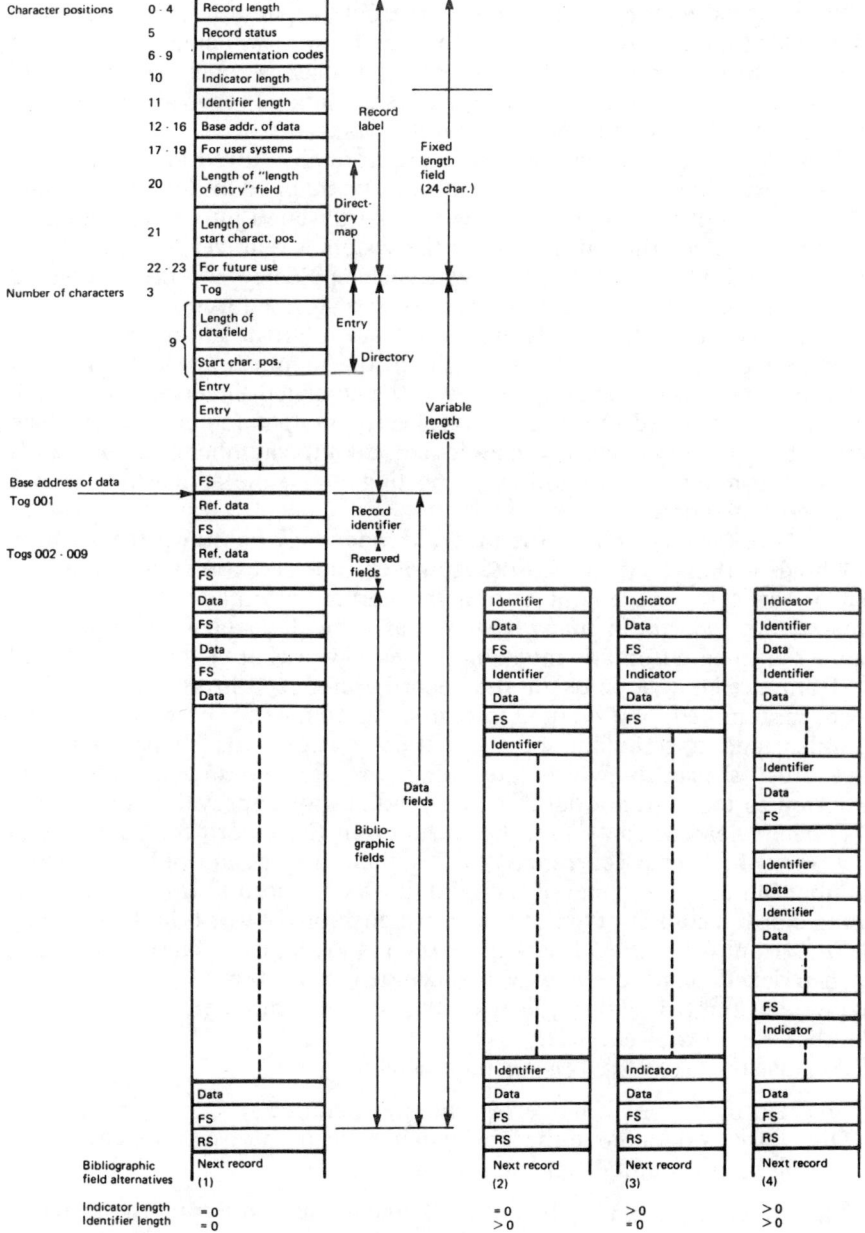

Figure 5.6 Bibliographic communications format

is a fixed-length leader (label) at the beginning of each record, indicating the total record length, its status (for example, new, amended), space for fixed-length codes to be implemented by the individual system, lengths of tags (indicator, identifier), the starting position of the data (base address), more fixed-length space for individual use, and details of the directory map. There is then a variable-length directory to the data in the record: for each field (entry) its tag is noted, the length of the field, and its starting position; the directory is concluded by a field separator (fs). A series of data fields then follows in sequence, the first few of which may be of fixed length and the remainder of variable length; each is concluded by a field separator. The first fixed data field carries the unique record-identification number. At the end is a record separator (rs).

Records of the kind just discussed are normally stored in direct access files on disc. The sequence of records may be mapped into the store using the record-identification number, which is translated into a store address by a hashing algorithm. If the size of the system is relatively small, a direct address method can be used in which a supplementary file is created linking the record-identification number to a store address.

To access the main file it is then necessary to create an index of search keys, each of which can be linked to the record numbers to which it relates. Most operational retrieval systems use the so-called 'inverted index'. All the keys are ordered sequentially (typically, in alphanumeric order). The record for each key generally includes a note of the number of data records to which it applies (the number of 'postings') and the actual data record numbers concerned.

The keys for inclusion in the inverted index may be drawn from search key fields within the data records. However, index creation may be carried out at this later stage, not during the earlier information analysis that created the record. In many systems, as each data record is input it is subjected to an automatic indexing process—words are extracted from all or from designated fields in the record, screened through a stop list, perhaps stemmed, and merged into an inverted index. There may even be at this stage a screening of the extracted words or stems against a thesaurus: thesaurus words are admitted into the index, others are reported to the system operator as candidates for approval or rejection.

Further elements may then be included in the record for each search key. First, for each occurrence of a key there may be not only the record number but also the name of the field in which it occurs. If the data fields being indexed consist of text, the relative positions of words in the text may be important for retrieval, as will be seen later. So for each occurrence of each indexed word there may be included in its record a note on the paragraph number within the text, the sentence number, and the word number within the sentence.

At this stage, the file organization is as follows:

Inverted index with data record number pointing to ...
Direct access data file, either through hashing or via a supplementary file linking record number and storage address

The inverted index may be held as a linear list, and during the retrieval process it may be searched sequentially or by a binary method. If the index is large, there is usually a hierarchical approach to it through further supplementary files (for example, a dictionary file pointing to letter pairs and a word file pointing to the inverted index):

Dictionary file:
    header—pointer to—pointer to—pointer to—etc.
            letter pair 1 letter pair 2 letter pair 3

Word file:
    letter pair 1
        word 1—pointer to inverted file
        word 2—pointer to inverted file
        etc.
    letter pair 2
        word 1—pointer to inverted file
        etc.
    etc.

5.6 Query formulation and searching

An 'information want' initially arises within the mind of an enquirer, who then expresses it in natural language either to himself or to a system operator (a so-called 'intermediary'). In order to carry out a matching process against index keys the natural-language expression must be transformed into an appropriately structured query. Such a query can differ from the natural-language statement in several ways:

(1) A query almost always uses a different type of syntax than the natural language;
(2) The query often substitutes for the significant words of the 'want' statement standardized terminology from a thesaurus;
(3) The query as initially stated may be an inadequate formulation of the want, and may need to be expanded or amended

The syntax of queries will be discussed in the next section, in relation to the file-searching process. A thesaurus is used in the ways already noted.

The formulation of a query so that it is an adequate expression of information want requires more than an understanding of its syntax and standard terminology. Knowledge of the subject area of the retrieval system is needed, so that the query topic can be accurately located within the subject structure; and also a knowledge of the ways in which the subject is organized within the database. To the casual user of a retrieval system query formulation may be a difficult and time-consuming process. Much current searching of large systems is carried out with the aid of an intermediary, an operator with a background knowledge of its subject area and good familiarity with the database structure.

After matching a query with the indexes of a system some sample output may be evaluated (as described later), and if it is not fully relevant to the want then the query may be reformulated in ways suggested by the nature of the output. This 'relevance feedback' may be carried out humanly by the enquirer and/or intermediary, or automatically by a computer program. It will be considered further in a later section.

In most retrieval systems the query syntax makes use of the Boolean operators AND, OR, NOT. To identify all records indexed by the terms 'information' and 'retrieval' the query INFORMATION AND RE-TRIEVAL is input to the system. Each term is individually searched in the inverted index and a report is made on the number of 'postings' for each:

SET 1   INFORMATION   m POSTINGS
SET 2   RETRIEVAL   n POSTINGS

The intersection of sets 1 and 2 is then reported—the number of items that have been indexed by both terms:

SET 3   1 AND 2   p POSTINGS

The record numbers in set 3 are then sought in the main file, and the records are appropriately displayed.

To identify all records concerned either with 'information retrieval' or with 'document retrieval', the following Boolean query could be input:

RETRIEVAL AND (INFORMATION OR DOCUMENT)

This would result in a display of

SET 4   INFORMATION   m POSTINGS
SET 5   DOCUMENT   q POSTINGS
SET 6   4 OR 5   r POSTINGS
SET 7   RETRIEVAL   n POSTINGS
SET 8   6 AND 7   s POSTINGS

Set 6 is the union of sets 4 and 5—the number of items indexed either by 'information' or by 'document' or by both. A search for RETRIEVAL NOT COMPUTER might be expected to identify a set of records indexed by 'retrieval' but not by 'computer' (set difference).

Most systems permit the use of right-hand truncation. A search for INFORM: might produce a report such as:

SET 9   INFORMATICS   t POSTINGS
SET 10   INFORMATION   m POSTINGS
SET 11   INFORMATIVE   u POSTINGS
SET 12   INFORMED   v POSTINGS

Such truncation is, of course, less needed if word stemming has already been carried out at the indexing stage. Left-hand truncation (for example, :COMPUTER to retrieve not only COMPUTER but also MICRO-COMPUTER and MINICOMPUTER) is less often available, being less sure in its operation and more costly to implement.

If the inverted index contains information as to the field in which a key occurs in each record it is possible to restrict search to particular named fields. For example, a search for WATER: (AU) might identify only authors whose names start with WATER and avoid other keys concerned with water occurring in other fields.

Where the data searched are numerical, systems may offer the possibility of range search, such as >97 AND <103. If the inverted index contains information about the relative positions of words in the records, as described earlier, then it is possible to carry out 'adjacency' searches. For example, the query INFORMATION (1W) RETRIEVAL (TI) might identify records which in their title fields had the words 'information' and 'retrieval' next to each other and in that sequence. The query RETRIEVAL (3W) INFORMATION (TI) might identify titles containing strings such as 'retrieval of information', 'retrieval of physics information', 'retrieval of current information'. A query such as INFORMATION (S) RETRIEVAL might restrict reports to records containing the two words in the same sentence, and INFORMATION (P) RETRIEVAL to those with the words in the same paragraph.

Many systems also offer the possibility of 'string search': the scanning of text fields for named strings of characters, even if these have not been specifically indexed. Since this is very costly in processing time it is usually restricted to small sets of records that have previously been identified by Boolean search.

It is often possible in retrieval systems to vary the display of retrieved records on terminal and/or printer. The fields and the sequence of items to be displayed may be varied. Some systems offer wide or even complete flexibility as to which of the many fields in the record are to be displayed. The default sequence of display may be the order in which the records were input to the system, or the reverse of this (in which case the most recent addition comes first). Other sequences may be achieved by sorting on named fields.

In an earlier section it was noted that automatic indexing may result in keys being assigned weights corrresponding to the weighting functions that have been used in selecting them for indexing. These weights may be used to rank retrieved records according to those of the search terms related to them. In principle, this can mean that records more likely to be relevant to the search query appear earlier in the display.

5.7 Evaluation of information output

The immediate output of a retrieval system is a set of messages that have been input to the system. As explained earlier, these messages may sometimes include the actual primary information (for example, in full-text systems or in databanks of numerical information). It is then immediately possible for the enquirer to judge whether the output satisfies his information want. In other cases, the output messages simply serve to identify the primary input, which is held in another store. If this store is not readily accessible, the enquirer must make an evaluation of the output from the retrieved messages alone. If the number of records in the retrieved set is large, it may be necessary to make the evaluation on the basis of a sample of these.

The procedure in an operational system is to examine each member of the set (or the sample) and to decide whether it is relevant to the information want; if a sufficiently high proportion of the set examined is judged to be relevant the whole retrieved set is accepted, and the enquirer may then proceed to locate the primary information which it identifies.

Ideally, an enquirer would like to ensure two things: first, that a high proportion of the retrieved set was relevant (the search achieved high 'precision'), and second, that the search had retrieved a high proportion of the potentially relevant items in the database (high 'recall'). Unfortunately, in an operational situation there is no simple way of determining whether the second criterion has been met. (One way of exploring the unretrieved bulk of the database is to formulate a query designed to retrieve a wider set than that already selected and see whether many more relevant records appear. This, of course, increases the time and cost of the retrieval process.)

A great deal of research effort has been expended on developing the theoretical basis of retrieval evaluation and on the testing of experimental systems in order to assess the relative performance of various indexing techniques and search strategies. Some of this work will be reviewed in Chapter 9. One very well-attested generalization that has emerged from this work is that precision and recall tend to vary inversely: a change in a query that results in improved precision (a higher proportion of the output is relevant) is likely to result in a loss in recall (few of the potentially relevant records in the database are retrieved), and vice versa. It is the constant aim of system design to achieve improved performance on both criteria.

5.8 Query modification

If a sufficiently high proportion of the sampled output is judged not to be relevant to the information want then there may be a reformulation of the query. Various aids can be used for this purpose. The thesaurus for the database being searched may be examined, to pick out broader, narrower, or otherwise related terms that may be substituted for the terms originally chosen. The initial search output may be examined: terms occurring in it (other than those used in the original query) may suggest an alternative search formulation. Finally, reference texts in the subject field of the query (dictionaries, encyclopedias, manuals, etc.) may suggest new search terms.

In a number of experimental retrieval systems various automatic methods of query modification have been tried. The simplest method is to widen the search by an automatic procedure. For example, if the original query is a Boolean intersection of terms A, B, and C a term may be dropped from the query to give an expression A AND B. Rules may be developed to determine which category of term should be dropped first. Again, in a Boolean search A AND B a thesaurus may be used to replace first A by its broader (BT) term, then B by its BT term, and finally both terms may be replaced.

More sophisticated forms of query modification are based on 'relevance feedback'. A sample of the inital output is evaluated as to relevance to the information want, and a subset D_R of the sample is identified as relevant and a subset D_N as non-relevant. The text/term matrix for these two sets is examined by program. According to specified rules, terms with high weights in the relevant set are added to the query formulation and terms with high weights in the non-relevant set are removed so that a modified query is constructed. This is then searched as before. Several such iterations may take place until a satisfactory output is achieved.

Most operational retrieval systems offer the user the following aids to query formulation and modification:

(1) A user manual, which contains a description of the databases accessible and an explanation of the command language in which searches are formulated, with examples;
(2) Help messages that can be called by program during the search, usually explanations of the command language;
(3) An interactive display of a chosen section of the index;
(4) Either a printed thesaurus or an interactive display of a chosen section of the thesaurus, or both.

Experimental systems, as already described, may also offer automatic query reformulation. Further intelligent aids that are being developed include:

(1) User interfaces that can accept natural language input of search questions and and transform this input into an appropriate Boolean or other search query;
(2) Interfaces that can further analyse the input search statement and evaluate its suitability as a query for the system: it may be outside the subject scope of the system, or contain words not present in the database index, or give insufficient information for formulation of a satisfactory query. In such cases, the interface may proceed to hold an interactive dialogue with the user in an attempt to achieve a more usable query;
(3) In systems comprising a set of databases an interface that can make a subject analysis of the query and on this basis select the most appropriate database for search.

Such intelligent aids will be discussed in a later chapter.

5.9 Primary information store

Where the information stored is brief—as in the case of numerical data or directory names and addresses—it may be included in the recorded messages in the retrieval system and so be immediately accessible to search. If the primary information comprises longer texts, or includes graphic material not readily stored in digital form, then the primary information store may consist of printed materials or microform reproductions of these. Some mainframe retrieval systems do include full texts within their records—this has been particularly developed for legal texts, so that access to any string of characters within the text is possible.

Automated access to primary information stores is taking a number of forms. The simplest is to provide the retrieval system with an electronic mail facility, so that after identification of records that relate to wanted information a message can be sent to a primary store (for example, a library) requesting provision of the primary texts. A method that has been used with microcomputer retrieval systems is to link the microcomputer with a videodisc player so that the retrieval program can call up required images from the videodisc.

The development known as 'electronic document delivery' consists of the storage in digital form of extended primary information, including both text and graphics. The text is converted to digital form by the usual methods of input (keyboarding, optical character recognition, etc.); the graphic material is scanned by facsimile camera which transforms images into digital form. The store can be accessed by electronic mail in just the same way as a library, and requested documents can then be transmitted electronically and converted to legible form by a digital facsimile display.

In the following two chapters we will explore two main aspects of information retrieval: first, the semantic problems associated with analysing messages, formulating queries, and matching queries to indexes; and second, the process of human interaction with retrieval systems.

Chapter 6

Semantics and retrieval

We have expressed the unit act of informative communication as:

$$S \relbar M(S) \relbar C \relbar M(C) \relbar I \relbar R$$

For an individual message emitted by a source and transmitted by a single channel, and from which information is assimilated by a single recipient, the diagram represents the essence of the matter. However, the social situation facing sources, channels, and recipients is more complex. A potential recipient with an information want may be aware of a variety of channels, each purveying a multiplicity of messages. Each channel has assembled the messages it transmits by selection from the many offered by sources—who, in turn, have selected channels to which messages will be offered. If we use the symbol Σ to signify a set of entities, and $\longleftrightarrow$ to represent selection from a set we can visualize the interactions taking place (*Figure 6.1*).

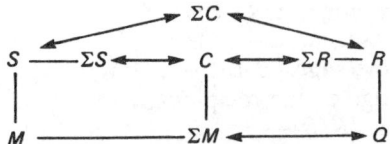

Figure 6.1 Interactions (1)

A source S emits a message; by mutual selection activities ($S \longleftrightarrow \Sigma C$ and $C \longleftrightarrow \Sigma S$) the message is incorporated by a channel C into its set of messages (ΣM). By mutual selection ($C \longleftrightarrow \Sigma R$ and $R \longleftrightarrow \Sigma C$) a recipient R is led to this set, and to satisfy a query Q he or she selects a message from it ($Q \longleftrightarrow \Sigma M$).

How are these selections carried out? The choice of a source, a channel, or a message must ultimately depend upon actual examination of the entity by the chooser. However, the elements of the information transfer chain are usually far too numerous to permit direct inspection of each possible choice. Each entity is normally assigned a 'designation', a meta-message that in some sense represents its content or nature. For example, texts have titles, sources and recipients have occupational labels, and sets of these may be assembled into indexes and directories.

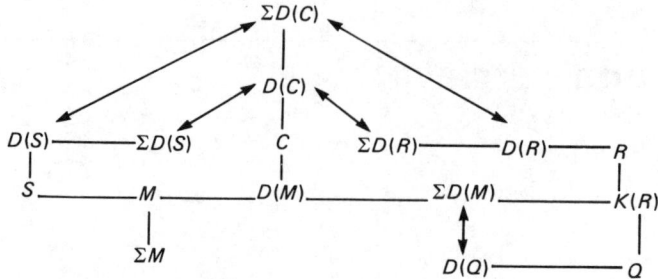

Figure 6.2 Interactions (2)

We use the word 'designation' (following Fairthorne, 1967) to express what may in other contexts be called index entry, bibliographic description, document representation, or surrogate in order to stress that it is designed, created by a human action to carry out a certain function. Our use of the term 'meta-message' implies that the designation is a message supplying information about another message. Our model is now more complicated (*Figure 6.2*). Each source, channel, and recipient has a designation $D(S)$, $D(C)$, and $D(R)$. These are assembled into sets (Σ) from which selections are made (for example, $D(S)\longleftrightarrow\Sigma D(C)$). Message M is incorporated by channel C into a set ΣM, and is assigned a designation $D(M)$ which is included in the set $\Sigma D(M)$. In the knowledge state of a recipient there is an information want that is expressed as a query (Q) and represented by a query statement $D(Q)$. By a selection process, $D(Q)\longleftrightarrow\Sigma D(M)$, relevant $D(M)$ and hence M are brought to the attention of the recipient.

In the total model we may now identify a series of problem areas:

(1) The emission of messages from sources, $S—M$;
(2) The incorporation of messages into public knowledge, $M—\Sigma M$;
(3) The changing structure of public knowledge, $\Sigma M—\Sigma M'$;
(4) The assignment of designations to messages, $M—D(M)$;
(5) The semantic organization of sets of messages, $D(M)—\Sigma D(M)$;
(6) The structure of the personal knowledge of the recipient, $K(R)$;
(7) The expression of an information want, $K(R)—Q$;
(8) The representation of an expressed want as a query statement, $Q—D(Q)$;
(9) Query modification, $D(Q)—D(Q)'$;
(10) The retrieval process, $D(Q)\longleftrightarrow\Sigma D(M)$;
(11) Eventually, the assimilation of information from a retrieved message by the recipient, $M—I(R)—K(R)$.

At first sight, these may appear to be relatively independent problems, but increasingly their underlying connections are being recognized. The structures of personal knowledge or memory, $K(R)$, and of public knowledge, ΣM, must in part be analogous, and certainly the study of each may throw light on the other. Thus cognitive psychology and the semantic organization of the populations of messages and meta-messages can fruitfully interact. All elements of the model are basically expressed in language, and consequently linguistics can provide insights into all problem areas.

6.1 Transfers of meaning

We may further look on the information communication process as a series of transfers of meaning, as suggested in *Figure 6.3*. At the stage we have called 'knowledge generation' a 'referent' in the human environment (an object, a phenomenon, a process, etc.) gives rise to a concept in the mind of the source. The concept is integrated into his or her personal knowledge structure, and is expressed in words or other linguistic symbols. To transmit information about the concept (and thus indirectly about the referent) linguistic symbols are emitted as a message or text. This is

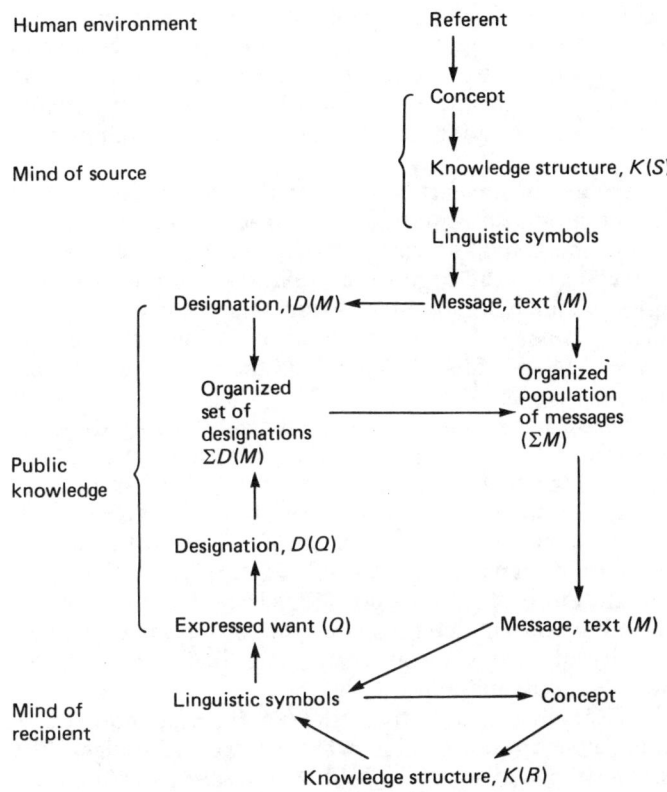

Figure 6.3 Transfers of meaning

integrated into the organized population of messages that constitutes public knowledge. The message is assigned (one or more) designations, and these are inserted into one or more organized sets of designations such as indexes. From the knowledge structure of the potential recipient a query emerges in linguistic form, and is assigned (one or more) designations. These are then matched with the sets of designations, and this leads to the retrieval of one or more messages from which concepts are extracted into the recipient's knowledge structure.

Each arrow in *Figure 6.3* may be said to represent a transfer of meaning, but the meaning of 'meaning' will vary according to the 'symbol situation', as pointed out many years ago by Ogden and Richards (1949). In the relation between referent and concept it is the percipient source who constructs a concept that is to be related to the referent, which in this sense constitutes the 'meaning' of the concept. The linguistic symbol 'stands for' or represents the concept, which thus constitutes the 'meaning' of the symbol; only indirectly can we say that the referent itself is the meaning of the symbol.

In an emitted message the meaning of a symbol may be regarded as (1) the concept to which the source intends to refer (hence indirectly standing for the referent to which he intends to refer) or (2) the concept (and hence the referent) to which he intends the recipient to refer. When this same symbol is assimilated by the recipient its meaning is (1) the concept (and hence the referent) to which the recipient believes the source to be referring or (2) the concept and referent to which the recipient actually refers when he or she uses this symbol. All these various meanings may differ from each other.

We have already argued in an earlier chapter that the meaning of a message to a recipient is the information he extracts from it and the consequent change in his personal knowledge structure. When we consider the arrow linking a message to the organized population of messages the meaning of 'meaning' is somewhat similar. From this point of view the meaning of an emitted message is the contribution it makes to public knowledge, the knowledge gap it fills, the change in the structure of public knowledge that it causes.

Lastly, let us consider designations. These are typically drawn from, or derived by, modification of a pre-existing set of designations—traditional 'subjects' and topics, standard lists of index terms, etc. In this context the 'meaning' of a message designation is a statement—by a source or a channel agent—as to how he or she believes the message to fit into an existing organized set of designations. This set, in turn, is believed to reflect the organized structure of public knowledge, wholly or in part. A query designation is intended to match those designations in the organized set that have been assigned to messages which, it is believed, will fill the information want in the recipient's mind.

Public knowledge (ΣM) has a structure that emerges spontaneously through the combined contributions of all who add to knowledge. The structures of personal knowledge, $K(S)$ and $K(R)$, are each unique, emerging in the life experience of each individual. One practical task of information transfer is to organize designations—particularly $D(M)$, $\Sigma D(M)$, and $D(Q)$—so that they effectively link personal knowledge structures with public knowledge.

6.2 The practice of subject retrieval

The practice of information retrieval has been outlined in the last chapter. Here we will examine it to identify subjects for subsequent discussion.

Let us first look at the assignment of designations to messages, $M - D(M)$, which in more conventional terminology is known as subject analysis and indexing. Designations such as index terms can be simply extracted from a text, as when the title of a publication is used as an index entry. Selective extraction of terms from title, abstract, headings, or full text is more usual. This extraction can be subjective (based on the knowledge and experience of the indexer) or it can be based on some statistical properties of the text indexed—for example, the most frequently occurring words (after exclusion of stop-list words). In either case the indexer (or an instructed computer) must work to some pre-established criteria, an indexing policy.

Extraction is often followed by assignation: that is, the selected terms are transformed into standard terms. One method is to stem them by application of a set of rules to strip off endings. A second method is to match each term against a synonym dictionary (such as a thesaurus) and to substitute preferred synonyms where necessary, or even standard codes such as classification symbols. A third method, less frequently used, is to analyse the meaning of each term into a combination of more elementary standard units (semantic factors). In each case there must be prior establishment of a standard (stemming rules, thesaurus, classification schedule, or semantic factors).

The result of these operations is that associated with each message is a set of extracted and/or assigned terms. This set may be used as the designation or further operations on it may be performed. One is to assign a 'weight' to each term to indicate its relative importance in the designation. Another is to link terms together to denote themes within the message, so that the designation becomes a set of 'subject strings', such as subject headings, class numbers, or semantic abstracts. Once again, there must be pre-established rules of weighting or synthesis.

One further complication needs to be mentioned. Machine-readable records serving as document representations often have several subject fields, each of which is an independent designation of the message. For example, the record may contain a title, a class number, a set of descriptors that may be weighted, and an abstract (a series of sentence-long strings). Each field has been created using different criteria (*Figure 6.4*).

The problems associated with message designations are mainly concerned with the prior establishment of standards: according to what principles should terms be stemmed, or treated as synonymous, or semantically factored, or weighted, or linked into strings? Above all, perhaps, what criteria should be adopted for selective extraction from text, and can rules for subjective and for statistical extraction be matched?

The individual message designations $D(M)$—each a set of terms, W, or subject strings, H—are next organized into a superset, $\Sigma D(M)$, that may be variously known as an index, subject catalogue, retrieval file, or database. The organization can take two forms. The first is to divide the total file into groups, classes, or clusters of designations, $GD(M)$, such that the designations within a group are more similar to each other than they are to the remainder of $\Sigma D(M)$. This grouping can be carried out by subjectively assigning each designation to a class, or designations can be clustered using some statistical properties of the distribution of terms W

6T. Toxicology

PROBLEMS IN AERIAL APPLICATION: DIRECTION OF MILD POISONING BY ORGANOPHOSPHORUS PESTICIDES USING AN AUTOMATED METHOD FOR CHOLINESTERASE ACTIVITY.
Civil Aeromedical Inst Oklahoma City Okla
Patsy R. Fowler, and Jess M. McKenzie, Apr 67, 15p
FAA-AM-67-5

Descriptors: (*Cholinesterase. Chemical analysis), Blood chemistry, Tissues (Biology), Toxicity, Pesticides, Insecticides, Automatic, Organic phosphorus compounds, Carbamic acids, Poisoning.

An automated method, capable of measuring cholinesterase activity in blood and tissue samples, was modified to provide increased reliability. The technique was evaluated as a means of detecting and measuring the inhibition of enzyme by organophosphorus and carbamate insecticides. As many as 200 specimens a day may be analyzed by the improved method, which provides precise estimates of cholinesterase activity in normal and poisoned samples. (Author)
AD-656211   HC$3.00MF$0.65

Figure 6.4 A bibliographic record

among designations $D(M)$. The subjective method requires the prior establishment of groups or classes; the alternative approach needs an agreed 'similarity measure' to create clusters.

This mode of organization, grouping, or clustering can be used instead of, or together with, a second mode, which is based on semantic relations among the terms, W, which may lead on to relations among the subject strings, H. The term relations are usually incorporated into a subjectively established thesaurus or classification schedule. They can, however, be established on the basis of patterns of co-occurrence of terms in designations.

The statistical methods used in the organization of $\Sigma D(M)$ are wholly dependent on the criteria adopted to produce the designations, but the subjective methods are based on additional operations, the establishment of group or class concepts, and of a semantic organization of terms and subject strings that we will denote as $K(W)$. The grouping concepts can be an integral part of $K(W)$, which is typically a thesaurus or classification schedule. The main problem associated with the organization of $\Sigma D(M)$ concerns this structure $K(W)$, its relation to the changing structure of public knowledge (ΣM) and to the personal knowledge structures of message recipients, $K(R)$.

The potential recipient, the enquirer, approaches the retrieval system with an information want. In much of the current practice of retrieval, little attention is paid to what we have called the recognition or expression of information wants, $K(R) - Q$, and for the present we will leave this to one side. The next step is to represent the want as a query statement, $Q - D(Q)$. This step may be left to the enquirer, who must find his own way into an index, which may be provided with some written 'guidelines'. Alternatively, the enquirer may be assisted by an intermediary (reference librarian, information officer, or whoever) who is familiar with $\Sigma D(M)$.

The minimum that must be done is to transform the questions posed by the enquirer into a form that can be matched with terms W and/or strings H

in $\Sigma D(M)$. The processes already described for deriving $D(M)$ must be employed to derive $D(Q)$. Only if the individual message designations $D(M)$ are very simple (a single W or H) will $D(Q)$ be in a form that exactly matches a particular $D(M)$. More usually, each $D(M)$ consists of a set of W or H, and a particular $D(Q)$ will call for a partial match with particular $D(M)$. This is achieved by specifying within $D(Q)$ what are acceptable matches. The 'search logic' normally used for this purpose specifies relations between terms—for example, logical product (*and*), logical sum (*or*), logical difference (*not*), juxtaposition in a string, occurrence within some specified field, etc.

Matching of the query may be restricted to particular groups within $\Sigma D(M)$, either subjectively specified or identified by relating the terms in $D(Q)$ to the $GD(M)$ clusters established in the file.

The query statement $D(Q)$ as initially formulated may not yield a result satisfactory to the enquirer—the $D(M)$ identified may be too few, too many, or be otherwise inadequate to satisfy the information want. General experience is that few questions can be satisfactorily searched as initially formulated, so there is usually a phase of question reformulation. This often involves a reconsideration of the information want itself—just what should be the content of Q? This aspect of the process will be discussed later. Here we will consider how the organization of $\Sigma D(M)$ is used to aid revision of $D(Q)$.

Such revision implies a change in the search logic, an alteration of the terms used, or both. Here we are considering changes of term. There are four sources of suggestions for a change:

(1) The subject knowledge of the enquirer (and perhaps also that of the intermediary);
(2) Terms found in those $D(M)$ that were identified in the initial search;
(3) Terms semantically linked in $K(W)$ to those used initially in $D(Q)$;
(4) Terms suggested by any other relevant subject document (dictionary, glossary, encyclopedia, etc.).

If the retrieval system is semantically organized, then $K(W)$ can be inspected by the enquirer (as a thesaurus, printed or online, as a classification schedule, etc.) and alternative terms chosen; some systems permit an automatic move from a given term to related terms. An alternative is to inspect the $D(M)$ already identified, select new terms appearing in those $D(M)$ that are judged relevant to the question, and eliminate terms that appear in those $D(M)$ judged to be not relevant. This operation can be carried out subjectively or statistically.

One last procedure may be noted: the enquirer may need to move from one retrieval file to another, from one semantic organization to another, in order to satisfy the enquiry. Any or all of the characteristics of $\Sigma D(M)$ may differ in the two systems; for example, indexing policy, mode of standardizing terms and of relating them within designations, semantic structures $K(W)$, search logic. In nearly all cases there is only one solution: for the enquirer (or intermediary) to learn the new system. There are possibilities of automating a switch between the standardized terms of the two systems or between their semantic structures.

6.3 Research in information retrieval

Retrieval problems, as exemplified by classification and indexing, have always been of central intellectual interest in library and information studies. We can distinguish a number of research traditions that have emerged.

The oldest theme has been the structure of classifications—in effect, the structure $K(W)$ by which message designations or actual messages (publications) should be organized (some well-known names in this field are Berwick Sayers, Bliss, Ranganathan). This whole tradition seeks to relate $K(W)$ to the perceived structure of public knowledge, ΣM. Often these perceptions have been influenced by philosophical theories as to the structure of reality, but the main criterion has been 'literary warrant'. By this is meant the belief that the semantic relations embodied in $K(W)$ should be those encountered in the texts that are to be organized.

A second tradition, less theoretically oriented, has been that of alphabetical indexing. Until relatively recently this work has only been concerned with semantic structure in a purely pragmatic way—introducing cross references between index entries as practical exigency suggested— and has been more occupied with matching entries to the perceived needs of the users. The orientation has therefore been towards the verbal habits of the enquirer, so as to minimize differences between the expressed want Q and the query statement $D(Q)$ that is needed to interrogate the index. More recently, this tradition and that of classification structure have begun to influence each other (Coates, Lancaster, Gilchrist, Vickery: in general, see A. C. Foskett, 1983).

A third tradition, much more recent than the others, is to interpret classifications and indexes as specialized languages designed to optimize retrieval, and to seek insights into their structure from the field of linguistics (Sparck Jones and Kay, 1973; Hutchins, 1975)

Fourth, there is the impact of the computer. Its manipulative capacities have led naturally to an exploration of the extent to which computation, based mainly on statistical features of text messages or designations, can derive $D(M)$ from M, structure $D(M)$, organize $D(M)$ into $\Sigma D(M)$, derive $D(Q)$ from Q, reformulate $D(Q)$, switch between different $\Sigma D(M)$, etc. One can regard this approach as in one sense an extreme application of 'literary warrant' in that the whole set of operations is, in principle, based on the statistical manipulation of text. However, the approach differs from the first tradition in that it often seeks to exclude subjective semantic considerations. As Fairthorne put it, the intention is to ascertain how far we can go by using ritual in place of understanding. Recent surveys of this field include books by van Rijsbergen (1979), Sparck Jones (1971), and Salton (1975).

The last research direction to be noted here cannot as yet be called a tradition. It aims to bring more into focus the knowledge structure of the enquirer, $K(R)$, as a factor that is relevant to the formulation and reformulation of $D(Q)$, and that should influence the structuring of $D(M)$ and $\Sigma D(M)$. More generally, all the elements of the retrieval process— queries, messages, designations, semantic structures $K(W)$—are the products of people, and are determined by the knowledge structures of people. It is not only the structure of public knowledge (however this may be perceived) but also the varied structures of personal knowledge that retrieval must take into account.

In our subsequent discussion we intend to pay considerable though not exclusive attention to this last theme in retrieval research. The other traditions must also be studied if a rounded view is to be obtained of retrieval in information science, and the interested reader is urged to follow up the references given above. The latest direction of research has not been as adequately documented within the context of information science, so we have chosen to give it more emphasis. The theme is also relevant to current trends within the computer field. To make computer-based retrieval systems more usable and more effective they must provide for greater interaction between the knowledge structure incorporated in $K(W)$ and the knowledge structures of their users. The computer tradition in retrieval is therefore turning to the study of artificial intelligence and expert systems, and is finding that an understanding of subjective knowledge structures is increasingly important for its own development.

6.4 Structures of public knowledge

Before turning to these matters we wish to take a brief look at some of the structures to be found in publicly recorded knowledge, some of the categories commonly encountered in published literature.

Relative position in space is a very common form of public knowledge, embodied in maps, charts, plans, detail drawings, etc. which can become of considerable complexity. Contemporaneity or succession in time is an equally general form of relation that may be displayed in diverse ways such as historical tables.

A more complex category than spatial relation is that of hierarchy, as defined, for example, by Simon (1969): 'A system composed of interrelated subsystems, each of the subsystems being in turn hierarchic in structure until we reach some lowest level of elementary subsystem.' The ubiquity of this form of structure is well displayed in a symposium edited by Whyte et al. (1969). Within a particular system the elements may be seen as in dynamic interaction.

More complex than temporal succession is the genetic relation, in which a later element is derived from or produced by an earlier, and this can be extended into an evolutionary structure or family tree, common in biological and historical knowledge.

The category of likeness between elements leads to the class–membership relation, and similarity among classes leads further to the generic or inclusion relation, application of which generates a classification, a form of structure that is found in most fields of knowledge.

Relations between classes yield propositions, and between propositions there may exist the relation of implication. The application of this leads to a set of interconnected propositions, a structure of theory.

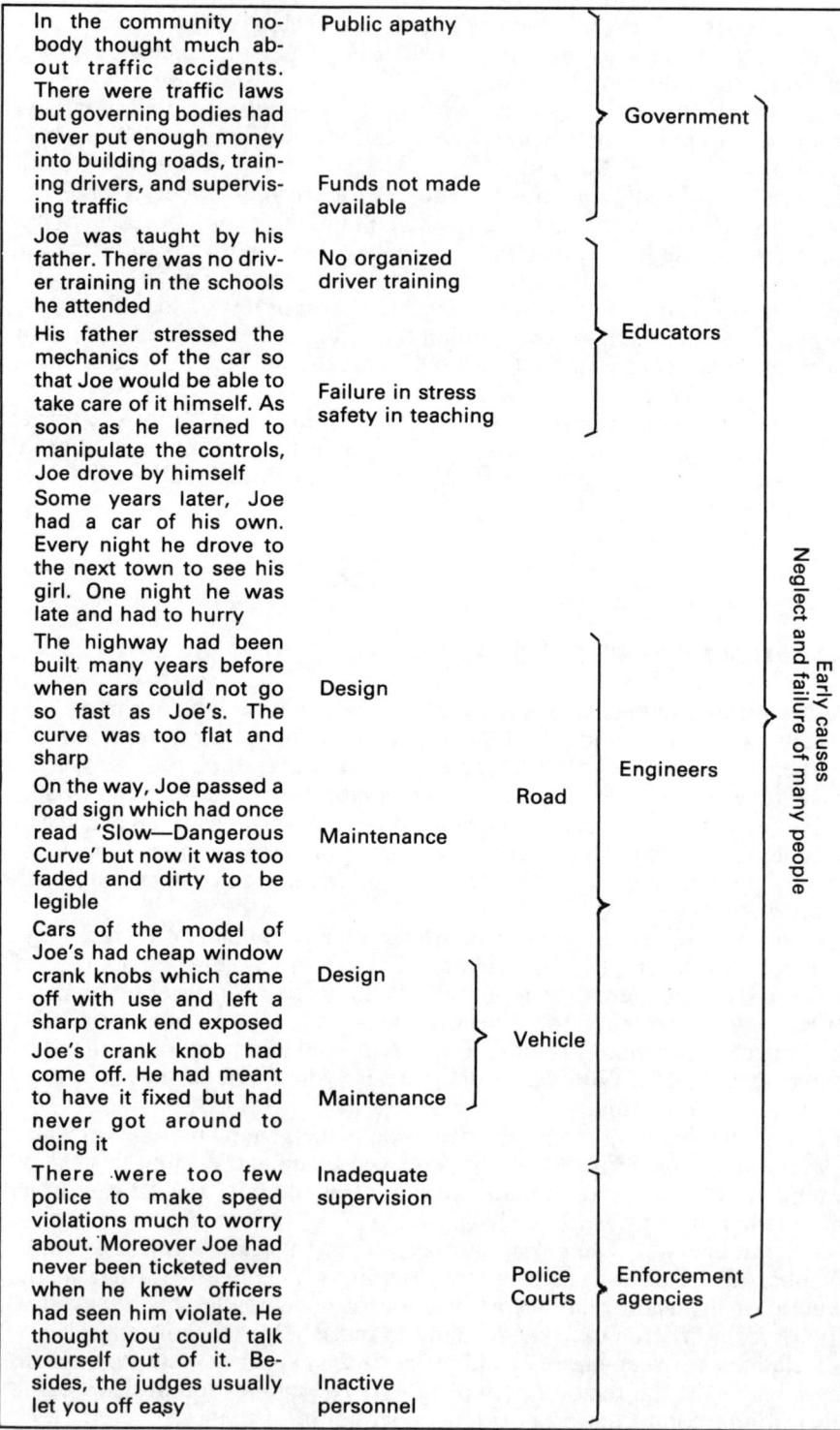

Narrative	Cause	Group	Super-group
In the community nobody thought much about traffic accidents. There were traffic laws but governing bodies had never put enough money into building roads, training drivers, and supervising traffic	Public apathy	Government	Early causes / Neglect and failure of many people
	Funds not made available		
Joe was taught by his father. There was no driver training in the schools he attended	No organized driver training	Educators	
His father stressed the mechanics of the car so that Joe would be able to take care of it himself. As soon as he learned to manipulate the controls, Joe drove by himself	Failure in stress safety in teaching		
Some years later, Joe had a car of his own. Every night he drove to the next town to see his girl. One night he was late and had to hurry			
The highway had been built many years before when cars could not go so fast as Joe's. The curve was too flat and sharp	Design	Road — Engineers	
On the way, Joe passed a road sign which had once read 'Slow—Dangerous Curve' but now it was too faded and dirty to be legible	Maintenance		
Cars of the model of Joe's had cheap window crank knobs which came off with use and left a sharp crank end exposed	Design	Vehicle	
Joe's crank knob had come off. He had meant to have it fixed but had never got around to doing it	Maintenance		
There were too few police to make speed violations much to worry about. Moreover Joe had never been ticketed even when he knew officers had seen him violate. He thought you could talk yourself out of it. Besides, the judges usually let you off easy	Inadequate supervision	Police Courts — Enforcement agencies	
	Inactive personnel		

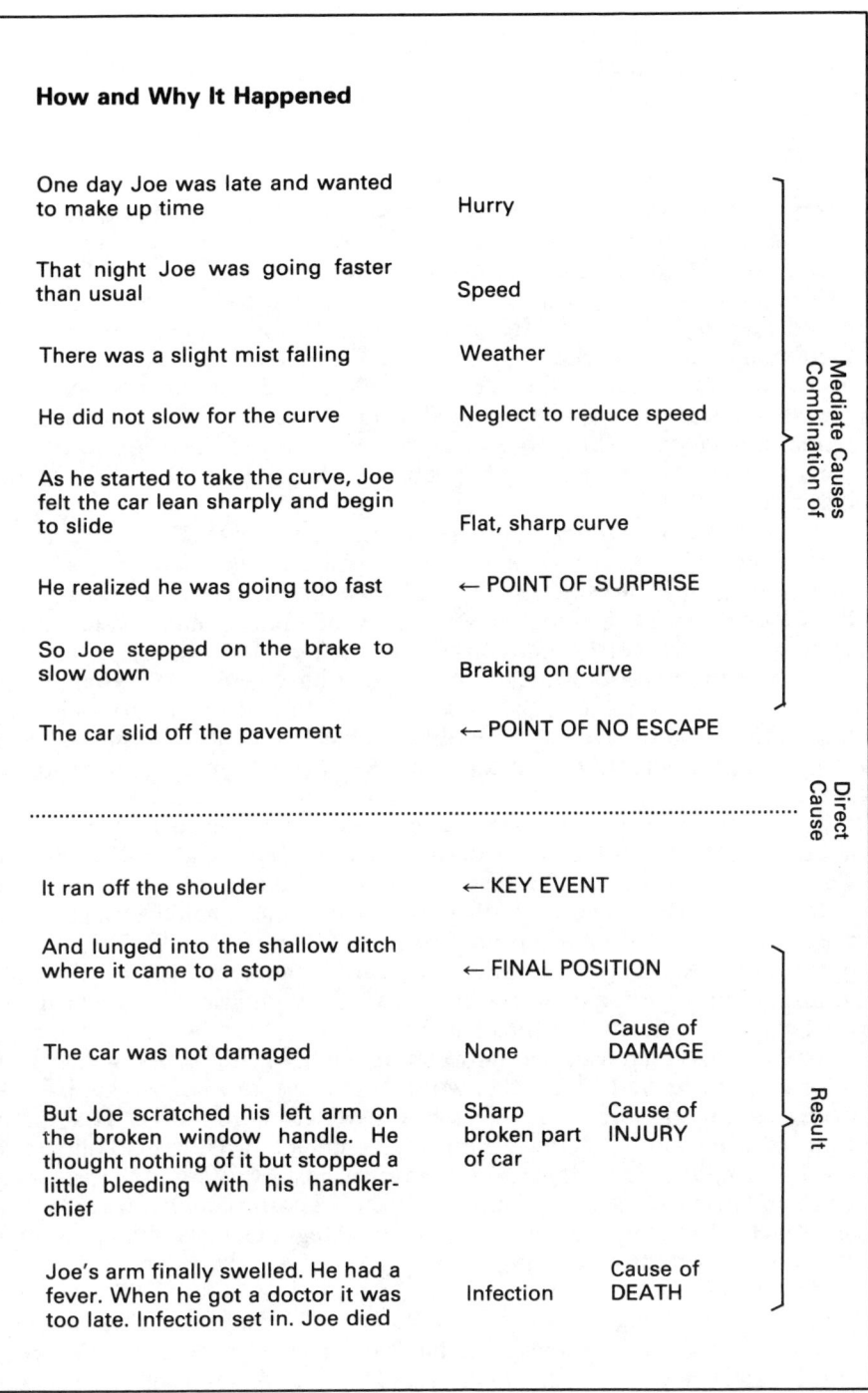

How and Why It Happened

One day Joe was late and wanted to make up time	Hurry	
That night Joe was going faster than usual	Speed	
There was a slight mist falling	Weather	
He did not slow for the curve	Neglect to reduce speed	
As he started to take the curve, Joe felt the car lean sharply and begin to slide	Flat, sharp curve	
He realized he was going too fast	← POINT OF SURPRISE	
So Joe stepped on the brake to slow down	Braking on curve	
The car slid off the pavement	← POINT OF NO ESCAPE	
It ran off the shoulder	← KEY EVENT	
And lunged into the shallow ditch where it came to a stop	← FINAL POSITION	
The car was not damaged	None	Cause of DAMAGE
But Joe scratched his left arm on the broken window handle. He thought nothing of it but stopped a little bleeding with his handkerchief	Sharp broken part of car	Cause of INJURY
Joe's arm finally swelled. He had a fever. When he got a doctor it was too late. Infection set in. Joe died	Infection	Cause of DEATH

Mediate Causes Combination of — Direct Cause — Result

Figure 6.5 Levels of causal relation

Causal relations among phenomena are relations asserted to be invariant between various elements of knowledge—the occurrence of one necessarily depending upon the occurrence of another. Causal relations can exist at many different levels, as illustrated in *Figure 6.5* (taken from Baker, 1955).

These are just some of the structures encountered in public and recorded knowledge—a brief indication of its complexity. We have also to take note of its dynamic characteristics.

The content and structure of public knowledge are continually changing. In social life every day there occur innumerable 'events'. Most of them are noted only by the immediate participants, who may store the details in their memories and perhaps note the significant items in diaries and letters. Many others come to the attention of only a few people. A small proportion is recorded, disseminated, communicated, and becomes part of public knowledge. The new events may give rise to the coinage of new names—technical jargon, colloquialisms, slang, journalese, or simple descriptive labels.

Social activity is continually generating new data that need to be communicated: new products, new trade names, new prices, new regulations, new institutions, etc. All this adds to the content of public knowledge—which includes a vast array of almost unintegrated detail upon which each person may, from time to time, have to draw.

Structured public knowledge, of which we have given a few examples, is the result of working over the mass of detail, organizing it into something more than bare events and data. One particular form of such processing—a scientific investigation—has been looked at in depth by Ravetz (1971).

The scientist in the laboratory or on field work collects a mass of data about the properties and behaviour of the natural or social entities studied. The raw data are analysed, summarized, integrated into conceptual 'information'. (Ravetz uses this word in a sense other than the usage in this book—as a stage in the transition from raw data to scientific 'fact'. There is, however, some relation with our use of the term, for it is usually 'information'—rather than raw data—which is published and which can then serve to 'inform' the recipient.)

The scientist then uses the 'information' he has generated, together with information derived from the work (writings) of other scientists, as evidence to support a conclusion on which he reports. His direct contribution to public knowledge is then completed. However, the use of his information as evidence in investigations by other scientists may gradually firm up his conclusion so that the scientific community accepts it as a 'fact'. The collective work of science integrates facts into conceptual systems supported by unifying theory.

As science—or any other area of integrated, structured knowledge—progresses, new 'facts' come to be accepted, old 'facts' lose their validity, and the conceptual systems that have been created begin to change—slowly, piecemeal, or at times rapidly and dramatically. Historical illustrations of such changes in structure may be found in a previous book, *Classification and Indexing in Science* (Vickery, 1975). Public knowledge is not static: it is a dynamic continuum, whose content is perpetually expanding and altering, and whose structures are continually being revised.

6.5 Personal knowledge

With this in mind we will now take a more extensive look at current views on personal knowledge structures as they have developed within cognitive psychology. We are concerned with the aspects of meaning transfer shown in *Figure 6.6*. The questions at issue are how knowledge of the world is assimilated, represented, stored, transformed, and accessed by the symbolic processing system of the mind.

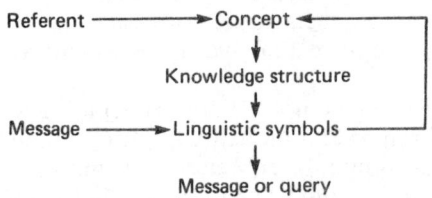

Figure 6.6 Meaning transfer and personal knowledge

Despite the amount of effort that has gone into the study of learning by children, Lindsay and Norman (1977) emphasize that studies of knowledge acquisition by adults are still relatively undeveloped. They suggest that the processes may be understood in the following way. Knowledge in the human mind is structured, organized into 'memory schemas' of various kinds, as will be discussed further below. Incoming information must either be fitted into existing schemas or new schemas must be developed. If a message relates to a topic for which there are already well-structured schemas the assimilated information can be linked on by accretion to the knowledge structure. If the information is mainly novel, its assimilation may require the restructuring of schemas to accommodate it. Brookes (1975) has expressed this as 'the fundamental equation of information science', $I + (K) \rightarrow (K')$: an increment of information, I, interacts with an existing knowledge structure, (K), which is thereby altered to a modified structure, (K').

There is little doubt that human cognition is very complex. The currently accepted view, as summarized, for example, by Loftus and Loftus (1976) or by Lindsay and Norman (1977), is that the impact of data into the mind can be illustrated as follows:

Environment
↓
Sensory store
↓
Short-term store with rehearsal buffer
↓
Long-term store for semantic and episodic memory

Although the following account refers to this series of 'stores' these are not necessarily physically separate areas of the brain but may be seen as stages or levels in the processing of incoming data.

There is evidence that data are first, as it were, held in a sensory store, comprising all the sense data momentarily impinging onto the body from the environment—a large quantity of messages indeed, but they decay quickly, and each datum is lost within a second or so unless it is transferred onward through the system. In any given situation the mind's attention is focused on a small proportion of the data in sensory store, and this is transferred to a short-term store of very limited capacity. Here it will decay and be lost in about 15 seconds unless there comes into play the 'rehearsal buffer' (as when one remembers a telephone number by repeatedly saying it to oneself). The final stage of the system is the long-term store, apparently of virtually unlimited capacity. A distinction has been made between its content of 'episodic' memories—records of individual life experiences—and the 'semantic memory', structured knowledge going beyond remembered episodes, though the two sets of memories are clearly interrelated. It is with the long-term memory that we are particularly concerned.

Insights into the organization of long-term memory are only beginning to emerge. As a physical mechanism the brain is enormously complex—about ten thousand million nerve cells in the human cerebral cortex, multiply interconnected. Perhaps we may say, following Young (1978), that each cell corresponds to '(1) a small part of one particular feature of change going on in the outside world, (2) some small part of a memory record of a past external change, or (3) some small part of the instructions for an action that can be done by the body, say to initiate the movement of a few fibres of one muscle', though his description deliberately simplifies the matter. Some mapping of the cortex to show the locality of different sensory and motor areas has been possible. No such mapping however, is yet possible for memory records—and indeed there is no physiological evidence that a specific memory is stored in a specific part of the brain: many brain areas seem to contribute to it (Lindsay and Norman, 1977).

6.6 Studies of memory

Clues to memory structure can only be provided by human behaviour—and in particular by verbal output. The knowledge expressed in behaviour, speech, and writing must be correlated in some way with the mental structure of the actor, speaker, or writer. For example, the sequences and relationships between concepts that are displayed in this book must reflect patterns in the minds of the authors. Analysis of speech or text, and of the structure of public knowledge, therefore gives an indication of memory structure. Experimentally, psychologists have sought clues from the responses of subjects to questions: for example, words commonly associated with a stimulus word or the speed of response to questions of the type, 'Is it true that an A is B?'. Examples below are taken from such texts as Kintsch (1977), Rumelhart (1977) Loftus and Loftus (1976), and Baddeley (1976). Admirable reviews of cognitive psychology from an information processing viewpoint are the book by the Lachmans (1979), and another by Anderson (1980).

Table 6.1 Responses to the word BUTTERFLY

	Moth	*Insect*	*Wing*	*Bird*	*Fly*	*Cocoon*
Moth	–	2	2	–	10	–
Insect	4	–	–	–	18	–
Wing	–	–	–	50	24	–
Bird	–	–	6	–	30	–
Fly	–	10	–	8	–	–
Cocoon	16	6	–	–	–	–

If the same word is presented to a large group of experimental subjects there is usually considerable consensus among them on the list of words spontaneously associated with the stimulus. For example, the words in *Table 6.1* are all likely to occur frequently among responses to the word BUTTERFLY. The table also shows the numbers of occasions on which each word was associated with each other in one particular study.

Such an association table suggests that a common pattern of association links in the mind is as shown in *Figure 6.7*. The numbers in *Table 6.1* give some indication of the 'strength' of association, the closeness with which two words are associated, their 'semantic distance'.

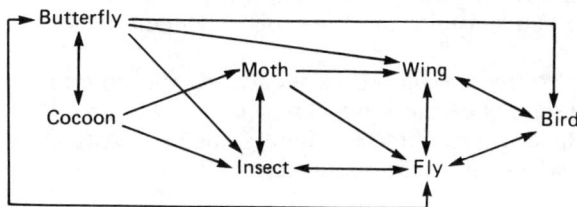

Figure 6.7 Association links

Strength of association has also been used as a measure of 'typicality'. If a number of people are asked to give a set of examples of BIRD, different birds will be mentioned with different frequency. In one experiment, frequencies such as the following were obtained.

Robin	377		Ostrich	17
Sparrow	237		Swan	14
Eagle	161	*but*	Crane	13
Crow	149		Geese	12
Canary	134		Pelican	11
Blackbird	89		Stork	10

The high-frequency items are more widely considered as 'typical' birds than the low-frequency ones, and are more readily recalled in response to the request 'Name a bird'.

Another approach to the indication of semantic distance is to ask subjects to rate the 'similarity of words'. For example, from a list of thirty mammals subjects were asked to rate each possible pair on a similarity scale between 1 (identical) and 10 (maximally different). In the course of the study it became clear that two criteria of similarity were seen as of most

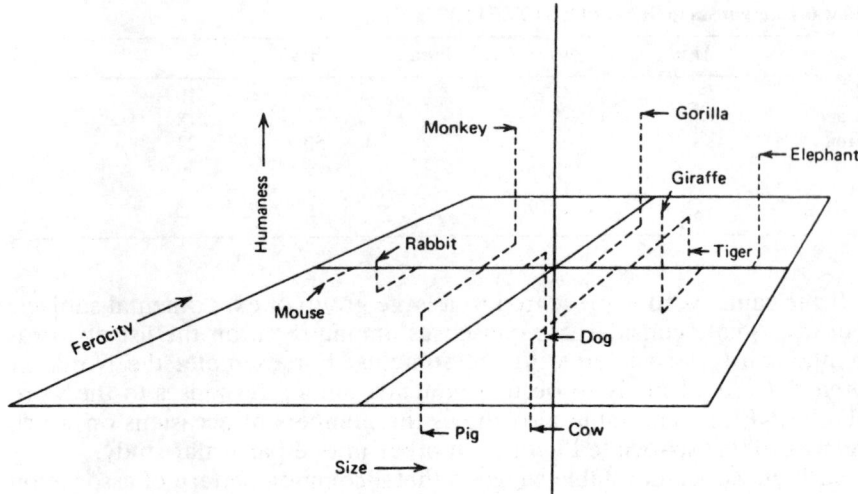

Figure 6.8 Representation of semantic distance

importance: how like or unlike a human the animal was judged to be, and how fierce. From the results a spatial representation of semantic distance was established (*Figure 6.8*).

Semantic distance has also been explored by measuring the time taken by a subject to verify statements of the kind 'An A is B—true or false?' Some representative results are given below, where *L* means 'verification of the previous word takes less time than verification of ...'

(1) Canary is a—bird *L* animal *L* fish;
(2) The following is a bird—canary *L* ostrich *L* butterfly;
(3) Collie is a—dog *L* animal *L* mammal;
(4) Canary is—yellow *L* flies *L* eats *L* has gills;
(5) Flower is a—chair *L* oak.

A simple interpretation of such results is to distinguish between entities (such as canary, bird, dog, chair) and properties (such as yellow, flies,

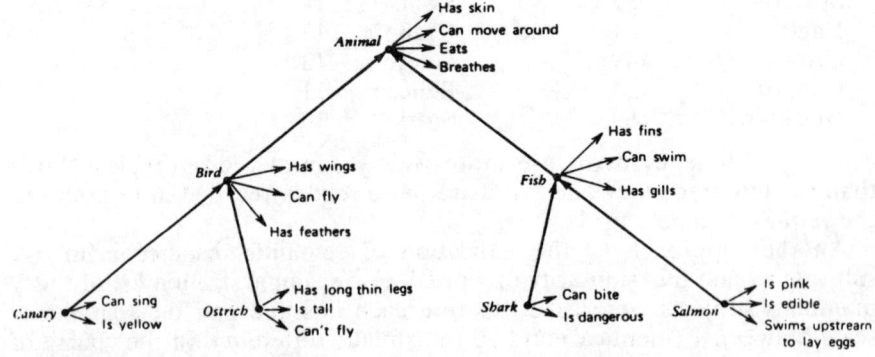

Figure 6.9 Hierarchical network

eats). The entities are linked hierarchically in a generic chain (animal–bird–canary–particular canaries), and at each link in the chain are attached properties specific to that level, but not properties common to entities at a higher level. An example of a hierarchical network from Collins and Quillian (1969) is shown in *Figure 6.9*.

It is assumed that to verify that A is B the mind accesses both A and B, and traces the chain of links between them: the longer the chain, the greater the response time. Thus 'canary is bird' takes less time than 'canary is animal', 'canary is yellow' less time than 'canary eats', and the latter less time than 'canary has gills'.

Some experimental results support the simple Collins and Quillian model, but others do not. Example (3) given above shows that 'collie is mammal', which should hierarchically come between dog and animal, takes longer to verify than either of the other statements about COLLIE, and this has been ascribed to the relative lack of familiarity of the term MAMMAL—i.e. it is less likely to be semantically close to COLLIE in a word-association experiment. Canary and ostrich are equidistant from bird in the model pictured in *Figure 6.9*, but example (2) shows that it takes longer to verify that ostrich is a bird—canary is more familiar, typical and closely associated. In example (5) flower and oak are in the same general area of knowledge, and the memory structure between them is explored to verify that a flower is not an oak, but the unrelated words FLOWER and CHAIR are more quickly assessed. It is evident that memory structure is more complex than the Collins and Quillian model, and in particular:

(1) Semantic distance is influenced by strength of association as well as by hierarchical links;
(2) We need not assume that a property is linked only to the highest level of entity to which it applies—for example, 'has wings' might be linked directly to a number of bird names; and
(3) The model makes no provision for direct linkages between properties.

An alternative model for memory does not stress hierarchical linkages but concentrates on associations. For example, we might have the sets of features associated with various concepts (*Table 6.2*). The nearer the top of a list, the stronger the association.

In response to the question whether A is B, the feature sets of A and B are compared. It is clear that CANARY—with four features in common with BIRD—is likely to be more readily verified as a bird than is OSTRICH. When BUTTERFLY is compared with BIRD there is an

Table 6.2 Concepts and features

Bird	Canary	Ostrich	Butterfly
Feathers	Sings	Neck	Wings
Wings	Yellow	Long legs	Flies
Flies	Cage	Beak	Flowers
Eggs	Wings	Runs	Nectar
Nests	Feathers	Feathers	Moth
Beak	Beak	Eggs	Coloured
Sings	Small		Insect
			Cocoon

overlap of two features and so there can be some initial doubt—hence perhaps the long response time in example (2) above. A feature model of this kind can be refined by distinguishing between 'defining' features (essential aspects of meaning) and other features, with the defining features playing a decisive role in cases of doubt. For example, if 'feathers' were a defining feature of BIRD it would act to include OSTRICH but exclude BUTTERFLY from the category of birds.

It snould be stressed here that the models discussed above are considered to represent the conceptual knowledge structure. It seems likely that there are in the mind also (1) a lexical structure of *words*, separate from though necessarily linked to the structure of concepts, and (2) a linked *image* store, since a sight, a sound, a smell calls up both a corresponding concept and its name. In the experimental work reported earlier, input stimuli in the form of words must first be matched in the lexical system before being transferred to the conceptual structure. Other experimental work has explored the structure of the lexicon itself by asking people to name pictures of objects and measuring the speed of response.

It has been found that the speed varies according to the frequency of occurrence of the name in general English usage—for example, the picture of a book or chair was more rapidly named than one of a bagpipe or gyroscope. There is another factor at work: everyone responds in the same way to a picture of a book ('It's a book'), but the names supplied for the picture of a gyroscope included spinner, top, whirler, circumrotator, and machine. As uncertainty about the name increases, so does the time taken to give a name, and this factor has been shown to be independent of the effect of usage frequency of the name. It appears that more frequently occurring names, and the names of more readily identified images, are both more easily accessed in the lexicon.

6.7 Language and logic

As well as cognitive psychologists, linguists also are concerned with words and meanings, and contribute their own insights into semantic relations. Consider a sentence such as 'He found that the thermometer reading was unexpectedly high'. It can be analysed into individual letters (or sounds, if it is spoken), words, phrases, clauses. Linguists further distinguish *lexemes*, vocabulary words that can take various forms—for example, the lexeme usually cited as 'find', one of whose other forms is 'found'. A *morpheme* is the smallest segment of a word that has semantic significance—for example, each part of 'un-expect-ed-ly'. A *sememe* is the concept represented by a lexeme or morpheme, and it can in principle be represented by another lexeme or morpheme or combination of them—for example, we might consider that the sememe underlying 'find' could also be represented by the lexeme 'discover', the two words being regarded as synonyms. Again, the sememe underlying 'thermometer' might be represented by 'temperature-measuring instrument'. In this case we can recognize that the sememe has a number of component features, 'semantic factors'.

For the discussion that follows a particularly relevant reference is the book by Hutchins (1975), and for a general introduction to linguistics the work by Bolinger (1975) is recommended.

There are two broad types of semantic relation to be considered. The first, known as paradigmatic, concerns sense relations between lexemes— for example, between 'lift' and 'elevator', or 'single' and 'married', or 'red' and 'blue', or 'orange' and 'fruit'. The second, known as syntagmatic, refers to relations between lexemes in the same phrase, clause, sentence, or text (for example, between the words in the sentence about a thermometer quoted above).

We will look first at paradigmatic relations. Linguists recognize at least five kinds:

(1) Synonymy—if the lexemes represent the same sememe and their mental associations are broadly similar;
(2) Quasi-synonymy—if the lexemes share a high proportion of common semantic components but do not fully overlap in meaning (for example, 'lighting' and 'illumination', or 'duration' and 'time');
(3) Complementarity—for example, 'single' and 'married', where a semantic component of one lexeme is logically incompatible with a component of the other;
(4) Scalar antonymy—if the lexemes represent sememes that are components on a scale (for example, 'biggest' and 'smallest');
(5) Hyponymy—if the sense of one lexeme is included in that of another (i.e. if the sememe of one is a component in the sememe of another, as 'flower' is to 'tulip', or 'instrument' is to 'thermometer').

The dictionary definition of a word may be a synonym, or a set of quasi-synonyms, or its representation as a combination of components:

Build: construct;
Mount: ascend, rise, go up;
Nail: hard terminal covering of finger and toe.

Many lexemes can be represented by a combination of semantic components, and some linguists seek to establish ever more 'primitive' components. For example, 'boy' can be specified as a 'male non-adult human'. A series of cooking terms may be represented by combining in various ways a much smaller set of 'primitive' semantic elements, as shown in *Table 6.3*.

We may turn now to the study of syntagmatic relations. In the form of syntax, parsing, word classes, this has a very long history. Classes such as noun, verb, adjective, and adverb are concerned with the functional relations of words in a sentence, and only indirectly with semantic relations between them. The two basic grammatical functions in a sentence are subject and predicate. However, writes Bolinger (1975), 'sentences are not uttered with the aim of expressing subjects and predicates but to convey something about entities and happenings ... The corresponding logical functions are participants, events and relations'. In the sentence 'Janet brought Mary' the two participating entities are Janet and Mary, the event is the act of bringing, and the relationships are that of 'actor' for Janet and

Table 6.3 Primitive semantic elements

	Non-fat liquid	Fat	Direct heat	Vigorous action	Long cooking time	Large amount of special substance	Other relevant parameters			Collocates with	
							Kind of utensil	Special ingredient	Additional special purpose	Liquids	Solids
Cook₃	+	−								+	+
Boil₁	+	−								+	+
Boil₂	+	−		+						+	+
Simmer	+	−		−					+Soften	−	+
Stew	+	−		−	+					−	+
Poach	+	−		−					+Preserve shape	−	+
Braise	+	−		−			+Lid			−	+
Parboil	+	−			−					−	+
Steam	+	−		+			+Rack, sieve, etc.			−	+
Reduce	+	−		+					+Reduce bulk	+	−
Fry	−	+					+Frying pan			−	+
Sauté	−	+				−				−	+
Pan-fry	−	+					+Frying pan			−	+
French-fry	−	+				+				−	+
Deep-fry	−	+				+				−	+
Broil	−	−	+							−	+
Grill	−	−	+	−			?(Griddle)			−	+
Barbecue	−	−	+					+BarBQ sauce		−	+
Charcoal	−	−	+							−	+
Plank	−	−	+				+Wooden board			−	+
Bake₂	−	−	−							−	+
Roast	−	−	±							−	+
Shirr	−	−	−				+Small dish			−	+
Scallop	−	−	−				+Shell	Cream sauce		−	+
Brown	−	−	+						+Brown surface	−	+
Burn	−	−			+					−	+
Toast	−	−							+Brown	−	+
Rissoler	−	+	−		+				+Brown	−	+
Sear	−	+	+		−				+Brown	−	+
Parch	−	−	−						+Brown	−	+
Flamber	−	−		−				+Alcohol	+Brown	−	+
Steam-bake	+	−								−	+
Pot-roast	+	−	−				(?)Lid			−	+
Oven-poach	+	−					+Frying pan			−	+

'patient' for Mary. It is such logical relations between lexemes in a sentence that linguists have more recently explored.

For example, some linguists identify four main types of verbal statement:

(1) State—as in 'the wood is dry';
(2) Process—as in 'the wood dried';
(3) Action—as in 'John runs';
(4) Action + Process—as in 'John dried the wood'.

The other words in each sentence subsist in various syntagmatic categories. Thus 'wood' in the above sentences is categorized as a Patient. In (3) and (4) 'John' is an Agent. In 'John is afraid', 'John' is regarded as an Experiencer, i.e. experiencing the state of fear. In 'John dried the wood over a fire', 'fire' is an Instrument, and in 'John made a table', 'table' is the Product of an action. The following categories or 'cases' are in common use in such analysis:

Act
Agent
Instrument
Recipient
Co-agent
Object, product
Beneficiary
Source
Goal
Location
Time

If we think now of the whole collection of sentences in a text we can see that it will have a complex relational structure. Within sentences, words will subsist as syntagmatic categories. Between sentences, words will be related paradigmatically. Beyond that, the sentences themselves will be related in such a way as to carry forward the discourse that is the content of the text. As Hutchins puts it:

Succeeding sentences build upon their predecessors by relating the new to what has already been conveyed... The new information represents a progression of the plot or argument, a further elaboration of one of the semantic threads. Various kinds of progression have been identified, such as general to specific, from whole to part, from past to present, from abstract to concrete, from cause to effect, from action to purpose, and so forth.

The modelling of textual discourse has been undertaken by researchers such as de Beaugrande (1980). A sample text he has analysed is as follows: 'A great black and yellow V2 rocket 46 feet long stood in a New Mexico desert. Empty, it weighed five tons. For fuel it carried eight tons of alcohol and liquid oxygen.' A suggested conceptual model is shown in *Figure 6.10*. The arrow labels represent some of the forty or so relational operators he uses to link events, actions, objects, and situations. For example, 'at' links an entity (such as 'rocket') and an attribute (such as 'yellow'); 'qu' stands

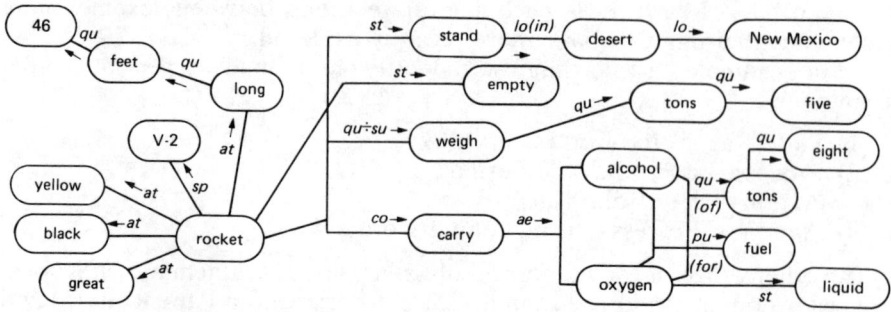

Figure 6.10 Conceptual model of text

for 'quantity'; 'st' points to the current condition of an entity (for example, the rocket 'stands'); 'lo' denotes location. De Beaugrande considers that the assimilation of a text by a reader involves the development within memory of some such conceptual model.

6.8 A global model of personal knowledge

After taking into account linguistic considerations such as these, cognitive psychologists have developed some considerably more complex—and more speculative—models of personal knowledge structures than we have so far reported. The Lachmans (1979) note a number of cognitive characteristics that a 'global' model must represent. People can quickly retrieve any one of a large number of facts. For example, an educated person has about 100 000 words in his/her productive vocabulary, yet while speaking he or she can locate and express about two concepts a second. A model must suggest how efficient search and retrieval is achieved. Second, the model must allow for rapid inference. If knowing X and Y makes possible inference Z, then something about the way X and Y are stored and linked to each other must contain the implicit information that Z is probably true. A model should also allow ready conversion of simple ideas into complex ones and provide for such abilities as classification and detection of similarities. Finally, it should permit accretion: the growth of knowledge by assimilation of external information and by generating new information.

Let us look at one particular global model of knowledge structure, that of the LNR research group as described by Lindsay and Norman (1977). They start with the hierarchical pattern previously illustrated (*Figure 6.11*). They go on to name the relations shown by the linking lines (class and property) and then to represent class membership by *isa* and property by *applies-to*. An example is given in *Figure 6.12*.

To take account of the fact that the lexical, image and conceptual structures seem to be separate though linked, the LNR model then represents concepts by numbered nodes, linked to lexical elements by the 'name' relation and also linked to images (*Figure 6.13*). Further, to take account of the 'typicality' effect, the group suggests that each familiar

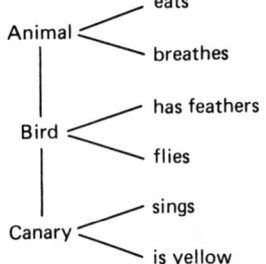

Figure 6.11 Hierarchical pattern of concepts

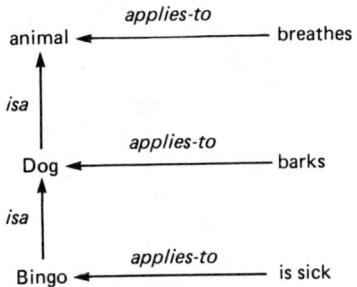

Figure 6.12 Hierarchy with named links

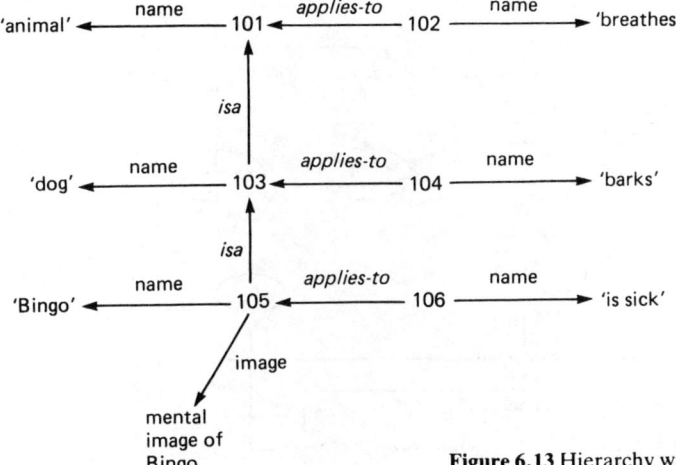

Figure 6.13 Hierarchy with nodes and names

concept might be associated with a 'prototype', as in *Figure 6.14*. The model implies that the more closely the characteristics of a particular bird match those of the prototype, the more readily would it be named or classed as a bird.

Lindsay and Norman accept the distinction between episodic and semantic memory—concepts in semantic memory are often accessed readily, without apparent search or effort, whereas it is often difficult to recall episodic information. Yet they see the two as intimately related. *Figure 6.15* is an example of the structure of personal knowledge as they

156

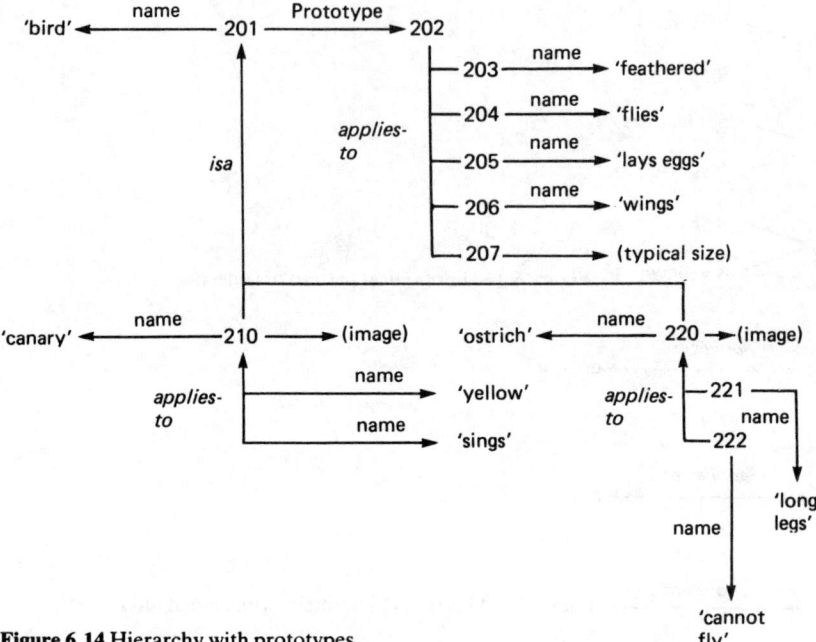

Figure 6.14 Hierarchy with prototypes

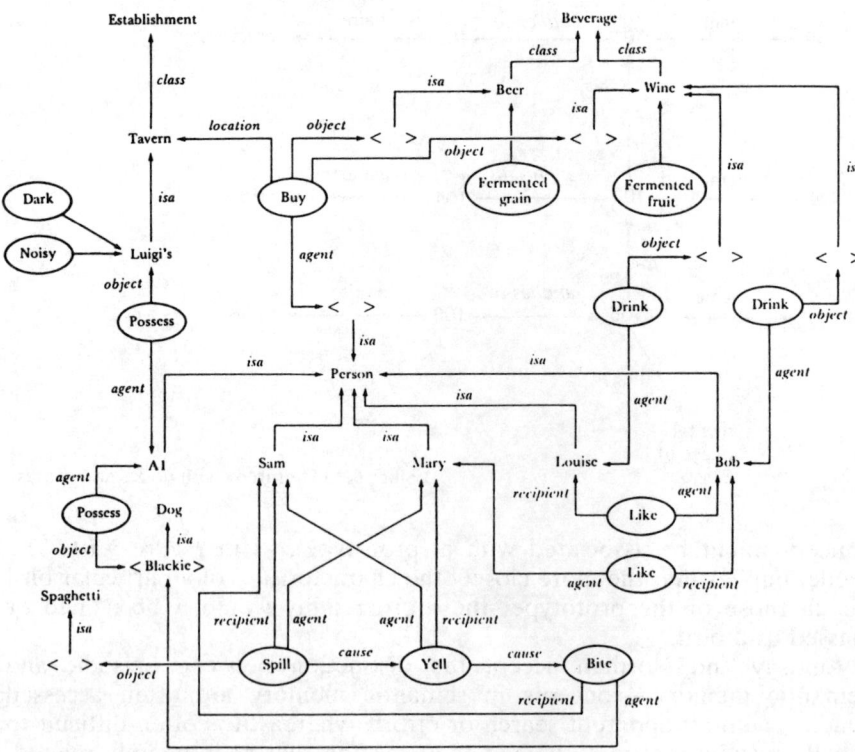

Figure 6.15 Personal knowledge structure

represent it (each concept and name has been coalesced into a name node to simplify the picture).

This figure represents some semantic information—beer and wine are beverages, made, respectively, from fermented grain and fermented fruit, a person can buy them from a tavern, such as Luigi's—but much more such information could be linked on. Embedded within this is the memory of an episode at Luigi's, where Bob and Louise were drinking wine, Mary spilled spaghetti on Sam, he yelled at her, and Blackie (the dog of Al, the owner of the tavern) bit Sam. To represent events, the LNR model uses the series of relations shown in *Table 6.4*.

Table 6.4 Relations used in representing events

Action	The event itself. In a sentence, the action is usually described by a verb: The diver was *bitten* by the shark.
Agent	The actor who has caused the action to take place: The diver was bitten by the *shark*.
Conditional	A logical condition that exists between two events: A shark is dangerous *only if* it is hungry. Linda flunked the test *because* she always sleeps in lectures.
Instrument	The thing or device that caused or implemented the event: The *wind* demolished the house.
Location	The place where the event takes place. Often two different locations are involved, one at the start of the event and one at the conclusion. These are identified as from and to locations: They hitchhiked *from* La Jolla *to* Del Mar. From the University, they hitchhiked *to* the beach.
Object	The thing that is affected by the action: The wind demolished the *house*.
Recipient	The person who is the receiver of the effect of the action: The crazy professor threw the blackboard at *Ross*.
Time	When an event takes place: The surf was up *yesterday*.
Truth	Used primarily for false statements: *No* special suits had to be worn.

Overall, then, Lindsay and Norman represent personal knowledge structures as a multiplicity of concept nodes, linked by various relations that are themselves concepts—*isa*, applies to, name, prototype, location, object, agent, etc. They visualize the memory system as an organized collection of pathways that specify possible routes through the database. Retrieving information from such a memory is going to be like running a maze. Starting off at a given node, there are many possible options available about the possible pathways to follow. Taking one of these paths leads to a series of crossroads, each going off to a different concept. Each new crossroads is like a brand-new maze, with a new set of choice points and a new set of pathways to follow. In principle, it is possible to start at any point in the database and, by taking the right sequence of turns through successive mazes, end up at any other point. Thus in the memory system all information is interconnected.

The system is continually modifying itself through active interaction with its environment. Thus our understanding of a concept continues to be elaborated and embellished, even though the concept may never directly be encountered again. Such an evolution is a natural property of the type of memory system we have been examining. As more information about the world is accumulated, the memory system's understanding continues to grow and become elaborated. As an automatic by-product of this changing structure, our knowledge continually changes.

The continual evolution of the stored knowledge within the memory system has very profound effects on the way that new information is acquired. It suggests that there must be a tremendous difference between the way a message is encoded into a child's memory and the way the same information is encoded by an adult. For children, each concept encountered has to be built up from scratch. A great deal of learning must take place during the initial construction of the database: understanding is only slowly elaborated as properties are accumulated, as examples are learned, and as the class relations evolve. At first, most of the concepts in memory will only be partially defined and will not be well integrated with the other stored information.

Later in life, when a great deal of information has been accumulated and organized into a richly interconnected database, learning should take on a different character. New things can be learned primarily by analogy to what is already known. The main problem becomes one of fitting a new concept into the pre-existing memory structure: once the right relationship has been established, the whole of past experience is automatically brought to bear on the interpretation and understanding of the new events.

For models of this type the development of individual differences and idiosyncratic systems should be the rule rather than the exception. Understanding evolves through a combination of the external evidence and the internal operations that manipulate and reorganize the incoming information. Two different memories would follow exactly the same path of development only if they received identical inputs in the identical order and used identical procedures for organizing them. Thus it is extremely unlikely that any two people will evolve exactly the same conceptual structure to represent the world they experience.

6.9 Knowledge representation in artificial intelligence

Artificial intelligence research, though related to cognitive psychology, is not itself directly concerned with models of the human mind: it is concerned with the design of computer systems that will behave 'intelligently'. Insights into the nature of the mind may be gained by studying the operation of computer programs, but the objective of AI research is usually to generate 'intelligent' behaviour, regardless of whether the means used in the computer are known to be the same as those used in the brain.

The aim is to build computer systems capable of performing tasks like playing chess, making logical deductions, analysing linguistic statements, diagnosing problem situations, learning from experience, planning. When we consider people doing such things we relate their intelligent action to their knowledge: one must know moves and strategies to play chess, one must know the structure of language to analyse it, one must have expertise to diagnose successfully. Consequently, AI research has included work on the representation of appropriate knowledge that can be used in a program to produce 'knowledgeable' behaviour. In this section we will review some of the schemes of knowledge representation that have been used, our prime sources being the *Handbook of Artificial Intelligence* edited by Barr *et al.* (1981/1982), and texts on the same subject by Rich (1983) and Winston (1984).

Public knowledge, as we have noted earlier, is multifarious, structured in many ways. What kinds of knowledge has AI research sought to represent? The categories usually encountered are:

(1) Objects—including classes of objects and properties of objects;
(2) Events and actions;
(3) Performance, procedures;
(4) Meta-knowledge, that is, knowledge about the scope and structure of the specific knowledge represented in the system.

Knowledge is stored in an AI system to be used by a computer program, the main kinds of use being (1) the acquisition of new knowledge (learning), (2) the retrieval of knowledge from store, and (3) inference (reasoning) from actual stored knowledge to other logically deducible knowledge. Some researchers (Schank, 1975; Wilks, 1972) have argued that these activities will be facilitated if knowledge is represented in terms of a small set of 'primitive' concepts, comparable with those mentioned in our section on linguistics. Others accept the concepts commonly used in the subject domain being represented but use a standard set of relational links betweeen them.

Semantic nets (*Figure 6.16*), comparable with those used in the personal knowledge structures proposed by Lindsay and Norman, are frequently used to represent objects, their properties, actions, and the relationships between these types of concept (Findler, 1979).

The 'conceptual dependency' structures developed by Schank provide a way of representing relationships among the components of an action. A set of primitive actions is used, shown in *Figure 6.17*, by means of which

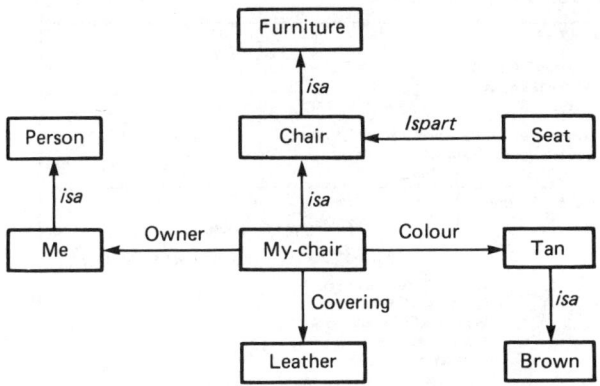

Figure 6.16 Semantic network

160

ATRANS	Transfer of an abstract relationship (e.g. give)
PTRANS	Transfer of the physical location of an object (e.g. go)
PROPEL	Application of physical force to an object (e.g. push)
MOVE	Movement of a body part by its owner (e.g. kick)
GRASP	Grasping of an object by an actor (e.g. throw)
INGEST	Ingesting of an object by an animal (e.g. eat)
EXPEL	Expulsion of something from the body of an animal (e.g. cry)
MTRANS	Transfer of mental information (e.g. tell)
MBUILD	Building new information out of old (e.g. decide)
SPEAK	Producing of sounds (e.g. say)
ATTEND	Focusing of a sense organ towards a stimulus (e.g. listen)

Figure 6.17 Primitive actions

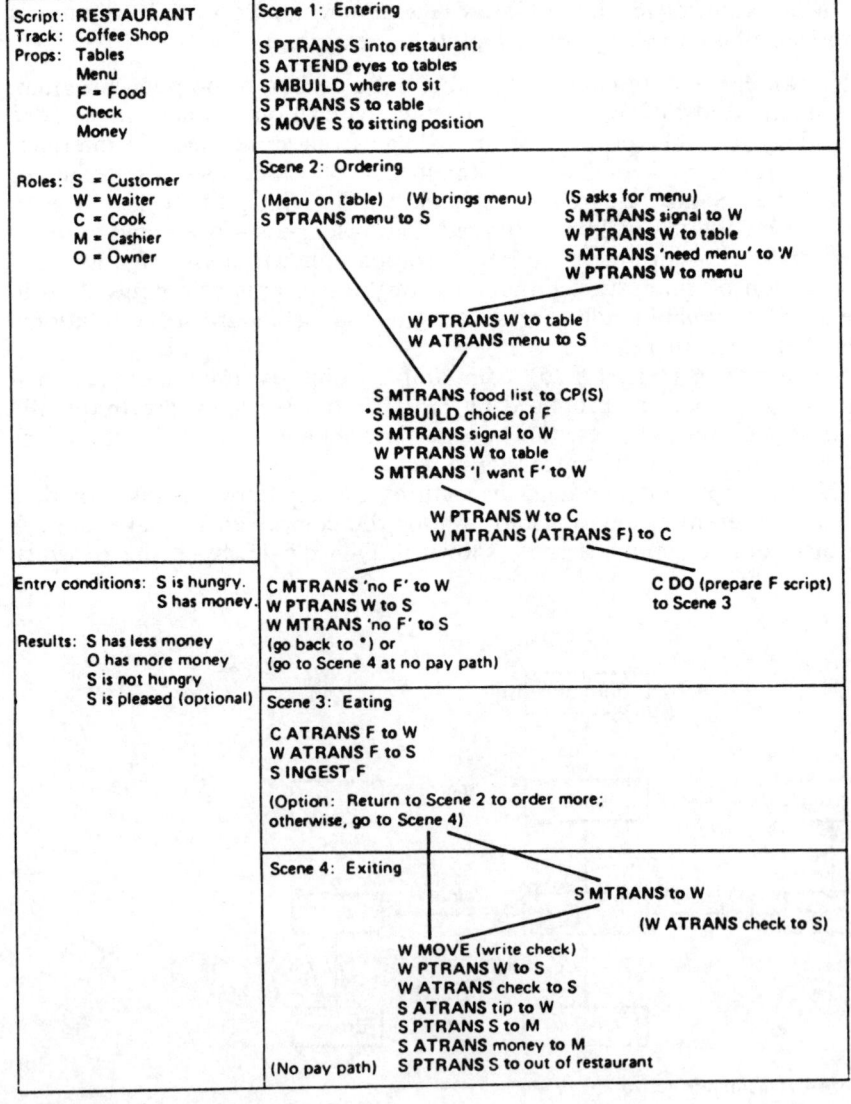

Figure 6.18 The restaurant script

specific actions can be represented. For example, 'Salesman gives parcel to customer' could be represented as:

$$\text{Salesman} \longleftrightarrow \text{ATRANS} \longleftarrow \text{parcel} \longleftarrow \begin{cases} \rightarrow \text{customer} \\ \searrow \text{salesman} \end{cases}$$

Schank and Abelson (1977) build conceptual dependencies into 'scripts'— stereotyped representations of sequences of events that are typical of a particular situation. For example, the much-cited 'restaurant script' represents the usual sequence of events in a visit to a restaurant (*Figure 6.18*).

Scripts are a particular example of a structure that brings together a set of concepts in a structured way. A more general structure of this kind is the 'frame' (Minsky, 1975). This has been used, for example, as in *Figure 6.19*.

A frame is instantiated for each term in a user question. The 'slots' in the frame are filled in during processing.

Term number
Term name
Semantic category
Class number
Synonym net
Input position
Associated categories (these will vary according to
                      the category of the term)

Figure 6.19 A frame in PLEXUS

Knowledge in an AI system can also be embodied in 'production rules' in which relationships between evidence and conclusions can be expressed. For example, in the system for medical diagnosis, MYCIN, there are many rules of the type:

'If the stain of the organism is gram-positive
and
the morphology of the organism is coccus,
and
the organism grows in clumps,
then there is 70 per cent probability that the organism is staphylococcus.'

Meta-knowledge has been discussed by Davis and Buchanan (1977). This is knowledge that the system has about the structure or pattern to which its specific knowledge content conforms. The primitive actions of Schank, and the frames of Minsky, can already be considered as providing generalized structures into which specific knowledge is incorporated, and in fact Davis and Buchanan use the frame (or 'schema') as an example of a structure representing meta-knowledge about objects. Production rules in a specific subject domain often tend to have characteristics in common— there are certain patterns of reasoning in the subject. A set of similar rules can be bracketed together by means of a 'rule model' that represents their typical structure. At a still higher level, there can be 'meta-rules' that embody general strategies of rule use. As an example from an AI system for investment decisions Davis and Buchanan quote:

'If you are attempting to determine the best stock for investment, and

the age of the client is over 60, and

there are rules about safe investment and

there are rules about speculative investment then there is 80 per cent probability that the safe rules should be used rather than the speculative ones.'

The last few sections of this chapter have sought to draw insights from cognitive psychology, linguistics, and artificial intelligence that may prove relevant to our understanding of the retrieval process and to the development of more effective retrieval systems. We will now resume a more direct discussion of retrieval problems.

6.10 Information wants and their expression

There is no ready-made answer to the question of how an information want may be represented in the human mind. In the most general terms, as we have seen, a personal knowledge structure probably consists of a number of elements between which there are various relations. Again in the most general terms, an information want may consist of some felt void in the knowledge structure—an awareness of missing elements and/or relations or of some uncertainty in the pattern of elements and relations. The acquisition of information may fill in the gap or lead to some reorganization of the pattern. Before the information is acquired how can the enquirer represent the felt void? Obviously not by stating exactly what will eventually fill it. At best, there can be a statement of the *kind* of elements and/or relations that seem to the enquirer to be likely candidates for filling the gap.

Consider a felt need to know 'the boiling point of mercury'. The search involves identifying a likely message or set of messages, and within this set locating the information that fills the gap. We may visualize the knowledge structures of both enquirer and message set as jigsaws, each with adjacent pieces labelled boiling point (BP) and mercury (Hg), and the latter with an interlocking piece giving the appropriate numerical data (*Figure 6.20*). The structures surrounding BP and Hg will almost certainly be different in enquirer and source message.

Now consider a need to know 'the highest melting point of any material known'. An edited extract from a verbalized search is given below (Carlson, 1961).

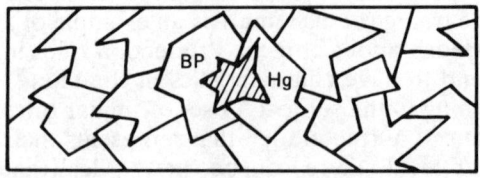

Figure 6.20 Gap in knowledge structure (1)

I will try the card catalog first, under the term 'melting point'. Here is a pamphlet on the melting points of the chemical elements. I will check it. The highest figure is for carbon, 3700°C. But an element is too specific. I will try this chemistry handbook. Here is a table headed 'melting and boiling temperatures', and it includes a column of 'temperatures of fusion'. Is that the same as melting point? The highest in the table is glass at 1100°C, so that is no good. I will check index entries under 'melting point': they include organic compounds, alloys. Nothing in those tables. Here in the index is a mention of ceramics—of course, ceramics in space vehicle nose cones, I saw a recent article about vehicle re-entry of the atmosphere, getting hot, nose-cone temperature—was it 7000 degrees? In the ceramics table, the highest is hafnium carbon at 4160°C. I will check the index for 'nose cones'—no luck. So here is a material with a high melting point, but is it the highest?

Here we see a search for source messages and browsing to gain some insight into the public knowledge relating to high-melting point materials. An internal association comes to the surface—ceramics in nose cones—and the information want is reformulated, but uncertainty still remains. The information void is here larger: knowledge of materials in general is not well structured in the searcher's mind (*Figure 6.21*).

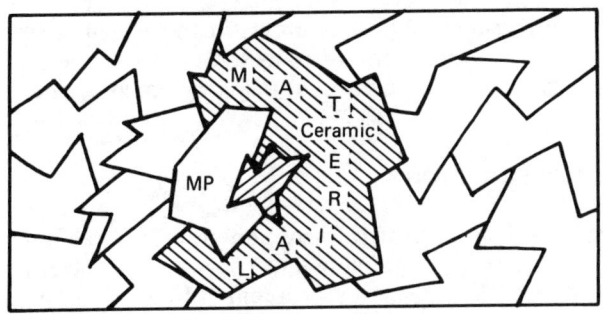

Figure 6.21 Gap in knowledge structure (2)

Let us now look at the information want discussed in this section: 'How may information want be represented?' Let us assume that the enquirer is familiar with information systems, subject indexing, search statements, retrieval, and the general use of designations assigned to messages and queries. The left-hand side of *Figure 6.22* is thus part of his personal knowledge structure.

However, the whole area of the jigsaw stretching out above and to the right of this is an information void, whose structure is for him very uncertain. Even to begin a search the enquirer must learn something of the structures of psychology, linguistics, computer systems, etc.

In sum, it seems that an information want can only be expressed in terms of its perceived *context* in a knowledge structure. The structure most readily accessible to the enquirer is his own, and this may be similar to the structure of a likely information source. However, if the information want is, so to say, at the edge of the enquirer's knowledge structure it may be

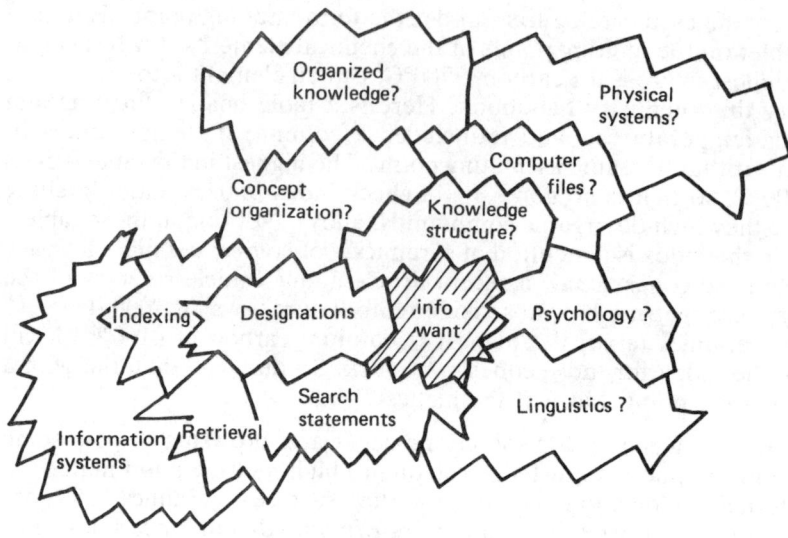

Figure 6.22 Context of an information want

necessary for him to search for sources with very different structures. He will then have to learn how to specify likely contexts in those structures. The problem for message designation is one of representing structure and context as well as the specific information content of particular messages.

6.11 The origin of designations

We have noted that the practical task of information transfer is how to organize designations so that they effectively link personal knowledge structures with public knowledge. The major problem is that of message designations, meta-messages, but it is helpful to look first at the designation of sources, channels, and recipients.

The designation of a person—whether source or recipient—is usually a social act. By this we mean that with respect to information transfer the relevant characteristic of a person is usually a social role he or she is performing: his occupation, or position in an organizational structure, or membership of an interest group. The names of such roles, which are used as designations, usually 'emerge' spontaneously in social discourse, rather than being specifically assigned by the act of an information transfer agent. During the early stages of its existence, the scope of a name may be unclear—for example, just exactly who should we designate as 'information scientists'? After a later period of clarity and stability, roles may start to change and diversify, so that an old designation still in use—say, 'engineer'—may no longer point to a homogeneous and well-defined group of people. There is therefore always some lack of precision in the designation of sources and recipients.

This vagueness is perhaps even greater for the designation of channels. Some typical channel designations are the names of periodical publications, of specialist publishers, of institutions that have an information-transfer function, of indexing services. Such names are often related to the role designations already considered—for example, there are periodicals, publishers, institutions, and indexes, all with the word 'philosophy' in their titles—but the scope of the channel may come to be very inadequately designated by its name (consider, for example, the physicochemical content of *The Philosophical Magazine*).

At first sight, it may seem that the designations of messages will not suffer from this lack of precision: an author gives his message a title, or an indexer gives it a subject heading—this is an individual assignment, not a spontaneous linguistic growth—and there may be no reason why it should not clearly designate what the message is 'about'. However, there is still a strong social element: the words used to entitle or index a message are drawn from a common stock, and may not adequately correspond to the content of the message.

To explore this possibility, let us look at how some message designations may originate. Let us consider a document that does contain information relevant to a particular enquirer's problem, and let it be published at time $t1$. It is likely that the author S has provided a title T as a designation, to express *his* image of what the document is about. This image is related to the way his knowledge $K(S)$ is structured at time $t1$. At some later time $t2$, the document is processed for a library, bibliography, or other retrieval system. An indexer C tries to assess what the document is about, and may frame this in terms of a designation $D(M)$ drawn from some standard schedule of indexing terms. The indexer may be influenced by the title T, but his image of the document is certainly dependent on the way his own knowledge $K(C)$ is structured at time $t2$, and he is constrained by the knowledge structure $K(W)$ embodied in the indexing schedule, that may have been first constructed at an earlier time $t0$.

The inquirer R at a still later time $t3$ has an image of his problem that is related to his knowledge structure $K(R)$, and he too must frame a designation $D(Q)$ of his question in terms of the schedule $K(W)$. The total interaction pattern is as in *Figure 6.23*.

The designations selected thus arise from the interactions of four knowledge structures, within different people at different points in time. Even if S, C, R and the schedule maker all graduated in the same subject at the same college on the same day, their subsequent experience will cause their knowledge structures to diverge. Moreover, the public and generally accepted structure of the subject field itself will be steadily changing

Time   Factors influencing designations $D(Q)$ and $D(M)$

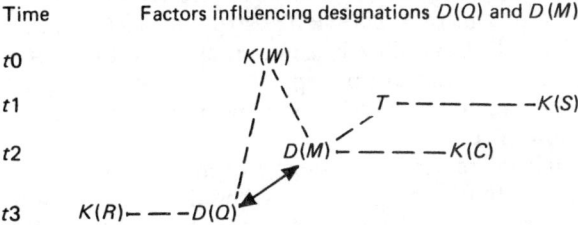

Figure 6.23 Interactions between knowledge structures

throughout the period $t0-t3$, so that even if both C and R are 'up-to-date', the dates concerned ($t2$ and $t3$) are different. For all these reasons, there is a definite probability that $D(Q)$ and $D(M)$ will not coincide even though the document is relevant to the query (or that they will coincide even though the document is not relevant).

6.12 Criteria for message designation

There are two basic approaches to the formulation of message designations. In the practice of indexing there is usually a distinction between 'derived' and 'assigned' terms. Index terms that have been extracted direct from the texts of messages are known as 'derived'. Those that have been selected from a standard schedule as representing the content of the message are known as 'assigned'. These distinctions are closely related to—though not identical with—the basic approaches considered here.

The approach corresponding to 'assigned' index terms starts from the position argued earlier that a potential recipient can only express his information want in terms of its perceived context in his own knowledge structure $K(R)$. It follows that his query designation $D(Q)$ will be in similar terms. This query $D(Q)$ will be matched against $\Sigma D(M)$ in the retrieval process, and it would seem that retrieval would be facilitated if $\Sigma D(M)$ tries to reflect $\Sigma K(R)$—i.e. if indexing is geared to the perceived information needs of particular groups of potential users.

We have earlier suggested that the 'meaning' of a message designation is a statement, by a source or channel agent, as to how he or she believes the message to fit into an existing organized set of such designations—i.e. that $D(M)$ is assigned in the context $\Sigma D(M)$, whose semantic structure may be represented by the schedule structure $K(W)$.

However, for a channel agent such as an indexer, the situation is more complex. First, there is his own perception of what the message is about: $M(S) \rightarrow I(C)$, where $I(C)$ is the information content of the source message as perceived by the channel agent. Second, there is his image of the knowledge structures of potential recipients—which we have called $\Sigma K(R)$. Third, there is the structure of the organized set of designations (the schedule) he uses, $\Sigma D(M)$ or $K(W)$. The indexer can thus ask himself 'How much, or what aspects of $I(C)$ are relevant to $\Sigma K(R)$, and how can I express these aspects within the context of $\Sigma D(M)$?' In such a case the indexer will try to optimize the assignment of message designations by (1) studying potential recipients ('user needs') so as to improve his image of $\Sigma K(R)$, and (2) using an indexing schedule whose structure $K(W)$ matches $\Sigma K(R)$. Ideally, he would mould his own knowledge structure $K(C)$ so that it matches $\Sigma K(R)$, so that he will think like his user audience. If this course is pursued it follows that each designation of a particular message will be different, depending on the particular indexer's view of its information content and its potential audience.

The alternative approach— related to 'derived' index terms— is suggested by the argument that, in general, schedule construction, indexing, and retrieval take place at different times, so it is unlikely that $K(W)$ at time $t0$, $K(C)$ at time $t2$, and $\Sigma K(R)$ at time $t3$ will match closely—

the indexer therefore cannot adequately predict the information needs of future users. Rather than indexing being geared to particular perceived information needs it should aim to provide a rounded and unbiased designation of the whole 'information content' of a message. The most reliable way of doing this could be to extract ('derive') a single designation directly from the text of the message. Such a designation should be able to cover the meaning of the message for all future enquirers, no matter what their knowledge structures.

Clearly, in a subject field where the structure of public knowledge is relatively stable, and well known to potential recipients (so that their personal knowledge structures match it), 'assigned' designations geared to $\Sigma K(R)$ would make for ready matching between $D(Q)$ and $\Sigma D(M)$. However, several features of the current situation oppose this approach:

(1) In many fields the structure of public knowledge develops and changes rapidly, so that the structure $K(W)$ of any index schedule soon begins to diverge from ΣM;
(2) Personal knowledge structures develop at different rates, not all keeping step with changes in ΣM, so that it is no longer easy to formulate a coherent $\Sigma K(R)$ for potential recipients in a particular subject field;
(3) The development of public knowledge gives rise to interdisciplinary enquiries, whereby recipients with different $K(R)$ may be seeking the same messages;
(4) The production of message designations is increasingly undertaken by channel agents not closely in touch with potential recipients—for example, by large international bibliographic services;
(5) The sheer cost of producing several designations for the same message—to meet several user audiences—makes this solution less possible. Despite the merits of a 'tailored' approach to the construction of designations, it is likely that 'neutral' and 'derived' designations will be the norm.

We have written above of the 'whole information content' of a message. What can we understand by that? In our usage, information (I) is what a recipient assimilates from a message that alters his personal knowledge structure. Each recipient reacts selectively to a particular message. Its total information content might be regarded as the sum of the information that all potential recipients draw from it (ΣI). To know this, an indexer would need to be aware of the knowledge structures of all such recipients—an impossible task. It seems then that the indexing process, $M \rightarrow D(M)$, cannot be regarded as wholly analogous to the process of being informed, $M \rightarrow I$, as implied earlier. Undoubtedly, the process $M(S) \rightarrow I(C)$ can and does occur, but it is not the whole story.

The process $M(S) \rightarrow I(R)$ is a transfer of *meaning*—we have earlier suggested that the meaning of a message symbol for the recipient is the concept (and hence the referent) to which the recipient believes the source is referring, or to which the recipient actually refers when using the symbol. However, it is possible to index a message without being aware of its meaning at this level: the indexer may have only an imperfect grasp of a concept in a text, and no experience of its referent, and yet be able to provide an acceptable message designation. This is possible by reason of the distinction by linguists between the *sense* and meaning of a text: meaning involves the identification of a referent, sense does not. 'The denormalization of the pi theorem for the quinification of alpha sets' may have no meaning for an indexer (or for anyone else), but it has a sense, and one could supply appropriate index entries. A designation could therefore legitimately aim to represent the whole sense of a message.

Here, however, we meet another difficulty. It is arguable that the best representation of the whole sense of a message is the message itself. Indeed, a 'full-text natural-language' retrieval system explicitly makes this assumption: in this case only the actual text of the message will do as its designation. However, in most information systems the aim is to construct compact designations that can be integrated into a set $\Sigma D(M)$. To do this, some selection from the total sense of the message is needed, some choice of its 'most significant' elements. It is evident that in this selection process the whole problem of meaning may again be introduced—that 'significant' could mean 'relevant to prospective enquirers'. It is not possible to exclude semantic issues from retrieval.

6.13 The standardization of designations

Earlier in this chapter, discussing the practice of retrieval, we have described in general terms the extraction or assignment of terms, W, from text messages, which may be linked to form subject strings, H. We noted that the problems associated with such designations were mainly concerned with standards. Here we take up the specific problem of deciding what kinds of semantic element should be included in designations, and how they may be represented in the form of standardized subject strings.

If the text messages for which designations are to be derived all lie within the same subject discipline the style of the texts may be reasonably standardized, and an indexing policy can specify the kinds of semantic element that should be extracted. For example, Hutchins (1977) suggests that scientific papers typically contain the following elements:

The problem: statement of current hypothesis
                tests of hypothesis
                disproof of hypothesis
                statement of problem
The solution: statement of new hypothesis
                tests of hypothesis
                proof of hypothesis
                statement of solution
Implications of solution

More concretely, the editorial guides of scientific abstracting publications recommend that the abstract include newly observed facts, conclusions of an experiment or argument, the essential parts of any new theory, treatment, apparatus or technique, the names of any new compound, mineral species, animal or plant, any new numerical data, new methods.

A second method for deriving a message designation has been based on frequencies of words occurring in the text, a technique pioneered by Luhn (see Schultz, 1968). Words of high frequency generally contribute little to information content, and may be filtered out of text by a stop list, such as was illustrated in *Table 5.1*. The variety of the remaining words may be further reduced by stripping them of suffixes (such as those listed in *Table 5.2*) to produce stems (see Porter, 1980). The number of occurrences of each stem is then counted, and the most frequent are extracted as index terms. Once again, subjective judgement (or trial and error) is necessary to decide how many such terms should be derived. All this analysis is, of course, feasible only if texts are in a form that can be processed by computer.

Human extraction of selected themes from texts can provide a set of strings (*H*) or of single words (*W*). The 'statistical' selection just described produces single stems. An extension of the automated technique can provide an equivalent to strings: phrases or sentences containing a number of high-frequency stems can be extracted.

There is one further step that may be taken in the derivation of message designations: the strings may be manipulated into a standardized form. Essentially, this involves the assignation of each word (or stem) in the string to a semantic category, and the display of the categorized words or stems in a structured way. This will be discussed in more detail in the next section.

We have earlier noted the development of syntagmatic categories in linguistics, and Sparck Jones (1979) describes computer text processors that make use of these—for example, the system of Schank and Abelson that produces normalized sentence strings. Sager and her colleagues (1978) have developed computer programs to analyse natural language text and transform it to semantic formats that are standardized within a specific subject field.

GL 641 2.2.1   More detailed studies of the effects of cardiac glycosides on sodium and potassium movements in red cells have been made by Kahn and Acheson (99), Solomon et al (168) and Glynn (67).

Human	V-study	Drug	V-cause	ARG1	V-phys	ARG2	Conj.
K and A (99) S et al (168) and G (67)	Have made more detailed studies of	{ Cardiac glycosides	Effect	Sodium	Move in	Red cells	and
				Potassium	[Move in]	[Red cells] }	

Figure 6.24 Formatted sentence (1)

A small example of such a semantic format is shown in *Figure 6.24*. Each column represents a word class, a semantic category of words that appears regularly in the subject field analysed. The entries in these classes have been obtained by use of a program that extracts words from the sentence shown above the table and allocates them to appropriate classes.

To achieve this, word classes in the subject field must first be identified. This is carried out by inputting a representative sample of subject texts into a clustering program. The program groups together words that occur frequently in similar textual environments (programs of this type are described and discussed by Salton and McGill, 1983). An example of noun

Table 6.5 Noun classes

Noun classes:

CG class	Cation class		
agent	Ca	ion	ion
cardiotonic glycoside	Ca	K	ˢubstance
CG	calcium		
compound	electrolyte		
digitalis	glucose		
drug	ion		
erythrophleum alkaloid	K		
inhibitor	Na		
ᵒuabain	potassium		
strophanthidin	sodium		
strophanthidin 3 bromoacetate			
strophanthin	Protein class		

Muscle class

actomyosin
cardiac

atrium
heart muscle   fiber
muscle   protein
ventricle

Enzyme class   SR class

Na+K+ATPase   sarcoplasmic reticulum
ATPase   SR
enzyme

False clusters

Myocardium   ADP
cell   El

LA 721 1.1.5 The possibility that administration of digitalis, through its inhibition of the $Na^+ - K^+$ coupled system, produces an increase in $Na^+ - Ca^{++}$ coupled transport and thereby an increase of influx of Ca^{++} to the myofilaments is discussed and is presented as a possible basis for the mechanism of digitalis action.

Human	V-study	Drug	V-cause	V-quant.	ARG1	V-phys.	ARG2	Conj.
[Author]	Discusses {{ 1 2	Digitalis (administration of)	Produces possibly	Increase	$Na^+ - Ca^{++}$ coupled	Transport		And thereby
		[Digitalis (administration of)]	[Produces]	Increase	Ca^{++}	Influx to	Myofilaments }₂	Throug
		[Digitalis] = its	Inhibition		$Na^· - K^·$ coupled system		}₁	And
[Author]	Presents	←——————————— [{ }]₁₁ ———————————→						As bas (possib
		Digitalis	Action mechanism					

Figure 6.25 Formatted sentence (2)

clusters constructed from pharmacology texts is shown in *Table 6.5*. A semantic 'grammar' for the subject is then developed by analysis of the co-occurrence patterns of the word classes in the texts, and this leads to the definition of a format into which the text can be transformed.

The output of the clustering program is therefore this format, and a lexicon of words encountered in the sample texts, with an indication of the format category of each. These data are available to the analysis program. New texts are fed into this program, which first identifies words not recorded in the lexicon: these are reported to a human editor for adding to the lexicon. The program then parses the text sentences in appropriate fashion, and maps the parse trees into the semantic format. A more elaborate example of the result is shown in *Figure 6.25*. Retrieval and question-answering systems based upon such formatted data have been developed.

6.14 The semantic structure of retrieval systems

The semantic structure of a set of message designations, $\Sigma D(M)$, has earlier been denoted as $K(W)$. A message designation is constructed in the first instance by selecting words, phrases, or longer strings of text from the message, as collectively representing its content. The strings so selected may then be processed in a number of ways—for example, by extracting morphemes (stripping suffixes and prefixes); by equating synonyms and quasisynonyms; or by semantic analysis into more 'primitive' components. The lexemes, morphemes, and sememes used may be drawn from a standard list, a 'controlled vocabulary' of permitted index terms. The terms so processed may again be linked into strings in which syntagmatic relations are expressed. Two extreme cases are illustrated below. Each may be regarded as arising from the selection from text of a key sentence 'the possibility is explored of changing the brittleness of cermet materials by modifying their microstructure'. In the first of the following examples the meta-message is an alphabetically arranged list of words extracted from text; in the second it is a coded string of semantic factors that express a variety of syntagmatic and paradigmatic relations:

> Example (1): brittleness, ceramics, cermet, crystals, metals, microstructure
> Example (2): KOV.CERM.2X.METL.001, KWV.KAP.PAPR.010, KAL.CIRS.MYTL.RANG.13X.001

In the second example, 'cermet' is represented by the coded compound CERM.METL, and 'microstructure' by the compound CIRS.MYTL. RANG, so that paradigmatic relations are established, for example, between 'metal' (METL or MYTL) and 'cermet' or 'microstructure'. The codes KOV, KWV, KAP, and KAL represent syntagmatic relations: for example, KOV means that a 'property is given for' cermet, and KWV identifies the property given (PAPR.010 = brittleness).

The individual meta-messages may be integrated into an organized set, $\Sigma D(M)$, by means of paradigmatic relations. In the simpler cases, these take the form of cross references between index terms, linking words with

172

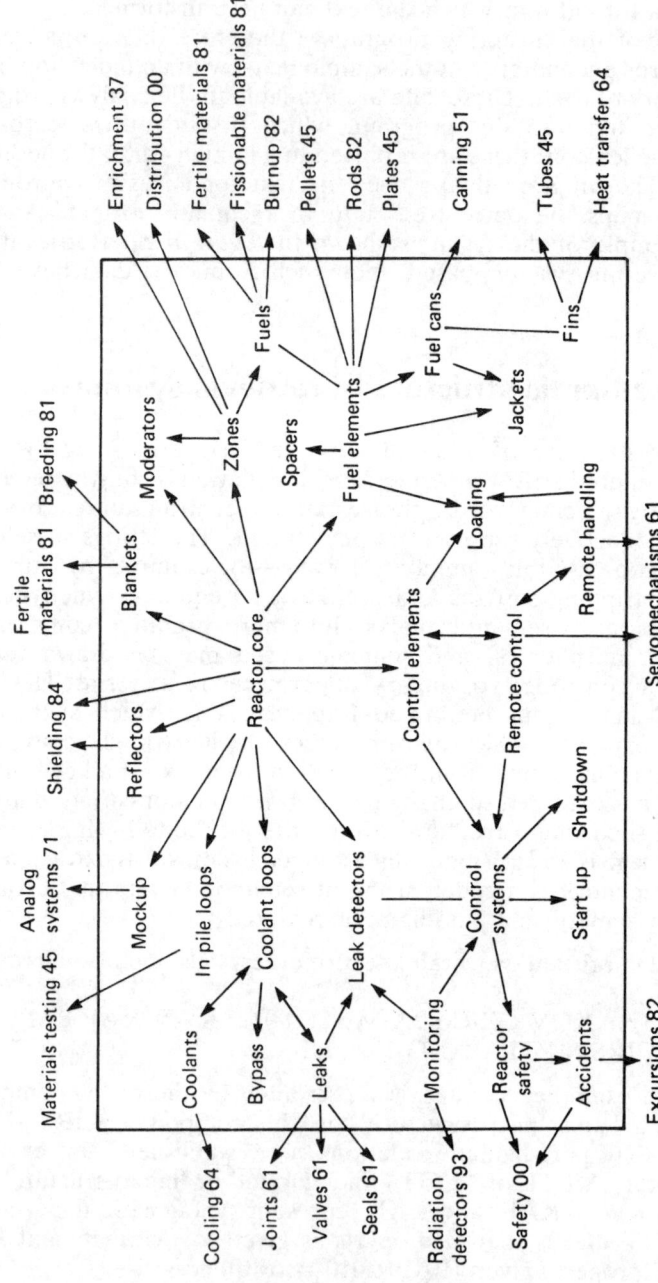

Figure 6.26 Arrow diagram of word relations

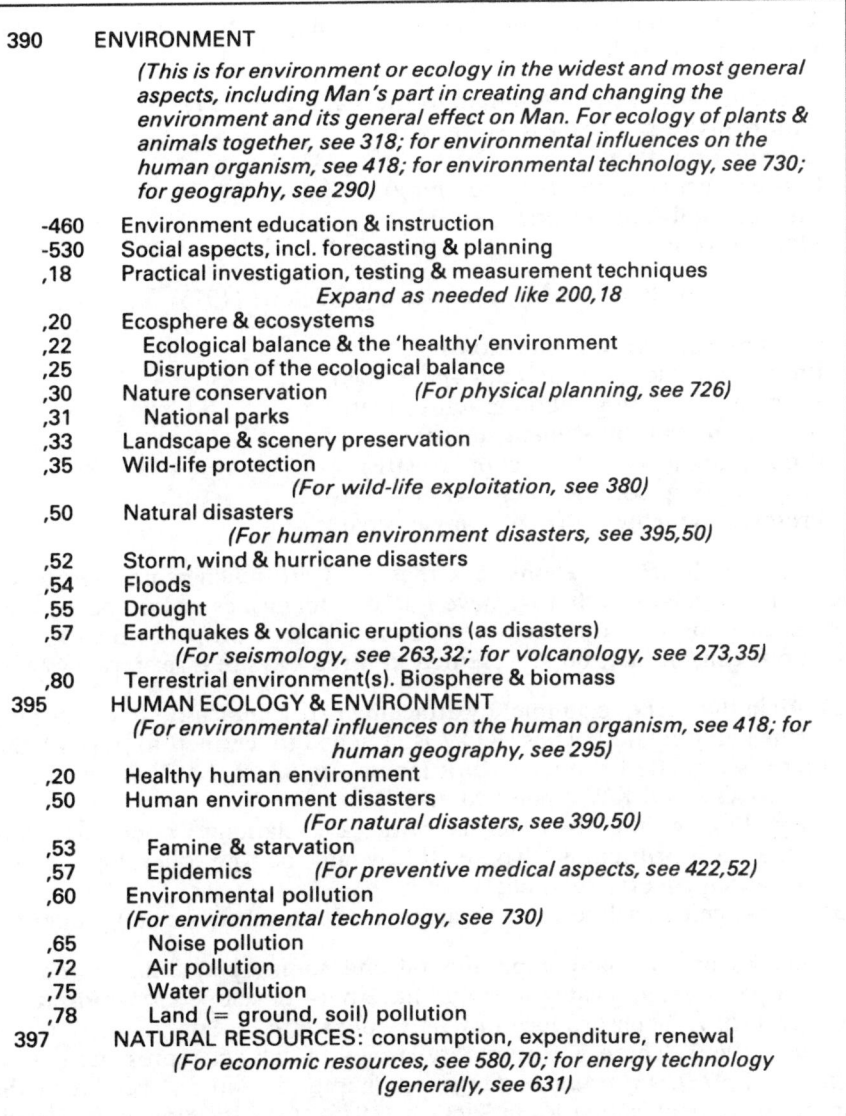

```
390      ENVIRONMENT
              (This is for environment or ecology in the widest and most general
              aspects, including Man's part in creating and changing the
              environment and its general effect on Man. For ecology of plants &
              animals together, see 318; for environmental influences on the
              human organism, see 418; for environmental technology, see 730;
              for geography, see 290)
  -460      Environment education & instruction
  -530      Social aspects, incl. forecasting & planning
  ,18       Practical investigation, testing & measurement techniques
                        Expand as needed like 200,18
  ,20       Ecosphere & ecosystems
  ,22         Ecological balance & the 'healthy' environment
  ,25         Disruption of the ecological balance
  ,30       Nature conservation        (For physical planning, see 726)
  ,31         National parks
  ,33       Landscape & scenery preservation
  ,35       Wild-life protection
                        (For wild-life exploitation, see 380)
  ,50       Natural disasters
                        (For human environment disasters, see 395,50)
  ,52       Storm, wind & hurricane disasters
  ,54       Floods
  ,55       Drought
  ,57       Earthquakes & volcanic eruptions (as disasters)
                        (For seismology, see 263,32; for volcanology, see 273,35)
  ,80       Terrestrial environment(s). Biosphere & biomass
395      HUMAN ECOLOGY & ENVIRONMENT
                   (For environmental influences on the human organism, see 418; for
                                  human geography, see 295)
  ,20       Healthy human environment
  ,50       Human environment disasters
                        (For natural disasters, see 390,50)
  ,53         Famine & starvation
  ,57         Epidemics       (For preventive medical aspects, see 422,52)
  ,60       Environmental pollution
              (For environmental technology, see 730)
  ,65         Noise pollution
  ,72         Air pollution
  ,75         Water pollution
  ,78         Land (= ground, soil) pollution
397      NATURAL RESOURCES: consumption, expenditure, renewal
                   (For economic resources, see 580,70; for energy technology
                                  (generally, see 631)
```

Figure 6.27 Part of a subject classification

some common semantic content. The links may be expanded into a
complex hierarchy or network of semantic relations, two particular
examples being shown in *Figures 6.26* and *6.27*.

Inspection of these examples shows that retrieval system semantics
comprise mainly (1) links between broader and narrower terms, thus
expressing the generic or class-membership relations, and (2) a heterogeneous collection of cross references to other 'related terms' (*RT*).

The British Standard on thesauri gives examples of the kinds of relation that may figure as *RT*:

> Coordinate terms (subordinate to the same generic term)
> Antonyms (e.g. hardness–softness)
> Genetic (e.g. father–son)
> Cause/effect (e.g. teaching–learning)
> Instrumental (e.g. writing–pencil)
> Material (e.g. books–paper)

Other relations found as *RT* are noted by Willetts (1975), such as:

> Measure (e.g. vision–threshold)
> Process/product (e.g. painting–paintings)
> Product/device (e.g. photograph–camera)
> Related roles (e.g. student–teacher)
> Product/application (e.g. copper–wire)
> Property (e.g. soil–permeability)
> Product/raw material (e.g. coal gas–coal)

Many of the *RT* relations in a thesaurus are much more akin to the syntagmatic relations that we have noted in linguistics and in the example at the beginning of this section (such as KWV = property given). Such relations can, in fact, be represented in three ways in a retrieval system:

(1) As in the earlier example, by attaching a 'role indicator' to each of two terms being related. Thus, KOV is attached to 'cermet' to indicate that there is a related property, 'brittleness', to which KWV is attached— thus, KOV and KWV point to each other;
(2) By linking the two terms with a 'relational operator', thus cermet–R3–brittleness, where R3 would be the operator for the substance/property relation;
(3) By assigning each term to a 'category' (here, substance and property).

Reviews of the many experimental and some operational systems of roles, operators, and categories that have been developed for information retrieval, have been produced by de Grolier (1962), Soergel (1967), and Coates (1960). There is a summary survey of subject representations in Vickery (1973), *Information Systems*, Chapter 5, and an account of the nature of subject categories in Vickery (1975), *Classification and Indexing in Science*, Appendix C. We will note here a set of categories or 'facets' that has been found to be generally useful in special classifications:

> Things, substances, entities
>   Naturally occurring
>   Products
>   Tools
>   Mental constructs
> Their parts
>   Constituents
>   Organs
> Systems of things

Attributes of things
  Qualities, properties, including
    Structure
    . Measures
  Processes, behaviour
Objects of action (patients)
Relations between things, interactions
  Effects
  Reactions
Operations on things
  Experimental
  Mental
Uses of things
Place, condition, environment
Time

6.15 Studies of index languages

A set of message designations, $\Sigma D(M)$, is thus in essence an organized assembly of words or other symbols. There is only one way to search it:

(1) To formulate a query designation $D(Q)$ as a word, phrase, or string in the form required by $\Sigma D(M)$;
(2) To locate in $\Sigma D(M)$ some designations that match $D(Q)$;
(3) To select messages that relate to the matching designations $D(M)$;
(4) To move from the initially chosen $D(Q)$ to alternative query designations—guided by the structure of $\Sigma D(M)$ or by other representations of the structure of public knowledge—and to repeat the message selection.

The enquirer therefore needs aid in the process $Q{\rightarrow}D'(Q){\rightarrow}D''(Q){\rightarrow}D'''(Q)$, etc., where the various $D(Q)$ represent different ways of designating the initial information want. This want is first formulated using terminology available to the enquirer. It states the *kind* of knowledge required, in the context perceived by the enquirer:

Query	$\Sigma D(M)$
Topic $T(R)$	Designation $D(M)$
Context $K(R)$	Context $K(W)$

If the words of the query topic $T(R)$ can be immediately located in $\Sigma D(M)$, a search can proceed through the semantic structure $K(W)$ of the set of message designations. If there is not found $D(M)$ corresponding to $T(R)$, some aspect of the context $K(R)$ of the search topic must be located in $K(W)$, so that likely $D(M)$ can be selected. The aid provided to the enquirer is therefore in the first instance the semantic structure $K(W)$ of the set of message designations.

How useful is this structure? This is a question to which we might expect an answer from experimental studies on index languages, which are instances of $K(W)$. There have been a number of such tests. The general pattern of each test is

(1) To use an experimental set of messages, all in the same subject area;
(2) to select from each message text statements that are believed to collectively represent the significant sense of the messages;
(3) To transform each selected statement into several forms (index languages) that differ in their paradigmatic and syntagmatic characteristics;
(4) To assemble into sets the designations constructed in each indexing language;
(5) To use a standard set of queries, and to search each $\Sigma D(M)$ to select message designations relevant to each query;
(6) To assess the relative success of each indexing language in providing relevant responses to the queries.

The technical problems of carrying out retrieval tests of this kind are many and complex—they will be briefly considered in Chapter 9, and are very thoroughly surveyed in a book edited by Sparck Jones *et al.* (1981). Here we will take them for granted, and consider only whether the results throw light on the utility of the structure of the set of message designations.

It must be admitted that the indications provided by the tests are far from clear. In an operational system, the searcher inspects the semantic structure $K(W)$—thesaurus, classification, or semantic map—in the region of his initially chosen $D(Q)$, and selects from it words or phrases that seem appropriate within his own knowledge context $K(R)$, in order to reformulate $D(Q)$. Most of the experimental tests have not created a situation of this kind, but have used a much more mechanical movement from one $D(Q)$ formulation to another.

For example, the Cranfield test on index language devices (Cleverdon, 1970) constructed two classifications, (1) of the concepts (phrases) used for indexing the test collection of documents, and (2) of the single words occurring in those phrases. From each classification, a set of index languages was constructed. Thus for concepts there were languages such as

    A. the initial concept alone
    B. A + synonyms
    C. B + concepts to which A was generic
    D. B + the concept generic to A
    E. B + other concepts to which D was generic
    F. C + D
    G. F + E

Each successive language therefore used $D(Q)$ broader, more embracing than those earlier in the set. A given question, formulated at first in terms of language A, was then reformulated as B, C ... G, and the performance of the system assessed for each search. (The performance measures used have been criticized, but we here leave this point aside.) The results of over two hundred queries were then averaged, and the seven languages indicated performed as follows:

    $G > F > C > D > E > B > A$

This appears to have demonstrated that the broader the conceptual search formulation, the better—a conclusion to which not all practical searchers would assent, and one which casts doubt on the criteria for success adopted in the test. However, the result does not throw much light on the help given by the semantic structure to the individual search.

Experiments carried out on the SMART test system (for example, those reported by Salton and Lesk, 1973) suggested that the relative performance of languages similar to those constructed at Cranfield was as follows: D > B > C or E > A. Only broadening by adding a generic term was sometimes more successful.

The tests at Case Western Research University (Saracevic, 1968) expanded initial search using (1) a system thesaurus, (2) other reference sources, and personal knowledge, and (3) a combination of these: success was most markedly improved by (2), and the semantic structure of the system had minor effect.

Various conclusions might be drawn from such results, for example:

(1) 'The problem explored in this section is illusory, and the initial formulation of queries is generally satisfactory'. All the tests would contradict this as far as the introduction of synonyms is concerned, and Saracevic explicitly claimed that 'questions cannot be searched as stated—the performance is too low. Expansion of question terms is needed as a rule'.
(2) 'The methods used in the experiments do not adequately test the issues under discussion here.' There is some truth in this argument. Analysis, question by question, of the effect of query expansion would throw more light on whether the structure $K(W)$ was of value.
(3) 'The semantic structures provided in the test systems were not the most appropriate.' This was suggested by Saracevic: 'Expansion through the system thesaurus alone does not add a sufficient number of related terms. It seems that expansion is best achieved when every tool available is used, including personal knowledge.' He did not go on to analyse what was supplied by reference tools and personal knowledge that was not available in the system thesaurus.

It is this last conclusion to which we draw attention here. The use of 'all available reference tools' implies the widest inspection of public knowledge recorded in them, and each personal knowledge structure reflects aspects of this public knowledge. Our brief discussion of public knowledge in section 6.4 suggests that it is considerably more complex than is normally represented in a thesaurus. It would seem that this could be a reason for the results obtained by Saracevic and his colleagues.

6.16 Conclusions

This chapter has focused on a number of semantic issues related to the retrieval of information from message stores, and here we will try to draw together some general conclusions.

(1) The essence of the retrieval process is the transfer of meaningful information from source to recipient, and the core problems are semantic.
(2) This information transfer is multiply mediated, and a number of differing semantic structures impinge on it—the designation of channels,

the organization of message stores, the knowledge structures of thesaurus or classification makers, of indexers and of reference librarians, and the personal knowledge of the recipient. The overall problem faced by all the mediating agencies is to link personal knowledge structures with public knowledge.

(3) This linking will be more effectively achieved if those concerned develop greater understanding of the complex structures of public knowledge and of the kinds of structure that are involved in personal knowledge.

(4) The structures of publicly recorded knowledge have been extensively studied by information science and embodied in classifications and thesauri. The insights so gained should be preserved and developed.

(5) Linguistic studies are progressively extending from pure syntax to semantics, and are providing insights into the microstructure of publicly recorded knowledge.

(6) Personal knowledge structures are now of central interest to cognitive psychology. The models of memory being developed—though still very tentative—can provide useful clues to those concerned with facilitating retrieval.

(7) Artificial intelligence is developing forms of knowledge representation that may prove of use in information retrieval.

(8) The research tradition in computer-aided retrieval is moving beyond the phase of purely statistical associations of concepts, and beginning to use such associations to derive semantic categories.

(9) Within all this work, some common themes are to be found:

(a) The use of semantic nets of one kind or another—whether as a classification or thesaurus in retrieval, or as a memory structure, or to model textual discourse, or as a representation of knowledge in an AI system,

(b) The use of a set of standard semantic categories—employed in the representation of events in episodic memory, or as the 'cases' of linguistic analysis, as relationships in thesauri, or as categories in 'faceted' classification,

(c) The use of 'meta-knowledge' about the knowledge structures used. The categories just mentioned are already an illustration of this. At a more detailed level we have in case grammar rules as to which cases are associated with each type of verbal statement; in classification, there are 'facet formulae'—rules as to what set and sequence of facets is typical of a given subject; and similar groupings of 'slots' associated with a particular frame category in AI.

(10) Despite these valuable advances and convergences, basic problems remain:

(a) There is still no clear evidence as to what semantic structures in retrieval systems can provide the most effective aid to the searcher;

(b) Such evidence as there is suggests that retrieval system structures do not adequately express the variety of semantic structures present in public knowledge, and are ineffective for this reason;

(c) It could equally well be argued that neither the memory structures nor the knowledge representations developed in AI studies yet match the complexity of personal and public knowledge;

(d) An over-elaborate retrieval system is not economically viable: the problem is to discover what is an appropriate minimum structure that can aid the searcher;

(e) Retrieval tests report on overall, average performance, but since each requester and each query is unique, the crux of the matter is to tailor each search to achieve optimum results. To achieve this, the retrieval 'system' needs to acquire understanding of (the relevant part of) the personal knowledge structure of the enquirer;

(f) This is made difficult by our limited understanding of personal knowledge structures and of how to represent information wants within them;

(g) For reasons explained earlier in the chapter it is unlikely that the semantic structures of retrieval systems can be tailored to the needs of the varied enquirers who will wish to use them. The emphasis must therefore be on iterative dialogue between system and user, to achieve a more effective match between the information want and the information available in the system. It is to this subject that we turn in the next chapter.

Chapter 7

Intermediaries and interfaces

Search of a retrieval system can be represented symbolically as:

$$K(R) \rightarrow Q \rightarrow D(Q) \longleftrightarrow \Sigma D(M) \rightarrow D(M \rightarrow I \rightarrow K(R)$$

An information want in the recipient is expressed as a query (Q), from which a query designation $D(Q)$ is developed. This is used to search the store of message designations, $\Sigma D(M)$, from which some may be selected as $D(M)$. There may then be reformulation of $D(Q)$, or even of Q, and iterative search. From the finally chosen $D(M)$ some information (I) is incorporated into the personal knowledge structure of the recipient. In the sequence of processes $Q—D(Q) \longleftrightarrow \Sigma D(M)—D(M)$, and in the feedback from $D(M)$, the recipient is interacting with the retrieval system.

The system may be wholly passive (for example, if it is a printed or card index). Its activity may be limited to message selection, $D(Q) \longleftrightarrow \Sigma D(M) \longleftrightarrow D(M)$, as is the case with most computer retrieval systems. The 'system' can be expanded to include a human intermediary, who actively helps the enquirer to clarify the query and to reformulate $D(Q)$. Finally, there is the possibility that such intermediary aid can be provided by a machine interface. This chapter is concerned with the functions of intermediaries and interfaces.

7.1 The reference process

We have seen in the previous chapter that in expressing an information want an enquirer can only state the kind of conceptual elements and/or relations that he perceives as likely candidates for filling the knowledge gap. His query is expressed in terms of its perceived context in a knowledge structure—the personal knowledge structure of the enquirer, and his perception of the public knowledge believed to be relevant. If the enquirer's understanding of the public knowledge in question is limited the expression of information want is likely to be imperfect. The first function of a reference intermediary or interface is therefore to 'clarify the query', to help the enquirer to a query statement that more closely matches the internally conceived information want.

The second stage of the reference process is to formulate a query designation—to express the query in a form that can be used to search the retrieval system. As seen in earlier chapters, this may require an understanding of the terminology used in the system (index keys may be drawn from a standard vocabulary); of the query syntax used (for example, Boolean operators); of the commands used to initiate system actions; and of the semantic organization of the message store, symbolized in the last chapter as $K(W)$. The enquirer may lack all this understanding and an intermediary or interface should provide it.

Matching of the query designation against the message store then takes place. This is not necessarily a purely clerical or mechanical process, but we will regard it here as separate from the basic intermediary functions. The result is an output of selected message designations, which may be used to extract the messages themselves from a primary store. The output is then evaluated as to relevance to the information want.

Evaluation in the last analysis can only be by the 'end user'—the recipient must assess whether the messages received provide (or seem likely to provide) the information needed to satisfy his 'want'. However, the intermediary or interface may carry out some preliminary evaluation— for example, screening out messages that have clearly been retrieved in error; selecting messages that more closely match the query in ways that could not adequately be expressed in the query designation; ranking the output in terms of probable relevance.

If the search output fails to satisfy the enquirer (or, indeed, the intermediary) the next stage of the process is to reformulate the query designation—or even perhaps the query. A first step here is to manipulate the initial query designation—for example, by dropping one or more terms, or relaxing syntactic constraints. The next step is more far-reaching. It may involve the selection of new terms and concepts from (1) the enquirer's mind, (2) the knowledge of the intermediary, (3) the semantic structure within the system, or (4) any representation of public knowledge—dictionary, encyclopedia, or other text. Search then iterates until a satisfactory (or wholly negative) output is achieved.

The role of the intermediary or interface is to use knowledge so as to improve the likelihood of retrieving messages that meet the recipient's information want. One way to consider the function is therefore to elucidate what knowledge is needed by an intermediary, and how it may be embodied in a machine interface. However, the other characteristic of the reference process is that it is an interactive dialogue between intermediary and enquirer, and we need to consider the nature of that dialogue, and how it could be performed by a machine interface.

7.2 What the intermediary should know

We will deal briefly with this question, since much of what was discussed in previous chapters is relevant. The intermediary or interface must 'know' (or have direct access to) such items as:

(1) Commands used to activate the retrieval system;

(2) Any standard terminology used in the system, and how these terms are related to non-standard vocabulary;
(3) Syntactic devices used in query designations, which govern the combination of terms;
(4) The semantic organization of the message store—whether this is in the form of thesaural relations between terms, cross references, classification structure, semantic factors, semantic networks, or any other;
(5) Features of the retrieved messages that may be used to make a preliminary evaluation of output—for example, literary form, intellectual level of message, date, size of message;
(6) Rules as to the most appropriate ways to modify a query designation (for example, which kind of term to drop first);
(7) Guidelines by which to assess the appropriateness of a query for the given retrieval system (for example, is it within the subject scope, is it too detailed or too general?);
(8) Guidelines by which to amplify or modify an inappropriate query, i.e. to help in query negotiation and reformulation.

In addition, the intermediary or interface must be able to build up some kind of model of the relevant personal knowledge of the enquirer so as to provide a context for query formulation and output evaluation. Such cognitive modelling is reviewed by Daniels (1986).

Finally, if an intermediary or interface is continually to improve in performance of his/her/its function there must be a capacity to learn, to enlarge on the knowledge available to him or her or it.

A human intermediary needs to understand how to conduct a dialogue with an enquirer so as to maximize the likelihood of providing the required aid. Such understanding must be built into the 'behaviour' of a machine interface. In the next few sections of this chapter we will present background studies related to questioning as a human process and to dialogue between humans, leading on to specific studies of the reference interview. In this presentation, and indeed in this chapter as a whole, we draw upon a review by Belkin and Vickery (1985).

7.3 The nature of questions

The purpose of a dialogue between enquirer and intermediary is to formulate a question, and the dialogue mainly proceeds by one or the other participant asking questions and proffering answers. It is on these elementary acts that we focus first. The study of questions has recently been reviewed by Swigger (1985).

Questions are usually recognizable from their spoken or written form, and Kearsley (1976) has provided a taxonomy of these forms (*Figure 7.1*). A distinction is made between verbal and non-verbal questions. Non-verbal questions may be overt or covert; overt questions are gestures, facial expressions, etc.; covert questions are internally directed questions, which we ask and answer ourselves. Verbal questions divide into direct and indirect questions. Direct questions are indicated in a verbal discourse by certain intonation patterns. They can be subdivided into two major groups, open questions and closed questions. Open questions usually have a falling

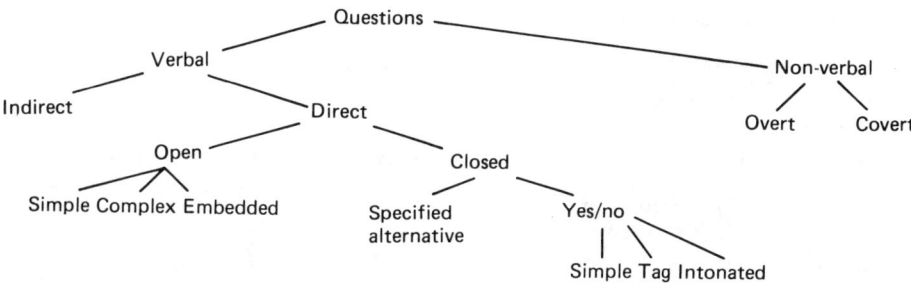

Figure 7.1 Taxonomy of question forms

intonation and are formed by the use of wh-constructions (WHO? WHY? WHOM? etc.) and hence are also called wh-questions. Closed questions have a rising intonation pattern and two subgroups: specified–alternative questions which list the alternatives acceptable in answer (for example, 'Do you want coffee, tea, or hot chocolate?'), and yes/no questions which require confirmation or denial of the assertion of the question. The yes/no questions have three subforms: simple yes/no questions formed by an auxiliary verb (for example, 'Is that dog dead?'); tag-type yes/no questions which involve inverted auxiliaries at the end of the question (for example, 'That dog is dead, isn't it?'); and intonated declaratives, created by raised intonation (for example, 'That dog is dead?').

This taxonomy of question forms may be useful for a descriptive analysis. However, a purely structural analysis neglects important functional differences between question types and needs to be supplemented by analysis of question functions.

The functional intent of each question is to elicit a verbal response from the addressee. However, questions may serve over and above the elicitation of verbal responses. *Figure 7.2* gives a classification of question functions developed by Kearsley (1976). While the categories of question form shown earlier are exclusive of each other, the categories that follow are not. A particular question may have two or more purposes simultaneously. Echoic questions are those which ask for the repetition of an utterance, or confirmation that the utterance has been interpreted as intended (for example, WHAT? PARDON? or sometimes a paraphrase of the original question—as distinguished from a literal repetition).

Epistemic questions serve the purpose of acquiring information. These have been subdivided into referential and evaluative questions. Referential questions seek to obtain contextual information about situations, events, actions, purposes, relationships, and properties. Evaluative questions are asked not for information but to establish the addressee's knowledge of the

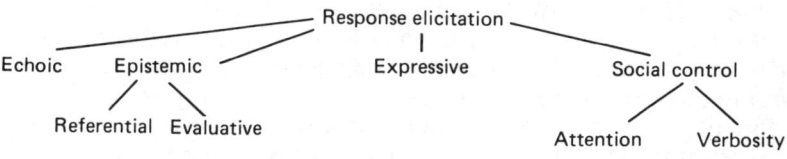

Figure 7.2 Taxonomy of question purposes

Table 7.1 Modes of wh-question

Wh-question	Mode	Example	Answer
Who (Whom)	(1) Unique person specification (2) Role specification	Who is that?	John The man
Where	(1) Geographical/common knowledge (2) Relative location (3) Shared private knowledge	Where does he live?	In Canada Two miles south Near your parents
When	(1) Objective date (2) Relative time (3) Personal age (4) Shared private knowledge	When were you there?	In 1975 Last year When I was 20 Before we met
How	(1) Evaluative (ascriptive) (2) Evaluative (nonascriptive) (3) Explanation of procedure (4) Justification	How are you? How many are there? How do you play this? How come I always lose?	
Why	(1) Justification of reasons (2) Puzzlement (3) Information (4) Explanation	Why did you do that? Why doesn't it work? Why do you ask? Why did it happen?	
What	(1) Specification of objects, activity, definition	What kind is that? What do you mean? What is he doing?	
Which	(1) Specification of objects, attributes	Which book do you want?	
Whose	(1) Specification of ownership	Whose car is it?	

answer. They are used in various test situations (examinations, interviews, discussions). All epistemic questions can make use of the wh-form of questions. *Table 7.1* lists each kind of wh-word and the modes of wh-questions compiled by Kearsley from Robinson and Rackstraw (1972).

An expressive question is independent of its information content. Particular syntactic patterns (and their intonation patterns) convey different expressive statements. The disjunctive form of a yes/no question usually expresses impatience (for example, 'Are you coming or aren't you?') while the question 'Aren't you coming?' uses the negative form of the auxiliary verb and indicates surprise or disbelief. The question 'You are coming, aren't you?', with the tag form of the auxiliary, expresses a state of doubt.

The social control purposes of questions are also independent of the information content. The meta-message of the 'attention' subgroup is 'listen to me' or 'think about this'. Questions with the characteristic of verbosity are asked only for the sake of politeness or to sustain conversation. These questions are asked in situations in which the interrogator may not be interested in an answer and may even not listen to one. They may serve to avoid embarrassing silences in conversation and maintain interaction between speakers.

The functional categories are not exclusive of each other; some questions are intended to serve only one purpose, others two or more purposes. The use of different purposes depends on various situational variables (for example, number of people involved in the discourse, degree of intimacy, peer pressures) and on individual variables (age, education, sex, etc.) There are simple and complex relationships between formal and functional categories. The two taxonomic schemes which classify questions on the basis of either form or function are useful for organizing and suggesting empirical studies about questions and may be helpful for discussing question processes.

7.4 Questions and answers

Belnap and Steel (1976) have sought to elaborate a set of concepts useful for categorizing, evaluating, and relating questions to answers. The aim of question analysis is to understand the meaning of a question—but there is still a need to come to an agreement between the query system and the user as to what counts as an answer to the question, regardless of how, or if, any answer is produced.

The notion of a direct answer to a question is basic in the logical analysis. A direct answer is a piece of language that completely, but just completely, answers the question. A direct question may be true or false. A question is an abstract thing, and the notation for it is an interrogative. An elementary question has two parts, a subject and a request. The subject presents a set of alternatives and the request identifies how many of the true alternatives are desired in the answer and what sort of claims for completeness and distinctness are to be made. Questions whose subjects present an explicit, finite list of alternatives are called 'whether' questions. Questions whose subjects present a set of alternatives that is possibly infinite are called 'which' questions.

The request can be analysed into three components. The first, selection–size–specification, is a quantifier-like indication of the number of true alternatives requested—for example, at least one, all, 5 per cent, etc. The second component of a request is a completeness–claim–specification, which indicates whether the questioner wishes the answer to include a claim concerning the degree to which the selection–size–specification is met. Finally, the distinctness–claim–specification is that component of the request that asks for an answer to address the issue of whether the alternatives are really distinct as opposed to being only nominally distinct—for example, '7' as opposed to 'VII'. It is not the case that all types of questions require all components of the request.

The kind of questions of relevance to retrieval are asked not so much to relieve a vaguely defined mental anxiety as to seek some definite piece of information. It is very hard to predict in advance just what kind of answer would satisfy the questioner. Sometimes he does not really know himself what he wants but, receiving a reply, will tell if the answer meets his need. Perhaps he will then ask a clearer question.

Investigators such as Belnap have concentrated on what may be called questions of standard inquiry, or standard questions. The term 'standard' refers to a situation in which the questioner knows exactly what his problem is and how to express it effectively. He knows the set of possible alternatives, he knows that one of these is true but he does not know which one. He wants to know which it is and he believes that the respondent will be able to help him. This is an ideal situation and, as Harrah (1973) expresses it: 'One need only ask such questions as: Does the questioner always want (need) the answer? Does the questioner always believe that the respondent will help him? Must the questioner also believe that he will receive help if and only if he asks the question? Can he merely believe these things, or must he know them? Wouldn't a "reasonable degree of confidence" suffice?' In view of these doubts it is best to regard the notion of standard question as very approximate.

7.5 Questions and problem solving

Kochen (1974) has explored the role of questions in the process of solving a problem. He divides this process into two stages—formulating the problem and seeking a solution. We might regard these as analogous to the clarification of a search query and its formulation into a designation. Kochen sees the two stages as involving rather different question qualities.

How a problem solver represents the task environment to himself is revealed by the questions he asks. If he is uncomfortable with the irrelevance or imprecision of his representation, he will tend to ask 'groping' questions. Later, during problem solution, when he has a more relevant and precise representation, he will tend to ask specific and generic yet precise and relevant questions.

At the stage of problem formulation three aspects of representation, three qualities of a question are of interest: relevance, precision, specificity. A question is specific if it yields information about a single noun object such that the information cannot be generalized to any other noun object or element in a class of noun objects; if a question yields information about a class of noun objects, then it is unspecific or generic. A question is relevant if it reveals information about the experimental problem state; if it does not, it is irrelevant. If the predicate of a question can be sharply defined, it is a precise question; otherwise it is fuzzy.

During problem formulation greater priority is given to relevance than to precision. An irrelevant but precise question is likely to elicit less information than a relevant but imprecise question. On the other hand, greater priority is given to precision than to specificity. By these criteria a precise but specific question during problem formulation is informationally more useful (of higher quality) than a generic but imprecise one. Of two questions equally precise and specific, the one that is more relevant to the representation of the problem the enquirer has in mind will be more useful, for without achieving relevance, problem formulation could never succeed. Of two questions both relevant and specific, the one which is more precise is of higher quality, for the interpretation of its answer will be less ambiguous and more unique than that of an imprecise one. Having two questions that are equally relevant and precise but differ in degree of specificity, the quality of the generic question should be greater because it has more potential for reducing uncertainty.

The criteria for quality of questions during the problem-solution stage are different from those described above. In the problem-formulation stage a subject is trying to understand his task. He terminates this stage when he gains a clear picture of the task. All stages beyond this first one belong to the problem-solution stage. The quality of a question in problem solution depends on the other questions the subject is asking, and on the representation on which it is based. By 'representation' Kochen means the view that the problem solver has of the range of possible solutions to the formulated task. Suppose that a particular representation admits a number N of possible hypotheses about the pattern of the eventual solution. If a hypothesis corresponding to a valid solution is in the representation, then it is among the N; if not, and the subject eventually reaches the solution, then a shift to another representation that includes the valid hypothesis must have occurred.

The function of questions in the problem-solution stage is to eliminate hypotheses from the representation or to reveal the need for hypotheses not yet included in the representation. A certain question may fail to eliminate any hypotheses in a given representation, no matter what the answer, because it does not apply to this representation. The ideal question is one that eliminates all but one of the set of hypotheses. If it did, it would be a perfect question early in the sequence, but we would recognize it as such only later, after the subject had asked more questions that reflected how he had eliminated all but one hypothesis. A question which elicits a contradiction as its answer is good because it eliminates a hypothesis. Likewise, a question that brings out the incompleteness of a representation is good. In brief, a question is good during problem solution to the extent to which it comes close to being one of the ideal questions just mentioned.

7.6 Questions in discourse

Questions are often used in dialogue as a means of maintaining control of the interaction. Mishler (1975) considers that question asking in discourse can be a mode of exerting authority or control. He suggests that the actual interrogative unit is not just question and answer but question, response, and confirmation.

Mishler identifies three modes by which questions may serve to connect dialogue units and thus produce a type of discourse that is both question initiated and question sustained. These are referred to as: chaining, in which the conversation is extended through successive questions by the initial questioner; arching, in which the response utterance contains a question; and embedding, in which there are two responses to a question. Chaining is used by the questioner to maintain control of the discourse; arching is used to regain control when asked a question; and embedding reflects a more equal power structure. Chaining and its different patterns could reflect role relationship between speakers. Mishler, who studied children's discourse in elementary schools, collected evidence that teachers use chaining and arching to maintain control over pupils and that children use these patterns to exert authority over each other. He suggests that through the act of questioning, one speaker defines the way in which the other is to continue with the conversation, and thus defines their relationship to each other along a dimension of power and authority.

He underlines that the control function of questioning may be obscured by the assumed equivalence of the term 'to ask' and 'to question'. Although often considered synonyms, they differ in their respective ranges of connotative meanings. According to Webster's *New International Dictionary* (2nd edition) the synonyms for 'ask' are: need, entreat, beseech, petition, implore. 'All of them suggest that the questioner is in a subordinate or subservient situation *vis-à-vis* the answerer.' However, the synonyms for 'question' include: challenge, demand, dispute, call into question, examine, charge, accuse, and doubt. 'Here the questioner is clearly in a superordinate or dominant position *vis-à-vis* the answerer.' A question may mean either 'ask' or 'question'.

An interaction between an enquirer and an information source (human or inanimate) is not just a technical transaction: it is a social situation, in which the enquirer is evaluating not only the messages received from the source but also the source itself—how expert and knowledgeable it appears to be, how authoritative, objective, and reliable.

When the source is human these perceptions are affected by the degree to which the interacting individuals share beliefs, values, educational background, language use, and social status. Individuals with strongly similar characteristics can communicate more easily. Enquirers often seek sources that are slightly more knowledgeable than themselves, but not too much so, in order to minimize 'heterophilic' differences (Rogers and Shoemaker, 1971).

Harrah (1961, 1963, 1973) has explored situations where an individual wants to acquire information, explore meaning, and evaluate the quality of information source. The enquirer assesses the value of resources in terms of how completely they answer his questions, how early in the message sequence the crucial one occurs. In Harrah's model, the enquirer is 'penalized' if the question asked is defective—i.e. if the source asks for it to be clarified, or gives an answer that is unhelpful. Both the enquirer and the respondent should be able to determine what answer counts as complete-and-just-sufficient for a particular question. The respondent must know how to put together something that the enquirer will accept as an answer.

A computer information system is a machine embodiment of expert knowledge, but it is subject to the same evaluative assessment by the enquirer as just described. If the interface puts questions to the enquirer (thus 'penalizing' him) it must appear understandable, reliable, sensible, and adjusted to the level of the enquirer.

7.7 Cooperative dialogue

It is clear from Mishler's analysis that there is an element of conflict in dialogue, a striving by each participant for control. Nevertheless, we must also consider the element of cooperation. In a reference interview there is a shared aim, to achieve a successful search. Some of the characteristics that are needed in a successful cooperative dialogue have been explored by Grice (1978). He proposes a general 'cooperative principle': 'Make your conversational contribution such as is required, at the stage at which it occurs, by the accepted purpose or direction of the talk exchange in which you are engaged.' He then proposes four sets of maxims needed for an effective cooperative dialogue:

(1a) Make your contribution as informative as is required for the current purposes of the exchange;
(1b) Do not make your contribution more informative than is required;
(2a) Try to make your contribution one that is true;
(2b) Do not say what you believe to be false;
(2c) Do not say that for which you lack adequate evidence;
(3)   Be relevant;
(4a) Avoid obscurity of expression;
(4b) Avoid ambiguity;
(4c) Be brief (avoid prolixity);
(4d) Be orderly.

A participant in a conversation, according to Grice, may fail to fulfil a maxim in various ways, for example, by quietly and inconspicuously violating a maxim (seeking to misinform); by opting out from a maxim and the cooperative principle; by finding there is a clash or by flouting a maxim. A readable introduction to the problems of cooperative dialogue is provided by Wardhaugh (1985).

7.8 Models of the other

A cognitive approach to cooperative dialogue has been explored by Hollnagel (1978). He stresses that for effective communication to take place each of the parties must have a model of the other, which almost certainly does not correspond to the other's model of himself. In Hollnagel's analysis one of the functions of communication can be to try to influence the model that the other participant has of one, explicitly for the purpose of making the communication more effective (at least from the sender's point of view). Hollnagel summarizes the conditions necessary for human communication as:

(1) The participants must have a common language or a common code;
(2) The participants must have a common understanding of essential parts of the environment;
(3) Each participant must have a model of the partner.

Hollnagel goes on to consider the third requirement in some detail, especially as it concerns the notions of credibility and intention. Credibility can be affective or cognitive; that is, based on trust or on knowledge, respectively. Although both are important in human to human communication, Hollnagel suggests that the former is not relevant to human–machine communication (which is his ultimate concern), and so concentrates upon describing the essentials of establishing cognitive credibility. One of the most important means to this end is that the partner is able to explain the structure of what he is attempting to communicate, and to explain why it is so. This explanation proves to the other partner that the sender does understand the subject matter. Another means to the end is by demonstrating, again usually by explanation, competence in the knowledge that is assumed to be shared by the participants. This type of communication Hollnagel calls secondary communication. That is, it is a sequence of questions and answers which are designed to increase credibility, and thus to corroborate the primary communication, the imparting of the information. Notice that secondary communication is concerned with affecting the model that one participant has of the other. Thus, in this sense, such models appear to be necessary for effective primary communication.

Hollnagel also suggests that knowledge of purpose and intention by each party of the other is useful in dialogues which are aimed at a single goal. Thus another function of secondary communication is to establish, in the model that A has of B, B's purposes and intentions in having engaged in the dialogue. The lack of such a model will seriously inhibit the successful conclusion of the dialogue in attainment of the goal. Hollnagel has suggested that one way to model purpose or intention is to understand the user's strategy in problem solving.

In later work directed more specifically towards human–computer interaction, Hollnagel and Woods (1983) suggest that for successful interaction a user needs to have a conceptual model of the overall retrieval system, and a mental model, meaning the user's own current, internal perception of the computer; and that the computer needs to have a model of the user. The viewpoint taken is that, to a large extent, successful interaction in complex tasks is dependent upon successful matching of the computer's model of the user and the user's own cognitive characteristics and upon adaptation to agreement upon one another's models.

7.9 The reference interview

The interaction between an enquirer and an intermediary is clearly a dialogue between two humans, within which may be embedded interaction with an information source such as an index or computer database. The dialogue has a shared goal, and to be effective must be cooperative. An annotated bibliography on reference interviews is provided by Norman (1979).

The first description of information-seeking behaviour based on an analytical investigation and not just personal impressions was written by Robert Taylor (1967). He considered the negotiation of reference questions as one of the most complex acts of human communication. 'In this act,' he writes, 'one person tries to describe for another person not something he knows, but rather something he does not know.' Taylor tried to reconstruct the negotiation process between a library user and the intermediary as follows:

(1) First of all there is a conscious or unconscious need for information not existing in the remembered experience of the enquirer.
(2) At the second level there is a conscious mental description of an ill-defined area of indecision. The enquirer may, at this stage, talk to someone else to sharpen his focus. He hopes and expects that a

conversation with a colleague may clear some ambiguities of the question.

(3) At the third stage an enquirer can form a qualified and rational statement of his question. He is now able to describe his area of doubt in concrete terms, and he may or may not be thinking within the context or constraints of the system from which he wants to extract information.

(4) At the fourth level the question is recast in anticipation of what the system can deliver.

Taylor suggests that four levels of question formation can be reformulated as shading into one another along a question spectrum:

(Q1) The visceral need—the actual but unexpressed need for information.

(Q2) The conscious need—the conscious, within-brain description of the need.

(Q3) The formalized need—the formal statement of the need, still within the enquirer's mind.

(Q4) The compromised need—the question as presented to the information system. The information need is expressed as a query submitted to the intermediary. Taylor calls it the 'compromised' need because the query asked may be modified by a reference negotiation between the enquirer and the intermediary.

It is the skill of the intermediary to work with the enquirer back from the compromised to the formalized and even to the conscious need so as to develop an appropriate search strategy. Thus, by funnelling the request for information through a series of filters, the intermediary helps the enquirer in understanding his information need. The filters listed by Taylor are as follows:

(1) Subject definition;
(2) Objective and motivation;
(3) Personal characteristics of enquirer;
(4) Relationship of enquiry description to file organization (the relationship of the query to the way the information is organized);
(5) Anticipated or acceptable answers.

The request for information passes through the above-mentioned filters and the intermediary selects significant data from each of the filters. This procedure helps in the completion of the search and in the ultimate provision of information.

7.10 Interviews for online search

When we refer to a negotiation process in the context of online interactive searching we refer not to a single process but rather to a series of complex interactions that may involve:

(1) A dyad consisting of an intermediary and a user interacting with each other;
(2) The intermediary reacting with the computer system;
(3) The intermediary or the user alone, reacting internally; or
(4) Reactions wholly within the computer system.

Overall, therefore, the negotiation process involves both human–human and human–machine interactions, each of them comprising many transactions, not all of which occur in all search processes. In addition, it is not yet clear how, or indeed whether, the negotiation process in online retrieval differs from the more traditional and more fully documented reference interview in the manual search for information. Nor is it yet clear what elements affect the user's ultimate satisfaction with the search, or how these factors may be separated out, measured, and related to the preceding elements of the search process (Auster, 1983).

Specifically, considering the interview for online search, Meadow and Cochrane (1981) consider the presearch interview as a process consisting of certain usually occurring steps:

(1) Clarifying and negotiating the information need and search objectives. It is now that it is determined whether high recall, high precision, or retrieving some specific relevant items is most important to the user;
(2) Identifying relevant online databases;
(3) Formulating basic search logic and planning search strategies;
(4) Compiling the search terms, whether from thesauri or free text, and deciding their sequence;
(5) Making output choices, and placing limits on the ultimate form of the printouts;
(6) Conceptualizing the search as input to the retrieval system: search terms are arranged into concepts using such features as truncation and word proximity, concept groups are arranged in order of importance;
(7) Reviewing search results and considering alternative strategies with possible recycling of steps (1)–(6);
(8) Evaluating final results and determining user satisfaction.

In her study of the behaviour of intermediaries in presearch interviews, Cochrane (1981) itemized tasks that other investigators had reported as taking place then, and developed a typology:

(1) Descriptive and tutorial tasks;
(2) Request clarification tasks;
(3) Request negotiation tasks;
(4) Vocabulary construction tasks;
(5) Search strategy tasks;
(6) Other activities (for example, administrative).

Somerville (1977) in a guide to the presearch interview divides its components into four groups: those common to all interviews; additional components if the user is unfamiliar with online searching; components if the user is present at the terminal during search; and components that can be omitted for frequent users.

The elements common to all interviews are:

(1) The use of interpersonal communication and negotiation skills;
(2) Discussion of the subject with the user;
(3) Determination whether a computer search is the appropriate way to answer the question;
(4) Ensuring that the searcher understands the question;
(5) Determining the comprehensiveness of the question;

(6) Identifying limits to the search;
(7) Selecting databases and systems;
(8) Identifying additional sources;
(9) Identifying main concepts and developing search strategy;
(10) Identifying potential problems;
(11) Determining alternative strategies;
(12) Discussing confidentiality;
(13) Conducting post-search review.

7.11 Interview techniques

Geraldine King (1972) suggested that the reference interview is composed of two chronological segments: one in which the intermediary encourages the enquirer to discuss fully the request, followed by one in which the intermediary asks questions to relate the request to materials available in the library (or in databases). She recognized that in the initial stage the intermediary asks open-ended questions to encourage the user to discuss his or her information needs, and avoids closed questions until the final stage of the interview. The 'openness' verses 'closedness' of the questions, and other signs of encouragement from the intermediary—silences, 'guggles', pauses between questions—she identified as especially important to successful negotiation.

Open questions, she suggested, were those prefaced by who? what? where? when? how?, and encourage the respondent to answer at length. Closed questions begin with words like is? do? can? will? and call for shorter responses. King stressed the need for intermediaries to be good interviewers, and advocated greater use of open questions to elicit fuller responses.

Lynch's (1983) examination of reference interviews in public libraries tried to analyse eight questions:

(1) How often does a reference librarian interview the user who presents a reference query?
(2) Does this frequency vary according to the type of transaction involved?
(3) Are interviews more frequent when the librarian is less busy?
(4) When an interview does occur, what gross categories or levels of information are sought by the librarian?
(5) How often does the librarian use open questions and how often closed questions?
(6) Does the reference librarian use the secondary questions (probes) used by interviewers in other situations?
(7) How does a librarian discover that the query first presented is not the query the enquirer wants answered?
(8) How many preliminary questions does the librarian ask the user in an interview?

The result of this study carried out in four public libraries, with 366 interviews recorded and 309 ultimately transcribed, revealed that open questions, i.e. those which allow flexibility in user response, were employed infrequently in the interview (8 per cent of all questions asked). Another 90 per cent were closed questions and 2 per cent were considered to fall into an intermediary category. Primary questions (questions by which the librarian introduces some aspect of the user's search for information and asks for content new to the interview) were infrequently used in the interview. About 52 per cent of the interviews involved only one question, and another 37 per cent had two or three questions.

Marylin White (1981) distinguishes four dimensions of the reference interview: structure, coherence, pace, and length: 'A dimension is a quality of the interview. It is affected by decisions made during the interview.'

7.11.1 Structure

Structure refers to the content of the interview and how the interview is arranged. The structure reflects the intermediary's goals for the interview. Goals are translated into tasks. Each task has its own information requirement, and requirements in turn affect the structure. During the interview the intermediary may address any or all the following topics:

(1) The problem creating the original question;
(2) The subject of the request;
(3) The nature of the service to be provided, i.e. answer requirements;
(4) Situational constraints likely to affect selection or use of information, such as deadline;
(5) Personal variables that constitute long-term constraints, such as intelligence and attitude;
(6) Prior search history, i.e. what the user has already done to locate the information.

Two basic approaches can be followed in the reference process, and both have implications for the structure of the interview: the systematic approach and the heuristic problem-solving mode. In a systematic approach the interview is a reasonably complete phase before the search. The interview preceding an online search without the user present at the actual search is an example of this type. In this situation the intermediary systematically covers all potentially relevant topics, perhaps gathering more information than actually is necessary, to provide a basis for decisions during the later search without the user.

In a heuristic problem-solving mode the interview is integrated more completely into the search phase. This approach combines personal interaction with trial lookup into sources, feedback from the sources, subsequent discussion with the user, additional search, etc. (a loop) until an acceptable solution is reached. In this situation the interview may be segmented into relatively small parts, interspersed throughout the search process. With the user being on the spot some interim relevance judgements can be made and fed into the negotiation system. This additional information can redirect the search at a different angle, usually resulting in a more successful yield.

7.11.2 Coherence

In some interviews the structure may be readily apparent to the user because it has an external logical validity or because it matches his own perception of an appropriate approach. In other cases an interview may be completely disjointed and reveal the intermediary's problems with determining goals, translating them into tasks, and identifying the informational requirements of those tasks. In still other interviews the interview may appear to be disjointed to the user but may indeed have a structure that matches the intermediary's image of an appropriate approach and thus have an internal, individual validity. Unless the user has tremendous confidence in the intermediary's ability to succeed despite apparent difficulties he is likely to begin to curtail cooperation if the structure is not apparent, since he cannot comprehend what is happening.

The case of the actually disjointed interview is the most serious one and can only be resolved by addressing goal-related problems. The third situation (apparently disjointed) can be resolved by altering another dimension of the reference interview—its coherence. Coherence refers to the user's perception of the structure and is dependent on systematic connection and integration of interview parts.

The user's cooperation is closely related to his understanding of what is taking place and agreeing with it. He will understand the order and plan of the interview better if the intermediary makes him aware of the context for individual questions or sequences of questions and thus allows him to see the relationships between and among the interview parts. The importance of context for comprehension is well known from research in psychology and linguistics.

White suggests that the intermediary can transmit his plan or framework to the user through some combination of the following stratagems:

(1) Outlining the framework early in the interview: 'Tell me how you plan to use the information and then we can determine which databases to use and which subject terms would be appropriate.'
(2) Making transitional statements to reveal relationships between or among questions or to place them within a broader framework: 'From what you have told me, I think I understand the topic you are working on, but let me ask you a few questions so I can determine what kinds of material to check.'
(3) Summarizing the information exchange: 'Now let me make sure I understand what you need. You want criticism—and particular form is now important—about Shelley's ode 'To a Skylark' that appeared over a seventy-five-year span after its publication.'

The most effective approach is likely to include a combination of at least two approaches, although this has not been tested and may vary among types of interviews, searchers, and users. Summary statements integrate the bits of information solicited in questions or inferred during the interview. They may reveal misconceptions or identify missing information.

'Coherence' thus refers to a perception, the perception of the user, not of the intermediary, which means that the latter consciously has to make an effort to ensure that order readily perceptible to him becomes perceptible to the enquirer.

7.11.3 Pace

Another dimension affected by procedures during the interview is its pace, which refers to the speed and efficiency of the question/response interchange. The intermediary has a direct control over the pace of the interview by:

(1) Selecting the type of questions;
(2) Determining the sequence of questions;
(3) Determining which information should serve as the basis for continued interaction;
(4) Determining the nature or method of providing feedback;
(5) Influencing the extent of digression tolerated or necessary within the interview.

The first decision 'type of question' refers to the distinction between open and closed questions. Sequencing refers to the arrangement of types of questions. In sequencing decisions the intermediary has three general approaches:

(1) The funnel sequence, moving from broad, open questions to closed, restrictive ones;
(2) The reverse funnel sequence, moving from closed to open questions;
(3) The tunnel sequence, using a series of the same type of questions, either open or closed.

Generally the funnel sequence is more effective if the enquirer knows his topic or problem well and can express himself effectively. By using probing questions, i.e. follow-up questions on specific points, the intermediary can expand or clarify any information gained through the open question. The inverted funnel allows the user to get involved slowly and is more likely to be effective when he needs to be motivated or when he cannot supply relevant information at an early stage. The tunnel sequence inhibits the user from volunteering information, but may be useful near the end of the interview, when rapport between the interviewer and the interviewee has been established.

Enquirer and intermediary are continually providing each other with feedback, sometimes in the form of verbal statement, at other times solely through non-verbal channels, such as posture, eye contact, gestures, facial expressions.

The pace of the interview may vary. In a common model for the reference interview the intermediary establishes a leisurely pace initially, using techniques already mentioned to make the user feel comfortable and to establish role expectations. As both participants become more involved in the problem and its solution the intermediary can turn to a faster pace, perhaps by asking closed questions. The final summary moderates the pace and allows both sides to evaluate the outcome and modify it if necessary before the search.

7.11.4 Length

Every decision the intermediary makes during the interview has implications for the use of time, and thus an effect on the length of the interview. Stringent time limitations, real and apparent, operate as constraints on the behaviour of both participants. An intermediary can establish some control over length by varying other dimensions, particularly structure and pace. Compromising coherence is risky.

To shorten the interview, the intermediary can modify the goals, his emphasis on them, the means of satisfying them and/or the sequence in which he addresses them. He can also accept the user's request as an accurate assessment of information need. This decision allows him to avoid the area of problem definition and the resultant need for explanations, digressions, or indirect approaches, all of which are time intensive. The intermediary can also rely more on information activated within his own mind without verifying it with the user.

7.12 Characteristics of enquirer/intermediary interaction

We have already looked at some semantic aspects of 'what the intermediary should know'. Here we summarize some behavioural features.

A prerequisite of any interaction is obviously that the intermediary should have the ability to understand the 'sense', even if not the referents, of each utterance by the enquirer. It is also necessary for the intermediary to recognize what is the formal mode and functional intent of any question put by the enquirer (Kearsley, 1976).

Second, the intermediary must be able to formulate questions, answers, and other statements that are informative, based on evidence, relevant, and lucid (Grice, 1978). Questions put by the intermediary should have the necessary qualities of relevance, precision, and specificity and seek eventually to eliminate all but one possible formulation of a query (Kochen, 1974). Open and closed questions should be used as appropriate (King, 1972). Throughout the interaction, the intermediary should aim to build up a model of the enquirer (Hollnagel, 1978).

The intermediary is not himself or herself a source of the information sought by the enquirer (nor indeed is the retrieval store the ultimate source). It is therefore necessary for the intermediary to demonstrate competence and credibility, in particular by providing reasons for the questions asked and the actions taken (Hollnagel). These explanations will also help the enquirer to perceive the interaction as coherent (White).

The intermediary, while not seeking to dominate the interview (Mishler, 1975), must nevertheless ensure that it is structured, and covers all the steps needed for successful search (as listed, for example, by Meadow and Cochrane, 1981, or Somerville, 1977). This feature, and the pace of the interview, is also related to the perception of coherence (White, 1981). The length of the interview must be kept as short as is compatible with its objective—remembering that every response demanded of the enquirer may be perceived as a 'penalty' (Harrah).

A consideration of the points made in this section, and in the earlier section on what the intermediary should know, makes it clear that the intermediary function is complex. The embodiment of this function in a machine interface is a very challenging prospect.

7.13 Machine interface for online search

It will be seen from the preceding discussion that a machine interface to carry out the functions of an intermediary must have several characteristics:

(1) It must have access to a variety of knowledge—about the procedures of the retrieval system with which it interfaces; about the semantic organization of the message store; about the message content; about strategies and tactics used by intermediaries.
(2) It must have sophisticated processing abilities—to analyse natural language input and extract the 'sense'; to emit to the enquirer appropriate responses, questions, and statements; to provide acceptable explanations of its activities; to translate user queries into a form searchable by the retrieval system and to analyse the output.

These characteristics serve to describe the type of expert system that is currently a major focus of interest in artificial intelligence studies, as one of the authors has explored in a recent paper (A. Vickery, 1984). Writing in more general terms, Bundy (1985) has discussed the 'intelligent front end', a user-friendly interface to a computer package (such as a retrieval system). Such an interface builds a model of the user's problem through a user-oriented dialogue, and from the model generates suitable coded instructions to activate the package. The typical architecture of the intelligent front-end is as follows:

$$
\text{USER} < \underset{\text{dialogue}}{- - - -} > \underset{\text{SPECIFICATION}}{\text{TASK}} < \underset{\text{interpretation}}{\overset{\text{synthesis}}{- - - - -}} > \text{PACKAGE}
$$

The interface requires expertise of three kinds:

(1) Knowledge representation—to represent models of the user, the task, and the package;
(2) Problem solving—to develop the task specification, to synthesize the package instructions, and to interpret its results;
(3) Natural-language understanding—to extract the sense of the user input.

Bundy gives references to a number of such interfaces that have been developed for various kinds of computer package.

Bates and Bobrow (1983) have described work on an interface that accepts natural-language queries, interprets them into an internal 'meaning representation language', then translates this representation into a query designation suitable for searching a particular database system. They noted that several other such projects had been reported at a Conference of Applied Natural Language Processing (Santa Monica, California, 1983). The organization of the Bates and Bobrow system is shown in *Figure 7.3*. The figure indicates a number of problem areas in interface design.

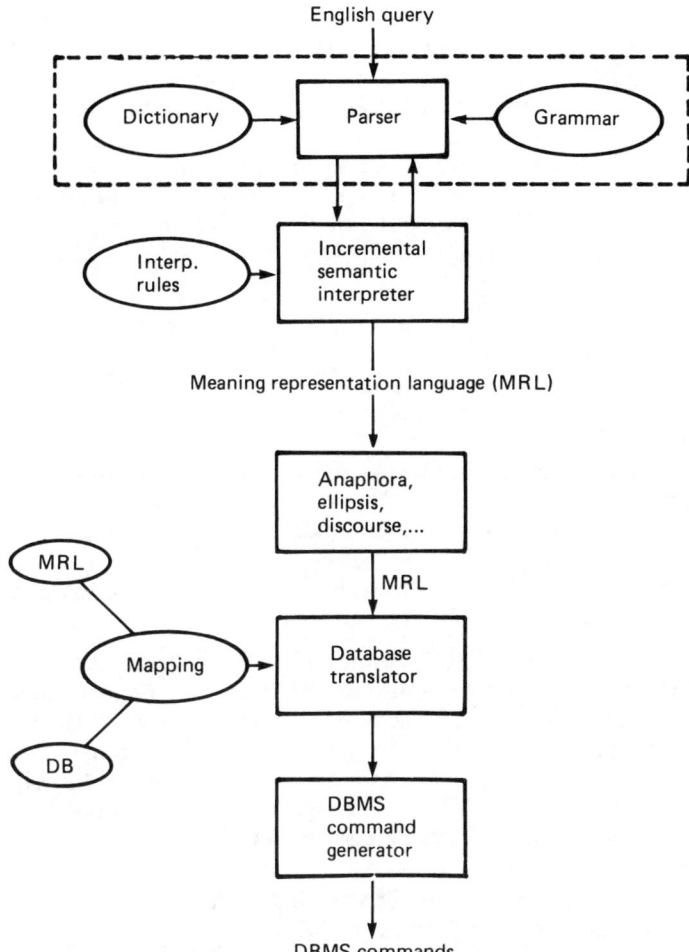

Figure 7.3 Organization of machine interface

Knowledge representation has been considered briefly in the previous chapter. Here we will discuss parsing in general terms.

7.14 Parsing

Introductions to the problems of parsing (extracting 'sense' from natural language) can be found in Salton and McGill (1983), and in books on artifical intelligence (e.g. by Winston, 1984, or Rich, 1983). As they all emphasize, for a computer system fully to 'understand' a natural-language statement or question is a difficult task, because of the complexity and variety of human utterances. This remains true even if the task is restricted to written (or keyboarded) text, avoiding the extra complications of speech.

Parsing can be reduced to simple pattern-matching: the interface can have a stored dictionary of words, stems, or strings, against which the input is matched. The parser then represents the meaning of the text as a set of identified words, stems, or strings as the basis for further processing by the interface.

A more sophisticated parser has a dictionary of words, against each of which is noted its 'part of speech', its syntactic category (noun, adjective, verb, preposition, etc.). Associated with the dictionary is a grammar, a set of rules about the syntactic structure of the language. A simple set of rules might be:

(1) S → NP VP-PPS: a sentence is composed of a noun phrase followed by 'VP-PPS', on which, see below;

(2) NP → DET ADJS-NOUN: a noun phrase is composed of a determiner (a, the, this, that) followed optionally by one or more adjectives, followed by a noun;

(3) VP-PPS: is a verb phrase followed optionally by one or more prepositional phrases;

(4) VP → VERB NP: a verb phrase is composed of a verb optionally followed by a noun phrase;

(5) PP → PREP NP: a prepositional phrase is composed of a preposition followed by a noun phrase.

One way that a parser may use such a grammar is to scan input text word by word, checking each in the dictionary to ascertain its category, and building up a 'parse tree' as long as the word sequence agrees with the syntactic rules (if it does not, a failure to parse must be reported). For example, take the text, 'The silly robot moved the red pyramid to the big table'. As each word is scanned, and recognized, and accepted as 'according to rule', it is replaced by its category, as follows:

```
The silly robot moved the red pyramid to the big table.
DET silly robot moved the red pyramid to the big table.
DET ADJ robot moved the red pyramid to the big table.
DET ADJ NOUN moved the red pyramid to the big table.
DET ADJS-NOUN moved the red pyramid to the big table.
NP moved the red pyramid to the big table.
NP VERB the red pyramid to the big table.
NP VERB DET red pyramid to the big table.
NP VERB DET ADJ pyramid to the big table.
NP VERB DET ADJ NOUN to the big table.
NP VERB DET ADJS-NOUN to the big table.
NP VERB NP to the big table.
NP VP to the big table.
NP VP-PPS to the big table.
NP VP-PPS PREP the big table.
NP VP-PPS PREP DET big table.
NP VP-PPS PREP DET ADJ table.
NP VP-PPS PREP DET ADJ NOUN.
NP VP-PPS PREP DET ADJS-NOUN.
NP VP-PPS PREP NP.
```

NP VP-PPS PP.
NP VP-PPS.
S.

A simplified 'parse tree' is shown in *Figure 7.4*.

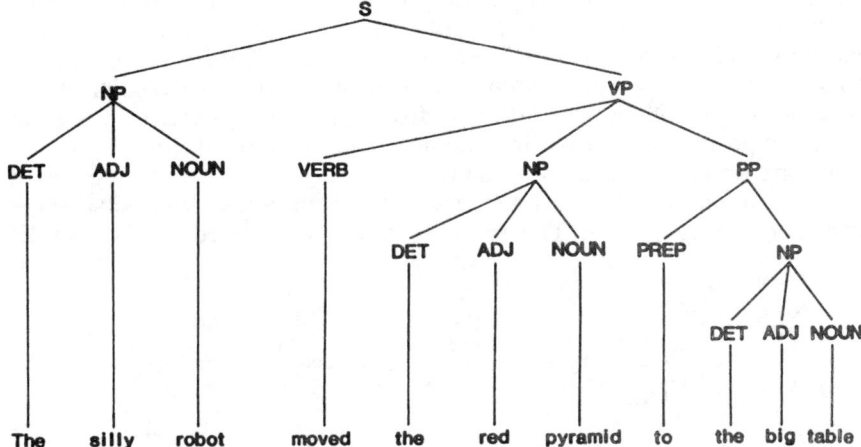

Figure 7.4 A parse tree

The English sentence structure represented by this grammar is relatively simple—too simple to capture real-life variety—and more sophisticated syntactic parsers introduce more rules and constraints. They have to be able to handle transformations—for example, texts such as 'Has the silly robot moved the red pyramid?' They recognize plurals and tenses, handle adverbs, conjunctions (and, or), and negations. They must cope with situations where a text word can belong to more than one category (the noun used adjectivally is a particular case of this). They must attach prepositional phrases correctly—which of the drawings in *Figure 7.5* is the interpretation of 'The man saw the pyramid on the hill with the telescope'?

Still other complexities are indicated in one of the boxes in *Figure 7.3*. Anaphora are pronouns referring to entities that appeared earlier in the

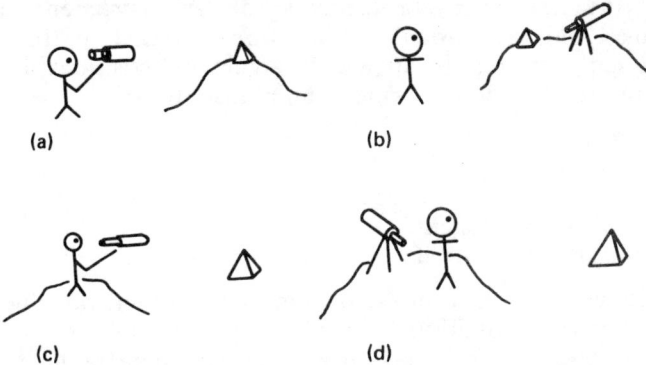

(a)   (b)

(c)   (d)

Figure 7.5 Some meanings of 'The man saw the pyramid on the hill with the telescope'

text, for example, 'these' in 'Some papers on information science are in Russian, and I want these'. Ellipsis refers to incomplete sentences that presuppose information given earlier—for example, 'I want all the Russian papers on information science. Also the Swedish'.

Syntactic parsers do not attempt to determine the semantic roles of words in text—to categorize 'pyramid' as the thematic object of the sentence, 'the man' as an agent of the act 'saw', 'hill' as a location, and 'telescope' (in *Figure 7.5*(a) or (c)) as an instrument. Semantic parsers aim to establish thematic roles. Some of them build upon the results of the syntactic parser, others work directly from input texts, using information about the positions of words in sentences and other constraints.

The grammar of a semantic parser must first of all specify the set of semantic categories to be used to assign thematic roles. A possible set is illustrated in *Figure 7.6*. The set chosen will be related to the subject

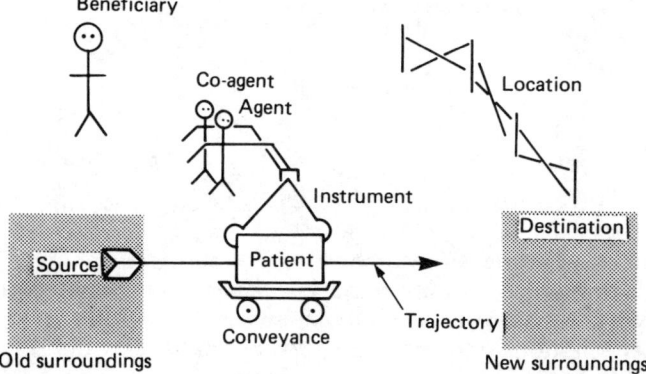

Figure 7.6 Some thematic roles

domain of the texts to be parsed—though some workers seek to establish a set of 'primitive' categories that will be usable in all domains. There are clear links here with our discussion of categories in the last chapter.

Semantic parsers are often based on verbs in the role of acts. Each verb in the system dictionary may be annotated as to the semantic categories with which it may be associated. For example, 'see' may be associated with a thematic object (the item seen), a seeing agent, an instrument, a location, and a time, and the normal relative word position of these categories within a sentence may be indicated. Again, prepositions are often indicators of the role of the following noun phrase, thus:

'from' implies source;
'to' implies destination;
'by' implies agent or conveyance or location;
'with' implies instrument or coagent;
'for' implies beneficiary or duration.

Nouns may themselves be tagged in the dictionary as to their possible roles—for example, 'man' cannot normally be a conveyance, a location, an instrument, or surroundings. Using all such clues and constraints, a semantic parser establishes the role of each sentence word. Such information can be much more useful for subsequent retrieval processing than the results of a purely syntactic parse.

It should be noted that system responses to a user rarely need such sophistication. They are usually generated from 'canned text' or 'prompts'—skeleton sentences stored in the system into which are slotted words appropriate to the particular response (words either previously elicited from the user or produced by the processing activities of the system).

7.15 Expert systems in general

An intelligent interface is an application of artificial intelligence, an 'expert system' that embodies knowledge and skills that are to be found among experts and that employs this knowledge to aid the less-expert user. A helpful introduction to the field is provided by Harmon and King (1985), and an extended and illuminating case history has been published by Buchanan and Shortliffe (1984). The potential for expert systems in retrieval is reviewed by Kehoe (1985).

Category	Problem addressed
Interpretation	Inferring situation descriptions from sensor data
Prediction	Inferring likely consequences of given situations
Diagnosis	Inferring system malfunctions from observables
Design	Configuring objects under constraints
Planning	Designing actions
Monitoring	Comparing observations to plan vulnerabilities
Debugging	Prescribing remedies for malfunctions
Repair	Executing a plan to administer a prescribed remedy
Instruction	Diagnosing, debugging, and repairing student behaviour
Control	Interpreting, predicting, repairing, and monitoring system behaviours

Figure 7.7 Tasks performed by expert systems

Expert systems can be visualized as performing any of the tasks shown in *Figure 7.7* (Hayes-Roth *et al.*, 1983). The most common form of 'ES' to date has been the system that is provided with data about a current situation, that makes a diagnosis or interpretation of that situation, and gives advice about possibly appropriate action. We can view an intelligent retrieval interface in a similar light—it receives data on an enquirer's information want, interprets this as a query designation for search by retrieval system, and passes back to the enquirer a response that may satisfy the want. It is typical of all such ES that they are not operating 'algorithmically', providing an assured and consistent output, but 'heuristically', using encoded judgement to provide responses that may or may not prove adequate.

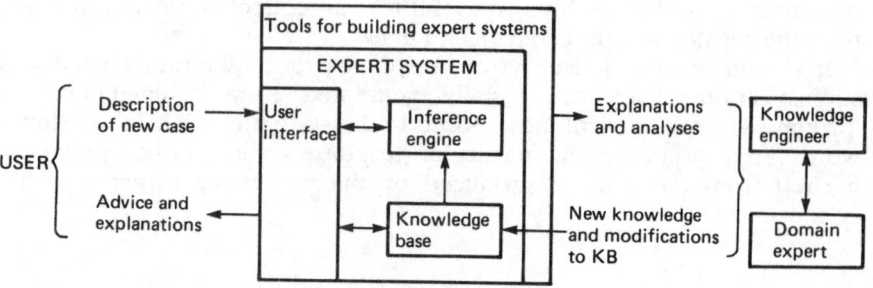

Figure 7.8 Overall pattern of expert system

The overall pattern of an advisory ES is shown in *Figure 7.8*. Experts in a subject domain, with the aid of the 'knowledge engineer' (a system designer) provide knowledge to build up a knowledge base. Once a prototype system is operating they are aided in this 'knowledge-acquisition' task by feedback from the system. Users interact with the system through a language interface, and the knowledge base is manipulated in response to user queries by the 'inference engine'. The ES outputs advice and explanations of its actions and conclusions. For a retrieval 'front end' we must visualize the inference engine passing query designations out to a retrieval system and receiving back search responses.

The knowledge base is, of course, wholly dependent on the subject domain. It embodies the expertise in a particular field.

In principle, the inference engine (the program that manipulates the knowledge base) can be independent of the specific knowledge handled, but a given program will only be usable for domains where the general structure of the knowledge embodied is the same as that for which the engine was initially constructed. Commercially available 'expert system shells' are inference engines, whose domain limitations need to be carefully specified.

The basic ES software is concerned with inference—relating input data to the knowledge base, interpreting it, drawing conclusions, and making recommendations. Supplementary software is concerned with (1) the language interface, (2) the provision of explanations, and (3) the acquisition of new knowledge to supplement the knowledge base. There can also be (4) a tutorial program to teach the principles upon which the inferencing is based, i.e. to transmit some of the expertise as well as the expert advice. To give a feel for the nature of expert systems we present a brief case history of what many regard as the 'grand-daddy' of them all.

7.16 The MYCIN story

MYCIN and its related computer programs were initiated in the early 1970s as an interactive computer system to provide physicians with advice on the choice of drugs to treat patients who had infectious diseases. As well as the main consultation program (MYCIN itself), the program TEIRESIAS provides facilities for explanation and knowledge acquisition,

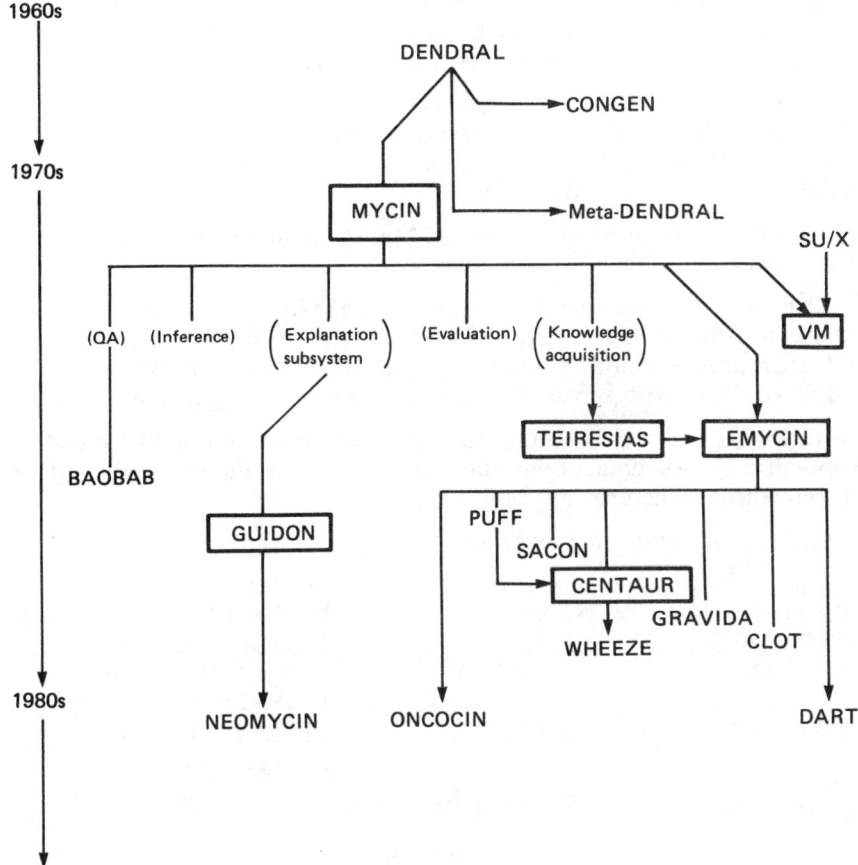

Figure 7.9 Programs related to MYCIN

BAOBAB is a recently developed language interface, GUIDON is a tutorial program for students (being further developed as NEOMYCIN), and EMYCIN is an ES 'shell' from which a number of other medical diagnostic systems have been developed (see *Figure 7.9*, taken from Buchanan and Shortliffe).

MYCIN deals with four main types of entity, so-called 'contexts': PERSONS (or PATIENTS), CULTURES, ORGANISMS, and DRUGS. Cultures are taken from patients (for example, from throat, blood, etc.); organisms are found in cultures; drugs affect organisms. Expert knowledge about the interrelationships among these entities is stored as about 500 'production rules', one of which has already been illustrated on page 161.

One characteristic feature of MYCIN is that each expert judgement is tagged with a 'certainty factor' that can vary from −1 to +1. It expresses the confidence that the expert attached to his THEN clause. As rules are combined to draw more general conclusions, their certainty factors are mathematically merged to produce joint certainties, so that the final conclusions of the program are also tagged in this way.

Associated with each context type are 'main parameters', attributes for which evidence must be obtained, either from the user or by inference from the data. Examples of such parameters are:

PATIENTS   : age, sex, allergies
CULTURES   : site, data, method of collection
ORGANISMS : identity, stain, morphology, aerobicity, portal
DRUGS   : duration of use

In addition to the production rules, MYCIN includes knowledge in the form of lists and tables, for example:

(1) List of all organisms known to MYCIN, with the staining characteristics, morphology, and aerobicity of each;
(2) List of different body sites, with organisms normally present;
(3) List of drugs with sensitivities to each of various organisms.

MYCIN collects information from the user by an interactive dialogue (Appendix 4). As data about the patient and his illness is elicited or inferred, three structures are built up.

(1) Patient data table; for example:

(object)	(parameter)	(value)
PATIENT-1	SEX	MALE 1.0
CULTURE-1	SITE	BLOOD 1.0
ORGANISM-1	IDENTITY	KLEBSIELLA 0.6
		HAFNIA 0.4
PATIENT-1	ALLERGY	PENICILLIN 1.0
		AMPICILLIN 0.5

(2) Context tree, structuring the patient data (*Figure 7.10*).

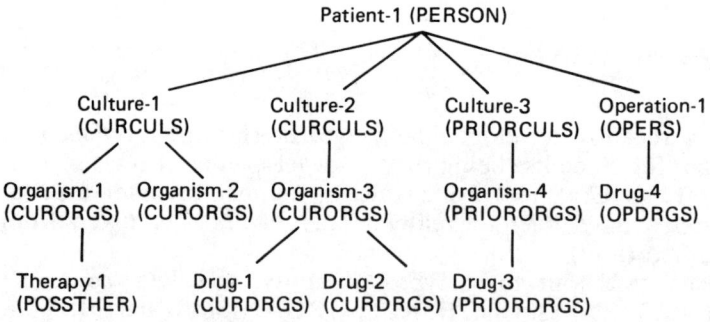

Figure 7.10 A context tree

(3) Goal tree, showing the production rules used and how inferences have been made (*Figure 7.11*).

At any time in the consultation the user can query the system as to WHY some data are demanded or HOW a conclusion has been reached. The TEIRESIAS module of the system provides an explanation (Appendix 5). This is achieved by climbing up and down the goal tree, identifying the rules that justify questions and conclusions.

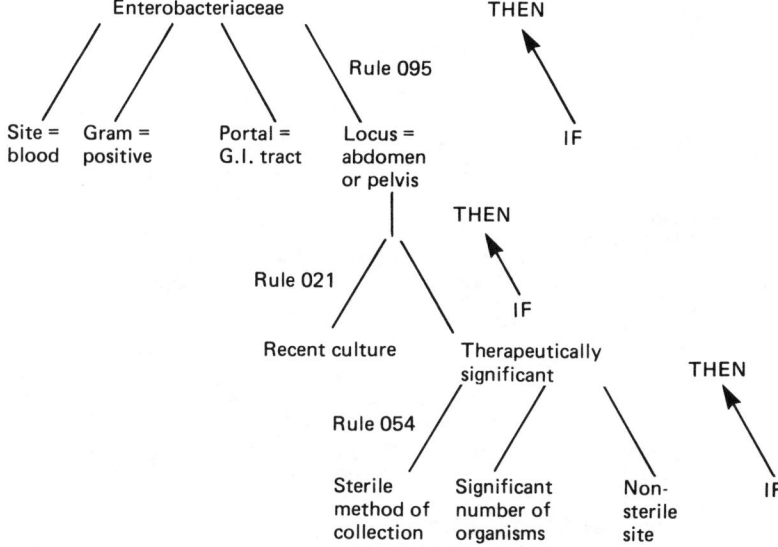

Figure 7.11 A goal tree

7.17 Expert system for referral

We now turn to an expert system, under development in the University of London, that is more directly relevant to the theme of this chapter. PLEXUS acts as a retrieval system for referral sources but is designed as an expert system to perform both the interface and search functions (Vickery *et al.*, 1986, 1987). It operates on a microcomputer with hard disc storage, and is intended for use by enquirers in a public library reference department. The prototype is restricted to the subject domain of gardening.

The enquirer keys in a query, and the system makes an assessment as to whether the query is appropriate for conversion into a query designation (search statement). If not, a dialogue with the user is conducted, to formulate an appropriate query. The query is then automatically converted into a Boolean statement which is used to search a database of referral sources (reference books and institutions to which the enquirer can be referred). Internal evaluation of the output may be followed by automatic modification of the search statement for further search. If no appropriate referral source can be identified further dialogue with the enquirer is conducted so as to reformulate the query, and searches are again performed. The overall system design is as in *Figure 7.12.*

The user interface handles dialogue with the enquirer. In the prototype PLEXUS system no parser is employed. Input text is screened through a stop list and the remaining words are stemmed and matched against the dictionary.

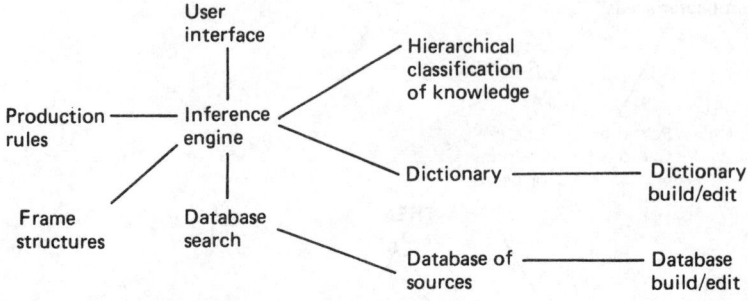

Figure 7.12 The design of PLEXUS

Each stem in the dictionary is assigned to a semantic category such as one of the following:

Object (e.g. plant, soil, insect, animal);
Part of object (e.g. flower, seed, topsoil);
Operation on object (e.g. prune, dig, rid);
Agent of operation (e.g. shears, spade, spray);
Attribute of object (e.g. dwarf, dormant, sandy);
Environment (e.g. indoors, shade);
Use (e.g. ornamental, windbreak);
Time (e.g. spring, Christmas);
Place (geographical).

The first function of the inference engine is to activate production rules that use this semantic information to build a model of the user problem statement (in a sense we can regard this as semantic parsing). The model consists of a set of completed frames, one for each stem accepted as part of the problem statement (an example of such a frame has been given on page 161). The inference engine then activates a second set of production rules to transform the problem statement into a Boolean statement, which is used to search the database. If search is unsuccessful, the inference engine activates production rules to modify the Boolean statement, and in the course of this may draw information from the hierarchical classification.

The database contents and the dictionary entries relate directly to the subject domain of the system. The hierarchical classification also relates to gardening, but it is drawn from a comprehensive general classification, the Broad System of Ordering, and thus can be extended to other domains. The production rules and frame structures could perhaps be used for any domain in which the chosen set of semantic categories is applicable—they would need amendment if the categories were altered. The inference engine is independent of subject domain, but, of course, is designed to manipulate a production rule system. The user interface is still unsophisticated and may need upgrading to cope with more varied user input. Limited explanation facilities have been provided. The database build/edit and search, the dictionary build/edit, the stop list, and the stemmer are domain independent.

7.18 Conclusion

In this chapter we have looked at the cognitive and behavioural problems of interaction between a recipient and a particular kind of channel—an information store. Because of the complexity of modern information stores and information systems, mediation between recipient and channel is often necessary, and the reference intermediary (whether in library or online search) is a well-established profession. The possibility of embodying the expertise of the intermediary in a machine interface has led to some penetrating studies of the reference process, which have laid bare its variety and complexity. Some first steps are being taken to create intelligent interfaces that can incorporate these intermediary skills (see Davies *et al.*, 1986). A brief account of recent developments in this field is provided in Appendix 6.

Chapter 8

Information systems

Linking the sources and recipients of informative communication are channels, carrying out functions which in Chapter 2 were broadly summarized as in *Figure 8.1*. In the most general sense, an information system is any organization of staff, materials, and equipment that is concerned with the formal execution of one or more of these channel functions. Examples already given in Chapter 2 are the telephone system, consultancies, publishers, booksellers, libraries, database producers, and database processors.

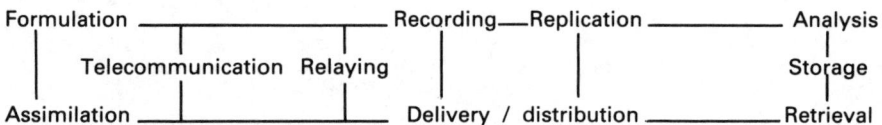

Figure 8.1 Channels of informative communication

The practical work of the information scientist is concerned with the development, operation, and management of information systems of all kinds, and with all the various techniques and technologies by which information may be transferred. In this book we lay more emphasis on the ways whereby information science can aid an understanding of information systems, their nature and variety, their design and evaluation, their dynamics and change under the impact of new technology. This understanding comes in four ways:

(1) By the adaptation of general systems principles to the particular characteristics of information systems;
(2) By the development of models of phenomena that information systems must take into account;
(3) By the devising of reliable and appropriate methods of system evaluation;
(4) By identification of the dynamic patterns of change displayed by information systems.

8.1 Typology of information systems

There are a number of criteria by which we may categorize information systems, apart from the one already noted, the function served. Considering information transfer as a whole, the broadest distinction to be made is between transient and recorded messages.

Transient messages cover both those spoken to an audience within hearing distance—a conversation, a lecture, a discussion—and messages broadcast by telecommunications, radio, or television. Conversation is direct, unmediated by any system (unless by telephone), but the other forms of transient message do indeed involve channel agencies that may be regarded as forms of information system: institutions that organize lectures and conferences; broadcasting organizations.

The vast majority of the information systems with which we are concerned handle *recorded* messages—and even ostensibly 'transient' agencies like the BBC increasingly rely on recorded material. However, there is another broad distinction we can introduce here that cuts across the one just discussed: it relates to the nature of the audience, whether individual or diffuse. At a given moment is there a mass audience for a particular message or a single recipient? The dissemination of messages to a diffuse audience is the function of the *mass media*—not only the broadcasting agencies but also publications such as newspapers and large-circulation magazines, leaflets, and advertising posters. In contrast, in a library each reader is using a different book.

The study of mass communication diverges in many ways from the informative communication problems considered in this book, although there are many points of contact. In subsequent analysis we will be primarily concerned with recorded messages for individual audiences.

The next distinction to be introduced is whether the audience is concentrated or dispersed. A *concentrated* audience is a group with a well-defined identity, homogeneous in at least some respects, all members of a single organization or institutional association, the number and names of the members usually being known. Examples are the employees of an industrial firm or a government department, or students and staff in an educational institution. Less concentrated, but still well defined, are the members of a professional or special-interest association. Examples of more *dispersed* audiences are those sharing a common subject interest even though in diverse employment—for example, people who are photographers—or, still less homogeneous, people interested in 'current affairs'.

Information systems exist for every kind of audience. The characteristics of concentration, homogeneity, known identity of the audience have a marked effect on the design features of a system serving them, in contrast to those of a system aimed at a dispersed, heterogeneous, largely unidentified audience.

Before information can be transferred to recipients it must first be collected from sources, and these too can be considered as concentrated or dispersed. At one extreme is an information system concerned only with disseminating information originating within its parent organization; at the other, a system trying to collect information from sources distributed worldwide.

Given dispersed sources and/or recipients, the information system itself may have various structures, *centralized* or *decentralized*. These characteristics can apply to:

(1) Acquisition points, through which information is collected from sources;

(2) Storage points;
(3) Access points, from which information is supplied to recipients.

A system decentralized in one or more of these ways has considerably different problems from a unitary centralized system.

The *orientation* of the recipient group has a marked effect on the nature of the information system. For example, services provided to administrators to aid managerial decision making differ considerably from those offered to researchers involved in scientific problem solving, and both will be different from a community service to help people cope with daily living.

The *form of information* provided is a further distinguishing characteristic. Broadly we can identify

(1) Documents themselves (as provided on library loan);
(2) References to documents (as provided by a bibliographical service);
(3) Data, facts, information in the strict sense; and
(4) Directory data—references to people and institutions that are themselves information sources.

A final criterion to be mentioned is the *medium* in which messages are delivered to the recipient (irrespective of how it may initially be recorded), and here we are thinking of three possibilities: orally, in written or other recorded form, or by electronic communication.

We have thus identified eight main criteria that can be used to construct a typology of information systems:

(1) Form of source message—transient or recorded;
(2) Nature of audience for a message—individual or mass;
(3) Distribution of recipients—concentrated or dispersed;
(4) Distribution of sources—concentrated or dispersed;
(5) Structure of acquisition, storage, and access activities—centralized or decentralized;
(6) Orientation of recipients;
(7) Form of information provided—documents, references, data, directory;
(8) Delivery medium—oral, recorded, online.

Each individual system can be characterized by some combination of these criteria. For example, a university library has the following 'profile': (1)—recorded; (2)—individual; (3)—reasonably concentrated; (4)—widely dispersed; (5)—often all three centralized; (6)—study and research; (7)—mainly documents, partly references; (8)—recorded.

A public viewdata system such as PRESTEL has the profile: (1)—recorded (though regular updating makes many records transient); (2)—individual; (3)—dispersed; (4)—reasonably dispersed; (5)—acquisition and access decentralized, storage mainly centralized; (6)—orientation diverse; (7)—mainly data and directory; (8)—online.

If we return now to consider *function*, this is a ninth criterion by which to characterize systems. Let us define the possible functions of a system handling recorded messages for individual audiences as:

(a) Recording basic information or data in documents of some kind;

Table 8.1 Agricultural abstracts and indexes

Services	Cumulated total	References per annum	Cumulated total	Percentage of the total
1	1	78 500	78 500	5.25
1	2	66 000	144 500	9.67
1	3	55 000	199 500	13.34
1	4	36 000	235 500	15.75
1	5	30 000	265 500	17.75
1	6	30 000	295 500	19.77
1	7	30 000	325 500	21.78
1	8	30 000	355 500	23.77
1	9	30 000	385 500	25.78
1	10	30 000	415 500	27.78
1	11	28 000	443 500	29.66
1	12	22 250	466 000	31.16
1	13	21 500	487 500	32.60
1	14	20 000	507 500	33.94
1	15	16 300	523 800	35.04
1	16	15 000	538 800	36.04
1	17	15 000	553 800	37.03
1	18	13 000	566 800	37.90
1	19	12 300	579 100	38.73
1	20	12 000	591 100	39.54
3	23	36 000	627 100	41.94
3	26	32 800	659 900	44.14
3	29	30 000	689 900	46.14
3	32	29 300	719 200	48.10
3	35	24 800	744 000	49.74
3	38	24 000	768 000	51.37
3	41	24 000	792 000	52.97
3	44	23 230	815 230	54.53
3	47	22 000	837 230	56.00
3	50	21 000	858 230	57.40
6	56	38 300	896 530	59.96
6	62	35 500	932 030	62.33
6	68	30 500	962 530	64.37
6	74	29 800	992 330	66.37
6	80	27 300	1 019 630	68.20
6	86	25 400	1 045 030	69.90
6	92	24 000	1 069 030	71.50
6	98	22 100	1 091 130	72.97
6	104	21 000	1 112 130	74.38
6	110	20 000	1 132 130	75.73
10	120	30 100	1 162 230	77.73
10	130	26 750	1 188 980	79.52
10	140	24 800	1 213 780	81.18
10	150	22 350	1 236 130	82.67
10	160	20 200	1 256 330	84.02
10	170	18 400	1 274 730	85.25
10	180	18 000	1 292 730	86.46
10	190	16 650	1 309 380	87.58
10	200	15 100	1 324 480	88.59
10	210	14 500	1 338 980	89.56
10	220	12 900	1 351 880	90.41
10	230	12 000	1 363 880	91.23
20	250	22 500	1 386 380	92.73
20	270	19 760	1 406 140	94.04
20	290	16 450	1 422 590	95.14
30	320	21 400	1 443 990	96.57
30	350	16 200	1 460 190	97.66
40	390	16 430	1 476 620	98.76
45	435	11 780	1 488 400	99.54
50	485	6 745	1 495 145	100.00

(b) Acquiring and collecting documents from sources;
(c) Analysis—description and indexing of documents;
(d) Storage of documents and/or analyses from stores;
(e) Retrieval of documents and/or analyses from stores;
(f) Processing the acquired or retrieved documents, e.g. by summary, translation, evalution (relaying);
(g) Delivery and distribution of information products.

A few information systems may carry out all these functions—for example, a company management information system. Others perform only one or two functions—for example, some database producers are concerned only with function (c), creating document analyses; database processors carry out (d), storage of analyses (references); and an online

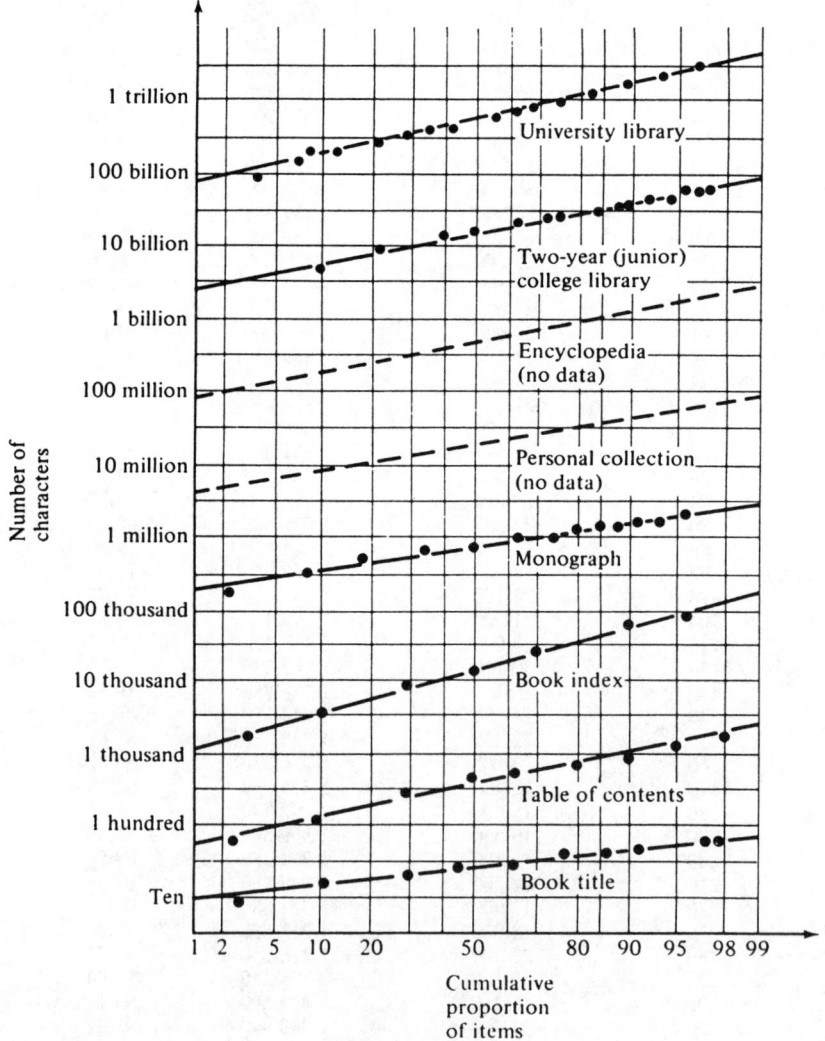

Figure 8.2 Range in size of bibliographic units

search service carries out (e), reference retrieval (using the search and delivery programs of the processor). In terms of function, a university library usually has the profile (b) + (c) + (d), since retrieval is normally carried out by the user, and PRESTEL itself does little more than (d) + (g).

The multiplicity of ways in which these nine criteria may be combined immediately suggests that there will be many types of information system, as indeed is the case. Even within a particular type, further diversity exists, and this may be illustrated by an example of the distribution of *system sizes*. *Table 8.1* shows the range of sizes of various agriculture abstracts and indexes in a survey carried out by Boyle and Buntrock (1973). *Figure 8.2* is an indication of the range in size of different 'bibliographic units', from individual book to university library (Resnikoff and Dolby, 1971).

8.2 The interconnection of systems

The figure with which we opened this chapter indicates that there is a number of linked functions involved in the whole process of information transfer. As already noted, organized information systems are associated with one or more individual functions. Only when the whole process takes place within one institution is it possible for all functions to be undertaken by a single information system—and even in those circumstances this is rare. Consequently if transfer from source to recipient—from generation to use, from formulation to assimilation—is to take place, a number of linked systems must participate. For example, a borrowed book has passed from author to publisher to bookseller to library before reaching the reader.

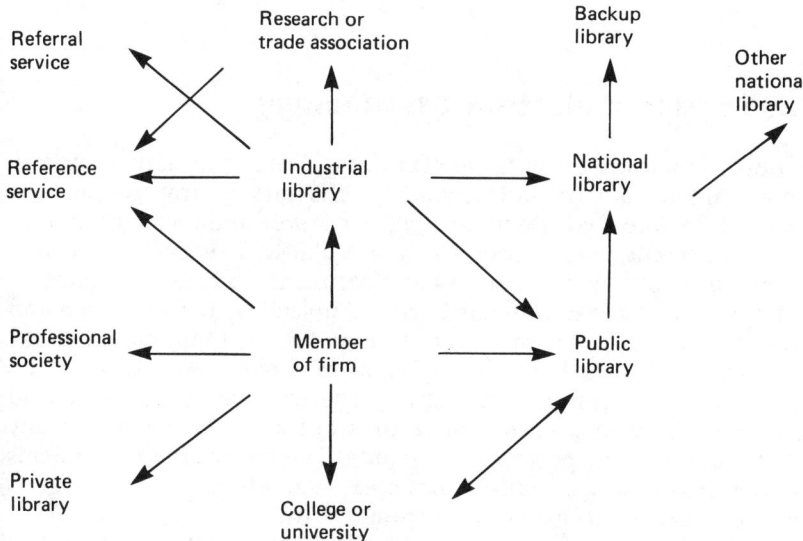

Figure 8.3 Sources tapped by industrial library

The consequence is that for each system in the information chain, immediately preceding systems are sources, and immediately following systems are recipients. Each system is typically in contact with many such intermediate sources and recipients. One pervasive feature of the whole cycle is search—each system seeking potential sources and recipients.

In terms of seeking recipients publishers search for booksellers to display their books, booksellers seek library customers as well as individual purchasers, libraries look for users. Search for libraries and booksellers as sources is carried out by readers, libraries seek booksellers and publishers, and publishers look for likely authors. If an information system aims to provide optimum service to its users it will extend the search for sources to other systems of the same kind. This is typically the case with libraries, which have developed interlibrary loan systems. Another form of system interconnection therefore exists. This is suggested in *Figure 8.3*, which shows sources that may be tapped by an industrial library on behalf of the members of the firm.

The overall system pattern is along the following lines:

Individual recipients—personal sources

Local sources, e.g. libraries,
                    booksellers,
                    other information systems

Distant sources, e.g. other libraries,
                    publishers,
                    other information systems

Original sources, e.g. authors

8.3 The impact of electronic technology

Information systems are created in order to facilitate information transfer between potential sources and recipients. Barriers to transfer include differences in the knowledge and language of source and recipient, and in the lack of information skills (literacy, search skills). However, the major barriers are the separation of sources and recipients in time and space.

The effect of time separation has been minimized by the recording and replication of messages. As Thomas Carlyle put it: 'All that mankind has done, thought, gained or been: it is lying as in magic preservation in the pages of books.' The printing of multiple copies, their transport to and storage in many diverse sites, makes records of human knowledge locally available to innumerable potential recipients. The interconnected systems we have described ensure that, in principle, 'the whole of knowledge is available for everyone to use' (Holmstrom, 1956).

However, it is logistically and economically impossible to ensure in this way that the whole of knowledge is everywhere *locally* available.

Information stores—whether those of an individual, a library, a bookseller, a work organization, an administrative department, or whatever—are inevitably selective and limited in relation to potential requirements. So total access is achievable only by links with other localities, other systems, to acquire information when needed—links involving the transport of recorded messages.

Before the advent of electrical communication the space barrier between sources, recipients, and information systems could be overcome only by the physical transport of documents to people or people to documents. This is still a major barrier, because transport or travel involves effort that has both monetary and psychological costs. The telegraph and telephone have had a considerable effect in speeding and simplifying the transfer of short messages—both those requisitioning information and those bearing substantive information.

Electronic technology—information technology, as it has come to be called, the coming together of computers and telecommunications—is likely to have a more profound effect because, in principle, it overcomes the space barrier for a much larger range of informative messages and greatly reduces the need for local information stores. Instead of the pattern previously illustrated there is the possibility of immediate access by each individual to *all* intermediate sources and even to original sources:

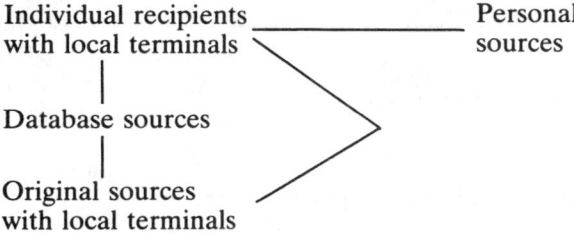

These implications will be discussed in more detail in our final chapter.

8.4 General system features

Now that we have briefly considered the nature and variety of information systems we can look at some of their characteristics.

A system of the kind considered in this book is a set of interacting components, under human control, operating together to achieve an intended purpose. A system carries out processing on inputs to produce required outputs and the agents of processing are men and machines. The inputs subjected to processing are those needed by the system to provide outputs—they are incoming data. However, a system also receives other inputs—policy information, funds and fees, demands and feedback from recipients of its outputs, requests from its sources, other information about the environment. As well as the results of processing, a system outputs reports on its functioning, issues demands and feedback to sources and requests to recipients, information directed generally to its environment, and perhaps monetary profit or loss to its funders (*Table 8.2*).

Table 8.2 A system's inputs and outputs

Inputs	Processing	Outputs
Source data	by man and	Results
Policies	machines	Reports
Funds, fees		Demands on sources
Recipient demands		Feedback to sources
Recipient feedback		Requests to recipients
Source requests		General publicity
Environmental information		Profits/losses

The way that a system works is a result of the interplay of all its inputs:

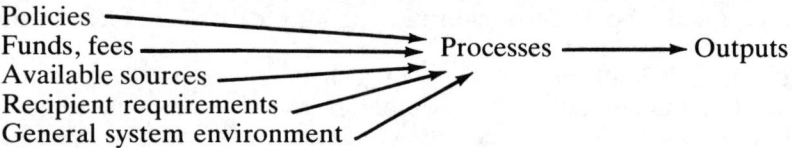

Because all the inputs are continually liable to change, so is the system: it is essentially a dynamic organism.

If we focus now more closely on information systems, relations with sources and recipients can be shown as in *Figure 8.4*. Source data are

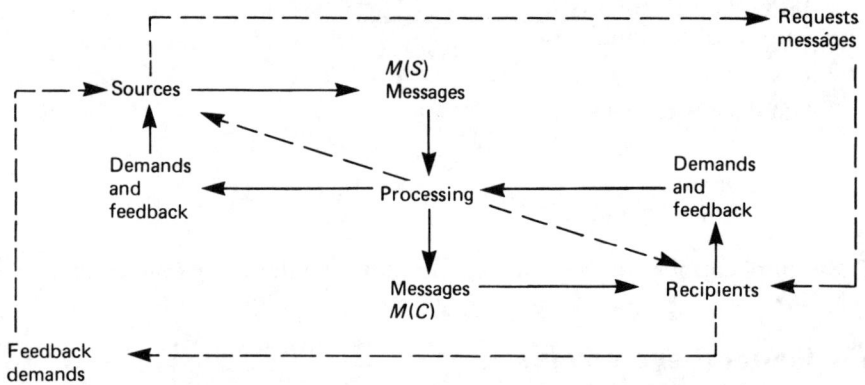

Figure 8.4 Systems, sources, and recipients (1)

input to the system via messages $M(S)$ and output messages $M(C)$ are issued to recipients. Demands and feedback flow from recipients to the system and from the system to sources. The inner dashed lines represent the ceaseless search by the system to identify new sources and new recipients. The outer dashed lines remind us that, outside the system, sources and recipients are passing information to each other through other channels.

The information system itself is here represented as a 'black box', Processing. The contents of the box, of course, depend on the functions and services of the particular system studied. In many cases a series of subsystems are involved. For example, we might show some of the processing activities of a publisher as:

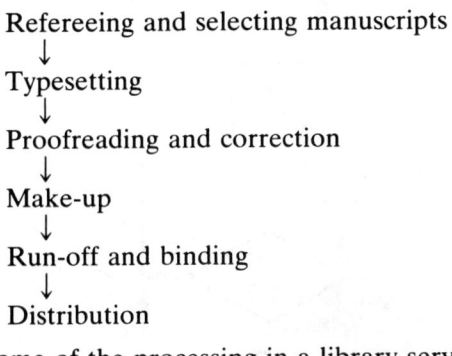

Refereeing and selecting manuscripts
↓
Typesetting
↓
Proofreading and correction
↓
Make-up
↓
Run-off and binding
↓
Distribution

Some of the processing in a library service could be charted as:

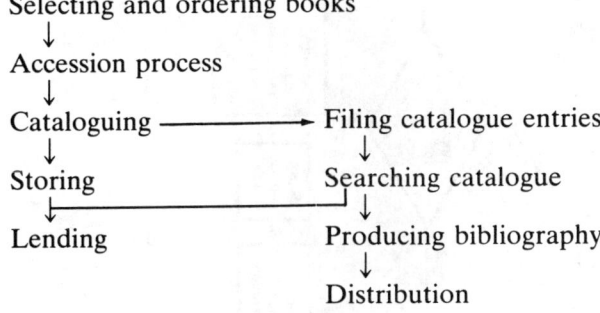

Selecting and ordering books
↓
Accession process
↓
Cataloguing ————————→ Filing catalogue entries
↓   ↓
Storing   Searching catalogue
↓   ↓
Lending   Producing bibliography
↓
Distribution

Practical systems development is concerned with the detailed analysis of individual information systems—existing or proposed—and their configuration so as to achieve a cost-effective design. Wherever possible, this design is based on data obtained directly from the environment in which the system is working or will work—the actual or expected volumes of material to be handled, variations in flowrate, size and frequency of demand, etc.

However, it is often the case that data specific to the particular system are hard to obtain. In this situation systems design must rely on data drawn from analogous systems or on models of the phenomena. These models have been developed by generalization from empirical observations made on other systems. If a model appears to describe a situation analogous to that in the system being designed it is safe to use it, at any rate as an initial assumption to be modified with experience.

It is the work of information science to collect generalized data, and to develop and test models of phenomena relevant to the design and operation of information systems. It is on this work that we will concentrate. A valuable review of models that are relevant to library planning—but also of use in the context of other information systems—is provided by Hamburg *et al.* (1974).

220

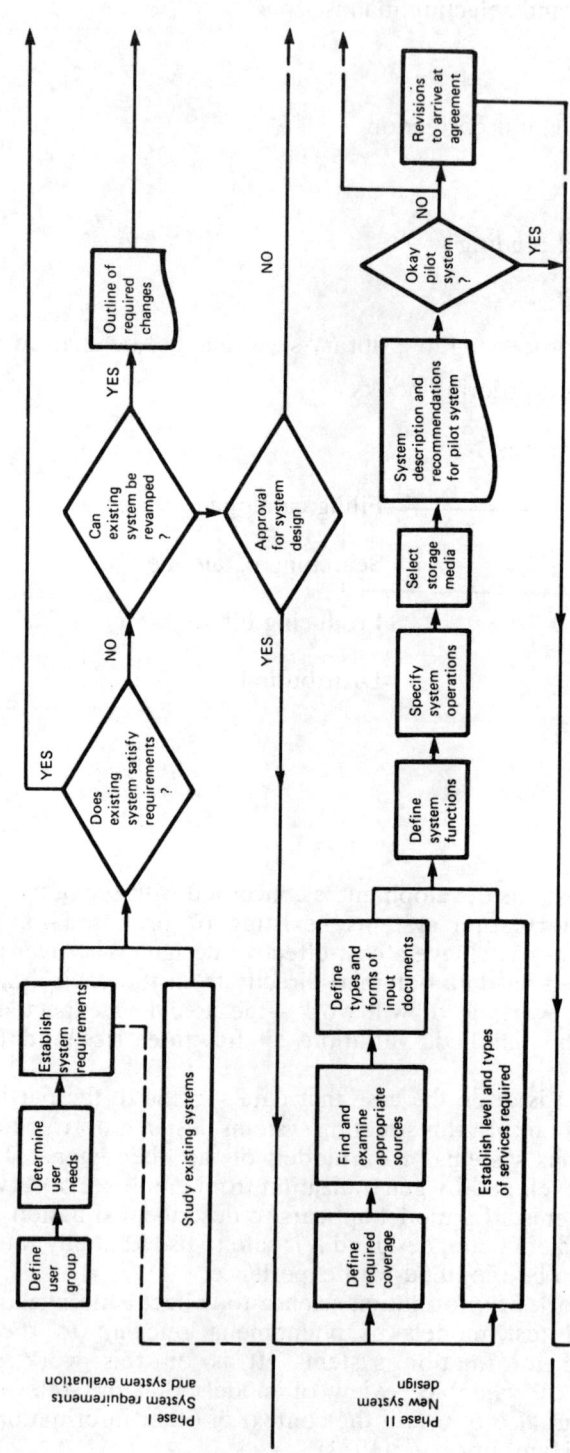

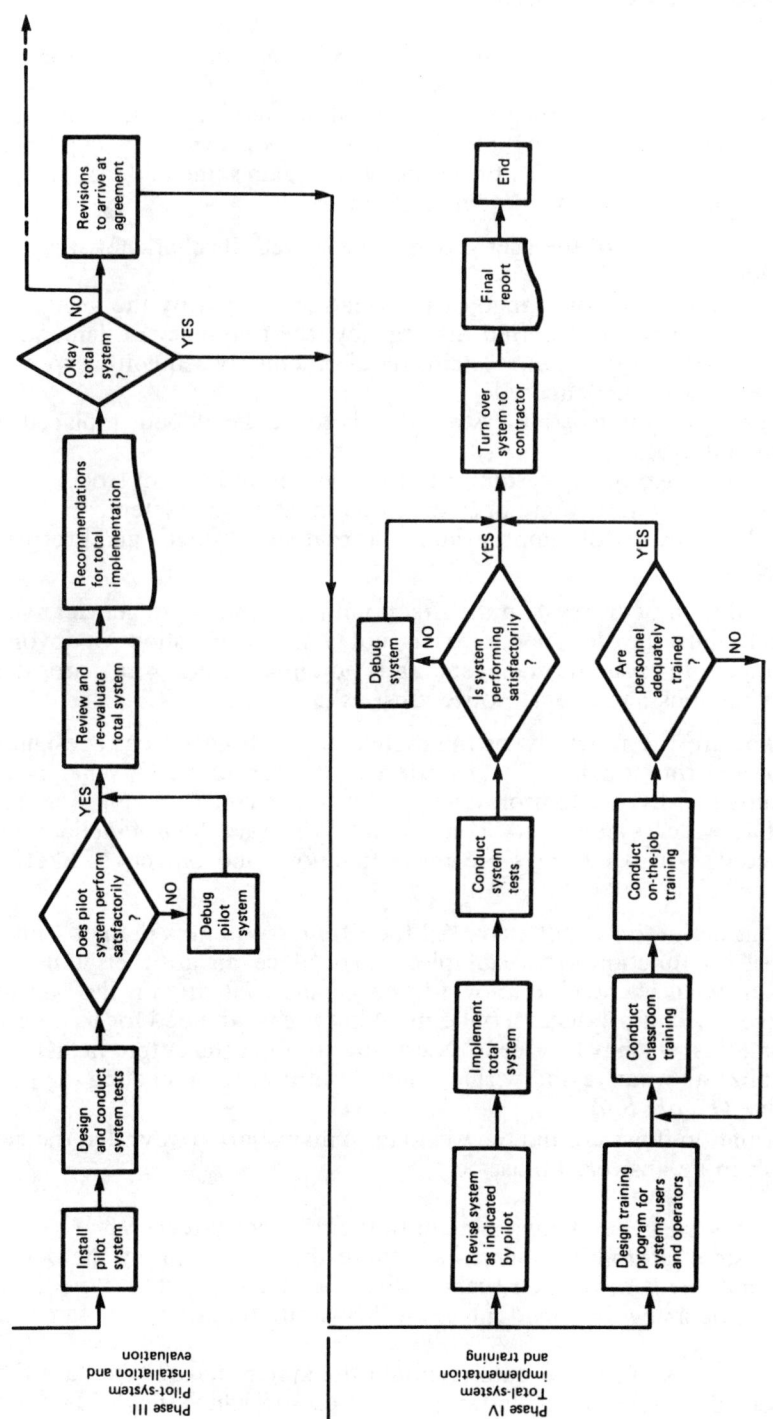

Figure 8.5 Systems development

8.5 System development

Although this book is not intended to be a practical guide to system analysis and design, to set our work in context it is useful to summarize the main features of the process of information systems development. A helpful diagram of one possible flow of work is provided in *Figure 8.5*, taken from Weisman (1972). From this we can gain some understanding of the kinds of data that the system designer needs:

(1) A specification of the user group to be served, its characteristics, size and location;
(2) A knowledge of the range of information needed by the group, the forms in which it is required, its urgency, the frequency of demand;
(3) An understanding of the systems requirements consequently expected, the services to be delivered;
(4) A grasp of any existing system that is to be developed, replaced, or competed against;
(5) The coverage of the system, i.e. the content and size of stock;
(6) The nature and volume of items to be input to the system;
(7) A knowledge of appropriate alternative storage and retrieval procedures.

In the design of any system the first point is, of course, to get clear what it is that must be designed. This is not a trivial question—it involves exploring with system managers and potential users what are their underlying aims and needs. So we must ask:

(1) What are the functions of the system to be designed or redesigned? What information is to be transferred or transformed? What is the objective—why is the information to be transferred?
(2) What wider systems are concerned? What are their functions and objectives? In what ways are these functions and objectives likely to change?

System definition is not easy. All too often a system is defined only in terms of its function—for example, 'to produce an abstracts bulletin'. However, what we need to know for design and evaluation is the system's objective—*why* it produces a bulletin. What *use* is intended for its output? Knowing this, we may be able to assess how useful is the output in fact, and to visualize alternative and perhaps more useful ways of meeting the same objective (*Figure 8.6*).

Information flows around the world in so many varied ways that the next question to be answered must be:

(3) What is the general environment of the defined system? What existing or possible alternative sources are there that might supply the desired information? What is their accessibility, quality, and cost? Is it necessary to develop a new system? Only if the answer to this last is Yes, can we go on:
(4) What kinds of service output should the system have? What are their preferred characteristics, in terms of the uses to which they will be put?
(5) What kinds of documentary input will be available to the system?

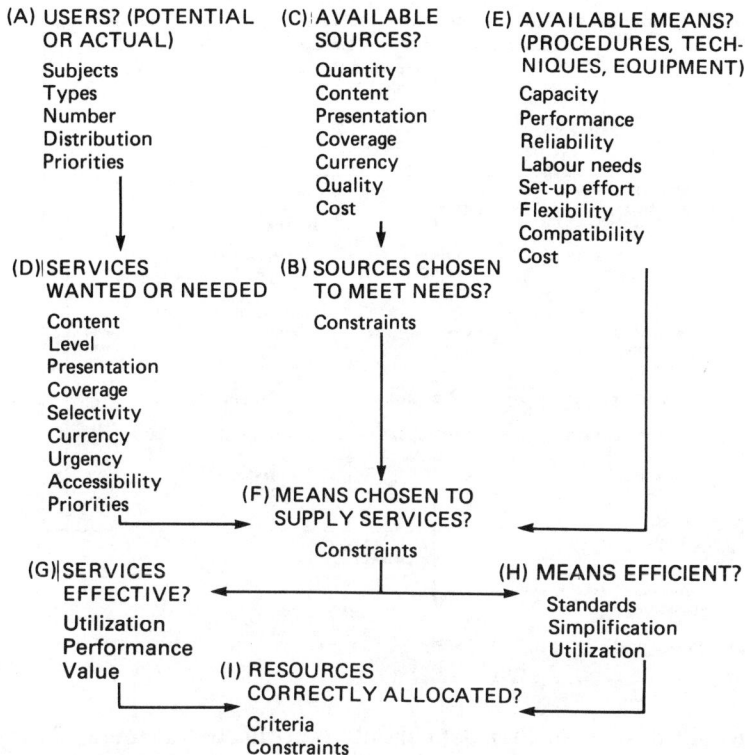

(A) USERS? (POTENTIAL
OR ACTUAL)

Subjects
Types
Number
Distribution
Priorities

(C) AVAILABLE
SOURCES?

Quantity
Content
Presentation
Coverage
Currency
Quality
Cost

(E) AVAILABLE MEANS?
(PROCEDURES, TECH-
NIQUES, EQUIPMENT)

Capacity
Performance
Reliability
Labour needs
Set-up effort
Flexibility
Compatibility
Cost

(D) SERVICES
WANTED OR NEEDED

Content
Level
Presentation
Coverage
Selectivity
Currency
Urgency
Accessibility
Priorities

(B) SOURCES CHOSEN
TO MEET NEEDS?

Constraints

(F) MEANS CHOSEN TO
SUPPLY SERVICES?

Constraints

(G) SERVICES
EFFECTIVE?

Utilization
Performance
Value

(H) MEANS EFFICIENT?

Standards
Simplification
Utilization

(I) RESOURCES
CORRECTLY ALLOCATED?

Criteria
Constraints

Figure 8.6 Some decisions in information system design

What are their characteristics? How are these related to preferred output characteristics?

In answering these two sets of questions, it is particularly important to consider the wider systems of which the defined system is a part. The designer should envisage all the possible uses of the files that may be created, in the hope that they can be made flexible enough to serve all these uses, or as many as is feasible.

As an example, consider *Figure 8.7*. The objective may be to design a new system to produce a set of abstracts journals for sale on subscription (the left-hand stream of processes in the figure). However, in the wider system are other possible or actual streams of activity—providing current notifications against profiles, bibliographies in response to queries, and photocopies on request. The same input (abstracts and index entries) could provide more than one output. Should the objectives of the design be widened to include these other outputs? With such points established, the next question is:

(6) What processes are necessary to transform inputs into outputs? At this stage specific procedures are not envisaged, but only the functional steps. It is important at this stage to generalize into functions, and to get away from specific procedures, so as to come to the design stage with as few procedural preconceptions as possible.

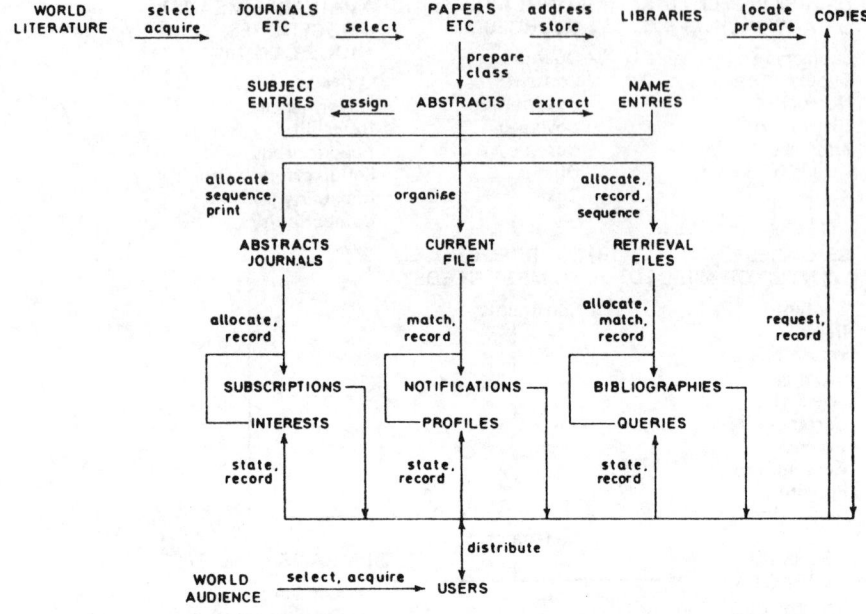

Figure 8.7 System inputs and outputs

In order to aid design, further data should be collected at the analysis stage:

(7) What are the expected volumes of input and output—for example, items processed per day, uses per hour, fluctuations in load? What sizes of records and files are to be expected? Quantitative considerations of this sort will be essential in deciding on the kind of equipment to be used. Since we will be designing for the future, it is also necessary to ask:

(8) What changes in volumes, or in the characteristics of inputs and desired outputs, can be forecast?

(9) What constraints are there on design—for example, as to choice of input, choice of machines, available personnel, cash? Must there be compatibility with other systems? What standard specifications should be adhered to? In practice, constraints of this kind have a very great effect. The choices open to the designer may be far fewer than are technically feasible. Yet since these constraints may also be open to question, it is important to take a wide view and to ask:

(10) What is the full range of technically feasible methods of carrying out the necessary processes? How reliable is each? What is its cost? What technical developments and costs can be forecast?

(11) What criteria are available to measure the performance of the system—as to both its effectiveness (how well it achieves its objective) and its efficiency (how economically it functions)? The very great difficulties of measuring information system performance are well

known, and will be discussed in the following chapter, but the analyst should put these questions, even if he is sometimes forced candidly to admit that he can only point to 'intangible benefits'.

The early phases of analysis should concentrate on gaining as wide a view as possible of the proposed system and its environment. Factors at first unrecognized are thus brought to light, that may significantly affect design decisions. As analysis proceeds, tentative design options will be formulated, and these will suggest where the analysis needs to go into further detail. It is wise not to embark on detailed analysis or surveys until a clear need for specific data is formulated—much time can be spent collecting data that prove irrelevant.

The most pervasive technique of analysis is individual and group discussion with the prospective managers, operators, and users of the system. As analysis proceeds, the interviews become more directed, more specific. They may be amplified by structured surveys of both operational staff and potential users. User survey is, of course, particularly important in order to ascertain required output characteristics and criteria of performance. Insights gained by general user studies, of the kind discussed in Chapter 4, should also serve as a guide. The characteristics of the input have to be analysed in detail—for example, the kinds of input documents and records, their structures, bibliographic elements, character sets. If an existing system is to be modified its structure may be carefully charted and costed. Familiarity with other existing or proposed systems must be extended through examination of published reports and visits to installations.

Particularly if a computer system is to be introduced into an information service for the first time, there should be the closest possible interaction from the very beginning of analysis with those who may later manage, operate, and use the new system. This is necesary to educate the designer as to system objectives, constraints, and environment, and to educate his 'clients' as to the new problems and opportunities that will face them.

We have tried above to sketch in the analysis procedure that must be followed by the designer who faces the problem of creating an information system. In the remainder of this chapter we look at data and models that can aid this design work.

8.6 Relevant data

The development of any kind of information system requires first, an understanding of the environment in which the system will operate. What kinds of message flow between the potential sources and recipients of the system? What are their typical behaviour patterns in providing and seeking information? What is the total volume of message movement? What is the typical time taken for messages to be transferred? Through what existing channels are they transferred?

Studies of the kind surveyed in Chapter 4 may provide background information on the behaviour of source and recipient groups analogous to those of interest to the system. An estimate of the likely volume of message flow may be obtained by inference from more general quantitative data. For instance, any information system using publications as input can draw conclusions from data on the current output of printed books, journals, and other forms of publication, and from forecasts of the volume of future output. An excellent example of an information science study that provided such data (for US scientific publication) is the report on statistical indicators by D.W. King *et al.* (1976). The figures in *Table 8.3* are derived from this. Overall descriptions of message transfer in the general field of interest of an information system can provide an understanding of the existing channels being used and their characteristics. Remaining with science, but this time in the UK, we may cite as an example the study by the Royal Society (1981), from which *Figure 8.8* is drawn.

The time intervals involved in the transmission of messages from source to recipient may be very relevant to the design of a system that hopes to speed transfer. Studies of the kind reported by Garvey (1979), and illustrated in *Figure 8.9*, can provide useful background knowledge.

Some estimate of the number of *potential* recipients of an information service can be obtained from census data on occupational employment in work areas of interest to the system, or from data on the membership of relevant professional or special-interest associations.

This section has given some examples of the kind of data that information science has provided that can be of use in system design. Many studies have been reported, and it is for the designer to seek out those that seem most relevant to the task in hand.

Table 8.3 US science publishing, 1960–1980

Year	Agriculture	Sociology and Economics	Medicine	Science	Technology	Philosophy and Psychology
1960	78	754	520	1089	698	240
1961	116	1613	776	1494	781	283
1962	142	2059	952	1743	931	327
1963	143	2487	1054	2211	1157	360
1964	143	3272	1211	2738	1125	383
1965	135	3242	1218	2562	1153	490
1966	144	3482	1446	2958	1333	446
1967	144	3611	1189	2367	1252	432
1968	125	4070	1277	2407	1262	473
1969	130	4462	1190	2353	1035	476
1970	133	5912	1476	2358	1141	640
1971	162	6095	1655	2697	1309	677
1972	195	6415	1839	2586	1425	582
1973	191	6565	2002	2714	1347	703
1974	196	6640	2281	3049	1593	684
		Projections				
1975	200	6858	1932	3148	1507	660
1976	224	7109	1714	3501	1582	667
1977	213	7285	1680	3576	1765	631
1978	206	7310	1956	3580	1834	654
1979	248	7413	1929	3859	1957	628
1980	230	7740	2055	4114	2109	666

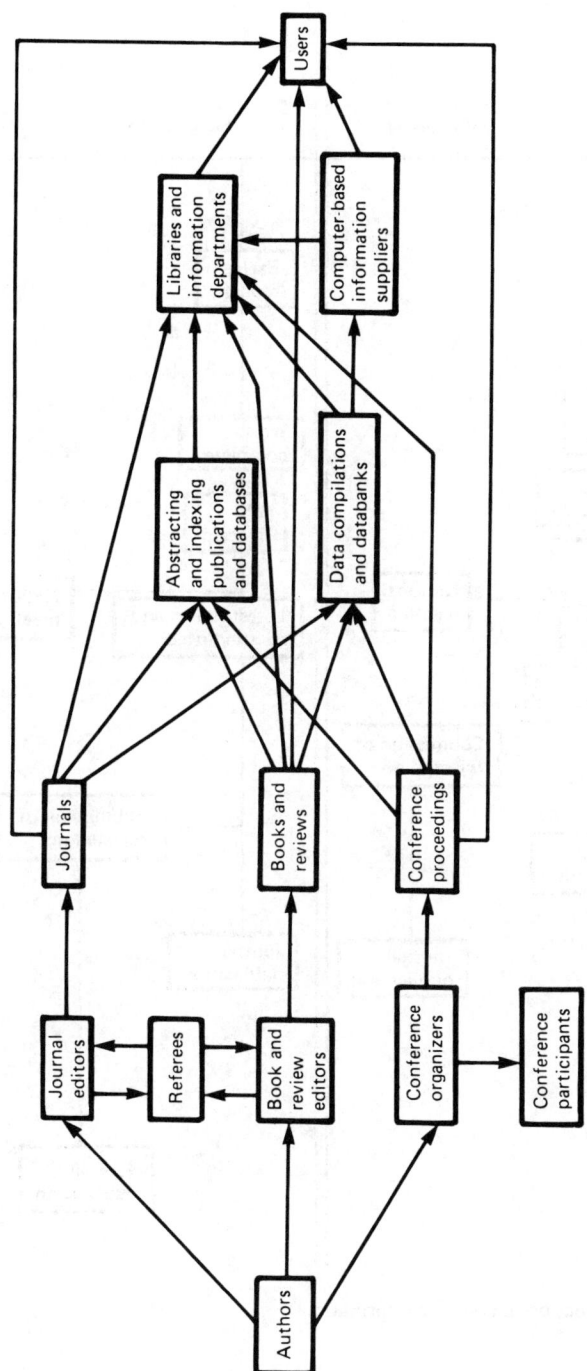

Figure 8.8 Science information flow

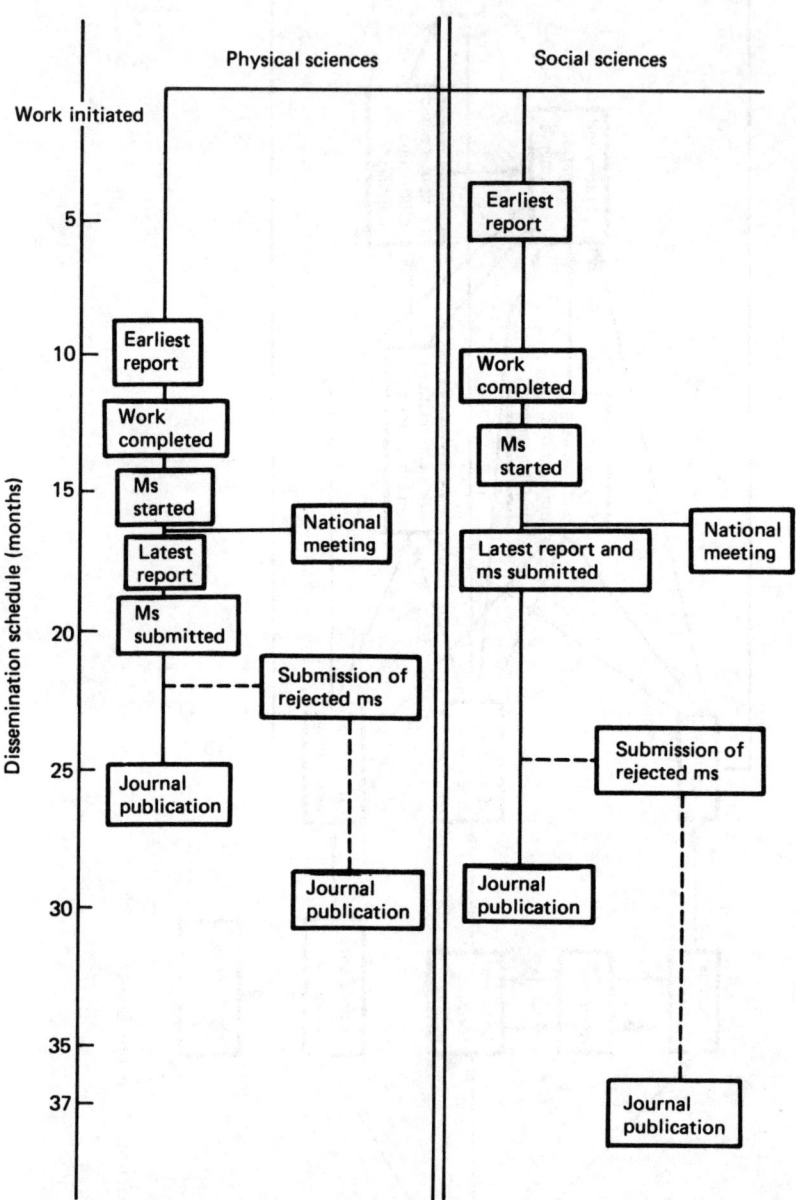

Figure 8.9 Dissemination of research information

8.7 The measurement of system use

Before we start to consider models relevant to systems design it will be as well to look briefly at ways in which data can be obtained that will lead to the formulation of quantitative models. Data about sources are relatively easy to assemble—in the very act of identifying and acquiring source messages. Data about the recipients of an information system may be much less easy to assemble, since recipients may be dispersed and unknown—or, even if they are concentrated, acts of use may not be adequately recorded.

Measurement of use can be direct or indirect. *Direct* measurement takes place when each use of an information system is recorded by the system. However, the detail of the record can vary. For example, a library turnstile simply counts the number of visitors (perhaps linked to a clock to give the time of visit); monitoring online connections to a computer system may do no more. If access to the system involves presentation of a user identifier of some kind, then the record can also give evidence of who uses the system. More detailed recording—for example, of library loan issues, or of file use and search outputs in an online service—provides data on what items of stock have been used by each recipient.

All these types of direct measurement are continuous and comprehensive—all uses are recorded. They can be supplemented or replaced by intermittent measurement. A sampling of use can be made—either of all uses during a limited period or of a proportion of uses over a longer period—in order to record detail that is not routinely collected.

In situations where no direct measures are available or obtainable—and this, of course, applies to a system under design—*indirect* measures can be employed as indicators of use. The most generally used form of indirect measure is the survey of potential recipients, in which questions are asked about specific incidents of information seeking—what was sought, where and how, with what success, how often, etc. This can build up both a qualitative and semi-quantitative picture of the likely demand on an information system.

A second form of indirect measure has been much used in the study of science information—the analysis of records made by recipients of items they have apparently received: in other words, analysis of the citations that authors make to other writings. Citation is at best only an indicator of use. Authors have not necessarily read all that they cite, and certainly do not cite all that they read. The source of the items cited is not apparent—and rarely will they all have come from one information system. So the details of citation analysis do not apply directly to the use or expected use of a particular system. However, citations can be fairly claimed to be a reasonable sampling of items used, and there is no reason to doubt that the general patterns displayed in citations can be regarded as analogous to patterns observed in direct use studies. Among the many discussions of citation analysis we draw attention to papers by Linda Smith (1981); Bensman (1982); Broadus (1983); Brittain and Line (1973).

8.8 Sources and recipients

Among the quantitative questions that need to be asked by information system designers are the following:

What is the expected annual volume of relevant messages?

Is the emission of source messages uniform over time, or are there likely to be regular or random variations?

How is the emission of messages likely to be distributed among the original source individuals?

Where these messages are recorded in publications, how may they be distributed among the total volume of published material?

How many recipients and demands may be expected?

What is the likely distribution of demands among recipients?

If a new service is to be offered, what is the likely pattern of 'market penetration', i.e. take-up of the service by potential recipients?

In the absence of firm data about the actual or intended sources and recipients a designer can draw upon established models that appear applicable to the system under development.

8.8.1 The volume of message production

If a particular form of information message is examined over time it is often found that overall the volume of messages emitted grows annually. To take an obvious example, the world production of book titles displays the trend shown in *Figure 8.10*. As with many figures in this chapter, because the range of one variable (in this case, book output) is large, it is plotted on a logarithmic scale. Such a trend as this derives from two factors—population growth (raising the number of potential authors) and the growth of literacy (increasing both the likelihood of authorship and the demand for books, that will stimulate authors to put pen to paper).

Viewed globally, as in this example, the output of a certain type of message often seems to be growing exponentially, at an ever-increasing rate. (On a logarithmic graph, exponential growth plots as a straight line). Any information system concerned to acquire such messages must envisage two alternatives: either an ever-increasing acquisition rate, or (if resources do not permit this) the acquisition of an ever-decreasing proportion of source outputs. Most libraries are in precisely this second situation.

A second pattern of message production is the logistic (see *Figure 8.11*). Outputs begins by rising exponentially but later flattens out to a steady rate. If the number of potential sources ceases to grow, and there is a limit to the 'productivity' of each source, a logistic pattern is to be expected. For an information system starting up when output has reached the plateau it will appear that the annual volume of messages is approximately constant. A system handling messages generated from an established parent organization may be in this situation.

A third pattern occurs if a system is concentrating on a rather specific subject area which is popular for a period and then declines. This can be the case for specialist research topics, as Goffman (1966) has shown, and the rising/falling curve (*Figure 8.11*) may be described by the same mathematical equations as are used in the theory of epidemics. In such a situation an information system must either accept the fact that it will be short lived, or regularly seek new emerging topics on which to base services. A 'current affairs' information service is in this situation.

It is clearly essential for a system designer to assess which of these situations is likely to apply to the system which is under study in order to identify an appropriate strategy for future development. The actual numbers of messages to be dealt with cannot, of course, be estimated from these models—at least some sample data from the system environment must be collected for this purpose.

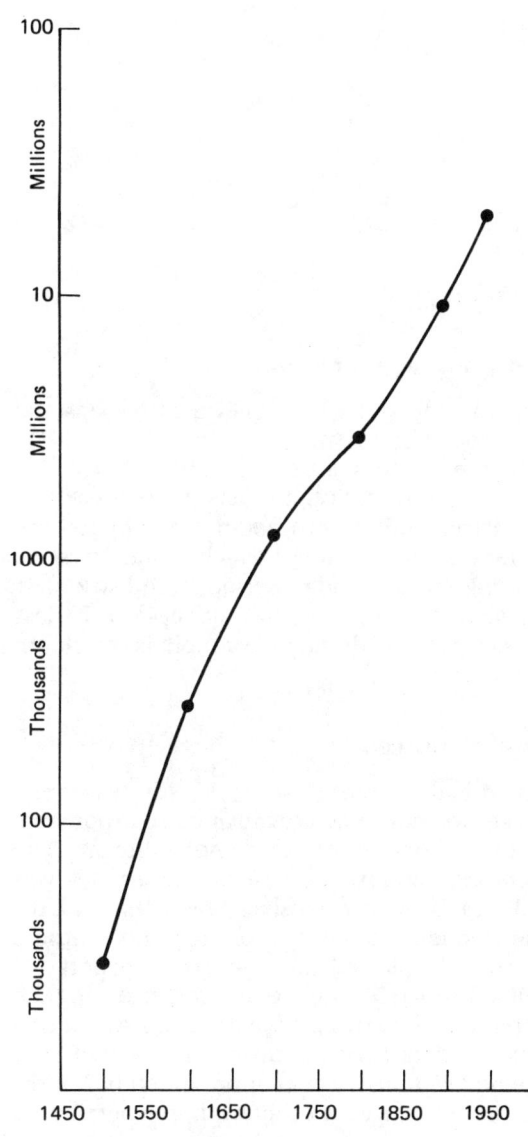

Figure 8.10 World production of book titles (Iwinski, 1911; Barr, 1971)

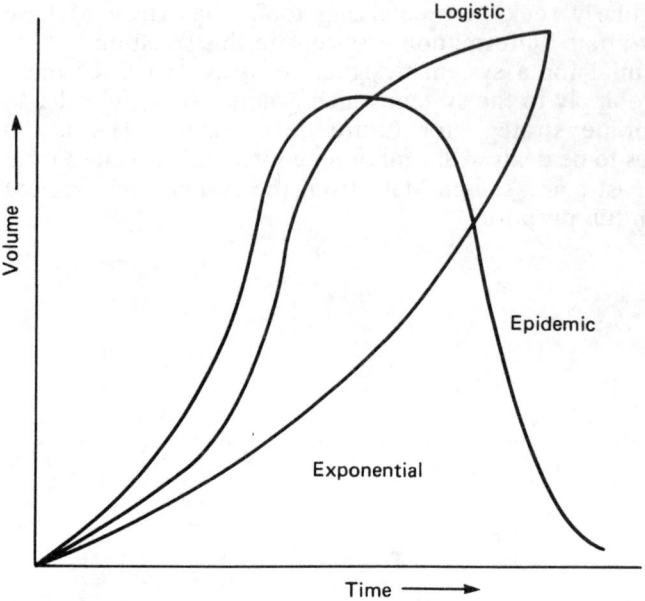

Figure 8.11 Exponential, logistic, and epidemic growth

8.8.2 Variations in the rate of message emission

The variations of most relevance to the system designer are the seasonal and those associated with major social upheaval.

Book publication is certainly subject to seasonal variation—with lulls intervening between publishers' spring lists, autumn lists, Christmas lists. Source messages in the form of Parliamentary proceedings do not emerge during periods when Parliament is not sitting. Much administrative communication tends to fall during major holiday periods. And so on.

The decline of message emission due to social disruption is less predictable, but is continually occurring. A dramatic example is the slump in scholarly publication during major wars.

8.8.3 Patterns of emission from sources

If we are dealing with individual message sources—for example, authors—common observation shows that some are much more productive than others. The distribution of authorship is 'skew', not uniform. The distribution of published papers among authors of scientific articles was studied quantitatively, originally, and most extensively by Lotka (1926). He examined, for example, the frequency of citation of individual authors in *Chemical Abstracts*, 1907-1916. He plotted the number of papers (x) against the percentage (y) of all authors publishing that number during the period of the survey (both plotted on a logarithmic scale). The straight line that approximately summarizes the data is of the form $x^n y = c$, where n and c are constants. In the data he examined, n was approximately 2 and c = 0.6. This last figure implies that 60 per cent of all authors contributed

Table 8.4 Authors in catalogue

Number of works	Number of authors	Percentage of total sample	Total number of entries
1	1489	63.50	1489
2	343	14.63	686
3	160	6.82	480
4	92	3.92	368
5	44	1.88	220
6	35	1.49	210
7	27	1.15	189
8	18	0.77	144
9	12	0.51	108
10	11	0.47	110
11	10	0.43	110
12	9	0.38	108
13	2	0.09	26
14	6	0.26	84
15	9	0.38	135
16	8	0.34	128
17	3	0.13	51
18	2	0.09	36
19	2	0.09	38
20	5	0.21	100
21	5	0.21	105
22	1	0.04	22
23	1	0.04	23
24	2	0.09	48
26	1	0.04	26
27	1	0.04	27
28	4	0.17	112
30	2	0.09	60
31	1	0.04	31
32	3	0.13	96
33	1	0.04	33
34	1	0.04	34
35	1	0.04	35
36	3	0.13	108
38	2	0.09	76
39	1	0.04	39
40	2	0.09	80
42	2	0.09	84
44	2	0.09	88

only one paper. A modification of his graph, with some later data added, is shown in *Figure 8.12*. Here, the numbers of papers (*x* or more) is plotted against the corresponding percentage of authors.

When $n = 2$ we can talk of 'an inverse square law of scientific productivity', and this is frequently spoken of as 'Lotka's law'. Some attempts have been made to establish whether it holds in other fields of authorship (see Potter, 1981; Pao, 1986). Two studies undertaken for the practical purposes of system management are of interest. Data based on a 0.5 per cent sample of the University of Illinois library catalogue are shown in *Table 8.4* and this closely fits the inverse square law (Potter, 1980). In *Table 8.5*, data from nearly 700 000 personal names on the Library of

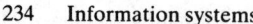

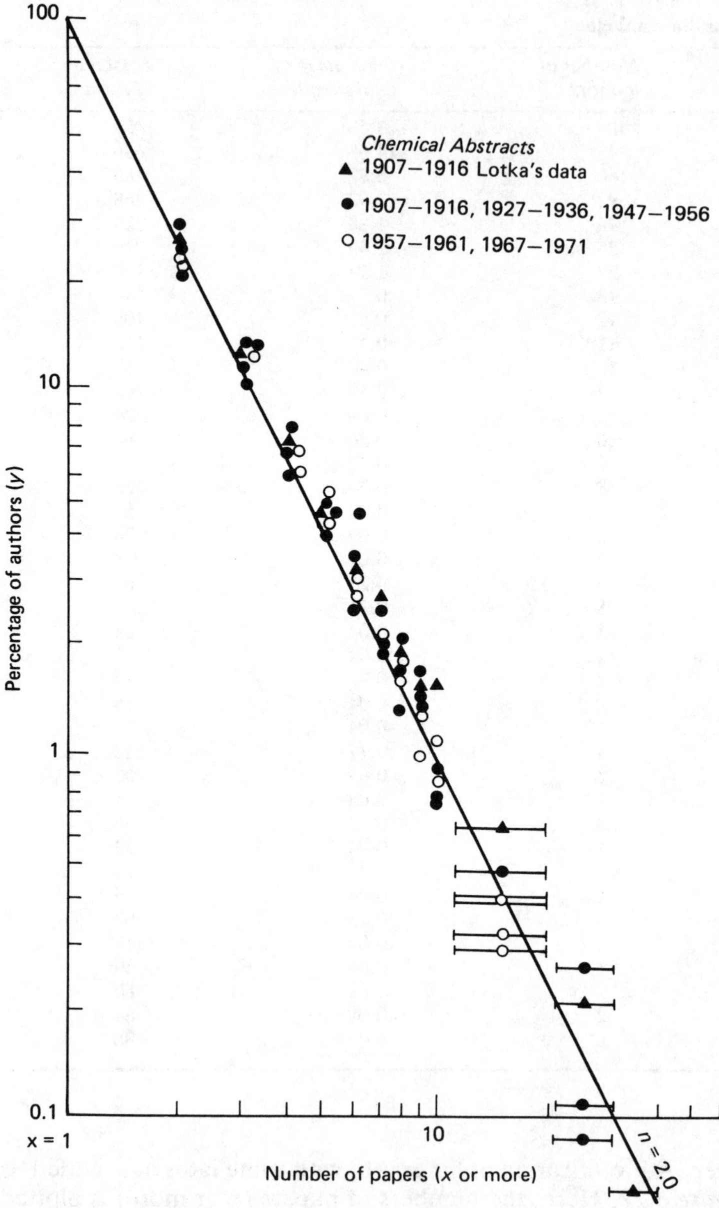

Figure 8.12 Distribution of scientific productivity

Congress MARC tapes are shown; here the fit is less good—*n* is about 2.35 (McCallum and Godwin, 1981). These results suggest that, although the value of *n* = 2 cannot be assumed, an author distribution of this general pattern can be expected. The proportion of authors making only a single contribution is likely to be within the range 50–75 per cent. Achieving complete coverage of these sources is sure to be very arduous.

Table 8.5 Names in MARC records

Number of occurrences	Distinct personal names		Distinct corporate names		Distinct conference names	
	Number	%	Number	%	Number	%
1	456 328	65.65	116 250	62.02	18 021	83.90
2	119 681	17.22	30 185	16.10	2 049	9.54
3	46 247	6.65	11 563	6.17	587	2.73
4	23 951	3.45	6 814	3.64	289	1.35
5	13 820	1.99	4 109	2.19	163	0.76
6	8 790	1.26	2 958	1.58	98	0.46
7	5 827	0.84	2 175	1.16	56	0.28
8	4 056	0.58	1 673	0.89	48	0.22
9	2 998	0.43	1 395	0.74	36	0.17
10	2 153	0.31	1 037	0.55	18	0.08
11–13	4 116	0.59	2 180	1.16	44	0.20
14–20	3 748	0.54	2 632	1.40	41	0.19
21–50	2 678	0.39	2 901	1.55	23	0.11
51–100	448	0.06	936	0.50	4	0.02
101–200	149	0.02	374	0.20	2	0.01
201–300	47	0.01	109	0.06	1	0.00
301–400	19	0.00	46	0.02	0	0.00
401–500	11	0.00	21	0.01	0	0.00
501–1000	5	0.00	53	0.03	0	0.00
1001+	2	0.00	18	0.01	0	0.00
Total	695 074	99.99	187 429	99.98	21 480	100.00

Table 8.6 Distribution of authored articles

Articles per year (A)	Titles (T)	A × T	Cumulative A × T	Cumulative T	Cumulative %A × T
1170	1	1170	1 170	1	3
912	1	912	2 082	2	5
792	1	792	2 874	3	7
780	1	780	3 654	4	9
676	1	676	4 330	5	11
624	1	624	4 954	6	13
605	1	605	5 559	7	14
600	1	600	6 159	8	16
552	1	552	6 711	9	17
520	2	1040	7 751	11	20
504	1	504	8 255	12	21
490	1	490	8 745	13	22
450	1	450	9 195	14	23
430	1	430	9 625	15	25
410	1	410	10 035	16	26
370	3	1110	11 145	19	28
330	1	330	11 475	20	29
310	1	310	11 785	21	30
270	1	270	12 055	22	31
250	3	750	12 805	25	33
210	4	840	13 645	29	35
190	5	950	14 595	34	37
170	3	510	15 105	37	38
150	19	2850	17 955	56	46
130	18	2340	20 295	74	52
110	18	1980	22 275	92	57
90	44	3960	26 235	136	67
70	55	3850	30 085	191	77
50	63	3150	33 235	254	85
30	116	3480	36 715	370	92
10	255	2550	39 265	625	100
0	493	0	39 265	1118	100

Let us think now of publishers as sources and individual journals as compound messages. In this case also there is markedly skew distribution. For example, among 400 UK society publishers, journals are emitted as follows:

No. of journals	1	2	3	4	5	8	9
No. of societies	355	29	11	1	1	2	1

A third situation relates to the occurrence of papers in periodicals. A periodical (journal, magazine) often contains a variety of message types—editorials, news items, 'letters to the editor', etc., as well as more substantial 'authored articles'. It is often only the last type that is of long-term interest in an information system. How are authored articles distributed among periodicals? A study by Vickery (1968) of a random sample of journal material in the UK National Lending Library for Science and Technology found that 44 per cent of the titles contained no authored articles. Half the articles occurred in 7 per cent of the sample (*Table 8.6*).

8.8.4 Distribution of source messages among publications

The system designer is normally concerned with published messages in a particular subject field. Are there models describing the expected distribution of these among the mass of periodical publications? The first to draw attention to such a model was Bradford (1934). He examined

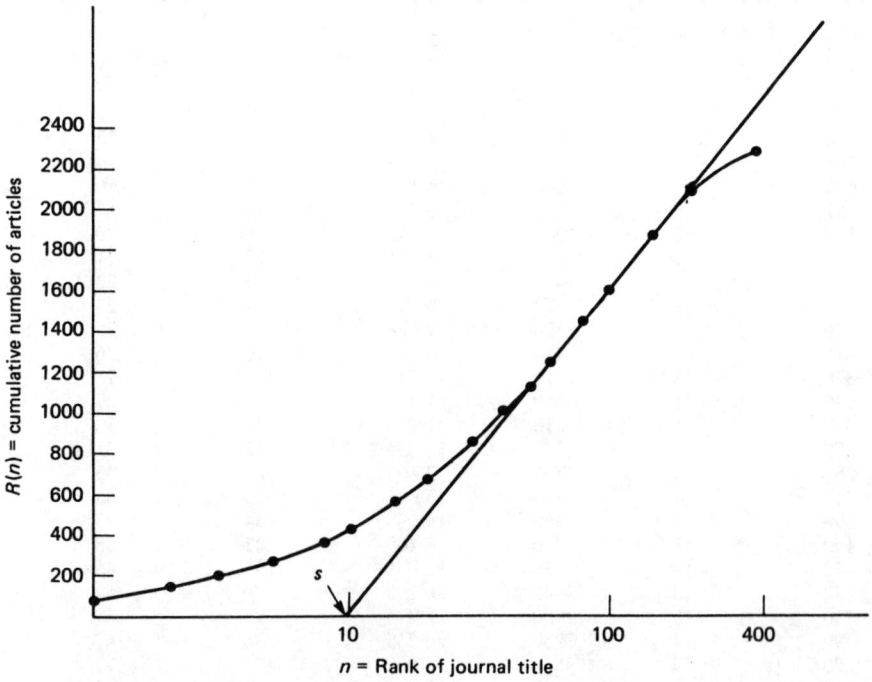

Figure 8.13 The Bradford distribution

several rather comprehensive bibliographies of scientific–technical specializations and recorded the frequency of occurrence of each individual journal title. An example of his method is as follows. After some experimentation, he ranked the titles in order of productivity (the most frequently occurring was ranked $n = 1$) and plotted the logarithm of n against the cumulative number of papers up to that point, $R(n)$. A plot of the form shown in *Figure 8.13* results.

The initial sloping portion of the curve is often called the 'core' or 'nuclear' zone. It may be regarded as represent the journals that are primarily devoted to the subject under investigation. The straight line then represents a wide range of titles, whose productivity declines as rank n increases. Often at the end of the curve there is a 'droop', a fall off from linearity.

This 'bibliograph', as it has been called, may be further illustrated by a numerical example. A survey of the 1970 literature of tropical agriculture

Table 8.7 Distribution of articles among periodicals

Articles/title	Number of titles	Cumulative titles, n	Cumulative articles. R (n)
80	1	1	80
70	1	2	150
51	1	3	201
41	1	4	242
33	1	5	275
32	1	6	307
31	2	8	369
30	2	10	429
29	1	11	458
28	2	13	514
27	2	15	568
26	1	16	584
25	1	17	609
24	1	18	633
22	1	19	655
21	1	20	676
20	2	22	716
19	3	25	773
18	3	28	827
17	1	29	844
16	7	36	956
15	3	39	1001
14	5	44	1071
13	3	47	1110
12	3	50	1146
11	10	60	1256
10	8	68	1336
9	11	79	1435
8	13	92	1539
7	11	103	1616
6	18	121	1724
5	25	146	1849
4	26	172	1953
3	40	212	2073
2	49	261	2171
1	113	374	2284

was made by Lawani (1973). In his bibliography, 374 periodical titles were encountered, between them providing 2284 articles. The data are summarized in *Table 8.7* and are plotted in *Figure 8.13*.

The clear conclusion to be drawn is that 85 per cent of the sources (1953 articles) are contained in 46 per cent of the journals (172 titles), and that achieving full coverage required the tracking down of 113 titles containing only one relevant article each during 1970.

Very many empirical analyses of this kind have been reported, all confirming the general pattern. The straight-line portion of the graph can be represented by the formula $R(n) = N \log (n/s)$, where s is the value of n at the point where the extended straight line cuts the horizontal axis of the graph. The slope of the straight line is given by the value of N. Sets of empirical data vary with respect to the values of N and s. For sets with similar values for N, smaller values of s imply fewer productive titles in the 'core'.

If we assume that the 'droop' at the top of the curve is anomalous—perhaps due to incompleteness, caused by missing some low-yield titles—then Brookes (1968) showed that N was an estimate of the total number of titles expected to contain relevant articles. For *Figure 8.13*, $N = 643$, which is considerably higher than the 374 titles in the survey. However, Praunlich and Kroll (1978) put forward a modification of the formula that provides mathematically for some degree of 'droop' and somewhat reduces the estimated total.

These formulae for the Bradford curve can be used by the system designer in the following ways. First, as already noted, it is abundantly clear that he can expect the general pattern to hold in any subject field. Second, if he has sufficient data to calculate the slope for relevant source material then some upper limit N can be placed on the number of journal titles. The same formula also permits an upper limit to be calculated for the number of articles, $R(N) = N \log (N/s)$. The designer thus has some estimate of the maximum volume of articles to be added to store (over the period to which his estimate of $R(N)$ applies), and the number of journal sources that will have to be identified to acquire them.

Apart from many empirical studies, the Bradford distribution has given rise to a considerable theoretical literature, exploring (1) the mathematical formulation of the observed curve, (2) its relation to other bibliometric distributions, and (3) its applicability to other social phenomena—see, for example, Fairthorne (1969), Naranan (1971), Leimkuhler (1977), Brookes (1977), Price (1976), Bookstein (1976), and Bensman (1982). For those with a mathematical bent, a good entry into this literature is the review by Hubert (1981).

8.8.5 Expected number of recipients and demands

This is one of the most vexing questions that the systems designer must face. Information sources—by and large—exist independently of a system, they can in principle be identified, and the only limit to accessing them is the effort which the system can devote to this task. The very fact that a source is a source—i.e. has information that he/she/it wishes to communicate—implies that in general he/she/it will respond to a request.

However, there is no guarantee that someone who is believed or even known to need information held by a system will in fact seek information from a particular system or respond to an offer. As well as making any overall estimate of those who *might* be interested in a service the systems designer must consider what factors will decide who will actually evince interest.

This is an area in which there are no clear quantitative models, but a good deal of evidence that the number of actual users of a system is always less—and sometimes considerably less—than the number of apparently potential users. To take an obvious example, the percentage of the adult population registered in the UK as public library users averages 25 per cent. A quite different example was studied by Blagden (1980). A system was set up to provide product information to architects and others working for London local government. There was a total target audience of 538 architects. From survey results it was estimated that 75 per cent would use the service sooner or later. But how much would they use it? Surveys indicated that these architects between them might seek 70000 items of information about construction products during a year, but only 7 per cent of these needs would result in demands on this information system. The bulk of the need was satisfied from personal data collections, information sources within architectural departments, and contacts with manufacturers.

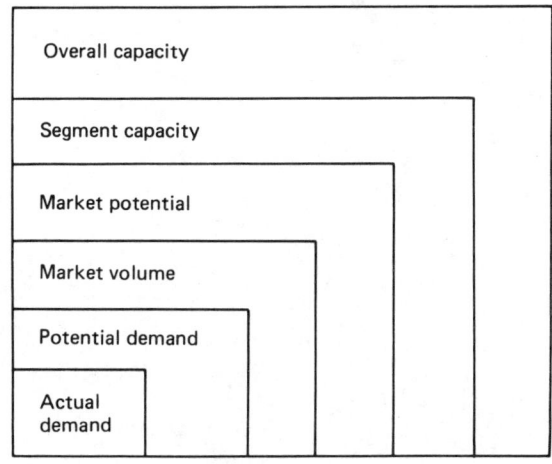

Figure 8.14 Model of the market

When considering markets in general, Bolt (1981) has distinguished a series of terms in which we may discuss the likely number of recipients for a service or product (*Figure 8.14*):

(1) The overall capacity of a market is the total volume of a certain kind of product or service that could be absorbed by all possible potential recipients;

(2) The segment capacity is the volume that could be absorbed by that segment of the market at which the information system under study is directed;

(3) The market potential is the effective demand of that segment given the price and other constraints (for example, accessibility) on the product or service;
(4) The market volume is the total number of actual demands, under these conditions, made to the set of systems supplying products or services of the kind considered;
(5) The potential demand is the number of demands that could be attracted by the specific system under consideration, if there were no constraints on its meeting these demands;
(6) The actual demand is the number of demands actually directed to the specific system under consideration.

Each quantity, as shown in the figure, is less than the preceding one. In the case of Blagden's architects, for example, it appears that the ratio of actual demand to segment capacity was 7 per cent. We will be looking later at some relations between the actual and potential demands on a system.

8.8.6 Distribution of demands among recipients

We have already seen in the last section that not all potential recipients of an information service will make use of it. Among those who do, there is a

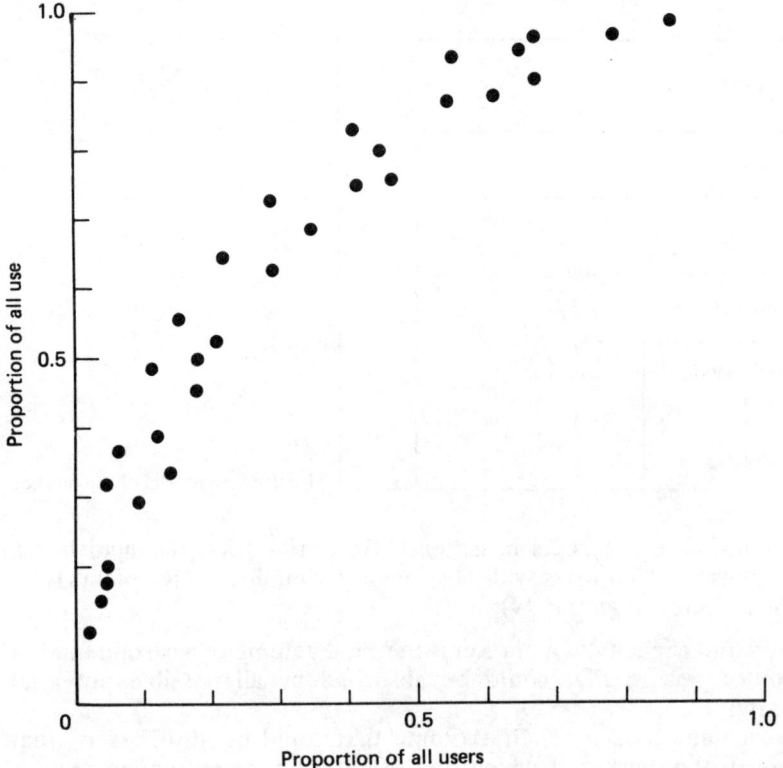

Figure 8.15 Borrowing pattern

marked inequality of use. A recent study was made by Wall (1980/1981) of student use of an academic library, and his results are included with others in *Figure 8.15*, taken from his paper. His figure includes data from seven different studies. If demand were equally distributed among all recipients, the plotted points would be on a straight diagonal from bottom left to top right. In fact, about 70 per cent of the demand is generated by 30 per cent of the users.

Although the shape of the curve will vary from one situation to another the system designer can expect that a somewhat similar pattern will occur. One consequence is that the extent of user experience will vary—frequent users will know a system and its services well, and will need little help in using it, but the many casual users will require more help. This has important implications for information systems, which must combine self-service features for the experienced user and user aids for the rest.

8.8.7 Rate of market penetration

Some comments on the degree of market penetration—i.e. the volume of use of a system by potential recipients—have been given in section 8.8.5 of this survey of sources and recipients. Here we are concerned with the rate at which, from the start up of a service, potential users become actual users.

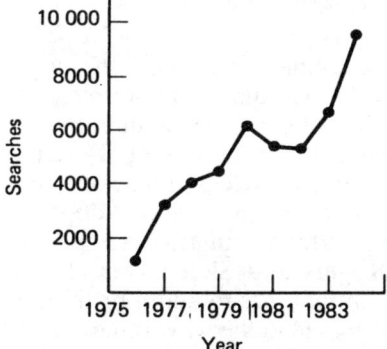

Figure 8.16 Growth of online searches

First, let us look at an actual example of the growth of demand. The University of London has, since 1975, provided a service for online search of remote bibliographic databases. Originally at one central point, it was decentralized over a period of years to thirty-six search stations. Total usage of the service is monitored and the number of online searches grew as follows (*Figure 8.16*):

1975	1200
6	3264
7	4104
8	4392
9	6108
1980	5520
1	5376
2	6756
3	9600

The cause of the fall-back in 1980-1981 was the onset of economic restrictions at the university. By 1983, the upward trend was again evident.

It is likely that for any information service or product there is some level at which the market is saturated. Even for a free library service, there is a limit to the volume of books that a given community will borrow. We could expect the ideal growth of demand over time to be S-shaped—an accelerating rise as potential recipients learn of and try out the product, then a gradual flattening out to a maximum (*Figure 8.17*). Evidently, after nine years of service, online searching at the University of London had not reached saturation level. The rate of market penetration in this case was slow.

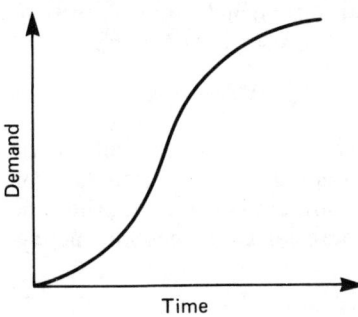

Figure 8.17 S-shaped demand curve

The case is far from being a 'pure' example. Although the user population has remained qualitatively much the same, the sources on which the service draws (online databases) have been growing in number, diversity, and size, thus becoming relevant to more potential users. Nevertheless, a slow take up of a new information service is quite common.

This has been found to be the case with innovations in general. Adoption generally follows an S-shaped curve, if we plot the cumulative number of adopters against time. To explain this, Rogers and Shoemaker (1971) postulate variations in the eagerness of potential users to adopt or try out something new: there are a few 'innovators' who lead the way, rather more 'early adopters', then a bulky majority, and last the 'laggards'. The cumulative numbers of adopters over time will be an S-shaped curve.

The pattern is discussed from a marketing viewpoint by Choffray and Lilien (1980). It is the growth pattern that may be expected by a new information system serving a 'captive' audience—for example, an academic library. However, a system offering its products and services in the marketplace will stimulate competitors to offer a similar service, and—in time—will be challenged by newer products that seek to replace it. In marketing the 'product life cycle' model has been developed, in which there comes a decline in demand after a period of saturation. *Figure 8.18* has been adapted from Bolt (1981).

In a study of the US sales of 'consumer hardware' Bass (1969) found that the time taken for demand to reach its peak P varied from seven years (steam irons, television sets) to 14 years (electric blankets). Clark (1985), in a more general survey of consumer goods, gives an estimate of 'the time required to judge the success or failure of a new product' (*Table 8.8*).

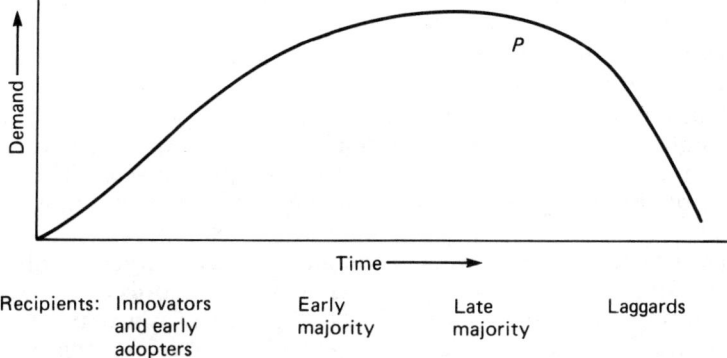

Figure 8.18 Product life cycle

Table 8.8 Time to success or failure of new products

Time (months)	Percentage of products
37–48	10
25–36	29
19–24	21
13–18	26
6–12	11
<6	9

If *Figure 8.18* is the expected pattern, the information system designer must foresee the eventual decline, and the need to generate new products or services if the system is to remain viable. A very general instance of this at present is the need that paper-based services now have to introduce electronically provided information.

8.9 Use of message stores

Most systems handling recorded information regularly collect messages from sources into a store (library, archive, database, etc.) which is searched in response to demands from recipients. System designers are interested in such problems as:

What is the amount of use per stored item that may on average be expected?
How is use likely to be distributed among stored items?
How may the use of an item vary with its age?

8.9.1 Use per stored item

The relation between the number of items in an information store, and the number of items selected from store to meet demand, is often not readily calculable from published figures. It will, of course, vary with the nature of the 'items' stored—whether they are documents, bibliographic references, factual data, directory entries, or whatever.

Public libraries in the UK in 1980/1981 had a stock of 131 million volumes, and issued 627 million loans—an average use of less than five issues per item per year. The main UK university libraries in 1978 held about 28 million volumes, and made about 11 million loans, so had an average use per item per year of about 0.4. However, if we take account of very considerable in-library use, the true university library figure may be nearer 1.0.

Now let us turn to publicly available online databases. In November 1981 *Monitor* estimated that they contained 116 million records of various kinds, and that there were then at least five million searches a year. How many records does an average search select? One figure for this was obtained by Vickery and Batten in an evaluation study at the University of London in 1978—about 50 references per search. We can therefore very crudely 'guesstimate' that the average annual accesses per record in 1980 was between two and three (perhaps it is higher now).

All these figures underline the fact that the volume of use of stored information items is, on average, low. The clear implication for system design is that the unit cost of storage must be kept to a minimum.

8.9.2 Distribution of use among items

The items in an information store are not equally used—far from it. In a study of library issues in a university library Kent *et al.* (1978) found the distribution as in *Table 8.9*.

Table 8.9 Distribution of existing issues

Times loaned	No. of items	Times loaned	No. of items
0	385961	9	275
1	63526	10	124
2	25653	11	68
3	11855	12	28
4	6055	13	13
5	3264	14	6
6	1727	15	9
7	931	16	4
8	497	17+	4

In a stock of half a million the average number of issues per year per item was 0.4, and 77 per cent of the books were not issued at all during the period. If we arbitrarily define 'heavy use' as 'issued seven or more times', this was restricted to less than 2000 items, 0.4 per cent of the stock.

Defining a stored item as 'a run of a periodical' (the length of run varying considerably), Urquhart (1959) examined the use of periodicals at the London Science Museum Library during 1956, with the following results:

Times used	0	1	2	3	4	5–9
No. of titles	4821	2190	791	403	283	714

Times used	10–19	20–29	30–39	40–49	50–99	100+
No. of titles	541	229	136	92	193	60

The average number of loan issues per year per title was 5.6, and 46 per cent of the titles were not issued at all during the period. About 250 titles (2.5 per cent) accounted for half the issues.

To take another example, Bulick *et al.* (1976) traced the issue history of 37 000 books acquired by a university library in 1969. By the end of 1975, only 60 per cent of these had ever been issued, and half the usage was accounted for by 10 per cent of the items. In the whole book collection of half a million items, 48 per cent were not issued during 1969-1975. At the same university, Flynn (1979) found that 63 per cent of the science journal titles held were not issued at all over the same period, and 12 per cent of the titles accounted for three quarters of the loans.

In all these library studies we must bear in mind that adding in-library use figures may considerably increase the actual volume of use, but it is unlikely to have much effect on the pattern.

If we accept citation by an author as an indicator of the use of an information item, we can take as evidence of the same pattern Garfield's (1979) sampling of a third of a million scientific articles published in 2200 journals during 1969. On average, each article cited about 12 references; among the resultant 3.85 million citations, half were to only 150 journal titles (about 1 per cent of the total number of science journals with 'authored articles' in 1969).

There are several implications of this kind of pattern for the system designer. First, unless a system is aiming at comprehensive acquisition because it has an archival function, the designer will seek to identify in advance the likehood of information items being demanded, and to minimize the input of items for which demand is likely to be low (or zero). Second, the use of the system needs to be monitored so that items not demanded can be removed from (primary) storage. Third, the designer may seek ways of storing items so that those most likely to be demanded are the most accessible, and vice versa.

8.9.3 Use versus age

It is commonly believed that recently emitted information messages are more likely to be demanded by recipients than are older messages. In any field where an information system serves as an aid to decision making about a current situation this is obviously true. Out-of-date timetables are of no use to the traveller, nor last month's share prices to the stockbroker. Publishers let many books go out of print because demand for them falls off. Is it generally true of information stores, that the volume of use is related to the age of the items sought? If so, age might be an attribute that could be used to guide the system decisions discussed at the end of the last section, relating to acquisition, relegation, and storage.

Many studies have been made of the 'obsolescence' of literature. One of the earliest reported (Barnard, 1938) was of the use of periodicals in a medical library, over a five-year period (1931-1935). The data obtained were as follows:

Years of publication	1931–1935	1926–1930	1921–1925	1916–1920	1911–1915
Uses (1931–1935)	2863	3278	1643	866	737

Years of publication	1906–1910	1901–1905	1896–1900	1891–1985	1886–1890
Uses (1931–1935)	495	324	174	84	62

If we leave aside the first figure (since all the 1931-1935 publications were not available for use throughout 1931-1935), we could assume that the usage of an item published during 1926-1930 was likely to be 53 times (3278/62) as great as usage of an item published during 1886-1890. However, the volume of 1886-1890 material in the library was much less than the volume of 1926-1930 material: no accurate figures are presented, but the ratio was certainly 1:6, and perhaps 1:10. At least part of the lower use of older material was simply due to the fact that there was less older material available to be used (see Line, 1970, with appended note by Vickery).

Most studies of 'obsolescence' do not take this factor into account—and this has led Line and Sandison (1974), in a very thorough review of the

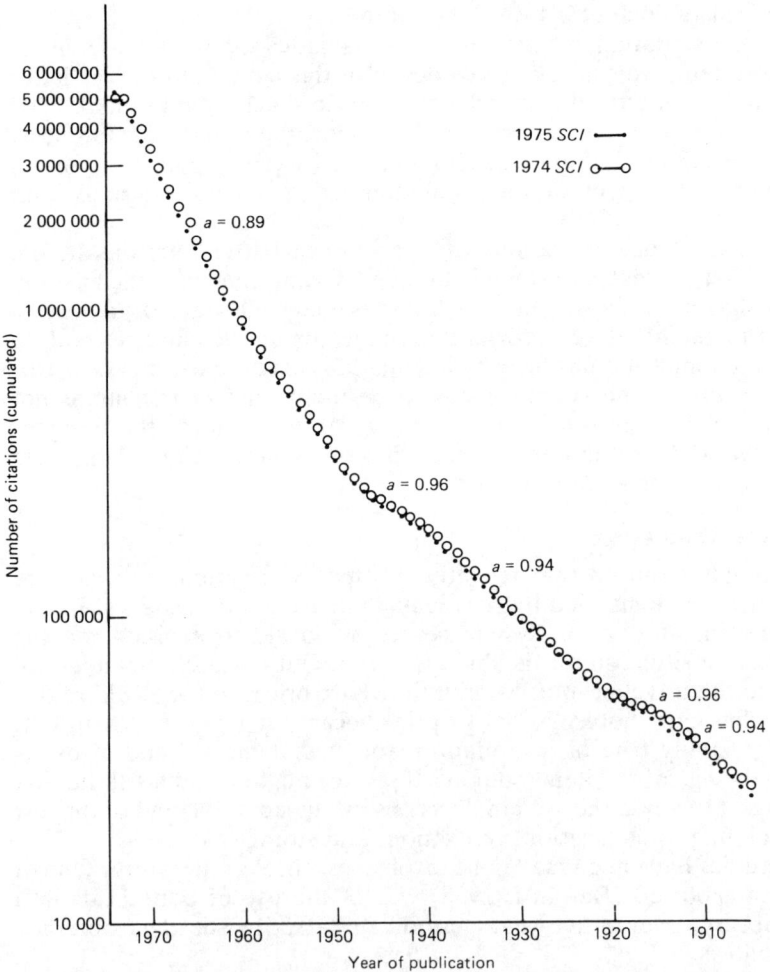

Figure 8.19 Ageing of literature. The number of citations received by all literature from the 1974 and 1975 *SCI* are plotted as described for the Brookes model in the text. Three different ageing rates are shown which correspond to the initial ageing phase, the disruptive effect of the two world wars, and long-term archival growth

subject, to cast doubt as to whether the hypothesis of 'obsolescence' has been unequivocally established. Yet most investigators would maintain that, by and large, the relative use of an item of information declines as it grows older.

As an example, we quote the careful experimental study by Griffith *et al.* (1979). They examined citations as an indicator of the use of scientific articles, and presented *Figure 8.19* as a guide to overall obsolescence. Roughly speaking, the number of citations to 1974 papers in 1975 was forty times the number of citations to 1934 papers. Although the exact growth rate of scientific literature is uncertain, no investigator would claim that it had increased anything like forty times in forty years (ten times is nearer the mark), so a good deal of the decrease in indicated use shown by the graph is genuinely due to obsolescence. In the figure the values of *a* indicate the rate of decline in use—a value of 1.0 would indicate no decline. The values at the lower end (0.96 and 0.94) correspond approximately to the estimated growth rate. This implies that the older literature is used fairly evenly, regardless of age: it is during the first 25 years that obsolescence occurs. More detailed studies in the Griffith paper demonstrate this for particular periodicals.

The system designer must therefore expect that as items of information in his store age, demand for them will decrease with the kind of logarithmic (exponential) pattern shown in the figure. The rate of decrease will vary greatly according to the nature of the information store. One further finding of the Griffith study is of interest: diffuse use of scientific literature by a diversified audience appears to show relatively slower ageing, whereas intensive use by a specialized audience shows much faster ageing. If generally true, this is a useful guideline for designers.

8.10 Access to information stores

User access to information in store is achieved, at one extreme, by personal visit to the actual site of the information (for example, taking the required book off a library shelf) or, at the other extreme, by delivery of information to the user at work or home by messenger, mail or telecommunications. There is every kind of intermediate situation, in which the user travels to some intermediate access/delivery point.

Whenever any amount of user travel is necessary some barrier to access is created that may in fact have the effect of limiting demand. This can be illustrated by studies of public library use. For example, a survey of selected public libraries was undertaken by the UK Department of Education and Science in 1972. The distances travelled to the libraries by the users surveyed are shown in *Figure 8.20*. Only a small percentage of the users travelled more than five miles. If we assumed that within one mile of a library the population was evenly distributed, the ratio between the cumulative percentages at one quarter mile and at one mile should be 1:16. There ratios were in fact as follows:

Whole survey	1:4
Central libraries	1:9.4

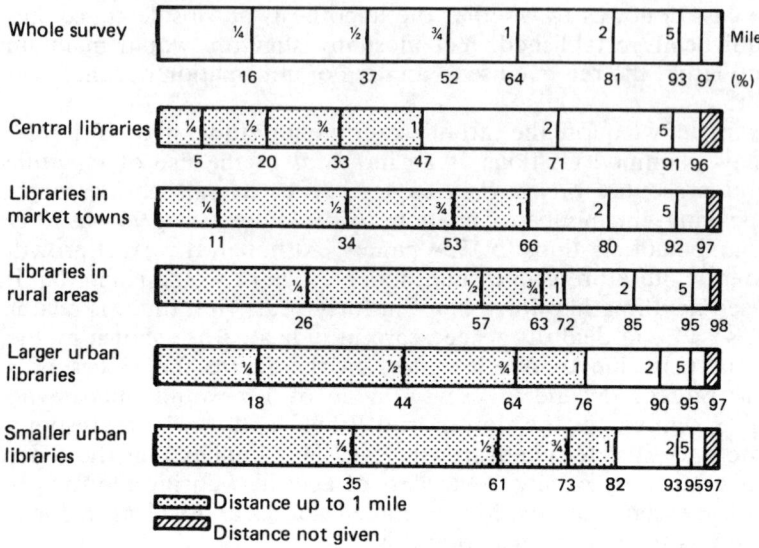

Figure 8.20 Distances travelled to library

Market towns	1:4.8
Rural areas	1:2.8
Larger urban	1:4.2
Smaller urban	1:2.4

This suggests that, even within a mile, a markedly smaller proportion of the more distant population used the library.

The fact that libraries attract use from a relatively small catchment area is well attested—as is indeed the case for many other social facilities, such as swimming pools (Cowling *et al.*, 1982)(*Table 8.10*).

Table 8.10 Catchment area for swimming pools

Distance travelled to pool (miles)	Cumulative percentage for conventional pool	Cumulative percentage for 'leisure' pool
<2	56	22
2–3	74	40
3–6	87	48
>6	100	100

These figures also demonstrate that a 'leisure' pool with special facilities attracts users from further afield. It is certainly the case that specialist information stores do the same.

Nevertheless, the size of catchment areas and the availability of local access points is a matter that is of concern to every information system. Even those that deliver information by electronic transmission have to consider the availability of local terminal equipment and telecommunication facilities. People—whether based during the day at work or at

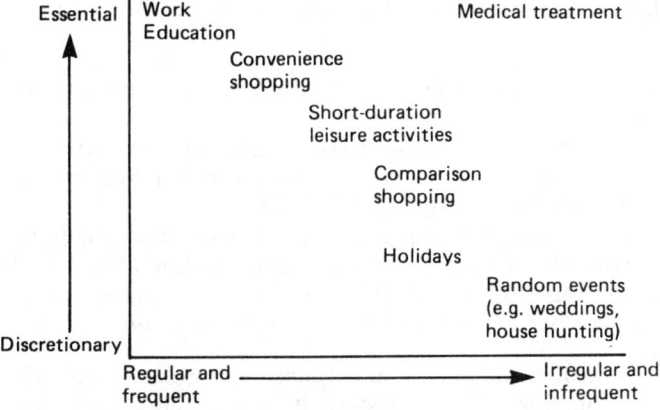

Figure 8.21 Activities involving travel

home—have limited time available for travel; the distance they can travel during that time is limited by transport facilities and costs; and there are various activities competing for the use of travel time, as suggested in *Figure 8.21* (Wood and Lee, 1980). Where access to information stores would fit into this figure depends on how essential and how regular is the individual recipient's need for information.

8.11 Probability distributions and modelling

In this chapter we have presented a series of frequency distributions:

(1) The range of sizes of information systems;
(2) Changes in the volume of publication over time;
(3) The distribution of publications among authors;
(4) The distribution of authored articles among journals;
(5) The distribution of demands among users;
(6) Changes in the number of demands over time;
(7) The distribution of use among stored messages;
(8) The decline in demand for items as they age.

Each set of empirical data seems to exhibit a general pattern, and we have at times suggested that the pattern can be represented by a mathematical relationship—exponential growth or decline, an S-curve, Lotka's law, the Bradford distribution. Such generalized relationships are known as 'probability distributions', and can be used in several ways:

(1) They provide a convenient and succinct summary statement of the observed patterns;
(2) By manipulation of their mathematical properties, conclusions may be drawn that are not evident from the raw data—thus from the Bradford distribution Brookes deduces values for N and $R(N)$;
(3) The mathematical relation may be used to introduce the observed pattern into models of more complex situations, as will be illustrated in the next section of this chapter.

The steps in the development of such generalized relations are as follows:

(1) Collect as wide a range of data as possible, each based upon samples sufficiently large to be but little affected by random variations (sample size criteria for 'Bradford' data are discussed by Brookes, 1969);
(2) Display the data in various ways to ascertain which mathematical relationship—or relationships—offers the best fit;
(3) Where several relationships seem possible, choose that which (a) offers the best possibility for mathematical manipulation from which conclusions may be drawn and/or (b) can best be linked to an explanation of the real-life factors underlying the relationship.

The possibility of fruitful mathematical manipulation is greater when the relation used is one that has been well studied by mathematicians and applied in other contexts. The book on library modelling by Hamburg *et al.* (1974) refers to a number of general probability distributions that have been used in information studies: the geometric, Poisson, normal, lognormal, binomial, negative binomial, exponential, hyperbolic.

'Probability' distributions are so called because they can be derived by mentally sampling at random a collection of entities (for example, information system sizes) and associating with each entity (in this case, each possible size) a probability of its occurrence. An observed frequency distribution can be regarded as a particular sample drawn from the total collection, the actual frequencies corresponding approximately to the theoretical probabilities. Let us take another example, and look back to *Figure 8.12.* We see the plotted actual percentage frequencies of authorship in *Chemical Abstracts* and the straight line that represents Lotka's theoretical distribution for $n = 2$. The theoretical distribution associates a probability of 1 per cent with ten authorships: the percentage frequency data for ten authorships range from about 0.75 to 1.5.

A probability distribution is not derived by just trying out all sorts of mathematical equations to find one that fits a good range of data. It is based upon reasoning about probabilities. The simplest probability situation is that of tossing a coin. It is postulated that there are only two outcomes—heads or tails; that the coin is unbiased; and that the outcomes are independent (the result of a toss is not related to the results of previous tosses). In such circumstances, the probability that any given toss is a head is $P = 0.5$, and the probability that three successive tosses will be heads is $P = 0.5 \times 0.5 \times 0.5 = 0.125$ (one chance in eight). Suppose now that we toss three coins together. There are four possible outcomes: HHH, HHT, HTT, TTT. The first and fourth can only occur in one way—if all coins are either H or T. However, the second and third can each occur in three ways—if any one of the three coins is a tail (second outcome) or a head (third outcome). So we have a probability distribution:

Outcome	P
HHH	0.125
HHT	0.375
HTT	0.375
TTT	0.125

If we choose other situations, with other postulates, we can derive other probability distributions. Thus most of the distributions mentioned by Hamburg can be derived from what is known as a 'Poisson process' (named after a nineteenth-century mathematician). A source (for example, an author) generates entities (in this case, papers) at a mean rate of m items per unit time. Each event (publication) occurs independently of the others, and the generation of entities by the source is not uniform over time—it occurs at random. The Poisson formula

$$p(x) = e^{-m}m^x/x!$$

represents the probability that the source will generate x items in a particular unit of time. (Readers with mathematical knowledge will recognise the meanings of e and the exclamation mark. Others can ignore them.) If the mean rate $m = 1$ (publication items per year) then the probability distribution in *Table 8.11* holds.

Table 8.11 Probability distribution

Items per year	P
0	0.3679
1	0.3679
2	0.1839
3	0.0613
4	0.0153
5	0.0031
6	0.0005
>6	0.0001

We may then consider N sources, each with a mean generation rate of m_r, these means themselves being distributed randomly according to the same formula. This model could then represent the set of authors considered by Lotka. His equation can be related to the 'mixed Poisson' model we have considered. The Poisson formula itself can be mathematically related back to the simple coin-tossing probabilities already considered.

The mixed Poisson model for the authorship of papers seems also a reasonable representation of the real factors at work—authors publishing at random time intervals, their mean productivities randomly distributed. So one could feel confidence in using a Lotka equation in a model that included author productivity. Empirical data would be needed to determine appropriate values of the constants in the formula for the particular situation being modelled.

It may happen that a relationship between variables is to be used in a model, and no appropriate theoretical distribution can be found—for example, the changes in demand during the 'product life cycle' (*Figure 8.18*) may not readily be generalized into a formula. In this case, an empirical frequency distribution (real or hypothesized) must be used instead.

We wish to make one more point about theoretical distributions and other generalized mathematical relations used in information science. Sometimes the situation is presented as though the mathematical relation is determinate—it is a law of gravity, imposes itself on the phenomena. If the observed data do not fit the relation there is an assumption that something is wrong with the data—they are incomplete, or the result of inadequate sampling, etc. Now it is perfectly in order to suspect data that diverge markedly from a generally found pattern, but in the last analysis, well-substantiated facts have to be respected. The phenomena studied by information science are not physical systems but human activities. As conditions change, so do the activities, and a previously observed 'law' may no longer apply. As with any social arrangement, we can change the pattern of human behaviour if we have the inclination to do so and the power to persuade others to conform. An observed deviation from a theoretical distribution is often of great significance, because it indicates that conditions have changed. So we must use theoretical relations only as convenient, approximate descriptions of information phenomena, always being prepared to find that in particular situations they do not reflect observed fact.

Probability distributions are, however, often stable despite varying conditions because they relate to features of the situation that do not change—for example, if a source continues to generate independent entities at rare intervals but at a constant average rate then the outcome will continue to be described by a Poisson distribution, no matter how other characteristics of the source may change. It is this generality of probability distributions that has made them so useful in the description of social situations.

The ensuing sections of this chapter will present some examples of models created to throw light on operational problems encountered in information systems. Useful reviews of this area are those of Rouse (1979), Kantor (1979), and Oswitch (1983).

8.12 Queueing

A very common problem in all kinds of system is that of queueing for service. In this section we will look at the matter in general terms and in the following section examine a particular instance. Discussions of queueing theory are to be found in most books on operational research. The problem can be visualized as comprising one or more service points, at which arrive individual entities (people, messages, or any other entity to be processed). It takes time to service each entity, so a queue of waiting arrivals may develop. After receiving service, entities leave the queue. If the patterns of arrival times and service times are known it is possible to predict values for such variables as the probability of having to queue, the average waiting time, or the proportion of time that a service point is busy. The values will depend upon such factors as the number of service points and queue discipline—is it first come, first served? Do all arrivals wait for service, or do some leave? In the simplest case, the following assumptions are made:

(1) The pattern of arrivals can be described by the Poisson formula

$$p(x) = e^{-m}m^x/x!$$

where m is the mean rate of arrival in unit time and $p(x)$ is the probability of x arrivals in unit time.

(2) The pattern of service times (at a single service point) can be described by the negative exponential distribution

$$p(t) = e^{-t/u}$$

where u is the mean service time and $p(t)$ is the probability that a service will take longer than t time units.
(3) The queue is first come, first served (and there are no simultaneous arrivals), and no arrival leaves the queue until served.

Mathematically it can then be shown that:

(1) The probablity of having to wait is $w = m/u$;
(2) The mean length of the queue is $l = m^2/u(u - m)$;
(3) The mean waiting time in the queue is $y = m/u(u - m)$.

So if we have a situation with $m = 6$ arrivals per hour, and $u = 8$ arrivals which can, on average, be served during an hour, then $w = 6/8 = 0.75$, i.e. there is a 75 per cent chance of having to wait; the average length of queue $l = 2.25$; and the average queueing time is $y = 0.375$ hours $= 22\frac{1}{2}$ minutes (plus the average service time of $7\frac{1}{2}$ minutes).

8.13 Collisions of demand

If two demands for the same item in a message store arrive simultaneously, or the second arrives before the first use is completed, one demand will not be met immediately. If its potential recipient is not prepared to join a queue the message will not be transmitted. Such collisions occur in many situations concerned with information systems—at the human level of user service and at machine level, when there is competition for access to an electronic device or transmission channel. The system designer needs to foresee the possibility that they will arise, seek to forecast their quantitative importance, and find ways to mitigate their effects.

The likelihood of collisions depends upon several factors: the average number of demands in unit time; the number of items in the store, and how demand is likely to be distributed among them; the pattern of arrival of demands over time; and the pattern of 'use periods'—i.e. how long an item is kept in use by a successful recipient. (In other contexts 'number of items in store' can be replaced by 'service points' or 'access points', and 'use periods' can be replaced by 'service times' or 'transaction times'.)

The distribution of use among items has already been discussed and some frequency data presented. Several probability distributions have been used to represent such data (in relation to the circulation of library books, see the articles by Burrell, 1980, Hindle and Worthington, 1980, and Bagust, 1983). There is considerable scope for differences of opinion, but a plausible choice is the negative binomial distribution. In many situations it has been found that arrival times at a service point can be described by the Poisson distribution. The pattern of use periods generally follows the negative exponential distribution. The last two distributions have been briefly introduced in the previous section. For the particular case of library book issues, one detailed study has been made by Morse

(1968, 1972), and we illustrate how his modelling can be used to implement a policy to reduce demand collision.

The gist of the suggested policy is that a second copy of a book should be acquired if its expected average annual use over the next ten years is greater than the average annual use of a recently purchased book—so that in terms of service the duplicate can be expected to be of more value than the average new purchase. The problem is to calculate these averages. The empirical input to the model is a sample of book issue data (in practice it may be necessary to sample each subject area separately, as issue patterns may vary between subjects). For each sampled book there is recorded the number of times issued during the last full year (L) and the same figure for the year previous to that (P). Data on the more recent books, which have no value P, are kept separately, and are used to calculate $R(1)$, the average annual use of recently purchased books: $R(1) = $ total L for recent books/number of recent books in sample.

To get from the observed values of L and P to a figure for D, the expected average annual use of a particular duplicate, Morse employs a model for the decline in use of books as they age. He postulates—basing his views on much experimental evidence from a university science library—that if the average annual circulation of a set of books in year t is $R(t)$, then the average for this set of books the following year is given by $R(t + 1) = A + B \times R(t)$. Note that these are averages—individual books in the set do not necessarily behave in this way—but in order to make a prediction about the future expected use of a particular book we must assume that it will behave in an 'average' way. Values of A and B must be obtained from the empirical data. The mathematical model developed by Morse indicates how the values can be calculated from the figures for L and P in the sample.

Morse then introduces a second model based upon queueing theory applied to collisions of demand. He assumes that the arrival of demands for a particular book is random, and that it can be described by a Poisson distribution; and further, that the times during which a book is retained on loan follow the exponential distribution. Mathematical manipulation of the appropriate equations indicates that if a book is issued R times in a year, then provision of a duplicate would permit R^2/M further issues. Here, $1/M$ is the fraction of a year during which a book is on average absent from the shelf during a single borrowing: for a 2-week loan period, M is about 24. So, if a book were issued 12 times a year, its duplicate would be issued 12 $\times$ 12/24 = 6 times. If R was very small, R^2/M would be too low to justify purchase of a duplicate.

There is some time lag between buying a new book, identifying that it is popular, and getting a duplicate on the shelf. A decision about duplication is better made if we have an estimate of its expected use over a number of years. Morse therefore combines his first model (use over time) with his second (collisions of demand). It turns out that if a book is issued $R(1)$ times its first year, its total circulation over the next 10 years is, on average, likely to be

$$S = (10A + B \times R(1)/(1 - B) - AB/(1 - B)^2$$

Using the formula R^2/M for the additional issues from a duplicate for each year, it is possible to compute a value for S', the total expected circulation of the duplicate over the next 10 years. Finally, we can calculate the expected annual average use of the duplicate over this period, $D = S'/10$.

Let us now consider a book issued L times during its first year. If $L = 12$, and our sample data shows that $A = 0.4$ and $B = 0.7$, then $S' = 10.25$ and $D = 1.025$, that is, that a duplicate is expected to be issued just over once a year for the next 10 years. If the average annual use of recently purchased books is less than 1, the proposed policy recommends purchase of the duplicate.

For details of this modelling, the reader is referred to Morse's publications. His 1972 paper provides helpful graphs to simplify the calculations required. Setting up such a model is mathematically complex, but its use in management is reasonably straightforward. In the next chapter we will be looking at another study of demand collision in the context of evaluating library performance.

8.14 Stock retention and discard

The variation of usage among stored items, and the decline in use with age, have been discussed earlier and utilized in the model just presented. Such data have also been employed to guide stock retention and discard policies—particularly as regards the storage of periodicals in libraries. Studies of this up to 1972 have been well reviewed by Hamburg *et al.* (1974) and a more recent review is that of Kraft (1979).

Given a collection of periodical runs—the choice of titles optimized by practical experience so that the collection meets most demands from users—and a need to limit the total collection size: on what criteria should material be selected for discard or removal to secondary storage? A given annual volume of a periodical may be little used (1) because the set to which it belongs is not very productive or (2) because the particular volume is old and its usage has declined.

The structure of journal usage has been illustrated by Buckland *et al.* (1970) as in *Figure 8.22*. Curve AB represents the Bradford distribution—journal titles ranked according to frequency of use in unit time (OA is the use per title, OP is journal rank). Curve AD represents exponential decline in use with age. It is assumed that the more productive a title, the longer time it is retained—so that the top-ranking journal is held until year x. Titles are retained until rank N (which is held for y years, less than x). The collection is represented by the volume ABCDxONE. The problem to be modelled is—in a given situation, how should N, x, and y be chosen so that the chance of meeting demand is maximized?

A somewhat simpler problem was first tackled by Cole (1962, 1963). He assumed that all titles would be held for the same length of time (x years). Given a maximum number (V) of volumes (title-years) to be retained, what choice of N and x is optimal? Cole expressed the Bradford distribution as follows:

$$R(n) = 1 + K \log (n/N)$$

Here, n is the rank of a title, $R(n)$ the cumulative number of demands up to

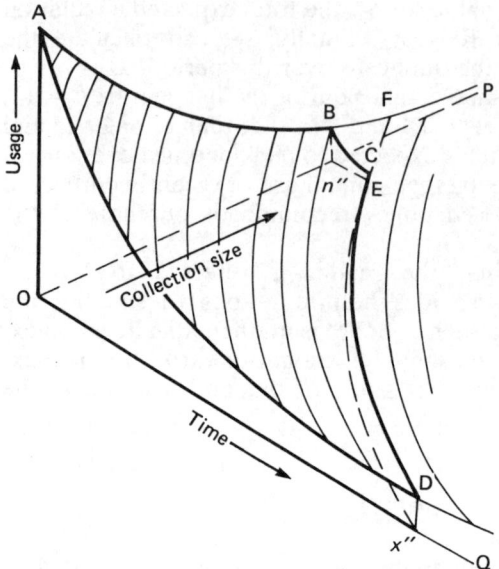

Figure 8.22 The structure of journal usage

that rank, and K a constant. He expressed the exponential decay of use with time as

$$R(x) = R(N) \times e^{-Lx}$$

where $R(x)$ is the number of demands older than x years, $R(N)$ is the total demand on the N titles, and L is a constant. Using these equations he was able to determine the value of N (and hence of $x = V/N$) for which the chance of meeting demand is maximized.

The more complex problem of varying retention periods has been studied by Brookes (1970c). He starts with exponential decline of use with age, and represents this as $R(x) = R(N) \times A^x$, where A is a constant called the 'ageing factor'. So $\log R(X) = \log R(N) + x \log A$. He then plots library use data as $\log R(x)$ against x, which yields a straight line of slope $\log A$ if decline in use is exponential, from which A can be determined. The 'utility' of a particular periodical volume is defined as the number of demands it can be expected to receive in the future. The utility at age x is $U(x) = IuA^x$, where I is the number of demands during the first year of the volume, and the 'utility factor' $u = 1/(1 - A)$. So for a given periodical, if we know A (its ageing factor) and I (the annual demand for the most recent volume), we can calculate the likely future demand $U(x)$ for a volume x years old. Library policy could be to discard a volume if its utility falls below some assigned critical level D.

8.15 Distributed storage

Evidence that usage of an information store declines sharply with its distance from the user base has already been presented. Rothenberg and

Ho (1977) have modelled the problem of optimizing the decentralization of access points for a dispersed population. They assume that the total collection may be held centrally, or be distributed among a number of substores, without any duplication of material, and that users are prepared, if necessary, to travel to any or all substores for information.

The geographical region to be serviced is divided into a convenient number G of grid areas (*Figure 8.23*) and each area is numbered, from $g = 1$ to G. The distance between any two areas, $d(g1 - g2)$, can be calculated from the grid. The number of potential users in each area is determined, $P(g)$. A constraint is introduced—M, the minimum allowable proportion of the collection to be located in any one area. If $M = 1$, the solution sought is the area in which a single centralized store should be located; if $M = 0$, there is no restriction on substore size; if $M = 0.1$, no substore should have less than 10 per cent of the collection. The mathematical analysis

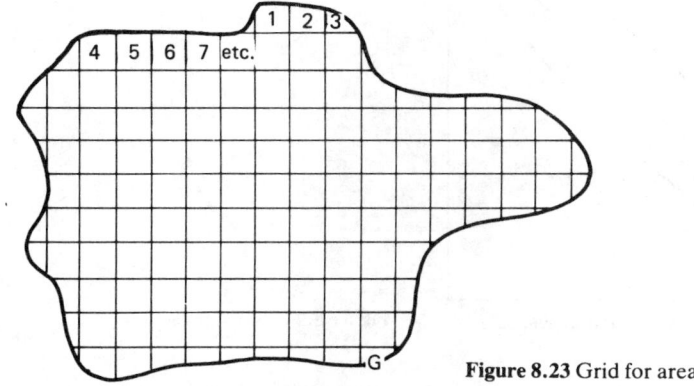

Figure 8.23 Grid for area served by library

proceeds by allocating proportions of the collection to each grid area in such a way as to minimize the total amount of travelling that needs to be done by all users to gain access to the collection as a whole. In a case study of mathematics information on a university campus, with $M = 0.25$, the model selected four particular areas in the region, each to house 25 per cent of the collection, as the best pattern of decentralization.

An important result derived from the modelling is that decentralization only reduces travel if a high proportion of each user's demand can be satisfied from a local substore. Consider *Figure 8.24*, plotting 'degree of satisfaction' S, against the proportion of collection available to the user A. The central straight line represents the situation when S is linearly related to A; along the upper curved line, S increases faster than A—for example, 30 per cent of the collection gives rise to 50 per cent of the satisfaction that the full collection would give; along the lower line, S increases more slowly than A. Only if the upper case holds true (S increasing faster than A) does distributed storage require less total travel than a single central store. The pattern of distribution of use among stored items—already illustrated—generally conforms to this requirement, so that on these grounds some degree of decentralization is justified.

This model seeks simply to minimize user travel effort, and does not take into account the relative costs of constructing and operating one or more stores.

A second approach to information access is to assume that a user can travel either to his or her local store or to a central store. We might have a central back-up library and local branch libraries—a two-stage hierarchy—which has been modelled by Brookes (1970a). He assumes that each local store holds material likely to be used by the local population, that the central store includes a duplicate copy of any item held locally, and that its stock is adequate to meet all demands.

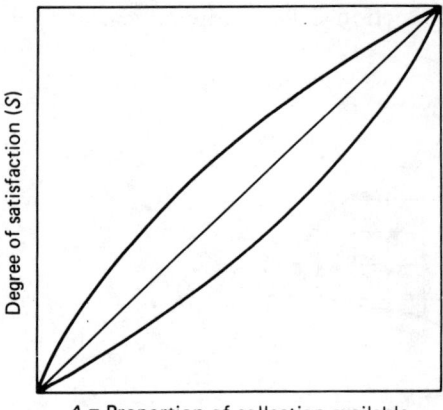

A = Proportion of collection available   **Figure 8.24** User satisfaction

The cost to the user (however expressed) of a visit to the local store is C units, and of a visit to the centre is AC, where $A > 1$. The local stocks are such that the probability of a demand being met is P. If the user were always to visit the central store first, with certain success, the average cost is AC units. The alternative strategy is always to visit the local store first. A successful visit to the local store costs C units, but this occurs only for the fraction P of user demands, so contributes PC to costs. Unsuccessful local visits account for $(1 - P)C$ costs, and must be followed by a visit to the centre, costing $(1 - P)AC$. The total average cost of the alternative strategy is $PC + (1 - P)C + (1 - P)AC = AC + C(1 - AP)$. This will be greater than AC if $AP < 1$. If the chance of local success is $P = 0.3$, and $A = 3$ (travel to the centre costs three times that of local travel), then $AP < 1$, and it is cheaper to ignore the local store. If the user knows well what the local store can provide he can adopt a third strategy and use the local store only when sure of success. Then average costs are $PC + (1 - P)AC$, which must always be less than with either of the other strategies. From the viewpoint of the system designer, if A is known, then P must be at least equal to $1/A$ if use of the local store is to be worthwhile even when the user cannot be sure of success there. Brookes (1970b) extends his analysis to a three-stage hierarchy.

8.16 Hierarchical provision

A third approach to access is to assume that the user travels only to a local store, and that demands not locally met are passed on to other stores, which transfer material to the local store concerned. Woodburn (1970) modelled a three-stage hierarchy of this kind (which could, for example, be academic department library, university library, national library). He assumes that the local store holds all items for which the expected number of demands per unit time, I, is greater than $R1$ (some marginal level of demand below which the item is not held). For each item, I could thus be the summed demand from all members of a particular department in a particular university. The expected demand for an item at the intermediate store is $J = \Sigma I$ for all the relevant local stores, for each item for which $I < R1$. It is assumed that the intermediate store holds all items for which $J > R2$ (a second marginal level). The expected demand at the central store is $K = \Sigma J$ for all the intermediate stores, for each item for which $J < R2$. It is assumed that all demanded items are held centrally. The values $R1$ and $R2$ thus constitute the storage policy of the system.

Woodburn used some factual data reported by Brown (1956) about demand for scientific journal titles. He modelled a situation with fifty intermediate stores (university libraries), each with eight local stores (departments), with a total annual demand of 42455 requests per year at each university, spread over 2736 journals, and with $R = R1 = R2$. His model shows how journals and successful demands would be distributed for various values of R. The figures in *Table 8.12* apply to each department and each university.

Table 8.12 Distribution and demands for journals

Marginal level R	Local store		Intermediate		Central	
	Titles held	Demands met	Titles held	Demands met	Titles held	Demands met
5000	NIL	NIL	NIL	NIL	2736	42455
1000	3	6762	NIL	NIL	2736	35693
200	38	18551	10	2940	2736	20964
50	135	27409	30	2169	2736	12877
10	568	36022	9	127	2736	6306

With $R1 = R2$, i.e. the marginal level of demand being set at the same figure in both local and intermediate stores, the latter play no significant role in meeting demand. A more realistic model might make $R2 > R1$, so that the intermediate stores would take up much more of the demand that otherwise goes to the central store. By making assumptions about the costs of transport between stores, and the 'cost' incurred by the user in waiting for interloan deliveries, Woodburn was able to suggest what value of R would give the most cost-effective distribution of journals among the three levels of store. A more elaborate model along the same lines has been developed by Elton and Orr (1973).

8.17 Some information system principles

We have tried in this chapter to draw together a number of the general characteristics of information systems, both qualitative and quantitative, that have been established by information science studies. Many other attempts at modelling are noted in the general references that have been cited.

We will conclude by setting out for consideration a list of principles that may guide the design and management of systems. Some of these principles can be related fairly readily to material presented in this chapter; others look towards the discussion of system performance that follows in the next chapter.

(1) Information is for use: the provision of information should be related to expected use.

(2) Information is for all (with right of access): information systems should take into account the information needs of all members of the community served.

(3) Every user his information: systems should ensure that each potential user can identify and gain access to sources of wanted information.

(4) Every source its user: the global information system should be organized so as to facilitate access to all recorded information.

(5) Supply creates demand: where a system judges that an item or range of information is needed, its provision often stimulates use.

(6) Save the time of the user: systems should minimize the effort needed to identify and access sources of information, and the time it takes to provide information.

(7) No information system can be self-sufficient: since the information needs of any user community are wider than any individual service can meet, there should be access for each user to the global information system.

(8) Each individual information service is only one channel of communication within the community served: it should take into account other complementary or competing channels;

(9) Documents, libraries, and information services have to be paid for: each possible supporting agency—public, corporate, or individual— should contribute funds in relation to the benefits it perceives.

(10) Individual systems should be cost effective: each service should seek an appropriate balance between performance and costs.

(11) The global information system should be cost effective: the distribution of functions and resources within the whole system should aim at a similar balance.

(12) Systems should adapt to change: since information needs, information materials, and social channels of communication are all continually changing, individual services and the system as a whole should look to the future—i.e. innovate and experiment.

Chapter 9

The evaluation of systems

In the social process of information transfer, $S - C - R$, the ultimate evaluation must be from the viewpoint of the potential recipients: have they received the information needed, wanted, demanded, and are the costs of this information provision personally or socially acceptable? There is also the question of evaluation from the viewpoint of the sources of information, who are concerned to know whether they have got their messages across, to whom and with what effect: this has been particularly the province of mass communication studies (see, for example, McQuail, 1975).

In this chapter we will concentrate on evaluation from the viewpoint of the individual information systems that act as channels—how effectively are they meeting the needs, wants, demands of their intended recipients, and are they achieving results in an economic way? The answers to these questions serve to guide the policies and procedures of the systems.

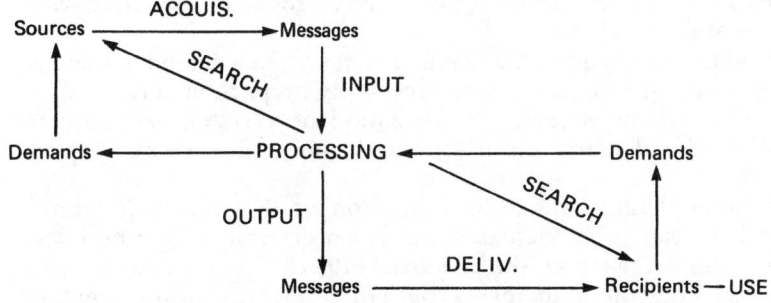

Figure 9.1 Systems, sources, and recipients (2)

Adapting an earlier diagram, we can express system activity as in *Figure 9.1*. Each system searches for potential sources and potential recipients; sends demands to sources that (hopefully) result in the acquisition of messages; inputs these messages to the processing system; receives demands from recipients and processes them (hopefully) to output messages; which are then delivered to the recipients. One further activity has been added—the use of the output messages by the recipient—for it is this use that determines whether the whole system has a real function. Evaluation can take place at any point along this chain of activities.

9.1 Criteria of evaluation

With respect to any activity, evaluation puts the questions: how well has it been performed? How much benefit is derived from it? Such questions can only be answered if criteria can be put forward against which the performance or value of the activity can be judged. There may be more than one criterion that appears relevant to a particular activity.

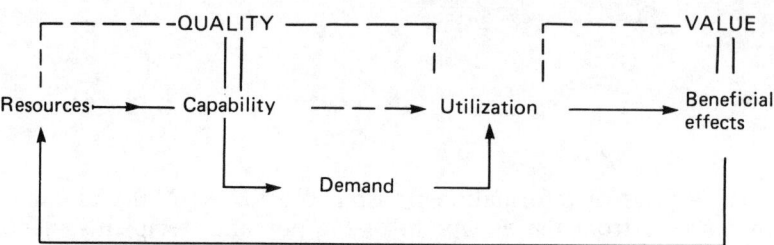

Figure 9.2 A model of evaluation

Orr (1973) presented a very general diagram of evaluation (*Figure 9.2*). Criteria related to performance he called 'quality', and those related to benefit he called 'value'.

The provision of resources to an information system results in its having a capability to provide various services; the utilization (use) of these services takes place when demands are made on the system; and the recipients may derive benefit from this use. The arrows in *Figure 9.2* represent the following propositions:

(1) Other things being equal, the capability of a system will tend to increase as resources devoted to it increase, but not necessarily proportionately;
(2) Other things being equal, the demand on a system will tend to increase as its capability increases, but not necessarily proportionately;
(3) Other things being equal, the utilization of a system will tend to increase as the demand on it increases, but not necessarily proportionately;
(4) Other things being equal, the utilization of a system will tend to increase as its capability increases, but not necessarily proportionately;
(5) Other things being equal, the beneficial effects of a system will tend to increase as its utilization increases, but not necessarily proportionately;
(6) Other things being equal, the resources available to a system will tend to increase as its beneficial effects increase, but not necessarily proportionately.

The repeated caveat, 'not necessarily proportionately', implies that there is always a limit to the extent that any factor in the sequence can be increased or improved. The second caveat, 'other things being equal', implies that many factors may counteract each suggested relationship: extra resources may be misused, and fail to increase capability; new capabilities may be irrelevant or ill marketed, and fail to increase utilization; extra uses may be trivial or may divert recipients away from real needs, and thus fail to produce beneficial effects; benefits received by users may not be perceived by or judged important by funders, and so not result in extra resources.

Criteria of 'quality' are directly related to the capabilities of the system: how well does a particular service perform—for example, what proportion of demands are satisfactorily met? Criteria of 'value' are directly related to the effects of using the system: how much does the recipient benefit—for example, how much of his or her time is saved?

It is not always easy to develop direct measures of quality and value. The dashed lines in Orr's diagram suggest indirect measures that are often used. For example, a system may point to an increase in capability (larger stock of information, more staff, bigger accommodation, etc.) as evidence of an increase in quality, thus basing itself on proposition (4) above; or the system may point to increases in use as evidence that its value must have increased, thus basing itself on proposition (5). Such proxy measures are only acceptable if indeed 'other things are equal'—including factors that affect demand. Orr pointed out that another proxy measure of increased value could be enlarged resources: if funders provide more money, they must have perceived the system as providing more value. This is in fact the argument that justifies a priced service: if recipients pay for it (thus contributing to resources) it must be of value to them. However persuasive such proxy measures may be to the practical manager of an information system, information science seeks to establish more clearly valid criteria of quality and value.

9.2 A framework for evaluation

Information systems process source messages for delivery via products and services to recipients. There are a number of ways in which we can picture this activity. First, let us consider the information made available to recipients by the system (*Figure 9.3*).

Of the whole universe of information messages only some are relevant to potential users of a particular system. Of these potentially relevant messages, most information systems manage to acquire only a proportion (and may well acquire some irrelevant material, suggested by the outer dashed line in *Figure 9.3*). Of the potentially relevant material in a system, only a proportion is provided to recipients on demand (and the output may

INFORMATION CONTENT

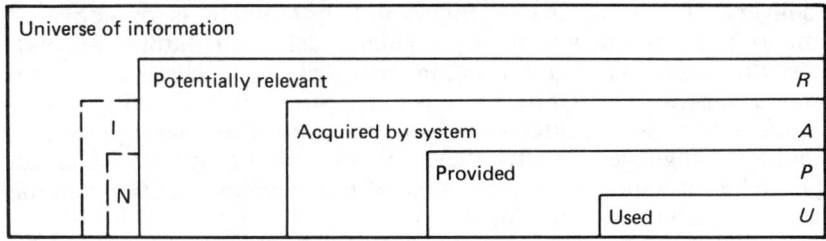

Figure 9.3 Information-provision model

well be mixed with irrelevant material, suggested by the inner dashed line). Lastly, of the messages provided, only a proportion may be actually used.

Comparisons between various boxes in *Figure 9.3* suggest various measures of quality. For example, the ratio A/R is a measure of the system coverage; the ratio of P (potentially relevant messages provided) to A (potentially relevant messages acquired) is a measure of how comprehensive is recall from the store; the ratio of N to P is a measure of how selectively the system extracts relevant material from its store (often called the precision); the ratio I/A would be a measure of irrelevant material acquired; the ratio U/P would measure redundancy in message provision.

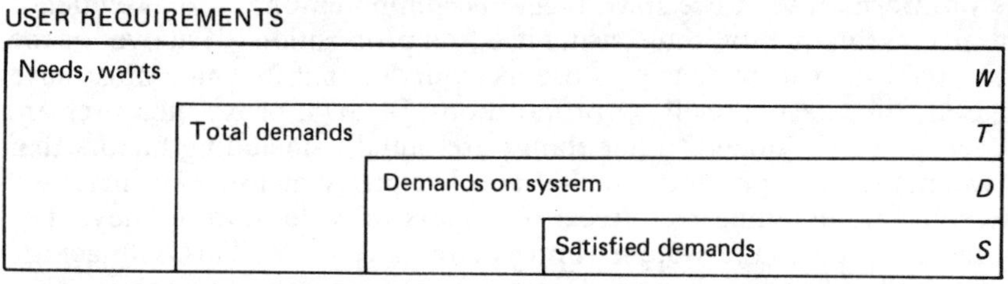

USER REQUIREMENTS

Needs, wants				W
	Total demands			T
		Demands on system		D
			Satisfied demands	S

Figure 9.4 User-satisfaction model

Now let us consider the process from the viewpoint of recipients (*Figure 9.4*). The distinctions made in *Figure 9.4* have been discussed by Orr (1973) and by Line (1974). A 'want' is an information need that is recognized as such by a potential recipient. There are also needs for information that can be identified by an observer of a work or life situation, but which may not be recognized as such by the participants. Of all the existing needs/wants, only a proportion result in positive action to acquire information, advancing beyond the wish, 'it would be nice to know'. This proportion is the total demand. Of this total, only some will be addressed to a particular information system, and only a fraction of these will be satisfactorily met. The ratio S/D is a direct measure of the quality of a service, the ratio D/T measures the extent to which a system is attracting active users (the market penetration); and T/W would measure the extent to which the global information system is reaching those who need/want information.

This analysis has identified a number of criteria by which the quality of an information system may be assessed. We can point to some further aspects of quality. The first is the pervasive importance of time in information provision: the time interval between initiation of a demand and delivery of output; the currency and up-to-dateness of delivered information; the frequency of any regularly delivered output. Second, there is the reliability of information provided—its accuracy, freedom from error, lack of bias. Third, there is the appropriateness of the form in which information is presented—for example, as regards quantity, format, terminology, language. Finally, there are the criteria against which all others can be set—the cost to the system of providing information and the cost to the recipient of obtaining it.

We end this discussion of a framework for evaluation by considering the kinds of data needed for the measures identified:

(1) Relevance assessments: coverage is measured by comparing the potentially relevant messages in the system with an estimate of those in the universe of information; recall compares those in the system with those provided to a recipient; precision assesses their proportion in the output provided. All these measures are thus based on assessments of relevance—judgements that a message is or is not of potential interest to an information need/want. A judgement as to the reliability of a message is an extension of this. Relevance assessments are therefore of key importance in evaluation.

(2) Recipient behaviour: measures of redundancy in output (messages provided but not used); of the successful meeting of demands; of market penetration; of the appropriateness of the form of presentation; of the cost of using a system—all these involve data about recipient behaviour: their use of outputs, the types and quantity of their demands, the way they react to message forms, the effort they must make to access a system. The study of recipient behaviour is therefore a second essential aspect of evaluation. We have examined many aspects of this in Chapter 4.

(3) System characteristics: delays between the initiation and meeting of a demand; or between the availability of information, its emission as a message, its acquisition by a system, and its delivery to a recipient; and the costs of information provision—all these are system characteristics, which are the third source of data for the evaluation of quality.

9.3 Relevance and its assessment

Relevance is defined by Saracevic (1970, 1975) in its most general terms as 'a measure of the effectiveness of the contact between a source and a destination (recipient) in a communication process'. If a message is emitted by a source and is assimilated by a recipient, causing some change to occur in the latter's knowledge structure, then the message can be said to be 'relevant' to the recipient, and there has been an effective communication of information. In this situation the recipient can make a relevance assessment of the message.

Only the ultimate recipient of an information message can make an unequivocal judgement: 'Yes, it is relevant—to me.' Yet at every stage of information transfer people are making hypothetical judgements. Generally speaking (and this qualification applies throughout), information is only generated if it is believed to be potentially relevant to known or hypothesized needs; it will only be recorded if a use later in time is foreseen; messages are only replicated if a publisher believes that there is an audience for whom they are relevant; published messages are only acquired and stored by an information system if judged relevant to actual or potential users of the system; in analysis (classification and indexing) document designations are created that seek to express the perceived relevance of each item to the hypothesized information needs of users; in retrieval, the search terms used are those judged to be relevant to the enquiry made.

Evaluations are often concerned with the comparison of relevance assessments. A study of the coverage of a system is, in effect, matching the relevance assessments made in the acquisition process against some more comprehensive assessment of the universe of information messages. A measurement of recall in a subject search is matching the relevance assessments made by the search system with more comprehensive assessment of the stock of messages in the system. A measurement of precision matches search system assessments against those of the recipient.

All relevance assessment is subjective and hence variable according to the assessor's understanding of the message content and understanding of the information need, his purpose in making the assessment, and the general context in which a particular assessment is made. Some of the practical difficulties involved will be considered when specific studies of coverage, recall, and precision are described.

9.4 Service qualities

The fact that information systems provide services to potential recipients means that their quality—as well as being measurable against the criteria so far identified—can also be judged in relation to more 'ineffable' characteristics.

The fact that a range of different services is available from a system is often attractive to users (as it is to customers of a supermarket). Even within a particular service, a menu of choices rather than a standard output is also perceived as a sign of quality. Because people have a wide spectrum of need, the possibility of going beyond the standard services offered, and receiving a 'tailor-made' output, is further evidence of good quality.

Simplicity of use of a system is a highly regarded quality because users may not have the time, inclination, or even ability to learn a procedure that is complex. If simplicity is operationally unachievable, then technical assistance in using the system is appreciated, and the provision of training facilities for those who do wish to learn. Another element that creates user wellbeing is explanation of what the system is doing, why there is an unavoidable delay, why output takes the form that it does, etc.

Lastly, there is the service characteristic that is most difficult to quantify, or even to define, its 'atmosphere': the attractiveness of the physical environment in which the user accesses the system, the courtesy and enthusiasm of information staff, the feeling of 'personal attention' that they impart.

All these 'ineffable' qualities can play a large part in affecting user reactions to an information system. Though they can rarely be formally evaluated, they should not be overlooked in assessing systems.

9.5 Evaluating performance

All measures of quality are concerned with comparing in some way what has actually been done with what could have been done in some ideal or optimal circumstances. Since actuality usually falls short of the ideal or optimal, evaluation may also wish to identify reasons for the shortfall. The decisions involved in establishing and using a measure of performance are therefore:

(1) What characteristic of the activity is the best measure of what has been or could have been done?
(2) What is the unit by which this characteristic will be measured?
(3) What other characteristics of the activity may throw light on the reasons for shortfall?
(4) How are the ideal or optimal circumstances to be specified?
(5) How are data on 'What has been done?' to be collected?
(6) How are data on 'What could have been done?' to be collected?
(7) How is the actual measure, relating these two sets of data, to be constructed?
(8) How are the values of the measure to be related to other data collected about the activity?

Orr (1973) has discussed some of the features that need to be considered in choosing a measure. Clearly, characteristics must be chosen on which data can be operationally obtained without too much difficulty, and with some certainty and reliability. A chosen measure should have an appearance of validity—being seen to be compatible with the criterion against which performance is being evaluated. Choice of the unit of measurement is important and often difficult. For example, just what should be counted as 'a relevant message' or as 'the use of a service'? Is waiting a week for an interlibrary loan $6 \times 24 \times 7 =$ about 1000 times as bad a delay as waiting 10 minutes for a book from the basement, and if not, in what units should delay be expressed?

The choice of other characteristics, that may help to identify reasons for shortfall, should be guided by developing a model of the possible causal relations that may affect the performance: in other words, by visualizing what can go wrong, what factors can impede success, and how they can be categorized and specified in each occurrence of the activity. The ideal or optimal circumstances in which an activity can take place are those in which nothing goes wrong, no factors impede success, so the modelling just noted also helps to specify these circumstances.

The kinds of data that may be needed in evaluation have been discussed earlier. Data collection can be carried out routinely, in the course of monitoring activities, or a special evaluation test can be carried out. The former method has some advantages in that it involves no extra work by any participant (human or machine), and thus keeps down the cost of evaluation. However, this method restricts the data obtainable to what happens to be routinely collected, and this may not be what is needed. The alternative is to devise a test that collects exactly what is sought, even though this is likely to cost more. It may also run the risk of disturbing the activity and its performance, by putting an extra burden on the system staff or users from or about whom data are sought, even causing them to modify their behaviour so that it is no longer typical.

The collection of data on 'what could have done ' may be easy or very difficult. It is one thing to specify an ideal situation, it is another to discover an example of it about which data can be obtained. It may be possible to hypothesize a mental model of the ideal system, in which nothing goes wrong and complete success is achieved. Alternatively, one may be able to identify some approximation to the ideal or optimal, and examine this. In this second case one cannot obtain an absolute measure of performance, only a relative measure (i.e. relative to 'the best we can find' rather than to the ideal).

A performance measure is a relation between some value derived from normal system activity and some corresponding value derived from the real or hypothesized activity of an 'optimal' system. Often, the relation used is a simple ratio (such as items received/items sought), but some other kind of relation may be more revealing of quality. There are situations when more than one measure can be used to characterize the performance of an activity, and here there arises the problem of combining these into some 'single-figure' measure of quality.

Lastly, we come to the identification of causes of less than ideal performance—'failure analysis', as it is often called. This requires a detailed investigation of individual cases, in which the observed characteristics of particular activities are examined to identify which affected performance.

Examples of this pattern of decisions will be given as we look at the evaluation of various activities in the system chain illustrated earlier. First, however, we will consider one last general point.

9.6 System efficiency: cost and cost effectiveness

The aim of every information system is to achieve maximum effectiveness in meeting the requirements of potential recipients. It can provide better or more wide-ranging services if it uses its resources wisely, and minimizes the costs of its activities. As well as effectiveness, systems therefore seek efficiency, and their aim is to be 'cost effective', as we noted in our statement of system principles at the end of the last chapter. Together with the assessment of quality and value must go estimates of effort and cost.

Costing is a far from simple activity. Some of its complexities are discussed in Vickery (1973, Chapter 6), Price (1974), and Wolfe (1974). Cost elements to be taken into account may include:

Labour
Expenditure on information materials acquired
Consumables (paper, storage media, etc.)
Use of equipment (depreciation, maintenance)
External charges (for processing, telecommunications, postage, transport, travel, etc.)
Service overheads (accommodation rent, rates, maintenance and insurance; water, power, heat; cleaning costs; general office services)
Administrative overheads (the costs of supervision, accounting, personnel, etc.)
Development (costs associated with developing the system may have to be recovered)

Costing must initially be applied to processes, the individual activities that are carried out within an information system. However, if we are to assess the cost effectiveness of a service then the costs of processes that contribute to that service must be allocated to it. If a particular process (for example, a retrieval search) contributes solely and directly to a particular service (such as an on-demand answer to an enquiry) cost allocation is simple. More difficult is the problem of allocating the cost of a process (such as information acquisition) that may contribute to several kinds of service.

One last general comment on costs: the analysis of the costs incurred by an information system may sometimes be difficult (and therefore in itself costly to perform), but it is always possible. A system is less well placed to estimate the cost incurred by a recipient in using a service, yet this also should figure in any valid assessment of cost effectiveness.

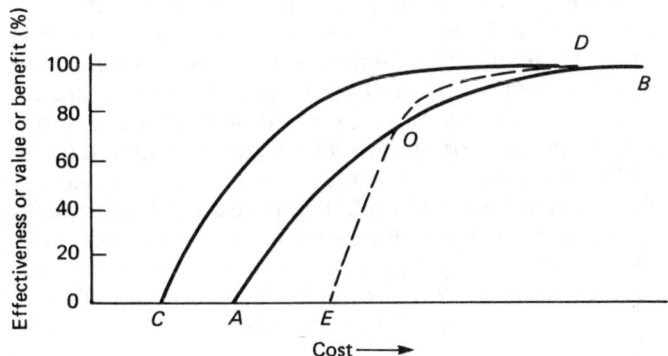

Figure 9.5 Cost-effectiveness curves

The meaning of 'cost effectiveness' can be displayed by considering *Figure 9.5*, which represents the typical situation encountered in an information system. General experience shows that the nearer one gets to peak effectiveness, the more costly it becomes to make further improvement. The *cost effectiveness* curve is like AB in the figure. To move from 50 per cent to 60 per cent effectiveness involves less extra cost than to move from 80 per cent to 90 per cent. There is some minimum cost, A, below which no performance can be obtained at all. A change of system may cause not just movement along the curve AB but shift to a new curve such as CD or ED. Curve CD is uniformly more cost effective than AB—at any level of effectiveness, the cost is less, so the new system is wholly to be preferred. Curve ED is only preferable to AB above point O, and the new system is only to be preferred if it will normally operate above that level of effectiveness. To be cost effective therefore means either (1) to be operating a system at a given level of performance as economically as is possible with the current system specification or (2) to be achieving as high a level of performance as possible with a given ceiling on costs.

9.7 Coverage in acquisition search

As noted earlier, information systems of every kind conduct a continual search for potential sources, and on locating them attempt to acquire their emitted messages. The coverage achieved is a measure of the success of this search process. In principle, coverage can be expressed as the simple ratio: source messages acquired/source messages emitted. Each particular type of information system can usually specify without difficulty an appropriate unit message—for example, author manuscript for a publisher, book or periodical title for a library, paper or report for an abstracts journal or database. Counting the acquired messages is usually straightforward.

It is much more difficult to devise a way of identifying emitted messages not acquired—after all, if one is identified, an attempt is made to acquire it. The ratio messages acquired/messages identified is a measure of success in the acquisition process, but is not a true measure of coverage. Some systems such as the British Library Lending Division, with a vigorous and well-funded acquisition activity, have gone so far as to say that if a journal cannot be acquired, then for all practical purposes it does not exist, so that the acquisition ratio and coverage ratio are both valueless in their context.

A less well-endowed system has the option of identifying a more comprehensive collection that covers its interests, and by comparison of stocks estimating a relative measure of coverage—and collections such as that of BLLD are often used as the standard of comparison. An alternative strategy is to identify one or more collections, each limited in subject scope but having the appearance of being comprehensive within that scope, and to compare system stock with each. If sufficiently many and diverse comparisons can be made, some overall relative measure of the coverage of one's own collection can be estimated.

Tests exemplifying this last method have been carried out by Martyn and Slater (1964). They identified about twenty comprehensive specialist bibliographies, and checked whether the items in them were to be found in a number of abstracting/indexing journals. In seven cases the journals tested included *Chemical Abstracts*. The coverage of *CA* in each case is shown in *Table 9.1*, together with the coverage achieved by the most productive abstracts journal in that particular test.

Thus, in no case did *CA* (the collection being tested) achieve 100 per cent coverage, and in five cases it was not the best of the collections tested.

Table 9.1 The coverage of *Chemical Abstracts*

Test	1	2	3	4	5	6	7
CA	87	80	16	20	18	70	42%
Best	87	80	21	65	20	91	86%

Table 9.2 The coverage of *Biological Abstracts*

Test	1	2	8	9	10	11	12	13	14
BA	29	20	33	19	33	66	55	57	68%
Best	87	80	81	53	59	83	71	86	90%

A similar set of figures for *Biological Abstracts* is as shown in *Table 9.2*. If the spread of tests over, say *BA* had been sufficiently wide and representative of its subject scope—this could not in fact be claimed in this case—then the overall coverage of *BA* could have been estimated from the sample data. As it is, we are merely left with an impression that the usual coverage of *BA* is somewhere between one third and one half.

An attempt at failure analysis was made. Characteristics selected as possible reasons for non-inclusion in the abstracting journals were

(1) Inferior quality of item;
(2) Obscure language;
(3) Uncommon form of publication.

However, no correlation with any of these factors could be established.

Let us look in more detail at one of the bibliographies used in these tests. The subject was radioactive fallout (Test 7 above), which listed 106 items. Martyn and Slater (1964, 1967) identified 98 of these in three abstracts journals:

Nuclear Science Abstracts—91 items
Chemical Abstracts—44 items
Index Medicus—25 items

The total is greater than 98 because of duplication. The compilers of the original bibliography also searched these journals—but, of course, via their subject indexes. In an article on the bibliographic work, Voress (1962) describes how there were also searched by subject eight other abstracting journals to pick up the remaining eight items not found by Martyn and Slater. The search effort needed to pick up the last 7.5 per cent of the bibliography was therefore considerable.

This leads us directly to consider the cost effectiveness of such search procedures. If an information system is seeking individually emitted source messages it is likely that the unit cost of actually acquiring each (once it has been identified) is approximately the same, but the unit cost of identification—as shown in the case of Voress—is likely to increase, perhaps exponentially. The cost/coverage curve will be of the form shown in *Figure 9.6*, the well-known 'law of diminishing returns'. If the system is looking for messages embedded in other source material—say, relevant articles in journals—then the Bradford distribution of messages among publications also plays a role: the unit acquisition cost per publication may remain approximately constant, but the yield of relevant items per publication declines, so the overall cost/coverage curve is stretched to the right—the cost of achieving a particular level of coverage is increased.

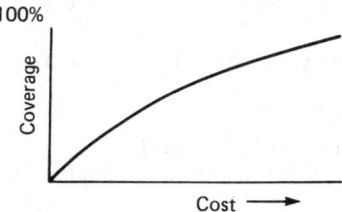

Figure 9.6 Cost-coverage curve

9.8 Retrieval from store

The evaluation of success in retrieving messages from a store, in response
to a user demand, has been the subject of much theoretical analysis and
practical experiment. The basic texts are those of Lancaster (1979), van
Rijsbergen (1979), and Sparck Jones (1981). Evaluation here centres
around the concept of relevance, already discussed, and makes use of the
following model:

	Relevant	Not relevant
Retrieved	Hits	Noise or waste
Not retrieved	Misses	Rejects

The box represents the collection of stored messages. Each act of retrieval
divides the store into two parts: items retrieved and those not retrieved.
Relevance assessment can then, in principle, divide each of these parts into
relevant and non-relevant portions. We are left with four quantities:
relevant items either hit or missed, irrelevant waste retrieved, and items
correctly rejected. Upon this foundation most evaluation of retrieval
performance has been based. The model clearly suggests two possible
criteria of quality: to minimize the number of misses and to minimize the
amount of waste retrieved. The ideal performance is one in which no
relevant messages are missed and no irrelevant messages are retrieved.
   The 'stores' from which messages are retrieved can be of different kinds:
a collection of documents arranged by subject; a verbal index to
documentary materials—printed or in a card catalogue; a database of
records containing references, data, directory information, or the full texts
of documents. Each type of store presents its own particular problems in
evaluation, but common to them all is the need for decision on the
following points:

(1) What should be the size of the test if it is to yield reliable results?
(2) What is to be the origin of queries that will form the basis of acts of
    retrieval?
(3) What is the definition of an 'act of retrieval'—the unit search whose
    quality is to be assessed? This involves such considerations as how a
    query is to be translated into a query designation (using terms
    appropriate to the retrieval system) and what modifications to the query
    designation will be permitted during the search.
(4) What will be the method of assessing the relevance of messages? Is a
    scale of relevance to be used?
(5) How will we identify what messages are retrieved? (This is not always
    as easy as it sounds.)
(6) How will we identify what relevant messages have been missed, or
    estimate their number?
(7) What performance measures will be used?
(8) How will each measure be calculated for each unit search?
(9) How will individual search performances be combined to give an
    overall test result?

(10) What variables are to be studied as possible influences on retrieval performance?
(11) How are data on each variable to be collected?
(12) How are these data to be related to the retrieval measures?
(13) What further information is to be collected to aid interpretation of the test results?

Two types of retrieval evaluation have been carried out—tests on the performance of operational systems and research studies on the behaviour of experimental systems. We have already considered some results obtained from experimental research in Chapter 6. Here we will examine three practical tests of computer-based retrieval systems and one large-scale experimental study.

9.9 The evaluation of MEDLARS

This investigation was carried out during 1966/1967 and is reported by Lancaster (1968, 1969). At that time MEDLARS (medical literature analysis and retrieval system) had a store of 700000 records relating to medical articles, held on magnetic tape that was serially searched, in batch mode, in response to user demands. Over 3000 searches were processed annually. Each article was indexed by subject headings, on average 6.7 per article (though the more important material averaged ten headings). The headings were drawn from a thesaurus (MeSH) that then contained about 7000 terms. The main objectives of the test were (1) to study user search requirements, (2) to determine how effectively and efficiently MEDLARS was meeting the requirements, (3) to identify factors adversely affecting performance, and (4) to discover ways to improve performance. Since this was the first major evaluation of an operating retrieval system we will examine it in some detail.

It was decided that a target of 300 evaluated queries was needed to provide an adequate test (the statistical basis for this judgement was not reported). The range of queries should, as far as possible, be representative of the normal demand. Representativeness was achieved by stratified sampling of the medical institutions from which demands had come during 1965, and processing queries received from the sample institutions over a 12-month period. Some 410 queries were received and processed, and eventually 300 of these were fully evaluated and used to assess performance. The queries processed were therefore those that arose naturally during the working life of the sampled users. The 300 queries used in analysis came from those requesters who proved willing to undertake relevance assessments.

Queries were submitted to MEDLARS by personal visit (which then resulted in a 'negotiation' of the request with information staff) or by mail. The request included the name, title, and institution of the user, a statement of the query ('Please be as specific as possible as to purpose, scope, definitions, limitations, etc.'), and suggestions as to medical terms pertinent to the query. From these data, MEDLARS staff prepared a search formulation (query designation) using an appropriate combination of MeSH headings. A computer search was then carried out 'in the normal way'. The 'act of retrieval', the unit search, was thus defined individually for each query according to the experience of the MEDLARS searcher (there was, of course, more than one searcher). At this stage each user was asked to submit a list of recent articles that he judged to be relevant to the query.

The result of a search was a computer printout of references. This was sent to the requester as a response to his query. If there was 30 or fewer items in the list a photocopy of each article listed was sent to the requester for evaluation; if more than 30, then about 25 items were selected randomly from the list, and photocopies of these were sent. The requester was asked to report about each article whether it was of major value (relevance), minor value, no value, or value not assessable (for example, in a foreign language). Relevance assessment was therefore carried out by the original requester, based on the full text of the message, and used the scale of relevance 'major–minor–nil'. The result of this operation was to provide an estimate of hits and waste: for example:

User number	1
Total retrieved	344
Photocopies sent	24
Major relevance	6 (25%)
Minor relevance	13 (54%)
Total relevant	19 (79%)

Since the 24 photocopies were selected randomly from the 344 retrieved references, the percentages shown are estimates of the proportions of those 344 items that could be relevant.

It was more difficult to obtain an estimate of the relevant items missed. There were two sources of information about articles judged to be relevant, other than the search itself. One was a list of recent articles submitted by the requester. The other was a list of articles found by searching the query in other information stores (not MEDLARS): photocopies of all these articles were also assessed by the user resulting in a small set of articles judged to be relevant. Any of these items not in the MEDLARS database were removed from this 'recall set'. After the search, the remaining 'recall set' was checked against the list of items retrieved. The result for user number 1 was as follows:

Items in 'recall set'	17
Major relevance	7
Minor relevance	10
Items retrieved	15
Major relevance	5
Minor relevance	10

For user number 1, considering total relevance (major plus minor) we have the following situation:

Items retrieved	344
Relevant retrieved (79% of 344)	272
Waste retrieved (21%)	72
Relevant not retrieved (2/15 of 272)	36

Two performance measures were now calculated. The recall ratio R is the proportion of hits to the total relevant items, 272/(272 + 36), or 88 per cent. The precision ratio P is the proportion of hits in the retrieved set, 79 per cent. The recall ratio is a measure of the success of the system in finding relevant items. The precision ratio measures its success in avoiding the retrieval of waste—irrelevant items. On these criteria, the 'ideal' system would yield $R = P = 100$ per cent.

This would not necessarily be ideal performance for all recipients—some do not want all the relevant messages but would 'ideally' like a judicious selection; some might even welcome a little non-relevant 'waste', because 'it could be interesting for some other purpose'. Some information systems try to meet these requirements by ranking the output of messages according to a criterion that hopefully is related to the ranking that 'judicious selection' would provide. Performance measures based on ranked output have been developed. However, we continue with a discussion of the MEDLARS evaluation.

The precision ratio for a single search is a clear-cut measure. The estimated recall ratio is more uncertain, being based (in the case of user number 1) on a recall set only 5 per cent of the size of the retrieved set. There are some problem situations if it has not been possible to find any items to put into the recall set, so $R = 0/0$:

(1) If the search also retrieves nothing, then $P = 0/0$. However, if there truly were no relevant items in the system, the search result was valid, so the test took $R = P = 100$ per cent.
(2) If the search retrieved X items, none relevant, then $P = 0/X$. Assuming once again that there were no relevant items in the system, $R = 100$ per cent, but the system had not avoided waste, so $P = 0$ per cent.
(3) If the search retrieved X, Y being relevant, then $P = Y/X$. A value can be given to precision, but how can recall be scored if there is no recall set? There were three results of this kind, which were simply dropped from the analysis.

If there was a recall set, but the system retrieved nothing, $R = 0$, and P was also set at zero. Because recall and precision were calculated from different sets of items, that might or might not overlap, the results of individual searches were sometimes anomalous—for example, user number 18 had 0/4 recalled, but 7/11 relevant in the system search; R is put at 0, even though 7 relevant items were retrieved.

Figure 9.7 is a scatter diagram of the results of the test searches, based on total relevant items retrieved. The points on the bottom line of the chart are of the anomalous type just noted. One search achieved 'ideal' performance (top right corner) and one was abysmal (bottom left). The extreme scatter was due to the problematic nature of the recall measure. The dashed line is a generalized performance curve, based upon some analysis to be presented in a moment. The actual average performance is roughly at the centre of the diagram, $R = 58$ per cent, $P = 50$ per cent. The implication is this: because of the way that the searchers on average defined 'the act of retrieval', the unit search, they were in effect choosing to operate the system at this average level of performance; if they altered their behaviour, and carried out searches to achieve either greater or less

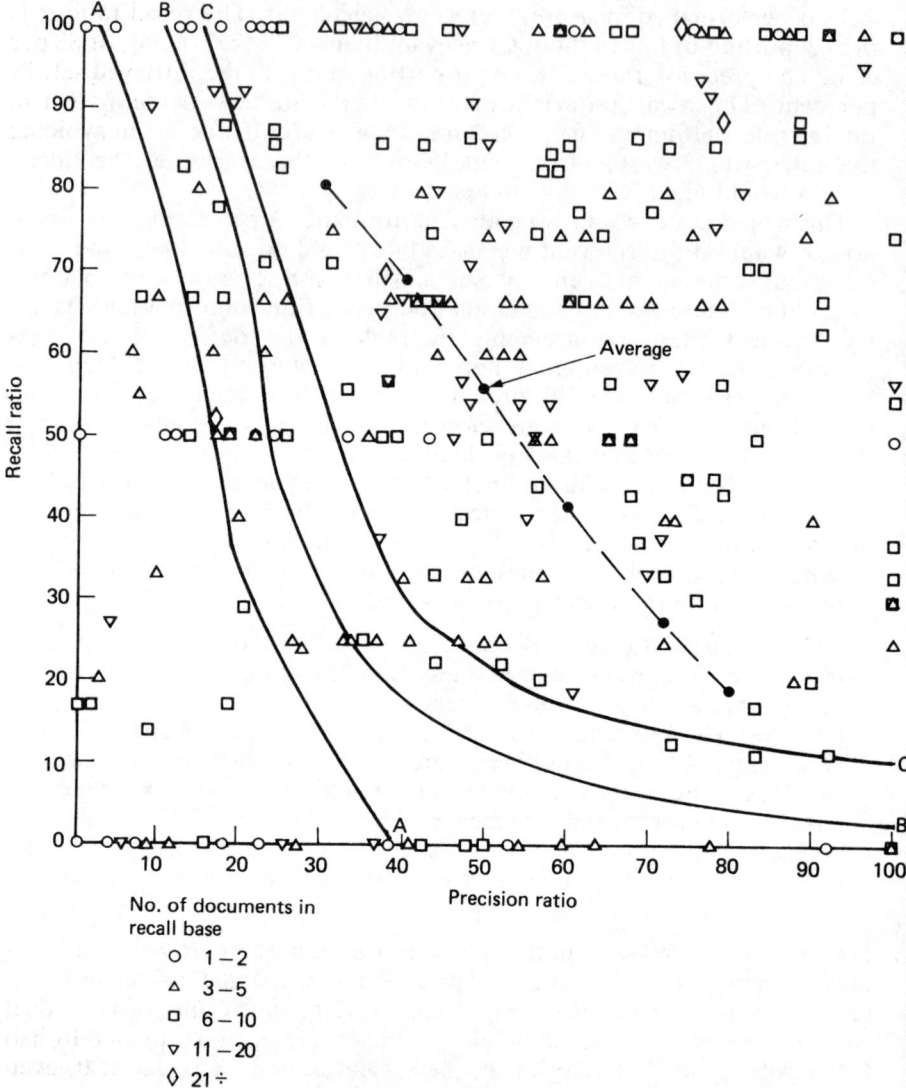

Figure 9.7 Scatter diagram of MEDLARS results. (A) 90 per cent guarantee that performance will not be worse than this; (B) 80 per cent guarantee that performance will not be worse than this; (C) 75 per cent guarantee that performance will be better than this

precision, it is expected that average performance would shift either down or up the dashed line. As can be seen, recall and precision are inversely related—on average, one can be improved only at the expense of the other.

The generalized performance curve was derived from analyses such as the following. Searchers were located at five different MEDLARS centres, and it was found that each centre had a different average definition of the 'act of retrieval'—for example, each used a different average number of terms in the search formulation (averages for each centre varied from 50 to 150). As a result, average performance differed:

Centre	I	II	III	IV	V	Total (%)
Precision	41	43	51	56	56	50
Recall	69	64	58	55	43	58

The inverse relation of recall and precision can be clearly seen. Such figures are the basis of the dashed line in *Figure 9.7*. The solid lines are statistical estimates derived from the generalized average curve and from the observed variability of individual results.

The next stage of the evaluation was an elaborate analysis of retrieval failures. The system was modelled in the following way (*Figure 9.8*).

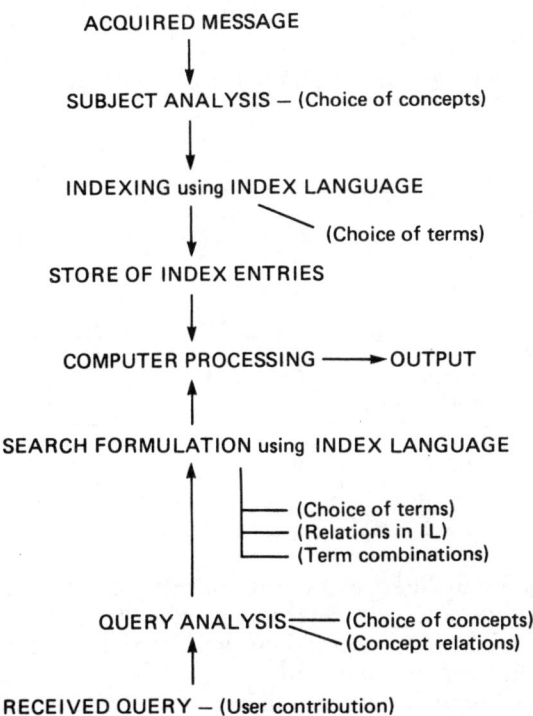

ACQUIRED MESSAGE

SUBJECT ANALYSIS — (Choice of concepts)

INDEXING using INDEX LANGUAGE

(Choice of terms)

STORE OF INDEX ENTRIES

COMPUTER PROCESSING ⟶ OUTPUT

SEARCH FORMULATION using INDEX LANGUAGE

— (Choice of terms)
— (Relations in IL)
— (Term combinations)

QUERY ANALYSIS— (Choice of concepts)
(Concept relations)

RECEIVED QUERY — (User contribution)

Figure 9.8 A model of the MEDLARS test

Each bracketed phrase in *Figure 9.8* represents a factor identified as potentially affecting the output. Messages acquired for recording in the MEDLARS system were analysed by subject, and the concepts chosen to designate them would determine what queries might retrieve them. The conceptual analyses were turned into index entries in the MeSH indexing language: the MeSH terms selected to represent the concepts would affect retrieval. At the search stage, the form of the received query could depend on how the user interacted with the system. Query analysis involved choice of concepts and of relations between them; search formulation translated these into terms in the indexing language (IL) and ways of combining them; all these would affect retrieval. More specifically, the following causes of failure were identified:

Indexing: too many concepts/terms chosen
             too few concepts/terms chosen
             important concept omitted
             inappropriate term chosen
             over-general term chosen
Index language: lack of appropriate specific terms
                   defects in IL relations
Searching: formulation too specific or too general
              formulation included too many or too few terms
              inappropriate terms or term combinations chosen
              incorrect relations between query concepts
User/system interaction distorts query

Data concerning failures were collected by examining, for each search:

(1) The request statement;
(2) The search formulation;
(3) The index entries for a sample of missed and waste items;
(4) The full texts of these items.

The results were as in *Table 9.3*.

Table 9.3 Data concerning failures

	Recall		Precision	
	Percentage of failures	*Percentage of searches*	*Percentage of failures*	*Percentage of searches*
Indexing	37.4	85.3	12.9	60.1
Index language	10.2	12.2	36.0	91.7
Searching	35.0	55.9	32.4	67.0
User/system	25.0	29.4	16.6	39.9

For example, the factors listed above in relation to indexing accounted for 37.4 per cent of the failures to recall particular items and 12.9 per cent of the waste items—and these failures were spread through 85 per cent and 60 per cent, respectively, of the searches analysed.

In about 29 per cent of the 302 searches, a recall failure was attributed to 'inadequate user–system interaction', and in about 40 per cent of the searches a precision failure was similarly attributed. A failure was attributed to inadequate interaction if a retrieved article was judged of no value by the requester, although it appeared to the evaluator to be within the scope of the stated request. The phenomenon implies that the stated request did not match the information need on which relevance assessment was based. The request may be narrower than the need (leading to low recall), broader than the need (leading to low precision), or partially overlapping the need (leading to both types of failure). The existence of the phenomenon is well known to librarians—the difficulty a user has in exactly stating his information requirements.

What is interesting is the way that this mismatch was related to user–system interaction. Four levels of interaction were recognized:

(1) Personal interaction—the requester visited a MEDLARS centre and discussed his information need personally with a system operator;

(2) Positive local interaction—a local librarian discussed the information need with the requester before transmitting the request;

(3) Negative local interaction—a local librarian simply transmitted the request;

(4) No local interaction—the requester mailed his request direct to MEDLARS.

Before the test it was hypothesized that the first group of requests would give the highest performance. The results were as in *Table 9.4*.

Table 9.4 User–system interaction

	No. of searches	Recall ratio %	Precision ratio %
All groups	302	57.7	50.4
(1) Personal interaction	109	56.4	49.3
(2) Positive local interaction	79	55.0	46.9
(3) Negative local interaction	65	60.6	53.2
(4) No local interaction	46	61.1	54.8

Both as regards recall and precision, the 'interactive' groups 1 and 2 performed worse than the 'neutral' groups 3 and 4. Lancaster commented:

It appears crucial to the success of a MEDLARS search that the requester be required to write down, in his own natural language, exactly what type of literature he is looking for. When he makes a personal visit to a MEDLARS center, or discusses with a local librarian, we do not normally have the benefit of this written, natural language statement. Rather, the requester is invited to discuss his need with a search analyst. Unfortunately, at this point, his information need tends to get distorted. The problem appears to be at least partly due to the fact that the requester's need is discussed in terms of, and unduly influenced by, MeSH. When the requester is writing down his request, he is forced to think of what exactly he is looking for. In this, he is not particularly influenced by the logical and linguistic constraints of the system. When, however, he approaches a MEDLARS center, if he has not already gone through the discipline of writing down his request, he has a less well-formed idea of what he is seeking (i.e. of the scope and constraints of the search). When this somewhat imprecise need is discussed with a search analyst, in terms of MeSH, it tends to become forced into the language and logic of the system. The final 'request' rather than representing what the requester wants, represents what he thinks the system can give him, phrased in a way that the system will search for it. In many cases the 'request', as recorded by a search analyst, is not a true request at all (at least it resembles nothing that a requester would submit in his own natural language terms). Rather, it is a 'pseudo-Boolean statement': a string of MeSH or MeSH-like terms put together in some relationship.

As a consequence of this analysis the evaluators were able to make recommendations concerning the future pattern of user/system interaction, the index language, indexing and search strategy, and the need to achieve greater integration of these various activities.

9.10 Operational current-awareness service

During 1970-1972 an evaluation was undertaken by Leggate *et al.* (1971, 1973) of several current-awareness services (SDI) provided by computer search of magnetic tapes containing references to scientific articles. The databases used were of American origin, and were constructed in the USA, but the tapes were processed in the UK under the control of the project team. The overall system could be illustrated as shown in *Figure 9.9*.

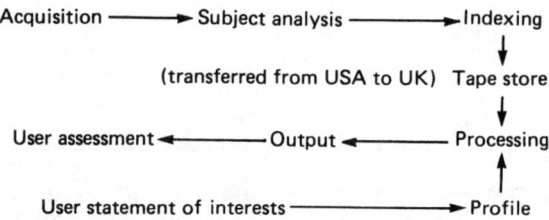

Figure 9.9 A model of the current-awareness test

The objective was to determine what effectiveness and efficiency could be achieved (given that the content of the databases was outside the UK's control). In the following account we will concentrate on the evaluation of one particular SDI service, *BA Previews*.

There was no prior population of users available for sampling—users had to be recruited by the offer of free service to scientists in academic, industrial, and government research. Some attempt was made to obtain a representative sample by recruiting a quota of users in each relevant subject area. Service was given for about a year to 300 users, half of whom agreed to take part in a more detailed phase of evaluation. This latter was based on more intensive analysis of about one month's service.

Each participant was interviewed at length to provide a narrative statement of his current literature requirements. From this, project staff created a search statement, a 'profile', consisting of search terms appropriately combined. Each profile was matched against the records on the current magnetic tape of *BA Previews* (there were three tapes each month). A printout of the matching references was sent to the user. During the general evaluation users could adjust their statements of requirements (and hence their profiles) to achieve better performance, but during the more detailed phase, profiles were held steady.

After receiving each printout the user reported on the number of items retrieved, the number of 'major value' (certainly related to interests), and the number of 'minor value' (of marginal interest). Relevance assessment was normally based on the references provided, not on the full documents. For the detailed evaluation, users were also asked to indicate, for each relevant reference, whether it was already known.

Both the general and the detailed evaluation phases permitted calculation of precision ratios, and these did not greatly differ (general phase 39.6 per cent, detailed phase 38.6 per cent, for total relevant). The detailed evaluation also permitted calculation of a novelty ratio (the proportion of relevant items not already known to the recipient): for items of major value 57 per cent, and for total relevant 77 per cent. This indicated that the *BA Previews* service was considerably less current than alternative sources scanned by the users (such as primary journals).

To estimate recall, each participant in the detailed evaluation was asked to provide a list of up to 30 relevant (major or minor value) references 'found by your normal methods of searching the current literature', from any source except *Biological Abstracts* (to which *BA Previews* is related). This sample was supplemented by a list of items found by project staff search of alternative databases, which was assessed by the user as to relevance. Overall results were as shown in *Table 9.5*.

Table 9.5 Estimation of recall

	User sample	Alternative sample	Total sample
Items in sample	1283	1478	2761
Items in *BA Previews*	950	1054	2004
Items in current *BA Previews*	705	795	1500
Items retrieved	414	460	874
Recall ratio	59%	58%	58%
Coverage ratio	74%	71%	73%

For estimating relative recall it was necessary to exclude from the recall set any items not in the current *BA Previews* tapes under test: recall is therefore the ratio between the fourth and third lines of the table. The same sample sets were used to give an estimate of relative coverage—the ratio between the second and first lines.

A subsidiary test was undertaken to ascertain whether relevance assessment would differ significantly if users were presented with full articles rather than just references. For the detailed evaluation phase, 7–12 English-language items were selected at random from the printout of each user and the corresponding articles submitted for assessment.

For references assessed as relevant, 90 per cent of the corresponding documents were similarly assessed; for references assessed as not relevant, 78 per cent of the documents were similarly assessed. In other words, 10 per cent of the references judged relevant were 'down-graded' on seeing the articles, but 22 per cent of the references judged not relevant were 'upgraded'. Overall, for 83 per cent of the items the assessment was the same.

Further assessment of the service was obtained by asking all participants (about midway through the year) to complete a questionnaire. Percentage responses included:

	%
Precision: Too many irrelevant references	43
Recall: Profile retrieves references I might not otherwise find	
—of major value	48

—of minor value	71
Misses too many relevant references	10
Coverage: Profile covers journals I would not normally see	78
Journal coverage is inadequate	9
Time saving: Service reduces time spent searching the literature	39
Delay: Too much delay between publication and appearance in *BAP*	47
Interest in a permanent service? Yes	69
No	17
Don't know	14
Service worth £50-75 per year? Yes	40
No	39
Don't know	21

The *BA Previews* project did not go on to analyse failures, primarily because relatively few variables were under the control of the search service—they could change the methods of eliciting statements of user interest and of profile construction but could not alter the acquisition, subject analysis, and indexing policies of the database producers, nor the time delay between article publication and delivery of the reference tape for search.

9.11 Online search service

In 1974 the University of London initiated a wide-ranging study to assess how best the University might make use of machine-readable sources of bibliographic information and data. Among other activities, an experimental central service was set up to provide online access to publicly available databases. During 1975/1976, the use of this service was formally monitored and evaluated (Vickery and Vickery, 1978; Vickery and Batten, 1978).

The chosen target population was the academic staff and postgraduates in science, engineering, and social science departments. This was a population of about 20000 working in over sixty institutions within the federal University. Administrative data were available showing their subject distribution within each institution, and these data were used to set up a sample list of eight institutions that, between them, would provide a representative range of potential users in the chosen subject fields. It was initially decided to concentrate on these institutions, though usage was not restricted to them: staff and postgraduates from other institutions requested service, and the medical schools in particular displayed an active interest. Eventually, users from 21 of the University's institutions provided over 2300 online search sessions for evaluation. The overall subject distribution of searches reasonably reflected the subject distribution of the parent population, though medical and biological usage was over-represented.

Queries were elicited in two ways:

(1) By advertising the existence of the central service to academic departments, academic boards and to academic staff individually;
(2) By taking a 'travelling workshop' on 96 visits to 20 institutions, each visit advertised to appropriate staff and postgraduates in the institution.

Most searches were carried out by the information officers employed on the project, in the presence of the enquirers. Each session was continued until searcher and enquirer agreed that no further online interaction was worthwhile, so the 'act of retrieval' was individually defined for each search.

In return for a free search with a printout of bibliographic references retrieved, each user was asked to provide the following: a relevance assessment of each reference, a subsequent report on his or her use of the references, a general comment on the search, and a statement as to whether the result justified the cost (which was reported to the user). The average results of an online session were as follows:

References displayed online	17
Assessed as relevant	9
Precision ratio	52%
Relevant references new to user	7
Novelty ratio	74%
References ordered offline	60
Precision ratio for these	53%
Novelty ratio for these	60%

A sample of respondents provided data on use of references: of an average of 18 new relevant references retrieved, 13 were subsequently read. The project did not attempt to measure recall or to undertake failure analysis. The expressed reactions of users to the search were: 37 per cent very satisfactory, 45 per cent satisfactory, 11 per cent could be satisfactory on another occasion, 7 per cent not satisfactory. A large amount of more detailed comment was collected.

In this evaluation the exact level of performance achieved was not of prime importance. The project sought to demonstrate (and did so to the satisfaction of the University authorities) that computer searches could provide relevant information that in many cases would otherwise either not be obtained or be obtained only by a considerable time investment in searching printed sources, and that the costs associated with the search were acceptable to those who would have to meet them.

9.12 Experimental study of retrieval

The Center for Documentation and Communication Research was set up at Case Western Reserve University in about 1955, and its Comparative Systems Laboratory was initiated late in 1963, with the specific task of systematically comparing the behaviour of various experimentally constructed information retrieval systems. After five years of work, to which over fifty people contributed at various times, they reported in 1968 (Saracevic, 1968).

The objectives of the research were to:

(1) Define the essential components of a reference retrieval system and to construct a system model;
(2) Identify variables affecting the performance of the system;

(3) Design a method of experimentally obtaining quantitative information on system performance;

(4) Construct an experimental system and assess its performance in relation to specified variables;

(5) Gain further understanding of the variables and processes within retrieval systems and of experimental methods for studying them.

The potentially variable components of a retrieval system were identified by intellectual analysis as:

(1) Subject field in which system operates;
(2) Type of users to be served;
(3) Size of the reference file;
(4) Method of selecting documents for analysis;
(5) Mode of reference file organization;
(6) Documentary source for subject analysis (title, abstract, full text);
(7) Indexing language used;
(8) Representation of index terms (English language or code);
(9) Source of terms for search statement;
(10) Width of search (narrow or broad);
(11) Format of output presented for relevance assessment (reference only, abstract, full text).

For the main experimental system it was decided to hold the first five variables and the last constant, and to vary the other five. With nine variant index languages (including variant documentary sources and term representations) and five types of search statements for a narrow search (only one for a broad search), there were in fact $9 \times 6 = 54$ configurations whose performance could be assessed.

At this stage in an experiment the choice of variables to examine depends upon (1) previous general experience of the system studied and (2) the results of any earlier experimentation. Width of experience is the only guarantee that important variables have not been overlooked or unwisely held constant; and that the range chosen for each variable suitably reflects possibilities. None of the five variables ((6)–(10) in the above list) was measured on a cardinal scale; for variables (6) and (10), ordinal scales were proposed.

The causal model postulated was that each of the chosen five variables, other conditions being held constant, would affect performance. The experiment aimed to test the postulate and to quantify the expected effects. Subsidiary tests did in fact look at other variables—such as indexer consistency.

The next problem was to decide how to measure system performance. The size of the system had to be decided (how many reference documents, how many test questions). Files were created for each of the 27 documentary source/index language combinations, and test questions posed by subject experts were searched in various ways. The objective was to maximize the retrieval of relevant references and to minimize the retrieval of irrelevant ones. Relevance was assessed by the subject experts, each of whom examined the references retrieved from all the searches for his question, and assigned a relevance to each such reference. For each search of each system configuration the usual data tabulation was constructed as in *Table 9.6* (numbers of references):

Table 9.6 References retrieved and relevant

	Relevant	Not relevant
Retrieved	a	b
Not retrieved	c	d

From these data three performance measures were derived, namely:

Sensitivity: $Se = a/(a+c) = \text{recall}$
Specificity: $Sp = d/(b+d) = \text{fallout}$
Effectiveness: $ES = Se+Sp-1$

The measure(s) chosen for a dependent variable must adequately reflect the performance objectives and be suitable for whatever mathematical manipulation may be desired. It is much to be preferred that, as in this case, they are on cardinal scales, since this permits more sophisticated manipulation.

To carry out the experiment it was necessary to set up index files in as controlled a manner as possible. Working procedures were established in relation to each of the eleven listed components. This involved the compilation of a set of procedure manuals covering (1) the use of index language, (2) the formulation of search statements, (3) the development of search strategy, and (4) interaction with subject experts. It was necessary to select and train indexers and question analysts, to develop work plans for them, and to prepare instructions on relevance assessment. Routines for searching the computer-held index files were compiled.

The practical details of the inquiry were as follows: 600 documents on tropical diseases were selected, and the title, abstract, and full text of each were separately indexed by five different indexing languages; 124 questions submitted by 25 specialist users were put to each index, varying the question analysis and search strategy; the output of each search was evaluated by users presented separately with the bibliographical citations, the abstracts, and then the full texts; the evaluations consisted of relevance assessments, and the total number of relevant items in the collection was taken to be that collectively retrieved by all searches.

The documents indexed were a random selection from the 1273 items abstracted during 1960 in the *Tropical Diseases Bulletin*, whose abstracts were used as one of the input sources. The 'indexing languages' used were: (1) 'telegraphic'—extracted or assigned terms, relations between terms being expressed by the use of role indicators and levels; (2) humanly extracted keywords; (3) keywords extracted by computer after exclusion of stop words; (4) the index entries prepared for the *Bulletin*; and (5) a 'meta-language' of abstract and concrete terms. The questions came from users actively engaged in research in tropical diseases. Each question was (i) analysed into unit concepts and was then expanded in two ways: (ii) using a locally prepared thesaurus; (iii) using any other tool (dictionary, reference work, etc.); then (iv) terms in (iii) were further expanded using the thesaurus, and (v) terms in (iv) were modified after consultation with the user. Two types of search strategy were used: in (1) all the concepts in the original question were retained (narrow search) and in (2) the coordination level was reduced to give 'the most general subject aspect' (broad search).

Let us look at some of the results. As already noted, three sources of input were separately indexed, thus leading to variation in depth or exhaustivity of indexing (*Table 9.7*).

Table 9.7 Variation in indexing

	Titles	Abstracts	Texts
Average words in source	5–9	250–400	2000–4000
Average terms in index	5–8	23–30	36–40

Index languages (1) and (2) were applied to all three sources, languages (3) and (5) only to titles. As exhaustivity increased, output and sensitivity rose, and 'specificity' fell, but 'effectiveness' was highest for abstracts. There seemed to be an optimum level of exhaustivity.

Comparisons using different indexing languages at the same level of exhaustivity gave no clear evidence that they significantly affected performance. This is not surprising, for the languages did not differ in any clearly defined way. Question expansion, however, did affect performance. The output, sensitivity, and 'effectiveness' was highest for expansion (iv), for which 'specificity' was the lowest. Of particular interest is the finding that expansion (iii) led to a much more marked change in performance than (ii)—i.e. the locally prepared thesaurus was a relatively inadequate tool of question expansion. The experimenters drew the conclusion that the prior preparation of a thesaurus may not have been worthwhile, but they did not conclude that expansion of the terms of a question was unnecessary: on the contrary, it was an essential step in improving recall and 'effectiveness'.

Other conclusions drawn were as follows: role indicators were of relatively little use; maximum recall could only be achieved by broad search strategy, and then only at the cost of very low precision; contact with users to amend question analysis was not beneficial; human decisions on indexing, question analysis, search strategy, etc. were the major influencing factors affecting performance.

What guidance, in broad terms, did the inquiry give to the designer of retrieval systems? It confirmed the interaction of indexing depth and performance; it told us nothing about the effect of index-language specificity; it stressed the importance and difficulty of question expansion and search strategy, but concluded that no general methods of optimizing them could yet be stated; it suggested that the effectiveness of retrieval systems was generally low—'a fact of life that (we) will have to learn to live with'.

Was this complex, lengthy, expensive, and involved project worthwhile? To all who took part in it, as an education in retrieval problems and in test design, it was undoubtedly valuable, and some of this educational value was passed on to the reader. However, the most general conclusion stated by CWRU was that, at present, real and productive testing of total retrieval systems was not feasible—it could do no more than uncover some gross effects and define problems. What was needed was more detailed experimentation on particular operations within the whole retrieval process—for example, on how to optimize question expansion. Despite the meagreness of its practical results, the CWRU inquiry brought us a little nearer to understanding how and on what to experiment. It was another step forward in the slow progress of our discipline towards science.

9.13 Availability on demand

The most immediate indication to a user of the performance of an information system is whether a demand for information can be met. When the sought information is embodied in particular documents that may or may not be in store we can speak of the availability of documents on demand. Repeated lack of availability will be interpreted subjectively by the user as poor performance. Delay in provision of documents or other services—lack of immediate availability on demand—will be similarly interpreted.

Non-availability of an item in a store may be absolute: it has never been put into the store. Evaluations of coverage, already discussed, assess this aspect of performance. An item may be in store but fail to be found when sought: this aspect of performance is assessed by an evaluation of recall in retrieval. When a document is physically removed from store for use, non-availability can be due to a collision of demands. This aspect has already been discussed from some points of view in the previous chapter, with particular reference to the modelling of book use. A wholly empirical study of demand collision will now be reported.

The most frequent way of using a library store is to look for particular books on the shelves. Each failure to find a sought book counts in the searcher's mind as an instance of non-availability. Because these searches are largely unobserved and unrecorded, the volume and nature of 'failure at the shelf' may be unknown to the library manager, yet it is a potent factor in user assessment of library performance. A technique to evaluate this aspect of availability was developed by Urquhart and Schofield (1971), and applied in academic libraries.

Readers were asked to record failures by completing a slip (taken from bundles hung at the shelves) and placing it on the shelf where they had sought the book. The slip recorded the call number of the book (or author and title if the call number was unknown), the date, and the status of the reader. Interviews with readers indicated that two thirds of them cooperated in the survey. All books used were reshelved by library staff, after noting where they had been (on loan, being bound, used within library), and matched against failure slips. At the end of the survey there was a check of all failure slips not yet matched.

The survey period was three months, during which time over 6000 failure slips were placed on the shelves: if all readers had cooperated fully, perhaps 9000 failures would have been recorded. Over the same period, 25000 books were borrowed and a number used in the library—regrettably not known, but perhaps between 10000 and 20000. If we put this last figure at 15 000, the total book use is estimated as 40 000, as against possibly 9000 failures, an overall success rate of 40/49, or about 80 per cent.

In the particular place first studied (Cambridge University Library), borrowing was allowed to those with MA status (graduate faculty), BA status (graduate research), and third year undergraduate. Other undergraduates were restricted to in-library use. The causes of the 6000 failures were analysed as follows:

		%
(1)	Borrowed by MA	26.9
(2)	by BA	6.5
(3)	by third year	20.6
(4)	In use in library	30.5
(5)	Binding	1.0
(6)	Book found on shelf	6.2
(7)	Book missing from stock	2.0
(8)	Cause not identified	6.3

Cause (6) could arise from reader oversight or looking at the wrong place on the shelf. A comparison between dates of failure and dates of reshelving gave estimates of the mean waiting times for books causing failure:

Type of borrower	MA	BA	Third-year	In-library
Mean time (days):	30.1	10.3	8.3	11.4

Often a book borrowed or used internally caused more than one failure (*Table 9.8*).

Table 9.8 Failure analysis

Fails	1	2	3	4	5+	Totals
Number of books:	2102	510	203	122	150	3087
Number of failures:	2102	1020	609	488	1098	5317

If we exclude the single fails, less than 1000 books accounted for about 60 per cent of recorded failures at the shelf—1000 out of a library collection of half a million books on open access. Judicious duplication could reduce the number of failures—even though in every three-month period it would not be exactly the same thousand books most in demand. The papers by Urquhart and Schofield give the results of more detailed analyses. A general survey of availability studies has been made by Mansbridge (1986).

9.14 Variables affecting availability

A study by Buckland *et al.* (1970) is particularly interesting from the viewpoint of system design. The investigator first examined issues from a short-term loan collection in a university library, from which books could be borrowed for up to four hours, there being four possible loan periods in a long working day. Because of heavy demand, individual books could be

Table 9.9 Short-loan availability table

Requests per day (s)	Copies provided = n									Copies required for		
	1	2	3	4	5	6	7	8	9	80%	90%	95%
0.4	95	100								1	1	1
0.5	94	100								1	1	2
0.6	93	100								1	1	2
0.7	92	100								1	1	2
0.8	91	99	100							1	1	2
0.9	90	99	100							1	1	2
1	88	99	100							1	2	2
2	79	97	100							2	2	2
3	70	93	99	100						2	2	3
4	63	90	98	100						2	2	3
5	57	86	96	99	100					2	3	3
6	52	81	94	98	100					2	3	4
7	47	77	92	97	99	100				3	3	4
8	43	73	89	96	99	100				3	4	4
9	40	69	86	95	98	99	100			3	4	4
10	37	65	83	93	98	99	100			3	4	5
12	32	58	78	89	96	98	99	100		4	5	5
14	28	52	72	85	93	97	99	100		4	5	6
16	25	47	66	80	90	95	98	99	100	4	5	6
18	22	43	61	76	86	93	97	98	99	5	6	7
20	20	39	57	71	82	90	95	98	99	5	6	7

This table shows percentage availability in relation to the request rate and the number of copies provided. The numbers have been rounded.

duplicated. Whether a request for a book could be satisfied depended on (1) the number n of copies of the book and (2) the number s of requests for it in a single loan period. It was assumed (with some experimental evidence) that the variation in numbers of requests for a book over several loan periods could be described by a Poisson distribution. From the formula developed on this basis it was possible to produce *Table 9.9* showing how availability on demand was affected by the provision of extra copies of a book, for various request rates. For example, if a book was, on average, requested twice a day, a single copy would be available only 79 per cent of the time, but adding another copy brought the availability up to 97 per cent, and with a third copy all requests would be met.

The only variable considered for change in this model is the number of copies held. In a more complex issue situation other variables can be manipulated—whether renewals are permitted or refused, whether books are recalled when reserved by a second potential user, and, above all, the official loan period, which correlates strongly with the use period (in this particular case, the 'use period' pattern was not negative exponential). An overview of the variables affecting user satisfaction is shown in *Figure 9.10*. Time of absence from the shelf is reduced by multiple copies, fewer books on loan (i.e. lower total demand), shorter loan periods, no renewals, recalls, lower frequency of demand per book, and low purchase of new books. In its turn, less absence from the shelf increases availability on demand, but decreases the total exposure of the user population to books. The overall situation is not static: if, for any reason, user satisfaction alters, this affects demand, and this in turn alters time of absence from the shelf.

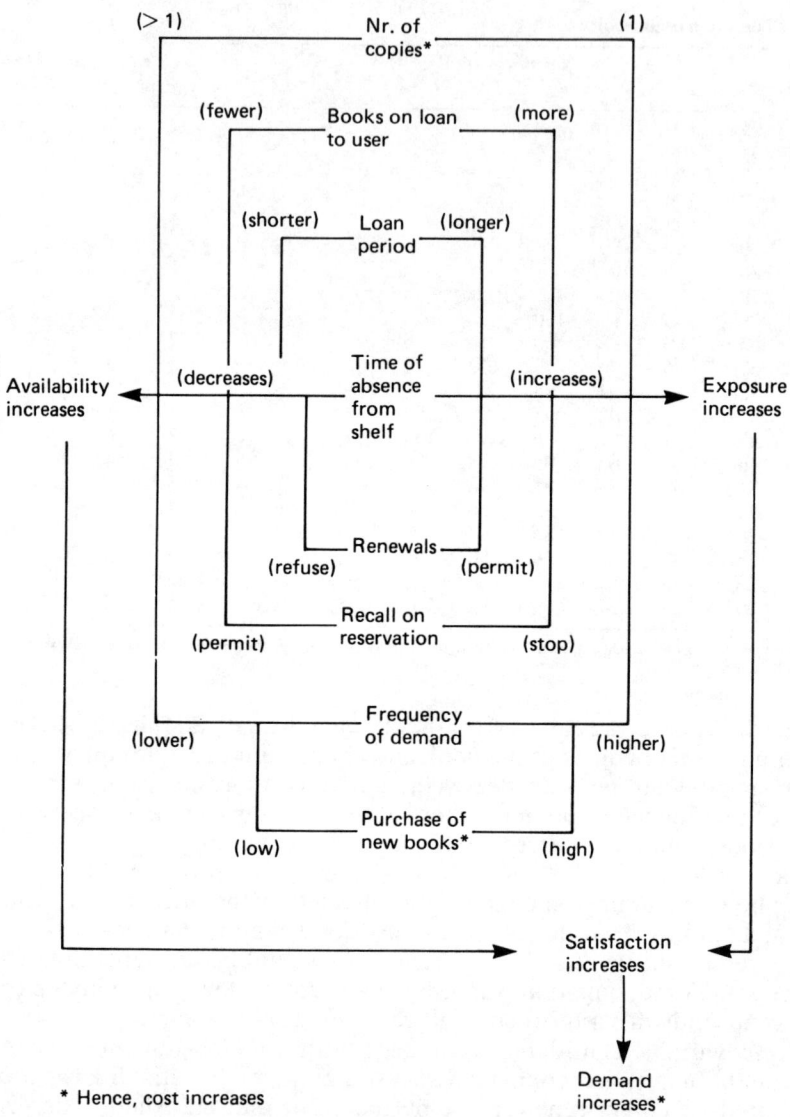

Figure 9.10 Variables affecting user satisfaction

This more complex situation was investigated by Buckland *et al.* (1970) using computer simulation. In the particular circumstances of the library studied (the University of Lancaster) it was decided to increase availability by a variable loan period (one week for the 10 per cent most popular books, three months for the rest). The effect was as shown in *Table 9.10*.

The change in loan policy (and subsequent further minor changes) increased availability from 62 per cent to 80 per cent; this raised user satisfaction and stimulated demand (from 32 issues per head to 51 and subsequently to 67). The increased demand resulted in increased time of absence from the shelf and brought availability down to its old level.

Table 9.10 Increase in availability

	Issues (1000)	Issues per user	Availability (%)
Old issue policy (1968/1969)	60	32	62
New policy (1969/1970)	125	51	80
(1970/1971)	167	57	?
(1971/1972)	186	64	?
(1972/1973)	202	67	60

One lesson for the information system designer is that collisions of demand may be minimized by (1) providing multiple copies of heavily demanded items of information, or permitting multiple simultaneous access to them, or (2) seeking ways of shortening use periods. A second lesson, to which we will return in a later section, is that user satisfaction and level of demand are interlinked. Changes in satisfaction can drive demand up (or down), and this in turn can affect satisfaction.

9.15 Document-delivery test

Evaluations of the availability on demand of items in a store, such as we have described, can be criticized from several points of view:

(1) Actual demand, as we have just noted, is affected by user perceptions. Users may not seek from a store items they believe not to be available in it or already in use. The actual demand, however recorded, is therefore unlikely to coincide with the total demand of the user community, and a performance measure based on it will overestimate the degree to which total demand is being catered for.
(2) Increasingly, libraries participate in interlending networks that can—in principle—give access to almost any sought document, provided that the recipient can accept some delay in supply. The overall ability of a library to make documents available is therefore a function not only of its own stock and procedures but also of its interconnections to the wider system of libraries. To measure this ability the criterion of success or failure to supply needs to be replaced by that of time taken to supply.

Based upon these considerations, Orr and his colleagues (1968) developed a 'document-delivery test' that involved the following steps:

(1) Create a set of demands that can be deemed to be representative of the total demand of a chosen user community;
(2) Check the 'availability state' of each item in the set at a chosen library;
(3) Find ways to determine or estimate the delivery time of each item;
(4) Combine the time data to produce a 'capability index' for the library.

The first step requires that the user community studied must be one whose use of documents can be identified independently of the demands they may make on the library under investigation. In practice, this has involved an indirect measure of use—the analysis of citations in the writings of a representative sample of the potential users (we have commented on this practice in the previous chapter). If the user community studied is 'concentrated' in a particular research institution, references in their published papers might be used to generate a sample set of items consulted. This could, however, still be biased towards what is readily available in their institution library. A more generally applicable set may be generated by the following procedure:

(1) Ask each member of a representative sample of the user community to list a number (x) of the most important journals in his subject;
(2) Combine the lists, and select the y highest-ranked titles;
(3) Examine the most recent annual volume of each selected journal and record all citations in it;
(4) Use this set, or a random sample from it, as representative of the total

Table 9.11 Document-delivery data sheet

Author(s) or Editor(s) (Books only)	/			Journal or book title	
Volume	/	Pages	/	Date	
Institutional source of citation: ____			Sample number ____	Case number ____	

1.
In medical library's collection?   (CIRCLE ONE)   No 1 → STOP   Yes 2 ↓

2.
On immediate premises?   (CIRCLE ONE)   No 1   (SPECIFY)   Yes 2 ↓
Storage site _____ (E.D.T. _____)
→ STOP

3.
On shelves?   (CIRCLE ONE)   No 1   Yes 2 ↓ STOP

4.   ↓ (CIRCLE ONE)

Off-shelf status		E.D.T.	Circulation 4	Can't locate in 1st search X
Bindery	1	(_____)		
In process	2	(available? Y N)		
In storage	3	(_____)		
Special location	5	(mediated? Y N____)		
To be shelved	6			
Recorded as missing	7			
Other known status	8	(_____)		

(SPECIFY _____)
→ STOP

5.   (CIRCLE ONE)
Circulation status   Loan period

Reserve	1	(____)	
Inter-library loan	2		
Faculty	3	(Recall? Y N) (____)	
Students	4	(Recall? Y N) (____)	
Other	5	(Recall? Y N) (____)	

(SPECIFY) _____
→ STOP

6.
Result of second search
On shelf	1
Can't locate	2
Other	3

(SPECIFY) _____
→ STOP

COMMENTS: (e.g. location tool problems)

demand generated by this kind of user community. A sample of 300 items is reckoned to be adequately reliable.

The delivery time for each item in the demand set could be obtained by presenting the demands to be met as part of the daily work routine of the chosen library. This is difficult to arrange, particularly if service is not to be biased by staff knowledge that a test is under way. A preferred method is to establish the 'availability state' of each item and the average delivery time for each state. A list of availability states applicable to an academic medical library is shown in *Table 9.11*. Observation, discussion with library staff, and examination of loan records are then used to assign to each availability state an average delivery time, using the speed indicators:

(1) Less than 10 minutes;
(2) From 10 minutes to 2 hours;
(3) From 2+ to 24 hours;
(4) From 1+ to 7 days;
(5) More than 7 days.

Each item in the set is thus assigned an indicator figure and these are then averaged to give a mean speed indicator. This is then normalized to give a 'capability index', using the formula:

$CI = 100 \times (5 - \text{mean speed})/4$

The *CI* is 100 if mean speed $= 1$, and is zero if mean speed $= 5$.

Penner (1972) conducted such a document-delivery test in two libraries concerned with librarianship, and presents a table incorporating his results and those of Orr's study of seven medical libraries (*Table 9.12*).

Table 9.12 Document-delivery test

	CI	Percentage owned
Librarianship X	56	49
Y	60	62
Medical A	86	89
B	81	88
C	81	84
D	83	83
E	76	73
F	75	71
G	67	58

The capability index is strongly correlated with the percentage of the test collection that is owned by the library. The value of *CI* does not make explicit the waiting times involved in supplying items, and it can usefully be supplemented by data on the proportion of demands subject to each delivery time, thus:

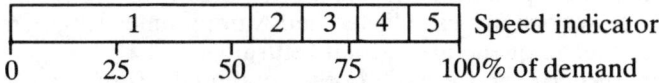

9.16 The effect of service delay

We have earlier made the point that in any kind of information service the time taken to provide service is regarded by recipients as an important aspect of its quality. In measuring delay, the emphasis—as in the document-delivery test—must be on the recipient's perception of elapsed time. There are often three time phases to be considered:

(1) Access: the time it takes for the prospective user to make contact with the information system;
(2) Queueing: the time between making contact and the actual start of service;
(3) Service: the time taken for a the system to provide the information sought.

For example, let us take the hypothetical case that a letter to a service requesting an online search receives an answer in five days (access time); the reply makes an appointment four days ahead (queueing time); travelling to and from the service takes 3 hours (more access time); the search process itself takes 45 minutes (service time). The online search may have taken only 15 minutes of connect time, but to the user the time between request and result is 10 days. The document-delivery test measures service delay. In this section we will consider the effect of queueing.

Every service agency, such as a post office, a bank, a restaurant, or a hospital casualty department, is aware of the impatience and frustration caused by queueing and may seek to speed service so as to reduce the length of queues and the waiting times. If the actual service time cannot be reduced the only alternative is to increase the number of service points—which means more staff or more self-service. If the number of service points is increased to meet peak demand at other times they will be idle, and this factor usually makes it uneconomic to eliminate queues altogether. In some such situations each customer may have an inescapable need for the service and no alternative but to wait. In others, waiting may prove intolerable and customers will in time quit the queue. Queueing theory, discussed in the previous chapter, has developed mathematical models of these situations.

Here we are concerned with the longer-term impact of queueing on demand, using the particular example of an information service offering online searches. This problem was first investigated by Lindquist (1978a,b). He started from the observation that newly formed services of this kind, after an initial period of expanding demand, then experienced a decline in use. On investigation, Lindquist concluded that the pattern could be explained by the following sequence of events:

Service offered with an initial work capacity
Demand builds up until it exceeds work capacity of service
Queues for service are established and waiting times lengthen
Customers leave queue and do not return
Rumours of poor service inhibit other potential customers
Demand declines to a level that can be handled by existing work capacity

Lindquist constructed a computer simulation model of the situation, using the method of 'system dynamics' (originated by Forrester, 1961).

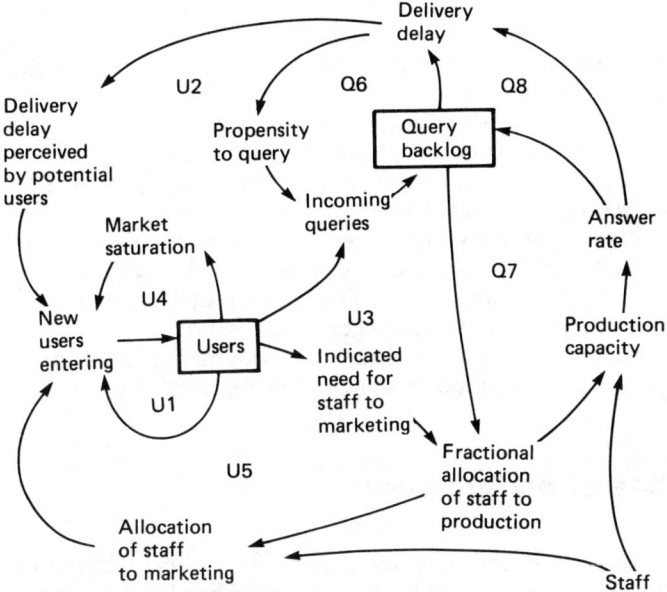

Figure 9.11 Influence diagram in system dynamics

This method develops an event sequence such as that shown above into an 'influence diagram' relating clearly defined variables, *Figure 9.11* being an example of this. Then, based on empirical or hypothesized data, quantitative relations between linked variables are established. The whole cycle of interaction is then represented in the form of a set of mathematical equations that can be fed into a system dynamics program and manipulated by computer. The quantitative values can be altered at will to explore the anticipated effects of varying assumptions or policies.

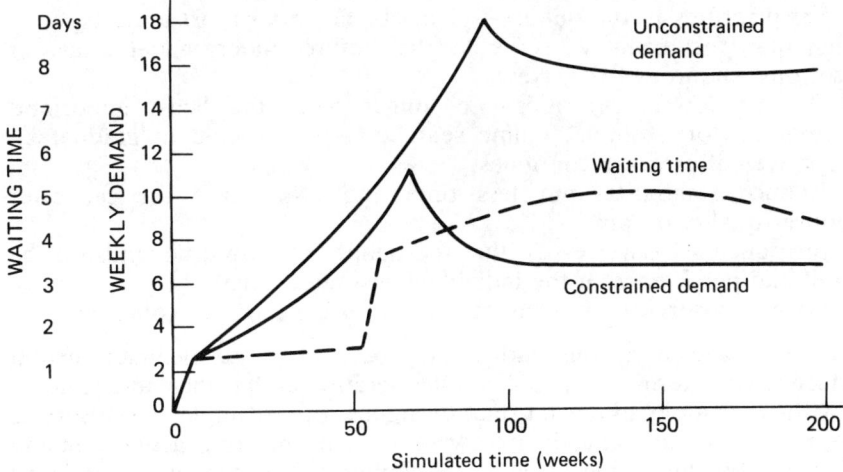

Figure 9.12 Effect of constraints on demand

Lindquist's work was taken further in a project at University College London, reported by Heseltine (1982) (and in more detail by Vickery *et al.*, 1984). The system dynamics program generates data on the changing values of its variables over time, and these can be displayed in tables or graphically. Typical results are incorporated in to *Figure 9.12*.

The top curve in *Figure 9.12* simulates how demand will develop if it is not constrained—if additional online staff and terminals are provided to keep pace with the growing demand. Eventually, the market is saturated, and demand settles down at a fairly high level. The lower curves simulate the situation when the initial low work capacity is not enhanced: waiting time increases, and demand remains well below the potential. That it is so far below may not be realized by the manager of the service.

Introductions to system dynamics techniques, and detailed discussions of the work outlined here, are provided in the references cited.

9.17 Degradation of performance

The situation just presented is one in which actual demand is inhibited by the lowered quality of service. An analogous situation has been analysed by Meier (1961, 1963), who hypothesized a growing service with an even more rapidly expanding set of customers, an irregular influx of messages with a strongly upward trend. As a typical example of such a communications system he examined a university library, and the 'messages' pouring in included publisher's announcements, items acquired, demands for loans, for seats, for reference information, for photocopies ... What happens when input begins to exceed work capacity? Performance starts to degrade, and Meier charted the course of this decline. Some of his policy stages are noted here:

(1) Queue inputs—with the possibility of the customer reactions just discussed. Then, as the pressure of demand increases,
(2) Set priorities in the queues—giving higher priority to some types of demand (for example, serve faculty before undergraduate; answer 'serious' enquiries first). Next,
(3) Destroy lowest priorities—no longer meet the 'least important' demands (for example, online searches are restricted to graduates). However, if pressure continues,
(4) Reduce standards—put less time and effort into service, offer poorer-quality output.
(5) Introduce self-service—so that the quality of output depends on the skill and persistence of the individual customer. Lastly,
(6) Withdraw service—we cannot cope, so it is not worth going on.

At any stage along this path it may be possible to evaluate current performance in terms of the policies in operation at that stage and to come up with what looks like a satisfactory figure. For example, a self-service information system may, in its own terms, be meeting actual demand effectively but be falling far short of coping with potential demand and the full needs of recipients. The implication is that a realistic assessment of performance has to take into account the policies in force and their impact on the satisfaction of user needs.

9.18 The value of information

Early in this chapter we distinguished (following the practice of Orr) between the quality of a service and its value to recipients. The subsequent discussion has almost entirely been concerned with quality—effectiveness and performance. It is now time to consider the more difficult problem of value. At this stage the focus of attention is on the reaction of the recipient to information provided. What characteristics of information messages are considered to be of value, and to what extent can value be quantified?

In considering retrieval from store, two qualities of information have been introduced—information provided must be relevant to the enquirer's want and it must be novel (previously unknown to the recipient). We have previously suggested other criteria: information must be current and up to date; it must be reliable, accurate, free from error and bias; it must be in a readily assimilable form (as regards language, terminology, format, quantity, etc.). Each of these qualities can be used to derive a measure of performance—precision ratio, novelty ratio, currency, standard error of data, readability of output, etc. However, can we assess what value these qualities have for the recipient?

Information received changes the personal knowledge structure of the recipient: if there were a way to assess the magnitude of this change we might use this as a measure of the value of the information delivered. However, there is no immediate prospect of making such an assessment—and certainly not in the context of routine information system evaluation. Failing this, we fall back on the recipient's own subjective assessment of the value of information, asking him or her questions such as 'How satisfied were you with the information provided?' or 'How important was the information to your intended use?' Responses to such questions rarely provide anything more than a general impression as to whether or not a service is meeting needs. Measures based on them ('53 per cent said they were very satisfied') have little or no objective meaning, since they are affected by so many arbitrary factors.

Information is often acquired for a particular purpose, so a measure of value might be the proportion of information provided that is actually used for that purpose. If all information provided to all recipients were used we might claim that the service was giving 100 per cent value in its response to the demands put by those recipients. For example, if we assume that the purpose of an online search is to provide documents for current reading, then the Vickery and Batten finding, that on average 13 out of 18 new relevant references retrieved were read within a few months, could suggest a value rating of $13/18 = 72$ per cent. We do not know, however, whether other references were noted down for reading at some later date, and still less do we know what proportion of the information received in the reading was actually used in the work of the recipient. Blagden (1980) made a small study of ten architects receiving design data documents. All ten read the documents (value rating 100 per cent on this criterion) but only seven used the data in a specific design (value rating 70 per cent on this criterion).

9.19   The perceived value of information service

A commercial service may judge that its products are perceived to be of value if its customers are willing to pay for them. Any separate estimate of value then appears to be superfluous. However, if a service is not priced its users can be asked to estimate its value in monetary terms. This approach was adopted by Wolfe in the late 1960s (Wolfe, 1974).

A sample was taken of 315 research and development staff in 93 UK firms in the following industries: agriculture, aircraft, chemicals, electrical engineering, and textiles. They were interviewed at length about their needs for and uses of information service. The majority of respondents spent 70 per cent of their time on R&D (some, 90–100 per cent of their time). Of the time spent on R&D, 10–35 per cent was on information activities, and 19–37 per cent of this was spent on using secondary information sources (abstracts journals, current titles, other current-awareness services, etc.). The importance of these published secondary services, relative to other information sources, was assessed by asking respondents to distribute 100 points among four types of information source, with the overall result as shown in *Table 9.13*.

Table 9.13 Importance of published secondary services

	Points
Published secondary sources	33.8
Trade literature	21.4
Personal contact inside firm	24.8
Personal contact outside firm	20.7

The perceived value of secondary sources was assessed by responses to the following questions:

(1) Compare the present situation in which you and your colleagues have access to all the secondary information services with the hypothetical one in which none of these is available to any of you.

If you had the choice of having your present job with secondary information services at your present salary, or the same job with no secondary information services and an increased salary, how much increase in salary would you require before choosing the situation where no secondary information services were available?

£0	£200–£300
£0–£10	£300–£400
£10–£20	£400–£500
£20–£30	£500–£600

£30–£40	£600–£700
£40–£50	£700–£800
£50–£100	£800–£900
£100–£200	£900–£1000

If greater than £1000, then £—.

(2) (a) In the same hypothetical situation, with none of the services available to you, you may choose to spend some extra time in doing your own information work, or you may choose to adjust to the situation in some other way.

In order to show what you would do, please indicate the changes which you would make in the number of hours you would devote to the following:

(i) Research and development work, not including information work;
(ii) Information work;
(iii) Other work.

(b) If you reduce your research time, this will presumably reduce your research output. How many hours extra would you have to put in to maintain your previous research output?

(c) Please indicate the weekly average number of hours which you work.

The money measures used were:

(1) Increase in salary required;
(2) Proportion of working time lost to R&D, × annual salary;
(3) Proportional increase in time spent on R&D, × annual salary.

The resulting ranges of values obtained were (1) £120–£620, (2) £8–£212, (3) £10–£215 (to be compared with the average salary at that time, £2261). If these results are accepted, it appears that the overall subjective reaction to loss of secondary services (measure (1)) was considerably greater than the perceived effects on work (measures (2) and '(3)).

Such subjective estimates of working time saved by the availability of information can be made more objective. When translated into salary money, time saved can be represented as a cash benefit to be set against the cost of information provision. Several studies of industrial information service have followed this approach (Mason, 1973; Magson, 1973).

9.20 Conclusion

During the last two decades increasingly sophisticated techniques of evaluation have been developed by information science and applied to experimental or operational services and systems. The range of procedures available has been well surveyed by Martyn and Lancaster (1981). All these studies have served to emphasize the complexity of the process of information transfer and the multiplicity of factors affecting performance. Evaluation continues to be a difficult and uncertain art.

Chapter 10

Information in society

The overall pattern of information transfer in society has been represented in the simplest way as $S - C - R$, where S is any source (individual, group, or institution), R is any recipient (similarly categorized), and C is any channel. The information needs and behaviour of many social groups have been explored in Chapter 4. Channels have been discussed from the viewpoint of systems analysis in Chapter 8. To conclude our survey of information science we wish to look at the overall pattern in sociological terms.

As is clear from earlier discussions, information systems are but one of the channels by which people acquire information. We could set them in the following context:

Foundation knowledge	*Continuing and current*	*On-demand information*
Family	Mass media	Friends
Education	Meetings	Colleagues
Training	Publications	Specialists
		Advisory agencies
		Information systems

An adequate understanding of information provision in society requires that attention be paid to the contribution of all such channels.

The sociology of communication in general is much better developed than corresponding approaches to informative communication. The study of mass communication, for example, asks questions about the social roles of the channel agents (newspaper, radio, television), whether the information they transmit is selective or biased, how such selectivity or bias may be related to the social positions of those who control the mass media, the extent to which the opinions and knowledge of recipients are influenced or even moulded by mass media messages. The sociology of education—a foundation activity closely linked to information provision—likewise discusses the social roles of educational agencies, possible limitations to the knowledge embodied in curricula, inequality of access to educational facilities, the economics of educational provision and how it should be financed. Questions of this kind are only beginning to be asked about information provision. Consequently the presentation in this chapter will be more concerned with identifying problem areas than with reporting the conclusions of research.

10.1 Information-transfer channels

Figure 10.1 is a broad representation of the formal channels via which informative messages are transmitted from sources to recipients. Expertise possessed by an individual (or collectively by a group or institution) can be communicated orally, face to face, by telephone, by a public presentation, or by using radio or television. A recorded message embodying expert knowledge can be communicated directly by mail (including electronic mail) or can be published and distributed to a number of recipients.

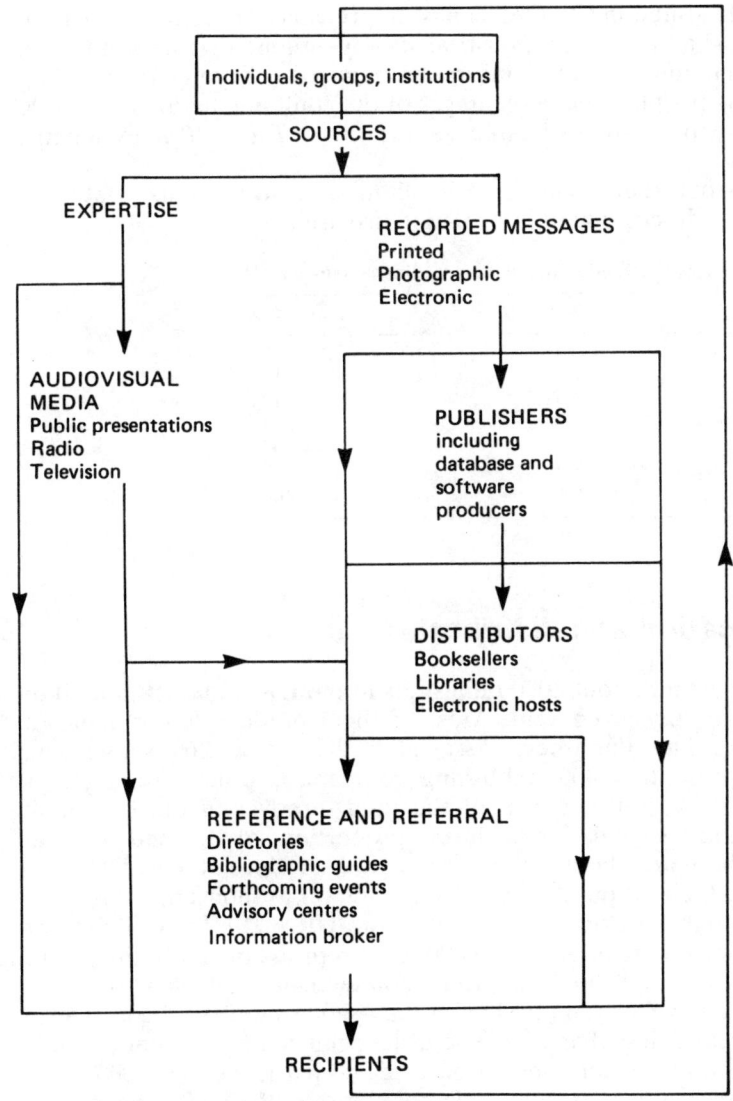

Figure 10.1 Formal information channels

Reference and referral agencies and their products can lead the enquirer to sources of expertise, to forthcoming public presentations and broadcasts, to messages (published and unpublished), to publishers, and to distributors. Recipients can themselves become sources. To make the discussion more concrete, recent data relating to UK channels will now be presented. We will describe first the various agencies handling printed materials, leaving until later some comments on the impact of information technology.

For five centuries, printed materials have grown in importance as the medium for the storage and transfer of informative messages. They were at first accessible only to a minority of the population, but the steady growth of literacy (illustrated in Chapter 1) has, in principle, brought them within reach of almost all people in industrial society—though we have noted in Chapter 4 that much printed information may be beyond the reading ability of some people. The percentages of the adult population of the UK reading newspapers are estimated as shown in *Table 10.1* (Williams, 1965).

Print on paper remains a basic medium, and justifies its continued importance in a description of information provision.

Table 10.1 Percentages of UK adult population reading newspapers

	Dailies	*Sundays*
1820	1	1
1860	3	12
1875	11½	19
1900	18	33
1920	54	→ 100
1930	75	→ 100
1947	→ 100	→ 100

10.2 Publication and distribution

There are altogether about 2000 publishers in the UK, although not all of them publish in any given year. Most of them produce fewer than ten books a year. The Publishers Association has some 260 subscribing members, representing 400 publishing companies, which are together responsible for over 90 per cent of the total turnover of the UK book publishing industry and for a large proportion of learned journal publishing. There are about 120 publishers that produce at least 50 books each year, and their output distribution in 1979 was as shown in *Table 10.2*.

The total number of titles published in the UK in 1981 was 43000, of which 34000 were new books and 9000 were reprints or new editions. In 1984, there were 375000 books in print, commercially available in the UK.

It is estimated by Curwen (1981) that the *average* number of copies sold per title per year is less than 300. The usual print run for a monograph is 1000–2000 copies, and for a textbook it is 500 hardback and 2000–3000 paperback copies. For a general paperback, a sale of 25000 is needed to cover costs.

Table 10.2 Publishers' output distribution

Number of new books	Number of publishers
600–700	2
500–600	1
400–500	4
300–400	6
200–300	4
100–200	45
50–100	60

The total annual turnover of the UK book publishing industry was reported by the Publishers Association in 1982 as £800 million, of which perhaps £100 million came from purchases by libraries. In an analysis of the 1978 net revenue of their 71 core members (who between them account for nearly 90 per cent of total turnover), the Publishers Association has provided the data for home sales (*Table 10.3*).

Table 10.3 Publishers' net revenue for home sales

Category of book	Percentage of net revenue
School texts	18.2
University:	
Science/Technology	4.6
Medicine	2.4
Business/Industry	1.3
Law	4.5
Humanities/Social Sciences	3.2
Journals	3.7
Specialized (encyclopedias, dictionaries, atlases, etc.)	8.6
General:	
Hardback	35.1
Paperback	18.4
	100.0

The terms 'periodicals' and 'serials' include newspapers, magazines, trade journals, and annual reports, as well as learned or scholarly journals. *Willings Press Guide* for 1982 lists 6551 UK periodicals plus 1895 annuals. Included in the guide is a list of 120 'leading publishers', who between them produce about 2500 titles. The range of subjects with serial publication is shown by the following 10 per cent sampling of the Willings 'classified index' (the bracketed figures are the numbers of UK titles in each subject):

Accountancy	(24)	Dentistry	(23)
Administration	(7)	Fancy goods	(13)
Advertising	(39)	Fashion	(12)
Africa	(35)	Films	(2)
Building	(102)	Finance	(84)
Building societies	(3)	Horticulture	(39)
Business management	(106)	Hospitals	(39)
Dancing	(10)	Hotels	(31)
Deaf and dumb	(7)	Machinery	(31)
Decoration	(12)	Market gardening	(5)
Defence	(23)	Marketing	(29)

Numismatics	(7)	Television	(2)
Nursing	(27)	Temperance	(8)
Nutrition	(11)	Tennis	(6)
Oceans	(15)	Textiles	(42)
Office management	(14)	Theatre	(27)
Offical reports	(12)	Theology	(25)
Oil and petrol	(32)	Woman's wear	(14)
Roman Catholic	(46)	Woodwork	(6)
Rubber	(12)	Work study	(15)
Rugby football	(8)	Yachting, etc.	(47)
Rural life	(60)	Youth	(33)
Safety	(24)		

In respect of learned or scholarly journals, considerable analysis has been carried out by Singleton (in Curwen). No clear picture emerges of the total number of such journals published in the UK. The number of UK serial titles received in 1978 at the BLLD was over 8000, but Singleton suggests that only half of these can be regarded as learned or scholarly journals.

There are many 'learned journal' publishers, a large number of whom publish only one title. There is one prolific publisher who accounts for more than 200 titles, but the next in size all have less than 100 titles. The prolific publishers are mainly commercial firms, although the journals they publish are often produced with the cooperation of a learned society. Over 500 societies are involved in journal publication—either directly or through a commercial firm—the distribution of journals among 400 of these societies being as follows:

| No. of journals | 1 | 2 | 3 | 4 | 5 | 8 | 9 |
| No. of societies | 355 | 29 | 11 | 1 | 1 | 2 | 1 |

Another survey of over 400 learned society journals has produced the circulation data shown in *Table 10.4*.

Table 10.4 Circulation of learned society journals

Subject area	Number of journals	Circulation	
		Mean	Median
Philosophy/Psychology	18	1950	1500
Social Sciences	51	6500	1500
Languages	4	2350	1450
Science	102	3045	1950
Medicine/Technology	168	6500	2900
Architecture/Arts	14	3700	1300
Literature	7	2200	230
Geography/History	67	1600	800

In many fields of information literature—for example, science and technology—foreign publications are important and much used in the UK. Indeed, many US publishers also appear under a London imprint. The total number of publishers and of items published that are relevant to UK information provision is therefore greater than is suggested here.

There are estimated to be about 36000 outlets in the UK for the sale of books, over half of them newsagents. About 3000 are members of the

Booksellers' Association and perhaps a thousand are real, stockholding bookshops. There is a core of 350 firms that are 'chartered' booksellers, who between them sold books to the value of £137 million in 1981.

Subscription agents play an important role in the distribution of scholarly journals. Probably a dozen agents account for half the turnover in this field, but there are many hundreds of small agents, often booksellers. It is estimated that sales by subscription agents in 1978 came to £31 million.

10.3 The press and broadcasting

There are eleven national daily newspapers in the UK, with circulations ranging from over 3 million to 25 000. It is estimated that, on average, three people look at each copy sold, so that the total 'readership' of these eleven papers is about 40 million. The circulation of the nine national Sunday newspapers is from nearly 4 million to over half a million; the total 'readership' is estimated at over 50 million. Most large towns have an evening paper (more than one in London), and there are a total of 85 of these. Outside London, 15 towns have morning newspapers, and five have Sundays. About a thousand weekly papers are produced in Britain (though there is much duplication of content, and there are only about 200 separate weekly newsrooms). All these papers are fed by a national news agency, the Press Association, and by international agencies (Reuters, AFP, UPI, UNS). In 1977, newspaper sales netted £676 million.

Apart from the four channels of BBC Radio there are over 40 local radio stations (half are BBC and half commercial), and there are, of course, the four television channels. *Figure 10.2* shows television and radio stations as of 1979. It is estimated that about 42 million people watch television each day and 25 million listen to radio. The average volume of viewing is 18 hours per week, and of radio listening, nine hours. (The material in this section has mainly been drawn from a survey by MacShane, 1979.)

10.4 Abstracting and indexing services

An analysis was made by East in 1979 of an inventory of abstracting and indexing services produced in the UK. At that time there were 339 identified services produced by 157 publishers, who between them published nearly 3 million bibliographic references annually. The publishers are commercial firms, learned or professional societies, government bodies, academic institutions, research associations, and some international agencies. The subject distribution of services was as shown in *Table 10.5*. Service sizes vary widely. The number of new references per year is distributed as shown in *Table 10.6*.

10.5 Libraries and information services

The Department of Education and Science census of library and information staff in the UK, 1981, presented the figures given in *Table*

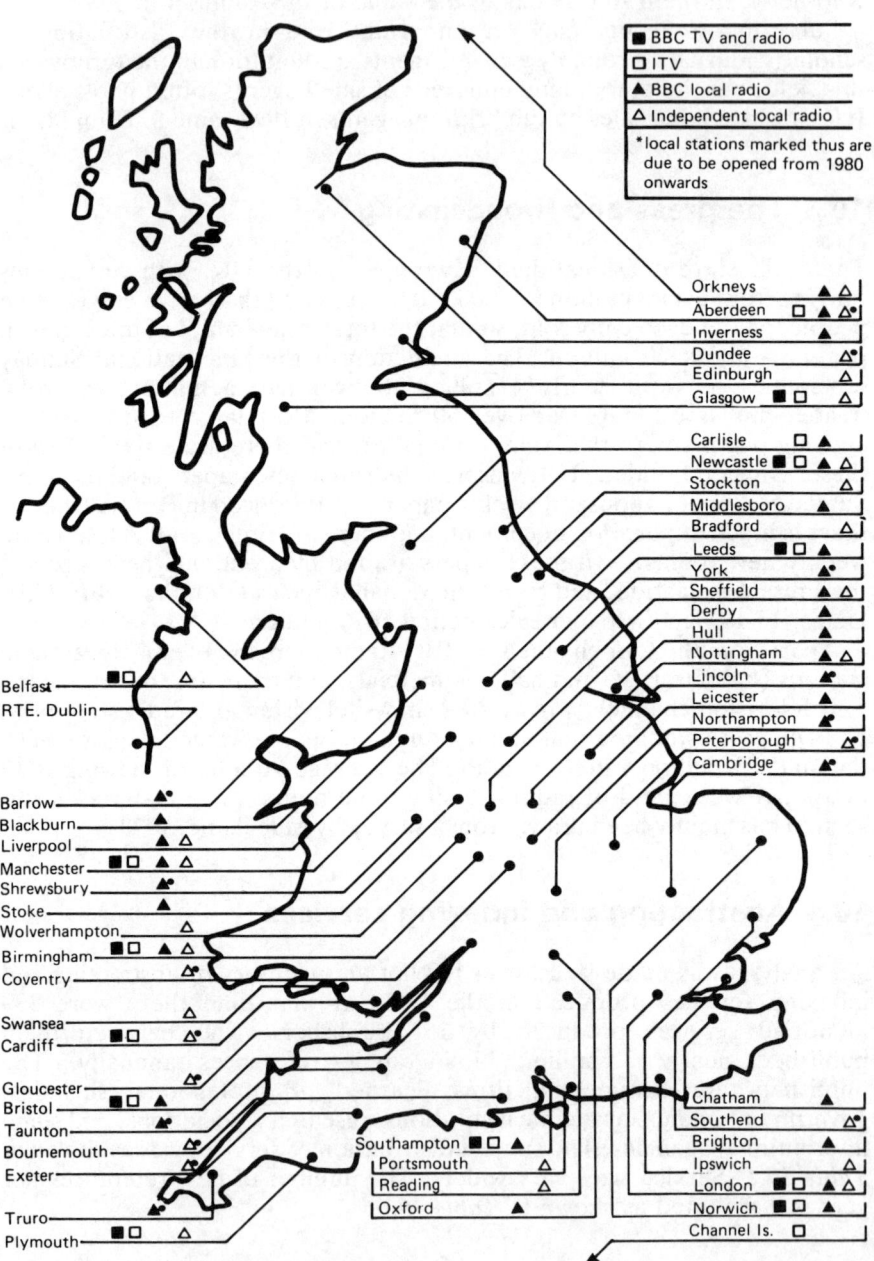

Figure 10.2 Television and radio stations in the UK

Table 10.5 Subject distribution of services

Subject area	%
General	4
Life Sciences	34
Physical Sciences	11
Engineering	31
Social Sciences	13
Arts, Humanities	7

Table 10.6 New references per year

	Percentage of services
Under 1000	22
1000–5000	40
5000–10000	17
10000–20000	10
20000–100000	6
Over 100000	5

Table 10.7 Census of UK library and information staff, 1981

Library type	Number of units	Number of staff Qualified	Other
Public library authorities	166	8328	16194
Other local government libraries	29	149	184
National	4	614	1780
University	195	1797	2488
Polytechnic	43	751	937
Other college	634	1296	1375
Government department	638	1058	1400
Public corporation	105	266	289
Industry and commerce	880	1625	1273
Learned and professional	132	399	236
Research and trade assoc.	101	295	239
Other	78	130	135
School	12	272	268
Totals	3017	16980	26798

10.7. Some of these figures are known to be too low: for example, about 2300 of the registered users of the British Library Lending Division are industrial or commercial organizations. The public library figure is misleading in that the unit is the statutory authority, not the physical library: there are in fact about 2700 full-time service points provided by public libraries. Some of the other 'units' figures (for example, for university or polytechnic libraries) can conceal multi-site situations; as can, indeed, the figure of four national libraries. The figures for school libraries are also much too small.

East (1984b) has estimated that the annual cost of UK libraries is of the order of £800 million (1982). The total available book stock is of the order of 250 million volumes, including about 20 million volumes in the national libraries (the British Library and the National Libraries of Scotland and Wales).

The varying average number of staff per unit, even allowing for multi-site situations, already indicates the considerable variation in library size, and this will be displayed in more detail below.

One important characteristic of nearly all types of library and information service is that their use is subsidized. The individual use of a public, academic, or special library or advice bureau is usually without charge. We will later be exploring this feature more closely.

10.6 Public libraries

There were in 1980/1981 some 160 public library authorities: 47 counties (England and Wales), 35 metropolitan districts, four non-metropolitan (Wales), 37 regions, districts or islands (Scotland), five boards (Northern Ireland) and 32 London Boroughs. Their total stock was 131 million volumes, and 637 million items were issued during the year (about 18 per cent of this was non-fiction, in some sense meeting an 'information' demand). About 13 million items were acquired, and a similar number of photocopy pages provided.

In terms of volumes of stock the size distribution of authorities in 1980/1981 was as given in *Table 10.8*. The number of books annually acquired was equally varied (*Table 10.9*). Total issues for each authority are not presented in the CIPFA statistics, but books on loan on a certain day are recorded. The average ratio of annual issues to the books on loan at one time is about 18 to 1 (*Table 10.10*).

Table 10.8 Volumes in stock, 1980/1981

Millions	Number of authorities
up to ¼	19
¼ to ½	43
½ to ¾	35
¾ to 1	19
1 to 1¼	13
1¼ to 1½	8
1½ to 1¾	8
1¾ to 2	3
2 to 3	7
over 3	4

Table 10.9 Number of books annually acquired

Thousands	Number of authorities
up to 25	19
25 to 50	36
50 to 75	47
75 to 100	18
100 to 125	15
125 to 150	5
150 to 175	7
175 to 200	1
200 to 300	8
over 300	3

Table 10.10 Average number of books on loan

Books on loan (thousands)	Number of authorities
up to 50	17
50–100	27
100–150	23
150–200	27
200–250	10
250–300	9
300–350	7
350–400	9
400–450	9
500–750	7
over 750	7

10.7 Educational libraries

There are nearly 60 university college libraries of 100 000 volumes or more, plus a considerable number of smaller college, institute, faculty, and medical school libraries in the larger universities. In terms of volumes of

Table 10.11 Size distribution of major libraries

Volumes (hundred thousands)	Number of libraries
1–2	13
2–3	7
3–4	12
4–5	4
5–6	4
6–7	7
7–8	2
8–9	2
9–10	0
Over 1 million	7

Table 10.12 Number of books annually acquired by major libraries

Acquisitions (thousands)	Number of libraries
up to 5	5
5–10	16
10–15	10
15–20	9
20–25	5
25–30	5
30 and over	5

Table 10.13 Loans to individuals per annum

Loans (thousands)	Number of libraries
up to 50	4
50–100	13
100–150	7
150–200	14
200–250	6
250–300	5
300–400	7
400 and over	5

stock, the size distribution of the major libraries in 1978 was as shown in *Table 10.11*. The number of books annually acquired was equally varied (*Table 10.12*). Loans to individuals per annum in the major libraries ranged as shown in *Table 10.13*.

There are about 800 other establishments of further education in the UK—polytechnics and other colleges. The 31 polytechnic libraries in 1979 had a total stock of about 9 million volumes, an average per library of about 300000. The average annual acquisition for each polytechnic was about 20000. Data on loans to individuals do not seem to be readily available.

Other colleges may be divided into four groups according to number of full-time-equivalent (FTE) students. The figures in *Table 10.14* refer to England, Wales, and Northern Ireland in 1979.

A 10 per cent sample of about 4000 secondary schools in England and Wales was surveyed by the Department of Education and Science in 1979. Most of the schools sampled maintain a library, the average stock being 7000 volumes.

Table 10.14 Library facilities for FTE students

FTE students	Number of libraries	Average stock	Average acquisitions
up to 500	152	18000	1000
500 to 1000	121	30000	2000
1000 to 2000	179	28000	2000
2000 and over	83	52000	4000

10.8 Special libraries and information services

The variety of special libraries has already been indicated by some of the categories in an earlier table: Government department, local government, public corporation, industry and commerce, learned or professional society, research and trade association. They vary widely in size, and in the intensity of information service provided to users.

If we consider only technical libraries, typical average stock sizes are as shown in *Table 10.15*.

Table 10.15 Average stock sizes in technical libraries

Type of library	Bookstock	Current periodicals
Industrial	3 000	250
Government	6 000	330
Non-profit	12 000	270

Apart from libraries, there are innumerable specialized institutions that provide information to their members, to *bona fide* enquirers, or to the general public. Their own stocks of materials may be small, but they are active users and purveyors of information. Many are listed in the *ASLIB Directory*.

Community information services have been described by Bunch (1982). Citizens Advice Bureaux, for example, now reckon to have an office in every town of population 30 000 and over, as well as in many smaller towns, and there were 900 such bureaux in 1981, handling 3 million enquiries per year. There were some 160 Housing Advice Centres in the UK in 1976, about 35 Law Centres in 1980, 150 Consumer Advice Centres, and many Neighbourhood Advice Centres.

10.9 Interlending and library cooperation

Interloan among libraries has steadily expanded over the last fifty years. Regional bureaux were formed at the beginning of that period. Their present pattern is shown in *Figure 10.3* (taken from Burkett, 1979), which gives the 1977 library membership of each region. (The numbers 1 to 27 represent locations of local cooperative library and information services.)

The majority of loans now come from the British Library Lending Division. In 1980/1981, 2.35 million requests were received there from UK users. During the same period, just over one million requests were received at the regional bureaux (59 per cent of these being supplied by BLLD).

In 1977 the BLLD carried out a national sample survey of interlending from which we may obtain a more detailed picture of the pattern then prevailing. Requests were directed by borrowing libraries as follows:

	%
To BLLD	78
To regional bureaux	9
To individual libraries	19

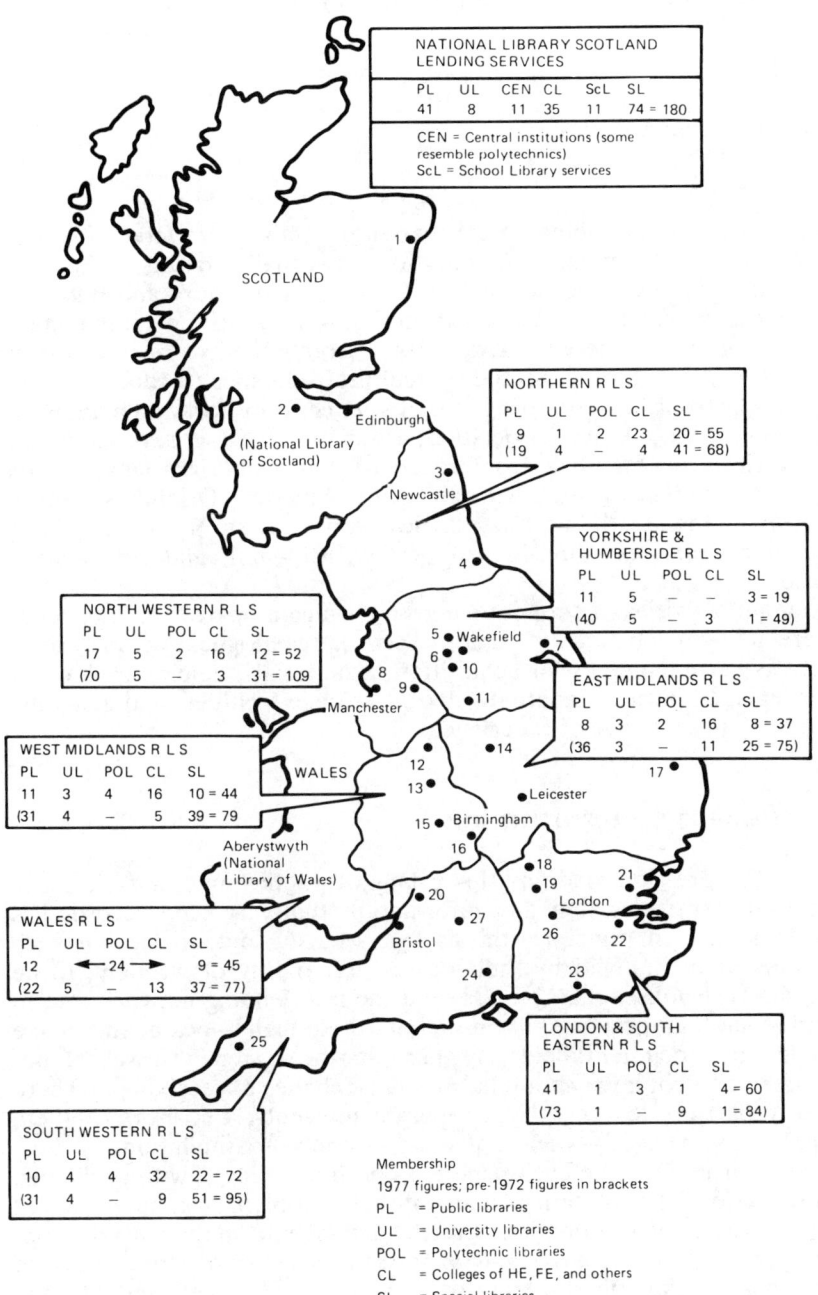

Figure 10.3 Regional library networks and local cooperatives

(Percentages total to over 100 because some requests went to more than one channel.) Requests were met from the following sources:

	%
By BLLD	70
By public libraries	10
By educational libraries	9
By other libraries	8
Not satisfied	3

Apart from interlending, libraries enter into a variety of other cooperative arrangements. Cooperation is usually based either on propinquity—for example, all the local cooperative library and information services, whose location is shown in *Figure 10.3*—or on commonality of subject or type of service. Examples of commonality are the subject groups of ASLIB (biological and agricultural; chemical; economics and business; electronics; engineering; social science; transport and planning); the sections of the Library Association; associations of law, education, and arts libraries; the Standing Conference of National Librarians and its groups (Slavonic and East European, Latin America, Orientalist, South Asia, China, Japan, Middle East, Africa, America, etc.): the Council of Polytechnic Libraries; the Council of City Research and Information Libraries.

The main activities of cooperative groups—again apart from interlending—are the production of union lists or catalogues of materials; cooperative arrangements for acquisition of materials; helping each other on reference enquiries; sometimes sharing storage facilities; and generally encouraging interchange of experience.

10.10 Access to information

The initial impression made by this galaxy of publications, libraries, and information centres is that any information that has been recorded is available to all. In principle, this is true (leaving out of account such documents as are judged by their possessors, rightly or wrongly, to be confidential). Booksellers, libraries, and the interlending network can, in principle—and in practice, if pushed hard enough—locate and make available any document held anywhere in the system. However, not everyone in need of information has the same chance of receiving it. There are many barriers to access, that operate unevenly. Let us trace them through the path: need—want—demand—supply—assimilation.

At work or in daily life each person is continually faced with problems, minor or major. The solution of many of these problems can be facilitated by the provision of information, but this actual information need is not always perceived to be such and expressed as a 'want'. In a study of information seeking by residents of New England, Chen and Hernon (1982) found that about 500 of 2900 respondents, though willing to participate, could not recall even one recent situation in which they needed to find an answer to a question, solve a problem, or make a decision. Perhaps these 500 had no such problems, but the investigators preferred to conclude that they experienced difficulty in seeing information needs and expressing them as wants. As compared with the 2400 who did identify at least one problem situation, the inarticulate tended to be less prosperous, older, and with a lower level of education.

Even when conscious of an information want, not everyone turns it into a 'demand'—i.e. actually asks a source or channel to supply the information. This can rarely be due to the non-existence of an appropriate channel, given the great variety of information agencies. More often it is due to the enquirer's not being able to identify an appropriate source or channel. There is inadequate knowledge of what information providers exist, of who can be approached. When asked what information providers they had consulted respondents to Chen and Hernon replied:

	%
Friend, neighbour, relative	57
Newspaper, magazine, book	45
Store, company, business	45
Co-worker	43
Professional (e.g. doctor or lawyer)	41
Government agency	27
Television or radio	21
Library	17
Telephone book	16
Social services	13
Religious leader	10
Other	3

(percentages total > 100 because multiple sources cited).

It seems clear that relatively few specific information sources were known to the respondents. This can reflect their general level of education.

There are other barriers to the translation of want into demand. There may be psychological reluctance to approaching other people or institutions for information. An appropriate source, though known to the enquirer, may be too distant for ready accessibility, particularly for someone who has a limited 'time budget'. About 15 per cent of Chen and Hernon's respondents mentioned 'cost in time' as the most important criterion that applied to choice of information provider. Any money price to be paid for information or incurred in accessing it is another deterrent to demand.

Not every demand put to an information provider results in supply. The source/channel may not accept the enquiry, or may give a perfunctory or misleading response, or may not have the information sought. The earlier analysis of library stocks shows the great variation in size of holdings within each category of library. Even if we assume that the stock of each library has been carefully chosen to match its average demand, it is evident that libraries will vary greatly in their ability to meet the needs of enquirers. The same will be true of all other types of information provider.

Failure to obtain information may also occur because no record of the required information exists—or, at any rate, not in the form sought by the enquirer. Another reason for lack of success in demand can be the inability of an enquirer to use a system successfully—for example, to conduct an information search. This too can be a reflection of the level of education.

The same factor applies directly to the last step in information provision—its assimilation by the enquirer. 'Understandability' was rated as an important criterion by some of Chen and Hernon's respondents (about 18 per cent in non-work problems, about 25 per cent in work problems), and sources labelled as unhelpful were criticized for providing information that was not relevant, accurate, reliable, and understandable. Once again, what is 'understandable' is related to the educational attainment of the enquirer.

Let us do a little calculation. If each of the four steps on the path need—want—demand—supply—assimilation is 90 per cent achieved, then two thirds of actual information needs result in the assimilation of information. An achievement of 80 per cent at each step leads to 40 per cent assimilation, and 70 per cent at each step means that only one quarter of the needs are satisfied by information provision. Can we be sure at what level of success our systems are working? Unfortunately, there is little evidence available.

10.11 Some lessons from educational research

The Advisory Council for Adult and Continuing Education, in developing plans for the expanded provision of these services in the UK, have found it necessary to explore some of the same barriers as we have noted above. Many of their arguments can be transferred to the problem of information provision. For example, they have addressed the issue of the need for improved educational provision:

It may be argued that this vision of an education service, systematically comprehending the needs of the whole adult population, cannot be realized for one simple reason—the lack of demand for education. Adults have after all always been free to choose to continue their education as and when they wanted. The market place analogy suggests that when demand is present, supply is forthcoming; and when demand is not manifest there is no reason to make provision for what is not wanted. But this argument misuses the term 'educational demand'. There are educational wants and needs, which are not easily translated into demands, and in the educational market place a lack of demand may mean nothing more than a lack of appropriate supply to stimulate the latent demand.

Many educators of adults consider that the present pattern of continuing education far from matches the educational needs and wants within the population. The public adult education sector in particular is generally only able, through its limited and diminishing resources, to meet the demand from those who are most able to articulate their wants and needs—in the main the most educated. The concept of a latent demand for education suggests that the provision of an appropriate supply would energize a demand from those who have not so far engaged in continuing education. The success of adult literacy work and the Open

University both support this view. Standing at either end of the education spectrum, each of these innovations has produced a sustained demand from those whose needs were previously unmet and largely unsuspected. Supply, made through a comprehensive and systematic system of continuing education, will trigger the demand to match the educational needs and wants of all sectors of the adult population.

In 1980 the Advisory Council carried out a structured survey of 2460 adults in England and Wales, aged 17 to 75. This enabled them to classify the educational history of the adult population, which is summarized in *Figure 10.4*. In this we can see that 39 per cent of adults have had no education since minimum school-leaving age and have taken no course of

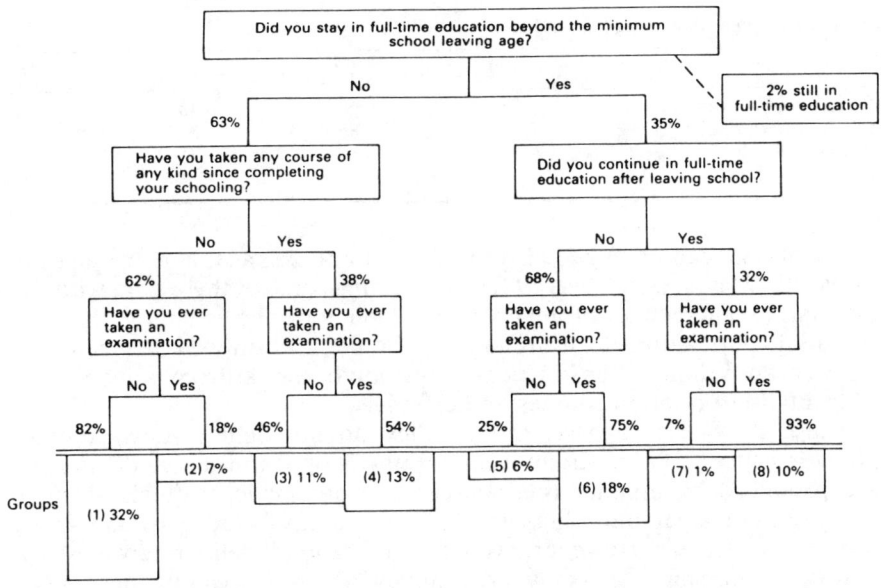

Figure 10.4 Educational history of adults

any kind. Another 24 per cent left school at the minimum permitted age but have subsequently taken a course. A further 24 per cent stayed at school beyond the minimum age, but have had no full-time post-school education. Only 11 per cent attended full-time education after school.

The Council commented on this situation in the following terms:

... there is one major problem which confronts people of all ages, and which is a fundamental barrier to participation in education of any sort (and equally, we add, to an educated use of information sources). Many adults are totally unprepared to enter much of our current education and training (and information) provision. The Council estimates that at least three million adults in Britain lack the fundamental skills necessary to enable them to function actively in a democratic society. Their poorly developed communication skills deny them the information, expertise and educational opportunities which are available to other adults.

The Council related level of educational attainment to social class as shown in *Table 10.16*, giving the percentages of men and women leaving full-time education by the age of 16:

Table 10.16 Percentages of men and women leaving full-time education

Social class	Percentage in population		Percentage leaving	
	M	W	M	W
AB (managerial, professional, administrative)	23	18	39	50
C1 (skilled non-manual)	12	38	68	65
C2 (skilled manual)	38	10	83	89
D (unskilled manual)	27	34	94	89

Table 10.17 Social classes and use of books

	AB	C1	C2	D
Read books at home	73	66	43	42
Buy hardback books	53	36	31	25
Buy paperbacks	69	56	46	39
Use a bookshop	25	13	7	5

Social class can be linked also to the use of books, as the percentages in *Table 10.17* show (see Reid, 1981). Combining some of these data with the population percentages of the preceding table it can be estimated that half the adult population do no reading at home, and only 12 per cent use 'proper' bookshops. This is a clear indication of the far from universal use of printed information sources and channels.

These data also suggest, though they do not demonstrate, another possible cause of failure in information provision. Informative documents are produced by innumerable sources and are made available through many hundreds of publishers in the UK, to say nothing of the many thousands overseas. However, even if a publication is deliberately aimed at a wide readership—as many are—it will almost inevitably have been composed or compiled by a member of social classes AB, managerial, professional or administrative. It is most likely to reflect the knowledge, interests, experience, and purposes of those social groups. It will often have emerged from a particular institutional environment—academic, industrial, governmental, professional, etc.—and be restricted primarily to information that is the special concern of the institution involved. For all these reasons, a particular publication may fail to provide the appropriate orientation, the right assemblage of information, to meet the needs of an enquirer from a different environment and with a different social experience.

10.12 Information technology

Technological developments during the last twenty years are causing significant changes in the pattern of information provision. The technology has arisen from the coming together of data processing by digital computer, with electrical telecommunications. It is becoming fashionable to call this combination 'telematics'. We do not wish to discuss the details of this technology—an excellent collection of significant papers related to computer information retrieval has been produced by Raitt *et al.* (1984). We will briefly indicate the functional components of telematic systems and their functional characteristics such as capacity, speed, and cost.

Telematics—computers and communications—may be used for many purposes—for example, renewal of driving licenses, remote medical diagnosis, teleconferencing, credit transactions, airline reservations. Our particular concern is its use in the provision of information on demand, whether the information is a bibliographic reference; a record of the availability of an item in a library, publisher's store, or database; a loan request or loan record; an acquisition order; directory information; factual data; full text; a facsimile; a computer program; or any other kind of recorded information that may be required. In this context we may distinguish at least the functional components shown in *Figure 10.5*.

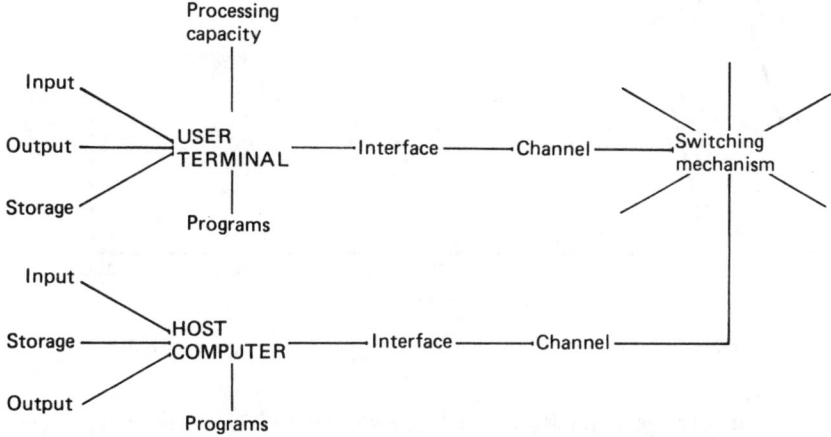

Figure 10.5 Functional components of telematic information provision

In all these functional areas there has been and is continuing to be incessant development in the volume of facilities available and their cost/performance. Here are some sample facts and figures.

The power of computers perpetually increases, and the unit cost of computation declines. In 1961 computers could carry out 5000 calculations per second, at a cost of £2 per calculation; in 1976, the figures were 2 million and 2 pence (Lewis, 1980). The expected improvement in cost/performance for four classes of computer, over the period 1977-1985, is shown in *Figure 10.6* (SITPRO, 1978, p. 43).

The cost of main memory storage, in dollars per month per megabyte, has fallen as follows: 1960, $22000; 1975, $3500; 1979, $250 (Lewis, 1980). In the late 1970s magnetic disc stores had a maximum capacity of 2×10^9 bits, an average access time of 5–10 microseconds, and a data transfer rate of 5–10 million bits per second. Future memory devices (such as magnetic bubble memories, holographic stores, video discs, charge-coupled devices)

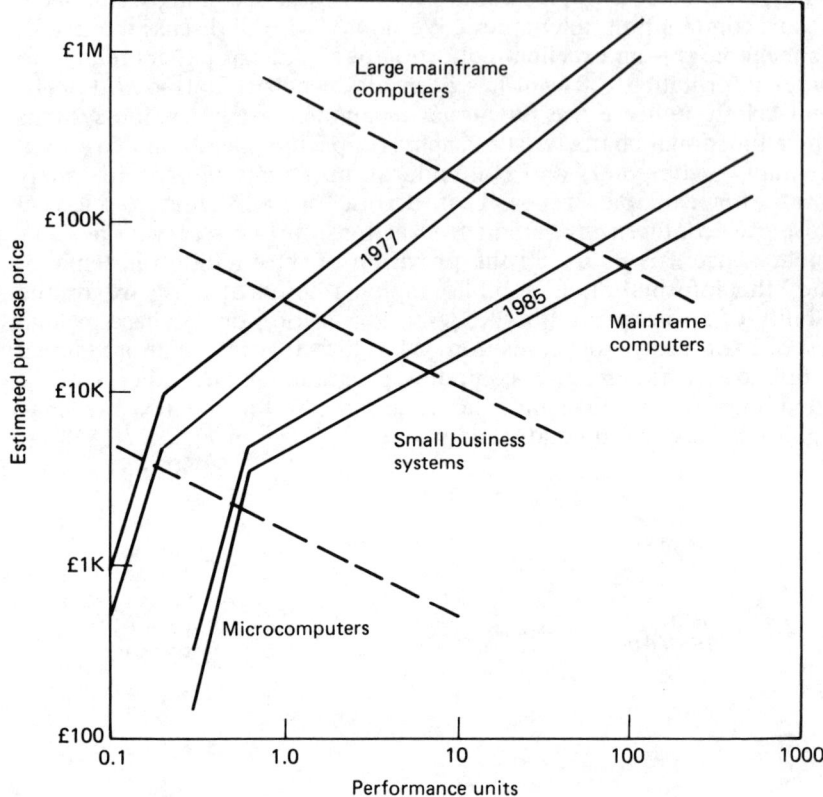

Figure 10.6 Estimated cost/performance of computers (CPU + memory prices only)

may push the storage capacity to 10^{11} or even 10^{13} bits, reduce the access time to one microsecond or less, and speed the data transfer rate.

At the user end of the telecommunication network there are an ever-increasing number of terminals (to say nothing of the use of adapted television sets). Estimates for the number of terminals are given by Lewis:

1965 USA—16 000
1979 USA—2 million, Europe—400 000, UK—1 000 000
1990 USA—10 million, Europe—4 million

Much more programming capacity and memory (the two being loosely termed 'intelligence') is being built into terminals, with cheap keyboards, printers, and local storage. Voice output and input are coming into use. Image transmission by videophone is developing.

The ever-increasing capacity of telecommunication channels is charted by Martin (1977, 1978) (*Figure 10.7*), and he indicates associated developments: a drop in the effect of distance on the cost of data transmission; easier and cheaper facsimile transmission of documents; cheap satellite links handling data and facsimile with facility. The lowered costs of data transmission are facilitated by developments in multiplexing

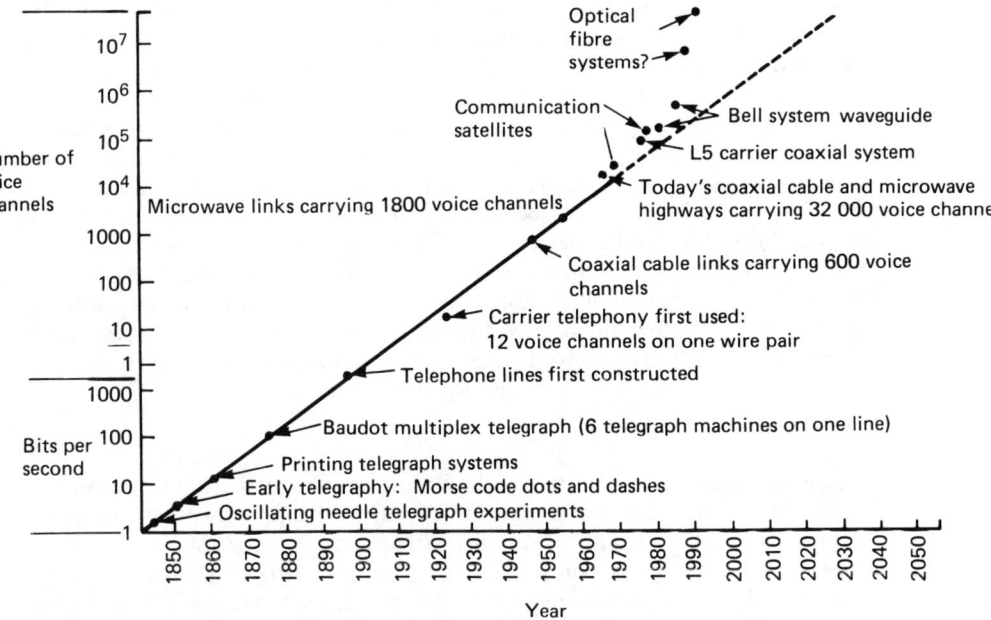

Figure 10.7 Capacity of telecommunication channels

and switching techniques, to permit large-scale sharing of transmission channels. At the user end, one coaxial cable into the home or office could serve all transmission needs.

Switching is necessary to link devices into networks. Freitag (1981) discusses possible network patterns of the 1990s based on satellite transmission, digital switching technology, and low-cost terminals, and hazards the estimate that the growth of data transmission in the USA will be as follows:

Year	1975	1980	1985	1990
Bits transmitted	1	5	9	15 (all $\times 10^{15}$)

Whether or not all the figures noted above are accurate does not affect the main point: there is a general consensus of great technological possibilities for improved information provision at lower cost, by the use of telematics. Some of these possibilities are further outlined by Martin.

During the 1980s

data banks with 10^{13} bits of directly accessible storage are fairly common. Such storage is used for photographs, drawings, and documents in image forms, as well as for digital data. Much telecommunication usage is for access to the numerous data banks rather than merely access to processing power which could be obtained from local minicomputers. The cost of storing alphanumeric data in large electronic storage units is now much cheaper than storing the data on paper in filing cabinets, or even in the form of printed books. And the cost per bit continues to fall. Information retrieval systems permitting a fast and efficient search of library databases—books, reports, corporate data, patents, legal documents, etc., are now in common use.

Major advances occur in the digitization of facsimile images. (Character recognition techniques are employed for print, and other techniques for corporate logos and signatures). Typical facsimile pages which used to be compressed into 200000 bits can now be compressed into 20000. LSI chips became available for this compression. Hence many documents are stored and transmitted in 'non-coded' image form. A terabit (10^{12} bit) storage can store 50 million pages of documents in image form. Hence massive information retrieval and library systems come into existence, many in government, which permit their users to carry out computerized searches for information.

By the end of the decade,

a new generation [of people] is now dominant which can communicate with the computers with ease over the various transmission links. Programming is taught at an early age in schools, and most well-educated persons under 30 can use one programming language fluently. The computer and software industries have spent much time and money developing the 'man–machine interface' so that the ubiquitous terminals are usable by the greatest number of people. Nevertheless, some minds seem naturally at home with the new technology whereas for others it is a struggle. Some persons seem to have a built-in hostility to this form of communication, which is becoming so vital in society.

A person who is well-adapted to the technology can carry out an amazing number of different functions from his home terminals. An ever-increasing world of computers, data banks, sound, film, and picture libraries is there to explore. Many authorities, however, still believe that the technology is only in its infancy. Certainly a vast amount of work lies ahead in building up the data banks, writing teaching programs, improving computer-assisted medical diagnosis, and so on. Many data bank uses that met with initial scepticism from the professional men they were designed for, are now gaining wide acceptance, but the work required to make them comprehensive is enormous.

Digital library storages are now available which store 100 terabits (10^{14} bits) on-line. These stores are used in data processing applications, for storing vast libraries of documents (hundreds of millions of facsimile pages), for large on-line music libraries, or for holding up to a thousand hours of randomly accessible television programing. Intelligence and police agencies use such stores for holding up to a million hours of recorded telephone conversations or conversations from bugging devices.

A study prepared for the US National Aeronautics and Space Administration offers estimates of US data record transmission (Hough, 1970) (*Table 10.18*). These figures give some idea of the 'telematic society' that technology seems to promise.

Table 10.18 Data transmission in the USA

		1950	1960	1970	1980	1990
Stolen vehicle information transfer	cases/yr $\times\ 10^3$	160	320	820	1950	4600
Facsimile transmission of 'mug shots', fingerprints, and court records	cases/yr $\times\ 10^6$	2	4	7	13	25
Stolen property information transfer	cases/yr $\times\ 10^3$	430	880	1700	3500	7000
Motor vehicle registration	items/yr $\times\ 10^6$	49	74	110	164	245
Driver's license renewal	items/yr $\times\ 10^6$	38	48	60	75	90
Remote library browsing	access/yr $\times\ 10^6$	0	0	Low	5	20
Remote title and abstract searches	searches/yr $\times\ 10^6$	0	0	Low	8	20
Interlibrary loans	books/yr $\times\ 10^6$	—	—	Low	40	100
Remote medical diagnosis	cases/yr $\times\ 10^6$	0	0	20	60	200
Remote medical browsing	access/yr $\times\ 10^6$	0	0	20	60	200
Electrocardiogram analysis	cases/yr $\times\ 10^6$	0	Low	20	60	200
Patent searches	searches/yr $\times\ 10^6$	6	6	6.5	7	7
Checks and credit transactions	trans/yr $\times\ 10^9$	11	25	56	135	340
Stock Exchange quotations	trans/yr $\times\ 10^9$	0	0	1	2	4
Stock transfers	trans/yr $\times\ 10^6$	290	580	1200	2500	4900
Airline reservations	pass/yr $\times\ 10^6$	19	62	193	500	1400
Auto rental reservations	reserv/yr $\times\ 10^6$	0	Low	10	20	40
Hotel/motel reservations	reserv/yr $\times\ 10^6$	—	—	25	50	100
Entertainment reservations	reserv/yr $\times\ 10^6$	—	—	100	140	200
National Crime Information Center	trans/yr $\times\ 10^6$	0	0	6	20	70
National Legal Information Center	trans/yr $\times\ 10^6$	0	0	Low	5	30

10.13 Institutional agencies

Let us look at the main institutional agencies connected with the telematic provision of information—database producers, network agencies, equipment and software vendors, intermediaries, and 'end users' (recipients).

The database producer (or information provider) is essentially a publisher providing information in machine-readable form for mounting in an online computer system. The database can consist of bibliographic records, quantitative data, factual information, full texts, directory data, computer programs, facsimile images, or other recorded information. The database is often a by-product of the process of producing a printed publication; but it may be specifically produced for online consultation. Any institution that already acts as a publisher—whether a commercial, governmental, or voluntary organization—is liable to become a database producer. New agencies for the production of databases are entering the field, in particular the so-called 'umbrella' information providers, who produce machine-readable data from information supplied by other institutions.

The database processor (host, online vendor, spinner, operator) acquires databases from producers (or the agency may itself also be a producer) and makes them available for online access on its own or a leased computer. The databases are manipulated by software developed by the processor (or acquired from someone else). We include in this category vendors who provide services such as book ordering, cataloguing, and book circulation, and who may store data contributed by cooperating libraries.

Within the field of information retrieval, *Monitor* (March 1981) distinguished three types of processor:

(1) The 'supermarkets' offering access to a large number of files, usually of a reference or bibliographic nature and aimed primarily at the library/documentation/information-centre market;
(2) The time sharers, usually offering data or statistical files and aiming at an engineer/R&D/management-planning market; and,
(3) Specialist services aimed at particular market segments and running their own files on their own machines. Examples of this would be Mead Data Central with its LEXIS service aimed at American lawyers, or Data Resources, Inc. (DRI), with its econometric and statistical models aimed at planners and economists.

Monitor commented that a fourth type had emerged in the form of the public information service offering viewdata and teletext.

Between the host processor and the user terminal is the physical communication channel, and this is provided by various types of carrier, using switching mechanisms to create networks. The 'common carriers' in Europe are the postal and telecommunication services (PTTS), such as the recently privatized British Telecom, who are responsible for the physical telephone, telegraph, telex, and digital data lines. Between countries there are submarine cables and satellite transmission. The international satellite systems INTELSAT and Intersputnik provide public telecommunication services in over 150 countries and territories. A regional European satellite system is being implemented, and the possibility of a UK system is being studied. Several US systems are operational or under development. In the USA the 'common carriers' have always been commercial.

The group known as 'value-added carriers' do not themselves construct physical communication links: they lease lines or satellite links from common carriers to create 'value-added networks' (VANS) with sophisticated computer control. Familiar in the UK are the two US 'VANS'— Telenet (owned by General Telephone and Electronics) and Tymnet Inc. In Europe, the PTTs have cooperatively provided a value-added service, Euronet. Private networks have been created by industrial and commercial firms. Martin gives examples of services that might be provided by value-added carriers:

Message delivery:	Telegrams
	Facsimile
	Mail
	Interactive computer data
	Batch computer data
	Interconnecting incompatible data machines
	One-way voice messages
	Monetary transfers
	Traffic when a bank card is used
Broadcasting:	Data broadcasting (like Britain's Ceefax and Oracle)
	Weather and marine forecast services
	News broadcasting by data, voice, or video

	Financial information services
	Music delivery
Message enhancement:	Adding forms to computer data
	Adding corporate logos and letterheads
	Adding signatures under tight security control
	Adding form letters to a transmitted recipient's name
	Message editing
	Word-processing functions
Message storage:	Document-filing services
	Secure storage service for vital records or audit trails
Message retrievals:	Library services
	Information retrieval and search services
	Financial information services
	Data bank services
	Newspaper morgue searching
	Music library

Software and equipment problems come in at every level of the information system. Host processors and network agencies must create or purchase appropriate programs and hardware, but their problems are not within the scope of this book. It is the equipment and software associated with terminals that are of particular relevance here. The variety of hardware that can be used for terminal access to host computers is continually growing, as is the local 'intelligence' with which the terminal may be endowed. The systems available run from those specific to and mandatory for a particular host processor, to those that purport to be adaptable to every online situation, including the capacity to 'stand alone' as a local processor or to enter into a 'local area network'. The continued emergence of new (or newly packaged) technical devices and systems makes choice very difficult. In the past the computer industry was not really involved in retail trade. Now there are springing up all kinds of terminal/microcomputer manufacturers and suppliers, and of 'software houses', large and small. Their claims and clamour fill the trade press, and the potential terminal user has somehow to come to terms with the situation.

Who, then, is or will be the terminal user? At present, terminals for information use are mostly acquired by and installed in institutions such as libraries, whose staff act as intermediaries in accessing online systems. However, there is much confident prediction of two other developments. First, new agencies may be set up to undertake an information search for a fee, the so-called information brokers. Second, end users with sufficiently frequent, urgent, or specialized information needs will use personal terminals, at work or at home. For access to quantitative and factual data, rather than bibliographic records, this is already the case.

10.14 Databases and database hosts

The pattern of provision of electronic information is very different from that of printed information. The logic of print on paper is local availability through multiple outlets of multiple copies of a particular document. Printing entails a multiplicity of local booksellers and libraries. The logic of the new information technology is quite different—it is that of multiple access via telecommunications networks to a single copy of a document held remotely in machine-readable form. Neither logic is implemented in a pure form—local book supplies are supplemented by interlending networks giving access to remote stores, and local forms of electronic store (for example, video discs) are becoming available. Nevertheless, the patterns are so markedly different that we have to focus on the provision of electronic information as an international phenomenon rather than one primarily national and local.

The number of publicly accessible databases is at present increasing all the time, and we do not attempt to provide an up-to-the-minute picture. An analysis of the situation in 1982 is given in *Tables 10.19* and *10.20* from *Euronet Diane News*. There were then internationally available over 1000 databases, including 345 covering between them 100 million bibliographic records. In 1984 it was estimated that there were 2450 online databases on 360 hosts, but usage was concentrated on about 250 of these databases.

Table 10.19 Distribution of databases, 1982

Origin of producers	Type of databases					
	Textual			Numerical		All categories of databases
	Biblio.	Factual	Mixed text/num.	Time series	Other numeric	
USA	155	83	105	140	87	570
EEC (CEC included)	113	71	21	29	30	264
Rest of the world	69	27	6	27	31	160
International organizations (CEC excluded)	8	3	2	16	3	32
All origins	345	184	134	212	151	1026

Table 10.20 Distribution of bibliographic records (× 1 000 000 records), 1982

Origin of producers	Private database producers	Public or non-profit database producers	All categories of producers
USA	33.2	41.9	75.1
EEC (CEC included)	4.9	16.3	21.2
Rest of the world	0.8	6.2	7.0
International organizations (CEC excluded)	—	1.5	1.5
All origins	38.9	65.9	104.8

An analysis was made earlier in 1982 of 714 unique databases technically and directly accessible in the UK (by Brown in Vickery *et al.*, 1984). Percentage distribution across subject area was then as shown in *Table 10.21*. The most common types of database were (1) numerical compilations in trade, finance and economics and (2) bibliographic compilations in science and technology. Much of the 'social science'

Table 10.21 Percentage distribution of databases across subject area, 1982

	Textual	Numerical	Both
Trade/financial/economic	6	31	2
Science/technology	27	6	2
Social science/law/humanities	15	2	0
Multidisciplinary	9	0	0

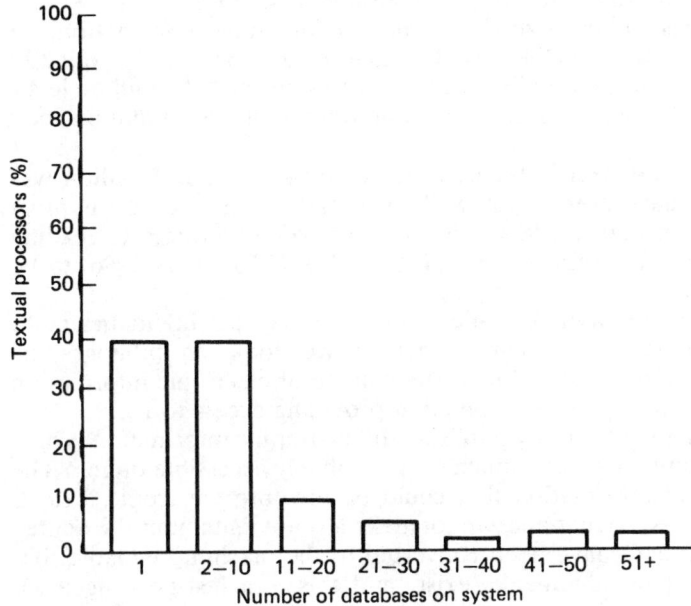

Figure 10.8 Textual data processors (100 per cent = 66)

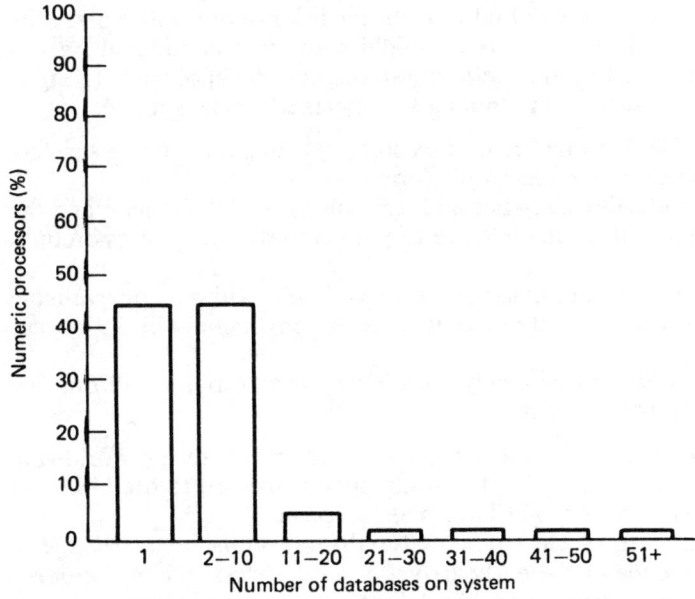

Figure 10.9 Numeric data processors (100 per cent = 82)

material related to law and jurisprudence. There was a small but growing amount of 'full-text' information online—journals, newspapers, encyclopedias.

At the time of Brown's analysis there were 66 hosts accessible from the UK handling textual (including bibliographic) databases and 82 handling numerical data. The number of databases per host varied widely, as shown in *Figures 10.8* and *10.9*. Only a small percentage of databases originate within the UK, and there are only a handful of UK hosts.

Reliable figures for the size of the market for online information are hard to come by. In 1980/1981 the UK market was probably about £30 million, but it is growing rapidly, and was in 1984 at the £100 million level. More than half the market is at present among the financial and business community.

In the USA it has been estimated that in 1984 about $3.5 billion was spent accessing databases—with well over half of this going on press services and stock market data. The numbers of subscribers to leading database services were reported by the *Guardian* (23 January 1986) to be as in *Table 10.22*.

The wide-ranging and ever-developing entry of telematics into information provision is clear. Whether we look at bibliographic references, factual data, or full text, the volume of electronic information grows as well as the agencies involved in providing access to it.

A high proportion of serially published bibliographic information is now in machine-readable form and much of it is publicly accessible online. The volume of factual information that could be put into electronic form is potentially limitless, so that one cannot make a statement about the degree to which printed data have been converted to the machine-readable, but already a good many databanks exist, and this is a fast-growing area. Full-text electronic information provision is still at an early stage of development.

Many now believe that eventually electronic information will replace the printed version, and in the USA a Delphi study was conducted on this point, posing queries to publishers, librarians, and technologists (King *et al.*, 1981). The following were among the specific forecasts made:

(1) By the year 2000, 50 per cent of existing indexing/abstracting services will be available only in electronic form.
(2) Existing periodicals (in science and technology, social sciences, and the humanities) will not reach even the 25 per cent level of conversion until after 2000.
(3) By 1990, 25 per cent of existing reference books will only be available in electronic form. The 50 per cent level of conversion will only occur after 2000.
(4) by 1995, 50 per cent of newly issued technical reports will only be available in electronic form.

It must be noted, however, that these forecasts relate to the worldwide production of publications. Had the study been restricted to the USA, an accelerated development might have been forecast.

Despite this growth of electronic materials and online access to them, there is little evidence of the early arrival of a 'paperless' society. Indexes and abstracts, specialized periodicals, reports, and reference books

Table 10.22 Subscribers to online database services

	1 Jan 1986
General interest	
CompuServe	259000
Western Union Easylink	127252
Source Telecomputing	60000
Official Airline Guides	23000
General Videotex (Delphi)	19000
Viewdata Corp of Am (Viewtron)	15000
GEISCO (GEnie)	2025
SUBTOTAL	505277
Financial	
Dow Jones News/Retrieval	235000
Quotron Financial Info	76665
Reuters Monitor	61000
Bunker Ramo Market Decision	31000
Telerate	31000
ADP Financial Info Services	25500
InnerLine	0
SUBTOTAL	460165
Sci/tech/professional	
Mead Data (Lexis, Nexis, Medis)	180000
Dialog Info Services	70000
Ip Sharp Online	37000
PRC Realty Multiple Listing Ser.	12500
One Point	8000
OCLC, Inc	6969
Knight-Ridder VU/Text	2350
Datatek DataTimes	2200
SUBTOTAL	319019
Credit reporting	
TRW Credit Data Service	40000
Equifax Financial Control Serv.	37000
Dun & Bradstreet DunSprint	23663
Chilton Credit Reporting	20000
SUBTOTAL	120663
News services	
Associated Press	16700
United Press International	14404
NewsNet	11000
Business Wire	800
SUBTOTAL	42904
TOTAL	1448028

constitute only a modest proportion of the total volume of print on paper. Moreover, though electronics may give access to them, text and data of any length or complexity are likely to need a printout (locally or centrally provided) if they are to be satisfactorily read and assimilated.

The main difference from the provision of printed information is that the channels of access to electronic information (the host processors) are not local but central, not national but international. Unlike libraries their use is rarely subsidized.

10.15 The context of information provision

There is a widely held belief that the development of new information technology will lead to an all-round improvement in the public availability of information. Access to all kinds of information, including bibliographic references, factual and numeric data, directory information and full text, will be enhanced and extended. Furthermore, it is implied that the benefits of this will be generally distributed: everyone will have the opportunity to take advantage of the wider access to information which new technology can provide.

Unfortunately, there is no necessary reason why this should be the case. It can be argued more plausibly that the benefits of any technological advance are likely to be distributed rather unequally. Under these conditions, any existing unevenness in the distribution of the products or services which the technology provides can be expected to increase. Indeed, the ability of one group to appropriate the benefits of a particular new technology may lead to an absolute reduction in the availability of products or services for those groups still dependent on the old technology. Technological innovation, in other words, takes place within specific institutional, economic, and political environments which determine the distribution of the benefits to be derived from that technology. In the case of information, therefore, it is quite possible that the development of new technology will only serve to widen the existing distance between the information rich and the information poor within a particular user community, or perhaps to change the identities of the rich and poor. This applies not only to individuals of course, but to broader social and functional groups, to those differently situated geographically, to different types of institution, to specific countries, and ultimately to the relations between the developed and underdeveloped worlds.

What is the institutional and economic environment of information provision? As already noted, librarians and information services (LIS) in the UK are mainly subsidized from public or institutional funds: for few of the services provided is a direct charge levied on recipients. LIS systems interact with the commercial world of publishers and booksellers, and many are now reconciled to cost-recovery charges to users for interloans and photocopies, but the profession largely thinks of itself as providing a personal service to particular user communities. However, LIS are only part of a very much wider 'information universe' and this is predominantly a commercial world.

In social analysis generally, the processing of information is no longer regarded simply as an ancillary (though necessary) accompaniment of more basic social activities. It is now seen as a substantial sector of economic activity. For many decades it has been customary to divide economic activity into three sectors: primary (extractive and agricultural industry), secondary (manufacture), and tertiary (services). The services have included transport, utilities (power, gas, electricity, water), repair, personal services, wholesale and retail trade. The proportion of economic activity devoted to the services sector has steadily grown in industrial societies. More recently, the processing of information has been identified as a quaternary sector. This is illustrated by *Figure 10.10*, taken from

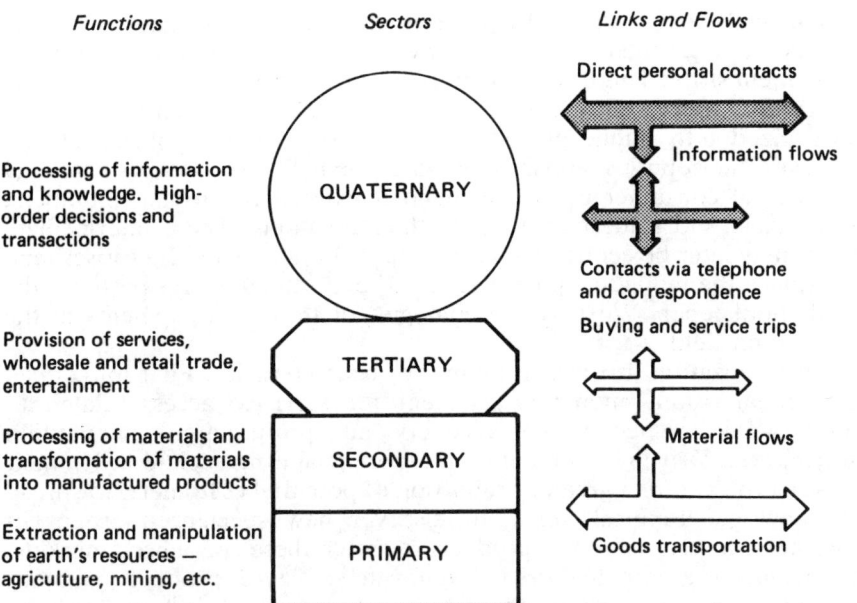

Figure 10.10 Economic sectors of society

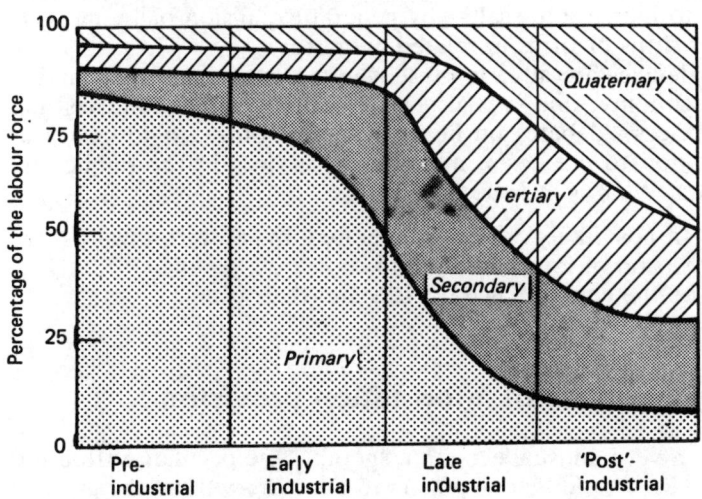

Figure 10.11 Sectoral shifts in the labour force

Dicken and Lloyd (1981), who also provide a broad picture of proportionate sectoral shifts over time (*Figure 10.11*).

In Western society every sector of social activity is potentially a candidate for industrialization. This has long been evident in the tertiary services sector of the economy. The personally owned horse and buggy is replaced by trains, buses, aircraft owned by large corporate enterprises, or by cars manufactured by similar enterprises. Coal fires, oil lamps, and garden wells are replaced by services from electricity, gas and water utilities. The cobbler is replaced by the repairs division of a large department store. This development is not, of course, the whole story. The electricity, water, and gas services, for example, centralized and reorganized into public plants, directly service millions of consumers. However, the countless apparatuses which mediate these sources of energy to the final consumer in turn demand individual repairmen, plumbers, electricians, and tradesmen to fulfil their functions. These intermediate agents may later be centralized in their turn. Large repair enterprises tend to displace the individual plumber, just as department stores push out the small shopkeeper. We may see analogies of these developments in the information field.

Industrialization involves a number of characteristics. First, of course, commercialization—monetary payment for services, access related to ability to pay, the need for cost recovery and a profit margin, competition for a market. Driven by competition, commercial firms seek to widen their markets, to capture a greater proportion of potential customers, to spread into new geographical areas, to discover new specialized groups of customers, to diversify their products to match these specialized markets. All this means a perpetual drive to innovate as regards products, methods of production, and ways of presenting or 'packaging' products, and this innovation involves the introduction of mechanization, to cheapen products and expand production. This in turn involves a constant tendency for production to increase in scale—by general expansion or by mergers between similar firms or firms in related areas.

All these tendencies are already present in the quaternary information sector of the economy, and can also be identified within libraries and information services—debates on library charges, outreach to new user groups, automation to cut costs, merging of services in the public and academic sectors. What is at issue here is this:

(1) Are these trends likely to be accelerated by a shift towards the electronic provision of information; and
(2) What may be the consequence for LIS and their users?

10.16 The economics of information provision

'Information' is a very unusual economic 'good'. One peculiar attribute is that it can be given or sold by one person to another, without the giver or seller losing continued use of it (although a particular physical embodiment of the information—book, pamphlet, magnetic tape, or whatever—may have been handed over to the recipient).

Equally important is the fact that 'information' is not the name of a well-defined product with a clearly specified area of use. Information is relevant to almost every human activity: its contents and uses are as diverse as the activities to which it may contribute. To talk of the economics of information in general may not be very illuminating. Here we are concentrating on the economics of services that provide, or are based on, recorded information (whether printed or electronic).

A third characteristic arises from the second—because of its universal relevance, information transfer is often not an autonomous activity but is contributory to some other activity. We buy food or medicines to keep alive and healthy, but we do not necessarily buy books just to 'keep informed'. There is certainly a proportion of information transfer for this purpose, but often the information is ancillary to solving a problem, taking a decision, working out an idea, helping a practical task.

What are some of the consequences of these characteristics?

(1) Because the giver is not a loser, information is often shared, informally and without charge, and so the transfer does not come into the economic marketplace. This undoubtedly contributes to the widespread belief that information should be 'free' unless there are non-economic reasons against this (such as national security, client confidentiality, or a threat from a business competitor).

(2) Because information and the occasions on which it is needed are so diverse it is a good about which there is likely to be much 'consumer ignorance' as to the best source. Although—and indeed because—there is a great variety of information sources, consumer knowledge of them is often very limited, and so there is little pressure on sources to be cost effective. (Among the economic conditions for 'perfect competition' is consumer treatment of all items on offer as equivalent. Since there is relatively limited substitutability among information items, competition among sources to provide 'best buys' occurs only within quite small groups of information products.)

(3) Because information transfer is so often secondary to another activity, its provision is often as a subsidiary to that activity, and is therefore subsidized. Industrial firms see information as leading to production and commercial benefits; educational institutions see libraries as contributing to teaching and research; government asserts the cultural benefit of public libraries. All these agencies treat information as a 'merit good'—whose consumption is stimulated because it is believed to generate both individual and social benefits. Newman (as cited by Levitan, 1982) goes so far as to distinguish such goods as 'institutional information', separate from 'market-supplied information'. Within institutional information he includes laws, regulations, customs, agreements established in both private and public sectors, as well as information transferred in the course of production, research and teaching.

We therefore see information as a good that is highly subsidized and with considerable consumer ignorance of the range and quality of its sources. The degree of specialization in provision leads to spatial restrictions—since only major conurbations can maintain a range of specialized services. The most widely dispersed general services—such as public libraries—are, in effect, in a monopoly position, and indeed in relation to the particular communities they serve, most libraries are at least partial monopolies.

Subsidy reduces the inequality of individual resources and thus helps to push demand up towards need; it increases individual benefit and social benefit. However, together with monopolistic aspects, spatial restrictions, and consumer ignorance, subsidy reduces the pressure on sources to maximize efficiency, so that the quality of provision is likely to be lower than it could be.

We are not going to attempt here any quantitative assessment of the extent to which provision of information achieves maximum social benefit. The data needed for such an assessment—and even agreement on ways to measure the benefits of information—are simply not available. What we do wish to explore is this: are there any indications as to whether a move from print on paper towards telematic access to electronic materials will increase or decrease social benefit in general, and opportunity of access to information in particular?

10.17 Economic trends associated with telematics

The introduction of electronic information provision creates new agencies concerned with information transfer and generates new functions within existing agencies. *Figure 10.12* looks at agencies and their activities. Online processors and networks for data transfer are the two main new types of agency involved in telematic provision. The boxed activities in the figure represent new functions undertaken by existing agencies such as primary publishers, bibliographic database and factual databank producers, LIS, and end users. These functions may, of course, also be undertaken by new agencies specially set up for the purpose.

The new agencies are basically commercial in nature: even if some of the online processors are not-for-profit institutions, they aim at least at cost recovery, with possibly some additional income to fund development. The networks and PTT are normally operating as commercial concerns, even if they are state agencies potentially in receipt of subsidies. The new agencies represent a further industrialization of information provision, and this is made very evident by the aggressive drive of processors for customers, often aiming at international markets, their competition, and price wars. The entry of multinational firms into the field indicates a hope of substantial profit. Other features of industrialization—mechanization, innovation, and increase in scale—are characteristic of the telematic scene.

From an overall viewpoint the new pattern implies a change in the flow of funds within the information 'system'. Let us look at the situation as it is represented in *Figure 10.13*.

Traditionally, information has been provided to users in three ways:

(1) Via *libraries* that have been funded either by national or local government (and thus from public funds) or by commercial organiza- tions (and thus from product sales) or by voluntary organizations (and thus from member subscriptions);

(2) Via *advisers* (e.g. lawyers or advice bureaux) that may be subsidized or receive commercial payments from clients;

(3) From *booksellers*, offering a commercial service.

There is a subsequent flow of funds between libraries, booksellers, publishers, and authors.

With the advent of online information services new fund flows emerge. The library may charge users. Libraries, individual users, advisers, may all

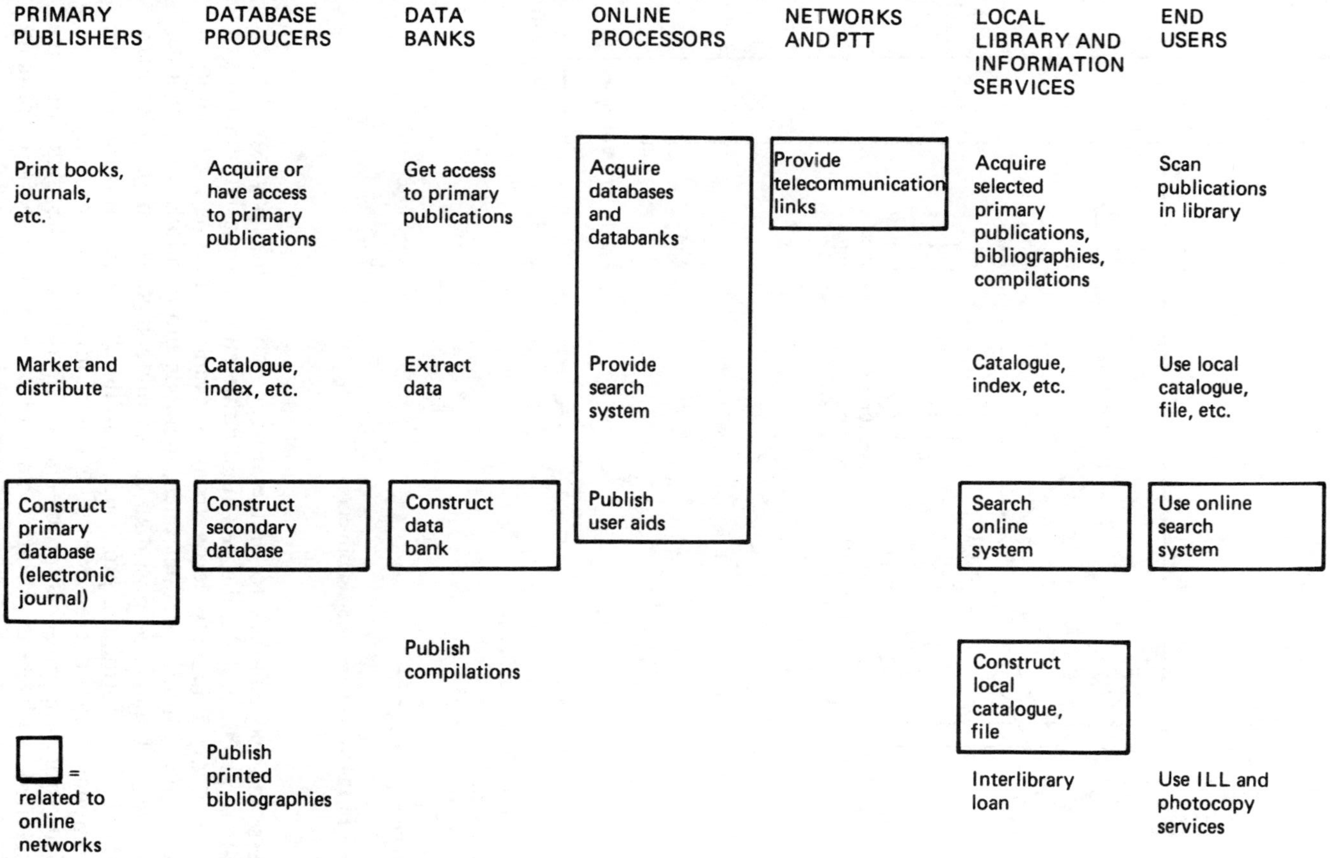

PRIMARY PUBLISHERS	DATABASE PRODUCERS	DATA BANKS	ONLINE PROCESSORS	NETWORKS AND PTT	LOCAL LIBRARY AND INFORMATION SERVICES	END USERS
Print books, journals, etc.	Acquire or have access to primary publications	Get access to primary publications	Acquire databases and databanks	Provide telecommunication links	Acquire selected primary publications, bibliographies, compilations	Scan publications in library
Market and distribute	Catalogue, index, etc.	Extract data	Provide search system		Catalogue, index, etc.	Use local catalogue, file, etc.
Construct primary database (electronic journal)	Construct secondary database	Construct data bank	Publish user aids		Search online system	Use online search system
	Publish printed bibliographies	Publish compilations			Construct local catalogue, file	
					Interlibrary loan	Use ILL and photocopy services

☐ = related to online networks

Figure 10.12 Main telematic information agencies

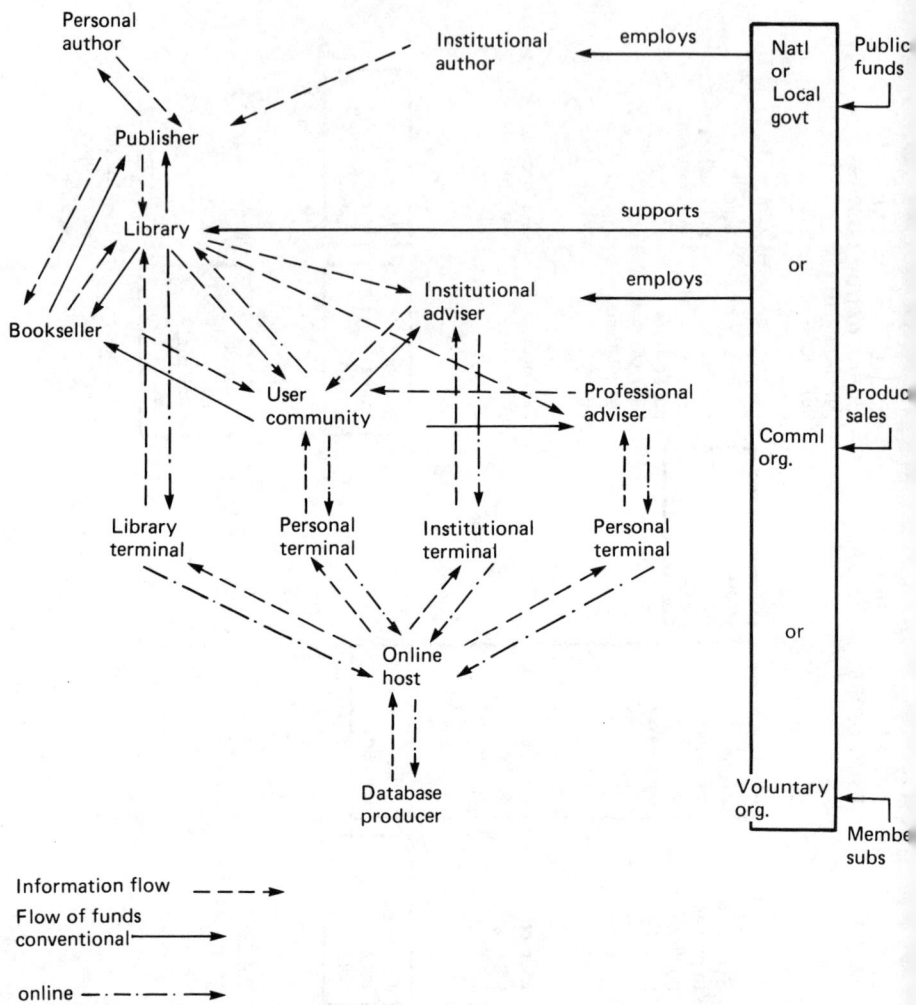

Figure 10.13 Flows of funds and information

access and pay charges to online hosts, who in turn pay royalties to database producers. All the new fund flows (shown as dash/dot arrows in *Figure 10.13*) ultimately derive from the same sources as the traditional flows—public funds, product sales, member subscriptions, or individual user funds. Unless we postulate an absolute increase in the resources available for information provision, fund flow for online services must be accompanied by a decrease in funds for traditional services.

This situation presents problems to all the agencies that are now concerned with both printed and electronic information—primary publishers, database and databank producers, LIS, and end users.

The funding of libraries by their parent institutions is unlikely to increase—indeed, during the economic recession it has been decreasing.

Rather than switch funds away from expenditure on printed materials many libraries charge users for online search (though the practice varies according to type of library). User communities must find extra funds if they are to access electronic information—whether directly through a personal terminal, via a library, or through an adviser (who in this context acts as an information broker). It is very likely that this will lead user communities to put pressure on funding agencies, so that these diminish their support for traditional print-on-paper services, and divert funds to electronic information provision.

The net effect of these various changes is that the environment of information provision will become less that of a subsidized service and more that of the marketplace. Economic theory predicts that a lessening of subsidy should (other things being equal) stimulate sources to improve their efficiency. However, the increased emphasis on monetary payment for access to information will mean that financial inequalities among users will play a more important role: for example, in academic institutions well-endowed departments will have more funds available for online search than those less affluent—a phenomenon that has already become apparent.

We have mentioned above that there is at present very considerable competition among host processors for customers. and this in theory should increase the user's freedom of choice, but it is likely that this competition may diminish. Collier (1981) has suggested that only large-scale host processors will continue to be economically viable, and that the market for online search will only support a few of these. This will strengthen any tendency to monopoly (or, at any rate, oligopoly) in provision, which would reduce freedom of choice.

We believe that this is an important issue upon which we must comment further. All the 2000 publishers in the UK have a chance to get their products to consumers (not necessarily an equal chance, since booksellers are selective in what they retail, and publishers vary in how much they can afford to advertise—but they can all make some sales). In principle, all potential users have access to any published document. This is not true for database producers, whose products are accessible only if mounted on computer by a processor. If there are a limited number of processors, and they are interested only in profitable high-use databases, consumer access to electronic materials may be much more limited than their access to printed materials.

Wessel and Kirkley (1982) make the following comment:

Many large corporations both in the US and abroad correctly see the new information era as an enormous opportunity and they are moving swiftly to position themselves to take advantage of the information bonanza that is fast becoming a reality. AT&T happily shed its operating companies in return for a premier position in the information marketplace. Merrill Lynch, McGraw-Hill, Dun & Bradstreet, and Citibank are just a few of the large companies jockeying for position in the information age. Many of these companies have come to realize that there is more to this information business than just making pots of money in the short term. They are acutely aware of the fact that information is power and that the actual control of the data is more important than the sophistication of the delivery system.

Writing more generally on concentration, MacBride (1980) concludes that

in the communication industry there is a relatively small number of predominant corporations which integrate all aspects of production and distribution, which are based on the leading developed countries and which have become transnational in their operations. Concentration of resources and infrastructures is not only a growing trend, but also a worrying phenomenon which may adversely affect the freedom and democratization of communication.

Overall, then, our arguments can be summed up as follows. Freedom in choice of source—and therefore individual benefit—may be increased by the stimulus of the marketplace and a lessening of spatial restrictions; but potential monopoly or oligopoly in provision and inequality of user funding may more than offset this increase. Any reduction in subsidized provision may lessen social benefits—for example, if online search by students and postgraduates is restricted because it is not subsidized, education and research may not benefit as much as they could. There is certainly no cut-and-dried assurance that telematic provision of information is a wholly beneficial development.

10.18 Factors affecting access to information

In order to gain further insight into the likely effect of telematics on social benefit we now present a more detailed comparison of the steps involved in information access using (1) exclusively printed sources housed in libraries and (2) exclusively electronic material available through host processors. We here include within this latter category all forms of material— bibliographic databases, factual databanks, full text. The two central columns of *Figure 10.14* represent successive steps in search, through printed sources on the left, through electronic sources on the right.

The steps of the printed source search are fairly obvious. The user must gain access to a library, select a suitable bibliography, scan it for references to relevant primary sources, locate their whereabouts, obtain access to them, and finally extract information from them. Electronic search involves gaining access to a terminal, selecting a suitable database (on an appropriate host), and searching it either for references to primary sources or for data; if the search yields only references, the next step is to locate a database containing the texts, get texts from the database, and finally extract information from them.

The success or quality of a search may be indicated by the range of information received, its pertinence, the time taken to complete the search, the cost to the user, or some combination of such criteria. Many factors influence success, and a number of these are listed in the first and fourth columns of *Figure 10.14*. There are strong likenesses between factors in the two columns, and it seems possible to conjecture, in general

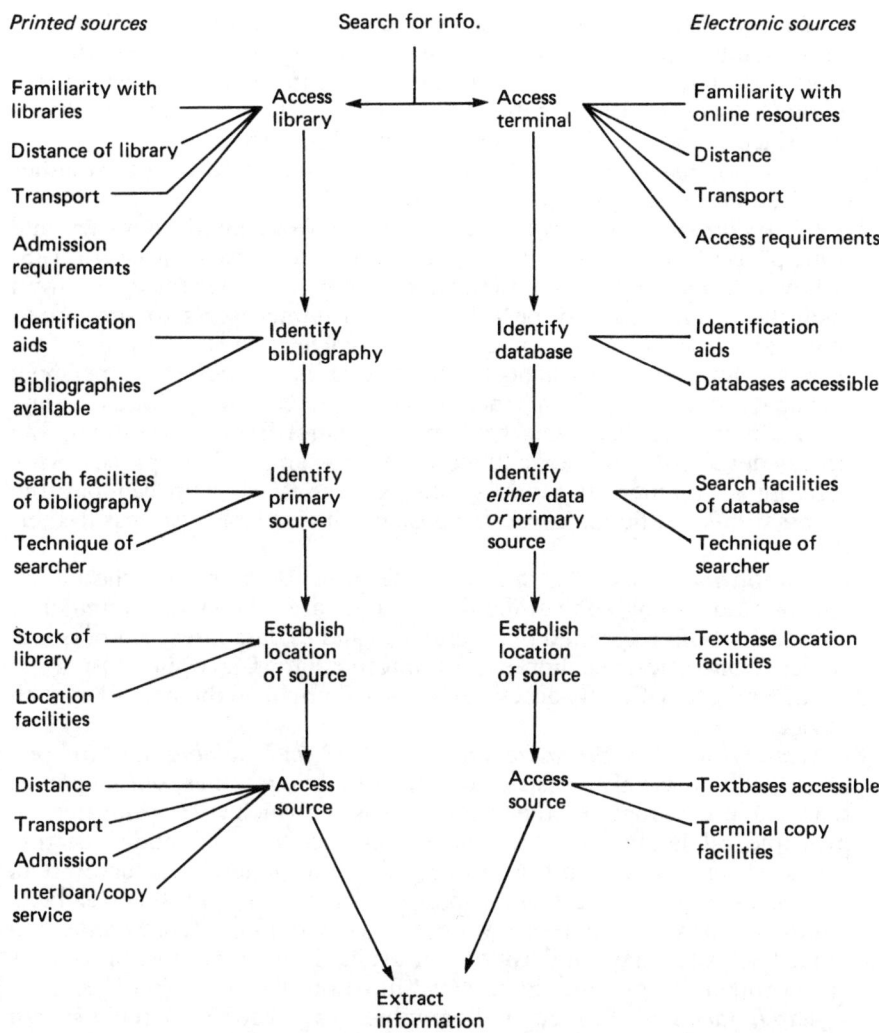

Figure 10.14 The search for information. The arrowed links represent successive steps in the search. The other links represent factors that may influence the quality of the search (range of information available, pertinence of information received, time to complete search, cost to user)

terms, what would be the relative effects of a particular type of factor on the success of search in printed or electronic sources:

(1) *Familiarity:* Libraries are used for a number of purposes besides formal information search, and it seems legitimate to presume that this will continue to be the case (not all reading materials will be electronic). Hence, familiarity with libraries may in general remain greater than familiarity with online resources—though this need not be so among users most likely to resort to online search.

(2) *Distance:* We have already suggested that a terminal may be more immediately available than an appropriate library. Distances will thus be short for direct end-user access to electronic information. However, for mediated access, distances may be even longer than for general library use, since not every library will have an online service.

(3) *Transport:* Facilities should not on average vary according to whether the destination is a printed book or terminal.

(4) *Admission or access requirements:* Apart from public libraries and some parts of the national library, there is not unrestricted access to LIS. Admission may depend on membership of or employment by a parent institution, and this may be a barrier to gaining access to specialized materials. Access to electronic sources involves two stages: access to a terminal and access to a host. Direct end-user access to a personal terminal obviously presents no problems. Access to a library online service may meet the same barriers as general library use, unless the library develops a brokerage function for this service. Host processors— offering a commercial service—offer access to all who can pay the necessary fee, although some database producers restrict access to their files.

(5) *Identification aids:* At this step the user is trying to choose an appropriate bibliography or database. There are, of course, a number of directories both to printed bibliographies and to databases, but personal advice from reference libraries or intermediaries is what most users need. End users directly accessing hosts will not have the benefit of such advice.

(6) *Availability of appropriate bibliographies and databases:* Any one library will have only a restricted range of bibliographies, but may have reasonable coverage for the subject areas on which it concentrates. In principle, all databases are accessible from each terminal, and restriction arises because some subject areas are likely to be less well served than others as regards electronic sources. Moreover, machine-readable databases for which there is low demand may not be offered online and older back files may similarly be not available. In fact, host processors are not likely to provide the archival function that libraries offer.

(7) *Search facilities:* Printed bibliographies vary widely in their search facilities—some having elaborate indexes, others being bare lists. Online databases usually offer far more search possibilities.

(8) *Technique of searcher:* Whether we consider manual or online search the same considerations apply: technique will depend on training and practice. It is likely that these are more important for online than for manual search, so that there is more chance of a poor quality search with the former.

(9) *Location of primary source:* A search for information in printed sources has the advantage that some of the identified primary sources are likely to be in the library being used—though for economic reasons it is likely that a growing proportion will not be locally available. In the latter case, identifying their location involves the use of directories, union lists, etc., and libraries vary considerably in the extent to which they make these available. A search of a bibliographic database may yield information about the location of printed documents, but if not,

then the same procedure is involved as for a printed bibliography search. In this case, direct end-user access to a bibliographic database must be followed by the use of a library to establish document locations. Since text databases for electronic document delivery are still in an early stage of development there is no experience of directories to establish the location of primary sources included in them.

(10) *Accessing source:* Obtaining a document not held in the library being used necessitates either travelling to a holding library (in which case distance, transport, and admission factors once again make their appearance) or use of an interloan service. Accessing a textbase—for example, to deliver a facsimile copy of a document—will involve additional equipment at the terminal and additional costs.

We have tried, in conjectural fashion, to indicate possible relative advantages of searches for information in printed sources and in electronic sources. Electronic search should have some clear advantages: the search point can be near at hand for direct end-user access; in principle, all databases are accessible from that point; and very flexible search is possible. Likely disadvantages are that the range of databases accessible online may not match the full range of bibliographic material available in libraries; the problems of locating and accessing primary sources may be aggravated rather than eased; and greater search skills are required.

10.19 The differential impact of new technology

Earlier in this chapter we suggested that the benefits of a new technology *could* be distributed unequally. Is there any indication from the arguments put forward above that this might be the case for telematic information provision?

A major shift towards the new technology will, we have suggested, have such features as:

(1) To those with ready access to terminals, a much wider range of bibliographic, factual, and (eventually) full-text material will be directly available than in a local library;
(2) To have a terminal available will involve the user (or the institution to which he is attached) in a cost;
(3) Access to information will increasingly be related to ability to pay;
(4) More skill will be needed to access information sources;
(5) Less funds will be available for print-on-paper sources and services;
(6) The databases available online will not match the range of material available in libraries taken collectively.

Recipients most likely to benefit are clearly those with ready access to a personal or institutional terminal; with personal or institutional funds available for information search; with a frequency of information need sufficient to maintain search skills; and with interests in subjects most likely to have databases available online.

Categories of recipient less likely to benefit from electronic information sources can readily be identified. Within the academic community, undergraduates and other students on taught courses will have less chance of access than postgraduate researchers and staff; the less wealthy departments and institutions will be similarly restricted. In scholarship generally, workers in the humanities are less likely to find a wide range of relevant materials, stretching back in time, available in electronic form. In scientific and technical research it is very possible that online search will be more readily subsidized by industry than by academic institutions.

There may also be bias within industry. Serafine and Andrieu (1981) report that 'small and medium-sized Canadian companies rely excessively on information suppliers who have a vested interest in selling a particular and perhaps inappropriate product as a source of technical information'. In general, they write, 'smaller businesses may be at a disadvantage in exploiting data accessible in data banks. At least initially, they will not be able to exploit the newly available data as effectively as large businesses that have the expertise to locate and interpret what they need'.

Lastly, we may turn to general community information needs. Ward (1981) comments that

> by the end of this century it is highly probable that having ready access to a data bank information service will be more significant in determining the quality of life you enjoy than having a healthy bank account. With this in mind it is clearly urgent that policies and programmes are devised to ensure that any member of the public, rich or poor, can gain access to such services ... Unless this is done there is every risk that their increasing use will only serve to widen in an unprecedented way the gulf between the haves and the haves nots.'

The possible future of information provision is perceived in very different ways. We will conclude this section by quoting the views of two observers. 'Throughout the 1980s,' writes Anthony Smith (1980) in *Goodbye to Gutenberg*, there will be a

> powerful growth in the business use of computer-based information systems; terminals and storage devices of many kinds are already pouring into the office blocks of large corporations, lawyers' offices, and educational institutions. Thousands of people will become more accustomed to the use of 'intelligent' typewriters, word processors replacing common typewriters, and other paraphernalia of the modern office. They will acquire experience in tapping into complex databases in order to extract business files, statistics, and salary information. Machines will be available in shops and stores and factories designed for non-specialist users, and even though these might not contain the material normally carried in the newspaper, they will familiarize both providers and readers with the special conceptual problems and skills involved in these forms of communication. Local advertising and local news will probably remain completely outside the computer based information systems for a long time to come, but people throughout the developed world will nonetheless frequently come into contact with vdt's and small computers in the course of their non-domestic lives. Real-estate agents will start to use viewdata-type services in Western Europe as travel agents already do in London. Customers will check the times of trains and planes, apply for holiday brochures, familiarize

themselves with the techniques of burrowing through a database in search of simple information, and perhaps find the task pleasant in itself and the information more clearly implanted in their minds afterwards.

For Ian Reinecke (1984) in *Electronic Illusions*, this development implies only that a new polarization in the possession of information will arise:

Compare, for instance, the information riches available to any ordinary individual and to a senior executive of an international company with a sophisticated computer network. So wide is the gap between the two that the ordinary citizen can, compared to the executive, be said in an important sense to be virtually illiterate. That description is not meant as an exaggeration. Before computers, literacy was a major requirement for human beings to possess information, apart from having access to the documents or books that contained it. Universal literacy, which began to spread in the United States and Britain in the second half of the nineteenth century, proved to be a great equalizer. The rise in literacy among Britain's rural and industrial poor was associated with increased pressure for democratic rights like voting and the right to form trade unions. Instead of information being held in the relatively few hands of those who could read, such as members of the aristocracy, merchants, and clergy, it was much more freely available. So dramatic are the changes that computers have brought to information handling that the inequalities of societies before universal literacy appear likely to be duplicated. Individual citizens compete unequally with private corporations and government agencies for electronically stored information. Their plight will be analogous to that of the illiterate working people of the early nineteenth century. The Information Society may see the rollback of benefits of the literacy programs that resulted from universal education.

10.20 Some final questions

As notified at the beginning of this chapter, our discussion has concentrated on displaying problem areas that deserve study by information science. Here we will try to summarize some of the questions that need investigation.

A general background to the issues considered here is provided by Halloran (1983), who works in mass communications research, and puts some of the queries that a sociologist in his field would raise:

Who needs information? What sort of information do different groups or the population as a whole need? Why do they need it? Who decides what is needed by whom? Who selects and presents what is provided? What are the aims and intentions of the providers? What use is made of what is provided? What are the consequences of that use for individuals, groups, institutions and societies? Could what is functional for one group be dysfunctional for others, or for society as a whole? What criteria are used in determining what is functional and dysfunctional?

There is a good deal of factual data available about printed information, its publication and dissemination. Data on available electronic information (databases) are less complete but are improving: knowledge of the volume and mode of access to electronic information is still very inadequate. There are few available data on the relative flow of funds among the component parts of the information system and how this flow is being affected by telematics. Studies on the differential impact of information provision facilities on particular social groups are virtually non-existent.

The subsidized nature of most libraries and information services has delayed the development of studies of the economics of information, and even now such studies are mostly concerned with the costs and benefits associated with particular products and services. The growing commercialization of information provision requires that the social basis of a policy of subsidy be more explicitly analysed. Who is receiving what financial benefits from the existing types of subsidy? What effects would arise from the removal or lessening of subsidy? What areas of information provision most deserve subsidy, on grounds of social benefit? What levels of subsidy are appropriate? Through what mechanisms can information provision be subsidized, now and in the future? Such questions as these can be closely linked to similar problems that arise in the field of adult and continuing education (discussed in the ACACE report).

The study of the communication of information in society, as explored in this book, has many facets. We have looked at the social contexts in which information needs arise, at people's behaviour in seeking information, at knowledge structures in man and machine, at the mechanisms and institutions by which and through which information is transferred, at their system characteristics and performance, at the problems of interfacing with these systems, at the position of this whole information transfer process in industrial society.

It can be seen that the set of problem areas for investigation is very heterogeneous. It may still be open to debate whether information science can become a homogeneous and autonomous discipline. The phenomenon that it aims to study—information transfer—is not in itself an autonomous social activity: it arises only because of other social activities that generate and use information. It is therefore inevitably influenced by and ultimately determined by this wider social context. It may turn out that information transfer can only be fruitfully studied in particular contexts in which information is generated and used, and that attempts to generalize more widely and independently of these contexts are not successful. Second, information transfer is a complex activity: in the communication process, the 'whole man' takes part, and to understand it we must take account of psychological, semantic, technical, system, economic, and social factors. This aspect is vividly illustrated on a wider scale by Colin Cherry's (1957, 1971) books on communication. Research in our field must necessarily be multidisciplinary. It is not yet clear whether the varied disciplinary approaches needed can merge into a new discipline with a distinctive viewpoint and methodology. This book is our imperfect report on progress made towards the emergence and coherence of information science.

We hope we have conveyed something of our own feelings about this field of study. As Octave Uzanne said of 'book hunting' a century ago: 'Of all impassioned pursuits, there is none more disturbing, more distressing in deception and hope, more intellectually absorbing, more obstinate in ill-success, more insatiable in triumph, more abundant in joys, noble, healthy and pure.'

References

ACKOFF, R. L. and HALBERT, M. H. (1958), *An Operations Research Study of the Scientific Activity of Chemists*, Case Institute of Technology

ACKOFF, R. L. *et al.* (1975), *The SCATT Report*, University of Pennsylvania

ADVISORY COUNCIL FOR ADULT AND CONTINUING EDUCATION (1982), *Continuing Education: from Policies to Practice*, Leicester

AFANASYEV, V. (1978), *Social Information and the Regulation of Social Development*, Moscow, Progress Publishers

AGUILAR, F. J. (1968), *Scanning the Business Environment*, London, Macmillan

ALLEN, T. J. (1966), *Managing the Flow of Scientific and Technical Information*, Massachusetts Institute of Technology, School of Management

ALLEN, T. J. (1970), 'Roles in technical communication networks', in Nelson, C., Pollock, D. *et al.*, *Communication among Scientists and Engineers*, Lexington (Mass.), Heath, pp. 191–208

ALLEN, T. J. and COHEN, S. I. (1969), 'Information flow in research and development laboratories', *Administrative Science Quarterly*, **14**, 12–19

ANDERSON, J. R. (1980), *Cognitive Psychology and its Implications*, London, W. H. Freeman

ARMSTRONG, C. J. and LARGE, J. A. (1988), *Manual of Online Search Strategies*, Gower

ARNOVICK, G. N. and GEE, L. G. (1978), 'Design and evaluation of information systems', *Information Processing and Management*, **14**, 369–380

ASHBY, W. R. (1956), *An Introduction to Cybernetics*, London, Chapman and Hall

ATHERTON, P. (1977), *Handbook of Information Systems and Services*, Paris, Unesco

ATKINSON, M. P. (1979), 'Database systems', *Journal of Documentation*, **35**, 49–91

AVRIEL, D. (1979), The effectiveness of information transfer from university to industrial projects in the pharmaceutical field in Israel, PhD Thesis, University of London

BADDELEY, A. D. (1976), *The Psychology of Memory*, New York, Harper and Row

BAGUST, A. (1983), 'Circulation model for busy public libraries', *Journal of Documentation*, **39**, 24–37

BAKER, J. S. (1972), 'Framework for assessment of causes', in Lazarsfeld, P. F. *et al.*, *Continuities in the Language of Social Research*, New York, Free Press, pp. 442–443

BALES, R. F. *et al.* (1951), 'Channels of communication in small groups', *American Sociological Review*, **16**, 461–468

BARNARD, C. C. (1938), 'The selection of periodicals for medical and scientific libraries', *Library Association Record*, **40**, 549–557

BARR, A. *et al.* (1981–1982), *Handbook of Artificial Intelligence*, Vols 1–3, Los Altos (Ca), Kaufman

BARR, D. (1971), *Book and Serial Publishing Trends, 1951–80*, National Libraries ADP Study, London

BARTON, A. H. (1955), 'The concept of property-space in social research', in Lazarsfeld, P. F. *et al.*, *The Language of Social Research*, New York, Free Press, pp. 40–53

BASS, F. M. (1969), 'New product growth model for consumer durables', *Management Science*,

15, No. 5

BATES, M. and BOBROW, R. J. (1983), 'Information retrieval using a transportable natural language interface', *Association for Computing Machinery, Special Interest Group on Information Retrieval*, **17**, 81–86

BELKIN, N. J. (1978), 'Information concepts for information science', *Journal of Documentation*, **34**, 55–85

BELKIN, N. J. and MARCHETTI, P. G. (1990), 'Determining the functionality and features of an intelligent interface to an information retrieval system', *ACM-SIGIR 90*, 13th International Conference on R&D in Information Retrieval

BELKIN, N. J. and ROBERTSON, S. E. (1976), 'Information science and the phenomenon of information', *Journal of the American Society for Information Science*, **27**, 197–204

BELKIN, N. J. and VICKERY, A. (1985), *Interaction in Information Systems*, London, British Library, Library and Information Research Report 35

BELL, D. (1976), *The Coming of Post-industrial Society*, Harmondsworth, Penguin Books

BELL, D. (1980), 'The information society' pp. 540–549 in T. Forester, *The Microelectronics Revolution*, Oxford, Blackwell

BELNAP, N. D. and STEELE, T. B. (1976), *The Logic of Questions and Answers*, London, Yale University Press

BENNION, B. C. and NEWTON, L. A. (1976), 'Epidemiology of research on anomalous water', *Journal of American Society for Information Science*, **27**, 53–56

BENSMAN, S. J. (1982), 'Bibliometric laws and library usage as social phenomena', *Library Research*, **4**, 279–312

BERELSON, B. and STEINER, G. A. (1964), *Human Behaviour*, New York, Harcourt, Brace

BERNAL, J. D. (1960), 'Scientific information and its users', *Aslib Proceedings*, **12**, 432–438

BERNIER, C. L. (1978), 'Reading overload and cogency', *Information Processing and Management*, **14**, 445–452

BERTALANFFY, L. VON (1971), *General System Theory*, Harmondsworth, Penguin Books

BERUL, L. H. *et al.* (1965), *Department of Defense User Needs Study*, Washington, Auerbach Corporation

BLAGDEN, J. (1980), *Do We Really Need Libraries?*, London, Saur/Bingley

BLAUG, M. (1972), *An Introduction to the Economics of Education*, Harmondsworth, Penguin Books

BLICK, A. R. (1977), 'Evaluating an in-house or bought-in service', *Aslib Proceedings*, **29**, 310–319

BLISS, H. E. (1929), *The Organization of Knowledge and the System of the Sciences*, New York, Holt

BOLINGER, D. (1975), *Aspects of Language*, 2nd edn., New York, Harcourt Brace Jovanovich

BOLT, G. J. (1981), *Market and Sales Forecasting*, 2nd edn, London, Kogan Page

BOOKSTEIN, A. (1976), 'The bibliometric distributions', *Library Quarterly*, **46**, 416–423

BOWER, C. A. (1976), 'Patterns of use of the serial literature at the BLLD', *BLL Review*, **4**, 31–36

BOYLE, P. J. and BUNTROCK, H. (1973), *Survey of World Agricultural Documentation Services*, Rome, FAO Documentation Centre

BRADFORD, S. C. (1934), 'Sources of information on specific subjects', *Engineering*, **137**, 85–86

BRAJNIK, G. *et al.* (1990), 'User modelling in expert man–machine interfaces', *IEEE Transactions on Systems, Man and Cybernetics*, **20**, 166–85

BRITTAIN, J. M. (1970), *Information and its Users*, Bath, Bath University Press

BRITTAIN, J. M. and LINE, M. B. (1973), 'Sources of citations and references for analysis purposes', *Journal of Documentation*, **29**, 72–80

BROAD SYSTEM OF ORDERING (1978), The Hague, Federation International de Documentation

BROADUS, R. N. (1983), 'Investigation of the validity of bibliographic citations', *Journal of American Society for Information Science*, **34**, 132–135

BRODIE, M. L. *et al.* (1983), *On Conceptual Modelling*, New York, Springer-Verlag

BROOKES, B. C. (1969), 'Bradford's law and the bibliography of science', *Nature*, **224**, 953–955

BROOKES, B. C. (1970a), 'Growth, utility and obsolescence of scientific periodical literature',

Journal of Documentation, **26**, 283–294

BROOKES, B. C. (1970b), 'Obsolescence of special library periodicals', *Journal of American Society for Information Science*, **21**, 320–329

BROOKES, B. C. (1970c), 'The design of cost-effective hierarchical information systems', *Information Storage and Retrieval*, **6**, 127–136

BROOKES, B. C. (1970d), 'The viability of branch libraries', *Journal of Librarianship*, **2**, 14–21

BROOKES, B. C. (1975), 'The fundamental equation of information science', in *Research on the Theoretical Basis of Information*, Moscow, International Federation for Documentation

BROOKES, B. C. (1977), 'Theory of the Bradford law', *Journal of Documentation*, **33**, 180–209

BROPHY, P. *et al.* (1976), *Reader in Operations Research in Libraries*, New York, Microcard

BRUCE, B. (1975), 'Case systems for natural language', *Artifical Intelligence*, **6**, 327–360

BRUTCHER, C. (1964), 'Cost accounting for the library', *LIbrary Resources and Technical Services*, **8**, 418–431

BUCHANAN, B. G. and SHORTLIFFE, E. H. (1984), *Rule-based Expert Systems*, Reading (Mass.), Addison-Wesley

BUCHANAN, R. H. (1976), *The World of Man*, London, Longman

BUCKLAND, M. K. *et al.* (1970), *Systems Analysis of a University Library*, Lancaster, University of Lancaster Library

BUCKLAND, M. K. (1975), *Book Availability and the Library User*, Oxford Pergamon Press

BUCKLAND, M. K. (1978), 'Ten years of progress in quantitative research on libraries', *Socio-economic Planning Sciences*, **12**, 333–339

BUCKLAND, M. K. (1983), *Library Services in Theory and Context*, Oxford, Pergamon Press

BULICK, S. *et al.* (1976). 'Use of library materials in terms of age', *Journal of American Society for Information Science'*, **27**, 175–178

BUNCH, A. (1982), *Community Information Services*, London, Bingley

BUNDY, A. (1985), 'Intelligent front ends', in Bramer (ed.) *Research and Deveopment in Expert Systems*, Cambridge, Cambridge University Press, pp. 193–203

BURKETT, J. (1979), *Library and Information Networks in the United Kingdom*, London, Aslib

BURRELL, Q. (1980), 'Simple stochastic model for library loans', *Journal of Documentation*, **36**, 115–132

BUSHA, C. H. and HARTER, S. P. (1980), *Research Methods in Librarianship*, London, Academic Press

CABINET OFFICE, INFORMATION TECHNOLOGY ADVISORY PROJECT (1981), *Making a Business of Information*, London, HMSO

CARLSON, G. (1961), *Report on the Organization of Large Files*, Los Angeles, Advanced Information Systems

CAWKELL, A. E. (1972), 'Cost effectiveness and benefits of SDI systems', *Information Scientist*, **6**, 143–148

CHAN, L. M. *et al.* (1985), *Theory of Subject Analysis*, Littleton, Libraries Unlimited Inc.

CHAPANIS, A. (1971), 'Prelude to 2001: explorations in human communication', *American Psychologist*, **26**, 949–961

CHARTERED INSTITUTE OF PUBLIC FINANCE AND ACCOUNTANCY (Annual), *Public Library Statistics—Actuals*, London

CHEN, C. C. and HERNON, P. (1982), *Information Seeking*, New York, Neal-Schuman

CHERRY, C. (1957), *On Human Communication*, New York, John Wiley

CHERRY, C. (1971), *World Communication: Threat or Promise?*, New York, Wiley-Interscience

CHILDERS, T. and POST, J. (1975), *The Information Poor in America*, Metuchen (NJ), Scarecrow Press

CHOFFRAY, J. M. and LILIEN, G. L. (1980), *Market Planning for New Industrial Products*, New York, Ronald Press

CIPOLLA, C. M. (1969), *Literacy and Devlopment in the West*, Harmondsworth, Penguin Books

CLARK, L. H. (ED.) (1985), *Consumer Behaviour*, New York, Harper

CLEMENTS, D. W. G. (1967), 'Use made of public reference libraries', *Journal of Documentation*, **23**, 131–145

CLEVERDON, C. W. (1970), 'Evaluation tests of information retrieval systems', *Journal of Documentation*, **26**, 55–67

COATES, E. J. (1960), *Subject Catalogues—Headings and Structure*, London, Library Association

COCHRANE, P. (1981), 'Study of events and tasks in pre-search interviews before online searching', in *Proceedings of 2nd National Online Meeting*, pp. 133–147

COLE, R. C. (1977), 'Lotka's frequency distribution of scientific activity', *Journal of American Society for Information Science*, **28**, 366–370

COLE, P. F. (1958), 'The analysis of reference question records as a guide to the information requirements of scientists', *Journal of Documentation*, **14**, 197–207

COLE, P. F. (1962), 'A new look at reference scattering', *Journal of Documentation*, **18**, 58–64

COLE, P. F. (1963), 'Journal usage versus age of journal', *Journal of Documentation*, **19**, 1–11

COLEMAN, J.S., KATZ, E. and MENZEL, H. (1966), *Medical Innovation: a Diffusion Study*, New York, Bobbs-Merrill

COLLIER, H. (1981), *Monitor*, No. 7, 10–12, September

COLLINS, A. M. and QUILLIAN, M. R. (1969), 'Retrieval time from semantic memory', *Journal of Verbal Learning and Verbal Behaviour*, **8**, 240–247

COOMBS, P. H. and AHMED, M. (1974), *Attacking Rural Poverty*, Johns Hopkins University Press

COOPER, M. D. (1978), 'Charging users for library service', *Information Processing and Management*, **14**, 419–428

COOPER, M. D. (1983), 'Economics of scale in academic libraries', *Library Research*, **5**, 207–219

COOVER, R. W. (1969), 'User needs and their effect on information centre administration', *Special Libraries*, **60**, 446–456

COWLING, D. et al. (1982), *Identifying the Market: Catchment Areas of Sports Centres and Swimming Pools*, London, Sports Council

CRAIG, G. M. (1979), *Information Systems in UK Agriculture*, British Library R and D Department Report 5469

CRANFIELD, G. A. (1978), *The Press and Society*, London, Longman

CRICKMAN, R. D. (1979), 'The emerging information professional', *Library Trends*, **28**, 311–327

CROFT, D. (1983), *Applied Statistics for Management Studies*, 3rd edn, London, MacDonald and Evans

CRONIN, B. (1982), 'Performance measurement and information management', *Aslib Proceedings*, **34**, 227–236

CRONIN, B. (1983), 'Post-industrial society: some manpower issues for the library and information profession', *Journal of Information Science*, **7**, 1–14

CURRAN, J. et al. (1977), *Mass Communication and Society*, London, Edward Arnold

CURWEN, P. J. (1981), *The UK Publishing Industry*, Oxford, Pergamon Press

CUTLIP, S. C. (1954), 'Content and flow of Associated Press news', *Journalism Quarterly*, **31**, 434–446

DANIELS, P. (1986). 'Cognitive models in information retrieval', *Journal of Documentation*, **42**, 272–304

DAVIES, R. (1985), 'Q-analysis', *Journal of Documentation*, **41**, 221–246

DAVIES, R. et al. (1986), *Intelligent Information Systems*, Chichester, Ellis Horwood

DAVIS, C. H. and RUSH, J. E. (1979), *Guide to Information Science*, Greenwood Press

DAVIS, R. and BUCHANAN, B. G. (1977), 'Meta-level knowledge', *Proceedings IJCAI-77*, 920–928

DE BEAUGRANDE, R. (1980), *Text, Discourse and Process*, Ablex Publishing Corp.

DE GENNARO, R. (1982), 'Libraries, technology and the information marketplace', *Library Journal*, 1045–1054

DE GROLIER, E. (1962), *A Study of General Categories*, Paris, Unesco

DEARBORN, D. C. and SIMON, H. A. (1958), 'Selective perception', *Sociometry*, **21**, 140–144

DEMBOWSKA, M. (1968), *Documentation and Scientific Information*, Warsaw, CISTEI

DEPARTMENT OF EDUCATION AND SCIENCE (1973), *Public Libraries and their Use*, London, HMSO

DEPARTMENT OF ENVIRONMENT (1978), *Education in Construction Industry Information*,

348   References

Glasgow, University of Strathclyde

DEPARTMENT OF ENVIRONMENT (1971), *Information System for the Construction Industry*, London, HMSO

DEPARTMENT OF ENVIRONMENT (1972), *Structuring Project Information*, London, HMSO

DEUTSCHMANN, P. J. and DANIELSON, W. (1960), 'Diffusion of knowledge of the major news story', *Journalism Quarterly*, **37**, 345–355

DICKEN, P. and LLOYD, P. E. (1981), *Modern Western Society*, New York, Harper and Row

D'OLIER, J. H. and DELMAS, B. (1975), *Planning National Infrastructures for Documentation, Libraries and Archives*, Paris, Unesco

DOUDS, C. F. (1971), 'The state of the art in the study of technology transfer', *R & D Management*, **1**, 125–131

DOYLE, L. B. (1975), *Information Retrieval and Processing*, Los Angeles, Melville

DROTT, M. C. (1981), 'Bradford's law', *Library Trends*, **30**, 41–52

DROTT, M. C. *et al.* (1979), 'Bradford's law and libraries', *Aslib Proceeding*, **31**, 296–304

DRUCKER, P. F. (1971), *The Age of Continuity*, London, Pan

DUNCAN, C. J. (1969), 'Survey of audiovisual equipment and methods', in Urwin, *Media and Methods*, New York, McGraw-Hill

DUNN, S. C. (1965), 'The management attitude to information', *Aslib Proceeding*, **17**, 286–296

EARLE, P. and VICKERY, B. C. (1969), 'Social science literature use in the UK as indicated by citations', *Journal of Documentation*, **25**, 123–141

EAST, H. (1979), *Some Statistical Indicators of UK Abstracting and Indexing Services*, British Library Research and Development Department Report 5488

EAST, H. (1983), 'Changes in the staffing of UK special libraries and information services in the decade 1972-81', *Journal of Documentation*, **39**, 247–265

EAST, H. (1984a), 'Special libraries and information services and the development of the UK information industry', *Aslib Proceeding*, **36**, 61–78

EAST, H. (1984b), *The UK Library and Information Service System*, Report to the British Library Research and Development Department

EFTHIMIADIS, E. (1990), 'Online searching aids', *Journal of Documentation*, **46**, 218–62

ELTON, M. J. C. and ORR, R. H. (1973), 'Document delivery service in a hierarchical system of libraries', *Communications Study Group*, University College London

ELTON, M. J. C. and VICKERY, B. C. (1973), 'Scope for operational research in the library and information field', *Aslib Proceedings*, **25**, 305–319

ESCARPIT, R. (1973), *L'écrit et la communication*, Paris, Presses Universitaires de France

EVANS, E. *et al.* (1972). 'Reviews of criteria used to measure effectiveness', *Bulletin of the Medical Library Association*, **5**, 102–110

FAHLMAN, S. E. (1979). *NETL: a System for Representing and Using Real-world Knowledge*, Cambridge (Mass.), MIT Press

FAIBISOFF, S. G. and ELY, D. P. (1976), 'Information and information needs', *Information Reports and Bibliographies*, **5**, No. 5

FAIRTHORNE, R. A. (1969), 'Empirical hyperbolic distributions (Bradford–Zipf–Mandelbrot) for bibliometric description and prediction', *Journal of Documentation*, **25**, 319–343

FAIRTHORNE, R. A. (1961), *Towards Information Retrieval*, London, Butterworths

FAIRTHORNE, R. A. (1967), 'Morphology of information flow', *Journal of Association for Computing Machinery*, **14**, 710–719

FARACE, R.V. and DANOWSKI, J. A. (1973), *Analyzing Human Communication Networks in Organizations*, Michigan State University, Department of Communications

FINDLER, N. V. *et al.* (1979), *Associative Networks: representation and use of knowledge by computer*, London, Academic Press

FISHENDEN, R. M. (1959), 'Methods by which research workers find information', in *International Conference on Scientific Information Proceedings*, Vol.1, , Washington (DC), National Academy of Sciences/National Research Council, pp. 163–180

FLOWERDEW, A. D. J. and WHITEHEAD, C. M. E. (1974), 'Cost-effectiveness and cost-benefit analyses in information science', London School of Economics, British Library Research and Development Report 5206

FLYNN, R. R. (1979), 'The University of Pittsburgh study of journal usage', *Serials Librarian*, 4, 23–33

FORRESTER, J. W. (1961), *Industrial Dynamics*, Cambridge (Mass.), MIT Press

FOSKETT, A. C. (1983), *The Subject Approach to Information*, 4th edn, London, Bingley

FOSKETT, D. J. (1970), 'Informatics', *Journal of Documentation*, 26, 340–369

FREITAG, J. (1981), 'Information utilities in the 1990s', *Information Reports and Bibliographies*, 10, No. 5, 3–24

GALTUNG, J. and RUGE, M. H. (1965), 'The structure of foreign news', *Journal of Peace Research*, 2, 64–90

GAPEN, K. D. and MILNER, S. P. (1981), 'Obsolescence', *Library Trends*, 30, 107–124

GARDIN, J. C. (1973), 'Document analysis and linguistic theory', *Journal of Documentation*, 29, 137–168

GARDNER, G. (1978), *Social Surveys for Social Planners*, Miton Keynes, Open University Press

GARFIELD, E. (1979), *Citation Indexing*, New York, John Wiley

GARVEY, W. D. (1979), *Communication: the Essence of Science*, Oxford, Pergamon Press

GARVEY, W. D. *et al.* (1972), 'Research studies in patterns of scientific communication. I–IV', *Information Storage and Retrieval*, 8, 111–112, 159–170, 207–222, 265–276

GARVEY, W. D. *et al.* (1974), 'The dynamic scientific-information user', *Information Storage and Retrieval*, 10, 115–131

GARVEY, W. D. and GOTTFREDSON, S. D. (1976), 'Changing the system: innovations in the interactive social system of scientific communication', *Information Processing and Management*, 12, 165–176

GARVEY, W. D. and GRIFFITH, B. C. (1972), 'Communication and information processing within scientific disciplines', *Information Storage and Retrieval*, 8, 123–136

GERBNER, G. (1956), 'Toward a general model of communication', *Audiovisual Communication Review*, 4, 171–199

GILCHRIST, A. (1971), *The Thesaurus in Retrieval*, London, Aslib

GILMORE, J. S. *et al.* (1967), *The Channels of Technology Acquisition in Commercial Firms*, Denver, Denver Research Institute

GODDARD, H. C. (1971), 'An economic analysis of library benefits', *Library Quarterly*, 41, 244–255

GOFFMAN, W. (1966). 'Mathematical approach to the spread of scientific ideas', *Nature*, 212, 449–452

GOFFMAN, W. and WARREN, K. S. (1980), *Scientific Information Systems and the Principle of Selectivity*, New York, Praeger

GOLDHABER, G. M. *et al.* (1978), 'Organization communication', *Human Communication Research*, 5, 76–96

GOWERS, E. and FRASER, B. (1973), *The Complete Plain Words*, London, HMSO

GRALEWSKA, A. (1970), *Evaluation Study of Rock Mechanics*, London, Imperial College Information Service

GRALEWSKA-VICKERY, A. (1976), 'Communication and information needs of earth science engineers', *Information Processing and Management*, 12, 251–282

GRALEWSKA-VICKERY, A. and ROSCOE, H. (1975), *Earth Science Engineers: Communication and Information Needs*, Imperial College Rock Mechanics Research Report No. 32, (OSTI Report 5226)

GREENBERG, B. S. (1964), 'Diffusion of news of the Kennedy assassination', *Public Opinion Quarterly*, 28, 225–232

GREGORY, R. L. (1984), *Mind in Science*, Harmondsworth, Penguin Books

GRICE, H. P. (1978), 'Logic and conversation', in Walker, D. E. (ed.), *Understanding Spoken Language*, Amsterdam, North-Holland, pp. 229–340

GRIFFITH, B. C. *et al.* (1979), 'Aging of scientific literature: a citation analysis', *Journal of Documentation*, 35, 179–196

GRIFFITH, B. C. (ed.) (1980), *Key Papers in Information Science*, White Plains (NY), Knowledge Industry Publications

GROSE, D. (1974), 'Some deprived information users', *Aslib Proceeding*, 26, 9–27

HAGSTROM, W. (1965), *The Scientific Community*, New York, Basic Books

HALBERT, M. H. and ACKOFF, R. L. (1959), 'An operations research study of dissemination of scientific information', in *International Conference on Scientific Information Proceedings*, Vol. 1, Washington (DC), National Academy of Sciences/National Research Council, pp. 97–130

HALLORAN, J. D. (1983), 'Information and communication', *Journal of Information Science, 7*, 159–167

HALSEY, A. H. *et al.* (1972), *Trends in British Society since 1900,* London, Macmillan

HAMBURG, M. *et al.* (1974), *Library Planning and Decision-making Systems*, Cambridge (Mass.), MIT Press

HARMON, P. and KING, D. (1985), *Expert Systems*, New York, John Wiley

HARRAH, D. (1961), 'A logic of questions and answers', *Philosophy of Science, 28*, 40–46

HARRAH, D. (1963), *Communication: a Logical Model*, Cambridge (Mass.), MIT Press

HARRAH, D. (1973), 'The logic of questions and its relevance to instructional science', *Instructional Science, 1*, 447–467

HAVELOCK, R. G. *et al.* (1969), *Comparative study of the literature on the dissemination and utilization of scientific knowledge*, Michigan University

HAYES-ROTH, F., WATERMAN, D. A. and LENAT, D. B. (1983), *Building Expert Systems*, Reading (Mass.), Addison-Wesley

HEAPS, H. S. (1978), *Information Retrieval: computational and theoretical aspects*, London, Academic Press

HENRY, W. M. *et al.* (1980), *Online Searching*, London, Butterworths

HERRING, C. (1973), 'Dissemination and use of information in physics', in *Physics in Perspective*, Vol. IIB, Washington (DC), National Academy of Sciences, pp. 1265–1452

HERTZLER, J. O. (1965), *Sociology of Language*, New York, Random House

HESELTINE, R. G. (1982), 'Some system dynamics modelling and the management of an online information service', *Journal of Librarianship, 14*, 247–265

HETMAN, F. (1973), *Society and the Assessment of Technology*, Paris, OECD

HINDLE, A. and WORTHINGTON, D. (1980), 'Simple stochastic models for library loans', *Journal of Documentation, 36*, 209–213

HJERPPE, R. (1978), *Outline of Bibliometrics and Citation Analysis*, Stockholm, Royal Institute of Technology Library

HOFFMAN, M. and WILLIAMS, A. (1977), *Using and Abusing Literacy*, Open University course on reading development, Book 3, Unit 12

HOLLNAGEL, E. (1978), *Qualitative Aspects of Man–machine Communication*, RISO National Laboratory

HOLLNAGEL, E. and WOODS, D. D. (1983), 'Cognitive systems engineering', *International Journal of Man–Machine Studies, 18*, 583–600

HOLMSTROM, J. E. (1956), *Records and Research in Engineering and Industrial Science*, 3rd edn, London, Chapman and Hall

HOLTON, G. (1962), 'Scientific research and scholarship', *Daedalus, 91*, 362–399

HOMANS, G. C. (1951), *The Human Group*, London, Routledge

HOUGH, R. W. (1980), ''Innovation transfer in 1990', *AIAA 3rd Communications Satellite System Conference*, Los Angeles

HUBEL, D. H. and WIESEL, T. N. (1976), 'Receptive fields', *Journal of Physiology, 195*, 215–243

HUBERT, J. J. (1981), 'General bibliometric methods', *Library Trends, 30*, 65–81

HUTCHINS, W. J. (1975), *Language of Indexing and Classification*, London, Peter Peregrinus

HUTCHINS, W. L. (1978), 'Machine translation and machine-aided translation', *Journal of Documentation, 34*, 119–159

INFORMATION HOTLINE (1977), 'Time line of developments in information and communication technology', April

INSTITUTE OF INFORMATION SCIENTISTS (1982), *Criteria for Information Science*, London, The Institute

INTERNATIONAL CONFERENCE ON SCIENTIFIC INFORMATION PROCEEDINGS (1959), Washington (DC), National Academy of Sciences/National Research Council

IWINSKI, M. B. (1911), 'Statistique internationale des imprimés', *Bulletin de l'Internationale Institut de Bibliographie*, **16**, 1

JACKSON, S. L. (1974), *Libraries and Librarianship in the West: a brief history*, New York, McGraw-Hill

JOHNSON-LAIRD, P. N. (1983), *Mental Models*, Cambridge, Cambridge University Press

KANTOR, P. B. (1976), 'Availability analysis', *Journal of American Society for Information Science*, **27**, 311–319

KANTOR, P. B. (1982), 'Evaluation of and feedback in information storage and retrieval systems', *Annual Review of Information Science and Technology*, **17**, Chap. 4

KANTOR, P. B. (1981), 'Quantitative evaluation of the reference process', *RQ*, **21**, No. 1, 43–52

KANTOR, P. B. (1979), 'Review of library operations research', *Library Research*, **1**, 295–345

KATZ, E. (1957), 'The two-step flow of communication', *Public Opinion Quarterly*, **21**, 61–78

KATZ, D. and KAHN, R. L. (1966), *Social Psychology of Organizations*, New York, John Wiley

KATZ, E. *et al.* (1963), 'Traditions of research in the diffusion of innovation', *American Sociological Review*, **28**, 237–252

KEARSLEY, G. P. (1976), 'Questions and question asking in verbal discourse', *Journal of Psychological Research*, **5**, 355–375

KEEN, E. M. (1973), 'The Aberystwyth index language test', *Journal of Documentation*, **29**, 1–35

KEHOE, C. A. (1985), 'Interfaces and expert systems for online retrieval', *Online Review*, **9**, 489–505

KENT, A. *et al.* (1978), *Cost Benefit Studies of some Critical Library Operations in Terms of Use of Materials*, University of Pittsburgh

KIEWITT, E. L. (1979), *Evaluating Information Retrieval Systems*, New York, Greenwood Press

KING, D. W. and PALMOUR, V. E. (1980), 'How needs are generated', *ASLIB/IIS/LA/Joint Conference*, Sheffield, London, Library Association, pp. 68–79

KING, D. W. *et al.* (1976), *Statistical Indicators of Scientific and Technical Communication, 1960–80*, National Science Foundation

KING, D. W. *et al.* (1981), *Telecommunications and Libraries*, New York, Knowledge Industry Publications

KING, G. B. (1972), 'Open and closed questions: the reference interviews', *RQ*, **12**, 157–160

KING, R. (1976), 'A comparison of the readability of abstracts with their source documents', *Journal of American Society for Information Science*, **27**, 118–121

KINTSCH, W. (1977), *Memory and Cognition*, New York, John Wiley

KOCHEN, M. (1972), WISE: a world information synthesis and encyclopaedia', *Journal of Documentation*, **28**, 322–343

KOCHEN, M. (1974) , *Principles of Information Retrieval*, Los Angeles, Melville

KOCHEN, M. and BADRE, A. N. (1974), 'Questions and shifts of representation in problem solving', *American Journal of Psychology*, **87**, 369–383

KOCHEN, M. and DONOHUE, J. (1976), *Information for the Community*, Chicago, American Library Association

KOCHEN, M. *et al.* (1967), *The Growth of Knowledge*, New York, John Wiley

KRAFT, D. H. (1979), 'Journal selection models', *Collection Management*, **3**, 163–185

KRECH, D. *et al.* (1962), *Individual in Society*, New York, McGraw-Hill

KUHN, A. (1966), *The Study of Society*, London, Tavistock

LACHMAN, R. and LACHMAN, J. L. (1979), *Cognitive Psychology and Information Processing*, New York, Lawrence Erlbaum

LAMBERTON, D. M. *et al.* (1971), *Economics of Information and Knowledge*, Harmondsworth, Penguin Books

LANCASTER, F. W. (1968), *Evaluation of the MEDLARS Demand Search Service*, Washington (DC), National Library of Medicine

LANCASTER, F. W. (1969), 'MEDLARS: a report on the evaluation of its operating efficiency', *American Documentation*, **20**, 119–142

LANCASTER, F. W. (1972), *Vocabulary Control for Information Retrieval*, Information Resources Press

LANCASTER, F. W. (1977), *The Measurement and Evaluation of Library Services*, Information

Resources Press

LANCASTER, F. W. (1978), *Guidelines for the Evaluation of Information Systems and Services*, Paris, Unesco

LANCASTER, F. W. (1979), *Information Retrieval Systems: characteristics, testing and evaluation*, 2nd edn, New York, Wiley-Interscience

LANGRISH, J. (1971), 'Technology transfer: some British data', *R and D Management*, **1**, 133–135

LAWANI, S. M. (1973), 'Bradford's law and the literature of agriculture', *International Library Review*, **5**, 341–350

LAZARSFELD, P. F. *et al.* (1955), *The Language of Social Research*, New York, Free Press

LAZARSFELD, P. F. *et al.* (1972), *Continuities in the Language of Social Research*, New York, Free Press

LE GRAND, J. and ROBINSON, R. (1976), *The Economics of Social Problems*, London, Macmillan

LEGGATE, P. (1971), *Evaluation of Operational Current Awareness Services*, Oxford, Experimental Information Unit

LEGGATE, P. *et al.* (1973), *The BA Previews Project*, Oxford, Experimental Information Unit

LEIMKUHLER, F. E. (1977), 'Operations analysis of library systems', *Information Processing and Management*, **13**, 79–93

LENSKI, G. and LENSKI, J. (1978), *Human Societies*, 3rd edn, New York, McGraw-Hill

LEVITAN, K. B. (1982a), 'Information resources as "goods" ', *Journal of American Society for Information Science*, **33**, 44–54

LEVITAN, K. B. (1982b), 'Information resources management', in *Annual Review of Information Science and Technology*, **17**

LEWIS, D. A. (1980), 'Today's challenge—tomorrow's choice', *Journal of Information Science*, **2**, 59–74

LIN, N. (1973), *The Study of Human Communication*, New York, Bobbs-Merrill

LINDQUIST, M. G. (1977), 'An explanation of the coming stagnation of information search services', *On-line Review*, **1**, 109–116

LINDQUIST, M. G. (1978a), 'Growth dynamics of information search services', *Journal of American Society for Information Science*, **29**, 67–76

LINDQUIST, M. G. (1978b), *The Dynamics of Information Search Services*, Stockholm, Royal Institute of Technology Library

LINDSAY, P. H. and NORMAN, D. A. (1977) *Human Information Processing*, 2nd edn, London, Academic Press

LINE, M. B. (1970), 'The half-life of periodical literature: apparent and real obsolescence', *Journal of Documentation*, **26**, 46–54

LINE, M. B. (1971), 'The information uses and needs of social scientists', *Aslib Proceedings*, **23**, 412–433

LINE, M. B. (1973), 'The ability of a university library to provide books wanted by researchers', *Journal of Librarianship*, **5**, 37–51

LINE, M. B. (1974), 'Draft definitions', *Aslib Proceedings*, **26**, 87

LINE, M. B. (1981), 'Libraries and information services in a post-technological society', *Journal of Library Automation*, **14**, 252–267

LINE, M. B. and SANDISON, A. (1974), 'Obsolescence and changes in the use of literature with time', *Journal of Documentation*, **30**, 283–350

LOFLAND, J. (1971), *Analysing Social Settings*, New York, Wadsworth

LOFTUS, G. R. and LOFTUS, E. F. (1976), *Human Memory*, New York, John Wiley

LOTKA, A. J. (1926), 'The frequency distribution of scientific productivity', *Journal of Washington Academy of Science*, **16**, 317–323

LYNCH, M. J. (1978), 'Reference interviews in public libraries', *Library Quarterly*, **48**, 119–142

LYNCH, M. J. (1983), 'Research in library reference information service', *Library Trends*, **31**, 401–420

MACBRIDE, S. (1980), *Many Voices, One World*, Paris, Unesco

MCCALL. G. J., SIMMONS, J. L. *et al.* (1969), *Issues in Participant Observation*, Reading (Mass.), Addison-Wesley

MCCALLUM, S. H. and GODWIN, J. L. (1981), 'Statistics on headings in the MARC file', *Journal of Library Automation*, **14**, 194–201

MCCLURE, C. R. (1978), 'The information rich employee and information for decision making', *Information Processing and Management*, **14**, 381–394

MCCLURE, C. R. and REIFSNYDER, B. (1984), 'Performance measures for corporate information centres', *Special Libraries*, **75**, 193–204

MCELROY, A. R. (1982), 'Library-information service evaluation', *Aslib Proceedings*, **34**, 249–265

MCFADYEN, D. (1975), 'The psychology of enquiry', *Journal of Librarianship*, **7**, 2–11

MACHLUP, F. *et al.* (1978–1980), *Information through the Printed Word*, Vols 1—4, New York, Praeger

MCLUHAN, M. (1967), *Understanding Media*, London, Sphere Books

MCNELLY, F. T. (1959), 'Intermediary communications in the international flow of news', *Journalism Quarterly*, **36**, 23–6

MCQUAIL, D. (1975), *Communication*, London, Longman

MCQUAIL, D. and WINDAHL, S. (1981), *Communication Models*, London, Longman

MACSHANE, D. (1979), *Using the Media*, London, Pluto Press

MADGE, J. (1953), *The Tools of Social Science*, London, Longman

MAGSON, M. S. (1973), 'Techniques for the measurement of cost-benefit in information centres', *Aslib Proceedings*, **25**, 164–185

MANSBRIDGE, J. (1986), 'Availability studies in libraries', *Library and Information Science Research*, **8**, 299–314

MANZER, B. M. (1977), *The Abstract Journal, 1790–1920*, Metuchen (NJ), Scarecrow Press

MARCH, J. G. and SIMON, H. A. (1958), *Organizations*, New York, John Wiley

MARKEY, K. (1981), 'Levels of question formulation in negotiation of information need during the online presearch interview', *Information Processing and Management*, **17**, 215–225

MARTIN, J. (1977), *Future Developments in Telecommunications*, 2nd edn, Englewood Cliffs (NJ), Prentice-Hall

MARTIN, J. (1978), *The Wired Society*, Englewood Cliffs (NJ), Prentice-Hall

MARTYN, J. (1975), 'Citation analysis', *Journal of Documentation*, **31**, 290–297

MARTYN, J. and LANCASTER, F. W. (1981), *Investigative Methods in Library and Information Science*, Los Angeles, Information Resources Press

MARTYN, J. and ROUSSEAU, G. (1984), 'Aspects of referral', *Aslib Proceedings*, **36**, 253–267

MARTYN, J. and SLATER, M. (1964, 1967), 'Tests on abstracts journals', *Journal of Documentation*, **20**, 212–235; 1967, **23**, 45–70

MASON, D. (1972), 'PPBS: application to an industrial information and library service', *Journal of Librarianship*, **4**, 95–101

MASON, D. (1973), 'Programmed budgeting and cost effectiveness', *Aslib Proceedings*, **25**, 100–110

MEADOW, C. T. (1970), *Man–machine Communication*, New York, Wiley-Interscience

MEADOW, C. T. (1973), *The Analysis of Information Systems*, 2nd edn, Melville

MEADOW, C. T. and COCHRANE, P. (1981), *Basics of Online Searching*, New York, John Wiley

MEADOWS, A. J. (1974), *Communication in Science*, London, Butterworths

MEIER, R. L. (1961), 'Efficiency criteria for the operation of large libraries', *Library Quarterly*, **31**, 215–234

MEIER, R. L. (1963), 'Information input overload: features of growth in communications-oriented institutions', *Libri*, **13**, 1–44

MENARD, H. W. (1971), *Science: Growth and Change*, Harvard University Press

MENZEL, H. *et al.* (1960), *Review of Studies in the Flow of Information among Scientists*, Columbia University, Bureau of Applied Social Research

MIKHAILOV, A. I. *et al.* (1984), *Scientific Communications and Informatics*, Los Angeles, Information Resources Press

MILLER, D. C. (1945), 'A research note on mass communication', *American Sociological Review*, **10**, 691–694

MILLER, G. A. (1968), *The Psychology of Communication*, Harmondsworth, Penguin Books

MINSKY, M. (1975), 'A framework for representing knowledge', in Winston, P. (ed.), *The Psychology of Computer Vision*, New York, McGraw-Hill

MISHLER, E. G.(1975), 'Studies in dialogue and discourse: II. Types of discourse initiated by and sustained through questioning', *Journal of Psycholinguistic Research*, **4**, 99–121

MOLES, A. *et al.* (1971), *La communication et les mass media*, Paris, Dictionnaire Marabout

MONTGOMERY, K. L. *et al.* (1976), 'Cost-benefit model of library acquisitions in terms of use', *Journal of the American Society for Information Science*, **27**, 73–74

MONTROLL, E. W. and BADGER, W. W. (1974), *Introduction to Quantitative Aspects of Social Phenomena*, London, Gordon and Breach

MORSE, P. M. (1968), *Library Effectiveness*, Reading (Mass.), MIT Press

MORSE, P. M. (1972), 'Measures of library effectiveness', *Library Quarterly*, **42**, 15–30

MOSER, C. A. and KALTON, G. (1971), *Survey Methods in Social Investigation*, 2nd edn, London Heinemann

MOTE, L. J. B. (1962), 'Reasons for the variations in the information needs of scientists', *Journal of Documentation*, **18**, 169–175

MOTE, L. J. B. and ANGEL, N. L. (1962), 'Survey of technical inquiry records at Thornton Research Centre', *Journal of Documentation*, **18**, 6–19

MUMFORD, L. (1966), *The City in History*, Harmondsworth, Penguin Books

MYLOPOULOS, J. and LEVESQUE, H. (1983), 'An overview of knowledge representation', in Brodie, M. L. *et al.*, *On Conceptual Modelling*, New York, Springer-Verlag

NARANAN, S. (1971), 'Power law relations in science bibliography', *Journal of Documentation*, **27**, 83–97

NARIN, F. *et al.* (1976), 'Structure of the biomedical literature', *Journal of the American Society for Information Science*, **27**, 25–45

NARIN, F. and MOLL, J. K. (1977), 'Bibliometrics', *Annual Review of Information Science and Technology*, **12**, 35–58

NEAL, H. E. (1963), *Communication from Stone Age to Space Age*, London, Phoenix House

NELSON, C., POLLOCK, D. *et al.* (1970), *Communication among Scientists and Engineers*, Lexington (Mass.), Heath

NEWCOMB, T. M. (1953), 'An approach to the study of communicative acts', *Psychological Review*, **60**, 393–404

NEWELL, A. (1982), 'The knowledge level', *Artificial Intelligence*, **18**, 87–127

NORMAN, O. G. (1979), 'The reference interview', *RSR*, **7**, 71–77

ODDY, R. N. (1977a), 'Information retrieval through man–machine dialogue', *Journal of Documentation*, **33**, 1–14

ODDY, R. N. (1977b), 'Retrieving references by dialogue rather than by query formulation', *Journal of Informatics*, **1**, 37–53

OGDEN, C. K. and RICHARDS, I. A. (1949), *The Meaning of Meaning*, 10th edn, London, Routledge and Kegan Paul

OLDMAN, C. M. (1976), 'The value of information services', *Management Bibliographies and Reviews*, **2**, 211–232

OLDMAN, C. M. (1978), *The Value of Academic Libraries*, PhD thesis, Cranfield Institute of Technology

OPPENHEIM, A. L. (1964), *Ancient Mesopotamia*, University Chicago Press

ORR, R. H. (1973), 'Measuring the goodness of library services', *Journal of Documentation*, **29**, 315–332

ORR, R. H. *et al.* (1968), 'Measuring a library's capability for providing documents', *Bulletin of the Medical Library Association*, **56**, 241–267

OSWITCH, P. A. (1983), 'Modelling information system dynamics', *Library Research*, **5**, 129–155

OVERHAGE, C. F. J. and REINTJES, J. F. (1974), 'Project INTREX: a general review', *Information Storage and Retrieval*, **10**, 157–188

PAISLEY, W. J. (1965), *The Flow of Behavioural Science Information*, Institute for Communication Research, Stanford University

PAISLEY, W. J. (1980), 'Information and work', *Progress in Communication Sciences*, **2**, 113–165

PALMER, E. S. (1981), 'The effect of distance on public library use', *Library Research*, **3**, 315–354

PAO, M.L. (1986), 'An empirical examination of Lotka's law', *Journal of the American Society for Information Science*, **37**, 26–33

PARK, R. (1967), 'News as a form of knowledge', in Turner, *On Social Control*, Chicago University Press, pp. 32–52

PASK, G. (1961), *An Approach to Cybernetics*, London, Hutchinson

PENNER, R. J. (1972), 'Measuring a library's capability', *Journal of Education for Librarianship*, **12**, 17–30

PENNIMAN, W. D. and DOMINICK, W. D. (1980), 'Monitoring and evaluation of on-line information system usage', *Information Processing and Management*, **16**, 17–35

PITERNICK, A. B. (1989), 'Functions and capabilities of online searching systems', *Online Review*, **13**, 457–76

POOL, I. DE S. (1983), 'Tracking the flow of information' *Science*, **227**, 609–613

POOL, I. DE S. *et al.* (1973), *Handbook of Communication* (including Pool on communication systems, Schramm on channels and audiences, Frey on communication and development), Chicago, Rand-McNally

POOL, I. DE S. *et al.* (1984), *Communication Flows: a Census in the US and Japan*, Amsterdam, North-Holland

POPPER, K. (1976), *Unended Quest*, London, Fontana

PORTER, M. F. (1980), 'An algorithm for suffix stripping', *Program*, **14**, 130–137

POTTER, W. G. (1980), 'When names collide', *Library Resources and Technical Services*, **24**, 3–16

POTTER, W. G. (1981), 'Lotka's law revisited', *Library Trends*, **30**, 21–39

POWELL, R. (1984), *Basic Research Methods for Librarians*, Norwood (Mass.), Ablex

POWELL, R. R. (1984), 'Reference effectiveness', *Library and Information Science Research*, **6**, 3–19

PRAUNLICH, P. and KROLL, M. (1978), 'Bradford's distribution: a new formulation', *Journal of American Society for Information Science*, **29**, 51–55

PRICE, D. J. DE S. (1976), 'General theory of bibliometric and other cumulative advantage processes', *Journal of American Society for Information Science*, **27**, 92–96

PRICE, D. S. (1974), 'Rational cost information', *Special Libraries*, **65**, 49–57

RAITT, D. *et al.* (1984), *An Introduction to Online Information Systems*, Oxford, Learned Information

RAMSEY, H. D. and GRIMES, J. D. (1983), 'Human factors in interactive computer dialog', *Annual Review of Information Science and Technology*, **18**, 29–59

RANGANATHAN, S. R. (1957), *The Five Laws of Library Science*, Madras Library Association, revised edn, Madras

RANGANATHAN, S. R. (1967), *Prolegomena to Library Classification*, 3rd edn, London, Asia Publishing House

RAVETZ, J. R. (1971), *Scientific Knowledge and its Social Problems*, Oxford, Oxford University Press

RAWSKI, C. H. *et al.* (1973), *Towards a Theory of Librarianship*, Metuchen (NJ), Scarecrow Press

REID, I. (1981), *Social Class Differences in Britain*, 2nd edn, London, Grant McIntyre

REINECKE, I. (1984), *Electronic Illusions*, Harmondsworth, Penguin Books

RESNIKOFF, H. L. and DOLBY, J. L. (1971), *Access to Information*, Los Angeles, R and D Consultants

REVANS, R. W. (1969), 'The structure of disorder', Chapter 17 in Rose, J. (ed.), *Survey of Cybernetics*, London, Iliffe

RICH, E. (1983), *Artificial Intelligence*, New York,, McGraw-Hill

ROBERTSON, A. (1973), 'Information flow and industrial innovation', *Aslib Proceedings*, **25**, 130–138

ROBERTSON, A. (1974), 'Behaviour patterns of scientists and engineers in information seeking for problem solving', *Aslib Proceedings*, **26**, 384–390

ROBERTSON, S. E. (1977), 'Theories and models in information retrieval', *Journal of Documentation*, **33**, 126–148

ROBERTSON, S. E. (1981), 'Methodology of information retrieval experiment', in Sparck Jones,

356   References

K. *et al.*, *Information Retrieval Experiment*, London, Butterworths

ROBERTSON, S. E. and HENSMAN, S. (1975), 'Journal acquisition by libraries: scatter and cost-effectiveness', *Journal of Documentation*, **31**, 273–282

ROBERTSON, W. P. and RACKSTRAW, S. J. (1972), *A Question of Answers*, London, Routledge and Kegan Paul

ROGERS, E. M. and ROGERS, R. A. (1976), *Communication in Organizations*, New York, Free Press

ROGERS, E. M. and SHOEMAKER, F. F. (1971), *Communication of Innovations*, 2nd edn, New York, Collier Macmillan

ROGERS, J. V. (1984), 'Networking: selected research studies 1979-83', *Library and Information Science Research*, **6**, 111–132

ROSENBLOOM, R. S. and WOLEK, F. W. (1967), *Technology, Information and Organization: Information Transfer in Industrial R and D*, Harvard Unversity, Graduate School of Business Administration

ROTHENBERG, D. H. and HO, D. Y. (1977), 'The geometrical location of information centres', *Information Processing and Management*, **13**, 317–327

ROUSE, W. B. (1975), 'Optimal resource allocation in library systems', *Journal of American Society for Information Science*, **26**, 157–165

ROUSE, W. B. (1976), 'Library network model', *Journal of American Society for Information Science*, **27**, 88–99

ROUSE, W. B. (1979), 'Mathematical modelling of library systems', *Journal of American Society for Information Science*, **30**, 181–191

ROYAL SOCIETY (1948), *Scientific Information Conference Report and Papers Submitted*, London

ROYAL SOCIETY (1981), *Study of Scientific Information System in the UK*, British Library Research and Development Department Report 5626

RUMELHART, D. E. (1977), *Introduction to Human Information Processing*, New York, John Wiley

RYDER, J. and SILVER, H. (1970), *Modern English Society*, London, Methuen

SAGER, N. (1978), 'Natural language information formatting', *Advances in Computers*, **17**, 89–162

SALTON, G. (1975), *Dynamic Information and Library Processing*, Englewood Cliffs (NJ), Prentice-Hall

SALTON, G. and LESK, M. E. (1973), 'Recent studies in automatic text analysis and information retrieval', *Journal of the Association of Computing Machinery*, **20**, 258–278

SALTON, G. and MCGILL, M. J. (1983), *Introduction to Modern Information Retrieval*, New York, McGraw-Hill

SARACEVIC, T. (1968), *An Enquiry into Testing of Information Retrieval Systems*, Comparative Systems Laboratory, Case Western Reserve University

SARACEVIC, T. (1970a), 'The concept of relevance in information science', in Saracevic, T. *et al.*, *Introduction to Information Science*, New York, Bowker, pp. 111–151

SARACEVIC, T. *et al.* (1970b), *Introduction to Information Science*, New York, Bowker

SARACEVIC, T. (1976), 'Relevance: a review of and framework for the thinking on the notion in information science', *Advances in Librarianship*, **6**, 79–138

SAYERS, W. C. B. (1967), *Manual of Classification*, 4th edn, London, Grafton Books

SCHANK, R. C. (1975), *Conceptual Information Processing*, Amsterdam, North-Holland

SCHANK, R. C. and ABELSON, R. P. (1977), *Script, Plans, Goals, and Understanding*, New York, Lawrence Erlbaum

SCHRAMM, W. (1964), *Mass Media and National Development*, Stanford (Ca.), Stanford University Press

SCHULTZ, C. K. (ed.)(1968), *H. P. Luhn: Selected Works*, New York, John Wiley

SEATON, J. (1975), 'Readability tests for UK professional journals', *Journal of Librarianship*, **7**, 69–83

SERAFINE, S. and ANDRIEU, M. (1981), *The Information Revolution and its Implications for Canada*, Government of Canada, Department of Communications

SHERA, J. H. (1972), *The Foundation of Education for Librarianship*, Becker and Hayes

SHERA, J. H. and CLEVELAND, D. B. (1977), 'History and foundations of information science', *Annual Review of Information Science and Technology*, **12**, 249–275

SHERIF, M. and SHERIF, C. W. (1969), *Social Psychology*, revised edn, New York, Harper

SHIBUTANI, T. (1955), 'Reference groups as perspectives', *American Journal of Sociology*, **60**, 562–569

SIMON, H. S. (1969), *The Sciences of the Artificial*, Cambridge (Mass.), MIT Press

SIMON, J. L. (1978), *Basic Research Methods in Social Science*, 2nd edn, New York, Random House

SINGLETON, A. (1976), 'Journal ranking and selection', *Journal of Documentation*, **32**, 258–289

SINHA, B. K. and CLELLAND, R. C. (1975), 'Modelling for the management of library collections', *Management Science*, **22**, 547–557

SITPRO (1978), *Future Trends in Computer and Communications Systems*, London, SITPRO

SLATER, M. *et al.* (1972), *Data and the Chemist*, London, Aslib

SLOMAN, A. (1978), *The Computer Revolution in Philosophy*, Brighton, Harvester Press

SMALL, H. (1980), 'Cocitation context analysis and the structure of paradigms', *Journal of Documentation*, **36**, 183–196

SMALL, H. and GRIFFITH, B. C. (1974), 'The use of scientific literatures, parts I and II', *Science Studies*, **4**, 17–40, 339–365

SMITH, A. (1980), *Goodbye to Gutenberg*, Oxford, Oxford University Press

SMITH, A.G. (1973), 'The ethic of the relay men', in Thayer, L. (ed.), *Communications: Ethical and Moral Issues*, New York, Gordon and Breach

SMITH, L. C. (1976), 'Artificial intelligence in information retrieval', *Information Processing and Management*, **12**, 189–222

SMITH, L. C. (1980), 'Artificial intelligence applications in information systems', *Annual Review of Information Science and Technology*, **15**, 67–105

SMITH, L. C. (1981), 'Citation analysis', *Library Trends*, **30**, 83–106

SMITH, L. C. and WARNER, A. J. (1984), 'Taxonomy of representations in IR system design', *Journal of Information Science*, **8**, 113–121

SOERGEL, D. (1967), 'Some remarks on information languages', *Information Storage and Retrieval*, **3**, 219–291

SOMERVILLE, A. N. (1977), 'The place of the reference interview in computer searching', *Online*, **1**, 14–23

SORMUNEN, E. (1989), *Analysis of Online Searching Knowledge for Intermediary Systems*, Research report 630, Technical Research Centre of Finland

SOWA, J. F. (1984), *Conceptual Structures*, Reading (Mass.), Addison-Wesley

SPARCK JONES, K. (1971), *Automatic Keyword Classification for Information Retrieval*, London, Butterworths

SPARCK JONES, K. *et al.* (1981), *Information Retrieval Experiment*, London, Butterworths

SPARCK JONES, K. and KAY, M. (1973), *Linguistics and Information Science*, London, Academic Press

STAUD, J. L. (1988), 'The universe of online databases: reality and models', *Journal of Information Science*, **14**, 141–58

STEINBERG, S. H. (1974), *Five Hundred Years of Printing*, 3rd edn, Harmondsworth, Penguin Books

STONE, L. (1969), 'Literacy and education in England, 1640–1900', *Past and Present*, No. 42, 120–121

STONE, S. *et al.* (1984), *CRUS Guides*, No. 1 onwards, Sheffield, Centre for Research on User Studies

SUCHMAN, E. (1967), *Evaluation Research: Principles and Practices in Public Service and Social Action Programs*, New York, Sage Foundation

SWANSON, R. N. (1975), 'Performance evaluation studies in information science', *Journal of American Society for Information Science*, **26**, 140–156

SWIGGER, K. (1985), 'Questions in library and information science', *Library and Information Science Research*, **7**, 369–383

358 References

TAGUE, J. *et al.* (1981), 'The law of exponential growth', *Library Trends*, **30**, 125–149

TAYLOR, R. S. (1967), *Question Negotiation and Information Seeking in Libraries*, Bethlehem (Pa.), Lehigh University

TAYLOR, R. S. (1968), 'Question negotiation and information seeking in libraries', *College and Research Libraries*, **29**, 178–194

TAYLOR, R. S. *et al.* (1973), *Economics of Information Dissemination*, New York, Syracuse University

THAYER, L. (1968), *Communication and Communication Systems*, Homewood (Il.), Irwin

THOMAS, P. A. and ROBERTSON, S. E. (1975), 'Computer simulation model of library operations', *Journal of Documentation*, **31**, 1–18

TOFFLER, A. (1971), *Future Shock*, London, Pan Books

UNISIST (1971), *Study Report on the Feasibility of a World Science Information System*, Paris, Unesco

UNWIN, D. *et al.* (1978), *Encyclopaedis of Educational Media Communications and Technology*, London, Macmillan

URQUHART, D. J. and BUNN, R. M. (1959), 'National loan policy for scientific serials', *Journal of Documentation*, **15**, 21–37

URQUHART, D. J. (1959), 'Use of scientific periodicals', in *International Conference on Scientific Information Proceedings*, Vol. 1, Washington (DC), National Academy of Sciences/National Research Council, pp. 287–300

URQUHART, J. A. and SCHOFIELD, J. L. (1971, 1972), 'Measuring readers' failure at the shelf', *Journal of Documentation*, 1971, **27**, 273–286; 1972, **28**, 233–241

UZANNE, O., The Book-hunter in Paris, quoted by Jackson, H. (1950), *The Anatomy of Bibliomania*, London, Faber

VAN RIJSBERGEN, C. J. (1976), 'File organization in library automation and information retrieval', *Journal of Documentation*, **32**, 299–317

VAN RIJSBERGEN, C. J. (1979), *Information Retrieval*, 2nd edn, London, Butterworths

VAN RIJSBERGEN, C.J. *et al.* (1984), *Research and Development in Information Retrieval*, Cambridge, Cambridge University Press

VAN SLYPE, G. (1979), *Conception et gestion des systèmes documentaires*, Paris, Editions d'Organisation

VICKERS, P. J. (1973), 'Cost survey of mechanized information systems', *Journal of Documentation*, **29**, 258–280

VICKERS, P. J. (1983), 'Common problems of documentary information transfer, storage, and retrieval in industrial organisations', *Journal of Documentation*, **39**, 217–229

VICKERY, A. (1984), 'An intelligent interface for online interaction', *Journal of Information Science*, **9**, 7–18

VICKERY, A. (1988), 'The experience of building expert search systems', *Online Information 88*, Oxford, Learned Information

VICKERY, A. *et al.* (1978), *Organisation and Impact of a Travelling Workshop for Online Information Retrieval*, University of London, Central Information Service

VICKERY, A. and BATTEN, A. M. (1978), *Large-scale Evaluation of Online and Batch Computer Information Services*, Library Resources Coordinating Committee, University of London

VICKERY, A., BROOKS, H., ROBINSON, B. and VICKERY, B. C. (1986), *Expert System for Referral, Final Report*, University of London, Central Information Service

VICKERY, A., BROOKS, H., ROBINSON, B. and VICKERY, B.C. (1987), 'A reference and referral system using expert system techniques', *Journal of Documentation*, **43**, March

VICKERY, B. C. (1948), 'Bradford's law of scattering', *Journal of Documentation*, **4**, 198–203

VICKERY, B. C. (1961), 'The use of scientific literature', *Library Association Record*, **63**, 263–269

VICKERY, B. C. (1963), 'Scientific information: problems and prospects', *Minerva*, **2**, 21–38

VICKERY, B. C. (1964), 'The present state of research into the communication of information', *Aslib Proceedings*, **16**, 79–91

VICKERY, B. C. (1965), *On Retrieval System Theory*, 2nd edn, London, Butterworths

VICKERY, B. C. (1968), 'Statistics of scientific and technical articles', *Journal of Documentation*,

24, 192–196

VICKERY, B. C. (1969), 'Indicators of the use of periodicals', *Journal of Librarianship*, **1**, 170–182

VICKERY, B. C. (1970a), 'Methodology in research', *Aslib Proceedings*, **22**, 597–606

VICKERY, B. C. (1970b), *Techniques of Information Retrieval*, London, Butterworths

VICKERY, B. C. (1971), 'Structure and function in retrieval languages', *Journal of Documentation*, **27**, 69–82

VICKERY, B. C. (1973), *Information Systems*, London, Butterworths

VICKERY, B. C. (1975), *Classification and Indexing in Science*, 3rd edn, London, Butterworths

VICKERY, B. C. (1978), 'Concepts of documentation', *Journal of Documentation*, **34**, 279–287

VICKERY, B. C. (1985), *Information Provision—Past, Present and Future*, University of London, Library Resources Coordinating Committee, Occasional Publication No. 4

VICKERY, B. C. (1986), 'Knowledge representation: a brief review', *Journal of Documentation*, **42**, 145–159

VICKERY, B. C. (1989), *Intelligent Interfaces: state-of-the-art survey*, London, Tome Associates

VICKERY, B. C. and EARLE, P. (1969), 'Subject relations in science/technology literature', *Aslib Proceedings*, **21**, 237–243

VICKERY, B. C. and EAST, H. (1971), *Computer Support for Parliamentary Information Service*, ASLIB Report

VICKERY, B. C., HESELTINE, R. G. and BROWN, C. (1984), 'Interactive information networks and UK libraries', *Journal of Documentation*, **40**, 36–49

VICKERY, B. C. et al. (1969), *Metals Information in Britain*, London, Aslib

VICKERY, B. C. et al. (1970), 'The analysis of library processes', *Journal of Documentation*, **26**, 30–45

VICKERY, B. C. and VICKERY, A. (1990), 'Intelligence and information systems', *Journal of Information Science*, **16**, 65–70

VICKERY, B. C. and VICKERY, A. (1992), 'An application of language processing for a search interface', *Journal of Documentation*, September issue

VORESS, H. E. (1962), 'Literature search on radioactive fallout', in *The Literature of Nuclear Science*, US Atomic Energy Commission, pp. 284–294

WADDINGTON, C. H. (1977), *Tools for Thought*, London, Paladin

WALL, T. (1980/1981), 'Distribution of use among users of an academic library collection', *Library Research*, **2**, 177–180

WAPLES, D. (1932), 'The relation of subject interests to actual reading', *Library Quarterly*, **2**, 42–70

WARD, J. (1981). 'Who needs to know', in ASLIB/IIS/LA Joint Conference, *The Nationwide Provision and Use of Information*, London, Library Association

WARDHAUGH, R. (1985), *How Conversation Works*, Oxford, Blackwell

WATERMAN, D. A. (1986), *Guide to Expert Systems*, Reading, Mass., Addison–Wesley

WEECH, T. L. (1974), 'Evaluation of adult reference service', *Library Trends*, **22**, 315–335

WEISMAN, H. M. (1972), *Information Systems, Services and Centers*, Los Angeles, Becker and Hayes

WESSEL, C. J. (1968), 'Criteria for evaluating technical library effectiveness', *Aslib Proceedings*, **20**, 455–481

WESSEL, M. R. and KIRKLEY, J. L. (1982), 'For a national information committee', *Datamation*, **28**, No. 10, 234–248

WHITE, D. M. (1950), 'The gatekeepers: a case study in the selection of news', *Journalism Quarterly*, **27**, 383–390

WHITE, M. (1981), 'Dimensions of the reference interview', *Reference Quarterly*, **20**, 373–381

WHITEHALL, T. (1980), 'User valuations and resource management for information services', *Aslib Proceedings*, **32**, 87–105

WHITLEY, R. and FROST, P. (1973), 'Task type and information transfer in a government research laboratory', *Human Relations*, **25**, 537–550

WHYTE, L. L. et al. (1969), *Hierarchical Structures*, New York, American Elsevier

WILKIN, A. (1977), 'Personal roles and barriers in information transfer', *Advances in Librarianship*, **7**, 257–297

WILKS, Y. A. (1972), *Grammar, Meaning, and the Machine Analysis of Language*, London, Routledge

WILLETTS, M. (1975), 'Investigation of the nature of the relations between terms in thesauri', *Journal of Documentation*, **31**, 158–184

WILLIAMS, A. (1976), *Reading and the Consumer*, London, Hodder and Stoughton

WILLIAMS, R. (1965), *The Long Revolution*, Harmondsworth, Penguin Books

WILLS, G. *et al.* (1972), *Technological Forecasting*, Harmondsworth, Penguin Books

WILLS, G. and CHRISTOPHER, M. (1970), 'Cost benefit analysis of company information needs', *Unesco Bulletin for Libraries*, **24**, 9–23

WILSON, T. D. (1975), 'Local library cooperation in the service of higher education', *Journal of Librarianship*, **7**, 143–152

WILSON, T. D. (1981a), 'Case study in qualitative research', *Social Science Information Studies*, **1**, 241–246

WILSON, T. D. (1981b), 'On user studies and information needs', *Journal of Documentation*, **37**, 3–15

WILSON, T. D. and STREATFIELD, D. R. (1981), 'Structured observation in the investigation of information needs', *Social Science Information Studies*, **1**, 173–184

WILSON, T. D. *et al.* (1977, 1979), 'Information needs in local authority social service departments', *Journal of Documentation*, 1977, **33**, 277–293; 1979, **35**, 120–136

WINSTON, P. H. (1984), *Artificial Intelligence*, 2nd edn, Reading (Mass.), Addison-Wesley

WOLEK, F. W. (1970), 'The complexity of messages in science and engineering', in Nelson, C., Pollock, D. *et al. Communication among Scientists and Engineers*, Lexington (Mass.), Heath

WOLFE, J.N. (1974), *Economics of Technical Information Systems*, New York, Praeger

WOOD, L. J. and LEE, T. R. (1980), 'Time–space convergence', *Area*, **12**, 217–222

WOODBURN, I. (1970), *Mathematical Model of a Hierarchical Library System*, University of Lancaster Library

WORTHEN, D. B. (1973), 'The epidemic process and the contagion model', *Journal of American Society for Information Science*, **24**, 343–346

WYLLYS, R. E. (1981), 'Empirical and theoretical bases of Zipf's law', *Library Trends*, **30**, 53–64

YOUNG, J. Z. (1971), *An Introduction to the Study of Man*, Oxford, Oxford University Press

YOUNG, J. Z. (1978), *Programs of the Brain*, Oxford, Oxford University Press

YOUNG, P. V. (1966), *Scientific Social Surveys and Research*, 4th edn, Englewood Cliffs (NJ), Prentice-Hall

ZELLDITCH, M. (1962), 'Some methodological problems of field studies', *American Journal of Sociology*, **67**, 566–576

Appendix 1

Criteria for information science
(Institute of Information Scientists)

Preamble

Information science is concerned with the science and practice of the provision of information. To this end, it includes the study of information from its generation to its exploitation, and of its transmission in a variety of forms through a variety of channels.

The Institute of Information Scientists, established in 1958, is the main body in the UK representing and bringing together those concerned with information science. There are large areas of knowledge relevant to the subject, whose broad study has resulted in the development of a variety of programmes of study and of examinations. The Institute, as an organization concerned with recognition of the breadth and depth of knowledge, and of the professional experience and competence to be expected of its members, has therefore described information science in terms of the appended Criteria.

These Criteria are intended to provide a guide to topics which may usefully and justifiably be included in a course of instruction in information science. It would normally be expected that, for acceptance by the Institute for corporate membership, a candidate would have good knowledge of the topics covered by Sections 1–7. Topics covered by the sections on ancillary skills may also be of value to an information scientist and therefore any of these may provide studies complementary to the core topics.

Whilst for convenience and clarity, the whole subject has been subdivided into sections, it is not intended that the sections should form self-contained divisions. This is particularly true in the case of technology. It is expected that whatever technology is appropriate, it be included in Sections 1–6. Section 7, on technology itself, has been kept brief for this reason, and also because the speed of development in new technology makes it unwise to be too specific about the sorts of technology that ought to be included. Therefore, a number of examples of the sort of technology that are considered appropriate is provided in Appendix A. This Appendix can be updated as required without having to change the Criteria themselves. The examples in the Appendix should NOT be construed as being exhaustive. It is essential that technology be integrated into the subjects referred to in Sections 1–6 as well as being considered in its own right.

The Criteria should not be construed as exhaustive. There may be other specialized contributions which educational institutions would consider might be usefully incorporated. There will certainly be developments in information science which are, at present, not foreseen. Therefore the Criteria as set out below may be modified from time to time to reflect the Institute's appreciation of changes of emphasis or widening scope of the subject. The current description simply represents the latest version of the Criteria to be formulated.

1 Knowledge and its communication

Creation and growth of knowledge (including bibliometrics). Nature, properties and characteristics of knowledge and information flows. Generation, transfer, and use of information. Information needs and information seeking and user behaviour and the impact of historical, social, psychological, economic, technical, and other factors on this behaviour. Communications systems theory, design and evaluation. Human communication from psychological and practical points of view. Communication in the corporate environment.

2 Sources of information

Primary sources of recorded information in their various media (e.g. textual material, computer files, machine-readable databases for online access, audiovisual and other records) and their information content, occurrences distribution, and use. Individuals and organizations (national and international) which collect, extract, and/or disseminate information (e.g. information brokers and consultants, expert individuals, libraries, information centres). Information sources in general and special subject fields. Major information services.

3 Theory of information storage and retrieval

Characterization of information problems and methods of dealing with them. Media for information storage and choice and organization of the media in store for various information types (e.g. full text, abstracts, numeric and tabular data, and audiovisual material, and combinations of these). Descriptive cataloguing. Theory and application of classification systems (e.g. enumerative and synthetic types and alphabetical schedules). Analysis of information content of sources. Theory and application of indexing of information content (e.g. coding by use of classification and indexing schedules—subject heading lists, thesauri; pre- and post-coordinate indexing; natural language and controlled vocabularies). Content and characteristics of secondary sources of information (e.g.

abstracts and indexes, publicly accessible computer files, library catalogues). Organization of small personal collections of information.

4 Systems for information storage and retrieval

User types, user patterns, finding user needs. Exploitation of resources—search methods and strategies and reference methods for information (e.g. references, data, full text, or combinations of these). Use of manual, mechanized, and mixed systems (e.g. paper files, card indexes, microfilm/fiche systems, word processing, computerized systems). Use of human and technical networks for retrieval. Internal and external systems, services and networks for retrieval (e.g. videotex, databases). Input, indexing, and output for successful retrieval. Evaluation of retrieval systems and secondary sources of information (e.g. effectiveness and efficiency).

5 Dissemination of information

Preparation of bibliographies and evaluated information reports. Effective writing. Proof reading, editing and presentation. Methods of reproduction. Networks (e.g. telecommunication networks).

6 Management

Information systems, internal and external environment, objectives and structure; moral and legal aspects (e.g. privacy, secrecy, copyright, health and safety, security). Implementation of information systems. Justification and cost/benefit/effectiveness analysis. General theory and techniques of management with particular reference to information systems, costing, budgeting, financial control; forecasting, policy making, planning; staff management and industrial relations; organization and methods, operational research. Systems approach (e.g. systems analysis and design). Characteristics of a good information scientist.

7 Technology and its applications

Technology for aiding information creation, acquisition, organization, transmission, retrieval, dissemination and management.

Examples of particular technologies that might be included are listed in Appendix A.

8 Ancillary skills

RESEARCH METHODS: historical research; deductive, inductive, hypothetico-inductive methods. Research proposal. Investigation, data collection and sampling. Evaluation of results, errors, validity. Conclusion, report.

MATHEMATICS: Appropriate mathematics and statistics.

LINGUISTICS: Natural and formal language. Linguistic classification. Semantics, syntactics, pragmatics. Relations of semantics and linguistics, psychology, logic and philosophy. The development of language.

FOREIGN LANGUAGES: Reading and comprehension of foreign languages. Translation. Preparation of abstracts, reports, etc. in English or the language of habitual usage. Use of foreign-language information sources.

Appendix A
Examples of appropriate technologies

Computer hardware, main components and their uses, types of input and output devices, storage devices, mainframes, minicomputers and micro-computers. Computer software: principles of operating systems, application programs; program packages; elementary programming. Computer processing: file design, record layout, file update. Communications: principles of standards, protocols, interfaces and types of equipment (e.g. modems). Computer projects: feasibility studies, specification, design, implementation, evaluation, documentation. Computers in information applications: e.g. information retrieval, viewdata, teletext, computer typesetting, computer output on microfilm (COM). Word processors: types (e.g. shared logic, stand-alone) and applications (e.g. input, information retrieval). Storage media and systems: e.g. video discs, automated microfiche systems. Electronic publishing and document delivery: e.g. Prestel, Ceefax, video scanning and digitizing of text, cable TV.

Areas of study in information science
(B. C. Vickery, 1982)

1 The role of information in society

(1) Factors giving rise to information demand and information provision: complexity of society, technological innovation, occupational specialization, educational level, cultural development, social administration.

(2) Main functions in information transfer: generation of information, recording, publication, distribution, analysis, storage, retrieval, relay, interpersonal transfer, reception, and use.

(3) Specific study of particular areas of information transfer—for example, science and technology, commerce, administration, social welfare, law. In each area: the natures of the occupations and activities leading to information need; typical institutional environments for such activities; modes of communication within the area; forms of document used; information sources and services; specialized features of information transfer in the area.

For example, in science and technology:

(4) The nature of scientific research, the development of team work, the kinds of institution that form the work environment of the researcher. Examples of such institutions. The development of institutionalized research since the seventeenth century. Main directories of research institutions and guides to research in progress.

(5) The importance of precise data, technical methods, and theories in research. Important sources of quantitative data and laboratory methods. Examples of data centres throughout the world.

(6) Science as a world community of scholars. The importance of quality control through publication and criticism by peers. Personal and professional characteristics of the scientific community.

(7) Technology and engineering in contrast to science. Its emergence and continuing link with craft practice. The increasing application of science to technology. The work environments of the technologist—for example, factory, oilfield, farm, nuclear reactor, computer centre. The main types and centres of technology. Directories to such centres.

(8) The importance of practical results to the technologist, and his consequent personal and professional characteristics. His use of raw data, practical recipes and procedures, materials and equipment.

Economic aspects of technological processes. Main sources of information on materials and equipment.

(9) Scientific and technical professional societies and associations; their development, their professional role, and their contributions to communication (publications, conferences, etc.).

(10) Modes of communication in science and technology: the importance of both formal and informal, oral and written sources. Characteristics of the various modes. The importance of intermediaries in the diffusion of scientific and technical information (gatekeepers, consultants, etc.).

(11) Forms of publication in science and technology: their development, characteristics, present state, quantity, and current problems.

(a) Monograph, journal, thesis, report, patent, drawing, map.

(b) Handbook, manual,standard, trade literature.

(c) Review paper, abstracts, indexing journal.

The main sources of information about current and past publications of each type. The main publishers of different types of materials. Main scientific and technical libraries and the services they offer.

(12) Linguistic and terminological problems in science and technology. Standard nomenclatures and glossaries. The languages in which material is published. The problems and availability of translations. Transliteration.

(13) Scientific information services: types, functions, and services, planning and management, staffing needs, problems. Services and directories to these services.

(14) Machine-based information services in science and technology. Database producers, processors, and purveyors, and the services they offer. Means of access to these services.

(15) National and international systems of scientific and technical information. The system in UK and its projected development. Other major national systems, the emerging international system—UNISIST and other agencies.

2 Computers and communications

The aim of a general course in this field will be to give the student (1) an understanding of the roles that computers and telecommunications can and will play in information systems and (2) a grasp of the specific skills needed for successful interaction with computers and communications systems. Beyond this, there will be need for special courses aimed at those more intimately concerned with the design and implementation of computer information systems.

A general course should impart understanding of:

(1) The distinction within information systems between intellectual operations, not at present reducible to decision rules, and clerical or formal operations. The possibility and advisability of using data-processing machines to carry out formal operations.

(2) The need for detailed systems and cost analysis of processes where data processing is to be introduced, to determine which operations can

economically be allocated to the machine. Study of examples of system and cost analysis.

(3) The digital computer as a data-processing machine. Its basic operations and characteristics. The kinds of operation suitable for computer manipulation. Typical examples outside the information field.

(4) The basic functional components of the computer: input, output, central processor and control, stores, conversational access. Practical handling of various input and conversational equipment. Demonstrations of output equipment, choice of input and output equipment for different types of application. Storage equipment.

(5) Coding data for computer handling. Bit codes. Character sets. Problems of mixed scripts.

(6) Instructing the computer: the nature of programming. Machine codes. High- and low-level languages. Compilers and interpreters. Operating systems. Training and practice in the use of a high-level language to write programs, input them with data, and observe output.

(7) Bibliographic records and files; practical analysis of the characteristics of a range of typical manual (visual) records and files—for example, catalogues, bibliographies, indexes. Elements within the record. Search access points.

(8) Adaption of bibliographic records for machine handling: record format. Practical work in preparing work sheets for input in standard format. Variations in format and the problems they create. Standardization.

(9) File organization: relationship between organization of manual (visual) file and of computer files. Logical and physical file organization. Types of organization.

(10) File-handling processes: sorting, merging, amending, updating, deleting, searching, extracting.

(11) Applications of computers to practical information processes: publication, acquisition, word processing, cataloguing, circulation, serials recording, accounting, management information, data management, machine translation, etc.

(12) Computer-based information retrieval. The kinds of subject element in database records (title, abstract, descriptors, subject codes, citations, etc.). Vocabulary control, free text. Access to searchable terms (word lists, thesauri, etc.). Search features (Boolean, weighting, truncation, within ranges, free text). Formulation of profiles and search statements. Current awareness (SDI) and retrospective search. Batch and online procedures. Man–machine interactions. Expert systems.

(13) Computer communications and networks. The purpose and value of linking computers. Types of data transmission channel. Terminal equipment. Protocols and interfaces. Varieties of network structure. The economics of networking. Administrative and political problems.

3 Information systems

The aim of a course in this area—the application of scientific method to practical information problems—is to give the student a grounding in the analysis, design, and evaluation of library and information systems, and in systematic methods of planning and management.

(1) The systems approach: the nature of systems, components and their interrelation, the importance of feedback, system environment, system purposes and functions, quantification.

(2) Levels of information system: international, national, individual library and information services, their sections, functional components, their elements.

(3) The basic components of information systems—for example, authors, documents, records, staff, equipment, processes, services, users. Their characteristics and interrelations. Individual student analysis of a particular library or information service into its components, quantified.

(4) The analysis of processes: flowcharting, method study, decision tables, work measurement, costing. Practice in using these techniques, applied to library and information processes.

(5) The design process. Specification of user needs, system management objectives, constraints (financial, human, equipment, other operational). Services to be provided, performance criteria, allowable margins of error. Available inputs (documents, records). Required outputs. Quantification. Processing required to produce outputs from inputs. Allocation of processing tasks between man and machine. Interactions between processes. Handling exceptions. Choice of equipment. Staffing needs. Costing the design. Teaching should be related to one or more specific and detailed case studies of systems design.

(6) The evaluation of library and information services. Efficiency, effectiveness, and value. Criteria, measures, methods of measurement. Types of measure for different services—for example, success rate, impact, recall, precision, coverage, delivery time. Cost effectiveness and cost benefit. Factors contributing to performance: experimental studies of systems. Interpretation of test results, application of results. Practical project to devise and carry out an evaluation test.

(7) Systems as organizations. Division of labour to carry out complex tasks. Organizational structure. Modes of departmentalization. Centralization and decentralization. Hierarchy of objectives, functions, policies, procedures, tasks. Consequences of the division of labour. Management by objectives and other methods of fostering coordination of work. Communication within the organization. Funding policy.

(8) Cooperation, collaboration, and networks. The rationale of resource sharing. Degrees of interdependence. Areas of cooperation among libraries and information services. Network patterns. Constraints on cooperation: administrative, legal, political. Standardization incurred. Network management.

(9) Forward planning for information systems. Monitoring the system environment: users (actual and potential), input (sources of information), technology (applicable to processing), the administrative metasystem (that controls and funds the information system), social developments. Trend prediction and forecasting.

4 Methods of information science

There is slowly emerging a distinctive discipline that may also be called 'information science', meaning the scientific study of the communication of information in society. As the science develops, its scope and content will change, and the indications given below will need revision. The aim of a course in this area is to give an understanding of the distinctive nature and methodologies of scientific research into the communication of information.

(1) Science and its research method. Data, hypothesis, theory. Observation and experiment. Measurement and quantification. Modes of investigation: description, comparison, correlation, causal analysis, analysis of complex systems. Use of mathematics and statistics. Research results and their presentation.

(2) The nature of information science. Its objects of study: people acquiring knowledge through documentary systems. Relationship to mass communication and personal communications. Methods of studying people, knowledge, documents, and systems are multidisciplinary. Methods specific to information science.

(3) Scientific methodologies of value in information science: techniques derived from sociology, psychology, linguistics, economics, operations research, etc. Examples: surveys of opinion, studies of behaviour, measurement of attitudes, study of social diffusion processes, analysis of knowledge and language patterns, welfare economics, communication theory, industrial dynamics.

(4) Analysis of publications and use records: for example, volumes of publication in different subjects, circulation and readership, distribution of topics among publications (Bradford–Zipf distributions), interrelations between subject fields (cluster analysis), obsolescence patterns of published literature.

(5) Social survey methods: for example, analysis of potential user groups and their work environments, information-use patterns of different social groups, expressed demands and attitudes of such groups, effects of information provision on user behaviour and attitudes, mechanisms of information transfer and diffusion.

(6) Information system dynamics: for example, identification of variables affecting information system development, prediction of trends in information provision and use, future effects of change on information systems.

(7) Statistical techniques of use in information science: distributions, averages, measures of dispersion, correlation, tests of significance, research design.

Appendix 3

Data questionnaire for chemists

(Margaret Slater, 1972)

Interviewer (name) ....

Interviewer No. ....

Sampling Point ....

Sampling Point No. ....

CLASSIFICATION

Organization	Respondent
Area	Name ....
Name	Department ....
Type E I NP	Job Title ....
Subject/industry	Subject field or discipline ....
....	Scientist ...... Technician ......

1. As a background, can you tell me a bit about the work you do?

2. What is your personal definition of data?
   (further questions if needed)
   —can you give me some examples of the kind of thing that you think of as data?
   —do you make any distinction between data and information?

3. (a) I'd like you to look at this list (present list X). It shows different definitions of data given by scientists interviewed earlier. Which of these statements comes closest to your opinion? (ring statement chosen)

   A   B   C   D

   None of them, sticks to definition given in answer to question 2
   ......

   None of them, gives a new 'other' answer (please record below)
   ......

(b) Here is another list (<u>present list Y</u>). Some people think that these things come under the heading data. What do you think?

	Data	Not data	D.K./Not sure
A	....	....	....
B	....	....	....
C	....	....	....
D	....	....	....

NOW FOR THE REST OF THE INTERVIEW I'D LIKE YOU TO FOCUS ON JUST ONE ASPECT OF DATA—THE KIND OF DATA INDICATED BY THE LAST TWO ITEMS ON <u>THIS</u> LIST (<u>present list X again</u>)—THAT'S NUMERICAL DATA.

4. In your work are you a producer of this kind of data, or a user of this kind of data, or both?

     Producer ....   User ....   Both ....

Ask Qs 5–7 to those who say they are Producers or Both at Q4

5. Can you give me some examples of the kind of data that you produce in your work?

6. How do you organize this data?

7. Who uses it?

Ask Qs 8–14 to those who say they are Users or Both at Q4

8. Can you give me some examples of the kind of data that you use in your work?

9. What are your main sources of data? are you satisfied with them?

10. Do you use any published data compilations? Which ones? Can you tell me about any particularly good, or particularly bad features of these compilations, from your point of view?

11. Is it necessary for you to have critically evaluated data?*

12 Is there any particular kind of data that's harder to obtain? Why's that?

13. How frequently are you using data?

14. When did you last need to search for some data?

15. Are there any other points you'd like to make about data—that haven't been covered by our questionnaire?

(c) <u>Data record sheets; a sampling of activity</u>

At the conclusion of the interview, respondents were given an adequate supply of 'data record sheets' and reply-paid envelopes. They were asked to fill in the sheets on the next working day after the interview. For every item of data sought on that day, the respondent completed a separate record sheet. If no data was needed, the respondent was asked to return a single sheet to us, clearly marked

---

*Critically evaluated data = data whose source and accuracy have been assessed or evaluated by experts in relevant subject fields.

'no data'. The aim in giving respondents this additional task was to obtain a record of data needs throughout one, presumably typical, working day. This would provide a useful quantitative supplement to the questions concerning 'typical examples' of data needed, which had been asked during the interview.

Response rate to the request to complete data record sheets was excellent—86.2% of data users co-operated. This high response rate is effective extra proof of the good impression left with respondents by the interviewers. A copy of the data record sheet itself is shown in section (d) below.

(d) *A data record sheet*

Interviewer _____

DATA RECORD SHEET

A record of data needs throughout one working day. Use it tomorrow (or the next working day if interviewed on Friday). Please record all instances where data was required during the day. Don't be concerned if the items seem trivial to you—they are still of interest to the study. The same applies if the day is not typical for you. Repeat questions 1–7 for all items of data sought, using spare forms supplied. Most of the questions can be answered by a tick in the appropriate box. If you don't need any data during the next working day, please send us a form marked 'no data'—as this will help us estimate incidence of data needs.

Please post forms back to Aslib in the envelope provided. Thank you for helping us.

DATA RECORD

1. Item of data required

2. Is it necessary that this data has been critically evaluated?
    - ☐ Yes
    - ☐ No
    - ☐ Other answer (please state) _____

3. Source(s) used:
    - ☐ published—please name book(s) etc. _____
    - ☐ person
    - ☐ own files/notes
    - ☐ other (please specify) _____
      _____

4. Total search time _____

5. Is this data central to/peripheral to your main area of study/work?
    - ☐ central
    - ☐ peripheral

6. Result of search:
    - ☐ satisfactory answer
    - ☐ unsatisfactory answer
    - ☐ failed to find anything

LIST X

A Data equals information, for practical purposes there is little or no difference

B Data is information in a stylised form; information without trimmings; information without theory or conclusions; includes facts as well as figures

C Data is primarily numerical material

D Data is primarily <u>reliable</u> numerical material

LIST Y

A Experimental results

B Facts about or descriptions of processes, methods, techniques

C Facts, descriptions <u>and</u> numerical information relating to equipment

D Purely numerical information relating to equipment

MYCIN at work

(Buchanan and Shortliffe, 1984)

Patient-1

(1) Patient's name: (first–last)
**Fred Smith
   *MYCIN collects some background data about the patient. The physician's
   responses follows the double asterisks.*
(2) Sex:
**Male
(3) Age:
**55
(4) Have you been able to obtain positive cultures from a site at which Fred
Smith has an infection?
**Yes

Infection-1

(5) What is the infection?
**Primary-bacteremia
(6) Please give the data and approximate time when signs or symptoms of
the primary-bacteremia (infection-1) first appeared (mo/da/yr).
**May 5 1980
The most recent positive culture associated with the primary-bacteremia
(infection-1) will be referred to as:

Culture-1

(7) From what site was the specimen for culture-1 taken?
**Blood
(8) Please give the date and time when this blood culture (culture-1) was
obtained (mo/da/yr).
**May 9 1980
The first significant organism from this blood culture (culture-1) will be
referred to as:

Organism-1

(9) Enter the identity of organism-1:
**Unknown

Typically, the identity of the organism is not known and, hence, must be inferred by MYCIN from various other pieces of laboratory and clinical information. MYCIN proceeds to ask questions that could help to determine the identity of the organism.

(10) Is organism-1 a rod, or coccus (etc.):
**Rod
(11) The gram stain of organism-1:
**Gramneg
(12) Have there been positive cultures from sites which are NOT associated with infections about which you are seeking advice?
**No
(13) Did organism-1 grow aerobically?
**Yes (.8)
(14) Did organism-1 grown anaerobically?
**Yes
(15) What is the suspected portal of entry of organism-1 into this sterile site?
**GI (.6)

More questions follow, to gather sufficient information for inferring possible identities of the infecting organisms.

My therapy recommendation will be based on the following probable infection(s) and potential causative organism(s):

INFECTION-1 is PRIMARY-BACTEREMIA
<Item 1> The identity of organism-1 may be PSEUDOMONAS-AERUGINOSA
<Item 2> The identity of organism-1 may be KLEBSIELLA-PNEUMONIAE
<Item 3> The identity of organism-1 may be E. COLI
<Item 4> The identity of organism-1 may be BACTEROIDES-FRAGILIS
<Item 5> The identity of organism-1 may be ENTEROBACTER
<Item 6> The identity of organism-1 may be PROTEUS-NON-MIRABILIS

(46) On a scale of 0 to 4, where higher numbers indicate increasing severity, how would you rate Fred Smith's degree of sickness?
**3
(47) Does Fred Smith have a clinically significant allergic reaction to any antimicrobial agent?
**No
(48) Fred Smith's weight in kilograms (or <number> pounds):
**70

Note that two drugs cover for six potential organisms.

[Rec 1] My preferred therapy recommendation is as follows:

In order to cover for Items <1 2 3 5 6>:
    Give: GENTAMICIN
    Dose: 119 mg (1.7 mg/kg) q8h IV [or IM] for 10 days
    Comments: Modify dose in renal failure
In order to cover for Item <4>:
    Give: CLINDAMYCIN
    Dose: 595 mg (8.5 mg/kg) q6h IV [or IM] for 14 days
    Comments: If diarrhea or other GI symptoms develop, patient should
            be evaluated for possible pseudomembranous colitis.
Do you wish to see the next-choice therapy?

Alternative choices are available.

**Yes
Which, if any, of the above drugs do you wish eliminated from
consideration?
**Clindamycin
[Rec 2] Next best therapy recommendation:
In order to cover for Items <2 3 4 5 6>:
    Give: CHLORAMPHENICOL
    Dose: 1 gm (15 mg/kg) q6h IV for 14 days
    Comments: Monitor patient's white count
In order to cover for Item <1>:
    Give: GENTAMICIN
    Dose: 119 mg (1.7 mg/kg) q8h IV [or IM] for 10 days
    Comments: Modify dose in renal failure

TEIRESIAS explains

(Buchanan and Shortliffe, 1984)

First, MYCIN's question:
What is the suspected portal of entry of organism-1 into this sterile site?
  The physician requests an explanation
**WHY
  Then TEIRESIAS proceeds to explain its 'reasoning'.
[I.e., why is it important to determine the suspected portal of entry of organism-1 into this sterile site?]

[3.0] ... in order to find out about an organism or class of organism for which therapy should cover.

It has already been established that
  [3.1] The site of the culture is blood
  [3.2] The stain of the organism is gram positive

Therefore if:
  [3.3] The portal of entry of the organism is G.I.
  [3.4] [Abdomen is the locus of infection, or Pelvis is the locus of
        infection]

Then
  There is strongly suggestive evidence (.9) that Enterobacteriaceae is the
  class of organisms for which therapy should cover.
[Rule 095]

In contrast to WHY, which spells out 'higher' nodes in the goal tree, the HOW command asks TEIRESIAS to explain the nodes lower down the tree that have been or will be expanded. For example, in the following exchange, the expert asks how MYCIN will determine whether the abdomen or the pelvis is the locus of infection:

** HOW [3.4]

  Note: [3.4] is the prefix of the statement of interest in the exchange above.

[I.e., how were you determining that the Abdomen is the locus of infection, or that the Pelvis is the locus of infection?]
[4.0] At that point Rule 021 was being used.
If the doctor now wants to see rule 21, he asks TEIRESIAS to explain HOW it was used, referring to the prefix [4.0] of the statement in which it was mentioned:

** HOW [4.0]

[I.e., how was Rule 021 used?]

    [5.0] It has already been established that

    [5.1] the culture is recent.

Therefore if:

    [5.2] There is therapeutically significant disease associated with the occurrence of this organism

Then

    It is definite (1.0) that the site of the culture is the locus of infection in the patient.

Intelligent search interfaces

During the years 1987–1991, there has been considerable research and development work on the construction of computer interfaces for online search of text databases. Reviews of such work have been produced by Vickery (1989), Belkin and Marchetti (1990) and Efthimiadis (1990).

The whole process of providing a user-friendly link to a variety of databases on a number of host computers has been analysed more closely. An intelligent search interface needs to provide at least the following functions:

(1) Interact with the user via an easy-to-use interface.
(2) Tailor its actions to individual user capabilities and preferences.
(3) Provide screen dialogue in the user's preferred language.
(4) Undertake linguistic analysis of user queries, in the language of the input.
(5) Give aid in the user selection of database(s) and host(s).
(6) Prompt the user in the clarification of queries.
(7) Automatically transform clarified queries into search statements in the form required by the host/database to be accessed, and if necessary in the language of the database.
(8) Perform automatically the telecommunication functions of dial-up, logon and so on.
(9) Automatically transmit search statements to the host, and download search output.
(10) Provide means for the user to evaluate search output.
(11) Give aid to the user in reformulating queries and/or search statements.
(12) Provide means for user to order documents online.
(13) Provide possibilities for post-processing of downloaded search output, in particular the relevance ranking of items.

A summary analysis of the knowledge required by an interface in order to perform these functions is set out below.

Of hosts: telecommunication links
               command languages
               output formats
               range of databases mounted
               available search facilities and search aids

Of databases: structural and content types
                  subject areas
                  field structures, searchable fields
                  indexes, thesauri, classifications
                  natural languages used
                  currency, updating policy
                  character sets

Of search strategies: search modes
                       reformulation techniques
                       relevance feedback techniques

Of users/uses: kinds, stereotypes
                capabilities
                individual preferences
                session contexts, including search purpose

Of subject domain: entities
                    relations between entities
                    modes of representing entities and relations

Of language: morphological analysis (stemming and truncation)
              lexical analysis (e.g. synonyms, compound words)
              grammar and syntactic analysis
              semantic analysis of queries, categories
              disambiguation of multimeaning and unknown words
              semantic relations between terms
              language equivalents of search terms

Of answer presentation: statistical and linguistic methods of ranking
                             elimination of duplicate responses

There has been much study of these varied areas of knowledge, and of the ways in which they can be embodied in computer interfaces. Particular attention has been paid to:

— search strategy (Armstrong and Large, 1988; Sormunen, 1989)
— host procedures and database structures (Piternick, 1989; Staud, 1988)
— language processing of user queries (Vickery and Vickery, 1992)

Less work has been done on user modelling (Brajnik *et al.*, 1990), and on making use of the lessons learnt about search interviews, that were discussed in chapter 7.

The outcome of these studies has been to indicate that an intelligent search interface should present functionality of the following kind to the user:

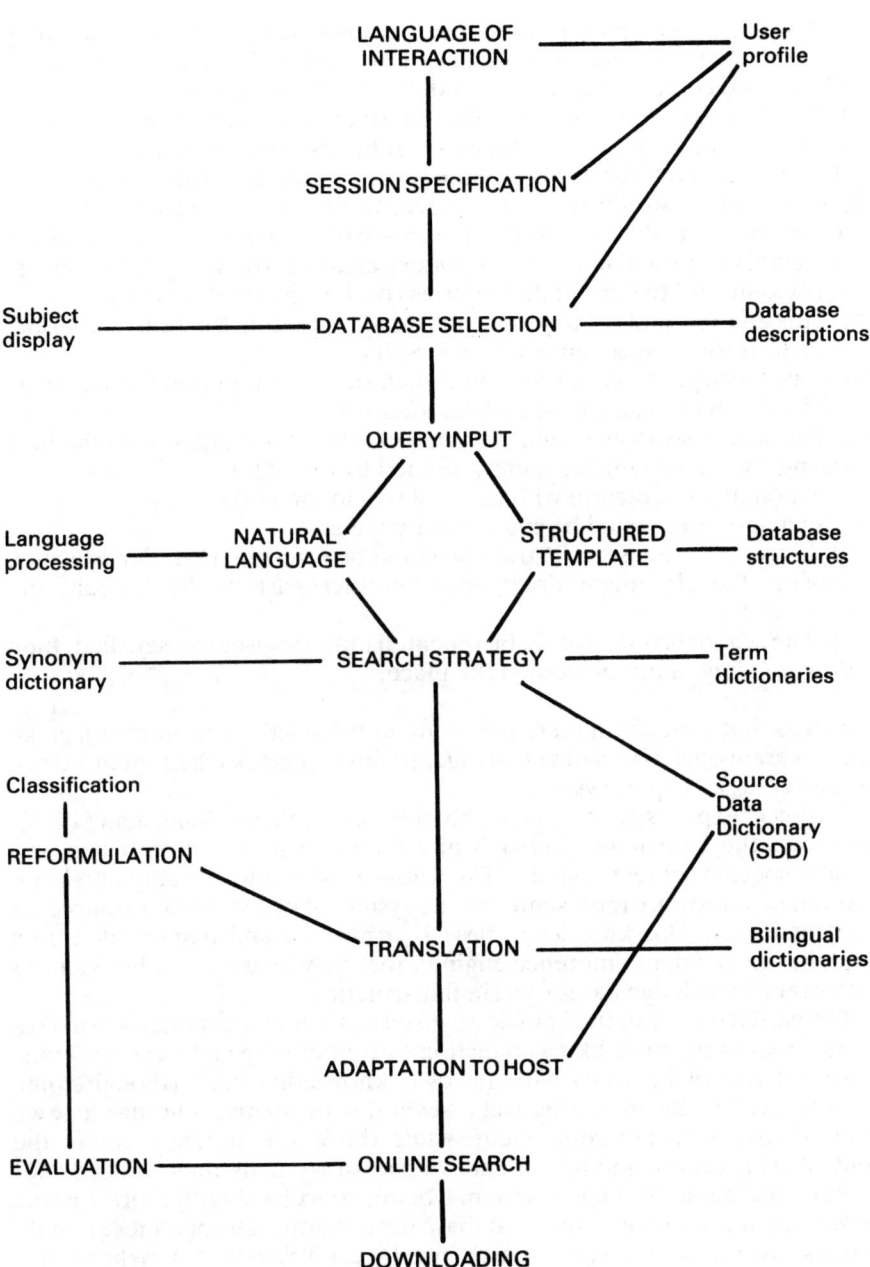

(1) A language of interaction would first be selected: this could be recorded as a default in the user profile. The profile would also hold any other characteristics making up a user model, that would guide later choices in processing. It would also hold specific details needed for host communications—telephone number for local access to telecommunications network, user passwords and host identifiers, etc.

(2) A session specification would then be supplied by the user, concerning types of data/document sought, date and language limitations, etc. Some of this also could be recorded as a default in the user profile.

(3) Database(s) would then be selected, drawing upon any defaults in the user profile, displays of database subjects and descriptions, other database characteristics, the session specification, user access rights, etc.

(4) Query input would then take place, the form of input offered being a function of the database chosen—with guidance from database structures recorded in the SDD. Query analysis would involve language processing and the use of dictionaries (part of the total lexicon).

(5) This analysis and processing would lead to the construction of a formal search strategy, again guided by the SDD.

(6) If necessary, search terms would then be translated into the language of the database, using bilingual dictionaries.

(7) The search strategy would then be put into a form adapted to the host (using command language, etc.), guided by the SDD.

(8) Automatic interaction with the host would then take place.

(9) Search output would be evaluated by the user.

(10) If required, the search strategy would be reformulated, during which process the IIS might draw upon another part of the lexicon, the classification.

(11) The search process would be repeated until the user was satisfied, then downloading of output could take place.

It is clear that to perform these functions an IIS must incorporate and make use of a great deal of varied knowledge. In this respect, such a search aid can be classed as an expert system.

A typical expert system, as described for example by Waterman (1986), embodies the knowledge and skill of a human expert in a particular and usually specific subject domain. The knowledge is often of only one kind, and can be uniformly represented in the system in one way (for example, as a set of rules). This knowledge base is controlled and manipulated by a domain-independent 'inference engine', that may be used in other systems with other knowledge bases of a similar structure.

The varied nature of the knowledge used in an intelligent interface makes it into something more like a collection of cooperating expert subsystems. Each subsystem operates with its own knowledge base (though some knowledge may be shared between several subsystems), and has its own manipulative software component, while the whole system is under the control of a central module. Some of the subsystems may, indeed, not deserve the name of 'expert system', being concerned with more routine tasks such as searching a file of database descriptions. Despite these qualifications, overall an intelligent search interface is a system that makes active use of embodied expert knowledge, and as such can be considered as a form of expert system.

A number of prototype and even operational systems of this kind has now been developed, but much remains to be done to solve all the problems that they present, and to produce robust interfaces acceptable to online users.

Index

This is an index to topics and names mentioned in the text. It does not include names occurring only in the references.

Abelson, 161
abstracting in UK, 305
abstracts, 90
access to information, 312, 336
access to stores, 247
Ackoff, 85
acquisition, 270
Advisory Council for Adult and Continuing Education, 314
aging of literature, 245
Allen, 53, 69
analysis of communication acts, 60
analysis of variables, 64
Anderson, 146
Andrieu, 340
animal communication, 29
answers, 185
Armstrong, 380
arrow diagram, 172
artificial intelligence, 158, 203
assignation of index terms, 137, 166
associations between concepts, 147
Auster, 192
authored articles, 235
automatic indexing, 121
automation, 33
availability, 287

Baddeley, 146
Bagust, 253
Baker, 144
Bales, 16, 53
Barnard, 245
Barr, A., 159
Barr, D., 231
Bass, 242
Bates, 198
Batten, 244, 282, 297
Belkin, 182, 379
Belnap, 185
Bensman, 229, 238
Berul, 81
bibliograph, 237
bibliographic records, 138, 324
Blagden, 239, 287
Bliss, 7, 140
Bobrow, 198
Bolinger, 151
Bolt, 239
book production, 232
book use, 316

booksellers in UK, 305
Bookstein, 238
Boolean operators, 128
borrowing pattern, 240
Bower, 74
Boyle, 215
Bradford, 7, 236
Brajnik, 380
Brittain, 229
Broad System of Ordering, 208
broadcasting in UK, 305
Broadus, 229
Brookes, 238, 250, 258
Brown, C., 324
Buchanan, 161, 203, 205
Buckland, 255, 288, 290
Bulick, 245
Bundy, 198
Buntrock, 215
Burrell, 253

Carlson, 162
Carlyle, 216
catchment area, 248
categories of concept, 62, 153, 174, 202
causal relations, 144
channel agent, 13
channels, 13, 22, 23, 70, 133, 164, 301
Chen, 107, 312
Cherry, 342
Choffray, 242
citations, 75, 245
citizen, 17
Clark, 242
classification, 140, 173
Clements, 64
Cleverdon, 176
Coates, 140, 174
Cochrane, 192
codes, 35
cognitive models, 189
Cole, P.F., 76, 255
Coleman, 59
Collier, 335
Collins, 149
collisions of demand, 253
communication, 13, 16, 300
communication incidents, 7
communicative acts, 81
community, 57

computer performance, 318
conceptual dependency, 159
construction industry, 106
Coombs, 95
cost effectiveness, 269
costing, 268
coverage, 270
Cowling, 248
current-awareness, 280
Curwen, 302
Cutlip, 57
Daniels, 182
Danowski, 55
data for analysis, 62, 82
data for evaluation, 264, 267
data transmission, 321
database processors, 321, 323
database producers, 321
databases, 323
Davies, 209
Davis, 161
de Beaugrande, 153
de Grolier, 174
Dearborn, 45
demand, 238, 253, 295, 313
Department of Education and Science, 247, 305
Department of the Environment, 106
derived terms, 166
designations, 134, 136, 137, 164, 166, 168
Deutschmann, 57
dialogue, 188
diaries, 78, 83
Dicken, 329
discourse, 153, 187
disposal of stock, 255
dissemination of research, 87, 228
document-delivery, 291
documentation, 7
documents, 36
Dolby, 215
Duncan, 49

Earle, 75
East, 305, 307
economics, 26, 330
education of adults, 315
education libraries in UK, 308
efficiency, 268
Efthimiadis, 379
electronic document delivery, 132
electronic information, 326
electronic mail, 131
electronic sources, 337
electronic technology, 117, 216, 316
Elton, 259
Ely, 112
engineers and information, 72, 99, 101, 105
epidemic growth, 232
episodic memory, 145, 155
Euronet Diane News, 324

evaluation of search, 129
evaluation of systems, 261
events, 157
Everyman, 107
expert systems, 203, 382
exponential growth, 232
extraction of index terms, 137

factory, 56
Faibisoff, 112
failure analysis, 278, 287
Fairthorne, 134, 140, 238
Farace, 55
features of concepts, 149
feedback, 33
Findler, 159
Fishenden, 83
Flynn, 245
Forrester, 294
Foskett, A.C., 140
frames, 161, 208
Freitag, 319
front-end, 198
funds for information, 334

Gardner, 84
Garfield, 245
Garvey, 59, 86, 91, 227
gatekeepers, 55, 57, 69
Gilchrist, 140
Godwin, 234
Goffman, 232
Gottfredson, 59, 91
Gowers, 47
Gralewska-Vickery, 51, 78, 99, 100
Greenberg, 57
Grice, 188
Griffith, xiii, 86, 247
group discussion, 16
groups, 53

Hagstrom, 69
Halbert, 85
Halloran, 341
Hamburg, 219, 250, 255
Harmon, 203
Harrah, 188
Havelock, 51, 98
Hayes-Roth, 203
Hernon, 107, 312
Hertzler, 47
Heseltine, 296
hierarchical storage, 258
Hindle, 253
Ho, 256
Hoffman, 47, 111
Hollnagel, 189
Holmstrom, 26, 216
Homans, 53
homophily, 51

Hough, 320
Hubel, 40
Hubert, 238
Hulme, 7
human information processing, 37
Hutchins, 140, 151, 153, 168

index languages, 175, 285
indexes of a characteristic, 68
indexing, 119, 137, 140, 166
indicators of a characteristic, 68
industrial society, 14
industrialization, 329
inference engine, 204
informal communication, 50, 100
information, 27, 30, 330
    analysis, 119
    contacts, 53
    demand, 4
    environment, 18
    functions, 10, 24
    needs, 17, 92
    overload, 20, 52
    provision, 263
    retrieval, 116
    science, 1, 9
    system, 9, 25, 210, 260
    technology, 316, 328
    transfer, 6, 28, 42, 301
    transfer cycle, 12
    want, 20, 134, 138, 162, 313
informative communication, 17, 28, 60, 210
innovations, 57, 98, 242
inputs, 219
Institute of Information Scientists, 11
interfaces, 180, 198, 204, 379
interlending in UK, 310
intermediaries, 51, 180, 197
interviews, 83, 193
inverted index, 126
isolates, 55
Iwinski, 231

jargon, 47
journal ranking, 64
journal use, 255
journals, 89, 303

Kantor, 252
Kay, 140
Kearsley, 182
Kehoe, 203
Kent, 244
King, D., 203
King, D.W., 107, 226, 326
King, G., 193
Kintsch, 146
Kirkley, 335
knowledge base, 204, 382
knowledge engineer, 204
knowledge generation, 22
knowledge representation, 158

knowledge structure, 21, 145, 162, 165
Kochen, 186
Kraft, 255
Kroll, 238

Lachman, 146, 154
Lancaster, 140, 272, 273, 299
language, 46, 150
Large, 380
Lawani, 238
laws of library science, 7
Lazarsfeld, 67, 70
Lee, 249
Leggate, 280
Leimkuhler, 238
Lenski, 2
Lesk, 177
Lewis, 317
liaisons, 55
libraries in UK, 305
library cooperation in UK, 310
Lilien, 242
Lindquist, 294
Lindsay, 39, 145, 154
Line, 114, 229, 246, 264
linguistics, 46, 140, 151
linkers, 51
literacy, 5
literary warrant, 140
Lloyd, 329
Loftus, 145
logic, 150
logistic growth, 232
Lotka, 232
Luhn, 168
Lynch, 193

MacBride, 335
MacShane, 305
machines, 33
Madge, 84
Magson, 299
Mansbridge, 288
MARC records, 235
market model, 239
market penetration, 241
Martin, 318, 322
Martyn, 270
Mason, 299
matching queries, 139
McCall, 84
McCallum, 234
McClure, 55
McGill, 117, 169, 199
McQuail, 51, 261
Meadow, 192
meaning, 135, 167
measure of performance, 267
measurement, 229
media, 48
MEDLARS, 273

meetings, 88
Meier, 296
memory, 146
Menzel, 81
message production, 230
messages, 19, 116, 133, 165, 166, 218
meta-knowledge, 161
meta-messages, 134
Miller, 57
Minsky, 161
Mishler, 187
modelling, 249
Morse, 253
Moser, 84
Mote, 77
Mumford, 4
MYCIN, 161, 204

Naranan, 238
news, 57
Norman, D.A., 39, 145, 154
Norman, O.G., 190
noun classes, 170
novelty, 281, 283

occupations, 15
Ogden, 136
online information, 332
online search, 191, 282, 294
online subscribers, 327
Oppenheim, 5
oral communication, 103
organizations, 55
Orr, 259, 262, 264, 267, 291, 297
Oswitch, 252
outputs, 218

Palmour, 107
Pao, 233
paradigmatic relations, 151
Park, 57
parsing, 199
participant observation, 83
Penner, 293
perceived value, 298
perception, 39
performance, 266
performance degradation, 296
personal knowledge, 134, 145, 154
phrase generation, 124
physicians and information, 59
Piternick, 380
PLEXUS, 207
Poisson process, 251
Pool, 49
population, 79
Porter, 169
Potter, 233
practitioners and information, 94
Praunlich, 238
precision, 130, 275, 281, 283
preprints, 89
press in UK, 305

Price, D.J., 238
Price, D.S., 268
printed sources, 337
probability distributions, 249
problem solving, 186
product life cycle, 243
production rules, 161, 205
productivity of authors, 233
professional orientation, 70
psychologists and information, 86
public knowledge, 134, 141, 167
public libraries in UK, 308
public library use, 64
publishing in UK, 302

quality, 262
quaternary sector, 328
query formulation, 127
query modification, 130, 286
query statement, 138
questionnaires, 83
questions, 182
queueing, 252, 294
Quillian, 149

Rackstraw, 184
radio in UK, 306
Raitt, 317
Ranganathan, 7, 140
Ravetz, 84, 144
readability, 46
reading, 111
recall, 130, 275
recipients, 13, 20, 133, 164, 218, 230, 238, 265
records of communication acts, 73
records in retrieval, 116, 124
reference interview, 190
reference process, 180
reference questions, 76
referral, 207
regional library network, 311
Reid, 316
Reinecke, 341
relationships between variables, 65
relative recall, 281
relays, 51
relevance, 272
relevance assessment, 265, 284
relevance feedback, 127
Resnikoff, 215
retrieval, 133
retrieval evaluation, 272
reviews, 90
Rich, 159, 199
Richards, 136
Robinson, 184
Rogers, 51, 55, 59, 242
Roscoe, 78, 100
Rosenbloom, 70
Rothenberg, 256
Rouse, 252
Royal Society, 226

Rumelhart, 146
rural information needs, 96
Sager, 169
Salton, 117, 140, 169, 177, 199
sample, 79
Sandison, 246
Saracevic, 9, 177, 265, 283
Sayers, 140
Schank, 159, 161
Schofield, 287
Schramm, 49, 63
Schultz, 169
scientific publication, 226
scientists and information, 59, 69, 84, 144, 227
scripts, 161
searching, 127
secondary publications, 90
selectivity, 39, 45
semantic categories, 208
semantic distance, 147
semantic elements, 151
semantic formats, 169
semantic memory, 145, 155
semantic nets, 148, 159
semantic organization, 138
semantic structure, 171
semantics, 133
sense, 168
Serafine, 340
service delay, 293
service qualities, 266
Sherif, 44
Shibutani, 46
Shoemaker, 51, 59, 242
Shortliffe, 203, 205
Simon, H.A., 141
Simon, J.L., 84
Singleton, 304
SITPRO, 317
size of systems, 215
Slater, 270
Sloman, 39
Smith, A., 340
Smith, A.G., 52
Smith, L., 229
social interaction, 44
Soergel, 174
Sommerville, 192
Sormunen, 380
sources, 13, 22, 93, 133, 164, 218, 230, 236
Sparck Jones, 140, 169, 176, 272
special libraries in UK, 310
Staud, 380
Steel, 185
stemming, 122, 169
stock retention, 255
Stone, 6
stop list, 122
stores of messages, 243, 256
subject retrieval, 136
subsidy, 331

Swigger, 182
syntagmatic relations, 151
system development, 221
system dynamics, 294
systems, 219
Taylor, 190
TEIRESIAS, 204
telecommunications, 318
telematics, 317, 332
television in UK, 306
Thayer, 19
thesaurus, 119, 174
time chart, 2
time spent on communication, 86
Toffler, 18
travel time, 249
Urquhart, D.J., 244
Urquhart, J.A., 287
use of journals, 244
use of system, 229
use per item, 243
use versus age, 245
user satisfaction, 264, 290
Uzanne, 342
value, 262, 297
van Rijsbergen, 140, 272
variables, 61
Vickery, A., 182, 198, 207, 244, 282, 297, 380
Vickery, B.C., 62, 75, 140, 144, 174, 268, 296, 324, 379
Voress, 271
Wall, 241
Waples, 7
Ward, 340
Waterman, 382
Wardhaugh, 189
weighting index terms, 120, 137
Weisman, 221
Wessel, 335
wh-questions, 184
White, H., xiii
White, M., 194
Whyte, 141
Wilkin, 95
Wilks, 159
Willetts, 174
Williams, A., 46, 111
Williams, R., 302
Winston, 159, 199
Wolek, 51, 61, 70
Wolfe, 268, 298
Wood, 249
Woodburn, 259
Woods, 189
word frequency, 121, 168
work orientation, 67
Worthington, 253
written communication, 102

Young, 33, 146